# COMPLEX INFORMATION PROCESSING

# PROCESSING

## The Impact of Herbert A. Simon

*21st Carnegie-Mellon Symposium
on Cognition*

# COMPLEX INFORMATION PROCESSING

## The Impact of Herbert A. Simon

Edited by

David Klahr

Kenneth Kotovsky

*Carnegie-Mellon University*

**Ψ Psychology Press**
Taylor & Francis Group

New York London

First Published by
Lawrence Erlbaum Associates, Inc., Publishers
10 Industrial Avenue
Mahwah, New Jersey 07430

Transferred to Digital Printing 2009 by Psychology Press
270 Madison Ave, New York NY 10016
27 Church Road, Hove, East Sussex, BN3 2FA

This work relates to Grant No. BSN-8620193 from the National Science Foundation.
However, the content does not necessarily reflect the position or policy of the National Science
Foundation or the government and no official endorsement should be inferred.

The United States Government has a royalty-free, nonexclusive and irrevocable license
throughout the world for Government purposes to publish, translate, reproduce, deliver, perform, dispose of, and to authorize other so to do, all or any portion of this work.

**Library of Congress Cataloging in Publication Data**

Complex information processing.
(21st Carnegie-Mellon Symposium on Cognition)
   Includes index.
   1. Human information processing.   2. Artificial intel-
ligence.   3. Problem solving.   4. Cognitive science.   5. Simon,
Herbert Alexander, 1916–     .   I. Simon, Herbert Alexander,
1916–     .   II. Klahr, David.   III. Kotovsky, Kenneth.
BF444.C66   1989        153 '.092 '4        88-31004
ISBN 0-8058-0178-2
ISBN 0-8058-0179-0 (pbk.)

To Herb,
for setting the common task

# Contents

**List of Contributors**    xiii

**Introduction**    xv

**PART I    REPRESENTATION AND CONSTRAINT
IN COMPLEX PROCESSING**    1

**1    The Lateralization of BRIAN: A Computational Theory
and Model of Visual Hemispheric Specialization**    3
*Stephen M. Kosslyn, Michael A. Sokolov,
and Jack C. Chen*

Introduction    *3*
High-Level Vision    *4*
Subsystems of High-Level
    Visual Recognition    *5*
Mechanisms of Hemispheric
    Differentiation    *11*
Lateralization Simulations    *16*
Results    *21*
Conclusions    *25*

**2    The Role of Working Memory in Language Comprehension**    31
*Patricia A. Carpenter and Marcel A. Just*

Working Memory From a Computational
    Viewpoint    *34*
Trade-Offs Among Processes
    in Working Memory    *42*

Syntactic Analysis and Working Memory    52
The Nature of Working Memory    59
A Final Note    66

**3    Representation and Transfer in Problem Solving**    69
*Kenneth Kotovsky and David Fallside*

Experimental Background: Problem
    Difficulty    71
Experimental Background: Transfer
    of Training and Problem Move Operators    77
Experiment 1: Representation
    and Transfer    81
Experiment 2: The Effects of Stimulus
    and Representational Similarity on Transfer    93
Discussion    104

**4    Developmental Differences in Scientific Discovery
Processes**    109
*Kevin Dunbar and David Klahr*

On the Origins of Discovery Processes    109
Developmental Issues in Scientific Reasoning    111
Studying the Discovery Process: General Procedure    113
Study 1: Adults Discovering a New Function    114
Study 2: Hypothesis-Space Search
    and Experimentation by Adults    125
Study 3: Scientific Reasoning in Children    127
A Dual-Search Model of Scientific Discovery    132
Discussion    137
Postscript: Acknowledgments to Herbert Simon    141

**5    Scientists of the Artificial**    145
*George A. Miller*

The Computational Nervous System    146
The Hard Working Memory    150
The Many Towers of Hanoi    153
Search and Research    158
Concluding Apology    160

**PART II    EXPERTISE IN HUMAN AND
ARTIFICIAL SYSTEMS**    163

**6    What Hath Simon Wrought?**    165
*Edward A. Feigenbaum*

Some Moments of Personal History    *166*
The Genesis of the Science
    (Early Life in the Search Space)    *166*
An Interlude: The Dimensions of Intelligence    *169*
The Exodus: From the Search-Based to the
    Knowledge-Based Paradigm    *172*
Leviticus: Laws in the Land of Promise    *178*
Conclusion: The Many Manifestations of Simon    *180*

**7    Expertise in Chess and Bridge    183**
*Neil Charness*

An Anecdote    *183*
Chess: A Drosophilia for Cognitive Psychology    *184*
Skill in Bridge    *193*
Lessons About Skill Acquisition    *204*

**8    Writing Research: The Analysis of a Very Complex Task    209**
*John R. Hayes*

Planning    *211*
Sentence Generation    *213*
Revision    *215*
Task Environment    *218*
The Writers' Knowledge    *224*
Conclusion    *231*

**9    Skilled Memory and Expertise: Mechanisms of
Exceptional Performance    235**
*K. Anders Ericsson and James J. Staszewski*

Expert Performance and the Paradox of Expertise    *236*
Skilled Memory Theory    *238*
Skilled Memory Theory and Exceptional
    Memory Performance    *241*
Skilled Memory Theory and Expertise    *245*
Concluding Remarks    *263*

**10    Expertise and Learning: How Do We Think About
Instructional Processes Now That We Have Discovered
Knowledge Structures?    269**
*Robert Glaser*

Components of Competent Performance    *271*
Approaches to Instruction    *275*
Comment and Questions    *278*

# PART III    INSTRUCTION AND SKILL ACQUISITION    283

**11    Situations, Mental Models, and Generative Knowledge    285**
*James G. Greeno*

A View of Semantics    *289*
Some Research on Meaning and Models    *296*
An Extended View of Semantics    *305*
Conclusions    *313*

**12    Display-Based Problem Solving    319**
*Jill H. Larkin*

Description of the Model    *323*
Illustrations of Using External Data
    Structures to Solve Problems    *326*
DiBS and Human Problem Solving    *331*
Potential Applications    *337*
Conclusion    *339*

**13    The Analogical Origins of Errors in Problem Solving    343**
*John R. Anderson*

The PUPS Theory of Learning    *345*
Sources of Errors in PUPS    *349*
Errors With the Lisp Tutor    *351*
Errors With the Geometry Tutor    *357*
Errors With the Algebra Tutor    *363*
Summary    *366*
Einstellung    *366*
Comparisons With VanLehn's Theories    *367*
Conclusions    *370*

# PART IV    SCIENCE AND THOUGHT    373

**14    The Scientist as Problem Solver    375**
*Herbert A. Simon*

Formulating Problems    *376*
Laws From Data    *379*
Representations    *383*
Finding an Explanatory Model    *386*
Designing Good Experiments    *388*
The Scientist as a Satisficer    *394*

**15    Putting It All Together**                                        **399**
*Allen Newell*

Herbert Simon          *400*
Unified Theories of Cognition      *402*
The Chapters of This Volume      *416*
Conclusion      *435*


**EPILOGUE**
**How It All Got Put Together**                                  **441**
*Allen Newell*

**Author Index      447**

**Subject Index      455**

# List of Contributors

**John R. Anderson**
*Carnegie-Mellon University*

**Patricia Carpenter**
*Carnegie-Mellon University*

**Neil Charness**
*University of Waterloo*

**Jack C. Chen**
*Harvard University*

**Kevin Dunbar**
*McGill University*

**K. Anders Ericsson**
*University of Colorado*

**David Fallside**
*Carnegie-Mellon University*

**Edward Feigenbaum**
*Stanford University*

**Robert Glaser**
*University of Pittsburgh*

**James Greeno**
*Stanford University*

**John R. Hayes**
*Carnegie-Mellon University*

**Marcel Just**
*Carnegie-Mellon University*

**David Klahr**
*Carnegie-Mellon University*

**Stephen Kosslyn**
*Harvard University*

**Kenneth Kotovsky**
*Community College of
Allegheny County*

**Jill H. Larkin**
*Carnegie-Mellon University*

**George A. Miller**
*Princeton University*

**Allen Newell**
*Carnegie-Mellon University*

**Herbert A. Simon**
*Carnegie-Mellon University*

**Michael A. Sokolov**
*Massachusetts Institute
of Technology*

**James J. Staszewski**
*University of South Carolina*

# Introduction

More than 40 years ago, Herbert Simon proposed a fundamental challenge to the dominant theories in both economics and psychology. In economics, he proposed a radical departure from the view of humans as completely rational decision makers toward a more realistic view of humans as creatures of limited rationality who use heuristic decision procedures to circumvent limitations of time and memory. For the contributions based on that work, Simon received, in 1978, the Alfred Nobel Memorial Prize in Economic Sciences. In psychology, he proposed an equally radical departure from the behaviorist "black box" approach that did not allow consideration of internal processes connecting stimuli to responses. Instead, he made these processes—the manipulation of symbolic structures—the focus of psychological investigation. Simon's steadfast commitment to this new focus became one of the driving forces behind the counterrevolution that returned psychology to the study of the mind. For the contributions based on those ideas, he received, in 1969, the Distinguished Scientific Contribution Award from the American Psychological Association, and in 1988, the Gold Medal Award for Psychological Science from the American Psychological Foundation. Simon's scientific contributions have been recognized in other areas as well, and his other awards include the A. M. Turing Award (1975) from the Association for Computing Machinery—for the first artificial intelligence program (with Allen Newell), the Distinguished Fellow Award (1976) from the American Economic Association, the Frederick Moser Award (1974) from the American Society of Public Administration, the James Madison Award (1984) from the American Political Science Society, the John von Neumann Theory Prize (1988) from the Operations Research Society of America and the Institute of Management Science, and the National Medal of Science (1986) from the President of the United States.

Simon is generally acknowledged to be a founder of the information-processing approach to cognitive psychology, an approach whose centrality is well-summarized by Palmer and Kimchi (1986):

> Of the many alternative approaches available for understanding cognition, the one that has dominated psychological investigation for the last decade or two is information processing. For better or worse, the information-processing approach has had an enormous impact on modern cognitive research, leaving its distinctive imprint on both the kinds of theories that have been proposed and the kinds of experiments that have been performed to test them. Its influence has been so pervasive, in fact, that some writers have argued that information processing has achieved the exalted status of a "Kuhnian paradigm" for cognitive psychology. (p. 37)

This pervasiveness—and its corresponding richness and diversity—should not obscure the initial unity inherent in the field's foundational ideas. We believe that this unity exists to a large extent because many of its critical ideas came from one person. Thus, this collection of papers on the state of cognitive science has a particular flavor, even though the topics vary widely: from imagery to memory to problem solving, from reading to computer programming, from experts playing chess and bridge to children learning about a toy robot. The real focus of the book is on Herb Simon's profound impact on the field of cognitive psychology.

Early in our careers, both of us had the privilege of having Herb as our dissertation advisor, and we are both deeply indebted to him for the kind of values, skills and attitudes that such an apprenticeship inculcates. Another thing we both learned long ago was to respect the dual-edged sword of Herb's rapid insight and equally rapid impatience with poor ideas. Thus, even two decades beyond our graduate student days, it was with some trepidation that we approached him with our plan for this volume. Would the whole idea strike him as tangential to the real business of science? It is clear from the book you hold in your hands that his general reaction was supportive, but he had two requests. First, he would not be a passive participant in his own Festschrift; at the age of 71, as always, the research was his focus and priority: and he wanted to present a paper on his current research program at the symposium. Of course, we were delighted with that idea, and we agreed. Second, he wanted us to instruct the other participants to "avoid hagiography." We agreed to that too. And so we left his office with his blessings, and without the slightest idea about what hagiography meant. (It was not the first time that we had left his office concealing our ignorance and scurrying off to remedy it.[1])

---

[1]Hagiography (hag-i-og-ra-fee) *n.* the writing and critical study of the lives of the saints.

Thus, our charge to the participants was to stick to the ideas, the first principles, the deep fundamentals. In general, the chapters are written within these constraints. The form ranges from personal recollections to straightforward descriptions of current research programs. Most of the authors have valiantly attempted to tell their stories in acceptable scientific format: with precision, clarity, logic, dispassion, and, as instructed, devoid of hagiography. However, one cannot read very far in many of these chapters before detecting indications of deep respect and poorly suppressed affection for the person who played such an influential role in the scientific agenda and scientific careers of all of the contributors to this volume, as well as an untold number of its readers.

In this edited collection, based on the 21st Carnegie-Mellon Symposium on Cognition, held in May 1987, the story of Simon's impact on the field is told somewhat indirectly, through descriptions of current research by a collection of cognitive scientists, some of whom are former students, some of whom are current colleagues, some of whom are contemporaneous pioneers who have shared with Herb the challenge of laying the foundations and pushing the frontiers of cognitive science. The substance of the story centers on what we currently know about complex human information processing, and the subtheme is how we came to know it: "we" meaning the field at large, and "we" meaning the particular set of scientists whose work is presented here.

The chapters are organized into four sets having somewhat arbitrary and overlapping boundaries. The first set focuses on representation and constraint in complex processing. In the opening chapter, Stephen Kosslyn, Michael Sokolov, and Jack Chen utilize an information-processing analysis of the various subsystems comprising the visual perceptual system to describe the process that yields lateralization out of visual experience. They use ideas of hierarchical decomposibility, adaptive response, and computational modeling to describe the system and its developing lateralization. In the next chapter, Patricia Carpenter and Marcel Just present evidence for the role of working memory as a workspace that accumulates the partial results of the computation involved in language comprehension. They argue that the temporary storage of intermediate computational results occurs in many types of cognitive activity. In the third chapter, Kenneth Kotovsky and David Fallside describe a two-phase model of problem solving. They show that what transfers from one problem to another is knowledge of the move operator which reduces the duration of the first phase and allows a rapid solution. They further demonstrate the primacy of representation in controlling the amount of interproblem transfer they obtain with isomorphs of the Tower of Hanoi problem. Next Kevin Dunbar and David Klahr present an analysis of the development of scientific discovery processes based on the performance of children and adults as they attempt to learn the rules governing the operation of a complex device. They found that people searched in two problem spaces in trying to solve the problem; a space of hypotheses, and a space of experiments, and that children differed from adults in their ability to remember and use the results of previous experiments to evaluate hypotheses. George Miller provides an integrative overview of this first set of chapters in which he traces the intellectual roots of the respective work to some of Herbert Simon's early ideas, particularly those summarized in *The Sciences of the Artificial* (Simon, 1981). Some of the major roots he considers are simulation as a way of testing computational models, hardware-software separability, computational approaches to comprehension, the centrality of representation, and the importance of heuristic search.

The second set of chapters deals with expertise in human and artificial systems. Edward Feigenbaum opens his chapter with a personal recollection of the beginnings of Artificial Intelligence during the mid-1950s when he was a student of Herb Simon. He goes on to present an analysis of the evolving relationship between heuristic search and knowledge in the development of AI. He argues that the relation between search and knowledge (culminating in the development of expert systems), should be viewed not as a "tradeoff," but instead as a "precipitation of search by knowledge." In the second chapter of this section, Neil Charness presents the results of a series of studies on the development of expertise in the games of chess and bridge. He, too, emphasizes the interrelationship of knowledge and search and demonstrates the importance of knowledge for expert level performance in both games. He refers to chess as the "Drosophila" of cognition as he traces the development of the wealth of work on pattern-based expert performance in chess. Charness notes that much of this research had its origins in the work done in collaboration with William Chase and Herb Simon. The chapter by J. R. Hayes describes the use of protocol based analyses of writing behavior to both understand writing as a complex cognitive process, and—foreshadowing the next section of the book—to develop the knowledge base from which to improve writing instruction. In addition, he analyzes expert-novice differences in writing, and the role played by various types of knowledge in the writing task. The chapter by Ericsson and Staszewski presents an analysis of the cognitive mechanisms that account for expert memory performance. They focus on the role of retrieval structures in accounting for expert-level memory performances in domains as diverse as chess, mental calculation, restaurant order taking, as well as in the storing and retrieving of random digit strings.

The third set of chapters deals with instruction and skill acquisition. Jim Greeno extends the knowledge theme by considering "generative knowledge," or knowledge as a relation between an individual and the social or physical situation in which that individual's activity takes places. He argues that the analyses based on symbolic knowledge and computation that have been able to account for school tasks must be extended to allow for the more relational application of knowledge that occurs in "highly situated" tasks. Jill

Larkin describes a computer simulation that accounts for the use of perceptual information in what she terms "display based problem solving." She uses her model to account for the reduction in memory load that occurs in problems where displays representing the current state of the problem and changes in that state are applicable. John Anderson presents an analysis of the errors that students make while using intelligent tutors to learn LISP, Geometry, and Algebra. A finding common to all three areas is the preponderance of analogical errors, where the student incorrectly applies a procedure from a recent example. The errors are modeled in the production system language, PUPS, which yields a precise analysis of the specific types of errors. In the final chapter of this section, Robert Glaser examines the importance of knowledge acquisition for instructional theory and design. He discusses the instructional implications of the shift in emphasis to the role of knowledge in expertise and examines the behaviors that characterize effective learners.

The final set consists of just two papers. One is an autobiographical account by Simon, describing how heuristic search guided one scientist along the road to some important discoveries. The other chapter is by Allen Newell, who travelled together with Herb on many parts of the search, and who tackles the monumental task of "putting it all together" at several levels. Finally, Newell's epilogue speaks eloquently for itself.

The chapters in this volume are written with an enthusiasm and optimism that bespeaks a vigorous and healthy field. Although the canons of scientific communication suggest a sober tone, we are happy to say that it is really fun to be a cognitive scientist. Is such a sentiment out of place in a serious volume like this? Hardly. Why deny the basic motivations and satisfactions associated with the work to which we have devoted so much of our lives? Herb put the issue this way:

> Man is a problem-solving, skill-using, social animal. Once he has satisfied his hunger, two main kinds of experiences are significant to him. One of his deepest needs is to apply his skills, whatever they be, to challenging tasks—to feel the exhilaration of the well-struck ball or the well-solved problem. The other need is to find meaningful and warm relations with a few other human beings—to love and be loved, to share experience, to respect and be respected, to work in common tasks." (Simon, 1965, p. 110)

As editors, we would like to take the liberty of speaking on behalf of all of the contributors to this volume in thanking Herb Simon not only for setting the common task, but also for creating the context in which so many of us have found exhilaration, meaning, respect, friendship, and warmth.

## ACKNOWLEDGMENTS

Funding for the symposium on which this book is based was provided in part by a generous grant from the Memory and Cognitive Processes Program of the National Science Foundation (BSN-8620193). Betty Boal and Sandy Curry assisted us in the organization of the symposium and the production of this volume. We thank them both for their tireless and able efforts. Our wives, Pam and Avis, gave us both the encouragement to do this project and the time to enjoy it. We thank them for their patience and support.

*David Klahr*
*Kenneth Kotovsky*

## REFERENCES

Palmer, S. E., & Kimchi, R. (1986). The information processing approach to cognition. In T. J. Knapp & L. C. Robertson (Eds.), *Approaches to cognition: Contrasts and controversies.* Hillsdale, NJ: Lawrence Erlbaum Associates.

Simon, H. A. (1965). *The shape of automation for men and management.* New York: Harper & Row.

Simon, H. A. (1981). *The sciences of the artificial* (2nd Edition). Cambridge, MA: MIT Press.

# I

## REPRESENTATION AND CONSTRAINT IN COMPLEX PROCESSING

# 1

# The Lateralization of BRIAN: A Computational Theory and Model of Visual Hemispheric Specialization

Stephen M. Kosslyn    Michael A. Sokolov
*Harvard University*    *Massachusetts Institute of Technology*

Jack C. Chen
*Harvard University*

> It is to physiology that we must turn for an explanation of the limits of adaptation. (Simon, 1981)

At first glance, a chapter on cerebral lateralization may seem out of place in this book. After all, this book is a tribute to Herbert Simon, who is not best known for his interest in neuropsychology. However, this apparent incongruity illustrates why it is entirely appropriate to have this chapter in this volume: Perhaps the most remarkable aspect of Professor Simon's career has been the very far-reaching impact of his ideas. This chapter is a good illustration of how far some of those ideas have spread beyond his original interests. Powerful ideas have a tendency to do that, and the idea of thought as computation, the concept of hierarchical and nearly decomposable systems, the emphasis on the importance of the requirements of the task in shaping cognitive processing, and so on, are very powerful ideas. We hope to demonstrate not only the applicability of these ideas to neuropsychology, but the added deductive and inferential power they confer.

## INTRODUCTION

It has been known at least since the middle of the nineteenth century that the two halves of the brain are not equally important in all tasks (e.g., see Jackson, 1932/1874). There is no question that the left cerebral hemisphere typically has a special role in language production and comprehension (e.g., see Milner & Rasmussen, 1966). Similarly, there is good evidence that the right cerebral hemisphere typically has a special role in perception (see De Renzi,

3

1982). However, these broad generalizations almost exhaust the consensus in the field. More precise and detailed characterizations of hemispheric specialization have eluded theorists (e.g., see Bradshaw & Nettleton, 1981; Bryden, 1982; Springer & Deutsch, 1981).

Part of the reason that theory has not progressed rapidly in neuropsychology is that experiments often do not replicate (e.g., for a typical review see White, 1969). Indeed, the failure to replicate is so pervasive that it seems unlikely that it is due merely to sloppy experimentation (cf. Hardyck, 1983). At least some of the difficulty may lie in differences among the subjects who were tested. If there are widespread individual differences, then the fact that experiments typically have small numbers of subjects would contribute to the variability in the reported results (see De Renzi, 1982). This chapter explores a computational theory of individual differences in the hemispheric specialization of visual processing. Very straightforward computational ideas allow us to understand how the two hemispheres can be specialized in a wide variety of ways.

The first part of this chapter is an overview of a theory of the processing subsystems of high-level vision. Following Simon's lead, we believe that computational theories of function are as necessary in neuropsychology as in cognitive psychology proper. If one does not have a reasonably clear idea of what is being done, it is rather difficult to discuss how it is done differently in the two hemispheres. The second part of this chapter is an overview of a simple mechanism that will produce lateralization of the system outlined in the first part. This mechanism accounts for how experience can produce individual differences in lateralization, depending on a person's innate predispositions for processing; this mechanism has four free parameters, the values of which can presumably differ from individual to individual. The third part of the chapter describes a computer simulation of the lateralization mechanism operating on the visual subsystems. This simulation is called BRIAN, short for Bilateral Recognition and Imagery Adaptive Networks (for a detailed description, see Kosslyn, Flynn, Amsterdam, & Wang, in press). We summarize here the results of computer simulations that explore the impact of varied individual differences parameter values on lateralization. These results illustrate how different qualitative phenomena can arise from underlying quantitative variation. Finally, we conclude with an examination of the virtues and drawbacks of the present approach.

## HIGH-LEVEL VISION

The processes that underlie object recognition can be divided into two sorts, *low-level* (or early) and *high-level* (or late). Low-level visual processes are concerned with segregating figure from ground on the basis of properties of the sensory input; these processes detect edges, grow regions of homogeneous values, derive structure from motion, derive depth from disparities in the images striking the two eyes, and so on (see chap. 3 of Marr, 1982). High-level visual processes involve the access or use of previously stored information. As such, high-level processes are used in recognition, where input is entered into memory and compared with previously stored representations; high-level processes are also used in navigation and mental imagery, but we shall not dwell on these topics here (see Kosslyn, 1987).

In this section we briefly summarize a theory of some of the processing subsystems used in high-level vision. Each subsystem is dedicated to carrying out one part of the information processing necessary to perform object recognition (cf. chap. 7 of Simon, 1981). Space limitations prevent our providing the full rationale for this particular decomposition; Kosslyn et al. (in press) develop detailed justification for this decomposition and also provide additional discussion of various issues raised by the theory and approach. As discussed in Kosslyn et al., in developing the theory we began by developing a taxonomy of the fundamental functional characteristics of the human recognition system, and then tried to ensure that the theory and model are not in principle incapable of producing these behaviors. Furthermore, we tried to ensure that the theory is consistent with the structure of the machine whose function we are describing, namely the brain. That is, we used brain anatomy and physiology as motivation for the theory (see Kosslyn, 1987; Kosslyn et al., in press for additional details; see also Feldman, 1985, for a similar project predating this one). In any event, the thrust of this chapter is not to develop or defend the theory of subsystems. Rather, we introduce the subsystems here only to allow us later to consider how they are affected by the lateralization mechanism.

## SUBSYSTEMS
## OF HIGH-LEVEL VISUAL RECOGNITION

The theory of subsystems is cast at a relatively coarse level of analysis; it specifies the nature of the constituent processing units used in high-level object recognition. We delineate subsystems by describing *what* they compute; we do not attempt to characterize *how* the subsystems actually carry out these computations (cf. Marr, 1982). The subsystems we formulate are not offered as the ultimate primitive processing units. Rather, we hypothesize that they delineate correct boundaries of separate subsystems at a macro level of analysis (cf. Simon, 1981). We have adopted a strong "hierarchical decomposition" constraint: Further subdivision must respect the boundaries posited at this coarser level; we cannot later posit more fine-grained subsystems that cut across the boundaries of those we hypothesize here.[1]

---

[1]The theory of subsystems summarized here is a refinement of that described by Kosslyn (1987). The further developments obey the hierarchical decomposition constraint; for example, the shape categorizer described previously now corresponds to the three ventral subsystems.

## Two Major Systems: What versus Where

One of the most remarkable functional properties of the visual system is its ability to recognize objects from different vantage points. It now appears that we know important aspects of the neural mechanism that underlies our ability to recognize objects when they appear in different positions in the visual field (so that the image falls on different parts of the retina). The neurons that apparently represent object properties (i.e., shape, color, texture) have very large receptive fields, responding when the stimulus falls in a wide range of positions. That is, the shape recognition system seems to ignore the location of objects (within a large range), which allows it to generalize over a range of positions (see Gross & Mishkin, 1977). This solution to the problem of recognizing objects in different positions requires a second system to represent location, given that we do in fact know where an object is. And there is now good evidence that information about "what" and "where" is processed separately in the high-level vision system. For example, Ungerleider and Mishkin (1982) summarized much evidence for the existence of "two cortical visual systems." Figure 1.1 illustrates the ventral system, which apparently analyzes object properties, and the dorsal system, which apparently analyzes location (for a brief summary of data supporting this distinction, see Kosslyn, 1987).

## Input to High-level Recognition Subsystems

The input to the shape and location systems is the output from the low-level vision system. This output is represented as patterns of activation in a series of retinotopic maps (see Cowey, 1985; Feldman, 1984; Van Essen, 1985; Van Essen & Maunsell, 1983). These maps preserve (roughly) the local geometry of the planar projection of the visible surface of an object (but with greater area typically being allocated to the foveal regions). We conceive of the circumstriate maps as a single functional structure, which we call the *visual buffer.*

## Attention Window

There is much more information in the visual buffer than can be processed at once; thus, one must select only some information for further processing. We posit an *attention window* that selects a region of space (within the visual buffer) for further processing; the location and scope of the window apparently can be varied (cf. Cave & Kosslyn, in press; Larsen & Bundesen, 1978; Treisman & Gelade, 1980). The contents of the window are sent to the ventral system for shape recognition, and to the dorsal system for location representation. This claim is consistent with results reported by Moran and Desimone (1985), who found that cells in the ventral system (in areas V4 and IT) were inhibited when the trigger stimulus fell outside the region being attended to, although it still fell within the cell's receptive field.

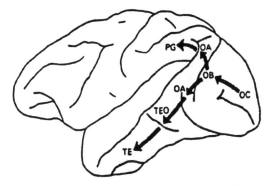

FIG. 1.1. The dorsal and ventral systems (modified from Mishkin, Ungerleider, & Macko, 1983). The inferior temporal lobe corresponds roughly to areas TE and TEO illustrated here. Reprinted by permission of author.

## Subsystems of the Ventral System

Kosslyn et al. (in press) argue that the ventral system can be decomposed into three types of subsystems, each of which is dedicated to performing a specific type of computation.

### Preprocessing

Objects must be recognized when they subtend different visual angles and are seen from different points of view. Lowe (1987a, 1987b) pointed out that some aspects of a stimulus (provided they are visible) remain invariant under translation, scale changes, and rotations. For example, parallel lines (representing parallel edges) remain roughly parallel, points at which lines meet are similarly preserved, and so on. The preprocessor highlights such invariant properties of the input and sends them to the pattern activation subsystem, where they serve as cues to access stored representations of shape.

### Pattern Activation

The information from the preprocessing subsystem is used to access stored representations of parts and global shapes of objects. A range of inputs will access the same representation, which allows the system to ignore irrelevant shape variations, such as those that occur when objects come in a variety of sizes and shapes (e.g., books, feet, or dinner forks).[2]

The cues from the preprocessing subsystem often may be sufficient to

---

[2]The pattern activation subsystem also can form an image by imposing a pattern into the visual buffer. This image generation process is useful in figure/ground segregation when an object is in a noisy environment (compare Cave and Kosslyn, in press, and Lowe, 1987a, 1987b).

activate a single shape representation, particularly if the object subtends a relatively small visual angle and is rigid (and hence does not vary from instance to instance).[3] However, such encodings may be insufficient if (a) the object subtends a relatively large visual angle, requiring multiple eye fixations to encode, or (b) the object is flexible, and hence its shape may not correspond to one stored in the pattern activation subsystem (e.g., a sleeping dog curled up oddly). In these cases, a more elaborate encoding process will be necessary, as will be discussed below.

### Feature Detection

Shape is not the only important property of objects, and some visual tasks do not involve encoding shapes into memory. Thus, there must be mechanisms that encode other properties of the input, such as color and texture. It is well known that brain damage can selectively disrupt color encoding without disrupting shape encoding per se; indeed, shape-color associations can be disrupted separately from color or shape encoding (e.g., see Benton, 1985).

### Subsystems in the Dorsal System

While an object's properties are being processed in the ventral system, its location is processed in the dorsal system. According to the Kosslyn et al. (in press) theory, this system has three major components.

### Spatiotopic Mapping

Locations in the visual buffer are specified relative to the retina, not space; such coordinates are useless for representing the locations of objects in space or the relative positions of parts of an object. This subsystem uses retinotopic position, eye position, head position, and body position to compute where an object or part is located in space. Andersen, Essick, and Siegel (1985) found cells in the inferior parietal lobule (part of the dorsal system) that respond selectively to location in space, gated by eye position; this finding is consistent with the inference that this structure is involved in computing spatiotopic coordinates.

### Categorical Relations Encoding

The spatial relations among objects or parts can be specified using categories, such as "connected to," "above," and so on. These kinds of categorical relations are useful for describing the spatial relations among parts of flexible objects, such as those of human figures; whereas the overall shape changes drastically, the nature of the parts and their connectivity does not change.

---

[3]When the attention window surrounds a multipart object, the spatial relations are implicit in the relative positions of the parts. In this case, then, both parts and (implicit) relations are encoded into the ventral system.

### Coordinate Relations Encoding

Although categorical representations are very useful for some problems, their virtues raise difficulties for others. For example, simply knowing that a given face has two eyes that are next to each other is not very useful because this is true of all faces. Similarly, two trees a specific distance apart near a bend in the trail may serve to define a landmark in the forest. For such stimuli, it is necessary to represent metric position information.

Because the two sorts of spatial representations are qualitatively distinct, we hypothesize that separate subsystems are dedicated to computing each type of representation. Whereas the categorical relations encoding subsystem assigns spatial relations between pairs of units into classes, the coordinate location encoding subsystem computes a representation of the locations of units in a coordinate space (which uses metric distances). Kosslyn (1987) summarized empirical support for this distinction.

## Multimodal Associative Memory

So far we have concentrated on two input streams, one encoding object properties and the other encoding location. At some point, these streams must come together. If a single object is being encoded over multiple fixations, the arrangement of its parts is critical (cf. Attneave, 1974). Thus, we posit an associative long-term memory, which plays several roles in object recognition (see Kosslyn et al., in press; also cf. Feldman, 1985). For present purposes, the most important role is in conjunction with another major system.

## Top-down Mechanisms

Because the fovea is so small, objects are often encoded over multiple eye movements. But how does one decide where to look next? It has long been argued that knowledge, belief, and expectation are used "top down" to drive sequences of attention shifts (e.g., see Gregory, 1970; Neisser, 1967, 1976). Particular cells in the parietal lobes seem to be involved in this top-down attention shifting process; these cells become active immediately before an attention shift, and do not become active if attention is not voluntarily shifted (e.g., see Lynch, Mountcastle, Talbot, & Yin, 1977; Yin & Mountcastle, 1977).

When a single object is being inspected, some object representations will be better satisfied by the input as shape and location information enter associative memory. These representations presumably become more highly activated. When a representation becomes more highly activated, the properties of the object become more easily accessed (indeed, this is almost definitional). Kosslyn et al. (in press) hypothesize that attention is then directed to the location of the most distinctive property of the most activated object. If the property is present, it will serve to further implicate the hypothesized object; if its weight is high enough, it may be sufficient to identify the object; otherwise, additional information must be sought in subsequent cycles. This sort of attention allocation involves moving the attention window to the specified location (as is discussed later) and priming the appropriate representation in the pattern activation subsystem, which biases it to access the stored representation that will confirm the hypothesis. This sort of priming is useful if one has a good guess about what one is seeing and wants to save time in making the match (it is also the basis of mental image formation, according to Kosslyn, 1987.

The hypothesis-testing process proposed here is necessarily serial at one level of analysis: The eyes and attention window can be moved to only one place in an image at any one point in time. However, it is not necessary that only a single part be encoded within the attention window. For example, if testing the hypothesis that one is seeing a dog, the entire head of the animal might be encoded as a single pattern. Alternatively, if testing whether one is viewing one's pet dog Sam, the snout, eyes, and ears might be encoded separately, affording higher-resolution encodings and more precise representation of spatial relations.

The following subsystems are posited to be used in top-down hypothesis testing. Although they do not compose a single subsystem at a coarser level of analysis (some are recruited in the service of other kinds of processing), it is convenient to group them together here.

### Coordinate Property Lookup

In order to test an hypothesis, one first must recall information about an object's properties. According to the Kosslyn et al. (in press) theory, several subsystems are involved in looking up distinctive properties of objects and their locations. We hypothesize a subsystem that accesses the names and locations of properties whose locations are specified in coordinates, which are useful for specifying the locations of parts of rigid objects (e.g., the mouth of the Mona Lisa is always in exactly the same place relative to the frame).

### Categorical Property Lookup

The coordinate property lookup subsystem has limited usefulness because many objects are not rigid. We also hypothesize a second lookup subsystem, which is specialized for looking up parts specified using categorical relations. Because such relations necessarily specify location relative to another part (e.g., the hand is "connected to" the wrist), one must locate the reference part in the image in order to know where to look for the hypothesized part.

### Categorical-Coordinate Conversion

Categorical relation representations are symbols that label a class of spatial relations; in order to use this sort of representation to direct attention, one must convert the categorical relation to a range of coordinates.

### Attention Shifting

Subsystems that actually shift one's attention must also exist. These subsystems not only reposition the attention window, but initiate eye, head, and body movements as appropriate (cf. Posner, Inhoff, Friedrich, & Cohen, 1985).

Finally, in order to test an hypothesis the expected properties must be compared with those subsequently encoded perceptually. Hence, when attention is properly located, a new perceptual unit is sent down the ventral system while its location is sent up the dorsal system. If this input corresponds to properties of the hypothesized object, one thereby has evidence in favor of the hypothesis being tested. If necessary, another property is then looked up and sought, and this cycle is repeated until the object's threshold is exceeded (i.e., enough "weights" accumulate from the encoded parts and relations; for details see Kosslyn et al., in press). (In addition, the threshold can be varied in different contexts, so that greater or lesser amounts of information are needed to decide that one is viewing a particular object. Similarly, when parts or relations that do not belong to an object are encoded, the threshold for that object can be raised.)

The subsystems and interconnections are illustrated in Fig. 1.2.

## MECHANISMS OF HEMISPHERIC DIFFERENTIATION

The mechanisms of lateralization proposed here are largely independent of the particular theory just described, but we need a theory of processing subsystems in order to test them; the results of our simulations apply to all theories of hierarchically organized subsystems with the properties described in this section.

One of the most striking properties of the brain is its plasticity. Indeed, even though roughly 95% of adults process speech in the left cerebral hemisphere (see Milner, & Rasumussen, 1966), if the left hemisphere is removed early enough during infancy (for medical reasons) the right hemisphere can assume language function. Although in these cases the right hemisphere does not become quite as proficient in language processing as the left typically does, it is remarkably able (see Dennis & Kohn, 1975; Dennis & Whitaker, 1976). Thus, it is plausible that even in normal brains there is considerable leeway in how functions become implemented in neural tissue. We have developed a theory of the way in which experience can contribute to individual differences in cerebral lateralization. This is a developmental theory, and is intended to describe events that take place during early childhood (cf. Annett, 1985; Kinsbourne & Hiscock, 1983; Lenneberg, 1967).

The present theory was initially proposed by Kosslyn (1987), who derived the mechanism from four macroproperties of the brain. The treatment here is slightly different, but captures the same principles discussed in the earlier paper. We now discuss the mechanisms in terms of three ideas. These ideas

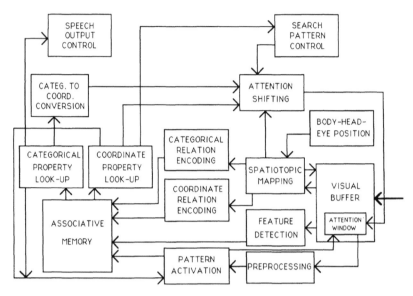

FIG. 1.2.    The subsystems hypothesized by the Kosslyn et al. theory.

lead to an account of how between-subjects variability in lateralization can arise.

## Adaptive Subsystems

We assume that each processing subsystem is capable of learning, if only the simplest sorts of improvement with practice. That is, we hypothesize that subsystems change with repeated use so that they more readily produce information that is utilized downstream. One possible mechanism that may allow subsystems to become so tuned is suggested by the neuroanatomy. A fundamental fact about the anatomy of the visual system is that, in all cases examined to date, every pair of visual areas that are connected by afferent pathways are also connected by efferent pathways (Van Essen, 1985; Van Essen & Maunsell, 1983). Indeed, the pathways running in each direction are typically of comparable size, which implies a rich exchange of information in both directions.

One role of the efferent pathways can be equated with a kind of training. This training allows the subsystem that received useful input to modify the sending subsystem so that it can produce this useful input more effectively in the future. More specifically, each subsystem is presumably implemented as a neural net (this must be true at some level of analysis), and such training would selectively alter the strength of the connections that were used to produce the output. If so, then it is clear why the pathways that feed back have such a broad bandwidth (cf. Hinton & Anderson, 1981; Rumelhart & McClelland, 1986). Training results in a subsystem's becoming selectively "stronger," which means it will produce the output faster and more reliably next time it is used in the same way.[4]

## Hemispheric Processing Inhibition

There is good evidence that information is less well processed when it has traversed from the other cerebral hemisphere. For example, it repeatedly has been found that shape-sensitive cells in the inferior temporal lobe respond more vigorously when the stimulus is presented in the contralateral visual field—and hence the information is delivered directly to that hemisphere—than when it is presented in the ipsilateral field—and hence the information must cross the commissures (particularly the corpus callosum) to reach the cell (e.g., see Gross, Rocha-Miranda, & Bender, 1972; Schwartz, Desimone, Albright, & Gross, 1984).

This result may reflect the allocation of attention over the two hemispheres. Holtzman and Gazzaniga (1982) presented evidence for this notion. They found that as more stimuli were stored in one hemisphere of a split-brain patient, fewer could be stored in the other hemisphere. This result is especially interesting because the hemispheres were completely isolated, and each had no knowledge of the information stored in the other hemisphere. This result makes sense if allocating attention to one hemisphere inhibits processing in the other (presumably via subcortical mechanisms); Hughes and Zimba (1985, 1987) presented evidence consistent with this notion (see also Kinsbourne, 1973, 1985; Moran & Desimone, 1985). This sort of allocation scheme would serve to minimize conflict when different information was being processed in the different hemispheres (e.g., as occurs when different stimuli fall in the two visual hemifields), and generally would minimize "cross talk" in this situation (Feldman, 1985).

The important idea is that when one hemisphere begins to process information before the other, processing is inhibited in the other hemisphere. This will apply not only to afferent input, moving downstream, but also to efferent information, providing feedback upstream. And here lies the heart of the mechanism that will differentiate the hemispheres: in this situation, training via feedback will not be as effective when it crosses to the other hemisphere. But under what circumstances will feedback originate in only a single side? Our third idea addresses this question.

---

[4]The present theory addresses only this one limited facet of learning; it does not address the questions of how representations are initially encoded, or how they are organized or reorganized.

### "Central" Bilateral Control

Each half of the brain typically controls the contralateral parts of the body. However, there are certain classes of activities that would best be directed by only a single hemisphere. These activities involve coordinating rapid sequences of precise, ordered operations that extend over both halves of the body. In these cases, each hemisphere cannot pursue its own agenda; a single set of commands is needed for both halves of the body. One possibility is that in such cases the commands are simply duplicated in each hemisphere, each copy being executed simultaneously. The problem here, however, is that it would be difficult to keep the subsystems synchronized across the two hemispheres. Another solution is to use only a single subsystem to control relatively rapid, ordered sequences of precise operations that are coordinated over both halves of the body. Kosslyn (1987) hypothesized that such "central" bilateral control subsystems are innately lateralized, which ensures that one locus will have control over both sides.[5] (For related ideas, see Gazzaniga & LeDoux, 1978; Geschwind, 1976; Kimura, 1976, 1977; Levy, 1969; Mateer, 1978; Nottebohm, 1970, 1979; Summers & Sharp, 1979; Sussman & Westbury, 1978; Zangwill, 1976.) However, although one side is innately dominant, if one hemisphere is removed at an early enough age, the nondominant analogous subsystem in the other hemisphere apparently is available to take over. We posit two such controllers, one for speech output control and one for bilateral search pattern control.

### Speech Output Control Subsystem

Speech is one example of a behavior consisting of precise, ordered operations coordinated over both halves of the body. Thus, we posit a unilateral speech output control subsystem. This claim is supported by much evidence, both from studies of brain-damaged persons and from studies of the suppression of activity during direct electrical stimulation of cortex. These studies demonstrate that the neurological area that controls speech output typically is on only one side of the brain (usually the left; e.g., see Benson, 1967; Mazzocchi & Vignolo, 1979; Naeser, Hayward, Laughlin, & Zatz, 1981). We assume that the speech output control subsystem is dominant on one side in children, but that residual capacity does exist on the other side (otherwise the plasticity evident following hemidecortication would not occur).

### Search Pattern Control Subsystem

The principle of central bilateral control also leads us to posit a unilateral search pattern control subsystem, which controls rapid search patterns that extend over both halves of space. This sort of visual search would be used

---

[5]Note that only the control subsystem is so localized; there are duplicate subsystems that actually perform the operations on each side of the body, which are treated as slave processes that are directed by the unilateral control subsystem.

whenever one is sampling without replacement over a scene, and would be used during navigation when one systematically examines the environment while one is moving. As was true in speech output, it again would be difficult to coordinate corresponding operations in the two sides of the brain. That is, a search pattern can extend over the midline, and hence be controlled by the contralateral hemisphere. As before, it is not effective if each hemisphere has its own agenda; one needs a single plan to search across the entire field. And again, as was true for speech control, it would be awkward to maintain tight synchronization between duplicate sets of instructions in the two hemispheres. The same argument offered previously leads us to hypothesize a single locus of control for rapid, coordinated programming of the "slave" subsystems that position attention in each hemisphere. (Note that this reasoning applies only to a rapid series of fixations; there is no reason why a number of different subsystems cannot program single shifts of attention; see Kosslyn, 1987, for more details on the argument and its implications.)

The claim that the right hemisphere has a special role in perception goes back at least to Jackson (1932/1874), and there is good evidence that damage to the right parietal lobe often disrupts search over both halves of space. However, it must be noted that the evidence for a right-sided unilateral locus for search pattern control is not as compelling as the evidence for a left-sided unilateral locus for speech output control (for a review of relevant evidence, see De Renzi, 1982).

## The Snowball Effect

We began with the idea that the subsystems adapt with "training" feedback, and then observed that feedback will be less effective when it crosses from a unilateral source to the other hemisphere. Given a unilateral source of feedback, then, these principles are sufficient to produce lateralization via a snowball effect. We explore this mechanism in depth is the following section, but let us illustrate the idea with a simple example: a baby making an utterance to express a thought (e.g., its wanting to be put down). Even a single-word utterance must be formed by sending instructions to the speech output control subsystem. Presumably, the concept is paired with a set of such instructions in associative memory. The categorical property lookup subsystem on the left side passes the instructions to the speech output control subsystem, as does the one on the right side (we assume that infants are of one mind in their to-be-expressed thoughts). The output from the lookup subsystem on the left side typically will not need to cross the callosum to reach the speech output control subsystem. But more important, when the control subsystem is used on the left side, it inhibits processing on the right side. Thus, feedback from the controller to the lookup subsystems will be less effective on the right side. And thus the lookup subsystem will be trained less effectively on the right side. With many trials, the categorical property lookup subsystem will become more effective on the left side.

And here begins the snowball: This subsystem will now fill the role of an innately unilateral subsystem. When in use it will inhibit processing on the other side, and hence the subsystems that feed it will in turn become better on the same side. And, subsystems that then feed these subsystems will in turn eventually become more efficient in the same hemisphere (for a similar idea, see Levine, 1982). This process will continue until plasticity decreases, and hence the subsystems will no longer exhibit large changes in effectiveness with practice (at about age 2 or so; cf. Lenneberg, 1967).

Thus, the lateralization mechanism rests on the ideas that (a) "central" control subsystems innately are biased to only one side; (b) processing subsystems that feed a control subsystem on the other side receive degraded feedback from the control subsystem (because processing in that hemisphere is inhibited); (c) thus, training is less effective than it is for the analogous subsystem on the same side; and (d) the subsystems that thereby come to be lateralized then serve as second-order seeds (in a catalytic sense), which provide more effective feedback to subsystems on the same side that provide them with input. This effect is compounded, percolating through the entire system until the subsystems become less mutable as the brain matures.

## LATERALIZATION SIMULATIONS

The implementation of the lateralization simulations is described in this section. Before reporting the results, we discuss the recognition tasks performed by BRIAN, the values of the four parameters that we expected to produce between-subjects variation, the feedback mechanism, and the measures of lateralization that were used.

### Simulated Tasks

The subsystems were implemented as separate procedures in object-oriented LISP, with each subsystem being duplicated (one in each hemisphere). Each subsystem was connected by data lines (also implemented as separate objects) to the analogous version on the other side and to the appropriate sending and receiving subsystems, as is illustrated in Fig. 1.2. Every feedforward line was accompanied by a feedback line (which is not illustrated in the figure). The visual buffer consisted of two arrays (16 × 16 pixels and 64 × 64 pixels), with parsed bitmaps (different letters being used for different parts) representing the input. The attention window was a 16 × 16 array that could be positioned over different parts of the visual buffer at high resolution, or over the entire buffer at low resolution. The contents of the attention window were sent to the preprocessing subsystem and then to the pattern activation subsystem while its location was being computed in the dorsal system, as described earlier. Kosslyn et al. (in press) provide details of the implementation.

In the experiments summarized here, the model performed two types of tasks, which tap different combinations of subsystems. The first task required BRIAN to answer the question "What is it?," to which it responded via the speech output control subsystem. In our simulations, the input was a picture of a sparrow, and the output was "It's a bird." We assume that the visual angle is so large that recognition of the bird cannot be achieved with confidence on the basis of the overall shape representation, and hence individual parts and relations are encoded. In the case of recognizing animals, categorical relations among the parts would be most useful (because they remain constant as the object assumes different postures and poses), and it is the categorical property lookup subsystem that feeds directly into the speech output control subsystem. Thus, we expected that—all other things being equal—this task would promote lateralization of categorical subsystems, and subsystems that feed them, to the same side as the dominant speech output control subsystem.

The second task required the model to answer the question "Do you know this person?," to which it responded by pressing (metaphorically speaking) a "yes" or "no" button. The input was a picture of a face, and we again assumed that the visual angle is so large that individual parts and the relations among them would be encoded during recognition. In this case, categorical relations are not useful, given that every face has two eyes "horizontally next to" each other, which are "above" the nose, and so on. Rather, the coordinate locations of the features are necessary to recognize a particular individual. In our model, the bottom-up processes lead to an initial categorization of the input as a face, and do not lead to an hypothesis about who it might be in particular. Thus, the search pattern control subsystem is invoked to direct a systematic search of the face. In order to scan over the proper region, the coordinate property lookup subsystem is used to access the size of the face being viewed; the size is encoded into associative memory via the coordinate relations encoding subsystem. Thus, we expected that—all other things being equal—this task would promote lateralization of coordinate subsystems, and subsystems that feed them, to the same side as the search pattern control subsystem.

The order in which the different subsystems are invoked in the two tasks is provided in Tables 1.1 and 1.2. As summarized earlier, this order is determined by logical prerequisites (e.g., the proprocessing subsystem produces the cues used by the pattern activation subsystem, spatiotopic mapping is necessary prior to computing spatial relations, and so on), and to some extent, information about the relevant neural pathways (see Kosslyn et al., in press, for additional details).

## Independent Variables

The present theory leads us to expect individual differences in lateralization to arise from four sources during early childhood:

TABLE 1.1
The Order in Which Subsystems Operate in the
Animal-Categorization Task

---

Visual Buffer
Preprocessing, Spatiotopic Mapping
Pattern Activation, Categorical Relations Encoding
Associative Memory
* Categorical Property Lookup
Categorical to Coordinate Conversion
Attention Shifting
Spatiotopic Mapping
Visual Buffer
Preprocessing, Spatiotopic Mapping
Pattern Activation, Categorical Relations Encoding
Associative Memory
[Return to * If Identification Threshold Not Reached]
Categorical Property Lookup
Speech Output Control

---

*Note.* Two names on the same line indicate parallel processing. The asterisk indicates where a loop begins if additional information must be encoded to reach threshold. The loop was not used in the present simulations.

### Innate Lateralization of Speech Output Control

We have been assuming that speech output control is completely lateralized to one side or the other. However, the argument for "central bilateral control" applies to individual behaviors; there is no reason why, in principle, one cannot have two controllers, with one sometimes in control and the other sometimes in control (for different utterances). Indeed, the plasticity evident in people who had one hemisphere removed early in life suggests that young children have (perhaps not equally effective) speech output control capacity in both hemispheres. Nevertheless, the data suggest that analogous left and right subsystems do not simply alternate control haphazardly. Rather, for the vast majority of people, the left-hemisphere speech output control subsystem is dominant, being used most of the time (however, there is also evidence that about 30% of left-handers have reversed laterality, with speech being produced in the right hemisphere; see Milner & Rasmussen, 1966). Furthermore, some people even have bilateral control of speech (interestingly, such people may stutter; see Jones, 1966). Thus, we posit a continuum of disparity in the innate "strengths" of left versus right speech output mechanisms, with most infants having a bias in favor of the left hemisphere (for further justification of this assumption, see Kosslyn, 1987).

### Innate Lateralization of Search Pattern Control

Similarly, we also posit a range of individual differences in the innate lateralization of the search pattern control subsystem. Although the relevant evidence is not conclusive, the literature suggests that a right-hemisphere bias for search control is not as pervasive as a left-hemisphere bias for speech output control. Hence, it is of particular interest to vary this parameter value in our computer simulations.

In our simulations, output bias and search bias each were specified as a number ranging from 0 to 100, representing (as a percentage) the probability that the left or right analogous control subsystem is dominant. Because the speech output control subsystem typically is innately dominant in the left hemisphere in humans, output bias is defined as the percentage of total speech outputs produced by the left speech output control subsystem. For example, if the output bias is 90, then the speech output control subsystem will operate with a probability of .9 on the left side, and with a probability of .1 on the right side. Conversely, the search pattern control subsystem presumably typically is dominant in the right hemisphere, and the search bias is thus defined as the percentage of total search patterns controlled by the right search pattern control subsystem. These biases determine how much more often the dominant control subsystem is used than its contralateral analog.

### Processing Inhibition

We also posit a processing inhibition parameter, which is relevant when attention is drawn to one hemisphere by a unilateral locus of activity. In this case, the active hemisphere inhibits processing in the other. Moran and Desimone (1985) found that attention to an object in one region inhibited the activity of extrastriate (visual) cortex cells to objects in other regions by an average factor of about .57. We assume that the amount of inhibition is

TABLE 1.2
The Order in Which Subsystems Operate in the
Face-Identification Task

| |
| --- |
| Visual Buffer |
| Preprocessing, Spatiotopic Mapping |
| Pattern Activation, Coordinate Relations Encoding |
| Associative Memory |
| * Coordinate Property Lookup |
| Search Pattern Control |
| Attention Shifting |
| Spatiotopic Mapping |
| Visual Buffer |
| Preprocessing, Spatiotopic Mapping |
| Pattern Activation, Coordinate Relations Encoding |
| Associative Memory |
| [Return to * If Identification Threshold Not Reached] |
| Response |

Note. Two names on the same line indicate parallel processing. The asterisk indicates where a loop begins if additional information must be encoded to reach threshold. The loop was not used in the present simulations.

an individual differences parameter, with values flanking this mean. Inhibition is defined to be a number between 1.0 and 0.0 (complete and none, respectively).

## The Relative Frequencies of Different Tasks

The relative frequency of experience with speech tasks and search tasks will affect how the system becomes lateralized. In the extreme case (e.g., a person who is blind, paralyzed from birth, and is forced to live in an iron lung), one may use the search pattern control subsystem infrequently if at all. In this case, tasks recruiting the speech output control subsystem might still arise relatively frequently, and this disparity in experience would presumably have a radical impact on how the system lateralized.

In sum, we examined three combinations of biases for the two control subsystems: 90/90, 90/10, and 50/50 (for speech and search, respectively). The first combination assumes that the left hemisphere controls speech output 90% of the time and the right hemisphere controls search patterns 90% of the time. However, the assumption that the right hemisphere is typically so specialized is not firmly established and thus we considered the case in which the left hemisphere simply is generally dominant, controlling both functions 90% of the time (the 90/10 case). Furthermore, as a baseline we considered the case in which each hemisphere controls both functions half the time (the 50/50 case). In addition, we combined these values with three values of inhibition: .75, .50, and .25, with greater inhibition acting to decrease the strength of feedback when it crosses to the other hemisphere. Finally, we combined these conditions with three task ratios: 1:1, 9:1, and 1:9, representing the relative frequencies of the two tasks.

## The Feedback Mechanism

Each subsystem sends training feedback to any subsystem that sends it information it uses. At each unit of simulated time, the subsystems that are active send feedback messages to all the subsystems that have just sent them interpretable information. The effect of training is equal to:

$$S' = S + (1-S)(1-I)(1-e^{-f})$$

where $S'$ is the new strength of the subsystem, $S$ is its current strength, $I$ is the amount of inhibition, and $f$ is the amount of feedback (equal to the strength of the subsystem providing training to this subsystem). Values of subsystem strength range from 0.0 to 1.0. Strength reflects the speed and accuracy of a subsystem when it is used, as well as the effectiveness of its outputs (both feedforward and feedback). The exponential function was chosen because it approximates the characteristic shape of a typical learning curve (note, however, that it is only an approximation to the correct function; see Mazur & Hastie, 1978). The strength of the feedback messages a subsystem sends is initially 0 for all except the control subsystems. As the snowball effect begins to take place, subsystem strength is adjusted by adding the increment from the feedback, modulated by the degree of inhibition, to the previous strength of the subsystem. Stronger subsystems will be more likely to win when outputs from different subsystems compete (e.g., for directing the attention shifting subsystem; see Kosslyn et al., in press).

In sum, feedback is used to train a subsystem, increasing its strength whenever it sends useful input to a subsystem downstream. The size of the increase in strength depends on the strength of the subsystem providing feedback, which hemisphere is more active, and the value of the inhibition parameter.

### Dependent Variable

We experimented with several different measures of lateralization and finally settled on the simplest: We defined the lateralization of a given subsystem to be the difference between its strength in the two hemispheres. Because the strength of a subsystem ranges from 0 to 1, lateralization ranges from -1 to 1, with negative values indicating that the subsystem has become stronger in the left hemisphere. This characterization initially seemed unsatisfactory because of the problem of scale. That is, the difference between .1 and .2 is in a sense more significant than the difference between .9 and 1; the former represents an increase of 100%, whereas the latter represents a change of merely 11%. However, on further reflection, we realized that this scaling effect was countered by the effect of the feedback function. The exponential feedback function implies that a strong subsystem requires a great deal of feedback to increase its strength still further, whereas a relatively weak subsystem will prosper when given even relatively meager reinforcement. Thus, the magnitude of the strength of the subsystem has already been normalized through the application of the feedback function.

In these preliminary investigations, we examine the system at the point when two subsystems achieved a strength of .9; two were chosen so that it was possible for one subsystem on each side to become maximally lateralized. (We assume that maturational changes actually dampen the snowball effect, but we have not tried to model such changes directly.)

### RESULTS

Let us begin by considering the left panel of Fig. 1.3, in which we examine mean lateralization. This is the standard measure of *hemisphericity*, in which one attempts to assess which hemisphere is generally dominant. As expected, the 90/10 bias case produced a general left-hemisphere dominance, and 90/90 bias produced left-hemisphere dominance when more animal-categorization tasks were performed, right-hemisphere dominance when more face-identification tasks were performed, and basically no overall lateralization for equal tasks ratios. In addition, the 50/50 bias produced essentially no lateralization. These effects were only moderately mitigated by the degree of inhibition.

The average asymmetry of all of the subsystems is a problematic measure in that if different subsystems are differently lateralized, their effects can cancel out. Thus, we also examined the absolute average asymmetry, ignoring the direction of the lateralization for each subsystem. Consider the corresponding absolute values in the middle panel of Fig. 1.3. it is clear that lateralization is in fact sensitive to the degree of inhibition in ways that are not intuitively obvious, as is evident by the crossing lines in the figure.

The right panel of Fig. 1.3 illustrates the number of tasks necessary before criterion (i.e., two subsystems with strengths of .9) was reached. This is an important measure because we do not know when the snowball effect stops. Presumably, the more tasks required to criterion, the less likely it is that strong lateralization will have occurred before the process ends. Note in the right panel of Fig. 1.3 that, in general, equal task ratios result in slower lateralization. Furthermore, the effects of variations in the degree of inhibition are greater with equal task ratios. In general, stronger inhibition results in faster lateralization in the 50/50 case, marginally faster lateralization in the 90/90 case, and has no effect in the 90/10 case. To the extent that bias promotes lateralization, the amount of inhibition is less important.

Much more insight can be gleaned from Fig. 1.4, which illustrates the lateralization of each subsystem in a variety of conditions. The white bars indicate the strengths of each subsystem, and the black bars indicate the difference between sides (i.e., the degree of lateralization itself). The combination of parameter values is noted below each bar graph. For example, in the leftmost panel of the top three displays of Fig. 1.4 we see what happened with 90/10 control biases, .75 inhibition, and 9 face-recognition tasks for every 1 animal-categorization task. Contrast this result with that illustrated in the rightmost panel of the top row, which had the same parameter values except that the search pattern control subsystem had a 90 bias on the right side. This one change was enough to lateralize all but one of the subsystems to the right side.

Both of these cases contrast with the center panel at the top of Fig. 1.4, which shows a distributed pattern of lateralization. The snowball effect operated as expected, lateralizing the categorical lookup and categorical encoding subsystems to the left and the coordinate lookup and coordinate encoding subsystems to the right; there was also weak lateralization of some other subsystems in ways that reflect quirks of the probablistic nature of the control subsystems. A very similar pattern arose when we changed only one

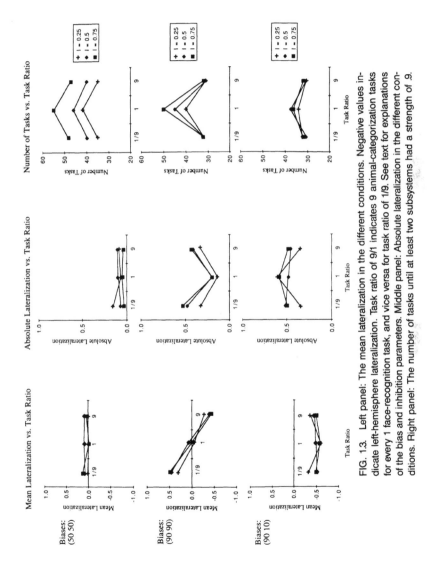

FIG. 1.3. Left panel: The mean lateralization in the different conditions. Negative values indicate left-hemisphere lateralization. Task ratio of 9/1 indicates 9 animal-categorization tasks for every 1 face-recognition task, and vice versa for task ratio of 1/9. See text for explanations of the bias and inhibition parameters. Middle panel: Absolute lateralization in the different conditions. Right panel: The number of tasks until at least two subsystems had a strength of .9.

Lateralization of Individual Subsystems
with Inhibition Model

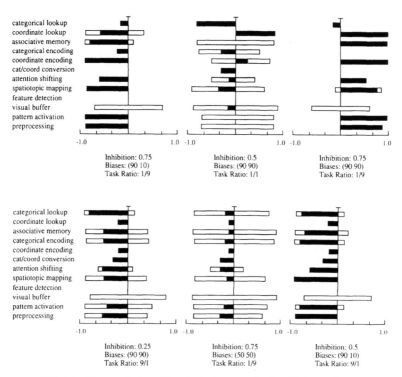

FIG. 1.4.   Some varieties of hemispheric specialization. Task ratio 9/1 indicates 9 animal-categorization tasks for every 1 face-recognition task, and vice versa for task ratio 1/9.

parameter value from those used in the condition for the rightmost display, using an equal task ratio.

The first important point illustrated by these figures is that the results are very different in the different conditions. Had we biased the speech output control subsystems to the right side (mimicking a reverse-lateralized left-hander), we would have produced mirror images of some of these results, further increasing the range of variation. Thus, if the present theory is even approximately correct, it is not surprising that there is so much variability in the literature.

The bottom row of Figure 1.4 illustrates some different patterns of essentially left-hemisphere specialization that can arise with different parameter values. Note that there are internal consistencies that cut across the various displays in Fig. 1.4, reflecting the operation of the snowball mechanism. As is evident, provided that no subsystem has reached saturation on both sides (i.e., .9 or greater possible strength, in our simulations) or has not lateralized at all, the preprocessing and pattern activation subsystems are always lateralized the same way, and so are the spatiotopic mapping and the attention shifting subsystems. Similarly, the categorical relations encoding and categorical property lookup subsystems typically are lateralized the same way (again, provided both are lateralized at all), and the coordinate relations encoding and coordinate property lookup subsystems typically are lateralized the same way. This underlying structure is a direct consequence of the operation of the snowball effect.

Note further that there are quantitative relations between subsystems in the degree of lateralization. For example, the pattern activation subsystem and the preprocessing subsystem tend to be lateralized to similar degrees, as do the spatiotopic mapping subsystem and the attention shifting subsystem. These preliminary results suggest that it may be possible to derive rules relating the quantitative degree of lateralization among the subsystems. If so, we will have very strong predictions to test empirically.

In short, armed with the theory behind the snowball effect, one should, in principle, be able to bring order to chaos. Unfortunately, previous work in the literature did not include tasks that allow us to sort out the contributions of the various subsystems, and hence new experimentation is required to test this theory.

## CONCLUSIONS

Consider the task of someone observing dozens of displays like those in Fig. 1.4, and trying to induce a theory of the regularities underlying them. This would be a difficult exercise. Now consider the task of someone who observes measures of left- and right-hemisphere performance in a variety of tasks, and tries to induce the underlying regularities. If one does not have a correct theory of subsystems, has no notion of a mechanism underlying how experience contributes to lateralization, is not aware of the existence of the key underlying parameters, and has no notion about the parameter values, this is probably a nearly impossible exercise. If the present theory is even approximately correct, it is no wonder that cerebral specialization is so poorly understood. The present results suggest that one must come to the situation armed with a theory not only of cognitive processing, but also with a theory of the mechanisms that underlie individual differences in hemispheric processing.

The present work is admittedly preliminary and exploratory. But even so, we believe that the computational approach has proven very useful. To summarize, the present observations have three straightforward implications for the study of laterality. First, rather than theorizing about left- and right-hemisphere specialization per se, one should ask about the lateralization of separate processing subsystems. Indeed, if we look only at mean lateralization, we might sometimes infer that there is no lateralization of function (e.g., when different types of tasks occur equally often, as in the left panel of Fig. 1.3), but looking at the lateralization of individual subsystems reveals a pattern of lateralization beneath the simple summary statement. Second, rather than drawing generalizations about the subsystems themselves (e.g., the categorical-coordinate conversion subsystem is stronger on one side), we have seen that one must also consider the values of several underlying parameters. Depending on these values, the system can become configured quite differently, not only in broad outline but also in the details of which subsystems are lateralized in which way and to what degree. Given the present results, attempts to characterize the functions of the hemispheres in terms of a dichotomy, or set of dichotomies, seem doomed to failure. Finally, even though lateralization can vary tremendously, there should be structure in how the system as a whole is lateralized. Thus, researchers should examine the fine-grained organization of subsystems, rather than simply characterizing the laterality of subsystems one at a time. Kosslyn (1987) described preliminary work in this direction, finding that subjects who were more strongly right-handed (which may reflect the speech output control subsystem bias) showed more extreme lateralization for the encoding of categorical versus coordinate spatial relations.

In summary, the following quote captures the essence of our project: ". . . both computer and brain, when engaged in thought, are adaptive systems, seeking to mold themselves to the shape of the task environment." This quote is, of course, from Herbert Simon (1981, p. 97).

## ACKNOWLEDGMENTS

This work was supported by ONR Contract N00014-85-K-0291. We thank John Daugman, Jerry Feldman, John Gabrieli, Lynn Hillger, and David Mumford for useful comments and criticisms. The editors also provided exceptionally constructive criticisms, and we are grateful for their careful and thoughtful reviews.

## REFERENCES

Andersen, R. A., Essick, G. K., & Siegel, R. M. (1985). Encoding of spatial location by posterior parietal neurons. *Science, 230,* 456–458.

Annett, J. (1985). *Left, right, hand and brain: The right shift theory.* Hillsdale, NJ: Lawrence Erlbaum Associates.

Attneave, F. (1974). How do you know? *American Psychologist, 29,* 493–499.

Benson, D. F. (1967). Fluency in aphasia: Correlation with radioactive scan localization, *Cortex, 3,* 373-394.

Benton, A. (1985). Visuoperceptual, visuospatial, and visuoconstructive disorders. In K. M. Heilman & E. Valenstein (Eds.), *Clinical Neuropsychology* (151-187). New York: Oxford University Press.

Bradshaw, J. L., & Nettleton, N. C. (1981). The nature of hemispheric specialization in man. *Behavioral and Brain Sciences, 4,* 51-91.

Bryden, M. P. (1982). *Laterality: Functional asymmetry in the intact brain.* New York: Academic Press.

Cave, K. R., & Kosslyn, S. M. (in press). Varieties of size-specific visual selection. *Journal of Experimental Psychology: General.*

Cowey, A. (1985). Aspects of cortical organization related to selective attention and selective impairments of visual perception: A tutorial review. In M. S. Posner & O. S. Marin (Eds.), *Attention and performance, XI.* Hillsdale, NJ: Lawrence Erlbaum Associates.

Dennis, M., & Kohn, B. (1975). Comprehension of syntax in infantile hemiplegics after cerebral hemidecortication: Left-hemisphere superiority. *Brain and Language, 2,* 472-482.

Dennis, M., & Whitaker, H. A. (1976). Language acquisition following hemidecortication: Linguistic superiority of the left over the right hemisphere. *Brain and Language, 3,* 404-433.

De Renzi, E. (1982). *Disorders of space exploration and cognition.* New York: Wiley.

De Renzi, E., & Faglioni, P. (1967). The relationship between visuo-spatial impairment and constructional apraxia. *Cortex, 3,* 327-342.

Feldman, J. A. (1985). Four frames suffice: A provisional model of vision and space. *Behavioral and Brain Sciences, 8,* 265-289.

Gazzaniga, M. S., & LeDoux, J. E. (1978). *The integrated mind.* New York: Plenum.

Geschwind, N. (1976). The apraxias: Neural mechanisms of disorders of learned movement. *American Scientist, 63,* 188-195.

Gregory, R. L. (1970). *The intelligent eye.* London: Weidenfeld & Nicholson.

Gross, C. G., & Mishkin, M. (1977). The neural basis of stimulus equivalence across retinal translation. In S. Harnad, R. Doty, J. Jaynes, L. Goldstein, & G. Krauthamer (Eds.), *Lateralization in the nervous system.* New York: Academic Press.

Gross, C. G., Rocha-Miranda, C. E., & Bender, D. B. (1972). Visual properties of neurons in inferotemporal cortex of the Macaque. *Journal of Neurophysiology, 35,* 96-111.

Hardyck, C. (1983). Seeing each other's points of view: Visual perceptual lateralization. In J. B. Hellige (Ed.), *Cerebral hemispheric asymmetry: Method, theory, and application.* New York: Praeger.

Hinton, G. E., & Anderson, J. A. (1981). *Parallel models of associative memory.* Hillsdale, NJ: Lawrence Erlbaum Associates.

Holtzman, J. D., & Gazzaniga, M. S. (1982). Dual task interactions due exclusively to limits in processing resources. *Science, 218,* 1325-1327.

Hughes, H. C., & Zimba, L. D. (1985). Spatial maps of directed visual attention. *Journal of Experimental Psychology: Human Perception and Performance, 11,* 409-430.

Hughes, H. C., & Zimba, L. D. (1987). Natural boundaries for the spatial spread of directed visual attention. *Neuropsychologia, 25,* 5-18.

Jackson, J. H. (1932). On the duality of the brain. In J. Taylor (Ed.), *Selected writings of John Hughlings Jackson.* London: Hodder & Stoughton. (Original work published 1874.)

Jones, R. K. (1966). Observations on stammering after localized cerebral injury. *Journal of Neurology, Neurosurgery and Psychiatry, 29,* 192-195.

Kimura, D. (1976). The neural basis of language qua gesture. In H. Whitaker & H. A. Whitaker (Eds.), *Studies in neurolinguistics* (Vol. 2). New York: Academic Press.

Kimura, D. (1977). Acquisition of a motor skill after left hemisphere damage. *Brain, 100,* 527-542.

Kinsbourne, M. (1973). The control of attention by interaction between the hemispheres. In S. Kornblum (Ed.), *Attention and performance, IV.* New York: Academic Press.

Kinsbourne, M. (1975). The mechanism of hemispheric control of the lateral gradient of attention. In P. M. A. Rabbitt & S. Dornic (Eds.), *Attention and performance, V.* New York: Academic Press.

Kinsbourne, M., & Hiscock, M. (1983). The normal and deviant development of functional lateralization of the brain. In P. Mussen, M. Haith, & J. Campos (Eds.), *Handbook of child psychology (4th Ed., Vol. 2).* New York: Wiley.

Kosslyn, S. M. (1987). Seeing and imagining in the cerebral hemispheres: A computational approach. *Psychological Review, 94,* 148–175.

Kosslyn, S. M., Flynn, R. A., Amsterdam, J. B., & Wang, G., (in press). Components of high-level vision: A cognitive neuroscience analysis and accounts of neurological syndromes. *Cognition.*

Larsen, A., & Bundesen, C. (1978). Size scaling in visual pattern recognition. *Journal of Experimental Psychology: Human Perception and Performance, 4,* 1–20.

Lenneberg, E. H. (1967). *Biological foundations of language.* New York: Wiley.

Levine, D. N. (1982). Visual agnosia in monkey and man. In D. J. Ingle, M. A. Goodale, & R. J. W. Mansfield (Eds.), *Analysis of visual behavior.* Cambridge, MA: MIT Press.

Levy, J. (1969). Possible basis for the evolution of lateral specialization of the human brain. *Nature, 224,* 614–615.

Lowe, D. G. (1987a). Three-dimensional object recognition from single two-dimensional images. *Artificial Intelligence, 31,* 355–395.

Lowe, D. G. (1987b). The viewpoint consistency constraint. *International Journal of Computer Vision, 1,* 57–72.

Lynch, J. C., Mountcastle, V. B., Talbot, W. H., & Yin, T. C. T. (1977). Parietal lobe mechanisms for directed visual attention. *Journal of Neurophysiology, 40,* 362–389.

Marr, D. (1982). *Vision.* San Francisco, CA: W. H. Freeman.

Mateer, C. (1978). Impairments of nonverbal oral movements after left hemisphere damage: A follow up of analysis of errors. *Brain and Language, 6,* 334–341.

Mazur, J. E., & Hastie, R. (1978). Learning as accumulation: A reexamination of the learning curve. *Psychological Bulletin, 85,* 1256–1274.

Mazzocchi, F., & Vignolo, L. A. (1979). Localisation of lesions in aphasia: Clinical-CT scan correlations in stroke patients. *Cortex, 15,* 627–654.

Milner, B., & Rasmussen, T. (1966). Evidence for bilateral speech representation in some non-right handers. *Transactions of the American Neurobiological Association, 91,* 306–308.

Mishkin, M., Ungerleider, L. G., & Macko, K. A. (1983). Object vision and spatial vision: Two cortical pathways. *Trends in Neurosciences, 6,* 414–417.

Moran, J., & Desimone, R. (1985). Selective attention gates visual processing in the extrastriate cortex. *Science, 229,* 782–784.

Naeser, M. A., Hayward, R. W., Laughlin, S. A., & Zatz, L. M. (1981). Quantitative CT scan studies in aphasia. I. Infarct size and CT numbers. *Brain and Language, 12,* 140–164.

Neisser, U. (1967). *Cognitive psychology.* New York: Appleton-Century-Crofts.

Neisser, U. (1976). *Cognition and reality.* San Francisco, CA: W. H. Freeman.

Nottebohm, F. (1970). Ontogeny of bird song. *Science, 167,* 950–956.

Nottebohm, F. (1979). Origins and mechanisms in the establishment of cerebral dominance. In M. S. Gazzaniga (Ed.), *Handbook of Behavioral Neurobiology (Vol. 2).* New York: Plenum.

Posner, M. I., Inhoff, A. W., Friedrich, F. J., & Cohen, A. (1985). *Isolating attentional systems: A cognitive-anatomical analysis.* Paper presented at the meetings of the Psychonomics Society, Boston, MA.

Rumelhart, D. E., & J. L. McClelland (Eds.). (1986). *Parallel distributed processing* (Vols. 1–2). Cambridge, MA: MIT Press.

Schwartz, E. L., Desimone, R., Albright, T. D., & Gross, C. G. (1984). Shape recognition and inferior temporal neurons. *Proceedings of the National Academy of Science USA, 80,* 5776–5778.

Simon, H. A. (1981). *The sciences of the artificial.* Cambridge, MA: MIT Press.

Springer, S. P., & Deutsch, G. (1981). *Left brain, right brain.* San Francisco, CA: W. H. Freeman.

Summers, J. J., & Sharp, C. A. (1979). Bilateral effects of concurrent verbal and spatial rehearsal on complex motor sequencing. *Neuropsychologia, 17,* 331–343.

Sussman, H. M., & Westbury, J. R. (1978). A laterality effect in isometric and isotonic labial tracking. *Journal of Speech and Hearing Research, 21,* 563–579.

Treisman, A. M., & Gelade, G. (1980). A feature integration theory of attention. *Cognitive Psychology, 12,* 97–136.

Ungerleider, L. G., & Mishkin, M. (1982). Two cortical visual systems. In D. J. Ingle, M. A. Goodale, & R. J. W. Mansfield (Eds.), *Analysis of visual behavior.* Cambridge, MA: MIT Press.

Van Essen, D. C. (1985). Functional organization of primate visual cortex. In A. Peters, & E. G. Jones (Eds.), *Cerebral cortex* (Vol. 3). New York: Plenum.

Van Essen, D. C., & Maunsell, J. H. R. (1983). Hierarchical organization and functional streams in visual cortex. *Trends in NeuroSciences, 6,* 370–375.

White, M. J. (1969). Laterality differences in perception: A review. *Psychological Bulletin, 72,* 387–405.

Yin, T. C. T., & Mountcastle, V. B. (1977). Visual input to the visuomotor mechanisms of the monkey's parietal lobe. *Science, 197,* 1381–1383.

Zangwill, O. (1976). Thought and the brain. *British Journal of Psychology, 67,* 301–314.

# 2

# The Role of Working Memory in Language Comprehension

Patricia A. Carpenter
Marcel A. Just
*Carnegie-Mellon University*

Much of what we think about flies past our consciousness, usually without us being aware of it. William James (1950/1890) said, "The mass of our thinking vanishes for ever, beyond hope of recovery, and psychology only gathers up a few of the crumbs that fall from the feast" (p. 276). This chapter deals with the site of that feast, namely, working memory. Even though the feast seemed inaccessible to James, recent studies of eye-fixations during complex thinking have begun to reveal some of the richness of the feast. These studies have revealed that considerable computation occurs during the 10 seconds that it takes to solve a simple analogy problem or during the 4 seconds that it takes to understand a sentence. The richness of the intermediate computations is evident in empirical measures of performance, as well as in the computer models that simulate the psychological processes. Computer simulation models of cognition have had to come to grips with the intermediate products of thought in order to generate the final products. Thus, simulation models have been forced to provide a tentative characterization of the organization of these computations in working memory.

Working memory plays a central role in all forms of complex thinking, such as reasoning, problem solving, and language comprehension. However, its necessity in language comprehension is especially evident. Because language processing must deal with a sequence of symbols that is produced and perceived over time, the temporary storage of information is an inherent part of comprehension. Working memory plays a central role in storing the partial and final products of our computations as we process a stream of words in a text, allowing us to mentally paste together ideas that are mentioned separately in the text or are only implied. This chapter examines how people comprehend language while simultaneously storing relevant information from the text. This focus treats working memory as a workspace that is used during comprehension and brings to light the purpose of working memory in the human processing architecture.

For the past 100 years, theories and research on working memory (or short-term memory, as it used to be called) have focused on the storage of information for retrieval after a brief interval. A familiar example used to illustrate the purpose of short-term memory is the storage of a telephone number between the time when it is looked up in a phone directory and the time when it is dialed. Short-term memory was typically conceptualized as a storage device, permitting a person to simply hold "items" until they were recalled. It was conceptualized and investigated in the context of retrieval, rather than in the context of performing a cognitive task such as reasoning, language understanding, or mental arithmetic. Another, related function attributed to short-term memory is its role as a stepping-stone on the path to long-term memory. In this view, short-term memory is the place where information is held while it is being memorized. Memorization might consist of rehearsal or some sort of elaboration, such as forming associations, chunks, or images. The studies of memorization and learning revealed a number of regularities concerning the capacity and nature of short-term memory. However, such studies had little to say about the role of short-term memory in other forms of cognition that are more computationally intensive. In any case, intentional memorization seldom occurs outside laboratories or formal study situations, so it is unlikely to have been the major purpose of short-term memory.

Then why did Mother Nature give us working memories, if we do not typically have to memorize unrelated items for either short or long periods of time? We argue that the major purpose of working memory is to provide temporary storage during thinking, such as the type of thinking that constitutes problem solving, planning, and language production and comprehension. In these tasks, the information that a person produces, or perceives, or uses is distributed over time. For example, in syllogistic reasoning, the premises are encountered one at a time and one of the major bottlenecks in the reasoning is in appropriately integrating the successive premises. In such tasks, successful performance requires actively considering more than one idea at a time. The activated elements that participate in the current stream of thought constitute working memory. These activated elements are the partial and final products of thought. They can originate from a perceptual encoding of an event in the outside world, or they can be a product of mental symbol manipulation. Thus, working memory is a computational arena or workspace, a proposal first made by Newell and Simon (1972).

An extreme view might hold that the driving force behind the evolution of working memory was the desirability of processing the seriality of speech, and that other forms of serial thinking evolved as a result of the increased working-memory capacity. It could be that language first evolved in those members of the species who happened to have larger working-memory capacities than the norm, because they could accommodate the sequences of distinguishable sounds (symbols) that the evolving articulatory system could produce. The adaptiveness of a larger working memory for holding the sequence in mind may have encouraged its continuing evolution. As a result of the larger working memory adapted to language, many other complex forms of thinking could have become possible, such as planning and problem solving. This proposal can also be stated in a much less extreme form, namely that working memory evolved in conjunction with the unrelenting seriality of all kinds of mental and physical events, including language. At any rate, the mental processes in reading comprehension can provide a window through which to examine the role of working memory in language comprehension.

The functioning of working memory in language comprehension brings into relief a different set of properties than those highlighted by tasks that involve little computation or that stress retrieval. It is in working memory that a reader stores the theme of the text he is reading, the representation of the situation to which it refers, the major propositions from preceding sentences, as well as a running, multilevel representation of the sentence he is currently reading. The storage and computational demands imposed by the reading of a text fluctuate from moment to moment, as a text introduces long-distance dependencies, digressions, or particularly demanding computations. In this regard, the management of information that occurs during comprehension may be paradigmatic of complex thinking, both of the linguistic and nonlinguistic type.

This chapter focuses on two aspects of working memory and comprehension. One focus of the chapter is on the transient computational and storage demands that typically arise during comprehension, and on the information management policies that attempt to satisfy those demands. We show how the component processes of comprehension operate within the constraints imposed by the limitations of working-memory resources. The organization of the comprehension processes tends to minimize storage requirements by minimizing the number of partial products that have to be stored. The minimization is accomplished by immediately digesting as much of the information from the text as possible (what we have called the immediacy of processing), rather than using a "wait-and-see" strategy.

A second focus is on the differences among individuals in their ability to maintain information in working memory during comprehension. We have found that such individual differences in working-memory capacity are closely related to large and stable individual differences in reading comprehension ability.

The chapter is organized into two main sections, which share both of these foci. In the first section, an overview of the role of working memory in comprehension from the computational framework of production systems is presented. In the second part, a number of recent studies that examine the trading relation between computation and storage in working memory during language comprehension are described. Although we analyze working memory in the context of language comprehension, we believe that this particular view reveals general properties of working memory.

## WORKING MEMORY FROM A COMPUTATIONAL VIEWPOINT

The main function of working memory is transient storage of partial results in the service of computation. This assumption underlies all computer simulation models of human thought that are cast as production systems, and it underlies our view of the human processing of language. The transient storage includes inputs, partial products, and final products to support the continuous flow of symbol manipulation in working memory. The distinction between partial and final products is not always sharp, because the information that is the final product of one computation may be the input or the partial product of another computation. The main function of working memory is not simple storage of inputs for subsequent retrieval.

When working memory is viewed as a computational arena, it becomes clear that its capacity should be construed not just as a storage capacity (perhaps measured in chunks), but as operational capacity, or throughput. By analogy, consider how the capacity of a hospital to perform surgery might be measured. Typically, we are interested in some measure of throughput, such as the number of surgical procedures of a given type that can be performed per day, rather than in a static measure, such as the number of surgical theatres. Of course, the surgical capacity of a hospital depends on what types of procedures are involved, what instrumentation is available, the skill of the surgeons and support personnel, and so on. So operational capacity must be specified in terms of the number of procedures of a given type per unit time, such as the number of appendectomies that can be performed per day. Similarly, any measure of working memory's operational capacity must take into account the nature of the information being processed and the nature of the operations that are being applied.

## Computational Assumptions of the Production System Approach

The nature of working memory is highlighted by computational models that provide a characterization of the intermediate products of comprehension. To illustrate how this approach characterizes working memory, we briefly describe the computational model of comprehension we have used, which is called READER. READER was designed to simulate a college student reading a short scientific text in order to summarize it. READER takes in the text from left to right, constructing the linguistic and referential representation as it goes. The time that READER spends on various parts of the text is proportional to the time that human readers spend, and the final recall or summary is similar to the ones generated by students. READER is a production system model derived from a family of production systems designed by Allen Newell and his colleagues (Forgy & McDermott, 1977; Newell, 1967; Newell & Simon, 1972). Consequently, many of the observations we make about the role of working memory in READER generalize to most other production systems.

Production systems are a particular kind of information-processing organization first advanced as a model of human thought by Newell and Simon (1972). In this type of model, procedural knowledge consists of a set of autonomous units called *productions*. Each production consists of a condition-action contingency that specifies what mental action is to be taken when a given information condition arises in working memory. Typically, the mental action of a production changes the contents of working memory, thereby enabling another production. For example, encoding the word *the* might enable a production that would add to working memory the knowledge that a noun phrase has been encountered. The knowledge that a noun phrase has been encountered might, in turn, enable another production that relates the new noun phrase to the rest of the syntactic structure of the sentence being read. All production systems share this basic organization, although there are interesting variations on the main theme (cf. Klahr, Langley, & Neches, 1987).

READER deviates in many important ways from conventional production systems. First, conventional production systems allow only one production to execute its actions on a given cycle; by contrast, READER allows all the productions whose conditions are satisfied to fire in parallel. Second, in conventional systems, elements are either present or absent from working memory; by contrast, in READER, elements can have varying degrees of activation. Thus the condition of a READER production specifies not just the presence of an element, but the minimum activation level (i.e., the threshold) at which the element satisfies the condition. Third, in conventional production systems, the productions create or delete elements in working memory. In READER, productions may also change the activation levels of elements by propagating activation from a condition element to an action element.

In the READER model, working memory consists of propositions whose activation levels are above a fixed threshold. Working memory elements can in effect be pointers to structures in long-term memory or they can be symbols that have been newly encoded or constructed during the process of thinking. The activation levels of the propositions affect their availability for various computations. A proposition is no longer part of working memory when its activation level falls below the threshold. In the nest section, we describe the relevance of these properties to the role of working memory in comprehension. A more detailed description of both the READER model and its production system environment (CAPS, for Concurrent, Activation-based Production System) can be found elsewhere (Just & Carpenter, 1987; Just & Thibadeau, 1984; Thibadeau, Just & Carpenter, 1982).

The same productions can fire reiteratively, over successive cycles, such that the activation levels of the output elements are successively incremented (or decremented) until they reach some threshold. Thus the symbolic manipulations occur not just as a one-shot firing, but a repeated action with cumulative effects. This regimen resembles that of a neural network, in which one unit can repeatedly activate or inhibit another. However, unlike some neural networks, CAPS permits dynamic connections between units (created by the relation between the condition and the action of a production). Also, the units can be pointers to arbitrarily large structures. Thus the flow of processing is under conventional production system control, but the nature of the processing consists to a large degree of propagation and accumulation of activation through a dynamically constructed network.

In the course of READER's processing of a text, its working memory accumulates information at several different levels of representation, such as the lexical, syntactic, and referential levels. Within a given level of representation, working memory provides the storage of elements whose onsets are separated in time but which must be processed as coarguments of some operation, such as a syntactic operation that relates the first word of a clause to the last word. Moreover, the multilevel representation of language in working memory provides a centralized repository in which information developed at one level of analysis (like the syntactic level) is available for potentially influencing another level (like the lexical level). This latter function is sometimes referred to as a blackboard model (Reddy, 1980), in which the metaphor for working memory is a shared blackboard on which different types of processes write their partial and final results and make them available to other processes.

## Capacity

As Newell and Simon (1972) pointed out, one of the attractions of production systems for modeling human thought is the potential correspondence between its working memory and human short-term memory. In most production system models that attempt to simulate human thought, including the READER model, the number of elements is very large, on the order of many tens of elements, and in some cases, hundreds of elements. In addition, each element can contain arbitrarily deep embeddings. In those production system models that make no pretense of cognitive simulation, the number of elements in working memory sometimes rises even higher, up to thousands of elements. To be sure, some of these large numbers occur because the modeler doesn't bother to clean up unneeded elements from working memory, and doesn't want to bother with the implementation of a forgetting mechanism, let alone a psychologically plausible forgetting mechanism. But even if unneeded elements were deleted from the working memory of existing models, the remaining number of elements would still be large. At least a few tens of elements in an activated state are needed to allow the computations to proceed. Contemporary cognitive simulation models typically attempt to describe a complex thought process that requires an orchestrated sequence of many computations. This kind of processing focuses on the necessity for storing many intermediate products and control information in working memory. Those few production system simulations whose knowledge elements have activation levels can make provision for decay of information from working memory by means of decrementing the elements' activation levels (e.g., Anderson, 1983). In general, however, computational models seldom take account of the type of capacity limitation of short-term memory described by Miller (1956) and incorporated into subsequent models of short-term memory (Atkinson & Shiffrin, 1968).

To illustrate the point in the case of language comprehension, consider the abbreviated description of the contents of READER's working memory (shown in Table 2.1) just after it has processed the simple four-word sentence: *Flywheels are mechanical devices.* The claim is that as a person reads and understands a complex sentence, there are many more than seven elements in working memory. Although the representation shown in Table 2.1 can be recast in many different ways, and the psychological reality of the propositions presented there cannot always be defended, both the numerosity of elements and the multiplicity of levels of representation would probably not change drastically under a different representation. Moreover, the numerosity of elements and multiplicity of levels probably characterize other forms of complex thought as well, such as problem solving and spatial thinking.

The READER model illustrates the fact that many elements must be activated during comprehension. However, the model does not provide an account of the constraints on working memory, except for the following. The slots that hold the words of a sentence are re-used for each successive sentence, so that the exact wording of a sentence is forgotten as the next sentence is read. This constraint on the storage of lexical information accounts for some of the human forgetting of exact wording that is discussed later in the chapter. An adequate model of the role of working memory in comprehension should specify the constraints that apply to all levels of comprehension.

Although complex thought requires transient storage of many symbols, nevertheless real limitations on our working memories do exist. We have only to try some mental arithmetic ($768 \times 536 = ?$) to experience the frustration caused by such limitations. The capacity limitations in short-term memory have been repeatedly demonstrated experimentally and characterized as a limit of approximately seven chunks (as first proposed by Miller, 1956, in his classic

TABLE 2.1
Some of the Propositions that Constitute the Representation of
the Sentence: *Flywheels are Mechanical Devices*

| Proposition | Processing Level |
| --- | --- |
| (WORD-1 :IS *flywheels*) | |
|     (WORD-1 :HAS *CONCEPT-1*) | lexical |
|     (*CONCEPT-1* :HAS REFERENT-1) | referential |
|         (REFERENT-1 :IS FLYWHEEL-1) | |
| (WORD-2 :IS *are*) | |
|     (WORD-2 :HAS CONCEPT-2) | lexical |
|     (WORD-2 :HAS SUBJECT-2) | syntactic |
|         (SUBJECT-2 :IS WORD-1) | |
|     (*CONCEPT-2* :IS CATEGORY-MEMBERSHIP-1) | |
|     (CATEGORY-MEMBERSHIP-1 :HAS SEMANTIC-SUBJECT-1) | semantic |
|         (SEMANTIC-SUBJECT-1 :IS FLYWHEEL-1) | |
| (WORD-3 :IS *mechanical*) | |
|     (WORD-3 :HAS ADJECTIVE'S-NOMINAL-3) | syntactic |
|         (ADJECTIVE'S-NOMINAL-3 :IS WORD-4) | |
| (WORD-4 :IS *devices*) | |
|     (WORD-4 :HAS *CONCEPT-4*) | lexical |
|     (WORD-4 :IS OBJECT-2) | |
|         (OBJECT-2 :HAS VERB-2) | syntactic |
|         (VERB-2 :IS WORD-2) | |
|     (WORD-4 :HAS REFERENT-4) | referential |
|         (REFERENT-4 :IS DEVICES-1) | |
|     (CATEGORY-MEMBERSHIP-1 :HAS SEMANTIC-OBJECT-1) | semantic |
|         (SEMANTIC-OBJECT-1 :IS DEVICES-1) | |

*Note.* Adapted from "A Model of the Time Course and Content of Reading" by R. Thibadeau, M. A. Just, & P. A. Carpenter, 1982, *Cognitive Science, 6,* Table 4, p. 173.

paper on the capacity of short-term memory). The theoretical problem raised by these limitations is to explain how people can reason, understand language, or solve problems in spite of these capacity limitations. A theory of working memory must describe the information management strategies (such as immediacy of comprehension) and the resource allocation policies that are invoked when the demand for working-memory resources outstrips the supply.

Conventional theories of short-term memory and theories of working memory differ not only in the capacities they attribute to the memory, but also in the stuff that is being stored. In a working memory, what is stored is not seven or five items, but a set of pointers that index relational datastructures. The relational structures can be quite large in some circumstances, and can be a part of long-term memory. In the course of performing some intellectual task, working memory holds *related* information that is sometimes configured as a network. The relatedness can be the result of prior association in long-term memory or the result of an integration performed by the ongoing computation. By contrast, short-term memory theories often focused on the storage of items that were unrelated to each other. Storing unrelated items is not the main purpose of working memory, although people occasionally do this sort of task, when they try to store a phone number or a short grocery list. Even then, they try to construct relations to help them remember the items. However, most of the time working memory stores the stuff of ongoing thought, which is generally a collection of interrelated concepts.

## The Need for Storage During Comprehension

Because language is a sequential communication channel, a reader or listener has to temporarily store early parts of the sequence in order to relate them to later parts. Consider the information a reader needs to process the following sentence: *A familiar example used to illustrate the function of short-term memory is the storage of a telephone number between the time when it is looked up in a phone directory and the time when it is dialed.* At the point of processing the phrase *is the storage,* the reader must keep in mind the noun phrase 9 words earlier that serves as the sentence subject *(a familiar example),* as well as information in the relative clause; the final pronoun *(it)* must be related to a referent that occurred 17 words earlier. As this example illustrates, ordinary prose, and particularly academic prose, imposes considerable storage demands. The demands can be increased further by interruptions, digressions, or long-distance dependencies. Furthermore, experimenters can add extraneous processing burdens by imposing additional demands, by requiring the reader to store some portions of the text verbatim, or to store some extraneous information, or to perform some additional task during comprehension.

This list of naturally occurring and laboratory events that can increase the need for storage during comprehension illustrates several points. The storage demands vary in the amount and kind of resources they require, they are imposed by a variety of sources, and they fluctuate from moment to moment. A theory of working memory must account for the way people rise to the challenge of such demands, or for the resulting difficulties when they fail to do so.

## Immediacy of Interpretation

The way that comprehenders deal with the sequential nature of language is to try to interpret each successive word of a text as soon as they encounter it, and integrate the new information with what they already know about the text and its subject matter. We have referred to this processing strategy as the *immediacy of interpretation.* A reader tries to digest each piece of the text as he encounters it (Just & Carpenter, 1980, 1987). The immediacy of interpretation entails many levels of comprehension: encoding the word, accessing its meaning, associating it with its referent, and determining its semantic and syntactic status in the sentence and the discourse. It is important to note that although the attempt at interpretation is immediate, the text can force postponement by withholding essential information. In such cases, the postponement is out of necessity rather than strategic choice. The default strategy is to interpret immediately.

The relation between immediate interpretation and working-memory capacity is straightforward. Immediate interpretation minimizes the storage of unanalyzed portions of text. The interpretive computations are applied as soon as the inputs are available. Low-level inputs (such as the shapes of individual words or phrases) generally do not have to be stored as a sequence of unrelated items while subsequent words and phrases are read. Instead, the interpreted representation is stored.

The immediacy of interpretation can be contrasted with a different strategy for dealing with the sequential nature of language, namely a wait-and-see strategy. A reader can always increase the probability of correctly interpreting a given word or phrase if she postpones interpreting it until she sees what follows in the sentence. Wait-and-see strategies have been proposed by several researchers (Kimball, 1973; Marcus, 1980). Comprehenders using the immediacy strategy still use the context that follows a piece of text to help interpret that piece, but they do so by elaborating or amending an already existing interpretation, rather than waiting for the context before making any interpretation.

The clearest evidence for the immediacy strategy is that the time spent looking at a word is strongly influenced by the characteristics of that word (e.g., Just & Carpenter, 1980; Carpenter & Just, 1983). The gaze duration on a word is directly related to the word's length (measured in number of letters), an effect we attribute to the encoding of the visual form of the word. Thus each word is encoded while it is being fixated. The gaze duration on a word is also related to the word's normative frequency in the language, an effect we attribute to the process of accessing the word's meaning in the mental lexicon (Just & Carpenter, 1987). Readers spend longer on a rare word like *sable* than on a common word like *table*. Thus the meaning of each word is being accessed while the word is being fixated. The downward slopes of the lines in Fig. 2.1 indicate the decrease in gaze duration with the logarithm of the word's frequency. Each of the lines in the figure corresponds to words of a particular length, and progression of lines (from bottom to top) indicates the increase in gaze duration with word length, independent of frequency.

Unusually long gaze durations can also be produced by words that present a difficulty because of their role in the syntax or semantics of a sentence. For example, a reader will pause longer on a semantically anomalous word compared to an appropriate word of comparable length and frequency; a reader will also pause longer on a word that requires a complex syntactic com-

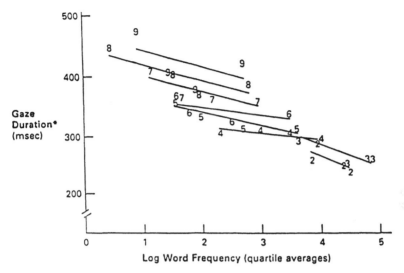

*Gaze duration averaged over fixated words only.

FIG. 2.1. The average time a reader spends looking at a word (in milliseconds), as a function of the logarithm of the word's frequency. More frequent words (those with a larger log frequency) are looked at for less time than less frequent words. The eight lines represent words of different lengths—words that are two letters long, three letters long, up to nine letters long. Each point represents the mean of a quartile of the words of that length. Word frequency has an effect on words of each length. Source: "What your eyes do while your mind is reading" by P. A. Carpenter & M. A. Just, 1983 (Fig. 17.2, p. 288). In K. Rayner (Ed.), *Eye movements in reading: Perceptual and language processing.* New York: Academic Press.

putation, compared to one that is syntactically less complex. These kinds of results indicate that the semantic and syntactic analyses of each word must be occurring while the word is being fixated. Thus the evidence indicates immediacy at several levels of interpretation, such as the lexical (Just & Carpenter, 1980; Just & Carpenter, 1983) syntactic (McDonald & Carpenter, 1981), and text levels (Dee-Lucas, Just, Carpenter, & Daneman, 1982). If a word introduces an increase in the processing load at any of these levels, there is an increased gaze duration on that word. All these results constitute strong support for the immediacy of interpretation. Thus the varying processing burden imposed by the successive words of a text is borne as soon as it is encountered. We show that this fluctuating computational burden draws on some of the same resources as the transient storage of information in working memory.

### Why Immediacy Works

There are two aspects of language use that minimize the costs and maximize the benefits of immediacy. The costs (such as making an incorrect interpretation) are low because it generally *is* possible to compute the correct interpretation of a word when it is first encountered. Wait-and-see proponents focus on contrived sentences presented without context, in which a reader has so little knowledge that he has no choice but to wait-and-see. However, normal context and normal sentences make it possible for the reader to develop strategies that succeed on an overwhelming proportion of the sentences people normally process. Readers use their knowledge of the context and their knowledge of relative frequencies of alternative interpretations in choosing the most likely interpretation. The benefit of immediacy is that it reduces the memory load of retaining information in an unprocessed form while waiting-and-seeing.

## TRADE-OFFS AMONG PROCESSES
## IN WORKING MEMORY

In the production system model of comprehension, working memory is the site at which productions collaborate and compete in calculating the intermediate and final products of comprehension. Although productions at many levels may be simultaneously involved in processing, there are some capacity limitations. Readers are usually not conscious of such limitations during normal comprehension. However, it is possible to construct a more demanding task, one in which comprehension processes must compete with other processes for working-memory resources. Baddeley and Hitch (1974) proposed that working memory was both a computational and a storage arena. They devised a number of tasks that indicated that the storage and processing capabilities of working memory tended to trade-off against each other, such that a large demand on one function would degrade performance on the other.

One such comprehension task was designed to require the reader to maintain an additional set of unrelated words in working memory while reading (Daneman & Carpenter, 1980). Readers normally maintain a great deal of information in an activated form while reading. However, the information that is activated during reading is maintained by virtue of its participation in the comprehension process. (In terms of the READER model, information is maintained by being acted upon by productions.) By contrast, maintaining even a small number of words in working memory that are extraneous to the text constitutes a considerable burden because their maintenance is not a natural outcome of normal processing. Rather, the subject must devise some extrinsic way of maintaining the items, such as rehearsing them.

Much of our research on the role of working memory in comprehension makes use of the reading span task developed by Daneman and Carpenter (1980). The task requires subjects to read a set of unrelated sentences and, at the end of the set, recall the final word of each sentence. For example, consider the following set of two sentences:

When at last his eyes opened, there was no gleam of triumph, no shade of *anger.*
The taxi turned up Michigan Avenue where they had a clear view of the *lake.*

After reading these two sentences, the subject was to recall the words *anger* and *lake.* Each subject was presented with sets containing from two to seven sentences, to determine the largest set size from which he could reliably recall all of the sentence-final words. The largest such set size was defined as his reading span. The rationale behind the test was that the comprehension processes used in reading the sentences would consume less of the working-memory resources of the better readers. This would leave the better readers with more capacity to store the sentence-final words.

This task has two important virtues. One virtue is that it measures performance when both the processing and storage capabilities of working memory are being used simultaneously. The second virtue is that the reading span assessed by this procedure provides an excellent index of an individual's reading comprehension ability, and consequently, is a useful psychometric instrument. By contrast, measures of passive short-term memory span, such as the ability to recall a list of digits or unrelated words, are not significantly correlated with reading comprehension performance.

The initial study demonstrated that skilled readers have greater working-memory capacity in reading than less skilled readers (Daneman & Carpenter, 1980). The greater capacity for computing and storing information may arise from a variety of sources, rather than a single one. For a good reader, many processes may be both faster and more automatic, including encoding, lexical access, and semantic and syntactic analysis. Working memory capacity is a property of the processing system that is the aggregate of several factors that could contribute to the individual differences in reading.

The reading spans of college students, which ranged from 2 to 5.5, were highly correlated with their reading comprehension test scores, with these correlations lying between 0.5 and 0.6 in various experiments. The correlation with reading span was even higher when specific comprehension abilities were considered individually. For example, the ability to answer a factual question about a passage was correlated between 0.7 and 0.9 with reading span in various studies. The correlation between conventional digit-span or word-span tests and reading comprehension was considerably lower, as it usually is.

A large working-memory capacity could facilitate particular facets of reading comprehension, such as interrelating facts that are referred to in separate sentences. Having a large working-memory capacity would permit a reader to store a greater number of recently processed propositions in an activated state. This would be an advantage whenever there was a need to relate a newly read proposition to another one earlier in the passage. To examine this hypothesis, college students read passages like the following one. Some of the passages contained a pronoun that had to be related to a referent that had been mentioned some number of sentences previously. The experiment manipulated the number of sentences that intervened between the mention of the referent and the pronoun.

Sitting with Richie, Archie, Walter and the rest of my gang in the Grill yesterday, I began to feel uneasy. Robbie had put a dime in the juke box. It was blaring one of the latest "Rock and Roll" favorites. I was studying, in horror, the reactions of my friends to the music. I was especially perturbed by the expression on my best friend's face. Wayne looked intense and was pounding the table furiously to the beat. Now, I like most of the things other teenager boys like. I like girls with soft blonde hair, girls with dark curly hair, in fact all girls. I like milkshakes, football games and beach parties. I like denim jeans, fancy T-shirts and sneakers. It is not that I dislike rock music but I think it is supposed to be fun and not taken too seriously. And here he was, "all shook up" and serious over the crazy music.

After reading the passage, the subjects were given comprehension questions, such as:

1. Who was "all shook up" and serious over the music?
2. Where was the gang sitting?
3. Who put money in the juke box?

Readers with larger reading spans were more accurate particularly at answering questions, like question 1, that interrogated the identity of a person referred to by a pronoun. That is, they were better at assigning the pronoun (such as the *he* in *and here he was, all shook up*) to the referent mentioned several sentences previously in the text *(Wayne looked intense and was pounding the table.)* More importantly, as shown in Fig. 2.2, the maximal distance across which a reader correctly assigned the pronoun was closely related to his reading span. Relating a pronoun to its referent is one type of integration process used in constructing a referential representation of the text. Readers with larger reading spans were better able to keep track of referential information. More generally, the conglomeration of processes that produces the larger reading span also produces a larger working-memory capacity that facilitates reading comprehension.

## Reading in the Span Task

Because the reading span test provides such a good index of reading ability, it is worthwhile to directly examine the reading behavior in the test itself, and

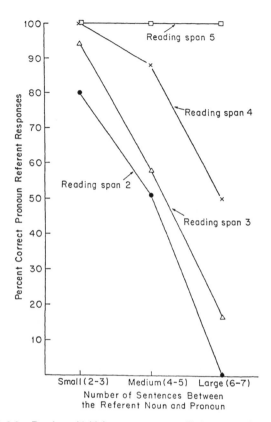

FIG. 2.2.    Readers with higher spans are more likely to correctly retrieve the pronoun's referent over a larger distance than readers with lower spans. The graph shows the percentage of correct responses as a function of the number of sentences intervening between a pronoun and its referent as a function of reading span. Source: "Individual differences in working memory and reading" by M. Daneman & P. A. Carpenter, 1980, *Journal of Verbal Learning and Verbal Behavior, 19,* Fig. 1, p. 456. Used with permission of Academic Press.

characterize the differences between subjects who are able to recall many words, typically four or five, and those who recall very few, typically two words. In particular, the eye fixation behavior has the potential of revealing which component processes of comprehension, such as word encoding or lexical access, distinguish among readers of differing spans and, by inference, differing levels of reading skill.

The procedure was similar to the usual administration of the span test. The subjects read a set of sentences aloud and tried to recall the final word of each sentence. To prevent the subjects from looking back at previously read sentences, the lines of display that he already read were removed from the display as he progressed down the screen. The number of sentences within a set varied from two to seven. A subject's span was the longest set in which he correctly recalled all the sentence-final words on at least 50% of the trials. The reading spans obtained in this study were 2, 3, or 4, with a mean of 2.9. Most of the analyses focus on the contrast between six low-span (2) and six high-span (4) subjects. The methodology involved intensive testing of these subjects, producing over 6,500 gaze durations.

### Eye Fixations in the Span Task

The general description of the eye fixation behavior was that the subjects read each sentence normally until they reached the last word of the sentence, at which time they tried to memorize that word. People with high spans read the sentences faster. The mean gaze duration on each word was 278 msec for the high-span subjects, and 355 msec for the low-span subjects. This result excludes the time on the final words in the sentences, where the subjects were memorizing as well as reading.

The findings of most interest were the individual differences in the way that word frequency modulated subjects' gaze durations, particularly when the subjects were reading while maintaining sentence-final words from previously read sentences. Most of the speed advantage of the high-span subjects came from faster lexical access rather than faster word encoding. This conclusion comes from the regression analysis relating gaze duration to word length and word frequency, for all but the final words in the sentences. The regression analysis produced very similar word length parameters for readers of all spans, but produced smaller word frequency parameters for readers with high spans. Specifically, the word frequency parameter (in msec per log unit of frequency) was 41 msec for the low-span subjects, and 28 msec for the high-span subjects. The word length parameter (in msec per letter) was 47 and 43 for the low and high groups respectively.

These results suggest that better readers read faster, partly because they can do lexical access faster, and they use their extra time for task-specific requirements. In this case, the task specific requirement is maintaining the storage of sentence-final words. The analyses reported further localized the effect of the load constituted by the sentence-final words on the reading of subsequent sentences.

Even though people with higher spans read faster, they spent more time on the sentence-final words. The mean gaze durations on the sentence-final words is 519 and 715 msec for the low and high-span subjects, respectively.

### Reading Under Load Versus No Load

While the first sentence of each screen is being read, there are no sentence-final words being stored. Thus the reading characteristics on the first sentence typify a normal no-load situation, in contrast to the reading of subsequent sentences. The interesting result is that the low-span subjects read very similarly under load and under no load, whereas the high-span subjects adapt to the load condition. In particular, the high-span subjects have a lower lexical access parameter under the load condition. The high-span subjects have a lexical access parameter of 38 (msec per log unit of frequency) on the first sentence on a screen (no load), but 22 on the remaining (load) sentences. The low-span subjects have similar parameters in the two situations (39 for the first sentence only, 48 for all the subsequent sentences). The upper left-hand panel of Fig. 2.3 shows the decrease in the lexical access parameter for the high-span subjects from the no-load to the load condition. The high and low span subjects differ reliably from each other in their lexical access parameters in the load condition ($F(3,5143) = 5.89$, $p < .01$, in a between-groups regression analysis in which the mean gaze durations for the two groups have been equated, and only the word-frequency parameters differ). By contrast, the two groups have similar word-frequency parameters in the no-load condition ($F(3,1400) = 1.17$, n.s.). The very same pattern of results (relating span to the word frequency parameter in load and no-load conditions of reading) was obtained in another study (described later), in which the sentence-final words constituted a sentence. The replication is shown in the upper right-hand panel of Fig. 2.3.

The effect of reading under load was selective, not just in which group of readers it affected, but also in the locus of the effect. Only the lexical access parameter, and not the word encoding parameter was affected by load. (Recall that the lexical access parameter relates gaze duration to word frequency, whereas the word encoding parameter relates gaze duration to word length.) As the lower panels of Fig. 2.3 show, the word encoding parameter remains approximately unchanged for both high- and low-span subjects under load or no load. The process of word encoding may be so automatic that it is not affected by the load imposed by storing a final word from a previous sentence. By contrast, the lexical access process does show the selective effect of load on the high-span subjects.

These results dovetail with the result previously reported, that a main difference between the high and the low span readers in the span task is in lexical access, with high-span subjects taking less time for it. During the reading of the first sentence only, a no-load situation, lexical access speed is similar for the high and low-span subjects. Thus the high-span subjects appear to change their reading under a memory load, such that lexical access takes less time. To be more precise, the relation between the word's frequency and its gaze duration is weakened under load. We interpret this result to indicate that high-span subjects activate less of the meaning of a word or activate the meaning to a lesser degree under load. This type of modification to "normal"

Replication 1                                      Replication 2

LEXICAL ACCESS PARAMETER

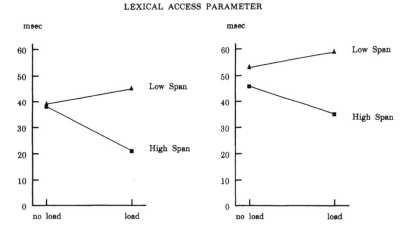

WORD ENCODING PARAMETER

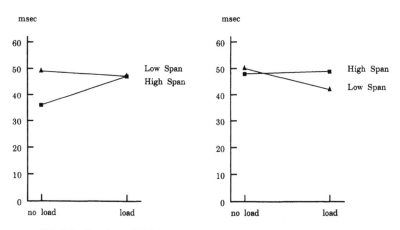

FIG. 2.3.   Readers with high spans show a lower lexical access parameter
(the top graphs) when reading with a memory load than readers with low
spans. By contrast, the word encoding parameter (the lower graphs) are
similar. Replication 1 represents data from the memory span task in which
the words were unrelated; replication 2 represents data from the memory
span task in which the words formed a sentence.

48

reading is similar to what we have observed in speed reading, during which the relation between word frequency and gaze duration is weakened more (see Just & Carpenter, 1987).

### Reading When the Sentence-Final Words Form a Sentence

Because it is generally easier to store and retrieve words that form a sentence, we constructed another form of the span task in which the sentence-final words formed a sentence. The following example illustrates how two sentence-final words form the sentence *Parcels arrived:*

I rushed to the door as the mailman approached and expected to receive several *parcels.*
A person resembling a poor clergyman or a poor actor *arrived.*

The right hand panels of Fig. 2.3. labeled *Replication 2,* present the data from the sentence condition. In general, this condition replicates the selective effect of memory load on the high-span subjects' lexical access time, and the lack of effect on their word encoding time.

The eye fixation behavior was generally similar in the two tasks. The overall reading rate was approximately the same (the mean gaze durations were 317 msec in the conventional task, and 344 msec in this new task, exclusive of sentence-final words). The subjects spent slightly less time on the sentence-final word (602 msec versus 565 msec) in the condition in which these words formed a sentence.

In passive memory span tasks, people can recall about seven unrelated words, but about twice as many if the words form a sentence. In this study, however, the mean recall of sentence-final words increased from 2.5 in the conventional reading span task to only 2.9 when the words formed a sentence. This slight increase in recall appears to have been purchased at the expense of a slightly slower reading speed during the reading of the sentences (excluding the time on the sentence-final word). It may be that the construction of the sentences formed by the sentence-final words (particularly the binding of the words to the syntactic structure) competes for some of the same resources as the parsing of the sentence that is being read.

The main result of this study is that the presence of a memory load affects only the lexical access process, not word encoding, and only for the high-span readers, not for low-span readers. This result reveals some of the detail of the trade-off between comprehension and storage when storage demand is manipulated, and pinpoints the flexibility of the better readers.

## The Trade-off Between Storage and Difficult Comprehension

Sentences can vary in many respects that affect how difficult they are to comprehend and this variation should affect the consumption of working-memory resources. Within the collection of stimulus sentences that are used in administering the reading span test, some sentences intuitively seem harder than others, because of a mixture of factors including vocabulary, syntax, the abstractness of the topic, and so on. Consistent with intuition, the reading speeds on the harder-looking sentences are generally slower than on easier-looking sentences (differing by a factor of almost two at the extremes of the distribution). Furthermore, the recall of sentence-final words on those sets of sentences that contain a particularly difficult sentence is often lower than on other sets. These informal observations relating judged sentence difficulty to reading speed and recall of sentence-final words support the view that more difficult sentences consume more processing resources, and hence leave fewer resources available for storage of sentence-final words.

In the experiment to be described later, we studied the trade-off between language processing and storage by systematically varying the number of difficult sentences in a set, and examining the resulting effect on the recall of sentence-final words. Because the previous experiment indicated that lexical access was a source of individual differences in reading comprehension, the words used in the difficult sentences were less frequent and less concrete. An example of an easy sentence was: I thought the gift would be a nice surprise, but he thought it was very strange. By contrast, an example of a difficult sentence was: The incorrigible child was reprimanded for his apathetic behavior toward the elders.

The kind of working memory we have proposed and installed in the READER model is of the blackboard variety, meaning that it is a site of interaction for processes from several levels—lexical, syntactic, semantic, and so on. Consequently, difficulties in comprehension at any level should manifest themselves in decreased storage capacity. In particular, we predicted that the comprehension of a difficult sentence in the reading span task should interfere with the ability to maintain the storage of sentence-final words from the preceding sentences in the set. The recall of sentence-final words should decrease as the number of difficult sentences in the set increases. However, these trade-offs are expected only when there is a competition for resources, that is, if the reader is operating at the limit of his working-memory capacity. For example, the presence of difficult sentences should be particularly damaging to a subject with a span of two when he is processing a set of three sentences. By contrast, difficult sentences should have no effect on a subject with a span of four when he is processing a set of two sentences.

The easy and hard stimulus sentences were combined into four different type of sets, varying in the number and location of difficult sentences that they contained. Some sets were composed exclusively of easy sentences and some exclusively of difficult sentences. There were also two intermediate conditions that contained only one difficult sentence, either in the second or in the last serial position of the set. The sentences were presented one at a time on a CRT. The subject controlled both when the sentence was initially presented and when it disappeared by pressing a button, thus providing a measure of the time taken to read each sentence.

Unlike previous studies, in which the criterion for measuring reading span entailed the comprehension of an uncontrolled mixture of hard and easy sentences, this study required a measure that took sentence difficulty into account. Each subject's span was defined here as the largest set of easy sentences for which he always recalled at least 80% of the sentence-final words. This criterion produced distributions of spans similar to those in earlier studies. After categorizing the subjects into high, medium, and low spans, we then examined their recall in sets of different sizes containing different numbers of difficult sentences.

The results confirmed that reading a difficult sentence did interfere with the ability to recall the sentence-final words of the set of sentences, involving the predicted interactions with individuals' span and the number of sentences in a set. Consider first the high-span subjects, particularly their recall of sets of four sentences, as shown in Fig. 2.4. In this situation, they are operating at the limit of their span. Their recall is best with sets that have no difficult sentences, and slightly impaired if a set of four sentences contains a difficult one among them. Their recall is substantially poorer if all four sentences in a set are difficult. In this case, their recall decreases to the level of set size 3. The increased processing burden imposed by the difficult sentences draws resources away from the task of retaining the set of sentence-final words. Although the high-span subjects are affected by the presence of difficult sentences in sets that push them to the limit of their span, they show no effect of sentence difficulty for sets below their span, producing a reliable interaction between the set size and the number of difficult sentences ($F(4,32)$ = 6.55, $p$ < .01). In situations in which they have working-memory capacity to spare, they use it to perform the additional processing without any consequence to their storage of sentence-final words.

Medium span subjects show interference effects for sets of length three and four, which are at or above their working-memory capacity. Their recall performance is poorer for sets composed of difficult sentences than sets composed of easier sentences. As with the high-span subjects, medium-span subjects show no interference effects for sets that are below their span, in this case, for sets of length two, producing a reliable interaction between the set size and the number of difficult sentences ($F(3,33)$ = 5.68, $p$ < .01). When they are operating below the limit of their span, the recall is the same irrespective of whether the sentences are all easy, have one difficult sentence, or are all difficult.

Finally, the low-span subjects show interference for sets of any length, because set sizes of 2, 3, or 4 are all either at or above their capacity. However, the effect is only marginally significant, $(F(3,21) = 2.36)$, perhaps because of a floor effect.

Thus, the experiment shows how language comprehension can interfere with storage, in a way that would be difficult to explain without the working-memory theory. It also demonstrates the clear differences among individuals and how the interference effects occur only when subjects are operating with sets that are at or above their working-memory span.

## Implications from the Span Task

Performance in the reading span task reflects the trade-off between computation and information maintenance in working memory, as well as providing a measure of differences among individuals in their working-memory capacity for language comprehension. The recent experiments provide a detailed account of the trade-off, indicating that it affects the different levels of comprehension selectively. The process of lexical access, the activation of a word's meaning, entered into the trade-off for high-span subjects who were reading under a memory load condition. By contrast, the process of encoding a word, recognizing the visual pattern it forms, did not enter into the trade-off, and always proceeded the same way, regardless of memory load.

The processing burden imposed by a difficult sentence manifests itself only if a subject is close to or above his span; otherwise, he has no need to trade away maintenance capacity to provide the additional computational resources required by a difficult sentence. Thus the effect of a difficult sentence is different for different readers, and is different for different memory load conditions.

The computations required to perform a complex but practiced task like language comprehension can be executed in the presence of other forms of thought, providing that both tasks together do not exceed the capacity of working memory. When competition for working-memory resources arises during language comprehension, more automatic comprehension processes appear to continue to execute without modification, while slightly higher level processes are modified to produce faster execution.

## SYNTACTIC ANALYSIS AND WORKING MEMORY

The reason that human language must have syntax is that a speaker can produce only one word at a time, so that an utterance must consist of a sequence of words. Syntactic organization allows us to build nonsequential grammatical structures out of a sequence of words. Even though an utterance must have a linear sequential structure, the underlying concepts are not linearly related

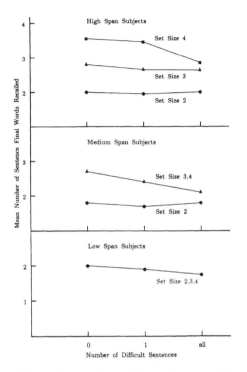

FIG. 2.4.   Readers show interference if the span contains difficult sentences
for set sizes that are at or above their span. The graph shows the number
of words recalled when there was 0, 1 or all difficult sentences in the set.
The high span subjects (the top graph) show interference with set size 4;
the medium span subjects (the middle graph) show interference with set
sizes 3 and 4; and the low span subjects (the lower graph) show interference
with all set sizes.

to each other, nor are the grammatical relations among the words strictly between adjacent words. Syntactic organization allows a sequence of words to
coalesce to form higher order constituents (phrases and clauses) that can bear
a variety of grammatical relations to each other. The syntactic organization
provides part of the temporary structure to organize the words until the
underlying concepts are understood. The coalescence occurs in working
memory, where the cumulating transient structure is held.

Syntactic processes help structure information so it can be held in working memory until the succeeding parts of the sentence are processed and while
other nonsyntactic processes are executed. If a series of words is unstructured,
readers have difficulty recalling even a small number of words that they have
read at a normal rate. Typically, a reader can recall no more than six or seven
unrelated words in order. Of course, a reader can understand and recall

sentences that are much longer than seven words because a sentence has an internal syntactic and semantic structure that helps circumvent this severe working-memory limitation. To measure the improvement in recall more precisely, we ran a simple experiment in which we asked subjects to read a single sentence aloud at a normal rate, and then immediately recall it (without access to the written version). The 18 stimulus sentences ranged in length from 8 to 22 words and in number of clauses from one to three.

The mean number of words recalled as a function of the number of words in the sentence is shown in Fig. 2.5. For sentences up to 20 words long, people recall a constant percentage of words (approximately 77%), with a lower percentage for 22-word sentences. The relatively constant proportion reflects the apparently paradoxical result that people can recall about 15 words of a 20-word sentence, but only about 8 words of a 10-word sentence. Of course, they spend approximately twice as much time reading the 20-word sentence, which accounts for some of the increased recall with sentence length.

The ability to recall a much larger number of words from a sentence than from a sequence of unrelated words suggests that the syntactic structure of a sentence provides a structure to which the words of a sentence can be bound during comprehension. This same structure can later provide a retrieval path at the time of recall. Thus the limitation in working memory applies particularly to information that cannot be interpreted, that is, cannot be bound to existing knowledge structures. So long as the binding that is the essence of normal comprehension occurs, about 77% of the words are stored well enough to be recalled. We do not know why the proportion of words recalled decreases at 22-word sentences, but it may be that the ends of sentences of such length are not being completely comprehended in the first place. It is plausible that the storage of the early part of such a long sentence consumes some of the resources necessary for the comprehension of the very late part.

Ericsson and Staszewski (chap. 9 in this volume; Ericsson, Chase, & Faloon, 1980) demonstrated the mnemonic power of binding isolated elements to a familiar structure. One of the most dramatic demonstrations of this power is the ability of college students to increase their recall for unrelated digits from 7 digits to almost 80 or 100 digits. These students, who happened to be runners, became skilled at relating sets of 3 and 4 digits to numbers that were already familiar, in their case, running times; then the running times would be linked to a hierarchical structure that enabled them to retrieve the items in the correct order. Memorizing a sequence of digits this way shares some properties of language comprehension, namely the circumvention of working-memory limitations by on-line binding of successive elements to a hierarchical knowledge structure. Of course, there are also some very important differences between the digit task and sentence comprehension. In the digit task, the knowledge structure to which the digits are bound is fairly inflexible and typically known before hand. By contrast, in sentence comprehension, the semantic and syntactic structure vary enormously from sentence to

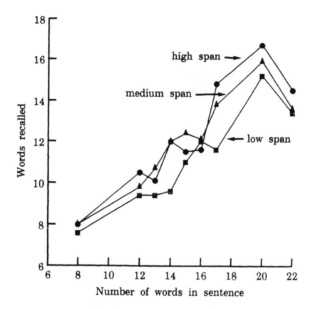

FIG. 2.5. Subjects are able to recall a large number of words that form a syntactically and semantically acceptable sentence. The graph shows the average number of words recalled as a function of the number of words in a sentence from 8 to 22 words, for subjects who tested as having low, medium, and high spans in the reading span task.

sentence, and they must be determined largely on the basis of the content of the input sequence of words. There is much more to comprehension than storage and retrieval.

The recall of words from single sentences also revealed small but systematic individual differences. The mean number of words recalled increased from low-, to medium-, to high-span subjects, with means of 11, 11.9, and 12.1, respectively. Thus, individual differences are found even if the recall is not in competition with comprehension, and even when the individual words form a meaningful sentence.

## The Working-Memory Load Imposed by Syntactic Processing

In this section, we consider not only how the presence of a syntactic structure can facilitate the storage of a sentence, but also how syntactic computations compete with the storage functions. In general, much of syntactic analysis in good readers appears to proceed without difficulty. Readers are seldom aware of syntactic difficulties during their processing of a well-written text.

However, the processing of certain unusual syntactic structures can tax working memory in a way that illuminates the trade-off between syntactic processing and working-memory storage in individuals of varying working-memory capacity.

One syntactic structure that has been studied extensively because of its unusual difficulty is a sentence with a center-embedded clause, such as the following: The salesman that the doctor met departed. Subjects who listen to sentences with a single center-embedded clause make errors in paraphrasing them about 15% of the time (Larkin & Burns, 1977). Errors rise to 58% (almost random pairing of nouns and verbs) if the sentence contains a double center-embedding, such as: The salesman that the doctor that the nurse despised met departed. Center-embedded sentences have been extensively studied precisely because they are one of the few structures that are genuinely difficult for a skilled adult to understand.

Several factors make center-embedded sentences difficult. First, the constituents of the outer clause (*the salesman* and *departed*) are interrupted by the embedded clause *(the doctor met),* so the reader must keep track of the initial noun phrase while he processes the embedded clause. The second factor is that *salesman* plays two different grammatical roles in the two clauses. *Salesman* is the grammatical subject of the main clause but the grammatical object of the embedded clause. Associating a single concept with two different syntactic roles *simultaneously* seems to be a source of difficulty (Bever, 1970). The difficulty does appear to be syntactic because the sentence is easier to comprehend if its structure is changed so that *salesman* is the grammatical subject of both clauses: The salesman that was met by the doctor departed.

One way to determine the nature of the processing difficulty is to compare the word-by-word processing time on center-embedded sentences with other types of sentences that share some of the same properties. For example, consider the following two sentences, the first of which contains a center-embedded clause, and the second contains a right-embedded clause:

Center embedded: The paper that the senator *attacked admitted the* error.

Right embedded: The paper that *attacked* the senator *admitted the* error.

In both sentence types, the embedded clause intervenes between the main subject and the main verb. However, in the right-embedding case, the main subject is also the subject of the relative clause, whereas it is the object of the relative clause in the case of the center-embedding. The sentences with center-embedding take longer to process, with the extra time being expended during the reading of the two verbs (Ford, 1983). The difficulty is probably attributable to the pairing up of the verbs and nouns that play different grammatical roles. The subject-verb pair of the outer clause is the same in both cases *(paper-admitted)*. But the process of putting this pair together is more difficult if *paper* has been playing the role of a grammatical object of the embedded clause in the meantime. The sheer memory load of retaining the first noun is not the problem. We know this because the word-by-word processing times increase only at the end of the embedded clause. Also, retention of the first noun in necessary in both center-embedded and right-embedded sentences, so that retention can't be the distinguishing problem. Thus, all the evidence points to the pairing process concurrently with the maintenance of the dual syntactic roles as the source of the difficulty.

In a more detailed examination of the parsing in these constructions, Jonathan King, a graduate student working in our laboratory, found that the difficulty is most severe for subjects with low working-memory spans, and that such subjects are particularly susceptible to interference from a concurrent memory load. The syntactic processing load imposed by center-embedded sentences was examined by pitting it against a memory load of 0, 3, or 5 digits that subjects were asked to store while they read the sentence. The sentences were read one word at a time in a self-paced "moving window" paradigm (Just, Carpenter, & Woolley, 1982), such that the subject had to press a button to enable the presentation of each succeeding word of a sentence. Only one word is displayed at a time, and the elapsed time during a word's display before the next button press indicates the subject's processing time on that word.

The readers with high spans tended to read faster and have less difficulty with center-embedding than those who were classified as having medium spans or low spans. Fig. 2.6 shows the time spent on reading each word of the center-embedded sentences in trials in which there were no extraneous digits to be stored during the reading. The high-span subjects had relatively little difficulty with the center-embedded sentences (or with right-embedded sentences, either). The medium- and low-span subjects, in contrast, took longer and showed noticeable elevations in reading times in the area that introduced the most complex syntactic computation.

The reading times on the center-embedded sentences were elevated particularly if the subjects were storing extraneous digits and if they were medium-span or low-span subjects. Moreover, the elevation occurred primarily on the critical verb. Figure 2.7 shows the results for the medium-span subjects, who present the clearest test of the proposal that storage resources compete with syntactic parsing resources, because the center-embedded sentences seem to lie at the limit of these subjects' normal processing capability. That is, the medium-span subjects have little difficulty processing the center-embedded sentences in the absence of an extraneous load, and their performance deteriorates as the extraneous load is increased. By contrast, the low-span subjects have difficulty with the center-embedded sentences even in the absence of an extraneous load, while the high-span subjects have little difficulty even in the presence of an extraneous load.

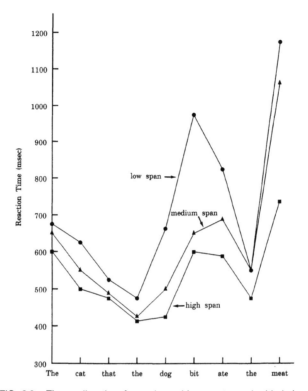

FIG. 2.6.  The reading time for each word in a center embedded clause
tends to peak at the verbs (as well as at the end of the sentence), indicating
that this is the locus of syntactic difficulty. The graph shows the reading
times when subjects were processing the sentences without any extraneous
memory load. The three graphs are for subjects who had tested as having
high, medium, and low spans in the reading span task. Low span subjects
have the longest reading time overall and show particular difficulty on the
verbs.

The variation in memory load makes its major impact on reading time
when the reader encounters the first verb, the first point in the sentence that
requires the difficult syntactic computations, as predicted by the immediacy
of interpretation. In the sample sentence used if Fig. 2.7, the first verb is *bit*.
The results also support the hypothesis that working-memory resources are
shared by many different kinds of processes. In this case, maintenance of the
digit load shares resources with the syntactic assignment process. Moreover,
the graded nature of the effect, from digit loads of 0 to 3 to 5, indicates some
degree of continuity of the sharing.

For the first time this study demonstrates that comprehension ability is
closely related to the ability to perform syntactic computations, and it links
this ability to storage and processing resources in working memory.

## THE NATURE OF WORKING MEMORY

In this section we describe what the computational approach tells us about the nature and capacity of working memory. Our claim is that this approach provides a different perspective on the nature of working memory than the older view that it is a passive buffer, with a capacity of seven chunks, whose primary role is information maintenance during learning.

### Working Memory as a Computational Arena

A major implication of the computational approach is that resources are shared among different component processes in performing a complex task, and that there are lawful trading relations among some of the processes that compete for resources. In particular, we have shown that lexical access and syntactic analysis are two of the comprehension processes whose resource needs can be traded away against the storage of information in working

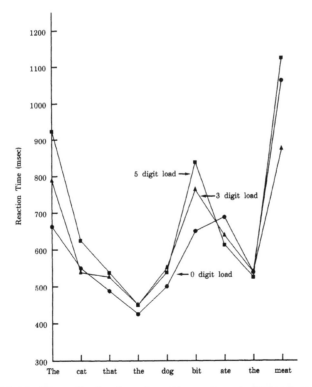

FIG. 2.7.   The reading time for each word in a center embedded sentence for medium span subjects with three memory loads: 0, 3, and 5 digits. The effect of the memory load is particularly apparent at the location of the verb.

memory. Symbol manipulation competes with symbol storage when capacity limitations are reached.

One of the important results is that there are systematic differences among individuals in their working-memory capacity for a given task. The trading relation came into play most clearly when readers' working memory was being taxed to capacity. Moreover, readers of different working-memory capacities begin to be taxed at different loads. The presence of difficult sentences in the reading span task affected the recall of sentence-final words only if the number of sentences in the set equaled or exceeded the subject's reading span. The experiments show that the trading function is different among individuals in at least two ways. The main result is that some subjects have a smaller pool within which to trade in this task. In other words, their working-memory capacity is small in the reading span task. The second result is that high-span subjects dynamically reallocate their resources in a task when an additional new demand is imposed. This result suggests the possibility that individual differences in working-memory capacity may be due in part to individual differences in the effectiveness with which working-memory resources are allocated. If this hypothesis is correct, it may be possible to modify working-memory capacity in some cases by telling subjects what allocation policy to use.

The trading functions are the manifestations of mental resource allocation policies, which indicate the resource pool within which the trades are made and the conditions under which resource allocations are changed. One small example of a resource allocation policy is the shift of resources away from lexical access among the high-span readers when sentence-final words have to be maintained in working memory. In this perspective, the trading functions indicate how people allocate their ability to think about more than one thing at a time. The competing "things" can be different component processes of a single complex task, or components of two different tasks.

Our new findings extend previous demonstrations of the effects of competition between processing and maintenance in working memory (Baddeley & Hitch, 1974; Baddeley, 1986; Case, 1985). Many of the Baddeley and Hitch studies showed that when memory load increases above some threshold, there are performance decrements on a concurrent task, such as the time to judge sentences as true or false. The current studies progress further by specifying the precise characteristics of the trading relation, that is, which language processes are traded off and which are not, the condition under which the trade-off occurs, and examining those processes that are sources of individual differences. These results tell us both about the nature of comprehension and about the nature of working memory.

## Readability and Working Memory

The experiments also provide a new perspective on text readability. The first atheoretical characterizations of text difficulty, such as the Flesch (1948) scale, attempted to predict readability in terms of a text's structural properties, such as the familiarity of the words and the lengths of the sentences. However, even if they have some predictive validity, such scales provide little insight into the psychological processes that are involved. The new perspective on readability gained from our considerations of working memory is that readability is not just a function of the difficulty of a given portion of text, but is also a function of how that difficultly impinges on the maintenance of other information. In other words, a difficult sentence can make a reader forget what he had previously read. In this perspective, an inherently difficult sentence should be more damaging to the comprehension of a text if it occurs at a time when the reader is storing lots of unfinished business (partial products).

Another recent insight is that anaphoric reference to a proposition that is no longer in an activated state in working memory decreases readability (Kintsch & Vipond, 1979). Kintsch and Vipond correctly predicted that a text that frequently referred to distantly mentioned topics would be more difficult to read. These two new considerations of the computational and storage requirements of comprehension help make readability a theoretically based measure of operational load rather than an inherent property of a text.

## Measuring Working Memory Capacity

Each of our reported experiments demonstrates that we can measure the relative working memory capacities of different subjects in a given domain. In this approach, working memory is measured in terms of operational capacity, rather than in terms of chunks of static storage. Working-memory capacity cannot be viewed as some general property of a fixed structure. Moreover, the operational approach suggests that there is no absolute measure of working-memory capacity; it can be measured only with respect to a set of mental operations in a given domain. In this view, it would not be surprising if working-memory capacity measured in one task was not predictive of performance in a different kind of task. Working-memory capacity will be specific to a particular person as well as specific to the processes in a particular domain.

Characterizing the resources of working memory in terms of operational capacity provides a new view of the benefits of chunking as it occurs during comprehension. It is well-known that if information has been organized into chunks, memory performance improves, decreasing the working-memory resources that are required for storage. But what about the use of the resources that perform the chunking? Chunking is not cost-free. The act of constructing a new chunk is time-consuming (Simon, 1974). The act of language comprehension can be viewed as recoding (chunking) an input string of symbols into an organized structure. If the chunking is particularly difficult, as is the case in the comprehension of center-embedded sentences, then it can create a competition for limited working-memory resources. We described how the comprehension of center-embedded sentences imposes a transient processing load at the point of a key syntactic computation (binding each of the noun–verb pairs that constitute a syntactic chunk). This result shows that chunking falls within the trading relation between working-memory storage and processing when the reader is performing at capacity. Chunking is an effective means to pack information into working memory, but it is effective only if there are working-memory resources available to do the packing. Working-memory capacity must be measured in terms of both chunks and the resources that are used to do the chunking.

The computational framework also highlights the fact that any complex task like language comprehension requires multiple levels of representation. Like READER, a human comprehender who encounters a given word of a text must have representations of letters, morphemes, the word pattern itself, the word-concept, the phrase and/or clause to which the word belongs, and a representation of the referential world. How can the multiplicity of levels be made congruent with the apparent limitation in capacity? The suggested resolution is that the limitation is specific to a particular level of representation. A person may only be able to hold a limited number of items at a particular level, but symbols from several levels can be stored simultaneously. This formulation is reminiscent of Miller's (1956) observations concerning the ability to make absolute judgments about a perceptual stimulus; as the number of varying dimensions of the stimuli increases, so does the performance, measured in information theoretic terms. To perform a complex task like language comprehension, the mind has evolved multiple overlapping and partially redundant levels of representation, increasing the total processing capacity.

## Levels of Processing and Their Time Course

The computational framework also provides a different perspective on the time course of different types of information in working memory. The time course of a given part of a representation may be determined by the computations that are being operated on it. The partial and final products of thought may persist only as long as they are being acted upon. Information that serves only as the input into an early computation may decay after serving its purpose.

The different types of information used in language comprehension, such as letter level, word level, or syntactic level, have different temporal profiles. They can differ in the time when they begin to become activated, when they actually reach the threshold state of activation, and how long they remain in the activated state. Not all levels have to be contemporaneously activated. The distinctive temporal profiles of the different levels means that they have different lifespans in working memory.

The main purpose of some of the earlier levels of representation is to enable a later level to operate (e.g., the letter level enables the word-percept). In at least two of the lower levels (word-percept, letter typecase), the evidence suggests that the representation is very brief, or if it persists, it does so at a low activation level. By contrast, memory for the higher-levels, such as the gist (the referential level), is long lasting.

### The Perceptual Level

The brevity of the representation of the typecase of a text has recently been demonstrated in an experiment that surreptitiously changed the case during a saccade that separated two successive fixations (McConkie & Zola, 1979). The typecase of a given word was sometimes changed while a reader made a saccade to see if he "remembered" it from one eye fixation to another. At all times the words of the text were composed of letters of alternating case (each letter was in a different case from the preceding letter). However, between some fixations, while the reader's eyes were in motion, the case of all the letters was changed from one state to the other. Each line of the example below shows how one line of the display looked during a given fixation, whose location and sequence number is indicated by the digits above the fixated text.

```
            1
    In ThE eStUaRiEs Of ThE fLoRiDa EvErGlAdEs ThE rEd MaNgRoVe
(case
change)              2
    iN tHe EsTuArIeS oF tHe FlOrIdA eVeRgLaDeS tHe ReD mAnGrOvE
                     3
    iN tHe EsTuArIeS oF tHe FlOrIdA eVeRgLaDeS tHe ReD mAnGrOvE
(case
change)                     4
    In ThE eStUaRiEs Of ThE fLoRiDa EvErGlAdEs ThE rEd MaNgRoVe
```

Changing the typecase of the letters between fixations produced no effect on the eye fixation behavior of a reader, neither on fixations nor on saccades. In fact, the display changes were not even visible nor detected. The lack of interference suggests that there is little memory for typecase from one fixation to the next. Once the word encoding processes have done their work, no other processes operate on the typecase information, hence it no longer needs to be maintained in working memory.

### The Lexical Level

The lexical level, namely the representation of the word meanings activated by the visual or auditory percept of a word, has a longer lifespan. Many word-percepts are associated with more than one word meaning; their relative lifespans are particularly distinguishable in the case of a homonymous word like *bank*. The word-percept activates both the intended and unintended meanings of *bank*. The unintended meanings of a word have a lifespan on the order of 300 msec. This result has been obtained in cross-modality priming experiments (Seidenberg, Tanenhaus, Leiman, & Bienkowski, 1982; Swinney, 1979). For example, during the comprehension of a sentence like *George went to withdraw some money from the bank last week*, the unintended meaning of *bank*, pertaining to the side of a river bed, is briefly activated. This lifespan of the unintended meaning provides a rough estimate of lexical activation that is not supported by other levels of processing. The unintended meaning does not enter into other levels of processing, and hence its representation is not maintained. By contrast, the intended meaning of a word remains activated for at least a second after the word has been encountered. The word meaning that receives collaborative activation from other sources becomes the selected interpretation of an ambiguous word. The main purpose of activating a word meaning during language comprehension is to enable higher level processes such as syntactic, semantic, and referential operations. The higher-level processes can prolong the life of a lower-level trace that would otherwise decay much sooner.

### The Syntactic Level

A seldom-cited point in a well-known article provides a useful insight into the time course of certain syntactic information (Jarvella, 1971). Jarvella's experiment examined how verbatim memory decays after a sentence boundary, by contrasting the recall of a target clause (e.g., *after he had returned to Manhattan*) when it was either part of the second-to-last sentence in a text (Condition A) or part of the last sentence (Condition B).

CONDITION A. Taylor did not reach a decision until *after he had returned to Manhattan.* He explained the offer to his wife.
CONDITION B. With this possibility, Taylor left the capital. *After he had returned to Manhattan,* he explained the offer to his wife.

As the subjects were processing the text, they were interrupted at the end of the second sentence, just after having been presented the word *wife*, and were asked to recall as much of the preceding text as they could. Recall of the last-processed clause *(he explained the offer to his wife)* was similarly high in Conditions A and B. The important data concerned the recall of the critical clause *(after he had returned to Manhattan)* that preceded the last-processed clause. Recall of this clause was much poorer when it was part of the preceding sentence (Condition A) than when it was part of the last sentence (Condition B). Moreover, recall dropped off abruptly at the sentence boundary, rather than gradually decreasing with the distance from the end of the sentence, providing evidence of the sharp decay of verbatim information at clause boundaries.

A seldom-cited aspect of Jarvella's study suggests that what drops off abruptly at clause boundaries is not just the knowledge of the words, but the knowledge of the word-order. In order to measure the recall of word order, Jarvella used a second, more strict scoring method that gave credit for recall of a word only if all the subsequent words were recalled in the correct order. Figure 2.8 contrasts the two scoring methods for Condition B, in which the critical clause was part of the last sentence. This strict scoring method shows that word order information from a previous clause drops off very sharply at the clause boundary. By contrast, the first, looser scoring method previously described shows that memory for the words themselves does not drop off as much at clause boundaries. The difference indicates that people have poor memory for the exact order of words in the preceding clause. Word order is a very important cue to syntactic analysis, and it may be that once the syntactic analysis has been done on a clause, the word order information is no longer retained. By contrast, while a clause is being processed, syntactic and semantic processes that relate the later words to earlier words help keep the precise words active, along with information that preserves word order.

There are several reasons why the exact wording of a preceding sentence or clause might be forgotten. One possibility is that after the syntactic analysis at the end of a clause has been performed, there may generally be little further need for retaining the exact wording information, and it may be intentionally purged. Another related possibility is that the syntactic computations that occur at the end of a major syntactic constituent are so demanding of resources that the exact wording information is displaced by the computations. Eye fixation studies consistently find an extra amount of time spent on the last word of a difficult sentence, and sometimes on the last word of a nonfinal clause (Just & Carpenter, 1980). We have attributed this extra time to wrap-up processing, tying up loose ends that have been unresolved until the end of the sentence. Some, but not all, of these loose ends are probably syntactic. The combined load of the leftover computations from several levels may cause forgetting of the exact wording information pertaining to syntax because of the computation-storage trade-off that we have described.

In this section, we have described how different types of information that are developed during the process of comprehension have different time courses in working memory. The time course of information in working memory may be a function of its participation in various component operations of comprehension. Thus, earlier levels of information (such as typecase) that do not directly contribute to the higher-levels of semantic and referential interpretation have a short lifespan. Similarly, the unselected meanings of ambiguous words persist for a relatively brief duration compared to the selected meanings of ambiguous words, because the latter meanings are acted upon by other productions involved in constructing the meaning of the text.

The idea that working memory serves as the arena for computations

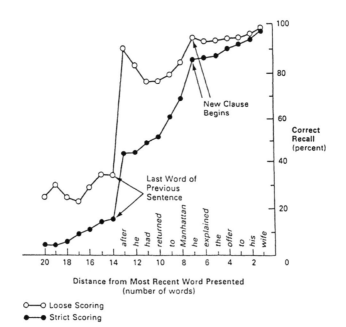

FIG. 2.8.   The contrast between two scoring methods suggest that memory for word order is responsible for some of the drastic decline at a sentence boundary. The graph contrasts the loose scoring criteria (open circles) in which any correct recall was credited with the strict scoring criteria (closed circles) in which words were only credited if subsequent words were in the correct order. Source: Adapted from "Syntactic processing of connected speech" by R. J. Jarvella, 1971, *Journal of Verbal Learning and Verbal Behavior,* Fig. 1, p. 411. Used with permission of Academic Press and the author.

that occur in the service of language processing provides a different perspective on the purpose, nature, and time source of representations. It becomes clear that the feast that William James described is an inherent part of any complex cognitive task and that working memory can be best understood when it is analyzed in the context of its role in such tasks.

## A FINAL NOTE

The approach to language comprehension taken in this chapter treats it as another part of the symbol manipulation that constitutes thought, rather than as a separate system. In most respects, the language processing we have described operates within the type of general cognitive architecture outlined by Herbert Simon and Allen Newell. To be sure, language processing has some distinctive characteristics, as does spatial processing or numerical processing. But they all function within a shared cognitive architecture, operating in coordination with each other. In many respects, language comprehension seems to provide a prototype rather than an exception to the way human thought relies on working memory. Language and working memory may have evolved together in the service of meaning transmission, and by so doing, may have provided some of the central resources of human thought.

## ACKNOWLEDGMENTS

This work was supported in part by contract number N00014-85-K-0584 from ONR, grant number MH-29617 from NIMH, and Research Scientist Development Awards MH-00661 and MH-00662 from NIMH.

We would like to thank both Ken Kotovsky and Dave Klahr for their valuable comments on an earlier version of the paper.

## REFERENCES

Anderson, J. R. (1983). *The architecture of cognition.* Cambridge, MA: Harvard University Press.

Atkinson, R. C., & Shiffrin, R. M. (1968). Human memory: A proposed system and its control processes. In K. W. Spence & J. T. Spence (Eds.), *The psychology of learning and motivation: Advances in research and theory* (Vol. 2). New York: Academic Press.

Baddeley, A. D. (1986). *Working memory.* New York: Oxford University Press.

Baddeley, A. D., & Hitch, G. (1974). Working memory. In G. H. Bower (Ed.), *The psychology of learning and motivation* (Vol. 8). New York: Academic Press.

Bever, T. G. (1970). The cognitive basis for linguistic structures. In J. R. Hayes (Ed.), *Cognition and the development of language.* New York: Wiley.

Carpenter, P. A., & Just, M. A. (1983). What your eyes do while your mind is reading. In K. Rayner (Ed.), *Eye movements in reading: Perceptual and language processing.* New York: Academic Press.

Case, R. (1985) *Intellectual development: Birth to adulthood.* Orlando, FL: Academic Press.

Daneman, M. & Carpenter, P. A. (1980). Individual differences in working memory and reading. *Journal of Verbal Learning and Verbal Behavior, 19,* 450–466.

Dee-Lucas, D., Just, M. A., Carpenter, P. A. & Daneman, M. (1982). What eye fixations tell us about the time course of text integration. In R. Groner & P. Fraisse (Eds.), *Cognitive processes and eye movements.* Amsterdam: Deutscher Verlag der Wissenschaften.

Ericsson, K. A., Chase, W. G., & Faloon, S. (1980). Acquisition of a memory skill. *Science, 208,* 1181–1182.

Flesch, R. F. (1948). A new readability yardstick. *Journal of Applied Psychology, 32,* 221–233.

Ford, M. (1983). A method for obtaining measures of local parsing complexity throughout sentences. *Journal of Verbal Learning and Verbal Behavior, 22,* 203–218.

Forgy, C., & McDermott, J. (1977). OPS: A domain-independent production system language. *Proceedings of the 5th International Joint Conference on Artificial Intelligence,* 933–939.

James, W. (1950). *The principles of psychology* (Vol. 1). New York: Dover. (Originally published by Henry Holt & Co. in 1890)

Jarvella, R. J. (1971). Syntactic processing of connected speech. *Journal of Verbal Learning and Verbal Behavior, 10,* 409–416.

Just, M. A., & Carpenter, P. A. (1980). A theory of reading: From eye fixations to comprehension. *Psychological Review, 87,* 329–354.

Just, M. A. & Carpenter, P. A. (1983). Reading skills and skilled reading in the comprehension of text. In H. Mandl, T. Trabasso, & N. Stein (Eds.), *Learning and comprehension of texts.* Hillsdale, NJ: Lawrence Erlbaum Associates.

Just, M. A., & Carpenter, P. A. (1987). *The psychology of reading and language comprehension.* Newton, MA: Allyn & Bacon.

Just, M. A., Carpenter, P. A., & Woolley, J. D. (1982). Paradigms and processes in reading comprehension. *Journal of Experimental Psychology: General, 111,* 228–238.

Just, M. A., & Thibadeau, R. H. (1984). Developing a computer model of reading times. In D. E. Kieras & M. A. Just (Eds.), *New methods in reading comprehension research.* Hillsdale, NJ: Lawrence Erlbaum Associates.

Kimball, J. P. (1973). Seven principles of surface structure parsing in natural language. *Cognition, 2,* 15–47.

Kintsch, W., & Vipond D. (1979). Reading comprehension and readability in educational practice and psychological theory. In L. G. Nilsson (Ed.), *Perspectives on memory research.* Hillsdale, NJ: Lawrence Erlbaum Associates.

Klahr, D., Langley, P., & Neches, R. (Eds.). (1987). *Production system models of learning and development.* Cambridge, MA: MIT Press.

Larkin, W., & Burns, D. (1977). Sentence comprehension and memory for embedded structure. *Memory & Cognition, 5,* 17–22.

Marcus, M. P. (1980) *A theory of syntactic recognition for natural language.* Cambridge, MA: MIT Press.

McConkie, G. W., & Zola, D. (1979). Is visual information integrated across successive fixations in reading? *Perception & Psychophysics, 25,* 221–224.

McDonald, J. L., & Carpenter, P. A. (1981). Simultaneous translation: Idiom interpretation and parsing heuristics. *Journal of Verbal Learning and Verbal Behavior, 20,* 231–247.

Miller, G. A. (1956). The magical number seven, plus or minus two: Some limits on our capacity for processing information. *Psychological Review, 63,* 81–97.

Newell, A. (1967). *Studies in problem solving: Subject 3 on the Crypt-Arithmetic task Donald + Gerald = Robert* (Technical Report). Pittsburgh: Carnegie Institute of Technology, Center for the Study of Information Processing.

Newell, A., & Simon, H. A. (1972). *Human problem solving.* Englewood Cliffs, NJ: Prentice-Hall.

Reddy, R. (1980). Machine models of speech perception. In R. A. Cole (Ed.), *Perception and production of fluent speech.* Hillsdale, NJ: Lawrence Erlbaum Associates.

Seidenberg, M. S., Tanenhaus, M. K., Leiman, J. M., & Bienkowski, M. (1982). Automatic access of the meanings of ambiguous words in context: Some limitations of knowledge-based processing. *Cognitive Psychology, 14,* 489–537.

Simon, H. A. (1974). How big is a chunk? *Science, 183,* 482–488.

Swinney, D. A. (1979). Lexical access during sentence comprehension: (Re)consideration of context effects. *Journal of Verbal Learning and Verbal Behavior, 18,* 645–659.

Thibideau, R., Just, M. A., & Carpenter, P. A. (1982). A model of the time course and content of reading. *Cognitive Science, 6,* 157–203.

# 3

## Representation and Transfer in Problem Solving

Kenneth Kotovsky
*Community College of Allegheny County*
*Carnegie-Mellon University*

David Fallside
*Carnegie-Mellon University*

The work reported here consists of two series of experiments that investigate the role of problem representation in transfer of skill from one problem to another. We first consider some previous work that resulted in the development of a two phase model of the problem solving process, and demonstrated the centrality of the problem move operator in the transition from the first to the second phase. Our first series of experiments is focused on the specific locus of transfer, and shows that transfer affects the learning of the move operator that normally takes place in the first phase of problem solving. A second series of experiments examines the relative influence of problem stimulus qualities and problem representation on transfer, and shows that representation is the controlling factor in transfer.

The investigation of the amount of transfer that is obtained in problem solving has been of great interest, both historically, (Judd, 1908; Katona, 1940; Ruger, 1910; Thorndike & Woodworth, 1901), and more recently as well, (Carver, 1986; Gentner, 1983; Gick & Holyoak, 1987; Hayes & Simon, 1977; Klahr & Carver, 1988; Papert, 1980; Singley & Anderson, 1985). The issue has been approached in recent work in a number of ways. It has been viewed as a task of finding and mapping higher-level analogies, (Gentner, 1983), a task of noticing problem similarity and abstracting a schema, (Gick & Holyoak, 1983), a task of mapping productions from source to target problem, (Gray & Orasanu, 1987; Kieras & Bovair, 1986), a task dependent on surface feature "remindings", (Ross, 1985), a task heavily influenced by problem difficulty, (Bhaskar & Simon, 1977; Hayes & Simon, 1977), a task involving interesting asymmetries in source and target problem transfer, (Bassock & Holyoak, in press), a task that is very sensitive to the amount of training on the source problem, (Smith, 1986), and a task that is dependent on move operator compatibility, (Kotovsky, Hayes, & Simon, 1985).

The attention that transfer has received is due not only to the theoretical issues surrounding transfer, but also to its practical importance. The pedagogical significance of transfer is that in many or most domains, the extent to which learning is generalizable (i.e., that positive transfer is attainable) is the extent to which learning is useful. Experimental and pedagogical experience suggests that it is hard (and often seemingly impossible) to teach/learn skills that are both specific enough to accomplish a given task, and general enough to be useful across the range of similar tasks the learner is likely to encounter. The importance of understanding transfer is thus based on both the richness of its theoretical conceptions and implications, and the practical importance of its utilization and control.

Given the value and importance of transfer, and the venerability of some of the inquiries into it, we might question the need to continue the investigation of such a basic phenomenon at this late date. We might reasonably expect that it would be a thoroughly understood phenomenon by now, a phenomenon that, at most, needs a cleaning up at the fringes. We take the position that there is still much to learn about transfer, and that our experiments demonstrate that to understand transfer we must first understand the effects of problem representation in both problem solving and transfer.

One embarrassment that any worker in the vineyard of problem solving faces is that of referencing work associated with one author, or more correctly perhaps, one pair of authors. It is sometimes hard to escape the belief that people will think you only had enough money for one book in 1972, or never did learn how to get past S in the author index of *Psychological Abstracts*. Modern research on problem solving is work on issues, and within conceptions, and utilizing research paradigms, that were generated by this symposium's honoree. Whether it is the idea of means-ends analysis, the task environment and problem search space, the importance of move operators, the use of verbal protocols, the value of computer simulation, and most importantly for the work we wish to discuss, the ideas of limited processing capacity and internal problem representation or problem space, (and thus the information processing approach in all its richness and fertility), the vintage is varietal Simon.

In their seminal book, *Human Problem Solving* (1972), Allan Newell and Herbert Simon introduced a theoretical framework for describing problem solving. Their theory describes problem solving as taking place in an external task environment with its associated objective search space. Out of the set of possible internal representations of that external task environment, the problem solver generates one (or more) problem spaces within which he or she operates. The problem space is the problem solver's internal representation of the problem. It includes the move operators together with the restrictions on their application (legality tests), and the set of knowledge states that he or she occupies on the way from start to goal. The examination of representational issues we undertake in this chapter builds on Newell and

Simon's concept of the problem space, and focuses on the internal representation as the determinant of transfer. The experiments we have done can only have been conceived and understood in the context of their approach. We would argue that the development of that approach was necessary before any reasonably complete understanding of transfer could be attained. Of course, the development of the "modern information processing approach" to problem solving has a rather direct relationship to the reason for the 1987 Carnegie Symposium; the honoring of the work of Herbert A. Simon. We turn now to a set of experiments that are an instantiation of that approach, and that form the immediate foundation for the new work we report here.

## EXPERIMENTAL BACKGROUND:
## PROBLEM DIFFICULTY

In 1974, Hayes and Simon published the first of a series of articles on isomorphs of the Tower of Hanoi problem. The large array of isomorphs they generated and investigated in that and later work consisted of problems that had the same problem search space as the three-disk Tower of Hanoi problem, the same number of move operators, the same starting position, and the same goal. A major class of such problems were termed *Monster* problems because they involved monsters passing globes back and forth, or changing the sizes of the globes they were holding. These two types of Monster problem were labelled the *Monster Move* and the *Monster Change* problems respectively. A major finding was that isomorphic problems could differ significantly in difficulty. In particular, they found that difficulty (solution time) ratios of 2:1 were obtained between Monster Change and Monster Move problems. Kotovsky, Hayes, and Simon (1985), extended the investigation to a broader array of problems, and obtained difficulty ratios of up to 16:1 for their hardest-easiest pair of problem isomorphs. Two findings that emerged from the latter work are the starting points for the research reported here. Those are: (a) the role of the move operator in determining problem difficulty and transfer, and (b) the discovery of a dichotomous pattern of moves as people moved through the problem space to reach a solution to the problem.

The problem search space[i] of most of the problems we used is identical to the problem search space of the problems used in the work of Kotovsky, Hayes, and Simon (1985), as well as the earlier work of Simon and Hayes (1976), and Hayes and Simon (1974, 1977). That search space is shown in Fig. 3.1 (after Nilsson, 1971).

The search space shown in Fig. 3.1 consists of 27 possible states joined

---

[i]Throughout the chapter we differentiate between the external problem search space and the internal representation by designating the former as the task environment or search space, and the latter as the problem space or representation.

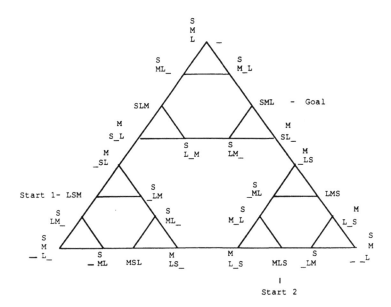

FIG. 3.1.    Problem search space. Tower of Hanoi isomorphs.

by links that represent legal moves. The labels on the states represent configurations of disks on pegs in the Tower of Hanoi problem, or configurations of globes held by monsters in the Monster problems. Each move involves transferring a disk from one peg to another. All but three of the states
have three possible legal moves associated with them. The three moves consist of a return to the previous state, or a move to one of two new states. The
three states from which only two legal moves are possible represent the cases
where all three disks are stacked on one peg. The different problems that share
this common problem space are defined by the internal problem representation including the move operators that define move legality. The internal
representation is engendered by either an external representation of important features of the problem such as the physical pegs and discs of the Tower
of Hanoi problem (Fig. 3.2), or a "cover story," such as the one that describes
the monsters and their globes in the Monster problems described in Table 3.1.

   One of the major findings to emerge from Kotovsky, Hayes, and Simon's
work was that problems differed greatly in difficulty. The hardest isomorph,
the Monster Change problem, took about 16 times longer to solve than the
easiest isomorph, the Tower of Hanoi problem. The differences in problem
difficulty were due to differences in the move operators. The more difficult
problems employed move operators that imposed more of a processing load.
The processing loads of the different move operators could be ranked in terms
of the number of entities (globes, monster loci) that had to be imaged in order

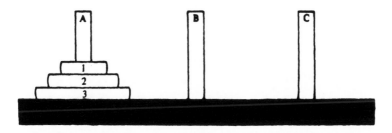

FIG. 3.2.   Tower of Hanoi problem. The goal is to move the three disks to the rightmost peg.

to test the legality of a move. This ranking was predictive of both the difficulty of making individual moves and also of overall problem difficulty. Thus, when subjects were asked to judge the legality of single moves that were presented tachistoscopically, their response latencies were correlated with the number of entities that had to be imaged in order to make the judgment. For example, in the Move problem, subjects' judgments were relatively fast when they compared the sizes of two globes held by the same monster, and relatively slow when they compared the sizes of two globes held by different monsters. An even harder comparison occurs in the Change problem where subjects had to imagine changing the size of a globe, and then test the imaged size against the size of another globe that was held by another monster. In that case, the imposed load was higher because of the need to imagine the size change together with the comparison at a distance. Hence there is evidence for a positive correlation between the processing load imposed by the move operators, operator application time, and problem difficulty.

Another major finding was that subjects' move making exhibited a surprisingly regular pattern. Their moves could be dichotomized into an initial, exploratory phase, and a subsequent "final path" phase. The exploratory moves were made slowly, they occupied the major phase of the problem solving time, and they were more difficult (took much longer) in the harder isomorphs. Furthermore, subjects were as far from the goal after making these moves as they were at the beginning of the problem. In contrast, the final path moves were relatively error free, were made very rapidly, were executed at a similar speed across all problem isomorphs, and led almost immediately to a problem solution. This dichotomous pattern of slow or difficult move making that made no net progress, and whose length reflected the relative difficulty of the problems, followed by a rapid dash to a solution in the last minute or so of the solution process, regardless of isomorph, was characteristic of a sizeable majority of the subjects. Thus, the exploratory moves seemed to bring the subjects to the point where they could move quickly and efficaciously towards a solution to the problem; that is, move along the final path.

This interpretation of the exploratory and final path phases provided a plausible link between move operator difficulty and problem difficulty. The issue was that although the processing load imposed by the move operators predicted the *ordering* of isomorph difficulty, the differences in move time were not great enough to account for the very large differences in problem solution time. For example, a relatively difficulty problem that subjects solved in an average of 15 moves might have a time-per-move that was 3 seconds longer than the time-per-move of an easier problem. However, instead of taking 45 seconds longer (the product of the number of moves and the time dif-

TABLE 3.1
Monster Problem Isomorphs: (a) The Rules for a Change Problem,
and (b) The Rules for a Move Problem

---

(a) Monster Change Problem

Three five-handed extra-terrestrial monsters were holding three crystal globes. Becausse of the quantum-mechanical peculiarities of their neighborhood, both monsters and globes come in exactly three sizes with no others permitted: small, medium, and large. The small monster was holding the medium-sized globe: the medium-sized monster was holding the large globe: and the large monster was holding the small globe. since this situation offended their keenly developed sense of symmetry, they proceeded to shrink and expand the globes so that each monster would have a globe proportionate to its own size.

Monster etiquette complicated the solution of the problem since it requires that:

1. only one globe may be changed at a time,

2. if two globes have the same size, only the globe held by the larger monster may be changed, and

3. a globe may not be changed to the same size as the globe of a larger monster.

By what sequence of changes could the monsters have solved this problem?

(b) Monster Move Problem

Three five-handed extra-terrestrial monsters were holding three crystal globes. Because of the quantum-mechanical peculiarities of their neighborhood, both monsters and globes come in exactly three sizes with no others permitted: small, medium, and large. The small monster was holding the large globe: the medium-sized monster was holding the small globe: and the large monster was holding the medium-sized globe. Since this situation offended their keenly developed sense of symmetry, they proceeded to transfer globes from one monster to another so that each monster would have a globe proportionate to its own size.

Monster etiquette complicated the solution of the problem since it requires that:

1. only one globe may be transferred at a time,

2. if a monster is holding two globes, only the larger of the two may be transferred, and

3. a globe may not be transferred to a monster who is holding a larger globe.

By what sequence of transfers could the monsters have solved this problem?

---

ferential), the harder problem actually took 10 or 15 minutes longer. To account for this discrepancy, the hypothesis was developed that move operator difficulty could prevent the planning of move sequences such as goal-subgoal pairs of moves, and that such planning is necessary for people to start the final path phase and solve the problem. To show that people do not solve the problem by randomly making moves, a random walk simulation was constructed and it used many more moves than the subjects in solving the problem. This was true even when the model was parameterized with the same bias against backtracking evidenced by human subjects. Furthermore, an information processing analysis of the load imposed in making goal-subgoal pairs of moves showed that the harder isomorphs, the Monster Change problems, imposed much higher memory loads than the Monster Move problems. The results of this analysis are presented in Table 3.2, in terms of the number of entities (globes, monster loci) that had to be simultaneously held in mind or imaged in order to make moves, or plan pairs of moves in the monster isomorphs. It can be seen that a move in the Monster Change problem always requires one more entity to be imaged than an equivalent move in the Monster Move problem. The direction of this difference is what would be expected from the pattern of move operator difficulties found for individual moves in the various isomorphs. Planning pairs of moves simply magnified the effects.

To test the hypothesis that subjects were planning their moves during the final path phase, the move latencies of the final path moves were analyzed for evidence of subgoal-goal pairs of moves.[2] The analysis indicated that the subjects solved these five-move-minimum path problems in two rapid sequences of moves. One sequence advanced them to within three moves of the goal, and a second sequence advanced them to the goal. The evidence for these distinct sequences were the patterns of move latencies, which were long-short and long-short-short. This is what we would expect if the subject attained the ability to plan and execute a subgoal-goal move pair, as contrasted with the pattern if they made individual moves, or planned and executed all five final path moves as a compiled whole. The long-short pattern of move latencies is presumably due to a planning-plus-move step, followed by a move step. The planning time for the subgoal-goal pair of moves occurs prior to the first move, and contributes to the "long" of the long-short pair of latencies. According to this analysis, the last move would be a fast one, either because it was part of the second planned chunk of moves, or because it is simply executed rapidly as a single move that requires no subgoal planning. Approximately two-thirds of the subjects for whom latencies were recorded exhibited the long-short and long-short-short temporal patterns.

---

[2]An example of a subgoal-goal move pair is that encountered in the Move problem when trying to move the medium globe to the medium monster when the medium monster is already holding the large globe. The completion of the move requires the subgoal of "clearing" the medium monster by moving the large globe elsewhere, followed by the goal move of moving the medium globe to the medium monster.

TABLE 3.2
Processing Load

|  | Test | Image | Image | Image |
|---|---|---|---|---|
| **Move Rules** | | | | |
| Rule 2 | X | | | |
| Rule 3 | X | X | | |
| **Move Planning** | | | | |
| Rule 2-Subgoal | X | X | | |
| Rule 3-Subgoal | X | X | X | |
| **Change Rules** | | | | |
| Rule 2 | X | X | | |
| Rule 3 | X | X | X | |
| **Change Planning** | | | | |
| Rule 2-Subgoal | X | X | X | |
| Rule 3-Subgoal | X | X | X | X |

Note: Each X represents an envisioned or imaged entity that must be kept in mind when planning moves.

The major conclusion drawn from these findings was that subjects were able to rapidly solve the problem only after they had automated move making enough to be able to plan a subgoal-goal pair of moves. Furthermore, differences in isomorph difficulty were due to differences in the demands imposed by the various isomorphs' move operators; differences that required varying amounts of time before the move making could be automated (or "compiled" or "proceduralized"). Another demonstration of this was that subjects who were given training on the move operators prior to the presentation of a problem were able to solve the problems rapidly, and without significant differences between the Monster isomorphs. According to this account of the results, once the processing load had been reduced through the automation of move-making, the Monster problems should have been about as difficult as isomorphs whose move making imposed minimal processing loads. The Tower of Hanoi is such an isomorph because the move operator restrictions are inherent to its external representation; the disks block each others' removal from the pegs, so that it is impossible to remove a larger disk first. Figure 3.3 shows the solution times for Monster isomorphs under a number of conditions, the final path times for those isomorphs, and the solution time for the Tower of Hanoi problem. The figure shows that the final path times, that is, the solution times once move making was automated, are about equal to the Tower of Hanoi solution time and are considerably less than the overall solution time for those isomorphs. These results provide further support for the conclusion that the processing load imposed by the move operators is minimal during the final path phase.

## EXPERIMENTAL BACKGROUND: TRANSFER
## OF TRAINING AND PROBLEM MOVE OPERATORS

If problem move operators are a major source of problem difficulty differences, the compatibility of the move operators of two problems should predict the amount of transfer that will be obtained between them. This idea was tested in an experiment reported in Kotovsky, Hayes, and Simon (1985) involving acrobats jumping between each others' shoulders on the tops of flagpoles, the acrobats corresponding to the disks of the Tower of Hanoi problem, or the globes of the Monster problems. As expected, the compatibility of the move operators was a major determinant of transfer. In one version of the experiment, the two problems were Monster Move problems in which the large spheres were free to move and blocked the small spheres from moving, and an Acrobat problem in which the move restriction was reversed; small acrobats were free to move and blocked large acrobats from moving. This

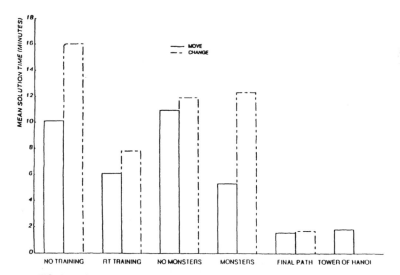

FIG. 3.3.   Solution times and final path times. The final path times for the Monster problems are close to the Tower problem solution time. Source: "Why are Some Problems Hard? Evidence From Tower of Hanoi," by K. Kotovsky, J. R. Hayes, & H. A. Simon, 1985, *Cognitive Psychology, 17,* 248–294.

move operator incompatibility resulted in relatively little transfer. In contrast, when the move operators were similar as in the Reverse Acrobat and Monster Move problems, where in both problems, large block small, there was positive transfer.

There were also interesting asymmetries between the problems in the amount of transfer that was obtained within pairs of problems. The amount of transfer from problem A to problem B was often different than the amount of transfer from B to A. Problem difficulty differences seemed to account for this asymmetry. If the source and target problems had different move oprators, such as in the Monster Move and Acrobat problem pair, then any information acquired from the source problem required transformation of the move operator information in order to be useful in solving the target problem. Such transformations should be more resource competing on more difficult target problems, and result in less transfer. This is consistent with the direction of the results obtained with the Acrobat problems. In the Monster Move-Acrobat problem pair, although the individual transfer effects did not reach significance, the direction of transfer from the hard to the easy problem tended to be positive ($+30\%$), whereas the transfer tendency from the easy to the hard problem was in the opposite direction ($-29\%$). On the other hand, in the Monster Move-Reverse Acrobat problem pair, where the move operators were compatible, this was not found. There was positive transfer in both directions. The amount of transfer from the easy to the hard problem was $+57\%$ and the amount of transfer from the hard to the easy was $+39\%$, with the former reaching significance as an individual effect. A similar tendency toward the occurrence of hard-easy asymmetry with more transfer to the easy target problem when move operators are not compatible has been found in a number of experiments (See for example the transfer results reported for the Move-Change pair of problems in Hayes & Simon, 1977).

In a similar vein, in an experiment described in Kotovsky, Hayes, and Simon (1985), Hayes measured the amount of transfer between three isomorphs of the Tower of Hanoi that embodied different amounts of move operator information. These problems consisted of a standard Tower of Hanoi problem with the substitution of styrofoam balls of various diameters for the more usual disks. In one isomorph, called the *Peg Move* problem, the balls had holes drilled in them so that they could be stacked on pegs that were inserted into holders. The move rules were the standard ones: (a) "only one ball may be moved at a time," (b) "if two balls are on a post, only the smaller is free to move," and (c) "a large ball may not be placed on top of a smaller one." The ability to stack the balls made the problem a standard Tower of Hanoi problem, and consequently, easy to solve because the second rule is built in to the external representation. Because the balls are stacked, only the top one is free to move, and the subject does not have to think about the second rule in making moves. A second isomorph, called the *Dish Move* problem, consisted of the same external representation, but without the pegs. The subjects in this version faced a more difficult task because they had to remember the second rule (as well as the others) because the balls could not be stacked. The third isomorph was called the *Dish Change* problem. Its external representation was similar to the Dish Move problem, with the modification that each dish had a reserve dish placed behind it that contained two balls in addition to the ball in the main dish. The balls in the reserve dish were of the two sizes not included in the main dish. These additional balls could be traded for the ball in the main dish if the subject wished to change its size. For example, if the main dish had a medium ball, and the subject wanted to make it large, he or she did so by trading the medium ball from the main dish with the large ball from the reserve dish. The Dish Change problem shared an important feature of the Move problems in that physically existent balls were moved back and forth between the main and reserve dishes. It was also similar to other Change problems in that objects had to be compared at a distance. Thus it was possible to predict the ranking of difficulty of the problems from easiest to hardest: Peg Move, Dish Move, and Dish Change, based on the amount of information load each problem imposed during move making.

The ranking of problem difficulty obtained from the experiment was as predicted. The median solution times of the Peg Move, the Dish Move, and the Dish Change problems were 160 seconds, 241 seconds, and 342 seconds respectively. The increasing solution times across the three problems reflects their increasing difficulty and the increasing information load of their move operators. The transfer results from this experiment, which have not been reported elsewhere, are presented in Table 3.3 in terms of percentage reduction in solution time (transfer scores). The transfer scores indicate a great deal of transfer between problems that have similar move operators, i.e., the Move problems. The only other case yielding a sizeable amount of transfer involved two problems that appear to be similar but have different move operators, namely the Dish Move and Dish Change problems, where the transfer is negative. The Dish Change problem took 59% more time when it followed a Dish Move problem than it did when it preceded the Dish Move problem. As in the Acrobat problems previously discussed, the more difficult target problem was not a good recipient of transferred skill if that skill had to be modified to be used. The Peg Move–Dish Change condition did not yield a similar result probably because of the large differences in the external representations (appearances) as well as the rule sets of those problems. It is likely that these differences were large enough so that attempts to transfer skill were not made.

An additional finding was that the Dish Change problem, in addition to being a poor recipient of positive transfer, was a poor source of transfer as well. Although part of this effect is no doubt due to the aforementioned difference in the move operators between it and the other problems, it did not even yield much self-transfer (reduction in solution time when the identical

TABLE 3.3
Transfer Scores Between Three Isomorphs of the Tower of Hanoi
That Vary in Difficulty and Similarity.

|  | Target Problem % Transfer= (T1 - T2) / T1 | | |
| --- | --- | --- | --- |
| Source Problem | Peg Move | Dish Move | Dish Change |
| Peg Move | 78 | 55 | 7 |
| Dish Move | 34 | 78 | -59 |
| Dish Change | -12 | -6 | 19 |

problem is administered twice)! This is quite opposite to the effect found with the other two problems, which both yielded large amounts of self-transfer. One possible interpretation of this finding is that less is learned from a single exposure to solving more difficult source problems (which are presumably more resource demanding), and therefore less is available for transfer, even to identical problems. The results of this experiment together with those of the Acrobat and Reverse Acrobat problems already discussed, support the conclusion that both move operator compatibility and problem difficulty are important and interacting determinants of transfer.

In summary, the results obtained by Kotovsky, Hayes, and Simon argue for two major conclusions. The first is that the problem solving, at least across the range of problems tested, is a two-phase process: (a) an initial phase that includes "problem exploration," during which people become expert enough at making moves to be able to plan, and (b) a subsequent "final path" phase during which people rapidly achieve a solution because they can plan move sequences that are within their processing limitations. The second conclusion is that move operator compatibility is a major determinant of transfer, with problem difficulty also having an effect on the ability to transform and apply a learned skill to a new problem. There was also an indication that problem similarity played a role in eliciting transfer, as in the Dish Move to Dish Change (but not the Peg Move to Dish Change) case. Given the demonstrated impact of problem representational issues on problem difficulty and transfer, we conducted an experiment to more precisely identify the effects of problem representation on transfer and difficulty, and to localize the effect of transfer within the problem solving process. Having identified planning move pairs as the skill acquired in the problem exploration phase of problem solving in the aforementioned work, we proceeded to test the hypothesis that transfer might perform a similar function, and thus substitute for problem exploration in problems having similar representations.

## EXPERIMENT 1:
## REPRESENTATION AND TRANSFER

In this experiment, we attempted to measure the effect of representational overlap on transfer and identify the locus of transfer within the problem solving process. A set of problems that differed in one or more features of their problem spaces was used to determine the effect these differences would have on transfer. We predicted that the greater the representational overlap, the greater the amount of transfer obtained. This prediction is thus consistent with the identical elements conception of transfer of Thorndike and Woodworth (1901), and the shared production conception of Kieras and Bovair (1986). The basic procedure was to present pairs of problems, and measure the difficulty of the second or target problem, as a function of which first or source problem it followed.

### Subjects

The subjects were 81 students at the Community College of Allegheny County who were given class credit for their participation.

### The Problems

The problems used in this experiment were Monster isomorphs of the three-disk Tower of Hanoi problem and were similar to the problems depicted in Table 3.1. The subjects' goal was to make moves in the problem space until each monster ended up with a globe whose size corresponded to his own. As is shown in that table, the Monster Change problem moves involved the monsters changing the sizes of their globes in accordance with Change problem rules, and the Monster Move problem moves involved the monsters passing their globes back and forth according to that problem's rules.

Within each problem type, the problems could differ in the starting position in the problem space. The two starting places used in the current experiment are depicted as Start1 and Start2 in the problem space presented in Fig. 3.1. Both starting positions are five moves from the goal. The problem space and the starting positions for the Change problem were chosen to be isomorphic to those for the corresponding Move problem. Two problems could also differ in the direction of the move operators (problem rules). There was a normal rule problem (depicted in Table 3.1) and a reverse rule problem. In a reverse rule problem, the smaller globes blocked the passing or changing of larger globes, in contrast to the standard problem in which larger globes blocked smaller globes. The rules for these reverse rule problems, although differing from the usual Monster Problem rules used by Hayes and Simon (1977), are more similar to the tower of Hanoi problem in which smaller disks block larger disks from moving. To summarize, problems could be similar or different in representation (Move or Change), problem rules (normal or reverse), and solution path (Start1 or Start2).

## Procedure

The problems were presented to the subjects on a MicroVAX computer, which displayed the stimuli, and recorded the responses and response latencies. The source and target problems were presented sequentially, with a short rest between. The subjects were run individually. Each subject was seated at the computer, given a brief introduction to the use of the mouse, and then given the first problem. Each problem was presented on the screen in three parts:

1. An introduction to the use of the mouse and instructions for "thinking out loud" while solving the problem.
2. Practice using the mouse with one "monster" on the screen. The procedure for making moves that S's practiced with one monster was identical to the procedure for making moves in the actual problem with three monsters.
3. A statement of the problem and the goal. These were very similar to the Change and Move problem instructions presented in Table 3.1, followed by the presentation of the problem itself (Fig. 3.4). Response latencies were measured from the time that the problem was presented. Figure 3.4 presents the problem display.

In the Move problem, a subject made moves by positioning the mouse pointer on the letter designating the size of the globe he wanted to move, in the box associated with the "destination" monster. On clicking the mouse, the desired globe moved to that destination box. In the Change problem, the subject made moves by positioning the pointer over the letter designating the size he wanted to change the globe into—the destination size—in the box of the monster whose globe he wanted to change. On clicking the mouse, the globe in that box changed to the desired size. The computer checked move legality. When the subject violated a rule, the computer displayed a warning message citing the rule number that had been violated, and asked the subject if he wanted to review the rules. The only move allowed after an illegal move was the retraction of the illegal move. The only display difference between a Change problem and a Move problem was that in the Change problem each monster's box held only one globe which changed in size, whereas in the Move problem, each monster's box could hold from zero to three globes, which could be moved from box to box.

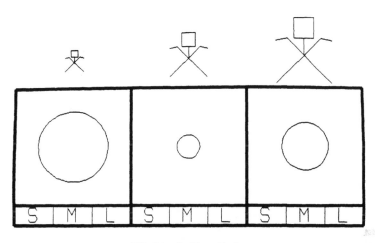

FIG. 3.4.   Problem display.

## Representational Overlap Between Problem Isomorphs

Of the total of six different problem isomorphs used in this experiment, three were isomorphs of the Monster Move problem, and three were isomorphs of the Monster Change problem. Within each major problem type (Move or Change), the source problems could differ from the target problem in a number of ways. These differences for the Change problem "Change 2 Regular" in target position are summarized in Table 3.4a, which shows the problems ranked in degree of overlap with the target problem. Change 2 Regular designates a Change problem with starting position 2, and regular (large blocks small) rules. The most overlap in problem representation occurred when the source and target problems were identical (Change 2 Regular followed by Change 2 Regular). Two problems that differed only in starting position were the next most related problems (Change 1 Regular followed by Change 2 Regular), problems that had similar rules that differed in their direction (normal rules vs. reverse rules) were next (Change 2 Reverse followed by Change 2 Regular), and problems that differed across the Move-Change category (Move 2 Regular followed by Change 2 Regular), differed the most. The main prediction was that the greater the representational similarity or overlap, the more transfer would be obtained. The problems all shared the same move sequence except for the Change 1 and Move 1 problems, which were not true isomorphs because of the different starting positions. Table 3.4a depicts the extent of the representational overlap of the four source problems with the target problem. Table 3.4b presents the same analysis for the Move target problem.

The features that determine representational similarity have been discussed

TABLE 3.4
Problem Representational Overlap: (a) Change Problem, (b) Move
Problem (An X in a column indicates that the source and target
problem share the representational feature or characteristic indicated
for that column.)

| (a) | Target Problem: Change 2 Regular | | | |
|---|---|---|---|---|
| Source Problem | General | Represent | Rule | Moves |
| Change 2 Reg. | X | X | X | X |
| Change 1 Reg. | X | X | X | |
| Change 2 Rev. | X | X | | |
| Move 2 Reg. | X | | | |

| (b) | Target Problem: Move 2 Regular | | | |
|---|---|---|---|---|
| Source Problem | General | Represent | Rule | Moves |
| Move 2 Reg. | X | X | X | X |
| Move 1 Reg. | X | X | X | |
| Move 2 Rev. | X | X | | |
| Change 2 Reg. | X | | | |

under methodology except for the first column labelled "general." This is a
residual category that includes all of the similarities that exist between the
problems that are not otherwise designated, such as: the use of the mouse,
the computer presentation, and the general style of problem (puzzle-like logic
problems). This category represents an attempt to account for the similarities
that exist even between the two most dissimilar problems.

## Results: Representational Overlap

We predicted that increasing the representational overlap between source and
target problem should lead to increasing amounts of transfer between the problems. The amount of transfer was determined by comparing the difficulty
of the target problem with the difficulty of the same target problem when
it was administered in the initial position (as a source problem for some other
target problem). In the following figures, we plot measures of target problem

difficulty as a function of its representational overlap with the source problem it followed, and for purposes of comparison, indicate the same measure for the target problem when it was solved in initial position.[3]

The transfer results from the Change and Move problems are presented in Fig. 3.5, which shows problem solving speed (the reciprocal of solution time) for the target problems, as a function of the amount of representational overlap. The abscissa depicts the amount of overlap as defined in Table 3.4, in the order of least to most. Fig. 3.5 shows that the target problems were solved more quickly as the amount of overlap increased.

The overall relation between representational overlap and problem solving speed is significant for the problems as a whole, $F(1,79) = 5.08, p < .05$, and marginally significant for the Change problems $F(1,39) = 2.97, p < .10$, and Move problems $F(1,38) = 2.78, p = .10$, taken as separate groups. Other measures of problem difficulty (moves, errors, solution times, average move latencies) tend to show similar effects of representational overlap on target problem difficulty, although this is more the case for Change problems than the Move problems that were affected by some fairly extreme solution times (and numbers of moves) in one condition.[4] By way of illustration, the time per move versus representational overlap data are presented in Fig. 3.6 for the Change and Move problems. The relation between these measures and representational overlap was significant for the problems taken as a group, $F(1,79) = 6.88, p < .025$, and marginal for Change problems $F(1,39) = 3.86$, $p < .06$, and Move problems, $F(1,38) = 3.27, p < .08$, taken as separate groups. Our overall conclusion is that increasing representational overlap is related to decreased target problem difficulty; that is, representational similarity increases positive transfer.

These results are in agreement with the previously discussed results of the Acrobat/Reverse Acrobat experiment, which also showed significant transfer in the condition having high move operator compatibility. In addition, the results agree with those of the Dish Experiment where again, there was a large amount of transfer between problems having similar move operators, and little transfer between problems having different move operators.

The general conclusion that emerges from these experiments is that prob-

---

[3]In figure 3.5, the Change and Move source problems have similar solution speeds. This is contrary to the usual finding that Change problems are more difficult (as indeed these were in the target position). If solution times rather than reciprocals are plotted, the Change problem–Move problem difference is more apparent, the times yielding a ratio of about 3:2. In contrast to speed measures, solution time measures are more influenced by slow subjects, i.e., those who find the problems difficult.

[4]A number of the measures in this experiment, particularly those that are responsive to extreme individual scores, exhibit a great deal of subject to subject variability both within, as well as across conditions, resulting in some marginally significant results. This contrasts with the findings presented in the next section of the discussion of results where we report on a phase of the problem solving process where the variability tends to disappear.

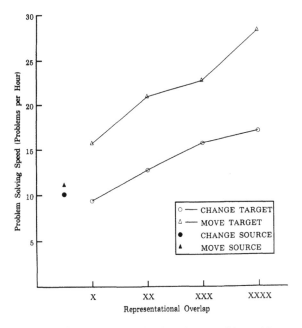

FIG. 3.5.   The effect of representational overlap on problem solving speed.

lem representation, in addition to exercising control over problem difficulty, is an important determinant of transfer. The results must be tempered by the realization that many factors affect target problem difficulty, and it therefore cannot be predicted as accurately as we would like solely on the basis of a subject's problem solving history, that is, on the basis of transfer. Nonetheless, these results suggest that a stronger prediction of target problem difficulty will become possible as we achieve the ability to further isolate the particular problem features that provide the source of transfer, more accurately localize the effects of transfer within the problem solving process, and thus more precisely specify the degree of representational overlap between two problems. We now turn to those issues.

## Results: Two Phase Solution Process

Although the transfer results presented clearly demonstrate the effects of representational overlap, the locus of such effects has not yet been determined. In an attempt to address this issue, we analyzed our transfer data in accordance with our previous characterization of the solution process as consisting of two phases: a nonprogress making exploratory phase, and a final path phase in which the subject rapidly advances to the goal.

The final path was defined as the set of moves made by each subject from their last occupation of a position five moves from the goal, to the attainment of a solution. A distance of five moves was chosen because it is the distance between the initial starting position and the goal, and thus consists of the subject traversing the entire start-to-goal distance. The move data was analyzed to determine the last occupancy of such a position, and the remaining moves and time were extracted from the move records. Kotovsky, Hayes, and Simon (1985) found that only a relatively small proportion of the problem solving time is spent on the final path, and its beginning is determined by the subjects acquiring the ability to compile moves, which allows them to plan ahead and thus quickly solve the problem. The current study constitutes the first test of that finding in a new problem situation. Furthermore, the entire set of move records is used, as opposed to using only those chosen by the additional criterion of temporal move patterns that evidence the attainment of move compilation ability. In this study, we simply take the end behavior of all the subjects to see if it exhibits the "mad dash to a solution" effect that was obtained in the earlier study.

The final path finding was replicated in this study. The subjects traversed the final path in a relatively short time and in relatively few moves. The median time to achieve a solution in the Change problem from the last occupancy of a position 5 moves from the goal was 83 seconds, with a median of 7 moves required to traverse the distance. This contrasts with the total solution results (the amount of time and number of moves to traverse the distance to the goal

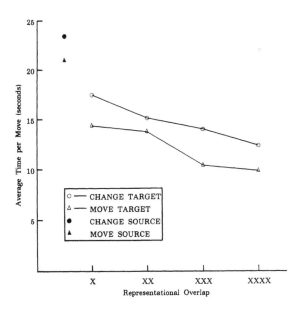

FIG. 3.6.   The effect of representational overlap on move latencies.

from the beginning of the problem) of 434 seconds, and 21 moves. For the Move problem, the results are similar: a final path median of 65 seconds and 7 moves, as compared to the total solution median of 350 seconds and 19 moves. (The mean number of moves for the final path and total solution respectively are 8.1 and 30.6 for the Change problem, and 8.1 and 24.7 for the Move problem. The mean times for final path and total solution are 104 and 630 seconds for the Change problem, and 108 and 441 seconds for the Move problem.) Thus the subjects do exhibit the predicted pattern of a large amount of exploratory behavior with no net progress toward the goal, followed by the very rapid attainment of a solution. The average time per move also reveals this dichotomous behavior: The average time per move being almost twice as fast during the final path phase of the solution process as it is during the exploratory phase.

The conclusion that the final path was achieved when subjects became able to plan and execute two move sequences was tested by searching for the temporal pattern of moves that suggested two goal-subgoal pairs of moves, followed by a quick final move. Because the planning of a goal-subgoal pair occurs prior to the first of the pair of moves, the expected pattern of move times is long-short, long-short. In addition, we expected a quick final move because minimal planning is required to move to the goal from a penultimate state. Table 3.5 presents the expected number of such temporal move patterns together with the number actually obtained from the final path records. In addition, the table shows the same measures obtained from the most immediately prior subgoal situation in the exploratory phase of the move records. For the exploratory moves, single subgoal situations were identified and the long-short temporal pattern was searched for. For the final path, only the occurrence of the entire long-short-long-short-short outcome was accepted as evidence of the ability to form and use subgoals, because on the final path we could be relatively certain what the subject was attempting. Even with this more stringent test, the evidence for subgoaling was extremely strong on the final path, and almost exactly at chance for the exploratory phase. Thus the conclusion is supported that the ability to plan and execute subgoal-goal pairs of moves is what differentiated the exploratory and final path phases.

## Results: Locus of the Transfer Effect

Having established the existence of these two different phases of the problem solving process, we can proceed to examine which phase is likely to facilitated by the prior solution of a similar problem. We predicted that the exploratory phase of the problem solving process would be shortened by the skill learned in solving the source problem. That is, the skill acquired on the earlier problem should reduce the exploratory phase of the process by helping the subject acquire the ability to plan and make moves. If the analysis of the solution process described in Kotovsky, Hayes, and Simon (1985) is correct, the

TABLE 3.5
Comparison of Subgoal Planning in the Final Path and Exploratory
Phases of Problem Solving

|  | Final Path | Exploratory |
|---|---|---|
| Pattern | L–S–L–S–S | L–S |
| Number Expected | 2.4 | 6 |
| Number Obtained | 14 | 5 |
| n | 24 | $12^1$ |
|  | $p < 0.0001$ | $p < 0.75$ |

Note: For each phase, the number of obtained move latency patterns consistent with subgoal planning is compared with the number expected by chance.

[1]In an additional 11 cases, the subject made an illegal move, thus offering further evidence of an inability to successfully plan and execute a subgoal-goal pair of moves in the exploratory phase.

locus of the transfer effect should be in the exploratory phase of the problem, because that is where the learning that is crucial for moving onto the final path occurs.

The final path performance measures for the target problems exhibit little variation regardless of the source problems. In contrast, our previous analyses of entire solutions exhibited significant variation in performance depending on the overlap of the source problems. Figure 3.7 shows that the target problems (and the source problems), have similar final path times. Although the total solution times might vary by 10 minutes or so, the final path times vary by less than 1 minute (much less, in the case of the Change problems). A similar result exists for the number of moves in the final path, which exhibit relatively little variation from one transfer condition to another, and are similar for source and target problems. These results, showing the relative equality of final path moves across conditions, are depicted in Fig. 3.8 for the Change and Move problems.

In contrast, the overall number of moves to a solution demonstrated the existence of a great deal of variability across problem conditions, with the means of the various overlap conditions ranging from 27.1 to 37.8 for Change problems, and 18.2 to 37.4 for Move problems. Of the measures used in this experiment, the one that is most descriptive of move operator application difficulty is time per move. In Figure 3.6 we showed that the time per move of the target problems varied with representational overlap. It is instructive to consider this move latency measure for the exploratory and final path phases

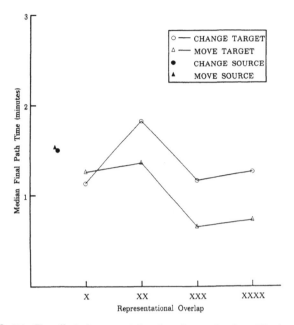

FIG. 3.7.   The effect of representational overlap on duration of final path.

separately. For exploratory moves, there were significant differences (one way anova) for all target problems, $F(1,79) = 4.47$, $p < .05$, as well as for the Change problems separately, $F(1,39) = 4.77$ $p < .05$, but not for the Move problems separately, $F(1,38) = 0.59$, $p < .45$. For the final path phase on the other hand, the time per move measure was not related to overlap. The corresponding figures for all target problems, Change problems, and Move problems were $F(1,79) = 1.13$, $p < .30$, $F(1,39) = 0.03$, $p < .89$, and $F(1,38) = 1.33$, $p < .26$, respectively; none approaching significance.

If the time per move for the first (source) problem is included, the result is even more striking, with large (and significant) differences in overall time per move and exploratory time per move, and no significant differences in final path time per move. For all problems (source and target) combined, the average time per move, exploratory time per move, and final path time per move yield $F$ ratios of 4.06, $p < .0001$, 3.1, $p < .0025$, and 1.19, $p = .3$, respectively. The corresponding values for Change problems alone are, average time per move, $F(4,56) = 6.61$, $p < .00025$, exploratory time per move, $F(4,56) = 4.72$, $p < .0025$, and final path time per move $F(4,56) = 1.29$, $p < .29$. For Move problems, the average time per move result is $F(4,55) = 3.84$, $p < .01$, exploratory time per move, $F(4,55) = 3.58$, $p < .025$, and final path time per move, $F(4,55) = 1.6$, $p < .2$. Thus the considerable variation that exists across problems is present in early parts of the problem solving process, but it is absent in the final path phase. The exploratory phase move latencies are depicted in Fig. 3.9 and the final path move latencies in Fig. 3.10. The average time per move results were presented earlier in Fig. 3.6.

*We conclude that the transfer that occurs between two problems acts by reducing the exploratory (move learning) phase of the problem solving process, while leaving the final path phase of the process essentially unchanged.* Stated in more general terms, these problems are solved in the last minute or minute and a half, whether or not a similar problem was solved immediately beforehand. Almost all of the variability in solution times occurs prior to this time. For example, the ratio of standard deviation to the mean for the final path times and moves is generally between ¼ and ½ of the ratio for the exploratory times and moves within each condition. Thus the within-condition as well as between-condition variation in times is greatly reduced in the final path behavior. Positive transfer enables subjects to reach the final path phase sooner than when there is no transfer. However, transfer does not affect the final path phase itself because at that point subjects have already achieved the ability to plan two moves, (through either the transferred skill or through practice in the exploratory phase), and thus rapidly achieve a solution. The analysis of move operator application time supports the conclu-

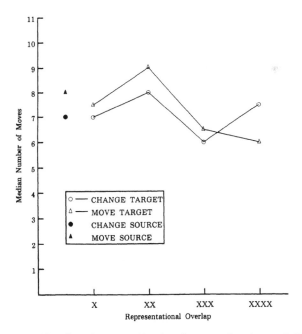

FIG. 3.8.    The effect of representational overlap on number of moves in final path phase.

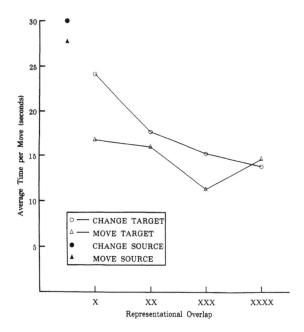

FIG. 3.9.    The effect of representational overlap on exploratory phase move latencies.

sion that it is move operator application that is learned during the exploratory phase of problem solving and that move operator application is also the target of transfer. The ability to easily make moves is, in this view, the key to being able to plan and execute goal-subgoal pairs of moves.

This first series of experiments has generated a number of conclusions about representation and transfer. These include:

1. Increased overlap in the representations of two problems increases the amount of skill that will transfer from the source problem to the target problem.

2. Replicating an earlier finding, the problem solving process can be divided into two phases. These are: (a) an exploratory phase during which the subject learns to make moves and compile two-move sequences, and (b) a final path phase during which the subject rapidly and efficaciously closes on the goal by planning and executing two-move sequences.

3. The target of transfer is learning to make moves. This learning can substitute for some of the learning that would normally occur during the exploratory phase of the solution process. Once subjects are on the final path, there is very little variation in move application times,

whether between target problems with quite different amounts of transfer from widely different source problems, or between the same problem in source and target position.

4. There is evidence of an interaction between target problem difficulty and transfer, such that increased target problem difficulty leads to less transfer from more distant problem isomorphs. Thus, information from a source problem that has to be transformed at the time of its application in a target problem can yield positive transfer, but is less likely to do so on harder problems that are more resource demanding.

## EXPERIMENT 2: THE EFFECTS OF STIMULUS AND REPRESENTATIONAL SIMILARITY ON TRANSFER

Experiment 1 demonstrated the influence of representation on transfer, and showed that the locus of transfer was in the exploratory phase rather than the final path phase of the search for a solution. The representational features that were included in that experiment exemplify the diversity of representational features that can affect transfer. The next series of experiments was

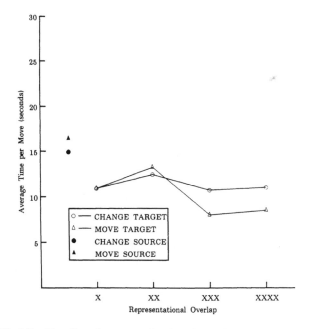

FIG. 3.10.   The effect of representational overlap on final path phase move latencies.

conducted to attempt to more precisely predict the transfer effects of representation, by separating the effects of internal representation from those of the external task environment, or problem "adequate stimulus." The strategy here was to control subjects' internal representation of the problem (i.e., their problem space), independently of the external problem presentation, in order to determine the effects of the internal representation on transfer.

One root of this line of investigation can be traced back to an interesting idea advanced by Charles Osgood (1949), who posited a relationship between stimulus similarity, response compatibility, and the amount of transfer that would be obtained in verbal learning situations. He formulated the "Osgood Transfer Surface" to describe the relationship. This transfer surface summarized a large portion of the data on transfer. Osgood posited that response compatibility would produce positive transfer, and response incompatibility would produce negative transfer. More importantly for the issues we are considering, he advanced the idea that high stimulus compatibility would produce large amounts of transfer (whose sign depends on the response compatibility/incompatibility), and low stimulus resemblance would produce small amounts of transfer. The work of Gick and Holyoak (1983, 1987) and others suggests that although the "large" might have to be qualified a bit, Osgood's analysis applies as well to problem solving.

Osgood's emphasis on stimulus similarity and response compatibility managed to both summarize a significant portion of the data on transfer, and fit into a more behaviorist zeitgeist. However, the current cognitive science view of the centrality of representation in cognition led us to consider an extension of his elegant analysis. Newell and Simon (1972) clearly differentiated the problem space or internal representation of the problem from the external task environment. This differentiation is essential to their analysis of problem solving, and impels us to focus our attention on the internal representational aspects of problem solving to achieve an understanding of the problem solving process. The question that we attempt to answer here is whether the same thing holds true for understanding transfer; that is, whether it is internal representational rather than external stimulus properties that are the important determinants of transfer.

The results of Experiment 1 argued for the importance of representation for transfer, but did not clearly differentiate between the relevance of stimulus overlap and internal representational overlap. The dimensions of representation that were manipulated, such as rule reversal and Move-Change problem representations, would be hard to map onto a stimulus similarity dimension in any reasonable way, although the representational differences are not totally independent of differences in the stimulus properties for some of the isomorphs. Thus, although normal rule and reverse rule problems have identical stimulus properties, Move and Change problems are not identical on the display screen of the MicroVAX even though they were constructed to minimize stimulus property differences. The major difference between the stimuli of a Move problem and a Change problem is that a monster in a Move problem can hold more than one globe, whereas a monster in the Change problem always holds only a single globe. This difference is one source of the move operator difficulty differences previously discussed, and thus is a potentially important difference between the two problems. In order to separate the effects of representation from those of stimulus similarity, the current series of experiments controlled for stimulus properties so that any differences in performance could be attributed to differences in representation.

## Experiment 2a

### The Problems

The basic experimental procedure used in this series of experiments was to sequentially present the subject with two problems to solve, both of which were isomorphs of the three-disk Tower of Hanoi problem. Four problem isomorphs were used: two Size problems and two Depth problems. The Size problems were very similar to the Change problems used in Experiment 1, with the exception of being presented in color. A black and white rendition of the display of the Size problem is given in Fig. 3.11. The displays consisted of three boxes (or so called "tunnels" in the Depth problem), each of which contained a sphere. The size of the sphere could be changed by positioning a cursor within the box, or tunnel, by means of a joystick, and pressing one of three keys on a keyboard that were labelled "small," "medium," or "large," in the Size problem, or "far," "middle," or "near" in the Depth problem. The display of the Depth problem was identical to the display of the Size problem in some versions of the experiment. In other versions, an additional detail, perspective "windows," was added to the Depth problem display in order to facilitate the illusion that the spheres moved in depth. A rendition of a Size problem display modified in this way is also given in Fig. 3.11. The inclusion or noninclusion of the windows is noted in the description of the individual experiments.

The move operator rules for making moves or changes in the Depth and Size isomorphs were made as similar as possible. They were always stated in terms of the darkness or lightness of the tunnel or box surrounding the sphere, instead of being stated in terms of sphere size and monster size as they were in Experiment 1. The text of the rules for a Depth problem are given in Table 3.6a and b. The corresponding rule set for a Size problem can be generated by substituting "change the size" for "change the position," and substituting "large," "medium," and "small," for "near," "middle," and "far," in that table.

To determine the effect of representational similarity on transfer from one problem to the other, subjects were presented with two problems that had identical (or very similar) stimulus properties, with instructions that induced either the same or different internal representations. Two Size problems and

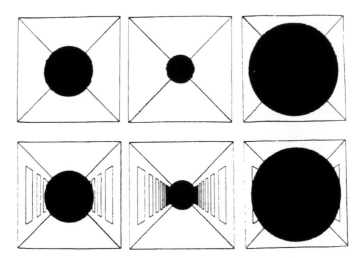

FIG. 3.11.   Experiment 2 displays shown with and without the windows that facilitated the depth illusion.

two Depth problems were used, the only difference between the two problems within each type was the starting position in the search space. The two types of problems were isomorphic, with Depth problem 1 (D1) having the same solution path as Size problem 1 (S1), and D2 the same path as S2. The difference between the Size and Depth problems was in the representation engendered in the subjects by the written problem statement. In contrast, the external representation (screen display) was either identical or very similar for all problems.

### Procedure

Subjects saw the problem displays on an AED graphics terminal driven by a MicroVAX computer, which also recorded their responses and response latencies. The subjects were seated at the terminal and the experimenter demonstrated the use of the joystick to control the cursor and the use of keyboard buttons to make moves. They were instructed to think aloud while solving the problems, and their verbal protocol was recorded. A general description of the problem was then given to the subject on a sheet of paper. When subjects were ready to begin, they turned over a second sheet that contained the specific problem statement. The description and problem statement given to subjects solving a Depth problem are given in Table 3.6a and b. Subjects' response latencies were measured from the time that they turned over the second sheet.

### The Subjects

The subjects were 64 students at Carnegie-Mellon University and the Community College of Allegheny County who were given course credit for their participation.

### Results

We predicted there would be more transfer between problems whose representations were the same than between problems whose representations were different. In the first of the experiments, the displays of the Size and Depth problems were identical. The stimuli on the screen consisted of three squares with diagonals drawn in to facilitate the depth effect. There was a

TABLE 3.6
Experiment 2 Problem Description: Change Problem Rules

---

**(a)**

This problem involves changing the positions of 3 identical spheres. Each sphere is in a separate 'tunnel' and the tunnels vary in how dark they are. You can move each sphere between three depths: Near, Middle, and Far.

To move a sphere, first position the black crosshair inside the sphere's tunnel using the silver joystick. Then hit one of the keys labelled Near, Middle, and Far to move the sphere to the desired depth.


**(b)**

Your task is to move the 3 spheres so that the sphere in the darkest tunnel is Near, the sphere in the next lightest tunnel is Middle, and the sphere in the lightest tunnel is Far. The 2 rules for moving the spheres are:

1) you may not change the position of a sphere if it is at the same depth as another sphere in a darker tunnel.

2) you may not change the position of a sphere if it will be at the same depth as another sphere in a darker tunnel.

If you break either rule, the computer will move the sphere but it will also ring a warning bell. If this happens, the only move you can make is the one that returns the sphere to its previous position.

---

large transfer effect; the target problem was much more rapidly solved than the source problem, $F(1,59) = 19.84$, $p < .001$. However, the effect of manipulating the representations of the source and target problems was not significant. Although it was in the direction of our prediction that there should be more transfer between problems whose representations were the same— two Size problems or two Depth problems—than between problems whose representations were different—a Size problem followed by a Depth problem or Depth followed by Size, $F(1,59) = 1.34$, $p < .26$.

In order for our hypothesis to be testable, it is necessary for subjects to form the intended internal representations of the problems. To check that subjects had formed the correct representations of the problems, we evaluated the verbal protocol statements that subjects made in announcing their moves. This analysis revealed that many subjects solving Depth problems did not perceive the spheres as moving in depth. The protocols showed that in these cases, the subjects often referred to depth moves as size changes. Thus, instead of saying "Now this one gets moved to near," or "Now change this to far," they would say "Now this one gets made large," and "Now change this to small." A subset (36 of 64 subjects) gave representationally correct references in announcing their moves, and the results from their data was closer to the predicted effect. However, this subset included very few subjects who solved a Size source problem and a Depth target problem. It seemed that once subjects had solved a source problem with the size interpretation, they had great difficulty forming a depth interpretation of the target problem. The analysis of the protocols indicates that subjects had difficulty forming the intended internal representation of the Depth problem, which may explain why we did not obtain the predicted effect.

In the next experiment we modified the display associated with the Depth problem to make it more perceptually viable, in the belief that this would increase its "availability" to the subject for further processing, or transfer. One useful result of this experiment is that it raised an issue we explore later, that is, the availability of a representation. The basic hypothesis, based on these preliminary findings, is that if it is difficult to achieve or maintain a representation of a problem, then that problem will not be useful as a source of transfer to subsequent similar problems.

## Experiment 2b

The second experiment used redesigned stimuli that were intended to be more easily perceivable as a depth display. To facilitate the achievement of a depth representation of the Depth problem, we introduced windows into the display associated with the Depth problem. These consisted of trapezoidally shaped windows in the walls of the tunnels of the display that helped produce the depth illusion and thus made it easier for the subjects to represent what they were doing as changing the position of spheres in the tunnels as opposed to changing their sizes. The experimental strategy was similar to that of Experiment 2a. To determine the effect of representational differences on transfer, problems were presented that had very similar stimulus properties, with rules that engendered either similar or different representations. We viewed the presence of the windows in the Depth condition, and their absence in the Size condition, as a minimal stimulus difference that would in itself not introduce a significant difference between the problems. The reason for this belief is that the windows were not a central feature of the displays, nor were they referred to in the statement of the problem or used as part of the problem move operators (This issue is investigated further in Experiment 2c).

### Subjects

The subjects in this and the following two experiments were students at the Community College of Allegheny County who were given class credit for their participation. Forty-four subjects were used in this experiment, 11 subjects in each of the 4 conditions: Size-Size, Size-Depth, Depth-Depth, Depth-Size.

### Results

As in Experiment 2a, there was massive transfer from the source to the target problem. The median solution times of the target problems are plotted for each condition in Fig. 3.12. The connected points in the figure show that target problems that were preceded by a source problem with a similar representation were solved more quickly than target problems that were preceded by a source problem with a different representation. The difference between the amounts of transfer obtained from the same and different conditions was significant, $p < .05$ (Mann–Whitney U test). The two unconnected points are results from two control experiments discussed later.

In addition to the predicted effect, the transfer results also exhibited a small (and nonsignificant) interaction that we tentatively attribute to different availabilities of the Size and Depth problems. The solution times in Fig. 3.12 suggest a greater difference in transfer between the Size-Size and the Size-Depth conditions than between the Depth-Depth and Depth-Size conditions. A possible explanation for this is that the Size representation is the more available of the two, and thus has the greater potential for transfer to similar problems. Depending on the measure, the interaction is at best marginally significant, but it does suggest further examination of the phenomenon, which we undertake in Experiment 2e.

We conclude that representation is a determinant of transfer, and that more transfer is obtained between problems sharing the same representation than between problems having different representations. One implication of this finding is that the Osgood transfer surface can be reinterpreted to refer to problem representation rather than stimulus similarity. That is, the similar-

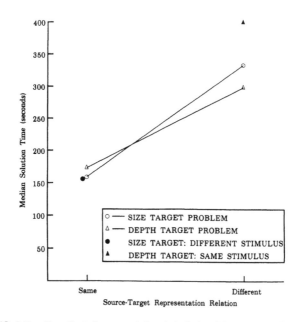

FIG. 3.12.   The effect of representational similarity of the source and target problems on solution times.

ity of the representations for two problems is the predictor of amount of transfer, rather than the similarity of the stimuli. This is not to argue that the similarity between the representations of two problems is totally independent of the similarity of their stimuli; we are not proposing a hallucinogenic model of problem representation. Rather, we argue that the representation the subject creates is the relevant variable, and it may be the product of several factors including the subjects' expectations (often induced by the problem instructions), and their problem solving history, as well as the stimulus qualities of the problem itself.

As was mentioned previously, the Size and Depth problem stimuli differed only slightly (via the presence or absence of windows), and by an amount that is unlikely to have produced the differential levels of transfer found between and within problem types. In order to rule out the possibility that these small stimulus differences somehow produced the different amounts of transfer that were obtained, we conducted two control experiments.

## Experiment 2c:
## Different Representations, Same Stimulus

The purpose of the first control experiment was to determine the effect of the small stimulus differences introduced by having windows present in some problems' displays. In this experiment, we measured the amount of transfer between two problems that had identical displays but different representations. Subjects solved a pair of problems with windows present in both problem displays, but with problem rules that defined the source problem as a Size problem and the target problem as a Depth problem. By making the stimuli identical, the *only* difference was the difference in representation engendered by the different rules. If the stimulus differences produced by the presence or absence of windows were responsible for the relatively small amount of transfer obtained in the Size-Depth and Depth-Size conditions of Experiment 2b, then the added stimulus similarity in the current experiment should result in more transfer than was previously obtained. Conversely, if the stimulus similarity (rather than representational similarity) was responsible for the relatively large amount of transfer obtained in the Size-Size and Depth-Depth conditions of Experiment 2b, then the identical displays used in the current experiment should yield a similarly large amount of transfer as in the equivalent conditions of the previous experiment.

The result was that the added stimulus similarity of having windows present in the displays of both problems had no effect on the amount of transfer. The eleven subjects in this control experiment exhibited relatively little transfer when compared to those in the Depth-Depth condition of Experiment 2b. They also exhibited no more transfer than subjects in the Size-Depth condition of Experiment 2b, as shown by the unconnected point in the different representation condition in Fig. 3.12. The increased stimulus similarity occasioned by having windows present in both problems' displays did not produce an increase in transfer; the control of transfer was in the representations. Comparing target problem times in the stimulus-different condition and the stimulus-similar condition (with size-depth representations in both cases), yielded an $F(1,20) = 0.3$, $p < .65$. The nonsignificant tendency was in the opposite direction to that predicted by a stimulus based model; if anything, the target problem took slightly longer in the stimulus-similar condition than in the stimulus-different condition. The unconnected data point reflecting this result is slightly above the stimulus-different comparison point in that figure, rather than below it. In other words, making the stimuli the same did not increase transfer.

The results indicate that the stimulus difference introduced by the presence or absence of windows in the Depth problem displays did not account for the transfer results we obtained. Rather, it was the difference in representations engendered by the problem rules that was the source of the different amounts of transfer obtained in the Size-Depth and the Depth-Depth conditions of Experiment 2b.

## Experiment 2d:
## Same Representation, Different Stimuli

In the second control experiment, we measured the amount of transfer between two problems that had identical representations but different displays. This differs from Experiment 2c in which we demonstrated that stimulus similarity did not produce transfer when there were different representations for the two problems. Here we were interested in finding any effects that stimulus differences might produce when representations are the same. The subjects in this experiment solved two Size problems similar to the Size-Size condition of Experiment 2a. The only difference was that there were windows present in the display of the source problem but no windows in the display of the target problem. The purpose was to investigate the effect of introducing the stimulus difference, as a further control on Experiment 2b.

### Results

There was no difference in the solution times for the target problem between the condition with the same representation and different stimuli, and the condition with the same representation and same stimuli. There was still massive transfer, with no significant difference between the two stimulus conditions. The results are depicted in Fig. 3.12 by the unconnected point in the same-representation condition. The figure shows that the introduction of the stimulus difference did not decrease the transfer. The results are almost identical to those obtained with the same representation and the same stimuli. The introduction of the slight stimulus difference between the two problems did not have the effect of reducing transfer. The fact that the representations of the two problems were the same (size-size), resulted in a great deal of transfer despite the difference in the problem stimuli introduced by the addition of the windows.

The overall conclusion about representation and transfer obtained from the second series of experiments is that the internal representation of a problem is the determining factor in transfer. The stimulus situation (in these experiments, the computer display of the problem) could make a difference in that it can influence the likelihood of forming and maintaining various representations, but it does not directly control the transfer of skill from problem to problem. If representation is controlled, the stimulus differences are not of consequence.

### Experiment 2e: An Independent Measurement of Representational Availability

At a number of points in this chapter we have argued that the representation of the Size problem was somehow more attainable, and therefore more available, than the representation of the Depth problem. Three results in particular have provided evidence for this argument. They are: (a) the contrast between the ambiguity of the results obtained from Experiment 2a and the stronger effect obtained in Experiment 2b, which used windows in the Depth problem display (to make that representation more attainable), (b) the slight interaction obtained in Experiment 2b that suggested more transfer from the more available representation, and (c) the increase in the strength of the main effect found in Experiment 2a when the subjects not attaining the desired representation were removed from the analysis. Most of these subjects were in a depth condition and did not maintain the depth representation. These results all argue for the difficulty of evoking or maintaining the depth representation, and for the influence of that difficulty on transfer. In this last experiment, we independently measured the relative availability of the two representations, and thus determined if availability is skewed in a direction consistent with the empirical results.

## Methodology

Subjects in this experiment were asked to step into a room and make a judgment about something they would be shown on a computer screen. The displays on the screen were identical to those used in Experiment 2b. The subject was shown either a Size problem display without windows, or a Depth problem display with windows. The experimenter then asked subjects to describe what they saw as he or she made the sphere change size/position. The experimenter noted whether their response referred to a size change or a position (depth) change. They were asked to rate, on a 5-point scale ranging from "not at all" to "totally," "how much it looks like the sphere is getting larger and smaller," if they had first described it as changing size, or to rate "how much it looks like the sphere is getting closer and farther away," if they had first described it as moving in depth. After making the rating on a written response form, subjects were prompted for the alternative representation by being told that "some people see the display as a sphere changing size, growing larger and smaller," if they had responded with a depth representation, or that "some people see the sphere as changing position by moving in and out of a tunnel," if they had reported the size representation. They were asked if they could see it that way, and to rate the alternative perception on the same 5-point scale.

## Subjects

The subjects were 40 students at the Community College of Allegheny County who were given a donut for their participation.

## Results

The results were strongly in the predicted direction; the depth representation was much harder to obtain than the size representation. All 20 subjects who were asked to describe the Size (no window) problem display described the sphere as changing in size. In contrast, only 9 of the 20 subjects who saw the Depth (window) problem display described the sphere as moving in depth, $\chi^2 = 11.61$, $(df = 1)$, $p < .001$. When asked if they could see it the other way, "Some people see it as moving in depth/changing in size, can you see it that way?" the subjects reported that they were able to. However, their ratings of the goodness of the display on the 5-point scale favored their first reported answer. Subjects who first perceived the sphere as changing position, when asked, gave that interpretation a higher rating than the size interpretation, whereas those who first perceived it changing in size, gave that interpretation a higher rating, even though all subjects reported being able to see it both ways. The overall preponderance of size interpretations over depth interpretations indicate that the size representation is more available from the Size problem display than the depth representation is from the Depth problem display. Furthermore, the consistency of the goodness ratings with the initial interpretations shows that once subjects have formed a representation of a display, they tend to stick with it, preferring it to the alternative representation of the same display.

The relative availability of the size and depth representations as measured in this experiment agrees with the predictions derived from the empirical transfer results. Hence, there is further evidence to support the tentative conclusion reached previously that the availability of a representation is a determinant of how readily it will transfer to other problems. The relative unavailability of the depth representation can explain the interaction between the size and depth conditions in Experiment 2b, in which the Size problems seemed to offer more transferable skill or knowledge than the Depth problems. Furthermore, it can explain why, without windows in the display, it was very difficult to obtain the depth representation after the size representation, and difficult to obtain cross representation transfer from depth to size, or even obtain within representation transfer from depth to depth. The ability to measure the availability of alternative representations, and use them to explain differences in transfer is a potentially useful addition to our findings about the role of representation in transfer.

## DISCUSSION

In total, these experiments demonstrate that transfer depends on the internal representation of problems. The first series of experiments, building on previous work, argued for the importance of representational similarity as a predictor of transfer. The amount of transfer obtained was shown to be related to the degree of representational overlap that existed between a pair of problems. Greater representational overlap resulted in increased transfer. The dimensions of overlap included features of the problem representation such as solution path, move operator rules, and Move-Change representational differences. The first series of experiments also showed that the locus of transfer was largely confined to the exploratory phase of the problem-solving process. By the time subjects were able to move efficaciously in the problem search space, they required very little time to solve the problem, and this was almost independent of the particular transfer condition or problem order. The final path time simply did not vary by very much, taking a minute or so in most target problem conditions. This finding about transfer is significant not only because it identifies the locus of the transfer effect, but also because of its relation to our understanding of the solution process. Kotovsky, Hayes, and Simon (1985) showed that subjects had to practice movemaking in order to be able to automate or compile the process of planning short (two move) sequences of moves before they could plan ahead. When the ability to plan two move sequences was attained, a solution was achieved in a very short period of time. In fact, all of the isomorphs considered there were solved in essentially the same time. A similar analysis was performed in the current experiment, and yielded the same conclusion; attaining the ability to plan and execute two move sequences was a precursor of the final path behavior.

Our findings about transfer are similar. The analysis of move operator application times strongly supports the view that the locus of transfer is in the exploratory phase and not the final path phase of problem solving. This analysis showed that the exploratory move application times exhibited significant variation with problem condition, whereas the final path move operator application times exhibited very little variation regardless of transfer history or problem order. The interesting implication of this result is that transfer seems to do what practice does. By automating move making, transfer allows enough move compilation to occur so that planning is possible. If this interpretation is accurate, then it is likely that the design of training materials can be targeted at those processes that allow such move automation to occur. By knowing how transfer occurs and what phase of the problem solving process it affects, it is possible that better practice regimens can be designed, and more effectively monitored to assess the progress of training.

The second series of experiments demonstrates that it is the internal representation of a problem that determines transfer, and this representation can operate independently of the stimulus features of problems. This finding indicates that models of transfer that try to predict the direction and magnitude of transfer on the basis of stimulus overlap and response compatibility should be translated into representational terms. Such a change might make them more effective, especially in situations where the stimulus properties are not predictive of the representations that will be evoked. In addition, by demonstrating that the availability of a representation can be directly and independently assessed, and that availability has a sizeable effect on transfer, we have suggested a methodology for assessing the likelihood of transfer, as well as a method for increasing the amount of transfer that will be attained. By modifying or initially designing problems to evoke particular representations, we can increase the likelihood of those representations that will produce positive transfer being available, evokable, and therefore usable in subsequent problem solving experiences. A question that arises from these considerations is to what extent these findings generalize to other domains both within problem solving, and in other areas as well. We very much hope that our findings about transfer transfer. Some work that has been reported by others suggests that this might be so. The work of Singley and Anderson (1985) on transfer of text editing skills is a particularly promising example of similar find-ings in a quite different domain.

The analysis we have presented is lodged within the view of problem solv-ing that Newell and Simon have developed over the last quarter century. It is a view predicated on the ability to understand problem solving not only as an externally observable process, but also one that is internally driven. It conceives that process as being dependent on an internal representation of the problem and its various components; a representation that is empirically measurable, computer modelable, and scientifically understandable. The key elements of that conception are predicated on a differentiation between the external task environment that problem solving takes place in, and an inter-nal representation of that environment that constitutes the problem space the subject works in as he or she moves from start to goal. The methodology of means-ends-analysis operates in that problem space, relying on move operators that make progress through it. By applying that type of analysis to transfer, we have tried to show that an understanding of transfer is not only possible within this kind of conception, but that this conception is necessary for the attainment of any complete understanding of transfer. This is particularly the case for the centrality of the representation of the move operator as a determinant of transfer across problems. According to this analysis, the manner in which people represent a problem determines the generalizable and transferable knowledge that they will attain. Furthermore, the availability of that representation is a determinant of the likely success of transfer. We have demonstrated that it is possible to measure which of a set of alternate representations particular problems elicit, that those represen-tations predict the direction of transfer, and that those representations can be empirically manipulated, so as to control transfer within a set of problems that are not only isomorphic but also virtually identical in their stimulus prop-erties. In doing so, we have extended the power of that analysis to a new area that is fully consistent with the work that has come before.

We have perused some of the vineyards sown by Herbert Simon and tasted a few of the grapes. Although the sign over the entrance proclaims a limited capacity, they come in many full-bodied varieties, and there are large bun-ches of them. We have gotten much sweetness out of them, and the seeds hold out the promise of much more to come.

## ACKNOWLEDGMENTS

This research was supported in part by the Personnel and Training Research Programs, Psychological Sciences Division, Office of Naval Research, under contract NK00014-85-K-0696. Reproduction in whole or in part is permitted for any purpose of the United States Government. We wish to express our gratitude to Herbert A. Simon and J. R. Hayes who have played a very active role in the conceptual development of the work reported in this chapter. The extent of their help and involvement makes them at the very least "unindicted co-conspirators" in the development of the research issues we report on. We also wish to thank Bela Banker and Patty Parry for conducting many of the experiments, and Nicholas Kushmerick for developing the programs that controlled the presentation of the problems and the recording and analysis of the subjects' behavior.

## REFERENCES

Bassok, M., & Holyoak, K. J. (in press). Interdomain transfer between Isomorphic topics in algebra and physics (Working Paper). *Journal of Experimental Psychology: Learning, Memory, and Cognition.*

Bhaskar, R., & Simon, H. A. (1977). Problem solving in semantically rich domains: An example of engineering themodynamics. *Cognitive Science, 1,* 193–215.

Carver, S. M. (1986). *LOGO debugging skills: Analysis, instruction and assessment.* Unpublished doctoral dissertation, Carnegie-Mellon University, Pittsburgh.

Gentner, D. (1983). Structure-Mapping: A theoretical framework for analogy. *Cognitive Science, 7,* 155–170.

Gick, M. L., & Holyoak, K. J. (1983). Schema induction and analogical transfer. *Cognitive Psychology, 15,* 1–38.

Gick, M. L., & Holyoak, K. J. (1987). The cognitive basis of knowledge transfer. In S. M. Cormier & J. D. Hagman (Eds.), *Transfer of learning: Contemporary research and applications.* New York: Academic Press.

Gray, W. D., & Orasanu, J. M. (1987). Transfer of cognitive Skills. In S. M. Cormier & J. D. Hagman (Eds.), *Transfer of learning: Contemporary research and applications.* New York: Academic Press.

Hayes, J. R., & Simon, H. A. (1974). Understanding written problem instructions. In L. W. Gregg (Ed.), *Knowledge and cognition.* Hillsdale, NJ: Lawrence Erlbaum Associates.

Hayes, J. R., & Simon, H. A. (1977). Psychological differences among problem isomorphs. In N. J. Castellan, D. B. Pisoni, G. R. Potts (Eds.), *Cognitive theory.* Hillsdale, NJ: Lawrence Erlbaum Associates.

Judd, C. H. (1908). The relation of special training to general intelligence. *Educational Review, 36,* 28–42.

Katona, G. (1940). *Organizing and memorizing.* New York: Columbia University Press.

Kieras, D., & Bovair, S. (1986). The acquisition of procedures from text: A production-system analysis of transfer of training. *Journal of Memory & Language, 25*(5), 507–524.

Klahr, D., & Carver, S. M. (in press). Cognitive objectives in a LOGO debuggin curriculum: Instruction , learning, and transfer. *Cognitive Psychology.*

Kotovsky, K., Hayes, J. R., & Simon, H. A. (1985). Why are some problems hard? Evidence from Tower of Hanoi. *Cognitive Psychology, 17,* 248–294.

Newell, A., & Simon, H. A. (1972). *Human problem solving.* Englewood Cliffs, NJ: Prentice-Hall.

Nilsson, N. J. (1971). *Problem-solving methods in artificial intelligence.* New York: McGraw-Hill.

Osgood, C. E. (1949). The simliarity paradox in human laerning: A resolution. *Psychological Review, 56,* 132–143.

Papert, Seymour. (1980). *Mindstorms: Children, computers, and powerful ideas.* New York: Basic Books.

Ross, B. H. (1985). Remindings and their effect on learning a cognitive skill. *Cognitive Psychology, 16*(1), 371–416.

Ruger, H. A. (1910). The psychology of efficiency. *Archives of Psychology, 2*(15), 1–88.

Singley, M. K., & Anderson, J. R. (1985). The transfer of text-editing skill. *International Journal of Man-Machine Studies, 22,* 403–423.

Simon, H. A., & Hayes, J. R. (1976). The understanding process: Problem isomorphs. *Cognitive Psychology, 8,* 165–190.

Smith, S. B. (1986). *An analysis of transfer between Tower of Hanoi isomorphs.* Unpublished doctoral dissertation, Carnegie-Mellon University, Pittsburgh.

Thorndike, E., & Woodworth, R. (1901). The influence of improvement in one mental function upon the efficiency of other functions. *Psychological Review, 8,* 247–261, 384–395, 553–564.

# Developmental Differences
# in Scientific Discovery Processes

Kevin Dunbar
David Klahr
*Carnegie–Mellon University*

## ON THE ORIGINS OF DISCOVERY PROCESSES

Questions about the origins of scientific reasoning have been posed by developmental psychologists many times throughout the last 60 years (e.g., Karmiloff-Smith & Inhelder, 1974; Kuhn, Amsel, & O'Loughlin, 1988; Piaget, 1928; Vygotsky, 1934). The context of developmental questions about scientific reasoning can be expanded to include a number of broader questions—both descriptive and normative—about the nature of science and scientific reasoning. Within psychology, one approach to these questions has been to consider science a form of problem solving (e.g., Bartlett, 1958; Simon, 1977). The science-as-problem-solving view is stated most explicitly in Herbert Simon's characterization of scientific discovery as a form of search and in his elucidation of many of the principles that guide this search. For example, he has used the notion of search in a problem space to analyze what science is (Simon, 1977), how scientists reason (Langley, Zytkow, Simon, & Bradshaw, 1986; Kulkarni & Simon, 1988), and how scientists should reason (Simon, 1973). In this chapter, we follow a similar path, and apply the notion of search to the development of scientific reasoning strategies.

A contrasting view treats scientific reasoning as a form of concept formation. In the paradigmatic investigation of science-as-concept-formation, subjects are given examples or instances of a concept and are then asked to discover what the concept is (e.g., Bruner, Goodnow, & Austin, 1962). The extensive body of literature accumulated using this approach has revealed many differences between the reasoning processes used by adults and children when forming concepts. However, other than simply asserting that scientific reasoning is a type of concept formation, psychologists have not formally specified how the cognitive processes involved in concept formation tasks are similar to those involved in scientific reasoning.

One way to specify this similarity is to build a model of the processes that are involved in both concept-formation tasks and problem solving. One model that has proved useful in this respect is Simon and Lea's (1974) Generalized Rule Inducer (GRI). Simon and Lea demonstrated how this single system encompasses both concept learning and problem solving. Within the GRI, concept learning requires search in two problem spaces: a space of instances and a space of rules. Instance selection requires search of an instance space, and rule generation requires search of a rule space. Simon and Lea's analysis also illustrates how information from each space guides search in the other. For example, information about previously generated rules may influence the generation of instances, and information about the classification of instances may determine the modification of rules.

A number of theorists (e.g., Cohen & Feigenbaum, 1983; Kulkarni & Simon, 1988; Lenat, 1977) have argued that the dual space search idea at the core of GRI can be extended to the domain of scientific reasoning, which takes place in a space of hypotheses and experiments. Using this idea, we developed a task that enables us to observe subjects' search paths in both spaces (cf. Klahr & Dunbar, 1988). Specifically, we studied the behavior of subjects who were attempting to extend their knowledge about a moderately complex device by proposing hypotheses about how it worked and then trying to determine whether or not the device behaved in accordance with their hypotheses. In this chapter, we use the task to investigate what components of the scientific reasoning process show a developmental course. Our goal is to understand how existing knowledge structures determine the initial hypotheses, experiments, and data analysis in a discovery task. Because we treat scientific reasoning as a search in two problem spaces, we explore the issue of whether there are developmental differences in how the two spaces are searched, and how search in one space affects search in the other.

Our subjects worked with a programmable, multifunctioned, computer-controlled robot whose basic functions they had previously mastered. We trained both adults and elementary-school children to the same criterion on basic knowledge in the domain before we asked them to extend that knowledge by experimentation. This training allowed us to analyze developmental differences among subjects who shared a common knowledge base with respect to the task domain. Our analysis focuses on their attempts to discover how a new function operates—that is, to extend their understanding about the device—without the benefit of any further instruction. In order to do this, our subjects had to formulate hypotheses and then design experiments to evaluate those hypotheses; the cycle ultimately terminated when they believed that they had discovered how to predict and control the behavior of the device.

The chapter is organized as follows. First, we briefly review some of the relevant literature on the development of scientific reasoning skills. Following this, we describe our task in detail, and then summarize two earlier studies using adult subjects.[1] These studies provide a context for the developmental questions. In the third study, we describe the performance of 8- to 11-year-old children on this task. On the basis of these three studies we propose a model for scientific reasoning, and then use it as a framwork for understanding the development of scientific reasoning strategies.

## DEVELOPMENTAL ISSUES
## IN SCIENTIFIC REASONING

We have reviewed research on scientific reasoning in adults elsewhere (cf. Klahr & Dunbar, 1988), and in this section we concentrate on developmental issues. Research on scientific reasoning has typically treated different aspects of the overall process in isolation. In the developmental literature this approach has tended toward a polarization of views about the ontogenesis of scientific thought. One position is that improvements in scientific reasoning abilities are a consequence of a knowledge base that grows as the child develops (e.g., Carey, 1985; Keil, 1981). For example, Carey (1984) stated that

> the acquisition and reorganization of strictly domain-specific knowledge (e.g., of the physical, biological and social worlds) probably account for most of the cognitive differences between 3-year-olds and adults. I have argued that in many cases developmental changes that have been taken to support format-level changes, or changes due to the acquisition of some tool that crosscuts domains, are in fact due to the acquisition of domain-specific knowledge. (p. 62)

Under this extreme view, the actual processes that children use only *appear* to be qualitatively different from that of adults because children do not have the necessary knowledge to perform at adult levels.

The other view, exemplified by the work of Piaget (1952), purports that although there are obviously changes in the knowledge base as children grow older, they are not the primary source of the radical differences in the behavior of children and adults. Rather, children have qualitatively different representations of the world and strategies for reasoning about it (e.g., Inhelder & Piaget, 1958; Kuhn & Phelps, 1982). Research in this tradition has used tasks in which the role of knowledge has been minimized and the different developmental strategies are made transparent. With respect to the development of scientific reasoning strategies, this latter view makes very specific claims. Flavell (1977) succinctly described the difference between the reasoning strategies of adults and children as follows:

---

[1]Reported in Klahr & Dunbar, 1988.

The formal-operational thinker inspects the problem data, *hypothesizes* that such and such a theory or explanation might be the correct one, deduces from it that so and so empirical phenomena ought logically to occur or not occur in reality, and then tests his theory by seeing if these predicted phenomena do in fact occur. . . . If you think you have just heard a description of textbook scientific reasoning, you are absolutely right. Because of its heavy trade in hypotheses and logical deduction from hypotheses, it is also called hypothetico-deductive reasoning, and it contrasts sharply with the much more nontheoretical and nonspeculative empirico-inductive reasoning of concrete-operational thinkers. (pp. 103–104).

Taken literally, this claim would lead to the conclusion that most adult subjects have not achieved the formal-operational level, because it has been well-established that adults find it extremely difficult to design experiments that provide a logical test of their hypothesis (e.g., Wason, 1968). Indeed, even well-trained scientists often draw invalid conclusions from the results of their experiments (e.g., Greenwald, Pratkanis, Leippe, & Baumgardner, 1986). Furthermore, the view of science as a hypothetico-deductive process is not consistent with recent descriptions of how scientists really work (cf. Harre, 1983; Kulkarni & Simon, 1988). Whether or not children's thinking is empirico-deductive is an open question. Although there has been a considerable amount of research on children's abilities to design experiments that test hypotheses, there has been little research that allows children to generate experimental results and then form hypotheses on the basis of these results. Therefore, one of the aims of our work with children was to discover what strategies they use in a scientific reasoning task, and how these strategies differ from those used by adults.

We believe that instead of framing the developmental question in terms of the dichotomy between a broadening of the knowledge base and a qualitative change in reasoning skills, it is more fruitful to provide a detailed characterization of the processes that are involved in scientific reasoning, and then to ask about the development of these processes. The specific approach in this chapter is based on the dual-space search idea introduced earlier, and our focus is on developmental differences in the search processes. By using the same task to investigate the types of hypotheses that subjects generate, and the types of experiments that they conduct, we avoid the problem of studying knowledge and strategies in isolation. This enables us to answer some more focused questions about the development of scientific reasoning skills.

## Development of Experimental Strategies

Many developmental investigators have looked at the ability to design informative experiments. One common approach is to allow children to design (or select) simple experiments that will reveal the cause of an event (cf. Case, 1974; Inhelder & Piaget, 1958; Kuhn & Phelps, 1982; Siegler & Liebert, 1975;

Tschirgi, 1980). For example, Kuhn and Phelps (1982) studied 10- to 11-year-old children attempting to isolate the critical ingredient in a mixture. They discovered that children's performance was severely impeded by "the power and persistence of invalid strategies," (i.e., experimental designs that were invalid, insufficient, or inefficient). Subjects commonly behaved as if their goal was not to find the cause of an effect, but rather to generate the effect. Tschirgi (1980) found that this tendency to generate a particular effect depends on whether the effect under investigation represents a good or a bad outcome. When the result of an experiment is undesirable (i.e., a bad outcome), subjects' tendency is to (correctly) vary *only* the hypothesized causal variable; in order to eliminate the bad outcome. However, for good outcomes, subjects tend to simultaneously vary *everything but* the hypothesized cause of the good outcome. Tschirgi found that adults were as likely to make this error as children.

Recent work on children's experimentation strategies by Kuhn and her co-researchers (Kuhn, Amsel, & O'Loughlin, 1988) showed some developmental changes in the ability to evaluate evidence. By presenting a large number of possible causes that might produce an effect and asking children to state what factor or combination of factors are the cause of the event, Kuhn and her colleagues discovered that children are more prone to ignore evidence that is inconsistent with their theory and are satisfied even when they know that their theory only accounts for some of the data. Furthermore, when children are asked to think of what data would be needed to disprove their theory, they have great difficulty. Taken as a whole, these studies suggest that children—and under some circumstances adults—frequently fail to distinguish between the goal of understanding a phenomenon and making it occur.

The approach to experimentation that we will take is one of discovering the strategies that subjects use to both design and evaluate the results of experiments. When experimentation is considered as a form of search it should be possible to delineate what types of cognitive processes govern the search of the experiment space and then specify the differences between adults and children with regard to these processes. In the following sections we describe the task and the type of hypothesis and experiment spaces that the subjects work in. This makes explicit the types of processes in which we expect to see developmental differences.

## STUDYING THE DISCOVERY PROCESS: GENERAL PROCEDURE

The device we use is a computer-controlled robot tank (called "BigTrak") that is programmed using a LOGO-like language.[2] It is a six-wheeled, battery-powered vehicle, approximately 30 cm long, 20 cm wide, and 15 cm high. The device is used by pressing various command keys on the keypad on the top

---

[2]This same device was first used in a study of "instructionless learning" (Shrager, 1985; Shrager & Klahr, 1986).

of the device, which is illustrated in Fig. 4.1. BigTrak is programmed by first clearing the memory with the **CLR** key and then entering a series of up to sixteen instructions, each consisting of a function key (the command) and a one- or two-digit number (the argument). When the **GO** key is pressed, BigTrak executes the program.

The effect of the argument depends on which command it follows. For forward (↑) and backward (↓) motion, each unit corresponds to approximately one foot. For left (←) and right (→) turns, the unit is a 6° rotation (corresponding to 1 minute on a clock face. Thus, a 90° turn is 15 minutes). The **HOLD** unit is a delay (or pause) of 0.1 seconds, and the **FIRE** unit is one audiovisual event: the firing of the cannon (indicated by appropriate sound and light effects). The other keys shown in Fig. 4.1 are **CLS**, **CK**, and **RPT**. **CLS** Clears the Last Step (i.e., the most recently entered instruction), and **CK** Checks the most recently entered instruction by executing it in isolation. Using **CK** does not affect the contents of memory. We describe **RPT** later. The **GO, CLR, CLS,** and **CK** commands do not take an argument. To illustrate, one might press the following series of keys:

$$\text{CLR} \uparrow 5 \leftarrow 7 \uparrow 3 \rightarrow 15 \text{ HOLD } 50 \text{ FIRE } 2 \downarrow 8 \text{ GO}$$

and BigTrak would do the following: move forward 5 feet, rotate counterclockwise 42 degrees, move forward 3 feet, rotate clockwise 90 degrees, pause for 5 seconds, fire twice, and backup 8 feet.

Certain combinations of keystrokes (e.g., a third numerical digit or two motion commands without an intervening numerical argument) are not permitted by the syntax of the programming language. With each syntactically legal key-stroke, BigTrak emits an immediate, confirmatory beep. Syntactically illegal key-strokes elicit no response, and they are not entered into program memory.

## STUDY 1:
## ADULTS DISCOVERING A NEW FUNCTION

In this study (we use the term *study* to distinguish our procedures from our subjects' "experiments"), we established a common knowledge base about the device for all subjects, prior to the discovery phase. We instructed subjects about how to use all function keys and special keys, except for one. All subjects were trained to criterion on the basic commands. Then the discovery phase started. Subjects were told that there is a "repeat" key, that it takes a numerical parameter, and that there can be only one **RPT** in a program. Then they were asked to discover how **RPT** works. (It repeats the previous *N* instructions once.)

FIG. 4.1.   Keypad from the BigTrak robot.

## Procedure

Twenty Carnegie-Mellon undergraduates participated in the experiment. All subjects had prior programming experience in at least one language. The study consisted of three phases. First, subjects were given instruction and practice in how to generate a good verbal protocol. Next, the subjects learned how to use the BigTrak. All subjects mastered the device within about 20 minutes.

The third—and focal—phase began when the experimenter pointed out the **RPT** key and asked the subject to "find out how the repeat key works." Subjects were asked to speak aloud, to say what they were thinking and what keys they were pressing. All subject behavior during this phase, including all key-strokes, was videotaped. At the outset of this phase, subjects had to state their first hypothesis about how **RPT** worked before using it in any programs. When subjects claimed that they were absolutely certain how the repeat key worked, or when 45 minutes had elapsed, the phase was terminated.

## Protocol Encoding

In this section we give a complete example of the kind of protocol that provides our basic source of data. (This listing, shown in Table 4.1, is one of our shortest, because it was generated by a subject who very rapidly discovered how **RPT** works.) At the outset, the subject (ML) forms the hypothesis that **RPT** $N$ will repeat the entire program $N$ times (003-004). (We call this kind of hypothesis *fully specified,* because both what will be repeated and the number of times it will be repeated are specified.) The prediction associated with the first "experiment" is that BigTrak will go forward 6 units (010-011). The prediction is consistent with the current hypothesis, but BigTrak does not behave as expected: it goes forward only 4 units, and the subject comments on the possibility of a failed prediction (013). This leads him to revise his hypothesis: **RPT** $N$ repeats only the last step (019). At this point, we do not have sufficient information to determine whether ML thinks there will be one or $N$ repetitions of the last step, and his next experiment (021) does not discriminate between the two possibilities. (We call this kind of hypothesis *partially specified,* because of the ambiguity. In contrast, the initial hypothesis stated earlier (003-004) is *fully specified.*) However, his subsequent comments (024-025) clarify the issue. The experiment at (021) produces results consistent with the hypothesis that there will be $N$ repetitions (BigTrak goes forward 2 units and turns left 60 units), and ML explicitly notes the confirming behavior (022). But the next experiment (026) disconfirms the hypothesis. Although he makes no explicit prediction, we infer from previous statements (023-025) that ML expected BigTrak to go forward 2 and turn left 120. Instead, it executes the entire ↑ **2** ← **30** sequence twice. ML finds this "strange" (028), and he repeats the experiment.

At this point, based on the results of only four distinct experiments, ML begins to formulate and verbalize the corect hypothesis—that **RPT** $N$ causes BigTrak to execute one repetition of the $N$ **instructions preceding the RPT** (030-034)—and he even correctly articulates the special case where $N$ exceeds the program length, in which case the entire program is repeated once (035-037). Note that whereas the earlier hypotheses revisions maintained the role of $N$ (it counted the number of times something was repeated), this final hypothesis gives $N$ a new role: it determines what gets repeated. ML then does a series of experiments where he only varies $N$ in order to be sure he is correct (038-046), and then he explores the issue of the order of execution of the repeated segment.

## Aggregate Results

### Overall Performance

Nineteen of the 20 subjects discovered how the **RPT** key works within the allotted 45 minutes. The mean time to solution (i.e., when the correct rule was finally stated) was 19.8 minutes. In the process of discovering how **RPT** worked, subjects generated, on average, 18.2 programs.

Of the 364 programs run by the 20 subjects, 304 were *experiments;* that is, they included a **RPT**. Another 51 programs were *control trials,* in which the subject wrote a program without a **RPT,** ran the program, then added **RPT,** and ran the program again. We label the initial program of the pair— as the one that does not include a **RPT**—as the control trial. Another seven programs we label as *calibration trials*: These were trials on which the subject attempted to determine (or remember) what physical unit is associated with **N** for a specific command (e.g., how far is ↑ 1). Only two programs that did not contain a **RPT** were unclassifiable.

We define a *common hypothesis* as a fully specified hypothesis that was proposed by at least two different subjects. Across all subjects, there were eight distinct common hypotheses. Protocols were encoded in terms of the fully specified hypotheses listed in Table 4.2. Subjects did not always express their hypotheses in exactly this form, but there was usually little ambiguity about the current hypothesis. We coded each experiment in terms of the

TABLE 4.1
Example of a Complete Protocol

| | | | | | | |
|---|---|---|---|---|---|---|
002 EXP: SO HOW DO YOU THINK IT MIGHT WORK?
003 Uh... it would repeat all of the steps before it, however many times
004 I told it to repeat it.
005 EXP: WELL... SO START WORKING ON IT NOW THEN.
006 Ok.
007 EXP: AND TELL ME EVERYTHING THAT'S GOING ON IN YOUR MIND.
008 Ok.
009 EXP: NOW PRESS CLEAR.
010 Ok, um... I'm gonna make it go
011 forward two, and then I'm gonna make it repeat that twice.

012 00:30 ↑ 2 RPT 2

**↑ 4**

013 Maybe not, uh....  ... repeat once

014 02:00 ↑ 1 ← 15 ↑ 1 HOLD 2 RPT 1

**↑ 1 ← 15 ↑ 1 HOLD 4**

015 Hmm.. guess that was it.
016 EXP: SO WHAT ARE YOU THINKING?
017 Um.. actually I have no idea now.
018 I'm trying to figure out what it is.
019 Um.. maybe it repeats the last step.
020 Ok, I'm gonna try that. ...... repeat once.

021 03:30 ↑ 2 ← 30 RPT 1

**↑ 2 ← 60**

022 All right, that backs up my theory.
023 Let me see if I can somehow make sure that that's what it does
024 is repeats the last step however many times that I tell it to,
025 so I'm gonna ... repeat it four times...

026 04:00 ↑ 2 ← 30 RPT 4

**↑ 2 ← 30 ↑ 2 ← 30**

027
028 That was strange, hmm... um... let me see that again.

029 04:30 ↑ 2 ← 30 RPT 4

**↑ 2 ← 30 ↑ 2 ← 30**

030 Ok, maybe it means repeat the last number...
031 however many steps before it that I put in,
032 that'll be the number after the repeat. For instance,
033 if I put repeat two, it'll repeat the last two steps.
034 If I put repeat five, it'll repeat the last five steps,
035 and if there's too many...
036 if the five is more than the number of steps in the program,
037 it'll just end it at whatever number of steps in the program,
038 so . . . repeat one, no, repeat two.

*Note:* CLR and GO commands have been deleted. BigTrak's behavior is shown in boldface type.

*(Continued)*

TABLE 4.1
*(Continued)*

| | | | | | | | | | |
|---|---|---|---|---|---|---|---|---|---|
| 039 | | | | | | | | | |
| 040 | 06:00 | ↑ 2 | ← 15 | ↑ 2 | FIRE 3 | RPT 2 | | | |
| | | **↑ 2** | **← 15** | **↑ 2** | **FIRE 3** | **↑ 2** | **FIRE 3** | | |
| 041 | All right, I think I might have gotten it. | | | | | | | | |
| 042 | | | | | | | | | |
| 043 | 06:30 | ↑ 2 | ← 15 | ↑ 2 | FIRE 3 | RPT 3 | | | |
| | | **↑ 2** | **← 15** | **↑ 2** | **FIRE 3** | **← 15** | **↑ 2 FIRE 3** | | |
| 044 | Ok, I think I've gotten it. I'm gonna make it repeat four times. | | | | | | | | |
| 045 | . . . wanna repeat four... | | | | | | | | |
| 046 | 07:30 | ↑ 2 | ← 15 | ↑ 2 | FIRE 3 | RPT 4 | | | |
| | | **↑ 2** | **← 15** | **↑ 2** | **FIRE 3** | **↑ 2** | **← 15** | **↑ 2** | **FIRE 3** |

047 Ok, now I'm trying to figure out which order the repeat step goes.
048 If it does the first part of the program or if it does...if it starts
049 from the last part of the program, where repeat...
050 if I say repeat one, does it repeat the first step in the program,
051 or does it repeat the last step I pressed in? Um...repeat that
052 step...
053

| | | | | | | | |
|---|---|---|---|---|---|---|---|
| 054 | 09:00 | ↑ 2 | ← 15 | ↑ 2 | FIRE 3 | RPT 1 | |
| | | **↑ 2** | **← 15** | **↑ 2** | **FIRE 6** | | |

055
056 It goes from the last step,
057 and I don't understand why it doesn't go backwards.
058 Maybe it counts back two steps.
059 If I put repeat two, it would count back two steps,
060 starting from there and go until the last step. Alright,
061 ...um...the last two steps were forward two and fire three,
062 so let me try and repeat that again.

| | | | | | | | |
|---|---|---|---|---|---|---|---|
| 063 | 10:00 | ↑ 2 | ← 15 | ↑ 2 | FIRE 3 | RPT 2 | |
| | | **↑ 2** | **← 15** | **↑ 2** | **FIRE 3** | **↑ 2** | **FIRE 3** |

064 All right, now if I ... repeat five...
065 so if I put repeat four, it should do the whole program over again.

| | | | | | | | | | |
|---|---|---|---|---|---|---|---|---|---|
| 066 | 11:00 | ↑ 2 | ← 15 | ↑ 2 | FIRE 3 | RPT 4 | | | |
| | | **↑ 2** | **← 15** | **↑ 2** | **FIRE 3** | **↑ 2** | **← 15** | **↑ 2** | **FIRE 3** |

067 Well, I think I figured out what it does.
068 EXP: SO HOW DOES IT WORK?
069 Ok, when you press the repeat key and then the number,
070 it comes back that many steps and then starts from there
071 and goes up to, uh...it proceeds up to the end of the program
072 and then it hits the repeat function again.
073 It can't go through it twice.
074 ......
075 EXP: GREAT.

*Note:* CLR and GO commands have been deleted. BigTrak's behavior is shown in boldface type.

TABLE 4.2
Common Hypotheses and Percentage of Experiments Conducted
Under Each

| HYPOTHESIS[4] | % EXPERIMENTS UNDER EACH HYPOTHESIS | |
|---|---|---|
| | Adults | Children |
| HS1: One repeat of last N instructions. | 02 | 00 |
| HS2: One repeat of first N instructions. | 04 | 00 |
| HS3: One repeat of the Nth instruction. | 03 | 01 |
| HN1: One repeat of entire program. | 06 | 03 |
| HN2: One repeat of the last instruction. | 04 | 05 |
| HC1: N repeats of entire program. | 14 | 21 |
| HC2: N repeats of the last instruction. | 20 | 08 |
| HC3: N repeats of subsequent steps. | 02 | 00 |
| HC4: N-1, N/2 or +N repeats. | 00 | 17 |
| HC5: N repeats of last 2 steps. | 00 | 07 |
| Partially specified | 03 | 27 |
| Idiosyncratic | 14 | 01 |
| No Hypothesis | 28 | 10 |
| | 100 | 100 |

[4]Hypotheses are labeled according to the role of **N**: HS - selector; HN - nil; HC - counter.

hypothesis held by the subject at the time of the experiment, and Table 4.2 shows the proportion of all experiments that were run in study 1 while an hypothesis was held.[3] (The final column in Table 4.2 refers to the children's performance in study 3, to be described in a later section.)

On average, subjects proposed 4.6 different hypotheses (including the correct one). Fifty-five percent of the experiments were conducted under one of the eight common hypotheses listed in Table 4.2. Partially specified hypotheses, which account for 3% of the experiments, are defined as those in which only some attributes of the common hypotheses were stated by the subject (e.g., "it will repeat it $N$ times."). An idiosyncratic hypothesis is defined as one that

---

[3]As noted earlier, HS1 in Table 4.2 is the way that BigTrak actually operates.

was generated by only one subject. Such hypotheses are not listed separately in Table 4.2. There were no stated hypotheses for 28% of the experiments.

## The Hypothesis Space

The eight common hypotheses—which account for over half of the experiments—can be described in terms of four attributes: The role of $N$, the type of element to be repeated, the boundaries of the repeated element, and the number of repetitions. The resulting *hypothesis space* is shown in Table 4.3, together with an abstract test program and an indication (in the rightmost column) of how BigTrak would execute the test program, if it operated according to the hypothesis in question.

This space can be represented in terms of *frames* (cf. Minsky, 1975). The basic frame for discovering how **RPT** works is depicted at the top of Fig. 4.2. It consists of four slots, corresponding to the four attributes listed: *n*-role, unit of repetition, number-of-repetitions, and boundaries-of-segment. A fully instantiated frame corresponds to a fully specified hypothesis, several of which are shown in Fig. 4.2. There are two principle subsidiary frames for **RPT**, $N$-role:*counter* and $N$-role:*selector*. Within each of these frames, hypotheses differing along only a single attribute are shown with arrows between them. All other pairs of hypotheses differ by more than one attribute. Note that the hypotheses are clustered according to the $N$-role frame in which they fall.

Recall that subjects were asked to state their hypothesis about **RPT** *before*

TABLE 4.3
Attribute-Value Representation of Fully-Specified Common Hypotheses[5]

| Rule | N-role | Rep-type | Bounds | # of reps | Prediction |
|------|--------|----------|--------|-----------|------------|
| HS1 | selector | segment | last N | 1 | abcdCDef |
| HS2 | selector | segment | first N | 1 | abcdABef |
| HS3 | selector | instruction | Nth fm start | 1 | abcdBef |
| HN1* | nil | segment | all | 1 | abcdABCDef |
| HN2* | nil | instruction | prior | 1 | abcdDef |
| HC1 | counter | segment | all | N | abcdABCDABCDef |
| HC2 | counter | instruction | prior | N | abcdDDef |
| HC3 | counter | segment | all following | N | abcdefEFEF |

Test Program: abcdRPT2ef

[5]1) * rules do not use N; 2) Uppercase letters in predictions show executions under control of RPT2; 3) Underlined letters reflect ambiguity in "repeat twice."

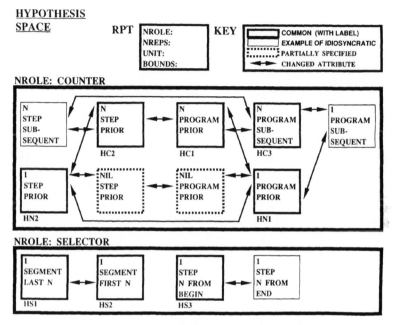

FIG. 4.2. Frames for hypotheses about how **RPT N** works. Heavy borders corresond to common hypotheses from Table 4.2; dashed borders correspond to partially specified hypotheses; arrows indicate a change in the value of a single attribute. (All possible hypotheses are not shown.)

actually using it in an experiment. This procedure enabled us to determine what frame is constructed by searching memory for relevant knowledge. No subject started off with the correct frame. Seventeen of the 20 subjects started with the *N*-role:*counter* frame. That is, subjects initially assume that the role of *N* is to specify the number of repetitions, and their initial hypotheses differed only in whether the repeated unit was the entire program or the single instruction preceding **RPT** (HC1 and HC2). This suggests that subjects drew their initial hypotheses by analogy from the regular command keys, where *N* determines the number of times that a command is executed.

Having proposed their initial hypotheses, subjects then began to revise them on the basis of experimental evidence. Subjects eventually changed from an N-role:*counter* frame to the *N*-role:*selector* frame. Fifteen of the subjects made only one frame change, and four of the remaining five made three or more frame changes. This suggests that subjects were following very different strategies for searching the hypothesis space. We discuss strategic variation later in this chapter.

### The Experiment Space

Subjects test their hypotheses by conducting experiments; by writing programs that include **RPT** and observing BigTrak's behavior. But it is not immediately obvious what constitutes a good or informative experiment. In constructing experiments, subjects are faced with a problem-solving task that parallels their effort to discover the correct hypotheses, except that in this case search is not in a space of hypotheses, but in a space of experiments.

A useful characterization of the experiment space is one that abstracts over the specific content of programs and refers to only two dimensions of their experiments. The first is the value of $N$—the argument that repeat takes. The second is $\lambda$—the length of the program preceding the **RPT**. Within the $N$-$\lambda$ space, we identify six distinct regions according to the relative value of $N$ and $\lambda$ and their limiting values. The regions are depicted in Fig. 4.3, together with illustrative programs. At the bottom of the figure, we indicate which of the common hypotheses would be confirmed by experiments in each region. Here we define the regions and indicate the general consequences of running experiments in each.

- Region I. One-step programs $N = 1$ or 2, (e.g., ↑ **1 RPT 1**, or ↑ **1 RPT 2**). although an incrementalist strategy would suggest that this is a good starting place for exploring the experiment space, such exepriments are totally undiscriminating: as shown in Fig. 4.3, they produce behavior consistent with all but HC3 in Table 4.2. Furthermore, the ambiguous distinction between "repeat once" and "repeat twice," mentioned earlier, is exacerbated with a one-step program. Regardless of whether the value of $N$ is 1 or 2, the command will be executed twice.

- Region II. Multistep programs with $N = 1$ (e.g., ↑ **1 FIRE 1 → 15 RPT 1**). Experiments in this region are consistent with hypotheses of the form "it repeats the previous step," such as HC2 and HN2. They rule out hypotheses that the entire program is repeated once (HN1) or $N$ times (HC1).

- Region III. Programs with at least three instructions and a value of $N$ less than $\lambda$ and greater than 1 (e.g., ↑ **1 Fire 1 → 15 RPT 2**). As long as no two adjacent instructions are identical, programs in this region are consistent only with HS1 (the correct hypothesis). For example, the program [↑ **2 → 15 FIRE 4 ← 30 RPT 3**] is inconsistent with every common hypothesis except HS1.

- Region IV. Here, $\lambda = N$ (e.g., ↑ **1 FIRE 1 → 15 RPT 3**). In addition to HS1, these experiments are consistent with hypotheses that **RPT** causes a repetition of the entire program (HN1), as well as with HS2 (Repeat first $N$ steps once).

- Region V. In this region, $N$ is greater than $\lambda$ (e.g., ↑ **1 FIRE 1 → 15 RPT 5**). In this situation, BigTrak effectively sets $N$ equal to $\lambda$, so experiments

## EXPERIMENT SPACE

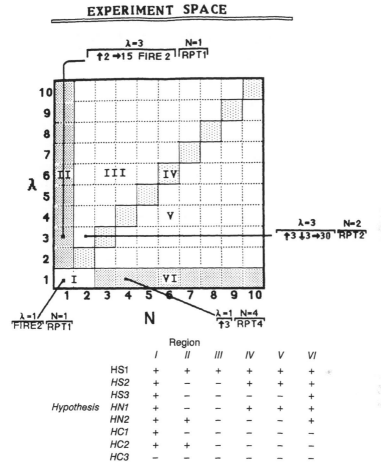

FIG. 4.3.  Regions of the Experiment Space, showing illustrative programs and confirmation/disconfirmation for each common hypothesis. (Shown here is only the 10 × 10 subspace for the ful 15 × 16 space.)

in this region tend to support the hypothesis that $N$ is irrelevant and that HN1 is the correct hypothesis.

- Region VI. Experiments in this region have one-instruction programs with values of $N$ greater than 2 (e.g., **FIRE 1 RPT 6**). This region is similar to Region V and also serves as the testing ground for hypotheses that $N$ corresponds to the number of repetitions (HC1-HC3). These hypotheses are disconfirmed in this region, but some subjects persevere here nevertheless.

Other formulations are possible, but we will use the $N$–$\lambda$ space in our analysis. We do not claim that subjects have this elaborated representation of the experiment space. Instead, it enables us to classify experiments according to the kinds of conclusions that they support.

## Strategic Variation in Scientific Discovery: Theorists and Experimenters

As noted earlier, subjects started with the wrong frame; thinking that $N$ functions as a counter. The most significant representational change occurred when subjects switched from the $N$-role:*counter* frame to the $N$-role:*selector* frame. Once subjects made this change, they quickly discovered how the **RPT** key works. Subjects used two different strategies to switch frames. Thirteen subjects were classified as experiment space searchers because they induced the correct frame from the result of an experiment in region III of the experiment space. For convenience, we refer to them as "Experimenters." The remaining seven subjects searched the hypothesis space for information to construct a frame that was consistent with the experimental data that they had observed. We call them "Theorists." Theorists did not have to conduct an experiment in region III of the experiment space to generate the correct frame.

### Experimenters: General Strategy

Experimenters went through two phases. During the first, they explicitly stated the hypothesis under consideration, and conducted experiments to evaluate it. They proposed a number of hypotheses within the $N$-role:*counter* frame, however they eventually realized that the $N$-role:*counter* frame was inadequate and they switched to a search of the experiment space. In this second phase, Experimenters conducted experiments without explicit statement of an hypothesis. Prior to the discovery of how the **RPT** works, Experimenters conducted, on average, six experiments without statement of an hypothesis. Furthermore, these experiments were usually accompanied by statements about what would happen if $N$ or $\lambda$ were changed. By pursuing the approach of changing $N$ and $\lambda$, Experimenters eventually conducted an experiment in region III of the experiment space. When the subjects conducted an experiment in this region, they noticed that the last $N$ steps were repeated and proposed HS1—the correct rule.

### Theorists: General Strategy

The strategy used by Theorists was to construct an initial frame, $N$-role: *counter,* and then to conduct experiments that tested the values of the frame. When they had gathered enough evidence to reject an hypothesis, Theorists switched to a new value of a slot in the frame. For example, a subject might switch from saying that the prior step is repeated $N$ times to saying that the prior program is repeated $N$ times. When a new hypothesis was proposed, it was always in the same frame, and it usually involved a change in only one attribute. These subjects eventually accumulated enough evidence to reject the $N$-role:*counter* frame entirely. Knowing that sometimes the previous step and sometimes the previous program was repeated, Theorists could infer that the unit of repetition was variable and that this ruled out all hypotheses in the $N$-role:*counter* frame—because those hypotheses all require a fixed unit of repetition. This realization enabled Theorists to constrain their search to an $N$-role that has a variable unit of repetition. As is shown in study 2, subjects can construct an $N$-role:*selector* frame without further experimentation. Following memory search, Theorists constructed the $N$-role: *selector* frame and proposed one of the hypotheses within it. They usually selected the correct one, but if they did not, they soon discovered it by changing one attribute of the frame as soon as their initial $N$-role:*selector* hypothesis was disproven.

Performance differences between Theorists and Experimenters are summarized in Table 4.4. The most important one is that Experimenters conduct more experiments than Theorists and that this extra experimentation is conducted without an explicit hypothesis statement. We have argued that this extra experimentation is indicative of searching the experiment space, and we have shown that Experimenters do indeed use more $N$-$\lambda$ combinations than the Theorists. Furthermore, we have argued that instead of conducting a search of the experiment space, Theorists search the hypothesis space for an appropriate role for $N$. This is an important claim for which there was no direct evidence in the protocols. Our second study tests the hypothesis that it is possible to think of an $N$-role:*selector* hypothesis without exploration of the experiment space.

## STUDY 2: HYPOTHESIS-SPACE SEARCH
## AND EXPERIMENTATION BY ADULTS

Our interpretation of subjects' behavior in Study 1 generated two related hypotheses: First, it should be possible for subjects to propose the correct rule without the benefit of any experimental outcomes. In Study 2, we tested this hypothesis by asking subjects to state not just one, but *several*, different ways that **RPT** might work, *before* doing any experiments. If subjects can think of the correct rule without any experimentation, then this can only be attributed to hypothesis space search because there is no experimental input. Second, if hypothesis-space search is unsuccessful, then subjects switch to a search of the experiment space. This hypothesis predicts that subjects who are unable to generate the correct rule in the hypothesis-space search phase will behave like the Experimenters of Study 1 and will discover the correct rule only after conducting an experiment in region III of the experiment space.

TABLE 4.4
Performance Summary of Experimenters and Theorists in Study 1

|  | Experimenters | Theorists | Combined |
|---|---|---|---|
| N | 13 | 7 | 20 |
| Time (minutes) | 24.46 | 11.40 | 19.40 |
| Experiments | 18.38 | 9.29 | 15.20 |
| Experiments with hypotheses | 12.30 | 8.57 | 11.00 |
| Experiments without hypotheses | 6.08 | 0.76 | 4.2 |
| Different hypotheses | 4.92 | 3.86 | 4.55 |
| Hypothesis switches | 4.76 | 3.00 | 4.15 |
| Experiment space verbalizations | 5.85 | 0.86 | 4.10 |
| $N\lambda$ combinations used | 9.9 | 5.7 | 8.45 |

## Method

Ten Carnegie–Mellon undergraduates participated in this study. The familiarization part of Study 2 was the same as described for Study 1; subjects learned how to use all the keys except the **RPT** key. Familiarization was followed by two phases: hypothesis-space search and experimentation.

The hypothesis-space search phase began when the subjects were asked to think of various ways that the **RPT** key might work. In an attempt to get a wide range of possible hypotheses from the subjects, we used three probes in the same fixed order:

1. How do you think the **RPT** key might work?
2. We've done this experiment with many people, and they've proposed a wide variety of hypotheses for how it might work. What do you think they may have proposed?
3. When BigTrak was being designed, the designers thought of many different ways it could be made to work. What ways do you think they may have considered?

After each question, the subject responded with as many hypotheses as could be generated. Then the next probe was used. Once the subjects had generated all the hypotheses that they could think of, the experimental phase began: The subjects were allowed to conduct experiments while attempting to discover how the **RPT** key works.

## Results and Discussion

Subjects proposed, on average, 4.2 different hypotheses. All but 2 subjects began with the N-role:*counter* frame, and 7 of the 10 subjects switched to the N-role:*selector* frame during Phase 1. The correct rule (HS1) was proposed by 5 of the 10 subjects. In the experimental phase all subjects were able to figure out how the **RPT** key works. Mean time to solution was 6.2 minutes, and subjects generated, on average, 5.7 experiments and proposed 2.4 different hypotheses.

The results of the hypothesis-space search phase of Study 2 show that it is possible for subjects to generate the correct hypothesis (among others) without conducting any experiments. This result is consistent with the view that the Theorists in Study 1 think of the correct rule by a search of the hypothesis space. The results of the experimental phase of Study 2 further support our interpretation of Study 1. All of the subjects who failed to generate the correct rule in the hypothesis-space search phase behaved like Experimenters in the experimental phase. They discovered the correct rule only after exploring region III of the experiment space. This finding is consistent with the view that when hypothesis-space search fails, subjects must turn to a search of the experiment space.

This study and the previous one have provided some initial answers to the question of how adults reason scientifically. The adults' performance provides a standard against which we can compare children's performance on the same task as was used in Study 1. Thus, in Study 3, children were given some initial training on how to use the BigTrak, and were then asked to find out how the **RPT** key works.

## STUDY 3:
## SCIENTIFIC REASONING IN CHILDREN

As a result of our work with adults we can now pose some more specific questions than those outlined earlier. One set of questions deals with searching the hypothesis space. First, given the same training experience as adults, will children think of the same initial hypotheses as adults? If they do, then this would suggest that the processes used to construct an initial frame are similar in both adults and children. Second, when children's initial hypotheses are disconfirmed will the children assign the same values to slots as the adults? That is, are the processes that are used to search the hypothesis space similar in both adults and children? Finally, will children be able to change frames or will they remain in the same frame? Given that some adults—Theorists— were able to construct frames from a search of memory, will children be able to do so too? Failing that, will they be able to switch their strategy to a search of the experiment space—as did the experimenters, or will they stay within their initial frame?

Another set of questions concerns children's search of the experiment space. Children may search different areas of the experiment space than the adults, or they may even construct a different type of experiment space. Such a finding would suggest that the strategies used to go from an hypothesis to a specific experiment are different in adults and children. Another possibility is that children may evaluate the results of experiments in a different way from adults. Kuhn and her colleagues' work suggests that the ability to evaluate experimental evidence is one of the major differences in reasoning strategies between adults and children. However, in her tasks, the opportunity for an interaction between data and theory is not present because the children cannot continually cycle from hypotheses to experiments.

## Method

### Subjects

Twenty-two third to sixth graders from a local private school participated in the study. All of the children had 45 hours of LOGO instruction prior to participating in this study. We selected this group partly as a matter of convenience, because they were participating in another study on the acquisition and transfer of debugging skills (Carver, 1986; Klahr & Carver, 1988). More importantly, because we will be contrasting the children's performance with adult subjects—all of whom had some programming experience—our subjects' experience provided at least a rough control for prior exposure to programming instruction. Furthermore, the subjects' age range (8;2 to 11;8) spans the putative period of the emergency of formal operational reasoning skills, the hallmark of which is, as noted earlier, the ability to "reason scientifically." Also, in a pilot study, we discovered that children with no programming experience had great difficulty understanding what was expected of them on the task.

### Procedure

As in study 1, the subjects were taught how to use the BigTrak and were then asked to discover how the **RPT** key works. The session ended when the child stated that he or she was satisfied that he or she had discovered how the **RPT** key works, or could not figure out how it worked. Two procedural modifications facilitated working with the children. First, if the children did not spontaneously state what they were thinking about, the experimenter asked them how they thought the **RPT** key worked. Second, if a subject persisted with the same incorrect hypothesis and did exactly the same type of experiment (i.e., $\lambda$ and $N$ were not changed) four times in a row, the experimenter asked the child what the purpose of the number with the **RPT** key was.

## Results

In this section, we first discuss the overall results. Then we describe the types of hypotheses and experiments that the children proposed. We also point to some of the more important differences between the strategies used by the children and the adults.

Only 2 of the 22 children discovered the correct rule. Fourteen children (including the 2 who were correct) asserted that they were absolutely certain that they had discovered how **RPT** works. Four gave up in confusion, and

4 thought that it worked in a particular way some of the time. The children spent, on average, 20 minutes trying to determine how the **RPT** key works. They generated an average of 13 programs. Of the 285 programs run by the subjects, 240 were experiments, 23 were control experiments, 1 was a calibration, and 21 were unclassifiable. Children proposed 3.3 different hypotheses during the course of a session. This is only about 1 less than the mean number of hypotheses proposed by adults; but as shown in the second columnn of Table 4.2, the relative frequency of experiments run under different hypotheses was very different. The following paragraphs discuss these differences.

### Partial Hypotheses

Nearly 30% of the children's experiments were conducted under partial hypotheses, whereas adults specified all but 3% of their experiments fully (see Table 4.2). Of those experiments children conducted under partial hypotheses, 51% did not mention the unit of repetition (i.e., whether it was a step, a program, or a segment), and 49% did not mention the number of repetitions that should occur. This statement of partial hypotheses could be the result of differences in the children's ability to articulate fully specified hypotheses, or it could result from the fact that the children often did not regard the attributes of number of repetitions and the unit of repetition as being salient attributes of the **RPT** key. With respect to the number of repetitions, the latter interpretation is supported by the finding that the children often failed to type in a number after pressing the **RPT** key, indicating that they did not see a number as being a necessary part of the **RPT** command. With respect to the segments, the issue is unclear. In any event, by not stating the unit of repetition or the number of repetitions, the children are indicating that they consider these attributes of the hypothesis to be secondary.

### Exploring Only One Frame

All of the 20 children who failed to discover how **RPT** works proposed hypotheses that were solely in the *N*-role:*counter* frame. Even though the children observed many experimental outcomes that were consistent with the *N*-role:*selector* frame and not with their current frame, none of the children were able to induce the selector frame. This suggests two things: First, the children did not have sufficient knowledge available to generate the *N*-role:*selector* frame by searching the hypothesis space. Second, the children did not use experiment-space search to induce a new frame. Instead, they used it to induce new slot values for their current frame. As a result, the children generated a number of hypotheses within the *N*-role:*counter* frame that were not generated by the adults.

Many of the children who originally had an hypothesis with *N*-role:*counter* abandoned it in favor of a nil role for *N* or invented a new number of repetitions to account for the data. Seventeen percent of their experiments were conducted using one of these hypotheses (HC4 in Table 4.2). These hypotheses were generated when the children were trying to account for the finding that **RPT** 2 only repeats the prior program once, not twice. These children either said that $N$ had no role, or tried to accommodate the number of repetitions slot to fit the data. The children stated that the program was repeated $N$-1 times, $N/2$ times, or stated that the value of $N$ replaced the value that was bound to the previous command (e.g., FIRE 3 RPT 8 will do a FIRE 3 FIRE 8). No adult generated such hypotheses.

Another type of hypothesis that appeared only in the children's data was that the last two steps of the program were repeated $N$ times. Three of the 22 children proposed this type of hypothesis after conducting an experiment in region III with $N = 2$. Thus, the children proposed an hypothesis that was within the $N$-role:*counter* frame, yet was consistent with the observation that the last two steps of a program were repeated.

Each of these hypotheses is a way of staying within the $N$-role:*counter* frame while accounting for the finding that there were not $N$ repetitions of a command or a program. These hypotheses were generated even though there was a large amount of evidence available that could disconfirm both the individual hypotheses and the frame itself. However, the children were content with hypotheses that could account for the results of the most recent outcome. That is, local consistency was sufficient, and global inconsistency was ignored.

### Search of the Experiment Space

One question that we raised earlier was whether children's search in the experiment space would be different from that of the adults. As can be seen from Table 4.5, the adults and children differed in the number of experiments run in regions I and V ($\chi_5^2 = 31.4$ $p < .05$). Children ran twice as many experiments as the adults in region I and about one third as many as the adults in region V. Experiments in region I confirm any hypothesis and merely show that something is repeated, without providing any information about number of repetitions or what is repeated. Experiments in region V suggest that $N$ is irrelevant, because they repeat the entire program once, whatever the value of $N$.

Although two thirds of the adult experiments were distributed over the experiment space in exactly the same way as the children's experiments, the hypotheses that they induced from these experiments were quite different. In particular, both adults and children conducted 17% of their programs in the (potentially) highly informative region III of the experiment space. Adults were able to induce the correct rule from experiments in this region, whereas children were not. Adults and children also conducted the same amount of experiments in region II of the experiment space yet reached different conclusions. Adults induced the hypothesis that the previous step was repeated,

TABLE 4.5
Percentage of Programs in Each Area of the Experiment Space
for Adults (Study 1) and Children (Study 3)

|          | I  | II | III | IV | V  | VI |
| -------- | -- | -- | --- | -- | -- | -- |
| Adults   | 15 | 25 | 17  | 10 | 20 | 13 |
| Children | 30 | 21 | 17  | 11 | 7  | 14 |

whereas the children did not; they maintained the hypothesis that it is the program that is repeated. In the following paragraphs we will explore these interactions between search of the Experiment and Hypothesis spaces in more detail.

### Differences in Search Strategies

Only two children generated the *N*-role:*selector* frame, so it is difficult to classify the other 20 children as either Experimenters or Theorists according to the same criteria used in Study 1. The earlier classification was based on how subjects switched from one frame to another. Clearly, when subjects only use one frame it is impossible to make this categorization. However, even without this criterion we can see that all 20 of the children who failed to generate the correct hypothesis can be classified as a type of Experimenter. The children were within the *N*-role:*counter* frame and their search of the hypothesis space consisted of changing the values of the slots within the *N*-role:*counter* frame. This was achieved by searching the experiment space to find values for the number of repetitions slot within the frame.

While the children were searching the experiment space to induce new hypotheses, their search was different from the adults: The adults searched the experiment space once they had abandoned the *N*-role:*counter* frame and the goal of their search was to induce a new frame. In contrast, the children used experiments to find new slot values within a frame that they were reluctant to abandon. Some experiments, because they were in uninformative regions of the experiment space, did confirm their incorrect hypotheses. Others did not, but children responded to disconfirmation either by misobservation or by ignoring the results and running yet another experiment that they were sure would confirm their prediction. This indicates that while the children were exploring both the Hypothesis and the experiment space, their search of the Hypothesis space was limited; their search of the Hypothesis space was constrained to staying within one frame—the *N*-role:*counter* frame.

### Summary

There were three main differences between adults and children. First, children proposed hypotheses that were different from adults. Furthermore, these different hypotheses were induced from the same type of data as the adult's hypotheses. Second, the children did not abandon their current frame and search the Hypothesis space for a new frame, or use the results of experiment space search to induce a new frame. Third, the children did not attempt to check whether their hypotheses were consistent with prior data. Even when children knew that there was earlier evidence against their current hypothesis, they said that the device *usually* worked according to their theory.

The analysis of the children's search strategies, as well as the earlier analysis of the adult group, have begun to yield a complex picture of the different ways that subjects can use experiments. In order to fully interpret these differences, it is necessary to introduce a theoretical framework that further explicates the distinction between the hypothesis space and the experiment space as well as the coordination of search in the two spaces. In the next section, we turn to that theoretical extension. Following that, we return to the comparative interpretation of our findings in terms of the framework.

## A DUAL-SEARCH MODEL OF SCIENTIFIC DISCOVERY

Our model of scientific reasoning is based on Simon and Lea's (1974) Generalized Rule Inducer (GRI). As noted earlier, in the GRI, concept formation tasks involve search in two problem spaces—a space of rules and a space of instances. Simon and his colleagues extended this original idea to the analysis of several important scientific discoveries (Kulkarni & Simon, 1988; Langley, Zytkow, Simon & Bradshaw, 1986), and we extended it to provide a framework for the interpretation of results from experimental studies of scientific reasoning in the laboratory. In this section, we describe our model of Scientific Discovery as Dual Search (SDDS), and in the following section we use SDDS as a basis for further discussion of developmental issues.

### SDDS: Summary[6]

The fundamental assumption is that scientific reasoning requires search in two related problem spaces: an hypothesis space, consisting of the hypotheses generated during the discovery process, and an experiment space, consisting of all possible experiments that could be conducted. Search in the hypothesis space is guided both by prior knowledge and by experimental results. Search in the experiment space may be guided by the current hypothesis, and it may be used to generate information to formulate hypotheses.

SDDS consists of a set of basic components that guide search within and between the two problem spaces. Initial hypotheses are constructed by a series of operations that result in the instantiation of a frame (cf. Minsky, 1975) with default values. Subsequent hypotheses within that frame are generated

---

[6]See Klahr and Dunbar (1988) for more detail.

by changes in values of particular slots, and changes to new frames are achieved either by a search of memory or by generalizing from experimental outcomes. Three main components control the entire process from the initial formulation of hypotheses, through their experimental evaluation, to the decision that there is sufficient evidence to accept an hypothesis. The three components, shown at the top of the hierarchy in Fig. 4.4 are SEARCH HYPOTHESIS SPACE, TEST HYPOTHESIS, AND EVALUATE EVIDENCE.

### SEARCH HYPOTHESIS SPACE

The goal of this process is to form a fully specified hypothesis, which provides the input to TEST HYPOTHESIS. This can be achieved in two ways. The first is by searching memory for a frame that could be used to generate an hypothesis (EVOKE FRAME). The second is by conducting experiments and inducing a new frame from the results of these experiments (INDUCE FRAME). Once a frame has been instantiated, the subject must assign specific values to the slots so that a specific hypothesis can be generated. Again, there are two ways that this can occur. One is by conducting further experiments to determine what the slot values should be (USE EXPERIMENTAL OUTCOMES), and the other is to fill in the slots with their default values (USE PRIOR KNOWLEDGE).

### TEST HYPOTHESIS

TEST HYPOTHESIS generates an experiment appropriate to the current hypothesis, makes a prediction, then runs and observes the result of the experiment. Experiments are designed in the E-SPACE MOVE process. This process consists of selecting a central focus for the experiment and then setting values for this focus. Once this is set the values of the other aspects of the experiment can be assigned. The output of TEST HYPOTHESIS is a description of evidence for or against the current hypothesis, based on the match between the prediction derived from the current hypothesis and the actual experimental result.

### EVALUATE EVIDENCE

EVALUATE EVIDENCE decides whether the cumulative evidence—as well as other considerations—warrants acceptance, rejection, or continued consideration of the current hypothesis.

### GENERATE OUTCOME

This process consists of an E-SPACE MOVE, which produces an experiment, RUNNING the experiment and OBSERVING the result. As we noted earlier the E-SPACE MOVE also occurs as a subprocess within SEARCH HYPOTHESIS SPACE.

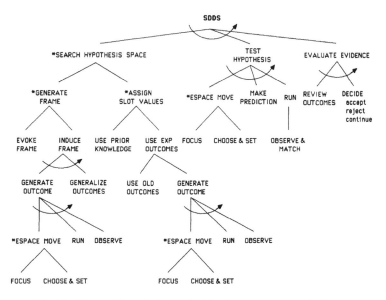

FIG. 4.4.    Process hierarchy for SDDS. All subprocesses connected by an arrow are executed in a sequential conjunctive fashion. All process names preceded by an asterisk include conditional tests for which subprocess to execute.

### E-SPACE MOVE

Experiments are designed by E-SPACE MOVE. The most imoprtant step is to FOCUS on some aspect of the current situation that the experiment is intended to illuminate. "Current situation" is not just a circumlocution for "current hypothesis," because there may be situations in which there is no current hypothesis, but in which E-SPACE MOVE must function nevertheless. (The multiple role played by experimentation is an important feature of the model, and is discussed further later.) If there is an hypothesis, then FOCUS determines that some aspect of it is the primary reason for the experiment. If there is a frame with open slot values, then FOCUS will select one of those slots as the most important thing to be resolved. If there is neither a frame nor an hypothesis—that is, if E-SPACE MOVE is being called by INDUCE FRAME—then FOCUS makes an arbitrary decision to focus on one aspect of the current situation.

Once the focal value has been determined, CHOOSE sets a value in the Experiment Space that will provide information relevant to it, and SET determines the values of the remaining, but less important, values necessary to produce a complete experiment.

## Memory Requirements

A variety of memory requirements are implicit in our description of SDDS and must, by implication, play an important role in the discovery process. Here we provide a brief indication of the kinds of information about experiments, outcomes, hypotheses, and discrepancies that SDDS must store and retrieve.

- Recall that GENERATE OUTCOME operates in two contexts. Under INDUCE FRAME, it is called when there is no active hypothesis and when the system is attempting to produce a set of behaviors that can then be analyzed by GENERALIZE OUTCOMES in order to produce a frame. Therefore, SDDS must be able to represent and store one or more experimental outcomes each time it executes INDUCE FRAME.
- Another type of memory demand comes from EVALUATE EVIDENCE. In order to be able to weight the cumulative evidence about the current hypothesis, REVIEW OUTCOMES must have access to the results produced by MATCH in TEST HYPOTHESIS. This evidence would include selected features of experiments, hypotheses, predictions, and outcomes.
- Similar information is accessed whenever ASSIGN SLOT VALUES calls on USE PRIOR KNOWLEDGE or USE OLD OUTCOMES to fill in unassigned slots in a frame.

At this point in the model's development, the precise role of memory remains an area for future research.

## The Multiple Roles of Experimentation in SDDS

Examination of the relations along all these processes and subprocesses, depicted in Fig. 4.4, reveals both the conventional and unconventional characteristics of the model. At the top level, the discovery process is characterized as a simple repeating cycle of generating hypotheses, testing hypotheses, and reviewing the outcomes of the test. However, below that level is a potentially complex interaction among the subprocesses. Of particular importance is the way in which E-SPACE MOVE occurs in three different places in the hierarchy:

1. As a subprocess deep with GENERATE FRAME, where the goal is to generate experimental evidence over which a frame can be induced. All of the Experimenters in study 1, and one of the children in study 3 used experiments for this purpose.
2. As a subprocess of ASSIGN SLOT VALUES where the purpose of the experiment is simply to resolve the unassigned slots in the current frame.

Both adults and children used this process, though it was used more extensively by children than by adults.

3. As a component of TEST HYPOTHESIS, where the experiment is designed to play its conventional role of generating an instance (usually positive) of the current hypothesis. This strategy was widely used by adults and children.

Note that the implication of the first two uses of E-SPACE MOVE is that in the absence of hypotheses, experiments can be used to generate hypotheses. Thus, experiments can be used for purposes other than the testing of hypotheses.

SDDS also elaborates the details of what can happen during the EVALUATE EVIDENCE process. Recall that three general outcomes are possible: the current hypothesis can be accepted, it can be rejected, or it can be considered further.

- In the first case, when there is sufficient evidence in favor of an hypothesis, the discovery process simply stops, and asserts that the current hypothesis is the true state of nature.

- In the second case, when an hypothesis has been rejected, the system returns to H-SPACE SEARCH, to either construct a new frame, or to fill in slot values of the currently active frame. If the entire *frame* has been rejected by EVALUATE EVIDENCE, then the model must attempt to generate a new frame using EVOKE FRAME. If the system cannot construct a new frame—as with the Experimenters and the children—then it will attempt to induce a new frame by running experiments. Having induced a new frame (which most of the children were unable to do), or having returned from EVALUATE EVIDENCE with a frame needing new slot values (i.e., a rejection of the hypothesis but not the frame), SDDS executes ASSIGN SLOT VALUES. Here too, if prior knowledge is inadequate to make slot assignments, the system may wind up making moves in the experiment space in an attempt to make the assignments. In both of these cases, the behavior would be the running of experiments without fully specified hypotheses. This was precisely what we saw in the second phase of the adult Experimenters' performance and for most of the children.

- In the third case, when there is not sufficient evidence to either accept or reject an hypothesis, SDDS returns to TEST HYPOTHESIS in order to further consider the current hypothesis. The experiments run in this context correspond to the conventional view of the role of experimentation. During MOVE IN E-SPACE, FOCUS selects particular aspects of the current hypothesis and designs an experiment to generate information about it.

## DISCUSSION

As outlined earlier, one of the major goals in theories of cognitive development has been to tease apart the relation between the development of the knowledge base and the strategies that are applied to this knowledge base. In this chapter, we have recast these questions in terms of scientific reasoning as a search in two problem spaces. This approach allows us to make some initial observations about the components of the processes that show developmental trends. Our model shows that if the prior knowledge is not available, then subjects will resort to searching the experiment space (Study 2). Because children do not have the requisite knowledge that would enable them to construct the correct frame by searching the Hypothesis space, they, like the adults, must switch to a search of the experiment space. But when children search the Experiment space, their strategies are different from those used by the adults. Although the children conduct experiments that are similar to the adults, they induce different types of hypotheses and also evaluate evidence in different ways.

### Different Experimental Strategies

#### Testing Hypotheses

Our model incorporates a goal that is central to the scientific process: testing hypotheses. The subjects also saw this as their goal. Over 70% of the experiments conducted by both the adults and the children were concerned with testing hypotheses. There were, however, some important differences in the hypothesis-testing strategies used by adults and children. Children often conducted a single experiment and then said that they had discovered how the device works, whereas adults conducted a number of experiments before they were convinced that an hypothesis was correct. Clearly, the criteria the children use for accepting hypotheses are very different from those used by adults.

The way children use disconfirming evidence differed substantially from that of adults. When an experiment produced disconfirming evidence, children attempted to conduct some new experiment that would confirm their hypothesis. Their goal was to generate some consistent outcomes, and their conclusion was that the device usually works the same way as their hypothesis. Thus, many of their experiments were designed to find evidence consistent with their hypothesis rather than to discover the correct hypothesis. Adults tended to be more sensitive to disconfirming evidence. Although adults did not abandon their hypothesis on the basis of a single disconfirming instance, they did attempt to understand inconsistencies. Children simply ignored them.

These findings are very similar to those reported by Kuhn et al. (1987). They found that when children have to judge what attributes of a ball make it produce a "good serve," they often proposed hypotheses that did not account for all of the data and were content with saying that the attribute sometimes makes a difference. Kuhn, Amsel, and O'Loughlin (1988) also discovered that children found it difficult to determine what evidence was sufficient to reject their current hypothesis. They argued that one of the reasons that children find it difficult to evaluate hypotheses is that they do not have the ability to reflect upon a theory in the abstract. What their results and ours suggest is that in the EVALUATE EVIDENCE processes there are a number of subprocesses that bias interpretation toward the currently favored hypothesis. This may be due to an inability to remember previous outcomes or to the use of different subprocesses by adults and children.

### Generating New Hypotheses

As our model indicates, another goal of experimentation is to generate new hypotheses when old ones have been disconfirmed. Again, there were many differences in how the children and adults did this. The adults tended to try only one or two hypotheses within a frame before abandoning the frame and switching to a search of the experiment space or searching memory for new frames. In contrast, all but two of the children stayed with the *N-role:counter* frame. These children proposed a number of hypotheses different from the adults as they attempted to reconcile experimental results with their hypotheses. They proposed a new hypothesis after only one experiment, they did not check to see if the results of the previous experiments were consistent with their hypothesis, and they were content with hypotheses that, from an adult's perspective, were highly implausible.

In terms of our model, these results suggest that the children's GENERATE OUTCOMES and GENERALIZE OUTCOMES processes do not include components specifying that a number of outcomes need to be generated and that the new hypothesis should be consistent with prior outcomes. Therefore, because of limitations in children's ability to GENERALIZE OUTCOMES, they tended to extract only the most local information from experiments. On the positive side, these results indicate that given a particular piece of experimental evidence, children are able to induce a rule that is consistent with the immediate result. Furthermore, children usually state the rule in a sufficiently abstract form so that it could account for a number of results. That is, they could state hypotheses in terms of any value of *N*, rather than in terms of the specific value that had been observed. However, although children of this age can induce new hypotheses from experimental data, the ability to correctly apply this inductive skill does not appear to be present.

### Generating New Frames

Our adult Experimenters spent a considerable amount of time conducting experiments without an hypothesis in an effort to generate a new frame. The notable features about this strategy were that subjects usually conducted three or four experiments before an hypothesis was proposed and that subjects proposed an hypothesis that was consistent with the results of the previous few experiments. Finally, the hypotheses that they proposed were plausible. Children rarely used this strategy. Recall that only 2 of the 22 children managed to evoke the correct frame from prior knowledge or induce it from experimental outcomes. It is clear that children rarely took the first main branch of SEARCH HYPOTHESIS SPACE once they had generated their initial frame.

Children's failure to propose more than one frame (*N*-role:*counter*), indicates that one of the major differences between adults and children is in the way that the results of previous experiments are used to evaluate evidence and to make new inductions. First, children did not use the information available to them to abandon their current frame. Rather, they spent much of their time using experimental results to ASSIGN SLOT VALUES to the *N*-role:*counter* frame. This suggests that either the children did not have the prior knowledge available to construct a new frame, or they could not deduce that the experimental evidence available disproved that the role of *N* was a counter, thereby allowing them to abandon that frame. A second major difference was that the types of inductions that the children generated from the data were not constrained by the results of prior experiments. Even those children who did discover that a segment of the program is repeated persisted in stating that the segment is repeated *N* times. The children either were unable to abandon their current frame, or did not have the knowledge available to construct a new frame that would be consistent with their results.

One of the central components of the previous analysis has been the idea that subjects search for information to construct frames. This search for new frames could occur in two ways. One way that subjects might construct a new frame is to search memory for information that allows them to construct a frame. This search process would be constrained by the problem specification, and by the results of prior experiments. A second possible way is to make some minor modification to a preexisting frame that already meets the task specifications. In the domain of machine learning, this idea has been used by Shrager (1985, 1987), and Falkenhainer (1987). Our model does not distinguish between these two possible ways of constructing frames, and subjects may have used either. Furthermore, it is possible that adults, having more knowledge available, may be able to import frames from other domains more readily than children.

## Scientific Reasoning Skills: What Develops?

It depends. The developmental story that is beginning to emerge has several layers. At the level of subjects' global behavior on this task, there is little difference between the children and the adults. Both groups clearly understand the nature of the task and realize that they can only discover how the device works by making it behave, observing that behavior, and generating a summary statement that captures the behavior in a universal and general fashion.

That is, both the children and the adults know what the scientific reasoning process is supposed to look like. However, viewed at the level of overall success rates, there are profound differences in the consequences of how this general orientation toward discovery is implemented. The adults had a 95% success rate, whereas 90% of the children failed. These differences do not lie in the ability to generate informative experiments, for, as we saw earlier, there were few differences in the regions of the E-space that were visited by children and adults. There appears to be a crucial difference in the *reason* that those experiments were generated and in the *inductions* that are made from the results of those experiments. In terms of the model, children tended to move in the E-space in order to generate some data to patch a faulty hypothesis or to produce a desired effect, whereas adults used E-space search to generate a data pattern over which they could induce a new frame. With respect to inductive differences, we discovered that although all the children could induce new hypotheses from experiments, none of them were able to use an experimental result to induce a new frame. Inductions were local rather than global.

Another possible reason for these differences is knowledge about how to evaluate hypotheses. More specifically, children tend to have much less stringent criteria for evaluating evidence than adults. Two consequences of these lax criteria are that children accept hypotheses on the basis of incomplete evidence and that they maintain them in the face of much inconsistency. As we argued earlier, successful performance on this task depends on memory for previous experimental results. Children appear to lack the knowledge that the results of earlier experiments must be considered when evaluating an hypothesis. Research on designing factorial experiments (Siegler & Liebert, 1975) has shown that many children do not spontaneously realize that they must keep track of the results of experiments. Kuhn et al. (1988) also argued that children do not have the metacognitive skills available to properly evaluate evidence. Thus, children's ability to test hypotheses will not be the same as adults until they are able to utilize such information.

## Conclusion

We have proposed that scientific reasoning requires search in two problem spaces and that the different strategies that we observed in children and in adults are caused by different patterns of search in these two problem spaces. We proposed SDDS as both a framework for interpreting these results and as a general model of scientific reasoning. Clearly, there are many aspects of the scientific reasoning process that we still do not fully understand, but we believe that SDDS offers a potentially fruitful framework for further exploration.

## POSTSCRIPT: ACKNOWLEDGMENTS TO HERBERT SIMON

We are pleased to include this work in a Simon Festschrift, because his influence is evident in nearly every important aspect: in the focus on scientific discovery (Langley et al., 1986), in the methodology of verbal protocol analysis (Ericsson & Simon 1984), in the conceptualization of scientific discovery as search in two spaces (Simon & Lea 1974; Simon, 1977), and most fundamentally, in the assumption that the scientific discovery process is subject to systematic investigation. As Simon (1986) recently commented on his own research program:

> The hypothesis that drives this research is that scientific discovery is a problem-solving activity like other problem-solving activities that human beings engage in, using the same basic information-processing mechanisms that have been identified in those other processes. This hypothesis rests, in turn, on the belief that the scientist does not stand outside the lawful scheme of Nature; he is part of that scheme, and it is an important goal of scientific research to undestand his mental processes, just as it is to understand the processes of a star, an atom, or a cell. (p. 168)

Indeed, Simon's pervasive influence is disquieting, for it threatens our need to believe that we have made our own modest but unique contribution to the area. We are at least gratified to know that Herb has stayed away from developmental studies in this area. And, for a while, we felt that we were unique in initiating experimental studies within the "scientific discovery as search" view, because Simon's work on computational models of the discovery process was confined to the analysis of the historical record of practicing scientists. However, he has recently extended his work on scientific discovery to the experimental laboratory as well! It is difficult enough to stand on the shoulders of giants, but when they persistently expand the frontiers of knowledge, it is a daunting task to keep ones eyes fixed on new discoveries. For such a challenge, we are deeply indebted to Simon.

## ACKNOWLEDGMENTS

This study was supported in part by the Personnel and Training Research Programs, Psychological Sciences Division, Office of Naval Research, under contract No. N00014-86K-0349. Reproduction in whole or in part is permitted for any purpose of the United States Government.

## REFERENCES

Bartlett, F. C. (1958). *Thinking.* New York: Basic Books.
Bruner, J. S., Goodnow, J. J., & Austin, G. A. (1962). *A study of thinking.* (science ed.). New York.
Carey, S. (1984). Cognitive development: The descriptive problem. In M. S. Gazzaniga (Ed. ), *Handbook of cognitive neurology.* Hillsdale, NJ: Lawrence Erlbaum Associates.

Carey, S. (1985). *Conceptual change in childhood.* Cambridge, MA: MIT Press.

Carver, S. M. (1986). *Transfer of LOGO debugging skill: Analysis, instruction and assessment.* Unpublished doctoral dissertation, Carnegie-Mellon University Pittsburgh.

Case, R. (1974). Structures and strictures: Some functional limitations on the course of cognitive growth. *Cognitive Psychology, 6,* 544-573.

Cohen, P. R., & Feigenbaum, E. A. (Eds.). (1983). *Handbook of artificial intelligence* (Vol. 3). Los Altos, CA: W. Kaufman, Inc.

Ericsson, K. A., & Simon, H. A. (1984). *Protocol analysis: Verbal reports as data.* Cambridge, MA: MIT Press.

Falkenhainer, B. (1987). Scientific theory formation through analogical inference. In *Proceedings of the 4th International Workshop on Machine Learning.* Los Altos, CA: Morgan Kaufmann.

Flavell, J. H. (1977). *Cognitive development.* Englewood Cliffs, NJ: Prentice-Hall.

Greenwald, A. G., Pratkanis, A. R., Leippe, M. R., & Baumgardner, M. H. (1986). Under what conditions does theory obstruct research progress? *Psychological Review, 93*(2), 216-229.

Harre, R. (1983). *Great scientific experiments: Twenty experiments that changed our view of the world.* New York: Oxford University Press.

Inhelder, B., & Piaget, J. (1958). *The growth of logical thinking from childhood to adolescence.* New York: Basic Books.

Karmiloff-Smith, A., & Inhelder, B. (1974). If you want to get ahead, get a theory. *Cognition, 3,* 195-212.

Keil, F. C. (1981). Constraints on knowledge and cognitive development. *Psychological Review, 88,* 197-227.

Klahr, D., & Carver, S. M. (in press). Cognitive objectives in a LOGO debugging curriculum: Instruction, learning, and transfer. *Cognitive Psychology.*

Klahr, D., & Dunbar, K. (1988). Dual space search during scientific reasoning. *Cognitive Science, 12*(1), 1-55.

Kuhn, D., & Phelps, E. (1982). The development of problem solving strategies. In H. W. Reese (Ed.), *Advances in child development and behavior.* New York: Academic Press.

Kuhn, D., Amsel, E., & O'Loughlin, M. (1988) *The development of scientific thinking skills.* Orlando, FL: Academic Press.

Kulkarni, D., & Simon, H. A. (in press). The processes of scientific discovery: The strategy of experimentation. *Cognitive Science.*

Langley, P., Bradshaw, G. L., & Simon, H. A. (1983). Rediscovering chemistry with the BACON system. In R. S. Michalski, J. G. Carbonell, & T. M. Mitchell (Eds.), *Machine learning: An artificial intelligence approach.* Palo Alto, CA: Tioga.

Langley, P., Zytkow, J. M., Simon, H. A., & Bradshaw, G. L. (1986). The search for regularity: Four aspects of scientific discovery. In R. S. Michaliski, J. G. Carbonell, & T. M. Mitchell (Eds.), *Machine learning: An artificial intelligence approach* (Vol. 2). Los Altos, CA: Morgan Kaufmann.

Lenat, D. (1977). On automated scientific theory formation: A case study using the AM program. In J. E. Hayes, D. Michie, & L. Mikulich (Eds.), *Machine Intelligence 9.* New York: Halsted.

Minsky, M. (1975). A framework for representing knowledge. In P. H. Winston (Ed.), *The psychology of computer vision.* New York: McGraw-Hill.

Piaget, J. (1928). *The child's conception of the world.* Boston: Routledge & Kegan Paul.

Piaget, J. (1952). *The origins of intelligence in children.* New York: International University Press.

Shrager, J. (1985). *Instructionless learning: Discovery of the mental model of a complex device.* Doctoral dissertation, Department of Psychology, Carnegie-Mellon University.

Shrager, J. (1987). Theory change via view application in instructionless learning. *Machine Learning, 2,* 247-276.

Shrager, J., & Klahr, D. (1986). Instructionless learning about a complex device. *International Journal of Man-Machine Studies, 25,* 153-189.

Siegler, R. S., & Liebert, R. M. (1975). Acquisition of formal scientific reasoning by 10- and 13-year-olds: Designing a factorial experiment. *Developmental Psychology, 11,* 401–402.

Simon, H. A. (1973). Does scientific discovery have a logic? *Philosophy of Science, 40*(4), 471–480.

Simon, H. A. (1977). *Models of discovery.* Dordrecht-Holland: D. Reidel Publishing.

Simon, H. A. (1986). Understanding the processes of sciences: The psychology of scientific discovery. In T. Gamelius (Ed.), *Progress in sciences and its social conditions.* Oxford, England: Pergamon Press.

Simon, H. A., & Lea, G. (1974). Problem solving and rule induction: A unified view. In L. W. Gregg (Ed.), *Knowledge and cognition.* Hillsdale, NJ: Lawrence Erlbaum Associates.

Tschirgi, J. E. (1980). Sensible reasoning: A hypothesis about hypotheses. *Child Development, 51,* 1–10.

Vygotsky, L. (1934). *Thought and language.* New York: Wiley.

Wason, P. C. (1968). Reasoning about a rule. *Quarterly Journal of Experimental Psychology, 20,* 273–281.

# 5

## Scientists of the Artificial

George A. Miller
*Princeton University*

This symposium is intended to honor Herbert A. Simon; if any queue is forming to honor Herbert A. Simon, I want to be in it. (I don't always get the
chance, of course—the king of Sweden neglected to invite me to the Big One.)
I am at least as interested in honoring Herbert A. Simon as in discussing what
the organizers of the symposium call "the current fruits of the intellectual
seeds sown by Simon over the past 30 years." But if all goes well, I may do
both at the same time.

His friends say that "Simon's pioneering contributions to cognitive
psychology have been fundamental." If you ask them privately, however, they
will tell you he is much more important than that. Not only has he contributed many of the basic insights on which the field is built, but he is also its
premier politician, able to recognize excellence and willing to create institu-
tional support for it, as well as its best public spokesman—clear, simple,
persuasive.

People sometimes ask me what they should read to find out about artificial
intelligence. Herbert A. Simon's book, *The Sciences of the Artificial* (1981)
is always on the list I give them. Every page issues a challenge to conventional thinking, and the layman who digests it well will certainly understand
what the field of artificial intelligence hopes to accomplish. I recommend
it in the same spirit that I recommend Freud to people who ask about
psychoanalysis, or Piaget to those who ask about child psychology: If you
want to learn about a subject, start by reading its founding fathers.

Although the second edition is twice the length of the first, *The Sciences
of the Artificial* is still a little book readable in the time available to busy
people. But it is also worthy of a slower reading, for nowhere else is Herbert
A. Simon's vision of this field set forth more succinctly. If there is any single

place where "the intellectual seeds sown by Simon over the past 30 years" are clearly on display, surely it is in *The Sciences of the Artificial*. I assume that everyone knows how important Herbert A. Simon is. And I assume everyone knows *The Sciences of the Artificial* as well as I do, if not better. My reason for mentioning these things is that I want to use the voice of Herbert A. Simon, as recorded in *The Sciences of the Artificial*, in order to comment on the four presentations just given. In that way I hope to focus on aspects of those papers that derive most directly from "the intellectual seeds" that Herbert A. Simon has "sown."[1]

## THE COMPUTATIONAL NERVOUS SYSTEM

First, what should be said about the claim by Kosslyn, Sokolov, and Chen that we need to be "armed with a theory not only of a cognitive process, but also with a theory of the mechanisms that underlie individual differences in hemispheric processing"? (chap. 1 in this volume). I want to approach the computational nervous system from a historical perspective.

The irony that it took a machine to arouse psychologists to an active interest in mental processes has been frequently noted. Cognitive psychology broke free from behavioristic psychology in the 1950s largely due to the growing recognition that mental phenomena can be analyzed using concepts that were developed to analyze electronic communication and control systems. In part, this realization was the result of the development of servomechanisms, which played a central role in cybernetic theories, and in part a result of increasing mathematical sophistication, thanks to mathematical theories of information, games, and learning, but mostly it was consequence of increased familiarity with the new computers and with the kinds of information processing of which they are capable. My favorite account of those early days is the historical appendix to Newell and Simon's *Human Problem Solving* (1972).[2]

In those early days many workers assumed that the similarity between brains and computers extended down to the level of their component parts. The great John von Neumann (1958) certainly made that assumption. Warren McCulloch and Walter Pitts (1943) even provided a logical calculus of neural activity that treated neurons in much the same way you would describe logical circuits in a computer. I think that many of those who synthesized neural networks and studied their behavior had a secret hope that if they could just put together enough imitation neurons and let them interact, something unex-

---

[1]If the voice of G.A. Miller sometimes breaks through the voice of H.A. Simon, I hope I will be forgiven. No simulation is perfect.

[2]The change in perspective that followed from these events has sometimes been called "the cognitive revolution," but the phrase is poorly chosen. Behaviorists were the real revolutionaries. Cognitivists were counter-revolutionaries, returning psychology to its traditional mission.

pected, wonderful, and intelligent might emerge. But the brain did not give up its secrets so easily. Interest in simulating neural networks never died out completely, but for about 25 years the study of neural nets was overshadowed by the information-processing approach to intelligent behavior.

Instead of drawing analogies between computers and brains, the information-processing approach took a more abstract view of the processes that intelligent systems must perform. As Simon and his colleagues were quick to see, computers offer an especially rich field for psychological theory. Not only do computer programming languages provide psychologists with notational systems in which to write psychological theories, but the machines themselves make it possible to immediately test the internal coherence and plausibility of those theories. As Simon says, because computer programs describe complex processes "in complete, painstaking detail, they are open to full inspection and analysis, or to trial by simulation" (1981, p. 156).

Trial by simulation helps to distinguish mere metaphors from serious hypotheses. If a theory is not sufficiently well-formed to run on a computer, it probably won't run on a brain either, but unless you actually try to run it, you can never know. Those who do not submit their ideas to trial by simulation can never learn anything from their untested models that they did not already know. As Simon says, "even when we have correct premises, it may be very difficult to discover what they imply" (1981, p. 19). By actually constructing and testing the model, it is often possible to discover unsuspected consequences of the basic premises.

To many psychologists in the 1960s, however, even an untested computational speculation seemed valuable if it led to hypotheses that could be tested experimentally. Today it is difficult for young psychologists to believe how constricted the behaviorist imagination really was, and what a relief it was to be able to talk about cognitive processes without feeling guilty of committing metaphysics. And so it came to pass that flow charts appeared in the publications of many psychologists who had who had no clear idea about how to convert them into computer programs.

That history is well-known and I remind you of it now only because I think it provides the proper context for discussing an important assumption underlying the information processing approach; an assumption so basic that it is seldom even mentioned, namely, the assumption that hardware and software can be treated separately. I call this the *separability assumption:* Information processing by computer assumes a principled distinction and a physical separation between the system that does the processing and the information that is processed. The hardware is distinct from the software in the same sense that a container is distinct from its contents.

Separability is fundamental. If the computer and its program of instructions could not be treated separately, every new kind of computation would require a new special-purpose computer, and there would be no possibility of mass producing a universal computer that could be programmed to compute anything and everything.

Separability permits reusability. Not only can the same hardware be used over and over, but so can the software. Early in the development of software technology the value of collecting libraries of reusable programs was recognized. The reduction in the cost of program development is obvious. Once the function to be computed can be defined abstractly, and not in terms of some special-purpose machine that is to perform the computation, then algorithms can be formulated with all the elegance of modern mathematics. Indeed, so much of what is regularly done with computers depends on separability that in most discussions it is simply presupposed without comment.

Separability is introduced differently in *The Sciences of the Artificial*, where a distinction is drawn between the outer and inner environments of an artifact. But it is the same idea under a different name. Simon says in a footnote: "A generalization of the argument made here for the separability of 'outer' from 'inner' environment shows that we should expect to find this separability, to a greater or lesser degree, in *all* large and complex systems, whether they are artificial or natural" (1981, p. 10). Personally, although I agree that the point Simon is making is extremely important, I find his choice of the terms *inner* and *outer* somewhat unfelicitous. They are too easily confused with the distinction between inside and outside the skin. A reader who makes that confusion will surely be surprised to find that short-term memory is one of the main limits of the *inner* environment (p. 77), whereas long-term memory is part of the *outer* environment (p. 65). Only if you think of short-term memory as a parameter determined by the hardware, and think of the contents of long-term memory as software acquired through long experience—only then will you understand what Simon means by inner and outer. Inner means hardware, outer means software.

Obviously, the inner environment should be designed to enable the artifact to function in its outer environment. The important point, however, is that we can understand one environment without understanding the other. In particular, Simon says, "We can often predict behavior from knowledge of the systems's goals and its outer environment, with only minimal assumptions about the inner environment. An instant corollary is that we often find quite different inner environments accomplishing identical or similar goals in identical or similar outer environments" (1981, p. 11). What he has in mind here, of course, is that computers and brains can achieve similar goals in similar environments, even though their inner environments are as different as transistors and neurons, or silicon and DNA. To put the idea slightly different, intelligent behavior can be adequately described in terms of functions so general that they will hold true of any system, animate or inanimate, that is capable of that behavior.

It is a strong claim. Simon says: "the possibility of building a mathematical theory of a system or of simulating that system does not depend on having an adequate microtheory of the natural laws that govern the system components. Such a microtheory might indeed by simply irrelevant" (1981, p.22). If true, this claim has exciting implications for the struggling young science of psychology, as he clearly saw. Simon says: "Psychology can move forward without awaiting the solutions by neurology of the problems of component design—however interesting and significant these components turn out to be" (1981, p. 26). At the price of a little abstractness, therefore, the realm of psychological theory could expand as rapidly as the psychological imagination could elaborate it. As indeed it has.

Cognitive science in general, and artificial intelligence in particular, have vigorously pursued this strategy of exploring the organization of the mind and ignoring the structure of the brain. Simon says: "the difference between the hardware of a computer and the 'hardware' of the brain has not prevented computers from simulating a wide spectrum of kinds of human thinking" (1981, p. 97). Moreover, separability is as relevant to visual imagery as it is to other cognitive functions. Simon says: "many of the phenomena of visualization do not depend in any detailed way upon underlying neurology but can be explained and predicted on the basis of quite general features of the organization of memory" (1981, p. 89).

One of his most beguiling propositions is that a science of behavior is possible because people are really very simple. Simon says: 'A man, viewed as a behaving system, is quite simple. The apparent complexity of his behavior over time is largely a reflection of the complexity of the environment in which he finds himself" (1981, pp. 65, 95, 126). He "hedges" this hypothesis with the disclaimers that (a) he is concerned with the thinking man, not the whole man, and that (b) he views the contents of long-term memory "less as part of the organism that as part of the environment to which it adapts" (1981, p. 65).

In other words, behavior only looks complicated because people have adapted to—been programmed by—a complicated environment. A person is really a simple information processing system that looks complicated because it—he, she—is running a complicated program. The hardware, the inner environment, Simon says, is quite simple: "There are only a few 'intrinsic' characteristics of the inner environment of thinking man that limit the adaptation of thought to the shape of the problem environment. All else in thinking and problem solving is artificial—is learned and is subject to improvement through the invention of improved designs and their storage in memory" (1981, p. 66). All you need to know about the brain is how many chunks of information per second it can process. Everything else is in the software.

But that does not mean that neuroscience is a waste of time. Neuroscience should explain the inner environment, the hardware. Simon says: "It is to physiology that we must turn for an explanation of the limits of adaptation: Why is short-term memory limited to four chunks; what is the physiological structure that corresponds to a 'chunk'; what goes on during the five seconds that a chunk is being fixated; how are associational structures realized in the brain?" (1981, p. 97). Unfortunately, these are not questions that brain scientists have been able to answer. And I suspect that there are good reasons why neurophysiological research is not answering questions about the limits of short-term memory.

Whatever else it may be, a brain is certainly not a general purpose computer. Yet the plausibility of the claim that people are simple information processing systems draws heavily on the assumption that the human nervous system is an extremely versatile, general purpose computer, and that the properties of that computer are separable from the properties of the programs it runs.

The assumption of separability has so long been so convenient for cognitive theorists that I am reluctant to question it in any way. But unless some question is raised it is all too easy to miss the power—not to say the daring—of Simon's claim. Perhaps the best way to introduce a different point of view is to quote a remark that I once heard from Norbert Wiener. "One difference between a brain and a computer," he said, "is that you only get one run on a brain."

Is this an irrelevant difference, as Simon might say, or is it crucially important, as some neurologists might claim? I take Wiener's point to be that hardware and software in a brain can be separated only in theory. You cannot load a program into the brain, run it, and then return to the original state by simply erasing the brain's memory. With brains, information is hard to get in and, once it does get in, it may never come out again. Moreover, when the constraints that the brain imposes on information processing are examined more closely, they are found to be anything but simple. Apparently the central nervous system is filled with a multitude of special purpose mechanisms.

Neurophysiology needs computational models just as surely as psychology needs them. How else is the neurophysiologist to know what functions the neural tissue must perform? Finding something you are looking for is hard enough; finding it when you don't know what you are looking for is probably impossible. But different claims need to be sorted out here. It is one thing to say that brain scientists need computational theories, but something very different to say that cognitive science cannot advance without better computational theories of nervous activity.

There are advantages to separating software from hardware, even if only in theory. The assumption of separability was a necessary first approximation, a way to start on an intellectual adventure that would otherwise have seemed too difficult to attempt. Even now, although admittedly counterfactual, theoretical separability still seems the best hope for continued development of the sciences of the artificial. Just as Herbert A. Simon knew it would be.

## THE HARD WORKING MEMORY

Let me turn now to Carpenter and Just's assumption that "the main function of working memory is transient storage of partial results in the service of computation" (chap. 2 in this volume). Its role in language comprehension is their special concern.

I. A. Richards once commented that "a book is a machine to think with" (1942, p. 9). If computers are machines who think, then books and computers should be an ideal match. That the two are not at all well matched proves, among other things, that two metaphors can be even worse than one.

Building a machine that can simply read and understand a book has turned out to be a far more difficult task than was originally expected—I will not try to list all the perceptual, lexical, morphological, syntactic, semantic, pragmatic, and conceptual problems that arise. Nevertheless, attempts to design such a machine have provided a framework in which to think about the complexity of the reading process. And thinking about reading in that framework has helped greatly to clarify what a psychological theory of comprehension should look like. Indeed, this approach has been so successful that the psychology of reading now threatens to swallow all of psycholinguistics in its theories.

Building machines to comprehend language, however, has proceeded much more slowly. Part of the problem is deciding what should count as evidence that a reading machine understands what it reads. As Simon said, "tests of whether a story has been 'understood' are ambiguous" (1981, p. 116). Human beings can demonstrate comprehension by answering questions, but that test presupposes an ability to generate well-formed language as well as to understand it. A machine might fail the question-answering test, not because it did not understand, but because it was unable to express what it understood as a well-formed verbal answer. Probably the simplest test is to issue a command in the form of an imperative sentence; if the command is correctly executed, the sentence must have been understood. But imperative sentences are a small part of what a true language comprehension system must be able to understand.

Hayes and Simon (see Simon, 1979, part 7) were able to enlarge the linguistic scope by asking the machine to solve problems that were phrased in English sentences. Their program, call UNDERSTAND, deals with language in two steps. Simon says that it first:

> parses the sentences of the problem instructions, and then constructs the representation from the information it has extracted from the parsed sentences. The task of analyzing natural-language sentences . . . involves inferring from the linear string of words the implied hierarchic structure of phrases and clauses. . . . The second phase (construction) is more interesting. Here, the parsed sentences are examined to discover what objects and sets of objects are being referred to, what properties of objects are mentioned and what are the relations among them, which of the predicates and relations describe *states* and which describe *moves,* and what the goal state is. (1981, pp. 112–113)

The program then proceeds to solve the problem: It constructs a format for representing states and generates programs for making legal moves by changing one state into another.

The goal of that research was to discover whether changes in the problem instructions would affect the way the problem was represented. Simon says: "The UNDERSTAND program predicts correctly the changes in problem representation that were induced by the changes in the problem instructions; but we do not have a satisfactory explanation of why the change in representation caused such a large change in problem difficulty" (1979, p. 448). More on problem difficulty in a moment. Here we are concerned with the kind of language comprehension that the program demonstrated.

I have been told that some philosophers deny that computers can understand human language; if so, their definition of understanding is narrower than mine. I do not object to saying that a machine that solves a complicated puzzle must understand the language in which the puzzle is posed. A much more interesting question is how that level of understanding has been achieved. In the case of UNDERSTAND, understanding consists of transforming English sentences into a representation that the problem solver can work with. When we examine that representation we find it is an organized collection of lists. Simon says: "Studies of visual perception and of tasks requiring use of natural language show with growing clarity that memory is indeed organized in associative fashion, but that the 'associations' have the properties of what, in the computer trade, are usually called 'list structures'" (1981, p. 96).

List structures are remarkably similar to linguistic structures. No doubt there are many reasons for this similarity, but some of the more compelling reasons derive from the biological nature of the human organism. Consider the following biological limitations.

First, human being can reliably produce and recognize only a limited variety of vocalizations. Because people have a great variety of things to communicate, this limited variety of vocal sounds could create a serious bottleneck. The bottleneck is broken by using rapid sequences of sounds: The variety of different sequences available to serve as messages increases exponentially with the length of the sequences.

Second, the length of the linguistic sequences that people can cope with is limited.[3] This second limit could also create a serious bottleneck; this time the bottleneck is broken by chunking, by grouping short sequences and labeling them. Then the labels can themselves be grouped and labeled. In this way speech sounds are chunked as syllables, syllables are chunked as words, words are chunked as phrases, and phrases are chunked as sentences.

The outcome of all this sequencing and chunking can be represented as a list structure. Consider the following sentence: A farmer shot a hawk. The list structure would be SENTENCE, which is the name of a list containing two items: SUBJECT and PREDICATE. SUBJECT, in turn, is the name of a list containing two words: *a* and *farmer,* and PREDICATE is the name of

---

[3]Ignore for the moment whether the limit is called immediate memory, short-term memory, or working memory, and whether its length is seven (Miller, 1956) or five (Simon, 1979, p. 51) units. The critical facts are that there is a limit, and that it is relatively short.

a list containing three words: *shot, a,* and *hawk.* And the words, in turn, are the names of lists of phonemes. Human beings have a remarkable capacity for processing such structures, so it is no accident that there is a remarkable parallelism between modern linguistic theory and information-processing theories of human thinking. Simon says: "Both postulate hierarchically organized list structures as basic principles of memory organization. Both are concerned with how a serially operating processor can convert strings of symbols into list structures or list structures into strings" (1981, p. 91).

Because the limited capacity for processing serial input seems to explain many of the structural properties of human memory, the nature of the limitation has been a topic for continued research and speculation for more than 30 years. At first it was assumed that short-term memory is a passive buffer, but the longer psychologists studied it, the more complicated it became.

Nothing seems to get into long-term memory without first passing through short-term memory. Some psychologists wanted to equate short-term memory with attention, but Sternberg (1966) quickly pointed out the trouble with that proposal. Sternberg showed that people can hold a list of digits in short-term memory while some other mechanism, presumably attention, "reads" the values serially and exhaustively. One response to such objections was to complicate the description of short-term memory by giving it powers not only to hold information but to perform operations on it. But these complications have made it necessary to refine terminology, and many psychologists now use *working memory* to distinguish the new, active short-term memory from the old, passive short-term memory.

Once the short-term memory was expanded to include attention, it was a natural step to adapt experimental techniques that had been developed to study attention in order to learn more about the computational capacity of working memory. Baddeley and Hitch (1974) reported experiments in which people were asked to divide their attention between remembering a string of digits and performing a reasoning task; they interpreted an interference effect to mean that working memory was required for reasoning.

Today, the theory of this remarkable mental organ has grown even more complex. If I understand the recent research correctly, however, it complicates but does not change the basic picture that Simon saw more than 25 years ago. If anything, the subsequent work has simply underscored Simon's early conviction that the management of attention is the key problem for cognitive simulation, and that studies of short-term memory provide the surest route to understanding attention.

## THE MANY TOWERS OF HANOI

Now I must consider Kotovosky and Fallside's claim (chap. 3 in this volume) that problem similarity is important for transfer to occur from one problem to the next.

One of my earliest insights as a graduate student was the recognition that similarity is a critical problem—at the time I saw it as *the* critical problem—of theoretical psychology. It seemed to stare back at me from the depths of every psychological phenomenon that I tried to understand.

I recall being puzzled that different people can utter the same word. That is to say, acoustic events that are easily distinguishable to the ear as different, are nevertheless perceived to be the same. Obviously, this ability to overlook differences serves us well in many situations. Without it, we could hardly profit from experience, for we would not recognize that a new situation is similar to a situation in which we already know what to do. The appreciation of similarity is propaedeutic to the formation of conceptual categories, and conceptual categories provide the basic building blocks for all cognitive structures. Wherever I turned, similarity was important. I once started to write a science fiction story about a child born without any appreciation for similarities, but such a mind was so foreign to anything I could imagine that I had to abandon the idea.

In the study of verbal learning, similarity is a critical variable governing transfer. I was taught to describe transfer in terms of similar stimuli and similar responses—in those days everything was discussed in terms of stimuli and responses. If you hold the response constant and explore a range of similar stimuli, you can get positive transfer. But if you hold the stimulus constant and explore a range of similar responses, you usually get negative transfer, or interference effects.

I had trouble remembering this generalization, so I rephrased it in terms of learning to use a typewriter. I imagined a person learning to type a particular document that is written in English, using the familiar QWERTY keyboard. When that person is asked to type a different document, also written in English (similar stimulus, same response), there is positive transfer: learning to type the first document facilitates typing the second document. On the other hand, when the transfer task is to type the first document on a typewriter with a different keyboard (same stimulus, similar response), there is interference: Learning the QWERTY keyboard interferes with learning a different keyboard, and the more the keys are relabeled and interchanged, the greater the interference. If both the stimulus and the response are different, of course, no interaction is observed: Learning to type neither facilitates nor interferes with learning to play the piano. Under that translation, the transfer-retroaction surface was reduced to simple common sense.

Memorizing generalizations about stimulus–response relations occupied much of my young manhood—years I might better have spent studying political science and economics. I now regard it as largely wasted effort. The problem is not that the generalizations were false, but rather that they did not seem to describe anything other than the particular experiments that gave rise to them. When attempts were made to apply them to practical problems, like how to increase positive transfer in the classroom, they were little help.

My perplexity over the role of similarity in the learning process was considerably reduced when I learned about representation, or, as I called it in those days, encoding. The difficulty of a new task depends less on the similarity of its stimuli and responses to the stimuli and responses of familiar tasks than it does on how the two tasks are represented. For example, when I tried to memorize which S→R connections facilitate and which interfere I could never keep them straight, but when I encoded the same information in terms of typing it was easy to remember.

It is now an old story, but I still believe that the recoding of binary into octal digits provides the simplest example of the value of a good representation (Miller, 1956). If people are asked to repeat a string of binary digits after hearing them once, they will be able to repeat eight or nine binary digits without error. But if they are trained to recode binaries as octals, they will be able to repeat about 24 binary digits without error. As far as the stimuli and responses are concerned, the task with and without recoding is unchanged, but when binaries are represented mnemonically as octals, the number of binary digits that can be recalled is tripled.

I recognized from the first that representing information to oneself is an important and ubiquitous psychological process. I also recognized that it completely changes all the questions I had been taught to ask about similarity. Consider these two strings of binary digits:

$$1\ 0\ 0\ 1\ 0\ 1\ 1\ 1\ 0$$
$$0\ 1\ 0\ 0\ 1\ 0\ 1\ 1\ 1$$

If you represent the second string as the same as the first, but with its final digit rotated to the front, the two strings look very similar indeed. But if you recode both strings as octals, they become 456 and 227, respectively, which have nothing in common. So, how similar are they? The question cannot be answered unless you know how they have been represented. Similarity, like beauty, is in the eye of the beholder.

But if similarity is subjective, how can it be studied objectively? For years American psychologists assumed that an objective science can study only objective phenomena. In order to make cognitive psychology scientifically respectable, it was necessary to prove that this assumption was wrong. Consequently, much time and energy was spent demonstrating something that we take for granted today.

The key is that objective events can have subjective causes. In particular, different mental representations can produce different behavioral consequences, and the consequences can be used to determine which representation a person happens to be using. Simon considers the following example, taken from McLean and Gregg (1967). A subject is asked to memorize a matrix of nine numbers:

| | | |
|---|---|---|
| 4 | 9 | 2 |
| 3 | 5 | 7 |
| 8 | 1 | 6 |

Then the stimulus is removed, a series of questions are asked, and response times are measured. It turns out that horizontal questions like, "What is to the right of 3?" are answered faster than vertical questions like, "What is above 1?" Why should that be? Simon says: "If the image stored in memory were isomorphic to a photograph of the stimulus, we should expect no large differences in the times required to answer the different questions. We must conclude that the stored image is organized quite differently from a photograph" (1981, p. 85). Simon assumed that the matrix will be stored in memory as a list structure, and the data indicate that the lists are organized horizontally. That is to say, apparently subjects first create a list consisting of TOP, MIDDLE, and BOTTOM. TOP is the name of the list consisting of 4, 9, and 2; MIDDLE is the name of the list consisting of 3, 5, and 7; and BOTTOM is the name of the list consisting of 8, 1, and 6. Given that form of representation, answering vertical questions becomes a much more complex process than answering horizontal questions.

No doubt such observations are boringly obvious to those who have been lucky enough to grow up in the present age of enlightenment, but to those of us who were raised to believe that all psychological truth has to be phrased in terms of objective stimuli, responses, and reinforcements, they came as a breath of spring, ending a long intellectual winter.

The difficulty of discussing mental imagery solely in terms of stimuli, responses, and reinforcements were apparent to me by 1955, but at that time I did not yet know what terms should replace them. What soon replaced them, of course, was the whole dictionary of cognitive psychology, some of it revived from prebehavioristic theories and the rest borrowed from the exciting new field of cognitive simulation, which eventually merged with artificial intelligence. It was fortunate for me that my simple experiments with binary digits had prepared me for the new ideas that Simon and his associates were developing.

In particular, I was prepared to appreciate the value of alternative representations. Simon saw the importance of representation even more clearly than I did. He pointed out, for example, that the theorems derived in formal systems are all implicit in the axioms of those systems, so the process of derivation can be viewed as a process of creating alternative representations, "making evident what was previously true but obscure" (1981, p. 153). Indeed, he even played with the idea that finding alternative representations is the essential component of all problem solving. Simon says: "This view can be extended to all of problem solving—solving a problem simply means representing it so as to make the solution transparent. If the problem solving could actually be organized in these terms, the issue of representation would indeed become central" (1981, p. 153).

An elegant example of what he had in mind is the game he called "number scrabble." It is played by two people with nine cards, the ace through nine, which are placed face up between them. Simon says: "The players draw alternately, one at a time, selecting any one of the cards that remain in the center. The aim of the game is for a player to make up a 'book,' that is, a set of exactly three cards whose spots add to 15, before his opponent can do so. The first player who makes a book wins; if all nine cards have been drawn without either player making a book, the game is a draw" (1981, p. 152). On first encounter most people fail to recognize that number scrabble is an isomorph of tic-tac-toe. To demonstrate the formal similarity, Simon arranged the nine cards as a magic square, where every row, column, and diagonal adds to 15.

| 4 | 9 | 2 |
|---|---|---|
| 3 | 5 | 7 |
| 8 | 1 | 6 |

In that representation, Simon says: "it is obvious that 'making a book' in number scrabble is equivalent to getting 'three in a row' in the game of tic-tac-toe" (1981, p. 152). Anyone who knows how to play tic-tac-toe well should never lose a game of number scrabble. As soon as the two games are given similar representations, transfer from the familiar to the novel game is complete and instantaneous.

So what does all this have to say about the importance of similarity? In my view, similarity is still an important problem for psychological theory, but now we know that the critical matter is neither stimulus similarity nor response compatibility, but representational similarity.[4]

Problem isomorphs have proved to be a valuable way to induce different mental representations of the same problem, and so to explore some of the invisible processes that mediate between the stimuli and the responses. We now have objective evidence about those subjective processes; we now have evidence that the way a person represents a problem determines not only the problem's difficulty, but also the transferability of the solution to similar problems.

Implicit in the observation that some representations are better than others is the assumption that a best representation exists for every problem. Simon says: "How complex or simple a structure is depends critically upon the way in which we describe it. Most of the complex structures found in the world are enormously redundant, and we can use this redundancy to simplify their description. But to use it, to achieve the simplification, we must find the right representation." (1981, p. 228). Surely, one reason we are honoring Herbert A. Simon if for his wonderful gift of finding the right representation.

---

[4]Note also that representational similarity has little to do with logical equivalence. In logic, deductions are valid by virtue of their form, not their content, yet it is their content that determines their mental representation, and thus their difficulty. For a set of problem isomorphs more easily reduced to a logical formalism, see the discussion of Wason's "four card problem" in Wason & Johnson-Laird (1972).

## SEARCH AND RESEARCH

Finally, what can I say about Klahr and Dunbar's proposal that "scientific reasoning requires search in two problem spaces"? (chap. 4 in this volume).

If I had to list in order all of the important things that Simon has taught me, the importance of search would be near the top of the list. In the early days it seemed that all intelligent behaviors could be described as searches through large combinatorial spaces. To play a game, search through all legal moves for moves that increase the chance of winning. To find the combination to a safe, search through all possible settings of the dials until the safe opens. To solve a crossword puzzle, search through all possible combinations of letters of the alphabet that will fill the white squares of the puzzle until a combination satisfies the clues provided. To prove a theorem, search through all possible derivations consistent with the axioms and the deductive rules. And so on and on.

As John McCarthy (1956) pointed out long ago, problems cannot be reformulated in terms of search unless they are well-defined: not only must the problem have a solution, but we must be able to recognize the solution when we see it. Once the problem space and goal state are known, a well-defined problem can be solved by searching exhaustively through that space until the goal state is discovered—and such searches are usually easy to mechanize.

This characterization might be interpreted to mean that well-defined problems are trivial and of little interest to psychology. But it is the very fact that people do not solve problems—even well-defined problems—by exhaustive search, that links psychology to the general theory of search. The cognitive processes that are involved in human problem solving can be described, therefore, as strategies to increase the efficiency of the search process.

In explaining his famous notion of satisficing, Simon says: "heuristic search can handle combinatorial problems . . . that are too large for exact solution even with the biggest computers. It is an especially powerful problem-solving and decision-making tool for people who are unassisted by any computers except their own minds, hence must make extensive simplifications in order to find even approximate solutions" (1981, p. 35).

How heuristic strategies can be characterized and incorporated into computer programs, and how those computer programs can be generalized to account for rule induction, is a story I will not try to tell. I would have to quote too extensively from *The Sciences of the Artificial,* for I could not improve on Simon's own account. Instead I simply express admiration for Newell and Simon for opening up this line of research, and gratitude to their colleagues and students for continuing to pursue it. Today there is a tendency to neglect the important topic of search, and to emphasize instead the study of systems with enough knowledge of their special domains to be able to avoid searching large spaces. I am glad that the topic is still alive and well in Pittsburgh.

The distinction drawn by Simon and Lea (1974) between searching through a space of rules and searching through a space of instances is a valuable idea. It can happen that a person knows how to perform some task efficiently yet has no communicable idea about the rules that govern the performance: Learning to perform successfully and learning the rule for successful performance are surely different tasks and deserve separate (but related) accounts. The distinction deserves to be developed and extended.

It can also happen, however, that a person who can perform a task correctly and can state the rule that must be followed in order to perform the task correctly is still unable to explain WHY the rule works. Indeed, it might be argued that some people value a persuasive explanation above either a skillful performance or a well-formed rule. I see no barrier to extending these powerful ideas to the question of how people search though still a third space, the space of possible explanations.

How many spaces can people search at the same time and how closely related must the outcomes of those searches be? If pursued with abandon, such questions can lead into all kinds of trouble. For example, Broadbent (1977) reported that people controlling a model of a city transportation system made more correct decisions after they had practiced the task, although practice had no effect on their ability to answer questions about relations within the system. Broadbent (1986) argued that such observations—and there are many of them in the journals of experimental psychology—mean that there are many situations in which the knowledge base on which performance depends and the knowledge base on which answering questions depends have little or nothing to do with one another.[5]

Before embracing a highly modular theory of multiple, independent spaces that are searched simultaneously, perhaps a simpler account should be considered. What look like independent processes to Broadbent might be made to look like different levels in a single hierarchical search process. Perhaps instances and rules could be viewed, not so much as independent spaces to be searched, but as two representations of a single problem space, seen from two different levels in a control hierarchy.

In *The Sciences of the Artificial,* Simon tells a parable about two watchmakers, Hora and Tempus. Hora prospered because he could make watches much faster than Tempus. Hora organized the manufacturing process hierarchically—he designed his watches "so that he could put together subassemblies of about ten elements each" (1981, p. 200)—whereas Tempus failed because he did not. Simon introduced the parable in order to argue that "complex systems will evolve from simple systems much more rapidly if there are stable intermediate forms than if there are not" (1981, p. 209).

Having made his point about evolution, he then applies the same lesson to problem solving. Simon says:

---

[5]What implications such modularity would hold for an experimental technique that relies on verbal descriptions of the mental representation that is governing performance is far too large a question to explore in this commentary.

A little reflection reveals that cues signaling progress play the same role in the problem-solving process that stable intermediate forms play in the biological evolutionary process. In fact we can take over the watchmaker parable and apply it also to problem solving. In problem solving, a partial result that represents recognizable progress toward a goal plays the role of stable subassembly. (1981, p. 206)

With this hint from Simon, it would not be difficult to develop hypotheses about the establishment of "partial results" at the level of overt performance before the higher level performance of hypothesis formation has been assembled. Such gradual progress at different levels of the hierarchy would only become apparent, of course, if the problem to be solved were very complex and difficult—like good problems at the frontiers of science.

Modules or hierarchies? The question remains open. There is still much left for future generations to do.

## CONCLUDING APOLOGY

I apologize if have said more about Herbert A. Simon's ideas than about the papers I was asked to comment on. If I have talked too much about a golden past when everything was clear and simple, I apologize for that, too.

But I don't feel apologetic. I feel that I *have* commented on each of today's papers by placing them—or, at least, trying to place them—in the context of a larger theory, a theory we owe to Herbert A. Simon. Given that goal, and given the time available, I could hardly do more than remind you of the clear and simple assumptions underlying that context.

Much of the power of Simon's ideas derives from the scope and coherence of the Big Picture of Thinking Man that he has painted for us. It is all too easy, when caught up with the details of this or that facet of the theory, to forget the Big Picture. Not that any of today's contributors would forget for a moment how much we all owe to Herbert A. Simon. But by pretending that they might have, I have managed to turn this occasion into an opportunity to acknowledge publicly my own appreciation for "Simon's pioneering contributions to cognitive psychology."

## ACKNOWLEDGMENT

Preparation of this article was supported in part by a grant to Princeton University from the James S. McDonnell Foundation.

# REFERENCES

Baddeley, A. D., & Hitch, G. (1974). Working memory. In G.H. Bower (Ed.), *The psychology of learning and motivation* (vol. 8). New York: Academic Press.

Broadbent, D. E. (1977). Levels, hierarchies, and the locus of control. *Quarterly Journal of Experimental Psychology, 29,* 181–201.

Broadbent, D. E. (1986). Implicit and explicit knowledge in the control of complex systems. *British Journal of Psychology, 77,* 33–50.

McCarthy, J. (1956). The inversion of functions defined by Turing machines. In C.E. Shannon & J. McCarthy (Eds.), *Automata studies, annals of mathematical studies.* Princeton, NJ: Princeton University Press. (pp. 177–181).

McCulloch, W. S., & Pitts, W. (1943). A logical calculus of the ideas immanent in nervous activity. *Bulletin of Mathematical Biophysics, 5,* 115–137.

McLean, R. S., & Gregg, L. W. (1967). Effects of induced chunking on temporal aspects of serial recitation. *Journal of Experimental Psychology, 74,* 455–459.

Miller, G. A. (1956). The magical number seven, plus or minus two: Some limits on our capacity for processing information. *Psychological Review, 63,* 81–97.

Neumann, J. von (1958). *The computer and the brain.* New Haven, CT: Yale University Press.

Newell, A., & Simon, H. A. (1972). *Human problem solving.* Englewood Cliffs, NJ: Prentice-Hall.

Richards, I. A. (1942). *How to read a page.* New York: Norton.

Simon, H. A. (1979). *Models of thought.* New Haven, CT: Yale University Press.

Simon, H. A. (1981). *The sciences of the artificial* (2nd ed.). Cambridge, MA: MIT Press.

Simon, H. A., & Lea, G. (1974). Problem solving and rule induction: A unified view. In L. W. Gregg (Ed.), *Knowledge and cognition.* Hillsdale, NJ: Lawrence Erlbaum Associates.

Sternberg, S. (1966). High-speed scanning in human memory. *Science, 153,* 652–654.

Wason, P. C. & Johnson-Laird, P. N. (1972). *Psychology of reasoning: Structure and content.* Cambridge, MA: Harvard University Press.

# II

## EXPERTISE IN HUMAN
## AND ARTIFICIAL SYSTEMS

# 6

# What Hath Simon Wrought?

Edward A. Feigenbaum
*Stanford University*

Sometimes it is luck that launches life's work. For me, it was an amazing piece of luck to both be at Carnegie Tech and be an undergraduate student of Professor Simon's, at the moment of the birth of the sibling sciences of artificial intelligence and information processing models of human thought! Luck was helped along by Herb Simon's always-open door. He led me in, to the most exciting of intellectual adventures.

Herb Simon once said to me: "Don't waste your time commenting on someone else's history. Wait until you write your own." This paper recounts some history[1]—careful, I hope, but not complete.[2] I want to reminisce a bit on this happy occasion, and acknowledge some personal debts. But I also want to expose some personal biases, developed over my half-a-lifetime of work in computer models of thought. And I want to discuss, perhaps even clarify, some basic issues that have arisen during the growth of the science and technology of artificial intelligence.

---

[1]The best history of the formative period of the science of artificial intelligence is that of McCorduck (1979).

[2]What a problem we amateur historians have (especially those of us who suffer the complexities of actually having been on the scene)! How do we sort out the Simon from the Newell? Following the allusion in my title, let's just say that there was one Word, and it came from God the Father and God the Son. Same God, two instances. Herb Simon once called our environment here "Athens," but perhaps it was Jerusalem.

## SOME MOMENTS OF PERSONAL HISTORY

In the mid-1950's, I was an undergraduate engineering student at Carnegie Tech, bored with thermodynamics and electric motors, sampling the excitement of behavioral science at a very new and very odd place on campus, the graduate school of industrial administration. I did experiments one summer with March and Simon on the decision-making behavior of small groups. The school year came and I signed up for a seminar Simon was giving—Mathematical Models in the Social Sciences. What we studied you can read in Simon's *Models of Man* (1957). Toward the end of the semester came the Christmas break and the New Year 1956.

The first session after the break brought an unforgettable moment. Herb Simon came into class and said "Over Christmas, Al Newell and I invented a thinking machine." Puzzled looks, from students contemplating an oxymoron. Machine? Thinking? Thinking Machine? What could that mean? He laid on the table some copies of an instruction manual for the IBM 701 Computer. I remember staying up all night, absorbing that manual, undergoing a conversion experience. What followed in class was LT and IPL-1 (Feigenbaum & Feldman, 1963) and then it was obvious what to do for graduate school (work with Simon and Newell) and what to do for the summer (learn to program real machines at IBM).

## THE GENESIS OF THE SCIENCE
## (EARLY LIFE IN THE SEARCH SPACE)

In the beginning . . . a science almost never has a unique beginning, so each of us can select our favorite candidate. In 1955–1956, around the time of the Logic Theorist, Simon wrote a pair of articles that I consider to be the seminal articles for the founding paradigm of AI research. These are the articles: "Behavioral Theory of Rational Choice"; and, "Rational Choice and the Structure of the Environment" (Simon, 1957). The BTRC is essentially a positive theoretical counterpoint to the theme that led to Simon's Nobel award: that omniscient Economic Man, the decision maker, with his immense (assumed) information processing power and prowess was an implausible fiction, unworthy of a place at the foundations of economic theory. In BTRC, Simon proposes a model of the decision maker characterized by limited information processing and information gathering capabilities; who therefore must be satisfied with decisions less than optimal; who uses strategies and tactics of thought (what later we would call heuristic processes) to achieve behaviors that are good enough in spite of the limitations on processing power. RCSE is Simon's first statement of the now-famous theme that the observed complexity of behavior arises not from the complexity of the goal-seeking and problem-solving mechanism but from the responses of an essentially simple mechanism to the complexities of the task environment. Later, this viewpoint was to be captured in metaphor as Simon's "ant on the beach" (Simon, 1970) and in this form became enshrined in AI's pantheon of powerful ideas. Unfortunately, in a young science, the culture is not always passed along systematically, so even today waves of new scientists waste the early parts of their careers designing ever-more-elaborate "reasoning engines," "planners," and so forth, ignoring complex task environments and the analysis and representation of their complexity.

### The Whole Man

With his view of the essential simplicity of the problem-solving mechanism—the simple goal-seeking ant on the complex beach—Simon assessed the experimental results of the Genesis period as indicating that we were approaching an understanding of the whole man (by which he meant Cognitive Man), an assessment that was not popular either inside or outside of AI. More than 20 years have passed since his assessment, and a great deal of system building and experimental work. The empirical evidence to date is that Simon was right. The essential structures and processes *are* simple. The model builder need not postulate much mechanism to make an experimental system work, that is, to build artifacts that behave intelligently with competence or to explain complex human cognitive phenomena.

Once again, the main theme: the apparent complexity of a cognitive system's behavior arises from its model of its world, its task environment, its *knowledge base*. To use the terms currently in vogue, the knowledge base of the intelligent system is large and rich with descriptions of objects, relations among them, and rules pertaining to them. The system's *inference engine* is small and simple.

### The Physical Symbol System Hypothesis

In the beginning (also) . . . was a credo, shared by all, but rarely articulated. It was later stated and named by Newell and Simon in their Turing Award lecture (Newell & Simon, 1976): *The physical symbol system hypothesis*. It states that "a physical symbol system has the necessary and sufficient means for general intelligent action." The PSSH was stated as an hypothesis, not a scientific law. It was (let me try various metaphors): an article of faith, a beacon. Believing it was a badge of belonging to the AI science. But it was *not,* at that time, an empirical generalization. Thus, we all believed it but we had not observed it.

### The Search Model

In the beginning (also) . . . was Search. The breakthrough model of problem-solving (exemplified by LT) was a model of guided and controlled search. We called it the "maze model of problem solving." The maze was the *prob-*

*lem space.* Solution states or solution paths were to be discovered by using (primarily) heuristics for pruning and steering the search. Problem-solving was conceived as the heroic struggle of the problem solver, with his limited information processing capability, against the dreaded monster exponential growth. The hero's crude but effective weapon was the heuristic.

## Heuristic Knowledge

So dominant was the concept of the heuristic that in computer science and operations research AI was sometimes called *heuristic programming*; and indeed even today the collection of research activities that I supervise is called the Heuristic Programming Project, now a part of the larger Knowledge Systems Laboratory at Stanford. *Heuristic* has been an ill-defined but powerful idea. In 1963, in the book *Computers and Thought,* I defined heuristic in terms of search reduction as previously sketched. From today's vantage point, can we assert that the essence of heuristic was and is knowledge? I believe the answer is "yes." The connection was rarely made explicit in early writings, because knowledge was rarely discussed explicitly. Here are two heuristics from early programs, that now we would call *experiential knowledge*:

LT: if the subgoal WFF contains more than $N$ negation signs in a row, prune it (rationale: shun the complexity of using not- not-$P$ implies $P$ to get rid of negation signs; try something else). $N$ could be set by the heuristic programmer.

Chess: "It's good to move rooks to open files."

## Search, in Its Prime

However, the focus of the scientific attention of the early years was *not* on the structure, codification, and representation of such knowledge but on problem-solving *processes* and *search.* To illustrate this:

The 1958 paper on the NSS Chess Player attends primarily to the processes for searching the game tree effectively. The words "a practical body of knowledge about . . . chess play" appear once, but in an incidental way, not woven into the main line of exposition. The table comparing the characteristics of various chess programs never mentions "amount of chess knowledge" as a characteristic, although all modern tables comparing expert systems would do just this.

In 1956, Simon told me that propositional calculus had been chosen as the first task environment because "the p's, q's, and r's carried no meaning" (i.e., the difficult problem of meaning could temporarily be factored out of the scientific problem of understanding problem solving as search).

Similarly, cryptarithmetic was chosen as a task environment because it allowed a careful study of problem solving as search. The knowledge employed was extremely simple and its representation and use played no important role in the research. In fact, there was a mildly humorous pun in adding DONALD to GERALD to get ROBERT, because the semantics associated with these symbol strings relates to digit assignment and not to people.

The design of GPS focused on the simplicity and elegance of the problem solving machinery for generating and selecting paths. What GPS *knew* about its task environment was relatively little, and was contained in an impoverished (by modern standards) knowledge base, the operator-difference table. One might think of the O-D table as a kind of "rule base," but even so it would be considered very small by today's standards. Newell and Simon were certainly aware of the issues relating to knowledge, but their scientific strategy did not lead them to attend to these issues.

Those AI scientists oriented toward mathematical models sharpened their pencils and proved theorems about best search strategies (A\*, etc.). Others who constructed models of problem solving using methods imported from mathematical logic were also concerned primarily with search and search-reduction techniques (primarily because the search trees generated by the resolution method were enormous for any problem of interesting scope, rendering the methods ineffective from a practical viewpoint).

In short, in the Genesis period (1956-1966), search and the search model of problem-solving dominated the research agenda of the science of computer models of thought. This was to change in the years that followed.

## AN INTERLUDE: THE DIMENSIONS OF INTELLIGENCE

Some AI programs solve problems with a level of competence equalled by only a few world-class experts, and yet critics claims that they are not "really" intelligent (sometimes expressed as not "truly" intelligent). What can this criticism possibly mean?

*Intelligence* is a broad-spectrum term that names a collection of different behaviors. Intelligence is clearly multidimensional. A critic viewing achievement along a dimension that is not his favorite says that the system is not really intelligent unless it achieves along the critic's favorite dimension. Several favorites have displayed their banners over the history of AI.

1. *Competence* (or *performance*). A system is intelligent if it displays a high level of competence in solving intellectually difficult problems. (This is the banner that I wave.)
2. *Learning*. A system is intelligent if it is able to increase its store of knowledge by reasoning or experience and thereby perform more competently over time.

3. *Generality*. A system is intelligent if its problem-solving processes are so adaptable that the problem solver can perform effectively over a broad span of tasks, using one unvarying set of mechanisms. (This banner was first inscribed with the initials GPS.)

4. *Common sense*. A variation of the generality dimension. A system is intelligent if it can perform cognitive acts over the full spectrum of the human knowledge and experience that we call "common sense." (From 1958, associated with John McCarthy, and currently very popular in AI.)

5. *Natural language understanding*. The essentially (perhaps uniquely) human cognitive act is communicating with language; hence the system is intelligent only to the extent that it is competent in the use of natural language for communication.

This may not be an exhaustive list but it will serve for the ensuing discussion.

Each of these dimensions of intelligence received investigative attention in the Genesis period. As I discuss later, the competence/performance dimension received the most attention. Learning, "adaptivity," was highly attractive but proved to be an early dead-end (but this is not the place to tell that story). It was put into a state of hibernation by a very significant paper by Newell (Newell, 1963) in which learning was correctly set in relation to performance processes. Learning research awoke again only when AI was able, with relative ease, to build programs of significant competence, whose performance could be improved by learning in the manner indicated by Newell in 1962 (Buchanan & Feigenbaum, 1978; Waterman, 1970).

## The Competence/Performance Dimension

The dimension of competence/performance has dominated the AI vision in myth and science. Chess playing programs occupied the early attention of Newell, Shaw, and Simon for a decade, and was attended by some startling predictions about achievable competence levels (world champion quality). The pioneering experiments of the NSS team with the Logic Theorist program were experiments about the scope of the program's competence (how many theorems of chapter 2 of Whitehead and Russell could it prove?) and the quality of its problem solving (the famous short proof that LT achieved). There was even a vigorous dispute between Newell and Simon and the mathematician Hao Wang over the competence level of LT versus that of Wang's algorithmic method.

Gelernter, with his Geometry Theorem Proving program (Gelernter, Hansen, & Loveland, 1963), was interested solely in the competence dimension, even to the extent of testing it with the New York State Regents Exam in plane geometry one year. And when Simon, speaking for Newell as well, made his oft-cited predictions at an ORSA meeting, very early in the Genesis period, the predictions focused on extraordinary performance on difficult tasks (that's what made the predictions so unpopular at the time).

## The Eclipse of the Competence/Performance View

Remarkably, the focus shifted, and the competence/performance dimension went into temporary eclipse. There were several reasons for this:

1. The GPS ideas commanded the attention of its generation of scientists. Working in the generality dimension had a "good scientific feeling" about it (a "romance" earlier seen in the learning programs, currently seen in the connectionist experiments).
2. The early success of the information processing models of human thought, for example the EPAM model of nonsense syllable learning and Feldman's model of binary choice decision making (Feigenbaum & Feldman, 1963). This work was exciting, important, and leading somewhere, but the somewhere was NOT high levels of competence/performance, but rather the detailed understanding of the microprocesses of human thought.
3. The early attempts at high levels of competence were difficult, troublesome, and not all that successful (e.g., after all the work invested, the actual competence in chess playing achieved by the NSS chess playing program was modest). With our current understanding of the role of knowledge as a source of power for problem solvers, we now understand why high levels of competence were difficult to achieve then.[3] Yet the early enthusiasm for the competence dimension diminished. Scientists found other pastures were greener.

## The Shift to the Knowledge-Based Paradigm

Yet, during this period of eclipse, the scientific ground work was being laid for the later return of the competence/performance dimension as AI's primary focus. In Minsky's lab at MIT, a generation of graduate students began work on semantic information processing. Moses began his important work on highly competent programs for performing symbolic integration tasks (McCorduck, 1979). The work at Carnegie in this 1961–1966 period was especially important: Quillian's work on semantic nets and the work of Newell and Simon on productions as the basis for problem-solving procedures. These, in my view, were the critical scientific events that would serve as prelude to the major shift in focus that was to occur in the 1966–1976 period, the change that was called (Goldstein & Papert, 1977) "the shift to the knowledge-based

---

[3]Ironically, chess turned out to be the major exception to the Knowledge is Power principle discussed later. Higher levels of competence were achieved by more and faster search.

paradigm." Because the power of programs to behave at high levels of competence derives from the knowledge the programs have about their respective
worlds, this shift was responsible for the reemergence of the competence/per-
formance dimension as the primary focus of the AI science (and now the
applied AI technology).

## THE EXODUS: FROM THE SEARCH-BASED
## TO THE KNOWLEDGE-BASED PARADIGM

The work of Newell and Simon impressed upon AI the methodological
paradigm of empirical science. The methodology dictates this "scientific loop":

1. Design: based on an information processing model.
2. Test: based on computer programs you write to represent your design.
3. Measure: based on actual computer runs of those programs (not "pencil-
   and-paper," not "armchair thinking," not "theorems").
4. Redesign : based upon the discoveries made about the behavior of the
   model.

This is the "coin of the realm, " as Newell labeled it recently. In AI, empirical
evidence really counts in shaping new directions.

### The Empirical Evidence

By 1966, a great deal of evidence from the first decade of Life in the Search
Space was in, and amounted to this: though the work had been enormously
fruitful in stimulating the development of the basic concepts of the field, it
produced almost no "powerful" programs, that is, programs that performed
intellectually difficult tasks at world-class levels of competence (performance).
The weak methods of the search paradigm were indeed weak in the sense of
not leading to high levels of competence on "big thinking tasks." The two-
handsful of problems that GPS had been able to solve were all relatively simple puzzles; the NSS Chess Player was not a strong player; and no one (except maybe Gelernter) had been able to do much better. Where now were
the visions of Simon's ORSA talk and his book *The Shape of Automation
for Men and Management* (1965; Simon, 1977)?

### The First Knowledge Engineer

The Genesis years laid the foundation for AI's next big move. The
methodological imprint already described was central, and the strength of
its impression is one of the greatest of the Newell-Simon contributions to
the field. Indeed, the concepts that were later to come to primary importance

could not and were not ignored during the Genesis period: concepts of knowledge representation, use, and acquisition. They were there, but they were not at the scholarly focus of attention.

The best example of this is to be recalled from the years of experiments with the NSS Chess Player by those (like me) who were witness. While Newell and Shaw were handling the issues of development and testing, Simon was deeply immersed in chess itself as a domain, reading chess books, studying chess lore, even playing an order of magnitude more chess himself than he had done before—all with the purpose of acquiring and codifying chess knowledge for use by the emerging program. These are the images I have in my mind when I think of Herb Simon as the first Knowledge Engineer (as such technologists are now called). Yet the papers on the NSS Chess Paper are mostly quiet on issues related to chess knowledge.

Why was this? The field's view of the role of knowledge in problem solving can perhaps be brought back to mind with a personal anecdote. The DENDRAL program, to be discussed later, solved problems in analytic chemistry. My first presentation of the results of DENDRAL was made at the 1966 DARPA Principal Investigators Conference. One of the smartest of the young AI scientists of the time, now a senior AI statesman, rose to ask this question: "It sounds like great Chemistry, but what does it have to do with AI?" As it turned out, I believe, a great deal, perhaps almost everything.

For we are all ants on beaches of knowledge.

## The View That Knowledge Is Power

The search paradigm, which had been leading the science, was also misleading it. First of all, there was the simple question of what issues should get priority of attention. As the knowledge-based programs of the Exodus era (beginning in 1966) were built, it became clear that the most simple, almost rudimentary, search techniques would suffice for the construction of high-performance systems. The backchaining of MYCIN was not more complicated than the backchaining of LT! In some cases, like MYCIN's, the search spaces were extremely small anyway and could be handled by exhaustive search.

Yet MYCIN was evaluated to have the competence level of nationally recognized physicians in infectious disease diagnosis and therapy. How come, with such rudimentary methods? Because the power of MYCIN (i.e., its competence) derived from the good and useful *knowledge* it had of blood and meningitis infections and antibiotic therapies (Buchanan, & Shortliffe, 1984). The same can be said for all the expert systems that are MYCIN clones (presently, thousands) and indeed for virtually all other expert systems. In fact, most system builders do not even bother to build their own search engine these days; they simply buy one off-the-shelf. The real system-building action is not in the search engine but in the knowledge and its representation.

*In the knowledge lies the power.* The polestar has shifted.

Even in subfields other than problem-solving systems, knowledge is the focus. The basis for understanding in image understanding, speech understanding, and natural language understanding is taken to mean: What does each program *know* about its particular world to guide its understanding of signals and symbols from that world?

I want to emphasize that the knowledge-is-power hypothesis is not sloganeering. It is an empirical hypothesis, within the imprint of the Newell-Simon methodology. It summarizes a very large body of evidence accumulated over 20 years. I return to this hypothesis in a later section.

## The Knowledge-Search Tradeoff

An objection that might be raised is based upon the knowledge-search tradeoff. This is a plausible and useful conception that was introduced in the early 1970s as an intellectual bridge between the search-based and knowledge-based paradigms. Imagine a two-dimensional space, knowledge $x$ search. The space is filled with "equal competence" curves. For each level of competence, more knowledge implies less search, and less knowledge more search. Hence, the objection would go, if a program lacks knowledge, it could always just substitute more search to maintain equivalent performance.

Because it leads to just this objection, the K-S tradeoff is misleading. It can not be said to be false because it is plausible at some abstract level. But it is misleading because it is not a good guide to system design and construction. It conceives too simplistically the relationship between knowledge and the control of search, assuming (without saying so) a simple transformation between knowledge applied and search nodes pruned. This conception works reasonably well for closed worlds, such as chess-playing or cryptarithmetic, with no variety of exogenous sources of knowledge that are potentially effective. But the conception fails for even as simple a case as MYCIN. There is no way that MYCIN can "trade off" *more* search of its space of diagnoses for *less* medical knowledge of presenting symptoms, disease states, characteristics of infecting organisms (e.g., their morphology, their staining characteristics) and so on. I give a more dramatic example later, with respect to nuclear magnetic resonance knowledge used by DENDRAL. But these are not isolated, peculiar cases. They are merely two (and early) instances of the *general* case.

It might be argued that in some globally conceived nesting of search spaces, knowledge can be traded for search. But such an argument is unfruitful (because it leads regressively through a hypothetical chain of search spaces in which eventually some fundamental knowledge really does trade for search);

and impractical (because, in any event, real systems are not built to work this way).[4]

Knowledge arises from a variety of sources exogenous to the problem solver that cannot be traded for: to mention a few examples, human pattern recognition ultimately transduced by a knowledge engineer into the knowledge base; statistical routines; books reporting a field's lore and facts, also transduced by a knowledge engineer.

The topic deserves an extended treatment, and this is not the right place. But perhaps a metaphor will help. The simplistic K-S tradeoff pictures a kind of bidirectional titration of knowledge and search, such as is found in cryptarithmetic solvers; the real situation is more like a unidirectional precipitation of search by knowledge, such as is found in MYCIN.

## DENDRAL As a Catalyst of Change

Among the events of early significance to this Exodus period were the DENDRAL experiments (Lindsay, Buchanan, Feigenbaum, & Lederberg, 1980) DENDRAL (1965-1983) was at the time of its demise, I think, the longest-lived continuous set of experiments in the history of AI, but the important experiments for the Exodus took place in the first several years. To recap briefly, DENDRAL was a program to solve problems of the induction of chemical structure hypotheses from spectral data (initially mass spectral data) and (optionally) the chemical formula. DENDRAL used several knowledge sources: valence (which gave the most basic topological knowledge); stability of molecules; mass spectral fragmentation processes; and some components of human judgment in mass spectrometry. It evolved through an intense collaboration with world-class experts in mass spectrometry, in a pattern that is now familiar and routine, but was rare for its time.

The DENDRAL team gave special attention to issues of knowledge representation, again for reasons that are now commonplace: (a) for "transparency," so that the chemist-collaborators could easily understand what the program was doing, and what it knew, (b) to facilitate knowledge acquisition, both human-to-machine and by a learning program (Meta-DENDRAL), (c) to simplify the symbolic manipulation that DENDRAL needed to do. The first two of these reflected a strategic decision that to model the behavior

---

[4]It is difficult to make this argument concisely. The key point is the difference between problem solving in a specific task (e.g., diagnosing a patient's infectious disease), and problem solving in more general spaces of concepts of the domain (e.g., discovering the relation between stains and infecting organisms). A doctor diagnosing a patient's condition, if he lacks knowledge of staining, does not shift his attention to the task of discovering the staining characteristics of organisms. If he knows it, he uses it. If not, his level of competence falls, This is different from the situation of the cryptarithmetic puzzle solver. If he doesn't know certain digit assignments, he can simply substitute more search to make up for that lack of knowledge.

of the chemists, maximizing their contribution, it was necessary to adhere closely to the concepts, structures, representations with which *they* understood their domain. List structures were, of course, ideal for representing the molecular graphs that chemists use. To represent other kinds of chemical knowledge (e.g., mass spectral fragmentation processes), we adapted the Newell-Simon productions into a style that we called production *rules*. This style later mutated several times in MYCIN and other systems we did at the Stanford Heuristic Programming Project. At Carnegie-Mellon, the Newell-Simon productions mutated into the OPS rule formalism, and together these two streams were the parents of today's technologies for rule-based systems.

What was the reason for the intensity of our focus on knowledge and its representation? The DENDRAL experiments began in late 1965, on simple tasks. As we proceeded to more complex problems, it became clear that search methods (our legacy from the AI's first period) were necessary but not sufficient. The only way to make progress was to add more and more of what the chemists knew specifically and in detail about their science and about the families of molecules they were observing. To overcome the lack of power (competence), knowledge was needed—not only to prune and steer, but also to define smaller search spaces for the particular problems presented.

### Enter NMR Knowledge, Exit Search

The most dramatic experimental result bearing on the knowledge-is-power hypothesis (also startling and totally unexpected) related to the analysis of the acyclic amines with many carbon atoms. Because of the large number of "branchy" carbon atoms, our search methods using only the knowledge of mass spectrometry were relatively powerless. For the twenty-carbon-atom case, the search space of "legal" candidates numbering approximately fifteen million could be pruned only to a set of approximately one million plausible candidates, unacceptably high for an "answer." Our methodology told us to "do what the chemists did" in this situation, which turned out to be straightforward: bring new knowledge (and data) to bear, in this case nuclear magnetic resonance (NMR). To make progress quickly without much up-front investment in the codification of NMR knowledge, and because our chemists were not NMR specialists, we codified only a very small and simple "theory" of NMR. Because it wasn't even a first approximation, we dubbed it our "half-order" theory. It was capable of giving DENDRAL only three inferences from the NMR spectral data: the total number of methyls ($CH_3$); the subset of these connected to carbon; and the subset connected to nitrogen. Surprise! With the addition of these three inferences, the "search" reduced from one million plausible candidates to *one* (i.e., no search; just assemble the answer). In terms of the metaphor I previously used, this was truly a "precipitation" of search by knowledge.

We packaged up the experimental results and the knowledge-is-power hypothesis into a paper (Feigenbaum, Buchanan, & Lederberg, 1971) whose title was designed to closely match the title of Ernst and Newell's GPS monograph (Ernst & Newell, 1969).

## Generality Achieved With Packages

The 1970s saw the development of a large number of these knowledge-based systems, solving problems in complex real-world task environments in medicine, signal understanding, and engineering. EMYCIN (late 1970s) was the grandfather of today's knowledge-based system development languages that give a clean separation between the domain knowledge and the problem-solving processes. It was a complete turn of the wheel, because Newell and Simon, seeking a model of generality in problem solving, had experimented with the same separation 15 years earlier in the GPS work. In a sense, their dream of the generality of problem-solving mechanism has been achieved, because today thousands of problem-solving programs, spanning an amazing range of human thinking tasks, have been built—built largely by students and by professionals who are not AI specialists, simply by engineering some task-specific knowledge (Feigenbaum, McCorduck, & Nii, 1988).

## Expert Systems and Their Economic Impact: A Living Monument to Simon's Work

Two years ago, the editor of the *Journal of Artificial Intelligence* collected opinions from well-known people in the field on a variety of issues concerning the development of AI, including an opinion concerning the most significant developments of the previous 10-year period (roughly 1975–1985). Newell responded: "There is no doubt, as far as I am concerned, that the development of expert systems is the major advance in the field during the last decade" (Bobrow, & Hayes, 1985).

I have recently been surveying the success stories, large and small, of this development (Feigenbaum, McCorduck, & Nii, 1988). The tasks cover such a broad range that it would be hopeless to itemize even the classes of tasks here. All the systems have this in common: the key ingredient is a good model of the heuristic knowledge of the judgment and experience needed to accomplish the task. Of course, factual knowledge supports the heuristic knowledge; and each program has a reasoning process, but usually a very simple one. Levels of competence approaching, and often exceeding, the levels of human experts in the tasks are routinely achieved. The economic payoff that has been realized is remarkable by any measure: magnitude of cost savings; return on investment in the system development; facilitation of the productivity of individual professionals and semiprofessionals; and the improvement of the quality of the work. In a trend not easily measurable now in monetary terms, the concept of the "organizational memory" has become real. Companies are capturing the knowledge of the expert skills important to them and using it to cushion problems of retirement, death, and job changing; as well as training and the immediate enhancement of the productivity of entry-level workers. Finally, an entirely new industry is now in place to serve and enhance this economic development.

There are several living monuments to Herb Simon's scientific insights, his visions of the future course of events, and his tireless championing of the fields of AI and cognitive science. The economic impact of the technology that is based on his science is one of those living monuments. As a champion of our collective work, he was prophetic in predicting the range of applications and importance of the economic impact (*The New Science of Management Decision; The Shape of Automation*). It is a source of joy for me that the realization of his predictions has occurred within his lifetime.

Along the dimension of intelligence that early dominated the attention of AI scientists—the dimension of competence/performance—we have entered the land promised by Simon. Perhaps we should call it the land of promise, for we have just entered and have not yet explored all the fruitful arbors.

## LEVITICUS: LAWS IN THE LAND OF PROMISE

By now there is a mass of empirical evidence regarding intelligent systems, in both the science and the applied technology, and it is time to reexamine the two hypotheses previously discussed: the physical symbol system hypothesis (PSSH) and the knowledge-is-power hypothesis (KPH). How much evidence must we require before these hypotheses can be regarded as confirmed? The answer to such an unanswerable question reveals one's scientific biases. So be it.

### The Physical Symbol System Hypothesis Transformed

The PSSH is framed in terms of "general intelligent action." As I discussed, the concept is multidimensional and very broad. If we ask, for example, whether general intelligent action involving commonsense reasoning has been empirically demonstrated, the answer is no. However, because I am inclined toward the dimension I called competence/performance, I assess the evidence as providing strong confirmation of the PSSH.

Though Newell and Simon were correct in calling this an hypothesis in 1976, I suggest a renaming of the PSSH, perhaps along these lines:

AI's First Law: the Law of Intelligence of Physical Symbol Systems

### The Knowledge-Is-Power Hypothesis Transformed

The KPH is not as all-encompassing a statement at the PSSH. It addresses itself specifically to the power or competence issue. The experimental evidence that has accumulated over the past 20 years has provided massive confirmation of the KPH, so much so that I feel it should now be renamed the *Knowledge Principle* (Lenat, & Feigenbaum, 1987). The Knowledge Principle states that a system exhibits intelligent understanding and action at a high level of competence primarily because of the specific knowledge that it can bring to bear: the concepts, representations, facts heuristics, models, and methods of its domain of endeavor. A corollary of the KP is that the reasoning processes of intelligent systems are generally weak and are not the primary source of power.

The KP should inform all decisions about what is possible in the AI science and with the AI technology. For example:

> It leads one to important observations and measurements, such as the one Simon made 2 decades ago: that chess masters get their masters' edge over less competent players not because they are more powerful reasoners but because they have stored about 50,000 "patterns" that arise in high-quality chess play.

> It leads to new directions in the design of problem-solving architectures, such as those called *memory-based,case-based*, or *analogy-based*.

> It leads away from the chase for raw speed in "logical inferences per second", because "knowledge-brought-to-bear per second" is much more powerful. Thus, it can shape and direct scientific mega-projects aimed at advancing the field of artificial intelligence, for example, the Japanese Fifth Generation Project (Feigenbaum & McCorduck, 1983).

> It facilitates assessments of new approaches and directions. For example:

> You say your new neural network will solve problems in Field X? What does it *know* about Field X? How will that knowledge be acquired? represented? deployed?

> You say you are building a "voicewriter" to do automatic transcription of dictation in business English? What does your system *know* about the things that are being said in business English?

> Performing learning tasks competently is no different from performing any other task competently. The learning must be supported by specific knowledge. Hence, learning can take place only at the "fringes" of what is already known by the system. Learning at the "fringes" of a very small kernal of knowledge will be very slow and difficult.[5]

---

[5]Continuing the example of diagnosis, the diagnosis of a case is an act of performance. Finding a rule to aid in diagnosis is an act of learning and discovery. It is part of the process of the development of expertise. How can a system develop the knowledge base needed for competent performance? By"being told" and by "learning from experience (data)." In learning tasks, there are usually far fewer knowledge-based constraints applicable; much more search must be done. Hence, search reenters the picture strongly at levels above the performance level. But even in learning tasks, knowledge plays a significant role in defining the space in which the search for new knowledge takes place, and in pruning and steering in that space. Learning itself is a knowledge-based task. Therefore, learning takes place at the fringes and interstices of what we already know. The more the learner knows, the easier it is to know more (Lenat & Feigenbaum, 1987).

It leads toward the construction of very large knowledge bases to handle the problem of commonsense reasoning in AI systems. For it asserts that there is no "magic bullet" in commonsense reasoning processes. There is only commonsense knowledge, undoubtedly many millions of things to know that are "common sense" about our world.

The point is clear, and more examples will not illuminate it further. The chaining methods, the means-ends analysis methods, the island-driving methods, generate-and-test methods, the theorem-proving methods, and others, that the AI science classes as "weak methods" are indeed weak and are not the important source of power for achieving high levels of competence in problem-solving.

The word *specific* in the knowledge principle is important. The reason was treated earlier in this paper, in the discussion of the knowledge-search tradeoff. The empirical evidence from the many systems that have been built is that the tradeoff is (in almost all cases, hence the general situation?) unidirectional, from specific knowledge to reduced search and higher quality in the selection of "satisfactory" solutions. Thus, with specific knowledge, better solutions are achieved faster; and with a given amount of information processing resources, more complex problems can be solved.

To repeat an old refrain, "The expert is the specialist, with a specialist's knowledge of his area and a specialist's methods and heuristics" (Feigenbaum, Buchanan, & Lederberg, 1971).

## CONCLUSION: THE MANY MANIFESTATIONS OF SIMON

Simon is not One. He is Many. To his grateful friends, former students, colleagues, and fellow scientists, he appears in several manifestations.

Simon as Monomaniac: Does he live in many fields?

Political science, administrative behavior, management science, operations research, psychology, computer science, philosophy of science, and (oh, I almost forgot) economics. Except for economics, each claims that he is *its* first Nobel laureate. When I arrived at Berkeley in 1960 (thoroughly Simonized by my graduate study) to teach administrative behavior in the business school, the school of public administration will *still* using Simon's textbook on municipal budgeting (how many of you know that Simon wrote such a book?). I asked him once how he managed such diversity. He denied the diversity. He said: "I am really a monomaniac. All my life I have been studying one thing: human decision making." This is the key to an understanding of what the Nobel Award committee was calling to the world's attention in the citation accompanying his award.

Simon as Pied Piper:

He attracted dozens of graduate students over the years to the study of behavioral science, cognitive psychology, and artificial intelligence.

Simon as Teacher and Colleague:

No one who has worked with him, as student or colleague, can ever forget the warm friendship, the openness, generosity, and of course the intellectual excitement. We can adequately repay our debt to him only by emulating his example, in our science and in our care for the generations of young people that will follow us.

Charles Darwin described his mentor and friend, the great geologist Charles Lyell, in words that describe our mentor and friend, Herb Simon: "His delight in science was ardent . . . He was very kind-hearted . . . and he felt the keenest interest in the future progress of mankind" (Boorstin, 1985, p. 468).

## REFERENCES

Bobrow, D., & Hayes, P. (1985). AI—Where are we? *Artificial Intelligence, 25,* 375–415.

Boorstin, D. (1985). *The discoverers.* New York: Vintage Books,

Buchanan, B. G., & Feigenbaum, E. A. (1978). DENDRAL and META-DENDRAL: Their applications dimension, *Artificial Intelligence, 11,* 5–24.

Buchanan, B. G., & Shortliffe, E. H. (1984). *Rule-based expert systems: The MYCIN experiments of the Stanford Heuristic Programming Project.* Reading, MA: Addison-Wesley.

Ernst, G. W., & Newell, A (1969) *GPS: A case study in generality and problem solving.* New York: Academic Press.

Feigenbaum, E. A., Buchanan, B. G., & Lederberg, J. (1971). On generality and problem solving: A case study using the DENDRAL program. In B. Meltzer, & D. Michie, *Machine intelligence 6.* Edinburgh: Edinburgh University Press.

Feigenbaum, E. A., & Feldman, J. A. (Eds.). (1963). *Computers and thought.* New York: McGraw-Hill.

Feigenbaum, E. A. & McCorduck, P. (1983). *The fifth generation.* Reading, MA: Addison-Wesley.

Feigenbaum, E. A., McCorduck, P., & Nii, H. P. (1988). *The rise of the expert company.* New York: Times Books.

Gelernter, H., Hansen, J. R., & Loveland, D. H. (1963). Empirical explorations of the Geometry Theorem Proving Machine. In E. Feigenbaum & J.Feldman, (Eds.) *Computers and thought.* New York: McGraw-Hill.

Goldstein, I., & Papert, S. (1977). Artificial intelligence, language, and the study of knowledge, *Cognitive Science,* 1(1).

Lenat, D., & Feigenbaum, E. A. (1987, August). On the thresholds of knowledge, *Proceedings of the International Joint Conference on Artificial Intelligence-87,* Milan, Italy.

Lindsay, R., Buchanan, B. G., Feigenbaum, E. A., & Lederberg, J. (1980). *Application of artificial intelligence for organic chemistry: The DENDRAL project.* New York: McGraw-Hill.

McCorduck, P. (1979) *Machines who think.* San Francisco, CA: W. H. Freeman.

Newell, A. (1963) Learning, generality, and problem solving. *Proceedings of the International Federation of Information Processing Congress, 62:* (pp. 407-412). Amsterdam: North-Holland.

Newell, A., & Simon, H. A. (1976, March). Computer science as empirical inquiry: Symbols and search, *Communications of the ACM,* 19(3) New York : Association For Computing Machinery.

Simon, H. A. (1957). *Models of man.* New York: Wiley.

Simon, H. A. (1965). *The shape of automation for men and management.* New York: Harper & Row.

Simon, H. A. (1970). *Sciences of the artificial.* Cambridge, MA: MIT Press.

Simon, H. A. (1977). *The new science of management decision* (3rd ed.). Englewood Cliffs, NJ: Prentice-Hall.

Waterman, D. A. (1970). Generalization learning techniques for automating the learning of heuristics. *Artificial Intelligence,* 1(1) 121-170.

# 7

## Expertise in Chess and Bridge

Neil Charness
*University of Waterloo*

### AN ANECDOTE

Many years ago, a young boy growing up in Milwaukee had occasion to play against Arpad Elo, a chess organizer in the area. He lost that game, but on doing his homework that night discovered that he could have beaten the master. On their next occasion of playing the youngster said "You know, I could have beaten you in that game," and showed him the analysis. "Yes", said Elo, "but that was yesterday." It was a good lesson for the young Herbert Simon, who later went on to somewhat greater feats outside the domain of chess (Simon, informal discussion, 1978). The question of how to measure chess skill was to preoccupy Elo, who eventually engineered the chess rating scale (Elo, 1978), now adopted universally, that bears his name. It seems equally true for cognitive analyses of skilled performance in "semantically-rich" (Simon, 1979) domains that the truths of yesterday, under closer analysis, may not apply quite so well today.

Simon suggested come time ago (Simon & Chase, 1973), that cognitive psychology needs a model organism to study, much as scientists interested in genetics selected organisms such as Drosophila. Despite its rather formidable complexity, chess playing seems a worthy candidate for such a role. Research on chess skill has been extremely influential for the understanding of skill in many other domains (Charness, 1988), and has attracted considerable attention from those studying artificial intelligence via the building of skillful chess programs (Berliner, 1978). As is the case in biology, different cognitive tasks are best suited to specific niches: chess is an excellent task to study search processes in problem solving. Later I discuss the advantages of the bridge planning task ("E-coli?") for examining pattern-driven planning behavior.

The chapter is organized into three main sections. The first examines skill in chess from the perspective of a case study of skill acquisition over a 9-year period. It explores how some of the markers of skill differences in cross-sectional studies (e.g., search depth, evaluation time, chunking in recall) apply to one player over time. A modest attempt is made to evaluate the concept of "chess talent."

The middle section examines the case of skill in bridge for planning the play of a bridge contract. I present evidence that bridge planning has more in common with medical diagnosis than with search in chess. But even here, knowledge seems to be organized around significant features of a bridge hand. A set of planning productions are proposed to account for differences between novice, intermediate, and master players. Both domains speak to the theme that "knowledge is power" (Feigenbaum, chap. 6 in this volume).

The final section deals speculatively with the issues of how motivation and instruction play a role in building up the knowledge base required for expert performance.

## CHESS: A DROSOPHILA
## FOR COGNITIVE PSYCHOLOGY

The history of understanding expert chess performance bears some parallels to the introductory anecdote, with Simon figuring prominently in both stories. The truisms of yesterday (e.g., de Groot, 1965/1978), that grandmasters do not search the tree of possibilities any more deeply than strong amateurs has given way to the significant relation observed between search depth and chess skill level (Charness, 1981b).

The cherished notion that the master's advantage springs primarily from a pattern recognition-based ability to select plausible moves (Chase & Simon, 1973a, 1973b) has been brought into question by Holding (1985). Holding argued that search efficiency differences are the key to expertise. He pointed, in part, to my work on search depth differences, and Holding and Reynolds' (1982) finding that with contrived chess positions, where there is no recall advantage for more skilled players, there is still an advantage in choosing the best move. A recognition-based theory of skill also has some difficulty accounting for age-related differences in recall ability among chess players equated in chess skill (Charness, 1981c).

The view that chess skill is due primarily to practice differences rather than genetic differences may be somewhat discomfited by the finding of significant speed advantages for more skilled players in piece detection tasks. This is even true when the positions are randomly arranged (Saariluoma, 1985), and where little advantage for the more skilled player would be expected.

What I hope to show in the first part of the chapter is the validity of earlier ideas about the preeminence of efficient pattern recognition in accounting for skill.

## Longitudinal Study
## of Chess Skill Acquisition by DH

All things come to those who wait.

In 1978, I gathered a considerable amount of data on the processes of search in chess, recall of chess positions, recognition confidence, and evaluation of endgame positions on a sample of 34 chess players varying in age (16–64 years) and skill (CFC rating 1,283–2,004) (Charness, 1981a, 1981b). (Chess ratings depend on a player's performance in organized tournaments, with points won or lost depending on the game outcome and the strength of the opposition. See Elo, 1978.) These studies were designed to explore how age and skill jointly determine performance in chess problem solving and chess memory.

The youngest player in my sample, DH, then almost 16, held a Chess Federation of Canada (CFC) rating of 1,570, (the mean value in the sample) putting him slightly above the mean of the Canadian chess playing population. In the following years, DH went on to reach the master level (a CFC rating of 2,200), and as of testing in the February–March 1987 interval, ranked seventh in Canada, with a rating of 2,423.

Given that the standard deviation (class interval) for chess ratings is 200 (Elo, 1978), this change in rating is in excess of four standard deviation units. In a match of 100 games between DH and someone who today has the same rating DH had 9 years ago, DH would be expected to win all 100 games.

His improvement function is shown in Fig. 7.1.

Ratings are provided bimonthly by the CFC for players who have been active during that interval. Some points are missing due to DH not having played in a rated tournament over a 2-month period. As Newell and Rosenbloom (1981) speculated, skill acquisition, even in a semantically rich domain such as chess, follows a (simple) power function. The linear fit is quite good (Rating = 1,613 + 7.656*Month, $r^2$ = .835), but the simple power fit is better (Rating = 895*Month$^{.211}$, $r^2$ = .920). The one significant deviation (months 37–39) was due in part to a rating deflation adjustment made by the CFC to everyone in the rating pool in 1980. This bonus award accounted for about 100 of the 300 rating points gained by DH. When queried about that particular summer interval, DH mentioned that he remembered having spent the entire summer playing in a large number of strong Canadian and U.S. tournaments.

DH, now a senior student in mathematics at the University of Waterloo, agreed to return to my lab, and we re-ran the same experiment, with new random orders for the experimental conditions. DH's memory for the earlier experiments was quite hazy. (For instance, he denied having been in two separate experiments, and had only very vague memory for any details.)

In part, this is due to the opportunity for massive interpolated interference by other chess positions over the 9-year interval. In July 1978 he reported

CHESS SKILL ACQUISITION BY DH: ESTABLISHED RATINGS

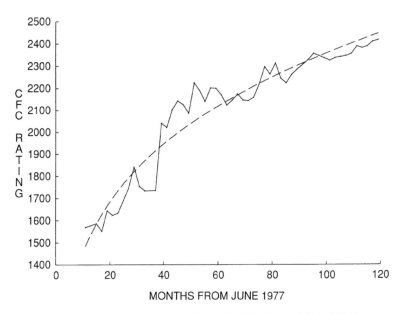

FIG. 7.1. Bi-monthly Chess Federation of Canada ratings for DH (solid line), and the power function fit (dashed line).

that he played 17 tournament games in the past year. In February 1987 he reported playing about 100 games in the past year. Despite the increase in tournament games, there was actually a decrease in the report of number of hours spent playing or studying chess per week: 14 hours in 1978 versus 10 in 1987.

It would be ideal to have a control subject for DH, someone with a similar initial skill level and age, who had also continued to play chess, but had not shown a very great improvement in skill level. Unfortunately, because of the small initial sample and the mobility of young people, no such candidate existed.

## Experimental Procedure

DH filled out a consent form, a short demographic questionnaire, and was given tape-recorded instructions for each task, identical to those given in 1978. In the first task, he was asked to choose the best move for White from each of four positions shown as slides on a screen, and to think aloud while doing so. Following this task, he was to evaluate as rapidly and accurately as possible 20 endgame positions as "win for White," "draw," "win for Black." These were also shown as slides. Then he was asked to attempt to reproduce the four choose-a-move chess positions by placing pieces on an empty board. Following the unexpected (incidental) recall task, he was asked to recognize the four positions from a set of 30 slides, and rate his confidence that a slide was a target slide.

A more detailed account of the procedure and materials is given in Charness (1981a). The only things that varied from the study 9 years earlier were the different research assistants administering the tasks, and some "aging" of the slides, probably making them a bit less distinct.

## Choose-a-Move Task

The recorded verbal protocols were transcribed, translated into problem behavior graphs, and analyzed for search statistics (Charness, 1981b). As seen in Table 7.1, DH now chose the optimal move in two positions, and less accurate moves in the other two. Nine years earlier he chose the correct move for only one position, though it was for one he chose an inferior move this time. Nine years earlier, he mentioned the correct base move for three of the positions in his protocols, and did so three times now. In short, there has not been an enormous change in accuracy for these four positions, which tends to argue against the idea that there was much carry-over from earlier testing.

More interesting are the statistics on depth and breadth of search. With

TABLE 7.1
Summary Statistics for Search in the 4 Choose-a-Move Positions
for the 1978 and 1987 Experiments With DH

| Position | Chose best Move | | Solution Time (sec) | | Unique Base moves | | Total moves | | Max Depth | |
|---|---|---|---|---|---|---|---|---|---|---|
| | 1978 | 1987 | 1978 | 1987 | 1978 | 1987 | 1978 | 1987 | 1978 | 1987 |
| Ending (N-d2) | yes | no | 499 | 321 | 1 | 1 | 27 | 18 | 6 | 5 |
| Quiet Middle (P-c5) | no | yes | 677 | 393 | 8 | 2 | 32 | 27 | 6 | 5 |
| Tactical Middle (Q-d4) | no | no | 715 | 780 | 7 | 6 | 69 | 52 | 9 | 9 |
| Tactical Opening (RxN) | no | yes | 556 | 531 | 3 | 3 | 52 | 53 | 7 | 9 |
| Mean | 1 | 2 | 612 | 506 | 4.75 | 3 | 45.0 | 37.5 | 7 | 7 |
| SD | .5 | .58 | 101 | 202 | 3.30 | 2.2 | 19.3 | 17.7 | 1.40 | 2.31 |

*Note.* The 1978 protocols have been reanalyzed to bring them in line with current scoring procedures resulting in slight changes to the total moves count and the unique base moves count.

only four positions being available for statistical analysis, there is very little power to detect changes, nonetheless, the trends are worth discussing. In general, DH took less time to choose a move now than earlier. He also tended to explore fewer unique base moves, that is, was more selective in generating first moves. The size of the search tree did not vary much, and mean maximum depth of search remained unchanged. There was a tendency for DH to search less deeply for the quiet positions and more deeply for the tactically active positions this time. If anything, DH exhibited a somewhat more compact search in 1987.

### Evaluation of Endgames

As seen in Table 7.2, DH assessed endgame positions more than twice as quickly $t(19) = 3.3$, $p < .01$.

He was nominally more accurate (75% vs. 70%, $t(19) = .44$). These results are consistent with the hypothesis that he was now able to evaluate the positions more by recognizing them, as opposed to doing search, particularly in view of the earlier results showing that search speed did not vary much from 9 years earlier.

### Chunking in recall

The issue of chunking is critical for theories of chess skill. Chase and Simon (1973a, 1973b) stressed, with de Groot (1965/1978,1966), that, because search statistics do not differentiate the highly skilled from their less-skilled counterparts, then the process of determining which moves get searched is critical. It has been assumed that a large repertoire of chess chunks underlies move selection, such that the master's internal representation of the position triggers the investigation of good moves.

DH generated virtually perfect incidental recall of chess positions 9 years ago: he had one error of omission for four positions. This time he recalled all positions perfectly. I used the Chase and Simon (1973a) technique of assigning chunk boundaries from pause times greater than 2 seconds for the videotapes of 1978, and used the same criterion to delineate chunks now. As Table 7.3 demonstrates, DH has changed in the direction of larger chunk

TABLE 7.2
Evaluation speed and accuracy for 20 endgame positions by DH in
1978 and 1987 (Standard Deviations in Parentheses)

| Year | Response Time (sec) | Proportion Correct |
|------|---------------------|--------------------|
| 1978 | 43.7 (33.8) | .70 (.47) |
| 1987 | 17.7 (14.05) | .75 (.44) |

TABLE 7.3
Incidental Recall Chunk Scores for DH in 1978 and 1987 for the Four
Choose-the-best-move Chess Positions
(Standard Deviations are in Parentheses).

| Year | Chunk features | | Piece placement RT (sec) | |
|------|----------------|---|--------------------------|---|
| | Mean pieces per chunk | Mean number per position | Mean median within chunk | Mean median between chunk |
| 1978 | 1.8 (.34) | 15.75 (4.5) | 1.24 (.256) | 5.05 (1.60) |
| 1987 | 2.7 (.58) | 9.0 (1.4) | 1.15 (.208) | 3.60 (0.90) |

sizes and smaller chunk numbers. His chunk size is 50% greater, $t(3) = 3.3$, $p < .05$, and necessarily, the number of chunks declines by 50%. (Because he placed almost the identical number of pieces then and now, the product of chunk number and chunk size is pretty much a constant.)

The increase in chunk size may be partially attributable to faster access to memory. Although there is no change in within chunk latencies ($t(3) = .84$), there is a marginal change in between chunk latencies ($t(3) = 2.62$, $p < .08$). This speed-up may mean that DH now accesses chunks from a hierarchical structure (e.g., as do the digit span experts: Ericsson, 1985; Ericsson & Staszewski, chap. 9 in this volume). If that structure has more than two levels, DH may have faster access to some chunks than to others.

It would have been preferable to derive the chunk boundary latency using Chase and Simon's (1973a) technique of examining both recall and perceptual reproduction placement patterns. Only recall was examined, so this option was not available.

Chase and Simon (1973a, 1973b) also showed that the number of shared chess relations (e.g., defence, proximity, color, type) between successively placed pieces was negatively correlated with interpiece latency. A multiple regression technique was used to assess how interpiece latency varied both with number of shared relations and with year of testing. Using each latency as a case for analysis tends to give somewhat undue weight to outliers, so conclusions must be viewed as tentative.

The initial regression showed no interaction between year of testing (1978–1987) and number of shared relations (0–4), implying that memory for the positions was organized the same way over time. Thus, an additive model was adopted. Both year of testing and number of relations were significant factors, $F(2,194) = 7.3$, $R^2 = .07$. Latencies declined at a rate of .35 seconds per year, and also dropped 1.6 seconds for each additional shared relation, replicating the Chase and Simon (1973a, 1973b) finding.

In summary, longitudinal changes in skill were most strongly associated with changes in chunking and evaluation speed rather than with search. Put another way, DH was already near ceiling for search depth as a moderately skilled player, and didn't show much improvement subsequently. The latter point buttresses an earlier speculation on why I obtained skill-related depth of search effects and de Groot did not (Charness, 1981b): Depth of search increases with skill at moderate levels but asymptotes at higher levels. A caveat should be emphasized. These generalizations are based on only four sampled chess positions.

## Chess Talent

I'd like to speculate now on another aspect of skill in chess: talent. The question is whether people are predisposed to become highly skilled at a particular activity. Folklore suggests that a talented player can be spotted early on the basis of unusually polished performance in some aspect of the domain, even though the skill has not yet been honed to a peak.

Naturally, with data from only a single subject, much of what follows must be treated with caution. One approach to identifying latent talent is to see whether DH was "advanced" on any marker of skill (chunking, evaluation speed, search depth). That is, did values of such variables in 1978 depart significantly from what would be expected for his skill level? To assess this question, we first need to predict how he should have performed.

Table 7.4 presents the predicted and observed values for DH in 1978 for variables that had significant relationships with age or skill in the chess sample (that is, for valid predictor variables). The predicted values are derived from the regression equations I published earlier relating search depth, chunking, evaluation, and other variables to skill and age in the sample (Charness, 1981a, 1981b). Predicted values indicate what would be expected for a 16-year-old player with a rating of 1,570. The standard error measure for each prediction equation was used to test whether DH's observed scores deviated significantly from his predicted scores.

Of the 18 variables, only 2 show him to depart significantly from the expected values for his level of skill in 1978, both at $p < .05$, two-tailed. He chose better moves in the choose-a-move task than would be expected, but he took significantly longer to generate an evaluation in the rapid evaluation task. Given that about one variable would be expected to be significant by chance for the 18 comparisons, we can tentatively conclude that his performance was not particularly unusual in 1978.

Specifically, for theoretically important variables such as depth of search, evaluation accuracy, and recall memory, there is no indication of latent talent. Obviously, one case study cannot rule out talent hypotheses. A further caveat on the talent hypothesis failure is that although DH is highly skilled with respect to the Canadian chess playing population, he is not (yet) among the ranks of the grandmasters that de Groot (1965/1978) examined (ratings of about 2,500+), those at the pinnacle of chess playing ability.

If talent does not account for skill, what does? Although hours of prac-

TABLE 7.4
Predicted and Observed Values for DH in 1978 on Variables
With Significant Age and Skill Relations

| Variable | Observed | Predicted | SE predicted | t value (df=33) |
|---|---|---|---|---|
| Move choice time (sec) | 612 | 490 | 188 | 0.65 |
| Rating of move | 6.75 | 4.4 | 1.12 | 2.098* |
| Correct moves mentioned (/4) | 3.0 | 2.14 | 1.01 | 0.85 |
| Percent correct (incidental recall) | 100 | 104 | 17.97 | 0.22 |
| Mean number of chunks | 15.75 | 12.3 | 3.21 | 1.07 |
| Mean number of pieces/chunk | 1.77 | 2.64 | .518 | 1.68 |
| Mean median between chunk latency | 5.05 | 4.13 | 1.02 | 0.90 |
| % correct endgame evaluations | 70.00 | 66.67 | 10.57 | 0.32 |
| Mean endgame evaluation RT | 43.7 | 19.82 | 9.55 | 2.50* |
| Mean search episodes | 12.25 | 9.19 | 3.072 | 1.00 |
| Terminal nodes | 15.75 | 12.68 | 4.69 | 0.65 |
| Total moves | 39.75 | 35.37 | 17.21 | 0.25 |
| Repeated base moves | 5.25 | 4.80 | 2.013 | 0.22 |
| Mean maximum depth of search | 6.75 | 6.64 | 2.096 | 0.05 |
| Mean mean depth of search | 3.72 | 3.24 | 0.893 | 0.54 |
| Repeated other moves | 4.25 | 4.84 | 3.69 | 0.16 |
| Unique base moves/minute | .435 | .74 | .321 | 0.95 |
| Unique base moves | 5.25 | 4.3 | 1.264 | 0.75 |

tice per week were not related to age or skill in the original sample, DH clearly was studying and playing chess much more intensively than the sample as a whole. He reported 14 hours per week when the sample reported 6.5 ($SD = 5$; $t(33) = 8.9$). In 1987 he reported playing or studying about 10 hours per week. Assume that a working year is about 50 weeks and that DH averaged 12 hours per week over the past 9 years. DH would have been playing or practicing chess for about 4,500 hours.

## Summary

Why are chess masters so good at chess? There are two popular views: Chess playing talent is innate, and chess masters are those with specialized circuitry that enables them to think more deeply about chess problems. The second view is that chess masters are made, not born. Their superior performance depends on a hard-won knowledge base that enables them to examine the most promising parts of the search space. Although, the latter hypothesis seems to have been adopted by most modern investigators, there continues to be controversy over the nature of the knowledge base. The relative contributions of search efficiency, evaluation accuracy, and a chunk-based pattern recognition system is still debatable (Holding, 1985).

The longitudinal investigation I report suggests that as a player gains in skill, rapid access to knowledge about endings increases, perceptual/memory chunk size increases, but search characteristics (e.g., depth of search) do not show much change. Given the size of the search space for choosing a move, and the human's limited capacity for retaining information about various search outcomes, it is obvious that selective search is the only reasonable way to choose a move. Search depth is likely to be more a consequence of increasing skill than a cause. Some reasonable evidence for this is provided by a related task, memory for sequences of chess moves. Chase and Simon (1973a) showed that accuracy in recall of the sequences, presented at the slow rate of 5 seconds per move, was strongly related to chess skill level. I doubt that telling a moderately skilled player to search more deeply will result in much improved levels of play, though that experiment has not yet been tried.

As difficult and expensive as they are, longitudinal studies of skill acquisition in semantically rich domains can be a useful adjunct to the traditional cross-sectional approaches. Skill acquisition takes a long time. DH reported that he first learned to play chess at age 11. He first played in rated tournament chess games at age 15. It was only at age 20, after 5 years of fairly intense tournament play, that he consistently performed at or above master level. As Simon and Chase (1973) pointed out, it takes at least 9–10 years to achieve grandmaster-level play.

It is probably not feasible to try to bring chess skill acquisition into the laboratory in the same way that, for instance, digit span acquisition has been studied (e.g., see Ericsson & Staszewski, chap. 9 in this volume). Chess skill is somewhat more difficult to decompose into component processes. What is needed is a more detailed look at how the pieces (recognition, evaluation, search) fit together into the package known as master-level play. Chess as Drosophila for cognitive psychology still seems a promising task environment, if only we could find a way to raise masters a little more quickly! Perhaps fittingly, that is probably the ultimate applied goal for understanding expert performance.

## SKILL IN BRIDGE

As a pastime bridge playing is probably more popular in North America than chess, at least insofar as newspaper column space is concerned. Bridge columns appear daily whereas chess columns appear once a week, if at all. Curiously, cognitive psychologists have had less interest in bridge than chess as a model environment for studying problem solving processes. Much as E-coli reproduces faster than Drosophila, bridge problem solving takes place more quickly than chess problem-solving, and as a result it will probably be considerably easier to map the patterns that the master bridge player uses than those on which the master chess player relies.

Only a few papers have been published concerning issues in skilled performance (Charness, 1979, 1983, 1987; Engle & Bukstel, 1978; Keren, 1987). Most of these deal with how players choose a bid in the initial stages of the game and how they incidentally or intentionally recall cards. Research has shown that higher skill levels are associated with faster and more accurate bidding, better choices for a line of play for a hand, superior intentional memory for structured but not for random bridge hands, and superior incidental memory for hands that are studied in a problem-solving context.

The Keren (1987) study showed that more expert players were better calibrated in their predictions of the outcome of a to-be-played bridge contract (showed a closer match between their generated a priori probabilities and the actual outcome). This result fits with a study by Holding and Pfau (1985) for chess players. More skilled players were more accurate in their evaluations of which side had the advantage in tactically active positions.

The pattern of results in the bridge studies cited is quite consistent with findings in the domain of chess skill. Skilled bridge players can recognize clusters of cards (primarily honor cards in a suit) as single chunks. Also, better players attend more successfully to "spot cards" (non-honors), as well as to the distribution of cards across suits (the shape of the hand). In bridge, because the skills of bidding and play can be independent, it is not yet clear what function the chunk has across the two tasks.

There is no gold standard for assessing bridge skill equivalent to Elo's chess skill rating system. Rather, bridge players compete in pairs, or as teams of four in tournaments (and more rarely, as individuals in events where they switch partners) and are awarded "Master points" based on their final standing in the field of competitors. There are different types of points available depending on the type of tournament (black for club games, red and gold points for regional and national events). Master points can be won, but never lost (in contrast to chess rating points).

If a player is persistent enough, or has sufficient financial resources to hire an expert partner, he or she can usually accumulate enough points to reach the title of Life Master. Thus, accumulated master points are sometimes more of a testimony to persistence than to skill level. One way to get around this scaling problem is to take the logarithm of master points, with the assumption that persistence but low skill level won't easily get you to the next scale point after an initial climb from novice levels to the 10-to-50-point range. See Charness (1979) for converging evidence on the utility of log master points.

Bridge involves two stages: bidding and play. A description of the bidding phase is given in Charness (1983) together with a model for the special case of the initial (opening) bid. This chapter concentrates on the issue of skill in playing out a contract.

After the contract has been won by one of the partnerships in the bidding phase, the player, termed declarer, from the successful partnership who first bid the agreed on suit (or no trump) plays out the hand, attempting to fulfil the contract (or in the case of a sacrifice, to minimize the loss). His or her partner becomes "dummy," and after the opening lead, places his or her hand face up on the table and plays no further part in the proceedings. Depending on the type of bridge competition (standard contract bridge, duplicate bridge, team of four event), the declarer will attempt to win as many tricks as possible, or find the safest way to make the contract and not worry about overtricks (excess tricks).

For convenience, and to follow the convention adopted in bridge books and newspaper columns, we can assign the positions of players to compass points, with declarer as South, dummy as North, and the opponents as West and East. Play of the hand proceeds as follows: West places the first card face up on the table, North, the declarer's partner, puts down his or her hand face-up on the table (called the dummy hand or "dummy"), and South, the declarer, chooses which card to play from the dummy. East plays his or her card, and the declarer plays a card from his or her hand. Whoever has the highest card wins the "trick," and leads the first card on the next round. Play continues until all 13 rounds have been completed (or a claim is made and evaluated).

Even given the restrictive rules of play (that players must play cards from the suit led, if they have any, or suffer penalties), the possible sequence of plays for a given hand is enormous. [For example, for Hand 1 (shown in Fig. 7.2), there are 372 unique first rounds alone, not counting illegal plays!] Here, as in other immense problem spaces (Newell & Simon, 1972), players must search selectively when planning their play. They use heuristics to narrow the search. Skilled players have an extensive knowledge base available to guide their search.

The goal for declarer is well-defined: capture the number of tricks you have bid plus the "book," six additional tricks. For a bid of 4 spades, declarer must capture 10 of the 13 tricks. A trick consists of a round of four cards, with the trick won by the side having the highest card (or trump card in the case where one or more players cannot follow to the suit led initially). The initial state is well-defined (you start with no tricks). The operators for winning tricks are relatively well-known as well (play the highest card in the suit if you are trying to win a trick, or a low card if you are not).

What makes the task challenging is the timing of plays. You may have many tricks to take in the dummy hand, but no way to reach dummy. You may have many tricks to take in your hand, but your opponents are on lead, and they take their tricks before you can take yours. In addition, at least in the early stages, you do not have perfect information about the distribution of your opponents cards, which is another critical feature of planning the play. (A good player, by keeping track of the cards already played, and prior bidding, can often infer what cards the opponents hold.)

Because bridge is a game of incomplete information, declarer must choose lines of play that have the highest probability of success against likely distributions of cards. Good players know these distributions and their associated probabilities (not necessarily precisely, but well enough to rank alternatives), and over a long sequence of hands, will win more often than those who choose less beneficial alternatives. It is of course possible to generate the probabilities of success of various lines of play "on line," but this may lead to very slow play. In tournament bridge, you can be penalized for slow play.

In the process of acquiring skill, players learn how to organize their play (both as declarer and as a defender), how to infer the card holdings in an opponent's hand, and a number of standard procedures for maximizing trick-taking ability with certain suit combinations (see Frey, Truscott, & Kearse (1976), p. 440–495, for the optimal lines of play for 656 important single suit combinations). It is probably fair to assume that highly skilled players recognize many of these suit combinations, and have the correct line of play associated with the description.

There are similar heuristics available for making use of the bidding in the auction preceding play, as well as for inferring card holdings of the opponents based on the opening lead. Analysis of the opening lead is not as mysterious as might be thought. In duplicate bridge, players fill out "convention cards," which list their agreed upon conventions for bidding and for play. (Stated conventions are guidelines, not absolute requirements. The only requirement is that partnerships are not allowed secret conventions. A player may depart from a convention when his or her partner is in no better condition than the opponents to detect such a violation.)

What is critical, however, is not just knowing individual suit plays, and likely card holdings in the unseen hands, but rather, how these can be combined to optimize trick-taking possibilities for the entire hand. A good analogy is the case of solving physics problems. Both novices and experts usually know the equations for the domain (Simon & Simon, 1978). Only the experts seem to know which equations are relevant on a given occasion. It appears that the conditions for applying a complex operator in bridge (execute a squeeze, execute a throw-in) are often ill-specified in bridge books. Rather, an example is given of the ideal situation late in play, and it is left to the player to recognize at the opening lead that the option exists and to plan accordingly. Simon and Simon (1978) noted that a similar problem exists with the style of instruction in physics textbooks.

My working hypothesis is that knowledge of specific card patterns and their associated play strategies is the major factor differentiating the skilled from the less-skilled bridge player. That is, the novice player starts out with general problem-solving rules. These become refined through experience garnered in play and study into much more specific rules, covering many concrete situations. (Hayes-Roth, Klahr, & Mostow, 1981, outline a set of possible mechanisms for such knowledge refinement in the game of Hearts.)

It is probably also reasonable to characterize this knowledge as a production system, with the condition side representing the encoded card combinations and the action side indicating the intended sequence of plays.

Readers with moderate bridge playing experience may already find this quite plausible. They probably can think back on their early training and remember that initially they were advised "When in a suit contract, first pull trumps." Later, the heuristic was probably revised to "When in a suit contract, pull trumps only if you don't need to ruff out losers first." It was probably revised again, to take into account other more specific cases (such as don't pull trump when you can lose control of the hand by virtue of the opponents shortening your trump holding by forcing you to ruff).

As these descriptions suggest, rules for planning involve more and more elaborate conditions for applicability. This idea parallels that of Anderson (1982), who argued that skill acquisition results from the compiling of simple productions into ones with complex condition and action sides.

It is to be expected that the expert also differs from the novice in the revision and successful execution of plans during play, when there is additional information available with each round of cards. The art of "card reading" (Engle & Bukstel, 1978) is already recognized in the folklore of bridge as a significant component of skilled play.

To evaluate these hypotheses, I attempted a detailed analysis of protocol data collected in a study of age and skill effects on bridge performance. A brief description of the experiment follows.

## Experimental Procedure

Forty-five bridge players varying in age and skill completed a set of experimental tasks (see Charness, 1987). In one task they were asked to think out loud while planning the best line of play for four bridge hands. The hands were selected from bridge columns by Easley Blackwood (1977a, 1977b), Edwin Kantar (1977), and Pedro Assumpcao (1977) in the *Contract Bridge Bulletin,* a monthly publication of the American Contract Bridge League.

Hands were presented on a computer screen, using symbolic displays, with North and South hands presented, the opening lead indicated, but with no bidding information available. (Bidding information was eliminated to ensure that all players started in the same knowledge state. Although this makes the task a bit artificial, there are many cases of bidding to a contract without the opponents intruding.)

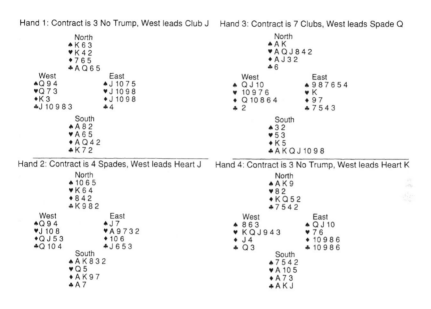

Hand 1: Contract is 3 No Trump, West leads Club J

**North**
♠ K 6 3
♥ K 4 2
♦ 7 6 5
♣ A Q 6 5

**West**
♠ Q 9 4
♥ Q 7 3
♦ K 3
♣ J 10 9 8 3

**East**
♠ J 10 7 5
♥ J 10 9 8
♦ J 10 9 8
♣ 4

**South**
♠ A 8 2
♥ A 6 5
♦ A Q 4 2
♣ K 7 2

Hand 3: Contract is 7 Clubs, West leads Spade Q

**North**
♠ A K
♥ A Q J 8 4 2
♦ A J 3 2
♣ 6

**West**
♠ Q J 10
♥ 10 9 7 6
♦ Q 10 8 6 4
♣ 2

**East**
♠ 9 8 7 6 5 4
♥ K
♦ 9 7
♣ 7 5 4 3

**South**
♠ 3 2
♥ 5 3
♦ K 5
♣ A K Q J 10 9 8

Hand 2: Contract is 4 Spades, West leads Heart J

**North**
♠ 10 6 5
♥ K 6 4
♦ 8 4 2
♣ K 9 8 2

**West**
♠ Q 9 4
♥ J 10 8
♦ Q J 5 3
♣ Q 10 4

**East**
♠ J 7
♥ A 9 7 3 2
♦ 10 6
♣ J 6 5 3

**South**
♠ A K 8 3 2
♥ Q 5
♦ A K 9 7
♣ A 7

Hand 4: Contract is 3 No Trump, West leads Heart K

**North**
♠ A K 9
♥ 8 2
♦ K Q 5 2
♣ 7 5 4 2

**West**
♠ 8 6 3
♥ K Q J 9 4 3
♦ J 4
♣ Q 3

**East**
♠ Q J 10
♥ 7 6
♦ 10 9 8 6
♣ 10 9 8 6

**South**
♠ 7 5 4 2
♥ A 10 5
♦ A 7 3
♣ A K J

FIG. 7.2. The four bridge hands used for the plan-a-line-of-play experiment. A hand consisted of the Contract, opening lead, and North/South card holdings only.

Players were instructed to think aloud and plan out the play of the hand. They were told that they were playing in a match point or rubber bridge style contest. This meant that they were to safeguard their contract, rather than worrying about over-tricks. They were told to take the usual amount of time to plan their line of play. The hands are given in Fig. 7.2, though players were presented only with the North-South hands.

Because the hands were not played out (players would take different lines of play, and their planning at each stage would diverge), the task can be seen as a form of diagnosis, akin to medical diagnosis (Patel & Groen, 1986), or possibly to classifying physics problems into different categories (Chi, Glaser, & Rees, 1982). The aim was to see whether the major problem in the hand was correctly identified.

To assess skill effects, holding age constant, the protocols from 6 players were selected: two masters (M1, M2), two intermediate players (I1, I2), and two novices (N1, N2). Calling the weakest players novices is somewhat misleading. Though they are relative novices as duplicate bridge players, they are generally quite experienced at playing informal (rubber) bridge. The players' ages, acquired master points, and performance on a bridge questionnaire are given in Table 7.5.

Cassette recordings of the verbal protocols were transcribed. Players took from 1 to 3 minutes per hand. A superficial examination of the transcripts does not give much support to the idea that players were doing extensive search. There is very little evidence of the type of thinking evident in chess search, where alternatives are considered for yourself, your opponent, yourself, and so forth. Rather, players launch into a line of play and pursue it more or less directly to an endpoint.

Think aloud protocols are incomplete records of someone's conscious though processes. They are reliable for what they contain, not what they omit (See Ericsson & Simon, 1984, for guidelines on protocol analysis). It is of course possible, for instance, that people would analyze the opening lead and not mention it. Unfortunately, this is probably more likely to occur for the highly skilled player who is likely to automate such inferences. If anything, we should obtain a conservative estimate of the master's inferences and reasoning.

Books of bridge instruction typically advise a player to plan the hand out at trick one. One popular acronym that players are advised to use is "ARCH": *A*nalyze the opening lead, *R*eview the bidding, *C*ount your winners and losers, *H*ow do you make the contract. We can take this as a schema for planning the line of play and evaluate first how well it describes the general content of the protocols for the players.

## Use of the ARCH Schema

Because no bidding was ever provided to the players, the planning schema becomes ACH. How often did players observe this ordering? For these 6 players, very little overt mention is made of any analysis of the opening lead: only 4 cases were observed for the 24 opportunities. (It is useful to recall the caveat about the incompleteness of protocols.) An analysis of the number of instances of the ordering ACH or CH, shows that for the novices, 3 of the 8 cases conformed. Intermediate players conformed for 4/8 cases, and experts conformed in 7/8 cases.

It appears that stronger players first try to count potential winners and losers, and then they use this information to plan out the play. Weaker players are more likely to plan how to take tricks, without first analyzing the exact needs for the hand. It should be recalled that this trend occurs for planning the play, not playing out the hand (though impulsive behavior during play probably differentiates the weak from the strong as well).

TABLE 7.5
Bridge Player Characteristics

| Player | Age (Sex) | Master Points | Bridge Quiz Score (/21) |
|---|---|---|---|
| Novice 1 | 36 (F) | 2 | 10 |
| Novice 2 | 30 (F) | 3 | 12 |
| Intermediate 1 | 32 (F) | 20 | 14 |
| Intermediate 2 | 32 (M) | 19 | 10 |
| Master 1 | 38 (M) | 1200 | 20 |
| Master 2 | 30 (M) | 1000 | 21 |

## A Planning Production System

The previous discussion concerns the ordering of plans, without concern for the content. What features of the hand trigger the specific plans being discussed?

What I present is a quasi-production system representing planning by novice, intermediate, and expert players. It attempts to predict the contents of planning (and only weakly their order). Because only four hands were presented, only a small portion of a player's knowledge base is available for simulation. We need considerably more exemplars to arrive at a definitive set of planning productions.

For this analysis I assume that players (even novices) are capable of estimating the number of definite winning tricks that they possess between dummy and declarer hands. (Counting of tricks was evident in almost every case.) Furthermore, I assume that the internal representation of a hand results in preferential treatment for "honor cards"—the Ace, King, Queen, Jack, and ten of a suit—as well as the distribution of cards to suits (the "shape" of the hand). There is compelling evidence that these features guide bridge bidding (Charness, 1979, 1983, 1987; Engle & Bukstel, 1978). Bridge bidding is predicated on the discovery of the best contract to play.

Productions consistent with the protocols are given in Table 7.6.

These productions were derived by starting with the novices and generating a hand-simulated production system that could account for their planning statements. I then applied the system to the intermediate players, and in cases of discrepancy coded a new production that could account for the deviant behaviors. Finally, the set of productions for both novices and intermediates was applied to the masters' protocols, and new productions were proposed to account for deviations.

The condition sides are probably specified too narrowly, because it is necessary to vary the hand types to generally establish how features are coded. It is probably fair to assume (based on recall data, Charness, 1979) that

Planning Productions for Novice, Intermediate, Master Bridge Players

A,K,Q,J,x are abbreviations for Ace, King, Queen, Jack, and any card less than
10, respectively.  Suit holdings are shown for North/South, with South as
declarer.  Where there is uncertainty in the protocols about the application of
a production it is shown in parentheses.

## Hand 1

N1    If lead is J and suit holding is AQxx/Kxx ---> set winners=3 and capture
     lead and plan to establish 4th card for winners=4

N1*   If lead is J and suit holding is AQxx/Kxx ---> infer suit split <>3-3 and
     set winners=3 and capture lead and abandon suit as low probability for
     winners=4

N2    If suit holding is Axx/Kxx ---> set winners=2 and abandon suit

N3    If suit holding is AQxx/xxx ---> set winners=1 and plan finesse for
     winners=2

I3    If suit holding is AQxx/xxx ---> set winners=1 and plan finesse for
     winners=2 and plan for suit split for winners=2

M3    If suit holding is AQxx/xxx and there is time to develop suit ---> set
     winners=1 and plan standard play for 2 winners (duck diamond, cash Ace,
     finesse Queen).

Applying to Novice 1: N1*, N2, N3
Applying to Novice 2: N1,  N2, N3
Applying to Inter  1: N1*, N2, I3
Applying to Inter  2: N1,  N2, N3 (I3)
Applying to Master 1: N1*, N2, M3
Applying to Master 2: N1*, N2, M3

## Hand 2

N4    If the lead is the J and suit holding is Kxx/Qx ---> play low card from
     dummy and infer losers=1

N5    If suit holding is Kxxx/Ax ---> plan to play A,K and ruff low cards

N6    If suit holding is xxx/AKxx ---> losers=1 with 3-3 split, else losers=2

M6    If suit holding is xxx/AKxx and you can't pull trump ---> losers=1 with 3-
     3 split, else losers=2 so plan to play A,K,x before pulling trump and ruff
     losing card.

M6*   If suit holding is xxx/AKxx and you can't pull trump ---> losers=1 with 3-
     3 split, else losers=2 so plan to play x,A,K before pulling trump and ruff
     losing card.

N7    If trump holding is 10xx/AKxxx ---> plan to finesse the 10 but infer 3-2
     split and losers=1

N7*   If trump holding is 10xx/AKxxx ---> plan to play A,K and set losers=1 else
     if doubleton Q,J losers=0

M7    If trump holding is 10xx/AKxxx ---> plan to play A,K and set losers=1 if 3-
     2 split, else set losers=2 if 4-1 split

*(Continued)*

TABLE 7.6
(Continued)

N8    If suit holding is Kxxx/Ax ---> set losers=1 or 2

Applying to Novice 1: N4, N5,  N7,  N6
Applying to Novice 2: N4, N7*, (N6),(N8)
Applying to Inter  1: N4, N7,  N5,  N6
Applying to Inter  2: N4, N7*, N5,  N6
Applying to Master 1: N4, M7,  M6
Applying to Master 2: N4, (N2,N2,N7*), M6*

#### Hand 3

N9    If trump holding is x/AKQJ1098 ---> set winners=7 and plan to pull trump

N10   If suit holding is AQJ842/xx (and you need a trick) ---> plan to finesse Q

N11   If suit holding is AJxx/Kx (and you need a trick) ---> plan to finesse J

N11*  If suit holding is AJxx/Kx ---> plan to play A,K, and ruff xx

M11   If suit holding is AJxx/Kx ---> plan to play A,K, and ruff x, hoping to drop the Queen

I4    If you plan 2 finesses ---> force opponents to discard by cashing winners

M4    If you plan 2 finesses ---> force opponents to discard by cashing winners and try for a show-out squeeze

Applying to Novice 1: N9,   N10,  (N11, N2, N2)
Applying to Novice 2: N9,   N11*, N10
Applying to Inter  1: N9,   N10,  N11, I4
Applying to Inter  2: N9,   N10,  (I4)
Applying to Master 1: (N9),N10,  N11, M11, M4
Applying to Master 2: (N9),N10,  N11, M4

#### Hand 4

N12   If lead is K and suit holding is xx/A10x (and contract is no trump) ---> hold off on lead until forced to take the A

M12   If lead is K and suit holding is xx/A10x (and contract is no trump) ---> hold off for 2 rounds if East doesn't signal doubleton and plan West throw-in

N13   If suit holding is xxx/AKJ ---> set winners=2 and plan to finesse

M13   If suit holding is xxx/AKJ (and you have contract-1 winners with other chances for winners) ---> plan to take A,K and hope Q drops

N14   If suit holding is KQxx/Axx ---> set winners to 3 and take A,K,Q hoping for 3-3 split to make winners 4

N15   If suit holding is AK9/xxxx ---> set winners to 2

M15   If suit holding is AK9/xxxx (and the goal is to avoid West) ---> set winners to 2 and plan to finesse the 9 and hope for a 3-3 split to make winners=3

M16   If sum of winners=contract-1 ---> plan a squeeze

Applying to Novice 1: N12, N13, (N14, N15)
Applying to Novice 2: N12, N13, N14,  N15
Applying to Inter  1: N12, N14, N13,  (N15)
Applying to Inter  2: N12, N14, N13   (N15)
Applying to Master 1: N12, M13, N14,  M15, M16
Applying to Master 2: M12, M16, (N13, N14, N15)

masters code the precise dummy-declarer suit holding, and that this is less true for the intermediate and novice players.

## Analysis of the Task Environment

The critical problem to be solved in hand 1 is how to get the ninth trick. There are eight tricks readily available in winning honors (two A-K pairs, one A-K-Q, and the A of diamonds). There are two obvious possibilities for the ninth trick. First, the club suit could be divided 3-3, so that the fourth low club will become a winner after the play of the A,K,Q. This is unlikely for two reasons: the opening lead of the J of clubs is probably from J,10,9,8 (assuming proper play from West); as well, when there are six cards divided among the opponents, the most likely split is 4-2 (48.5% of the time), not 3-3 (35.5%).

The second possibility is to get an additional trick from the diamond suit. One candidate is to finesse the Queen. (Reach the Dummy; lead a small diamond and when East plays a low diamond, play the Queen.) This is precisely what the novice players plan to do. The simple finesse is a 50% chance. Another possibility is for the diamond suit to split 3-3, even if the finesse does not work. One intermediate player mentions this explicitly, and it is weakly implied in the protocol of the other by the expected trick count. The best line of play, however, will produce the needed extra trick 77% of the time (see Frey et al., 1976, p. 467). It involves playing a low diamond from both dummy and declarer, then playing the Ace, then leading to the Queen. One master generates this plan more or less automatically (e.g., through recognition). The other appears to work it out on line (via means-ends reasoning after noting the possibility of a diamond split or a diamond finesse, but wanting to improve on those options).

What we can conclude about skill differences, tentatively, is that the masters both recognized that when there is a suit distribution of AQxx/xxx in a no trump contract, and there is time to develop the suit, there exists a standard play to optimize winning two tricks. Intermediate and novice players both considered only a simple finesse or at best a finesse and a suit split. This is reflected in the differences between productions N3, I3, and M3. There were apparently also differences related to analyzing the opening lead, but these were somewhat inconsistent across skill levels.

In hand 2, the critical feature is timing. Players should note that the problem in the hand is how to avoid losing more than one diamond trick. This involves ensuring that one diamond can be trumped by Dummy. It is necessary to give up a diamond trick early before playing the Ace and King of spades to prevent the opponents either from pulling Dummy's last spade, or over-trumping Dummy by playing the fourth round of diamonds before Declarer has pulled all the trumps.

One master recognizes the problem and the solution almost immediately. The other recognizes the problem, proposes a partially correct solution, recognizes the flaw, but fails to search for an improvement. Neither the novices nor the intermediate players even realize that there is a problem with the diamond suit for this hand, and they all plan to take their winning tricks and hope for good things to happen. Skill differences seem to be captured in terms of a more sophisticated production being available to the master (M6 or M6* vs. N6).

In hand 3, the critical feature is again timing. There is a need to find an additional trick, with three good possibilities: the heart finesse, the diamond finesse, or ruffing out the diamond Queen. With appropriate timing there is the additional chance of producing a "show-out squeeze," so that the heart finesse can be avoided. Both masters recognize the squeeze possibility after first debating which finesse to take, although only one plans for it accurately. Both intermediate players recognize the need to try to gather information from the discards their opponents make before trying one of the finesses, but neither see the squeeze possibility. Both novices fixate on the heart finesse possibility, but one recognizes the need to gather information on opponents' discards and maybe try something in the diamond suit instead of the heart finesse. These differences are captured by N11 versus M11, and the masters having M4 versus I4.

In hand 4, the critical feature is to create a ninth trick without allowing West into the lead where he or she can set the contract by cashing winning heart tricks. This involves ducking (avoiding the win of a trick) two rounds of hearts to prevent East from reaching West with a heart lead, and arranging to play suits such that any tricks are lost to East.

Declarer then has many possibilities for creating the ninth trick: trying to finesse the spade 9, hoping to lose the trick to East, and also hoping the spade suite will split 3-3, allowing South's small spade to become the ninth trick. If the spades don't split, then declarer can still try the club finesse, or possibly discover that the club Queen can be dropped after the Ace and King are played. Diamonds might split 3-3. There are also squeeze play opportunities. The key is again timing, to allow for all of these opportunities.

One novice recognizes the need to duck the heart, but then relies solely on the club finesse. The second novice plans to duck the heart once, and then assumes either that diamonds will split or that a club finesse will be necessary. Both intermediate players choose the same plan as the second novice, although both recognize that they will need to duck two heart tricks before winning the third. One master decides to duck one heart, take the A on the second round (if East follows to the second round and does not indicate a doubleton by signalling), and then allow West to cash hearts and lead to him, hoping for a squeeze, or at worst a diamond break or club finesse. The other master plans to win the third round of hearts, and hope for a squeeze, a diamond split, or at worst a club finesse. In short, only the master plans for the possibility of a squeeze (M16).

### Conclusions About Bridge Planning

Apparently, across these bridge hands, skill differences in planning are associated with more sophisticated productions. It appears that the masters have both more productions (e.g., plan a squeeze productions), and better tuned ones (e.g., the greater number of tests and actions within some productions). Skill in planning is a function of both quantity and quality of stored information.

There are some important parallels between skilled play in bridge and in chess. For one thing, the less skilled bridge player often fails to perceive the critical problem in the hand. This is somewhat reminiscent of the way in which weak chess players fail even to explore the relevant base moves, let along choose them. It can be assumed that good bridge players recognize the critical features of a hand, and that at least some of the time, have specific lines of play directly associated with their internal representations of the hand.

Similar to the idea that for skilled chess players, patterns lead to plausible moves, for skilled bridge players, patterns lead to plans with high probabilities of success.

Planning involves abstracting away enough detail to enable reasonable goal-setting. If all possible interactions had to be represented, there would be no advantage to planning, because the problem space would be as large as that for which no planning took place. Experts clearly generate more detailed plans than do the weaker players. The reason that they can support a more complex planning space probably lies in their chunking advantage. For them, sets of suit combinations are probably chunkable. Support for this idea is that only the experts appear to have mastered the concept of a squeeze play. A squeeze involves the coordination of threat cards, entries, squeeze cards, and correct timing: by definition, a multisuit pattern.

Pattern recognition enables good problem solvers to evoke fairly sophisticated plans. They substitute knowledge for search in domains like chess, and sophisticated plans for primitive ones in bridge. It is probably fair to characterize knowledge acquisition in bridge as the process of both adding new productions and refining existing ones to cover more precise card combinations. To enable such productions to operate in a limited capacity information processing system, it is necessary that the conditions be easily recognized chunks.

Thus, we have a partial answer for why chunking lies at the heart of skilled performance. It bypasses the bottleneck of a limited capacity working memory, enabling a problem solver to tailor his or her behavior to a complex, yet often predictable environment.

## LESSONS ABOUT SKILL ACQUISITION

What lessons can be drawn about the acquisition process in domains such as bridge and chess? As Feigenbaum (chap. 6 in this volume) argues, knowledge is power. (Or at the least, it is the result of a power law!) The expert knows more than the novice, and this knowledge enables him or her to avoid fruitless search paths in an objectively enormous problem space. The expert has learned to glean useful information from the patterns in the environment so that he or she virtually "sees" a different problem.

How does someone become an expert? It is no longer satisfying to conclude with the pious refrain that if you keep someone at the task for the required 1,000 hours, they can be assured of a fair degree of mastery. There are two primary unresolved problems: motivation and instruction.

We know all too little about what are effective motivators for keeping people working at a task for the extended period of time necessary to acquire a large knowledge base. We do know a little about what does *not* work. Studies indicate that external sources of motivation are inferior to intrinsic ones in maintaining interest in a task (Deci & Ryan, 1985). This includes the case of chess problem-solving on a short-term basis (Pritchard, Campbell, & Campbell, 1977).

Need for achievement and anxiety level have long been considered important factors in predicting task performance (Atkinson, 1983), but there are no studies that I am aware of that have contrasted people of different skill levels to see whether such factors account for any of the skill variance beyond that explained by knowledge base differences. Perhaps it is time to try. There are enough intriguing interview data to suggest that those who reach the top levels have a very high degree of drive and commitment to the field that they master, and in many cases are very competitive (Bloom, 1985).

The issue of what constitutes effective instructional techniques is one that occupies many educators, though the experimental work is most likely to concentrate on very small knowledge bases and usually contrasts two or more broad teaching techniques. It is clear that trying to train a novice with an expert's representation of domain knowledge is doomed to fail. Put bluntly, there is almost no way for the novice to parse the condition side of an expert's production, because the concepts or patterns denoting it are too large to fit working memory. The tailoring of the knowledge base to the level of the learner is probably what distinguishes the excellent teacher or coach from the good one. As Bloom (1985) pointed out, superior coaching and parental support seem to be important ingredients for success in many domains.

On the other hand, the acceptance of the theoretical importance of domain-related patterns leaves some hope to the educator. It stresses the need for more attention to defining the conditions of application for various actions or operators. When describing a squeeze in bridge, it is going to be helpful to teach the minimal squeeze position (a three-card ending) in conjunction with the full position at trick one, pointing out the reasons why a squeeze, as opposed to a throw-in or finesse might be considered. It is going to be necessary to push the novice to consider a finesse as a device of last resort (not first), after a throw-in or squeeze is ruled out.

Although it is useful to teach the basic principles first, then advanced play later, perhaps the novice needs to be warned that the basic principles have side conditions attached, so that they leave some slots open in their play schemas.

Because much of the expert's knowledge is pattern-indexed, textbooks and instructors ought to be concentrating more on teaching the novice to recognize the differences between patterns, possibly by displaying them overtly and pointing out why one rather than the other applies. Too often the correct action is pointed out for the correct pattern, but it is left to the learner to generalize or particularize from the one example. If we are to take learning mechanisms like EPAM (Feigenbaum & Simon, 1984) seriously, then helping the novice to make the appropriate discriminations becomes one of the first orders of business.

There is also the issue of how much overt, intentional learning is needed to acquire expertise, and how much accrues automatically, by virtue of attention to domain information. A skill acquisition theory such as Anderson's (1982) seems to imply that automatic processes hunt down environmental constants and compose the necessary new productions.

Taking the domains of chess and bridge, it is quite possible to see frequency of occurrence information registering automatically (Hasher & Zacks, 1979), and influencing plans or moves. There were successful gamblers long before probability theory was worked out, and there are undoubtedly many bridge players who do not know probability theory, yet have independently discovered the optimal strategies for play.

On the other hand, there is much anecdotal evidence that those who master semantically rich domains spend many hours "burning the midnight oil," intentionally learning bridge bidding conventions and suit plays, or in chess, opening sequences and endgame techniques, from instructional texts. Assessing the relative weight of intentional and incidental learning in mastery may be a useful task.

The ultimate challenge for those in both the theory and the applied side of cognitive psychology remains. We need to find efficient ways to uncover and describe the knowledge base that the expert uses, as well as the means to transmit it efficiently to the novice. The study of skilled performers in model domains such as chess and bridge represents a promising path toward the attainment of that ambitious goal.

Simon once proposed that the apparent complexity of the ant's path on the beach was more a testimony to the intricacy of the beach than the ant. Tasks such as chess and bridge represent equally complex environments for the study of the human-environment interaction. Even if we solve that problem, we'll still be left with a tantalizing puzzle: Why do humans insist on spending significant portions of their lives mastering the geography of such beaches? Perhaps we'll have to look more closely at Simon than at the ant.

## ACKNOWLEDGMENTS

This work was supported by NSERC grant A0790. It was inspired by work done by Herbert A. Simon and the Late William G. Chase. I am grateful to Paul Barton and Danica Lavoie for assisting in collecting and transcribing the bridge data, and to Frank Huntley for collecting the recent chess data, as well as to DH, and the bridge players for participating in these studies.

## REFERENCES

Anderson, J. R. (1982). Acquisition of cognitive skill. *Psychological Review, 89,* 369–406.

Assumpcao, P. P. (1977). Secret is in timing. *The Contract Bridge Bulletin, 43,* (6), 73–75.

Atkinson, J. W. (1983). *Personality, motivation, and action: Selected papers.* New York: Praeger.

Berliner, H. (1978). A chronology of computer chess and its literature. *Artificial Intelligence, 10,* 201–214.

Blackwood, E. (1977a). Basic play. *The Contract Bridge Bulletin, 43* (7), 79–80.

Blackwood, E. (1977b). Basic play. *The Contract Bridge Bulletin, 43* (8), 65–66.

Bloom, B. S. (Ed.). (1985). *Developing talent in young people.* New York: Ballentine.

Charness, N. (1979). Components of skill in bridge. *Canadian Journal of Psychology, 33,* 1–16.

Charness, N. (1981a). Aging and skilled problem solving. *Journal of Experimental Psychology: General, 110,* 21–38.

Charness, N. (1981b). Search in chess: Age and skill differences. *Journal of Experimental Psychology: Human Perception and Performance, 7,* 467–476.

Charness, N. (1981c). Visual short-term memory and aging in chess players. *Journal of Gerontology, 36,* 615–619.

Charness, N. (1983). Age, skill, and bridge bidding: A chronometric analysis. *Journal of Verbal Learning and Verbal Behavior, 22,* 406–416.

Charness, N. (1987). Component processes in bridge bidding and novel problem-solving tasks. *Canadian Journal of Psychology, 41,* 223–243.

Charness, N. (1988). Expertise in chess, music, and physics: A cognitive perspective. In L. K. Obler & D. A. Fein (Eds.), *The exceptional brain: The neuropsychology of talent and special abilities.* New York: Guilford Press.

Chase, W. G., & Simon, H. A. (1973a). The mind's eye in chess. In W. G. Chase (Ed.), *Visual information processing.* New York: Academic Press.

Chase, W. G., & Simon, H. A. (1973b). Perception in chess. *Cognitive Psychology, 4,* 55–81.

Chi, M. T. H., Glaser, R., & Rees, E. (1982). Expertise in problem solving. In R. J. Sternberg (Ed.), *Advances in the psychology of human intelligence.* Hillsdale, NJ: Lawrence Erlbaum Associates.

Deci, E. L., & Ryan, R. M. (1985). *Intrinsic motivation and self-determination in human behavior.* New York: Plenum.

de Groot, A. D. (1978). *Thought and choice in chess (2nd ed.)* The Hague: Mouton. (Original work published in 1965).

de Groot, A. D. (1966). Perception and memory versus thought: Some old ideas and recent findings. In B. Kleinmuntz (Ed.), *Problem solving: Research, method and theory.* New York: Wiley.

Elo, A. E. (1978). *The rating of chessplayers, past and present.* New York: Arco.

Engle, R. W., & Bukstel, L. (1978). Memory processes among bridge players of differing expertise. *American Journal of Psychology, 91,* 673–689.

Ericsson, K. A. (1985). Memory skill. *Canadian Journal of Psychology, 39,* 188–231.

Ericsson, K. A., & Simon, H. A. (1984). *Protocol analysis.* Cambridge, MA: Bradford Books.

Feigenbaum, E. A., & Simon, H. A. (1984). EPAM-like models of recognition and learning. *Cognitive Science, 8,* 305–336.

Frey, R. L, Truscott, A. F., & Kearse, A. L. (Eds.). (1976). *The official encyclopedia of bridge (3rd ed.).* New York: Crown.

Hasher, L., & Zacks, R. T. (1979). Automatic and effortful processes in memory. *Journal of Experimental Psychology: General, 108,* 356–388.

Hayes-Roth, F., Klahr, P., & Mostow, D. J. (1981). Advice taking and knowledge refinement: An iterative view of skill acquisition. In J. R. Anderson (Ed.), *Cognitive skills and their acquisition*. Hillsdale, NJ: Lawrence Erlbaum Associates.

Holding, D. H. (1985). *The psychology of chess skill.* Hillsdale, NJ: Lawrence Erlbaum Associates.

Holding, D. H., & Pfau, H. D. (1985). Thinking ahead in chess. *American Journal of Psychology, 98,* 271–282.

Holding, D. H., & Reynolds, R. I. (1982) Recall or evaluation of chess positions as determinants of chess skill. *Memory & Cognition, 10,* 237–242.

Kantar, E. (1977). Test your play. *The Contract Bridge Bulletin, 43* (6), 75–76.

Keren, G. (1987). Facing uncertainty in the game of bridge: A calibration study. *Organizational Behavior and Human Decision Processes, 39,* 98–114.

Newell, A., & Rosenbloom, P. S. (1981). Mechanisms of skill acquisition and the law of practice. In J. R. Anderson (Ed.), *Cognitive skills and their acquisition*. Hillsdale, NJ: Lawrence Erlbaum Associates.

Newell, A, & Simon, H. A. (1972). *Human problem solving*. Englewood Cliffs, NJ: Prentice-Hall.

Patel, V. L., & Groen, G. J. (1986). Knowledge based solution strategies in medical reasoning. *Cognitive Science, 10,* 91–116.

Pritchard, R. D., Campbell, K. M., & Campbell, D. J. (1977). Effects of extrinsic financial rewards on intrinsic motivation. *Journal of Applied Psychology, 62,* 9–15.

Saariluoma, P. (1985). Chess players' intake of task-relevant cues. *Memory and Cognition, 13,* 385–391.

Simon, H. A. (1979). Information-processing models of cognition. *Annual Review of Psychology, 30,* 363–396.

Simon, H. A., & Chase, W. G. (1973). Skill in chess. *American Scientist, 61,* 394–403.

Simon, D. P., & Simon, H. A. (1978). Individual differences in solving physics problems. In R. Siegler (Ed.), *Children's thinking: What develops?* Hillsdale, NJ: Lawrence Erlbaum Associates.

# 8

## Writing Research: The Analysis of a Very Complex Task

John R. Hayes
*Carnegie-Mellon University*

Writing is a task with many properties that should attract the attention of cognitive scientists. First, it is a real rather than a 'toy' task. It is a frequent and important part of everyday life. Second, it is a complex natural language task involving lexical, grammatical, semantic, and pragmatic aspects of language. Third, it is a generative task, which distinguishes it from reading, a much more frequently studied natural language task. Finally, it is a task that has interesting parallels and contrasts with computer programming, a task that has already attracted considerable attention from cognitive scientists.

Research on cognitive processes in writing is relatively new. Janet Emig's (1971) case study of 12th grade writers is often cited as the first example of this sort of research. Linda Flower and I began our writing research about 10 years ago. Since that time we have conducted a large number of studies and have collaborated with many colleagues whose names appear throughout this chapter; most of them in the English department at Carnegie-Mellon University.

As our initial approach, we chose to analyze thinking aloud protocols of writers at work in order to identify the overall organization of writing processes. On the basis of this early work (Hayes & Flower, 1980), we proposed the descriptive framework shown in Fig. 8.1. The important features of the descriptive framework are:

1. A division of the writing task into parts for easier analysis. The division we chose is modeled on that used by Newell and Simon (1972, p. 89) for the analysis of problem solving.

   (a) The task environment including the writing assignment, and the text produced so far.

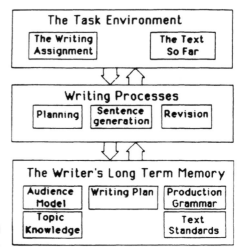

FIG. 8.1.    The Hayes–Flower model
of composition.

(b) The writers long-term memory including content knowledge, knowledge of genre, and knowledge of audience.

(c) The writing processes

2. A division of the writing processes into three major subprocesses: planning, sentence generation, and revision.

Our division of the writing process into three parts was based on evidence obtained by analyzing protocols of adult writers. However, planning and revision become prominent parts of the writing process only as the writer matures. Bereiter and Scardamalia (1987), summarizing their extensive research on planning in developing writers, pointed out:

> In the beginning years of composition, children's mental activity is so closely tied to producing the written composition that it is difficult to identify much in the way of separate thinking that can be called planning. Gradually, as writing ability develops, there is a separation of the problem of finding content for a composition from the problem of actually writing the composition. At this point, clearly identifiable planning can be seen, but the planning remains at the same time tied to the content needs of text production, so the plan that is generated consists of a listing of content possibilities. In adolescence, planning starts to become sufficiently differentiated from production that we begin to see the plan as having properties and containing elements that have only an indirect bearing on the content of the text. (p. 193)

Revision also depends on the stage of development of the writer. Bracewell, Scardamalia, and Bereiter (1978) found that 4th graders hardly revise at all, that 8th graders' revisions hurt more than they help, and that for 12th graders, helpful revisions narrowly outnumbered harmful ones. Our description of writing processes, therefore, is clearly a description of *adult* writing processes.

We have relied heavily on this descriptive framework to guide our subsequent work. Many of our early studies were exploratory in nature. In later work, to the extent that we have been able, we have tried to find experimental tests of the hypotheses we derived from exploration. In this chapter, I report studies that we have carried out on planning, on sentence generation, on revision, and on the impact of various aspects of the task environment and long-term memory on these writing processes.

## PLANNING

Planning is widely recognized as an important aid to performance in many areas of human action (Miller, Galanter, & Pribram, 1960). But what is planning in writing? In a theoretical article, Flower and Hayes (1984) proposed that the primary function of the planning process is to produce a writing plan consisting of at least three sorts of elements:

1. Goals to express content knowledge that may be stored in a variety of forms such as episodes (e.g., "Tell them about the first day of class last year") or visual images (e.g., "Describe how she looked when she opened the envelope").
2. Noncontent related goals such as goals to influence the audience in particular ways (e.g., "I want to make them think that I am one of them") and goals concerning form (e.g., "Add an introduction").
3. Goals to use particular words that the writer finds felicitous.

The goals to express content knowledge appear to correspond to the early developing plans for content described by Bereiter and Scardamalia (1987). In a protocol study of planning and text generation, to be described in detail later, Kaufer, Hayes, and Flower (1986) observed writers constructing plans such as those described by Flower and Hayes (1984) and turning goals in those plans into text.

Does planning facilitate writing? Carey, Flower, Hayes, Schriver, and Haas (1987) found that the more successful writers planned their writing objectives more completely before beginning to write that less succcessful writers. Carey and her colleagues (1987) explored the relationship between the quantity and quality of the plans writers made before they began to write and the quality of the resulting text. The subjects of the study, five experienced writers and seven undergraduates, were asked to give thinking aloud protocols while they wrote expository essays. Although on the average the expert subjects did perform better than the novices, there was sufficient overlap between the groups that analysis of expert-novice differences did not seem profitable. Instead, analysis was performed on data for the combined group of subjects.

Specifically, subjects were asked to spend about an hour writing an essay on "My job" for a teenage audience. The resulting essays ranged in length from about 300 to 900 words. The protocols were divided into clauses and coded for all planning activities that occurred before the writers produced their first written sentence. The numbers of clauses in the part of the protocol before writing started ranged from 8 to 209 with an average of 70. The number of clauses involving planning was used as the measure of the amount of planning. Examples of clauses that were judged to include planning are "I'll write to these kids about what they should look for in a job" and "Don't forget the audience." The quality of planning was judged by two experienced writers who independently rated the protocols for the quality of three types of planning:

- planning to adapt the text to the audience
- planning to develop a focus, point, or purpose for text
- planning to provide structure for the text

Overall planning quality was measured by the sum of these ratings. Inter-rater reliability for overall quality was moderately high ($r = 81$.)

The quality of the texts was judged by four experienced writers (different from those who evaluated the protocols) who independently rated the texts on the following dimensions:

- How well is the text adapted to the audience?
- To what extent does the text have a clear focus, point, or purpose?
- How well structured is the text in terms of overall organization and coherence?

The sum of these ratings was taken as a measure of the overall quality of the texts. The average inter-rater reliability of these scores was .39. The sums of these scores for all four rates were used in the comparisons reported in the following paragraphs.

Comparison of the planning and text measures revealed four correlations significant at the .01 level: The correlation between the amount of planning and the quality of the text was 0.67; the correlation between the quality of planning and the quality of the text was 0.87; the correlation between the quality of planning for audience and adaptation of the text to the audience was 0.78; and the correlation between the quality of planning for focus and focus in the text was 0.74. The correlation between the quality of plans for structure and structure in the text, $r = 0.49$, was not significant.

Although these results are consistent with our commonsense notion that planning is important in writing and suggest that quality of planning may be more important than quantity, they do not demonstrate a causal relation between planning and text quality. Experiments exploring that causal link would be very informative.

## SENTENCE GENERATION

How are plans turned into text? Kaufer et al. (1986) conducted a series of studies exploring several aspects of this question. In their first study, they analyzed protocols of 12 writers either planning to write or in the process of writing essays on the same topic and for the same audience as in the Carey et al. (1987) study. Six of the writers were college graduates and six were experienced writers. The data for these two studies overlap because five of the protocols of the experienced writers analyzed in Kaufer, Hayes, and Flower's study were the same as those examined in the Carey et al. study. However, the focus of analysis was quite different in the two studies. In this study, the researchers found that the work involved in translating plans into text is substantial. They compared the lengths of writers' outlines with the lengths of their essays. Even for the most extensive outliners, the ideas noted in the outline were expanded on the average by a factor of eight in the final essay. Thus, even after the writing plan has been completed, the task of formulating words to express the plan is still largely undone.

A second finding of the study was that writers compose sentences in parts. Sentence parts were defined by pauses in the thinking-aloud protocols and averaged between 7 and 12 words in length. The following is a typical sentence generating episode observed by Kaufer and his colleagues. The dashes indicate pauses of 2 seconds or more in the composing process. The writer is trying to describe her job.

The best thing about it is (1)—what?(2)Something about using my mind(3)—it allows me the opportunity to(4)—uh—I want to write something about my ideas.(5)—to put ideas into action(6)—or—to develop my ideas into(7)— what?(8)—into a meaningful form?(9)Oh, bleh!—say it allows me(10)—to use(11)—Na—allows me—scratch that. The best thing about it is it allows me to use(12)—my mind and ideas in a productive way.(13)

The proposed sentence parts in this episode were fragments 1, 4, 6, 7, 9, 11 and 13. Fragments 2 and 8, which reflect the writer's uncertainty about what should be written next, indicate that these sentences are in the process of being composed. They are not being transcribed from a preformed verbatim plan for the text. Fragments 12 and 13 comprised the finished sentence that the writer included in her essay.

A third finding of the study was that experts proposed significantly ($p <$ .05 by Mann–Whitney test) longer sentence parts (11.2 words per part) than average adult writers (7.3 words per part). The authors proposed that this difference in sentence part length may reflect a difference in sentence pattern knowledge parallel to the difference in pattern knowledge observed by Simon and Chase (1983) in expert and novice chess players. Simon and Chase found that expert chess players knew both more and larger chess patterns than novices. Kaufer et al. suggested that larger sentence part lengths may correspond to knowledge of more and larger sentence patterns and that this knowledge may, in turn, account for the experts' greater fluency in writing.

In the second study of this series, the researchers explored how sentences are constructed from parts. Two graduate students, one in psychology and one in English, who were considered competent but not professional writers, were the subjects. Each writer provided think aloud protocols as they wrote essays for a teenage audience on the topics: "My job," "Abortion: pro and con," and "Women's role in business." The authors identified all of the sentence parts that the writers proposed for inclusion in their essays whether or not these parts were later written down. The proposed sentence parts for the 145 sentences in the six essays were classified as being at the leading edge or not at the leading edge of the sentence as follows: If a proposed sentence part was either to be added to the right of the current rightmost sentence or was a replacement or revision of that part, then the part was classified as being at the leading edge. If the part was to be placed anywhere else in the sentence or was a replacement or revision of any but the rightmost part, then it was classified as not at the leading edge. The first part in each sentence was not scored.

The authors found that 342 of the proposed parts were at the leading edge and 30 were not. Thus, the sentences were constructed very largely in left to right fashion. Furthermore, the authors estimated that 80% of parts at the leading edge contributed new meaning, whereas only 20% of the parts not at the leading edge did so. Thus, 98% of new meanings were added at the leading edge as sentences were being constructed.

In the third study of the series, Kaufer and his colleagues attempted to determine if sentence parts had special grammatical properties. In particular, they wondered if the ends of sentence parts tended to fall at phrase or clause boundaries in the sentence being constructed. To obtain evidence on this point, they examined a selected set of the sentence parts identified in study 2. The rule of selection was that only those sentence parts were included that were beginnings or continuations of sentences and were themselves followed by continuations of sentences. The selection eliminated sentence parts that were revisions of other sentence parts and sentence parts that may have been interrupted by revision processes. In addition, the selection insured that there was sufficient context to determine whether or not a sentence part ended on a clause or phrase boundary.

The selection procedure identified 205 sentence parts that were contained in 1,420 words of proposed text. Each space between words was classified either as a clause boundary, a phrase boundary, or as other. The text contained 193 clause boundaries, 293 phrase boundaries, and 933 spaces classified as other. Sentence parts ended on 38% of the clause boundaries, 18% of the phrase boundaries, and only 8.5% of the spaces classified as other. These results strongly suggest a relation between clausal units and the writer's production grammar.

Currently, there is little research on the processes by which writers produce sentences. The work of Kaufer and his colleagues indicates that sentence generation involves highly structured processes for creating sentence parts and for assembling them into sentences and that there are interesting differences in these processes between more and less skilled writers. The topic appears to be a very promising one for continued research.

Friedlander (1987) measured sentence part lengths in advanced Chinese ESL students writing one to two page letters in Chinese and in English. Letter topics were counterbalanced over languages. Each of six students provided think aloud protocols as they wrote one letter in Chinese and one in English. The Chinese protocols and letters were translated into English and sentence parts were then identified by the same methods used by Kaufer and his colleagues. The average sentence part lengths and the average number of sentence parts considered for each sentence composed are shown in Table 8.1. For each of the students, average sentence part length was greater for the Chinese letters than for the English letters and average parts per sentence were less for the Chinese letters than for the English letters. Friedlander's results appear to confirm the suggestion by Kaufer and his colleagues that sentence part length is an index of the writers facility with grammatical structures in the language.

## REVISION

To revise a text for an audience is a very complex task. It requires the revisor to comprehend the goals of the text, to predict how well the text will accomplish those goals for the intended audience, and to propose better ways to accomplish those goals when the revisor perceives the text to be faulty. Writers differ a great deal in their revision skills. Hayes, Flower, Schriver, Stratman, and Carey (1987) compared seven expert writers with seven freshman writers in protocol study of the revision process. All of the writers were asked to revise the same poorly written two-page letter for a freshman audience. Hayes et al. (1987) found three major differences between experts and freshmen.

First, freshman writers defined revision as a word or sentence level task. Thus, freshmen typically dealt with the text one sentence at a time, fixing spelling and grammar problems but ignoring problems of transition, organization, and focus. The experts, in contrast, attended much more to global problems such as problems of organization and purpose and might well defer attending to sentence level problems on the grounds that the whole text needed to be reorganized and rewritten. Evidence of differences between experts and freshmen in attending to global problems was obtained as follows: Two ex-

TABLE 8.1
Measures of Sentence Parts Composed by Chinese Writers Writing
in English and Chinese

| Language | words/part | parts/sentence |
|----------|------------|----------------|
| English | 2.31 | 7.03 |
| Chinese | 6.33 | 2.55 |

pert and two freshman protocols were selected at random and divided into problem-solving episodes. (Judges can identify such episodes quite reliably.) Typically, the episodes corresponded to a single problem-solving event, for example, "Wait, 'naive' may sound condescending. Better delete it."

After the protocols were divided into episodes, each episode was evaluated to determine if it was concerned with a problem above the sentence level or with a problem at or below the sentence level. For the freshmen, only 15% of the episodes involved problems above the sentence level in contrast to 42% for the experts.

Second, the freshmen writers were persistently insensitive to text problems that the more experienced writers detected immediately. For example, the letter to be revised contained the sentence, "in sports like fencing for a long time many of our varsity team members had no previous experience anyway." Several of the freshman students read this sentence between four and eight times in the course of the revision task without finding fault with it. One of them commented, "Freshmen would like that." Overall, freshmen detected only 62% as many problems as the experts.

And third, when they did detect problems, freshmen were much less likely to diagnose them than the more experienced writers. Writers may be said to detect a problem when they become aware that there is some fault in the text even though they may not know the cause of the problem. For example, they might comment, "This sentence just doesn't sound right." Writers may be said to diagnose a problem when they assign a cause to it. For example, they might say, "The subject and verb don't agree here." Experts diagnosed 74% of the problems they detected, whereas freshmen diagnosed only 41%.

Although experts are clearly more skilled than freshmen in revising texts, it is not obvious that even expert revisors operating on their intuitions can accomplish this task optimally. Duffy, Curran, and Sass (1983) found that when professional writing firms revised documents for clarity, the results were frequently disappointing when the original and revised documents were compared in tests of comprehension. Swaney, Janik, Bond, and Hayes (1981) asked a group of four document designers to revise four public documents (a warranty, a notice, a sales agreement, and part of an insurance policy) so that they could be understood by a general audience. The designers, working separately and together, invested about 100 hours in the project. Comprehension tests on the original and the revised documents showed that the designers efforts had improved the comprehensibility of three of the documents but made the fourth one worse. Swaney et al. then revised this last document using reader protocols. That is, they collected thinking aloud protocols of readers attempting to comprehend the document and used these protocols to identify features of the text requiring improvement. The document was then revised in the light of the protocols. They called this procedure *protocol-aided revision*. After three revision cycles, the protocols revealed no further problems in the text. Comprehension tests showed that the text was now significantly clearer than the original (16% errors vs. 46% errors). This result is both a sensible one and a very practical one. Going directly to the audience for information about readers' comprehension needs rather than relying on the writer's intuition eliminates one potentially faulty step in making inferences about the reader. It is a very practical result because it can be applied directly to the improvement of documents.

Schriver (1984) noticed that writers who use protocol-aided revision claimed that it changed their writing. They claimed that repeated exposure to protocols had made them so familiar with how readers respond to text that they could now predict readers' problems without protocols. To explore the implications of this observation, Schriver conducted an extensive teaching study. The objective of this study was to determine if teaching writers to anticipate readers' needs through exposing them to readers' responses via protocols could increase their ability to detect aspects of texts that confuse readers. First, Schriver created a training text (Schriver, 1984) consisting of 10 lessons designed to engage the writer with reader protocols. Each lesson contained two parts:

1. *A problematic first draft of a text,* that is, one that will give the intended audience difficulties in understanding it. These draft texts did not contain spelling and grammatical errors, but rather had poor definitions, unclear procedures, missing examples, ambiguities, and other "above the word or phrase" level problems. They were instructional texts—elementary lessons in operating a word processing system on a university computing system and they were all written for a lay reader—freshman, secretaries, and staff.

2. *A think-aloud reading protocol of a person trying to understand the draft text.* For each of the 10 texts, a protocol was collected from a different member of the actual audience. The protocols revealed a wide variety of understanding and usability problems.

To evaluate the effectiveness of these training materials, Schriver (1987) used a pretest–posttest design. In pretest and posttest, the participants task was to predict those aspects of the text that would create comprehension problems for a lay reader, that is, someone without topic knowledge of the text's content. The pretest and posttest materials consisted of six half-page passages that were excerpts from the science and medicine sections of *Time* and *Newsweek* magazines. To determine the accuracy of writers' predictions of readers' problems during pretest and posttest, it was necessary to determine exactly what problems the stimulus texts created for lay readers. To identify the problems, Schriver collected think-aloud reading protocols from 30 freshmen trying to understand each of the six texts. The presence of a problem was revealed by readers' comments that indicated confusion, for example, "Isn't something missing here?" "I don't understand," and "What does this mean?" Two coders independently evaluated readers' comments on the 180 protocols and agreed in identifying the locus of comprehension problems in 95% of cases. Table 8.2 shows a portion of one of the texts, "Flywheels," indicating the text elements that caused problems, and showing how many of the 30 freshmen had trouble with the text element.

The participants in the study were 117 college juniors and seniors enrolled in ten intact classes in professional writing. Five classes served as the experimental group and five as the control group. Writers in the experimental group were taught using "readers' responses to poorly written text." For each of the ten lessons, writers first predicted the location and nature of a lay reader's problem with the draft text. Then they read and evaluated the think-aloud protocol to revise and discover readers' problems they missed in their initial predictions. Training with the reader protocol materials took place over a period of 3 weeks. Writers in the control group were trained in traditional audience analysis heuristics and peer response methods including peer critiquing, role playing, identifying demographic features of audience, and others.

The results of the study were quite dramatic. Figure 8.2 shows the hit rates (the mean number of times participants correctly predicted a reader problem) for experimental and control groups on pretest and posttest. After training, the experimental group correctly identified 62% more reader problems than before. Analysis of variance indicates that the improvement of the experimental group due to training is statistically significant ($p < .005$). In addition, the pretest differences between experimental and control groups and the pretest–posttest differences for the control group are not significant.

Schriver's training method, then, has proved quite successful in teaching writers to detect and diagnose text features that will cause problems for the reader. Moreover, results indicate that writers' knowledge of audience acquired through the experimental teaching method transferred from the domain in which it was acquired (instructional text) to another kind of text (expository science text). This line of work not only has considerable promise for writers but for training in "audience sensitivity" more generally—such as for training speakers how their talks will be received and for training literature teachers how their students will respond to assigned texts.

## TASK ENVIRONMENT

### The Physical Environment of Writing

Haas (1987) investigated the planning processes of writers who were composing with computer or pen and paper. She collected thinking aloud protocols from

TABLE 8.2
One Text Used in Pre- and Post-Tests

## Flywheels

Flywheels [6] are one of the oldest mechanical devices known to man. Every internal-combustion engine contains a small flywheel [3] that converts the jerky motion [4] of the pistons [4] into the smooth flow of energy that powers the drive shaft. [4] The greater the mass of the flywheel [5] and the faster it spins, [3] the more energy can be stored in it. But its maximum spinning speed [3] is limited by the strength of the material [6] it is made from. If it spins too fast for its mass, [7] any flywheel will fly apart. [3] One type of flywheel [3] consists of round sandwiches of fiberglass [12] and rubber providing the maximum possible storage of energy [3] when the wheel is confined in a small space as in an automobile. Another type, the "superflywheel" [3] consists of a series of rimless spokes. [6] This flywheel [13] stores [6] the maximum energy [7] when space [6] is unlimited. [3]

*Note:* Numbers of students who had difficulty with a text segment are shown below the segment.

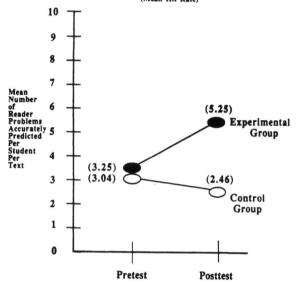

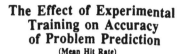

The Effect of Experimental
Training on Accuracy
of Problem Prediction
(Mean Hit Rate)

N = 5 classes (43 students) in experimental group
N = 5 classes (74 students) in control group

FIG. 8.2.   Mean hit rates for experimental and control groups.

10 students and 10 experienced writers, each of whom composed an essay using only a computer and another using only pen and paper. Haas divided the protocols into clause units and identified those clauses that reflected planning activities such as proposing content for the essay, considering the needs of the audience, proposing organization, and so forth. Although experienced writers planned much more than students, both groups showed a greater proportion of planning clauses to total clauses in the pen and paper condition than in the computer condition. Furthermore, writers planned more before starting to write in the pen and paper condition than in the computer condition. These results are shown in Table 8.3.

In addition, Haas found that the kind of planning that the writers did was influenced by the instrument they used to write. Haas divided planning clauses into several categories including those concerned with sentence level issues, such as proposing wording for sentences, and those concerned with conceptual issues, such as "Let's see . . . I need to tie this all together in a concluding paragraph." Haas found a significantly higher proportion of sentence level plans and a significantly lower proportion of conceptual plans when writers used the computer than when they used pen and paper. Mean proportions of total plan-

TABLE 8.3

The Impact of the Medium (Pen and Paper vs. Computer) on
Total Planning Clauses and on Planning Clauses Before Writing
in Writing Protocols

|  | Condition | |
| --- | --- | --- |
|  | pen and paper | computer |
| Number of planning clauses in protocol divided by total clauses in protocol | .339 | .272 |
| Proportion of planning clauses in protocol which occur before anything is written | .426 | .283 |

TABLE 8.4

Impact of the Medium (Pen and Paper vs. Computer) on the Proportion of
Planning for Writing at the Sentence Level and the Conceptual Level

|  | sentence level | | conceptual | |
| --- | --- | --- | --- | --- |
|  | pen | computer | pen | computer |
| expert | 27.9 | 36.9 | 66.2 | 53.7 |
| novice | 22.4 | 35.4 | 69.4 | 50.2 |

ning clauses are shown in Table 8.4. In summary, Haas found that when writers wrote with a computer they planned less overall, planned less before beginning to write, and planned less at a conceptual level than when they wrote using pen and paper. These findings are clearly of great importance for education and practice in writing. Further research is very definitely in order.

Writers who work with word processing systems, of course, are not constrained to do their writing entirely on the computer. In fact, a study of 16 experienced computer writers by Haas and Hayes (1986) showed that nearly all of these writers made some use of hardcopy while composing. To determine what it was that writers were using the hardcopy for, Haas (1987) studied six freshmen and five experienced writers over a 4-month period. During that time, the writers were asked to keep process logs when they used word processors to write. They were asked to note especially when they used hardcopy and what they used it for. In addition, they were observed while writing in their natural environments. Haas found four major uses of hardcopy:

1. Formatting. In many word processing systems, the screen format is different from the hardcopy format.
2. Proofreading. Many writers found it easier to search for spelling and punctuation problems with hard copy than online.
3. Reorganizing. Writers expressed a need to examine hardcopy to assure themselves that reorganizations done online had had the desired effect on the text.
4. Critical reading. Many writers felt that they could not adequately evaluate the development of their text or "get a sense of the text" unless they read it in hardcopy.

Haas found that the distribution of these uses of hardcopy by experienced writers was quite different from the distribution for freshmen, as is shown in Table 8.5. Freshmen were much more likely to use hardcopy to check format and spelling, whereas more experienced writers were more likely to use it to evaluate organization and meaning.

Haas divided data for the experienced writers into two sets: one set for long texts and one set for short texts. The distribution of hardcopy use for the short texts resembled that for novice writers, whereas the distribution for long texts resembled that for the experienced writers. Consequently, the use of hardcopy to evaluate organization and meaning appeared to be restricted to long texts.

## The Social Environment of Writing

In a series of studies of students writing in natural college environments, Nelson and Hayes (in press) showed that the social context can shape the writing process in dramatic ways. The authors selected a random sample of eight

TABLE 8.5
The Distribution of Uses of Hard Copy by Students and Experienced
Writers

## Uses of Hard Copy

|  | Students | Experienced Writers |
|---|---|---|
| Formatting | 75% | 31% |
| Proofreading | 13% | 9% |
| Reorganizing | 8% | 21% |
| "Text Sense" | 4% | 39% |

students in classes that had been assigned to write research papers. These students were asked to keep daily logs of all of the activities involved in writing their assigned papers, including library research, planning, conversations with peers, and the actual production of text. The diaries were collected by the researchers at least every other day.

The results indicated that the students differed markedly in their approaches to the assignments, falling into two general groups. Three students who employed a low-effort strategy and five students who employed a high-effort strategy. The following are the key features of the low effort strategy:

1. Students didn't start reading for their assignment until the week before the paper was due. (For the three low-effort students, reading began 6, 1, and 7 days before the due date.) Students didn't start writing until a day or two before the due date. (For the three low-effort students, writing began 2, 1, and 1 days before the due date.)

2. Topic choice was based on the easy availability of information rather than on the student's personal interest in the topic.

3. Students made an average of 1.67 trips to the library (the numbers of visits by the low effort students were 1, 2, and 2). Once writing began, no further sources were examined. Thus, the information collected during this one trip determined what the paper could be about.

4. Students summarized and paraphrased sources page by page and one source at a time.

5. Writing, which was accomplished in one or two sittings, consisted of arranging chunks of notes, each chunk corresponding to a source text.

There was little or no global revision. Most revision involved changes at the word or sentence level.

6. Students disliked the writing assignment, often characterizing it as "boring" or "tedious."

The following features of the high-effort strategy contrast sharply with those of the low-effort strategy:

1. Students started reading for their assignment 3 weeks to 6 weeks before the due date. (For the five high-effort students, reading started 41, 23, 32, 44, and 54 days before the due date.) Students started writing from 1 to 3 weeks before the assignment was due. (For the five high-effort students, writing started 10, 11, 26, 10, and 25 days before the due date.)

2. Topics were chosen on the basis of personal interest.

3. Students visited the library on average of 5.8 times (the numbers of visits by the five high-investment students was 4, 8, 6, 6, and 5). Searching for information often included "broad background reading" not accompanied by note taking.

4. Notes were typically organized around a predetermined plan rather than summarizing one source at a time.

5. Writing, which was completed over several days or even weeks, showed little direct correspondence with the writer's notes. There was considerable global revision with some students completely abandoning early drafts to start anew.

6. Students did not complain about the writing task or characterized it as "fun" or "interesting."

These differences between students' use of high- and low-effort strategies corresponded to differences in the way the teachers of the students managed the writing assignments. Teachers of low-effort students simply specified the assigned topic and the due date. Teachers of high-effort students also did one or more of the following things: specified required references, required students to submit drafts, or required students to give in-class talks on their topics. Diary entries suggested that the requirement to give a talk had an important impact on the students. When he learned he would have to give a talk, one student commented, "I can't just write a paper. I've got to understand this topic."

## THE WRITERS' KNOWLEDGE

Figure 8.1 suggests that knowledge of many sorts are involved in writing: Knowledge of topic, knowledge of audience, knowledge of the structure of language, and so forth. Some of the studies previously reviewed provide information about the role of knowledge in writing. The Schriver (1987) study indicated the importance of audience knowledge in revision. The studies by Kaufer, Hayes, and Flower (1986) and Friedlander (1987) suggest that variations in knowledge of language structures influence the way people compose sentences. In this section, I review three studies. The first is by Voss, Tyler, and Yengo (1983). Although this study does not involve writing, it has clear implications about the role of topic knowledge in writing. The second study, by Wishbow (1988), suggests that knowledge plays a critical role in the composing processes of eminent poets. The third, by Hayes, Schriver, Spilka, and Blaustein (1986) shows that topic knowledge can make it difficult for people to adjust their writing to the needs of the reader.

Voss, Tyler, and Yengo (1983) studied how people with different amounts of topic knowledge solved the following social science problem: "Assume you are the head of the Soviet Ministry of Agriculture and assume that crop productivity has been low over the past several years. You now have the responsibility of increasing crop production. How would you go about doing this?" Their subjects were four social science faculty members who were experts on the Soviet Union and six undergraduates entering a course on Soviet domestic policy. In addition, because faculty members and undergraduates differ in more than topic knowledge, Voss and his colleagues also studied four social science faculty who were experts in subjects other than the Soviet Union (e.g., Latin America, and four chemistry faculty members). All subjects gave thinking aloud protocols as they attempted to solve the problem.

I discuss four of the measures Voss and his colleagues used. Several of these measures are based on Toulmin's (1958) analysis of argument. According to Toulmin, an argument consists of a claim based on data. For example, "Low productivity on Soviet farms [Data] results from lack of incentives for the farmer [Claim]." The belief or principle that justifies drawing the claim from the data is called a *warrant* (e.g., "Lack of incentives generally leads to poor performance"). *Backing* is a statement supporting a warrant (e.g., "I remember how I felt working for minimum wage"). Voss, Tyler, and Yengo measured:

1. The amount of backing subjects provided for their arguments. They used this as an index of argument development.
2. The length of argument chains, e.g., the number of links in arguments of the form "A implies B, B implies C, etc."
3. The source of knowledge the subjects use for warrants, e.g., knowledge of Soviet Union, economics, agriculture, etc.
4. The proportion of the protocol devoted to developing the problem representation. Developing the problem representation involves identifying constraints on problem solutions based on ideology, history, climate, etc.

There was evidence in the Voss, Tyler, and Yengo data that social scientists may share some knowledge other than topic knowledge that influenced the way they approached the problem. They found that the Soviet experts devoted 24% of their protocols, the other social scientists, 16% of their protocols, and the other two groups almost none of their protocols, to developing their problem representations. However, the structure of the argument that the subjects produced seemed to depend primarily on topic knowledge. Table 8.6 shows that the Soviet experts developed their arguments much more fully and constructed longer argument chains than any other subject group. Furthermore, the Soviet experts were the only group for whom knowledge of the Soviet Union was the primary source of warrants for their arguments. Topic knowledge, then, influenced both the structure and the content of the arguments that the subjects constructed in solving the Soviet agriculture problem. It is easy to believe that very similar results would have been obtained if the subjects had been asked to write their arguments down.

Wishbow (1988) explored the relation of preparation and productivity in the careers of eminent poets. The purpose of her study was to determine if poets, like the chess players studied by Simon and Chase (1973) and the composers and painters studied by Hayes (1985), required a long period of preparation before they began to produce notable works. In this study, she explored the careers of 66 poets who met the following two criteria:

1. Their poetry was noteworthy as indicated by inclusion in the Norton Anthology of Poetry (1970).
2. There was sufficient biographical information to determine when they first became seriously interested in poetry.

For each of the poets, she determined how many years elapsed between the time when the poet became seriously interested in poetry and the time they wrote the first of their poems included in the *Norton Anthology*. Wishbow found that the elapsed time was never less than 5 years and for 55 of the 66 poets, it was 10 years or more. Consequently, poets, just as composers and painters, appear to require a considerable period of preparation before they become creatively productive.

Although Wishbow's data indicates that a period of preparation is necessary for creative productivity, it doesn't tell us why. Simon and Chase's (1973) analysis of performance in chess provides a very interesting hint. On the basis of their analysis of expert and novice performance in chess tasks, Simon and Chase concluded that grandmaster chess players have a larger store of chess pattern knowledge than weaker players and that this knowledge is essential for world-class performance. Grandmasters acquire this store of pattern knowledge, they suggest, through thousands of hours of practice, that is, through years of playing and studying chess.

Simon and Chase's "window" on chess players knowledge was a chess

TABLE 8.6
Properties of Arguments Proposed by Soviet Union Experts and Others
in Attempting to Solving the Soviet Agriculture Problem

| Group | Argument Development | Argument Length | Warrents |
|---|---|---|---|
| Soviet Experts | 8.8 | 7.1 | Knowledge of USSR |
| Other Social Scientists | 0.8 | 3.6 | Knowledge of Government |
| Chemists | 1.2 | 2.6 | Knowledge of Agriculture |
| Students | 2.3 | 2.6 | Knowledge of Psychology |

memory task. The Dutch psychologist, de Groot (1965) noticed that grand-master chess players were much better than weaker players at remembering chess games they had glimpsed only briefly. Simon and Chase (1973) used this window to examine expert chess knowledge. In her second study, Wishbow (1988) explored two tasks to see if they might provide comparable windows on poetic knowledge. The first was a knowledge-of-poetry task in which subjects were shown a sequence of poems and asked to name the poem, the poet, and the century in which the poem was composed. The second was a lexical choice task in which the subjects were shown a list of poems, each with one word deleted. The subjects were asked to select the word from a list of synonyms that they thought the composer of the poem would have chosen to fill the blank.

Wishbow's (1988) subjects for the knowledge-of-poetry task were 19 poets nominated for excellence by expert informers, 14 faculty members in literature, and 9 computer science graduate students. The poets and the professors of literature scored about equally well (64.2% and 62.4% correct respectively) and both outscored the computer scientists (who answered 30.6% of questions correctly). Differences among the three groups were highly reliable by analysis of variance ($F = 23.96$, $df = 2, 39$, $p < .0001$).

In the lexical choice task, the subjects were 8 poets, 10 literature professors, and 9 computer science graduate students. In this task, the poets scored 58.5% correct, the literature professors, 48.2% correct, and the computer scientists, 43.9% correct. The differences between the poets and the other two groups were significant ($p < .05$) by the Newman–Keuls test. These results suggest that tasks such as the lexical choice task can be found that differentiate between poets and others and may provide us with useful information about the nature of poetic skill.

In the studies just described, greater knowledge was associated with better performance. This is the sort of effect we would expect knowledge to have. However, in the study I am about to describe, greater knowledge actually leads to poorer performance.

It is widely believed that if a person is familiar with a topic, this very familarity may make it difficult for the person to explain the topic to another. Moreover, research on revision has suggested a mechanism whereby knowledge might make it more difficult to write clearly. Hayes and his colleagues (1987) proposed that "evaluation is best viewed as an extension of the familiar process of reading for comprehension" (p. 202). In particular, they proposed that writers detect problems in text by attending to failures of their own comprehension processes. Any special condition of the writer that makes comprehension easier, such as familiarity with the subject matter, will make it more difficult for the writer to identify parts of the text that might confuse the intended reader. Hayes, Schriver, Spilka, and Blaustein (1986) called this the *knowledge effect* and examined it in a series of studies.

In study 1, 88 undergraduates were asked to read four two-page texts, a clear and an unclear version on each of two topics: autism and statistics. The clear autism and the unclear statistics texts were naturally occurring texts. The statistics text was rewritten to be clear and the autism text to be unclear. For example, in the autism text, the phrase, "Autistic children look normal" was replaced by "Autistic patients in childhood appear asymptomatic." Observations of study 2, to be described later, confirmed that the clear texts did indeed present fewer comprehension problems to the readers than the unclear texts. The subjects were then asked to predict reader troubles by underlining those parts they thought would confuse another student. This is called the *prediction task*. The design of the study is shown in Table 8.7.

Half of the subjects, the high knowledge group, had read and evaluated a clear version of the text before they read the unclear version. As a result, they had knowledge about the content of the unclear version when they were trying to predict what parts of it would be unclear to other readers. The other half of the subjects, the low knowledge group, had not read the clear version and therefore had little knowledge of the content of the unclear version when they were making their predictions. The results, shown in Table 8.8, indicate that knowledge of the text had a strong effect in reducing the numbers of text problems predicted. The low knowledge group identified about 60% more text items as being problematic than the high knowledge group. Statistically, this difference between the two groups is highly reliable ($F = 13.7$; $df = 1,88$; $p < .001$).

Hayes and his colleagues (1986) also explored the effect of a short delay between acquiring topic information and evaluating the unclear text. They

TABLE 8.7
Design of the Knowledge Effect Study

| Knowledge | Texts | |
|-----------|-------|--------|
| High | Clear Autism | Unclear Autism |
| Low | ------ | Unclear Autism |
| High | Clear Graph | Unclear Graph |
| Low | ----- | Unclear Graph |

reasoned that if the subjects read information about a topic very recently, coming across that topic in the unclear text might remind them that they had just learned it and, perhaps, sensitize them to the possibility that their audience is unfamiliar with the topic. For the half of the subjects in the delay condition, the subjects read and evaluated a third text in the interval between reading the clear text and reading the unclear text. For the half of the subjects in the no delay condition, the unclear text was presented immediately after the subject had read and evaluated the clear text.

Table 8.9 shows that subjects in the delay condition identified approximately 25% fewer problems in the texts than subjects in the no delay condition. Although this difference is not statistically reliable, it does suggest that delay may intensify the knowledge effect. A subsequent study by Levine (1987) showed that a delay of 1 week resulted in an additional reduction of 25% in the number of text problems predicted.

Study 1 showed that the low knowledge group predicted more text problems than the high knowledge group. However, it might be that the predictions of the low knowledge group were poorer in quality than those of the high knowledge group. That is, the low knowledge subjects may have been less successful than the high knowledge subjects in predicting problems that readers actually have. Study 2 was conducted to answer the quality question by determining what things undergraduates actually found confusing about the unclear texts.

In study 2, 20 undergraduates were asked to read the unclear texts sentence by sentence and explain the meaning of each one as if to another student who had not read the text. This is called the *explanation task*. The purpose of the explanation task was to learn what freshmen actually understood in the texts. If subjects overlooked any points or explained them ambiguously, the experimenter questioned them until it was clear whether or not the point was understood. Half of the subjects read a clear version of the text before

TABLE 8.8
The Effect of Knowledge on the Numbers of Predictions That Other
Readers Will Have Trouble With the Text

**Knowledge**

|  | Low | High |
|---|---|---|
| **Autism** | 267 | 161 |
| **Graph** | 127 | 83 |
| **Total** | 394 | 244 |

TABLE 8.9
The Effect of Delay on the Numbers of Predictions Other Readers Will
Have Trouble With the Text

**Delay Condition**

|  | Immediate | Delayed |
|---|---|---|
| **Autism** | 87 | 74 |
| **Graph** | 53 | 30 |
| **Total** | 140 | 104 |

TABLE 8.10
The Effect of Knowledge on Sensitivity in Predicting Reader Problems
Measured by Signal Detection Analysis

**Knowledge**

|  | Low | High |
|---|---|---|
| **Autism** | .80 | .65 |
| **Graph** | .56 | .32 |

they attempted to explain the unclear version. These subjects were comparable to the high knowledge subjects in study 1. The other half of the subjects, who did not read the clear version of the text before attempting to explain the unclear text, were thus comparable to the low knowledge subjects in study 1.

The data of study 2 served two functions in the investigation. First, they identified the aspects of the unclear texts that low knowledge readers actually have difficulty in understanding. These results together with the subjects' predictions in study 1 were used to perform a signal detection analysis to compare the ability of subjects in study 1 to predict readers' comprehension problems. Table 8.10 shows $d$-prime values for high and low knowledge subjects.

Second, the data study 2 indicated which items of the unclear text were understood better by high knowledge than low knowledge subjects. This was of interest because a knowledge effect should apply only to those items for which prior reading of the clear text improved the subject's understanding. The items in the unclear texts were divided into three categories: the *positive learning* category, consisting of the 31 items that high knowledge subjects understood better than low knowledge subjects; the *zero learning* category, consisting of the 66 items that were equally well-understood by high and low knowledge subjects; and the *negative learning* category, consisting of 15 items better understood by the low knowledge than the high knowledge subjects.

Table 8.11 shows the percentage of items in each category for which more low knowledge subjects predicted reader troubles than high knowledge subjects. These results suggest that the knowledge effect really is an effect of knowledge.

## CONCLUSION

In this chapter, I have reviewed a variety of research efforts that have explored many facets of the writing process. These facets include the relation of planning to writing quality, the way in which sentences are constructed from sentence parts, the roles of task definition and of detection and diagnosis in revision, the effects of reader feedback in teaching writers to attend to their audience's comprehension needs, the impact of word processing on planning in writing, the influence of variations in the writing assignment on student's commitment of effort to the writing task, the role knowledge has in facilitating creative processes in poets, and the negative effect of topic knowledge on the writer's perception of what readers can understand.

Each of these studies illuminates the complex task of writing at widely separated points, like Lilliputian lamps searching out the shape of the giant Gulliver. Not much is visible as yet, but what can be seen is sufficiently interesting to suggest that further search can yield important results for cognitive science.

TABLE 8.11
Predictions of Reader Difficulties for Three Types of Items
in the Unclear Text

| | Positive Learning n=31 | Zero Learning n=66 | Negative Learning n=15 |
|---|---|---|---|
| **% of Items for which more low knowledge S's predicted difficulties** | 61.3% | 48.5% | 46.7% |

## Post-script

When I began work on writing with Linda Flower in 1977, I had been working with Herb Simon for about 6 years on the UNDERSTAND project (Hayes & Simon, 1974, 1977; Simon & Hayes, 1976). In this project, we were trying to describe how problem solvers managed to derive internal representations of problems from written problem statements. I was also involved in a closely related comprehension project in which Don Waterman and I, in consultation with Herb, were trying to describe how readers identified relevant elements in a problem text. I certainly owe my orientation to studying problems of language use to Herb. Much more important than that, I, and I suspect many of us owe our willingness to consider really complex problems to Herb's example. example. My early training in psychology was as a Skinnerian. We were taught to laugh at social psychologists with their fuzzy thinking about attitudes and other nonoperationally defined mysteries. The major sin of the social psychologists and others well beyond the pale, such as anthropologists, was their willingness to consider complex problems involving humans. We were taught to study simple things first and that meant studying simple responses of simple organisms. To be scientific was to build step-by-step on a firm foundation. Scientists were, in Vigotsky's term, to stay within their zone of proximal development. To be scientific certainly didn't mean to be adventurous or to take on complex problems. I've changed a lot since that time and so has psychology. I think that we owe much of our renewed spirit of scientific adventure to Herb Simon.

## REFERENCES

Bereiter, C., & Scardamalia, M. (1987). *The psychology of written composition.* Hillsdale, NJ: Lawrence Erlbaum Associates.

Bracewell, R. J., Scardamalia, M., & Bereiter, C. (1978). *The development of audience awareness in writing.* (ERIC Document Reproduction Service No. ED 154 433)

Carey, L., Flower, L., Hayes, J. R., Schriver, K., & Haas, C. (1987). *Differences in writers' initial task representations* (Office of Naval Research Technical Report 2). Pittsburgh, PA: Carnegie-Mellon University.

de Groot, A. D. (1965). *Thought and choice in chess.* The Hague: Mouton.

Duffy, T., Curran, T., & Sass, D. (1983). Document design for technical job tasks: An evaluation. *Human Factors, 25,* 143–160.

Emig, J. (1971). *The composing process of twelfth graders.* Urbana, Ill: National Council of Teachers of English.

Flower, L. S., & Hayes, J. R. (1984). Images, plans, and prose: The representation of meaning in writing. *Written Communication, 1,* 120–160.

Friedlander, A. (1987). *The writer stumbles: Constraints on composing in English as a second language.* Unpublished doctoral dissertation in rhetoric. Pittsburgh, PA: Carnegie-Mellon University.

Haas, C. (1987). *How the writing medium shapes the writing process: Studies of writers composing with pen and paper and with word processing.* Doctoral dissertation in rhetoric. Pittsburgh, PA: Carnegie-Melon University.

Haas, C., & Hayes, J. R. (1986). What did I just say? Reading problems in writing with the machine. *Research in the Teaching of English, 20* (1), 22–35.

Hayes, J. R. (1985). Three problems in teaching general skills. In S. F. Chipman, J. W. Segal, & Glaser (Eds.), *Thinking and learning skills, volume 2: Research and open questions.* Hillsdale, NJ: Lawrence Erlbaum Associates.

Hayes, J. R., & Flower, L. S. (1980). Identifying the organization of writing processes. In L. Gregg & E. Steinberg (Eds.), *Cognitive processes in writing: An interdisciplinary approach.* Hillsdale, NJ: Lawrence Erlbaum Associates.

Hayes, J. R., Flower, L. S., Schriver, K. A., Stratman, J., & Carey, L. (1987). Cognitive processes in revision. In S. Rosenberg (Ed.), *Advances in psycholinguistics, volume II: Reading, writing, and languages processing.* Cambridge, England: Cambridge University Press.

Hayes, J. R., Schriver, K. A., Spilka, R., & Blaustein, A. (1986). *If its clear to me it must be clear to them.* Paper presented at the Conference on College Composition and Communication, New Orleans, LA.

Hayes, J. R., & Simon, H. A. (1974). Understanding written problem instructions. In L. Gregg (Ed.), *Knowledge and cognition.* Hillsdale, NJ: Lawrence Erlbaum Associates.

Hayes, J. R., & Simon, H. A. (1977). Psychological differences among problem isomorphs. In N. J. Castellan, D. B. Pisoni, & G. R. Potts (Eds.), *Cognitive theory* (vol. 2, pp. 22–41). Hillsdale, NJ: Lawrence Erlbaum Associates.

Kaufer, D., Hayes, J. R., & Flower, L. S. (1986). Composing written sentences. *Research in the Teaching of English, 20,* 121–140.

Levine, L. (1987). Personal communication.

Miller, G. A., Galanter, E., & Pribram, K. (1960). *Plans and the structure of behavior.* New York: Holt, Rinehart & Winston.

Nelson, J., & Hayes, J. R. (in press). *How the writing context shapes students' strategies for writing from sources.* Technical report for the Center for the Study of Writing at Carnegie-Mellon University and the University of California at Berkeley, Berkeley, Ca.

Newell, A. & Simon, H. A. (1972). *Human problem solving.* Englewood Cliffs, NJ: Prentice-Hall.

Schriver, K. A. (1984). *Revising computer documentation for comprehension: Ten lessons in protocol-aided revision* (Tech. Rep. No. 14). Pittsburgh, PA: Carnegie-Mellon University, Communication Design Center.

Schriver, K. A. (1987). *Teaching writers to anticipate the reader's needs: Empirically based instruction.* Unpublished doctoral dissertation in rhetoric. Pittsburgh, PA: Carnegie-Mellon University.

Simon, H. A., & Chase, W. G. (1973). Skill in chess. *American Scientist, 61,* 394–403.

Simon, H. A., & Hayes, J. R. (1976). The understanding process: Problem Isomorphs, *Cognitive Psychology, 8,* 165–190.

Swaney, J. H., Janik, C. J., Bond, S. J., & Hayes, J. R. (1981). *Editing for comprehension: Improving the process through reading protocols* (Tech. Rep. No. 14). Carnegie-Mellon University, Document Design Project.

Toulmin, S. E. (1958). *The uses of argument.* London: Academic Press.

Voss, J. F., Tyler, S. W., & Yengo, L. A. (1983). Individual differences in the solving of social science problems. In R. Dillon & R. Schmech (Eds.), *Individual differences in cognition.* New York: Academic Press.

Wishbow, N. (1988). *Studies of creativity in poets.* Unpublished doctoral dissertation in rhetoric. Pittsburgh, PA: Carnegie-Mellon University.

# 9

## Skilled Memory and Expertise: Mechanisms of Exceptional Performance

K. Anders Ericsson
*University of Colorado at Boulder*

James J. Staszewski
*University of South Carolina*

The knowledge that intelligent systems bring to a particular task is a major determinant of task performance. Some of the most compelling support for this broad claim can be found in studies of human expertise. Since the pioneering studies of chess experts performed by de Groot (1966, 1978) and Chase and Simon (1973a, 1973b; Simon & Chase, 1973), a considerable body of experimental evidence has accumulated that relates experience (i.e., practice) in a particular task domain or discipline to superior performance. Experience has often been measured in years, even decades; and performance has been observed in widely varying tasks, including memory (Ericsson, Chase, & Faloon, 1980; Chase & Ericsson, 1982), comprehension (Chiesi, Spilich, & Voss, 1979; Spilich, Vesonder, Chiesi, & Voss, 1979), academic problem solving (Chi, Feltovich, & Glaser, 1981; Larkin, McDermott, Simon, & Simon, 1980), and practical tasks (Anderson, Farrell, & Sauers, 1984; Ericsson & Polson, 1988, in press; Hayes & Flower, 1986; Jeffries, Turner, Polson, & Atwood, 1981; Lesgold, 1984). These studies as well as studies of artificial intelligence (Feigenbaum, chap. 6 in this volume) show that "knowledge is power."

A growing number of researchers are now attempting to understand the relation between expert knowledge and exceptional performance in terms of cognitive structures and processes. The fundamental problem in this broad endeavor is to describe what it is that experts know and how they use their knowledge to achieve performance that most people assume requires extreme or extraordinary ability.

This chapter explores how experts use knowledge efficiently. As Bartlett (1932) noted, experts not only succeed at what they do more frequently than novices, they also achieve their goals more efficiently. If this characterization of expertise is accurate, it becomes necessary to reconcile experts' efficient use of vast amounts of knowledge with well-established capacity limits on human information processing. In short, we ask what enables experts to be fast and accurate.

We approach this issue by first reviewing the early studies of the skilled memory effect, (i.e., experts' superior short-term memory for information within the domain of their expertise) along with Chase and Simon's (1973a, 1973b) theoretical account of this phenomenon. We then discuss Chase and Ericsson's (1982) skilled memory theory, a more recent theory of expert memory, which postulates that acquired memory skills enable expert subjects to store and retrieve large amounts of information in long-term memory both reliably and efficiently. Next we review the empirical support for skilled memory theory that comes from studies of memory experts (i.e., mnemonists), outlining the mechanisms these individuals employ to perform exceptional mnemonic feats. We then address the generality of skilled memory theory by presenting data showing that mechanisms like those used by the expert mnemonists also mediate the remarkable skills of a waiter with exceptional memory for dinner orders, three "lightning" mental calculators, and an expert blindfold chess player. We conclude that a common set of mechanisms enables experts in these different domains to manage the memory demands of their respective tasks and perform effectively and efficiently. We suggest that skilled memory theory may characterize how experts from other domains quickly organize, encode, and retrieve large amounts of information to enhance their information processing capabilities and achieve exceptional performance.

## EXPERT PERFORMANCE AND THE PARADOX
## OF EXPERTISE

Knowledge is information acquired through experience and stored more or less permanently in long-term memory (LTM). The appeal to knowledge to explain the vast differences in performance between experts and novices has considerable empirical support (see Chi, Glaser, & Farr, in press). However, this explanation also poses theoretical problems, one of the most thorny being the paradox of expertise (Barsalou & Bower, 1984; Smith, Adams, & Schorr, 1978). Experts use enormous amounts of knowledge to achieve superior levels of performance. For example, Simon and Chase (1973) estimated that grandmasters rely on a knowledge base containing some 50,000 familiar chess patterns to guide the selection of moves. At the same time, experts are presumably subject to the same basic information processing constraints that all humans face, including limited attentional capacity (Broadbent, 1958), limited short-term memory (STM) capacity (Baddeley, 1976; Miller, 1956; Newell & Simon, 1972), and relatively slow LTM storage and retrieval processes (Simon, 1976). How is it that experts bring more knowledge to bear on problem solving and skilled performance than novices and at the same time perform more quickly and accurately? We postulate that experts develop skilled memory. That is, experts acquire not only content knowledge through long hours of practice, they also develop skills that enable them to efficiently apply their knowledge.

The clearest evidence for experts' reliance on acquired knowledge to recognize, encode, and retain large amounts of information is the skilled memory effect. This phenomenon has been experimentally demonstrated in a wide variety of domains (see Chase, 1986). It refers to experts' ability to recall large amounts of material displayed for only brief study intervals, provided that the material comes from their domain of expertise. In contrast, novices' recall of the same material under identical presentation conditions is typically quite poor. However, it is significant to note that when unfamiliar material is presented to experts, their recall is no better than that of novices. This latter finding shows that experts do not possess general memory capabilities that novices lack.

The theoretical role of LTM in the skilled memory effect was first articulated by Chase and Simon in their classic studies of chess expertise (Chase & Simon, 1973a, 1973b; Simon & Chase, 1973). Their theory fixed the primary locus of this effect in LTM, asserting that organized patterns of information stored in LTM, that is chunks, mediated experts' rapid encoding and superior retention of chessboard displays. They theorized that experts encoded gamelike arrangements of pieces not in terms of individual pieces, but in terms of familiar, integrated patterns of pieces learned through years of practice. Labels corresponding to these chunks of information in LTM were held in STM and subsequently used to retrieve each chunk, whose constituent elements could then be "unpacked." Novices, on the other hand, lacking such structured knowledge representations and the ability to quickly transfer information about individual pieces and their board positions from STM to LTM, could retain only a very limited amount of information.

Analyses of the temporal structure found in the recall protocols of both experts and novices support this view. Both experts and novices reconstructed board configurations in bursts of activity during which pieces were placed on the board in rapid succession, followed by clear pauses. Examination of the contents of the chunks revealed the source of the experts' advantage. All subjects retrieved about the same number of chunks, but the size of chunks varied with subjects' prior experience, experts' chunks containing more individual pieces than those of novices. Thus, Chase and Simon concluded that experts' use of an organized body of knowledge, acquired through years of chess playing and used to recognize and encode familiar patterns of information, gave them domain-specific memory capabilities that far exceeded those of novices.

Subsequent studies of experts in many domains (see Chase & Ericsson, 1982; Chase, 1986, for good reviews of these studies) have both established the generality of the skilled memory effect and supported most of the major premises of the Chase–Simon theory. However, Chase and Ericsson (1982) noted one premise of this theory that is challenged by two empirical facts. First, the number of chunks recalled by Chase and Simon's (1973b) chess expert exceeded revised estimates of the working capacity of STM (Broadbent, 1975; Chase & Ericsson, 1982; Glanzer & Razel, 1974; Simon, 1976). Second, studies by Charness (1976) indicated that experts' reconstruction of board displays is minimally affected by a STM interference task. Together, these findings challenge the proposal that, in the recall tasks that establish the skilled memory effect, experts retrieve chunks of information held in LTM by maintaining the appropriate cues in STM. These findings also raise questions about how experts find, distinguish, and retrieve the "right" chunks from the vast number they hold in LTM without a lengthy search. Thus, although the Chase–Simon theory gives a tenable account of how experts rapidly encode large amounts of information, the paradox of expertise is reflected in its inability to explain how information encoded in an extensive knowledge base is easily retrieved.

## SKILLED MEMORY THEORY

A theoretical alternative to the Chase–Simon theory that can better explain experts' speedy storage and retrieval of large amounts of information is skilled memory theory (Chase & Ericsson, 1982). This theory has evolved from Chase and Ericsson's (1981, 1982; Ericsson & Chase, 1982; Ericsson, Chase, & Faloon, 1980) studies of expert mnemonists and is based primarily on detailed analyses of individuals who increased their digit spans far beyond the well-known limit of seven plus-or-minus two digits (Miller, 1956). Overall, skilled memory theory offers a more detailed characterization of the knowledge experts possess than the Chase–Simon theory. Essentially, it states that acquired LTM encoding and retrieval skills give experts an information processing advantage that novices lack: an expanded working memory capacity for materials within the area of their expertise. Novices' performance in most complex tasks is constrained by (a) the sharply limited capacity of STM and (b) relatively slow LTM storage and retrieval processes (Anderson, 1987; Hitch, 1978; Newell & Simon, 1972). In contrast, experts' efficient use of LTM to store information enables them to access amounts of information that far exceed the capacity of STM and to do so with the speed and reliability normally associated with STM encoding and retrieval. The resulting computational efficiency contributes to the superior task performance that typically differentiates experts from novices. From this theoretical perspective, the skilled memory effect, that is, experts' superior recall for familiar materials, is viewed as a natural by-product of experts' use of LTM to maintain information in an easily accessible state for processing in complex tasks.

Chase and Ericsson (1982) characterized experts' efficient use of LTM in terms of three principles originally drawn from their analyses of a single subject, SF, who expanded his digit span to 84 digits over the course of 2 years of observed laboratory practice (Chase & Ericsson, 1981; Ericsson, Chase, & Faloon, 1980).

The first principle of skilled memory, the *meaningful encoding principle*, states that experts exploit prior knowledge to durably encode information needed to perform a familiar task successfully. By encoding information in terms of a familiar, well-organized body of concepts and relations represented in LTM as meaningful units (i.e., chunks), experts form more elaborate and accessible memory representations than novices. Consistent with this view, experimental evidence shows that SF did not increase his capacity to hold digits in STM through practice. Instead, his verbal reports indicated that he grouped together short, random sequences of digits and encoded these groups in terms of their meaning as running times, dates, and ages. For instance, he would encode the sequence 3492 as "3 minutes, 49.2 seconds"—a near world-record time for the 1-mile run. In general, SF used his elaborately structured knowledge about running times help him retain the meaningless sequences of digits presented on digit-span trials. Over the course of his practice he augmented his knowledge base with categories for ages (798 would be coded as a "79.8-year-old man"), and dates, (e.g., 1860, 1963) to accommodate digit sequences not easily encoded as running times. The important point is that his strategy exploited both the content and structure of an elaborate semantic memory network to create meaningful memory codes that created multiple potential cues and avenues for retrieval.

The second principle, the *retrieval structure principle*, states that experts develop memory mechanisms called retrieval structures to facilitate the retrieval of information stored in LTM. Significantly, these mechanisms operate in a fashion consistent with the encoding specificity principle (Tulving & Thomson, 1973) in that retrieval structures are used strategically to encode information in LTM with cues that can later be regenerated to retrieve the stored information efficiently without a lengthy search. As opposed to a less foresighted strategy for maintaining information in memory, these abstract, hierarchically organized mechanisms reflect (a) experts' sensitivity to that information that is critical to future processing activities, and (b) the systematic methods experts apply to temporarily maintain such information in an easily accessible state. Both protocol data and chronometric studies of SF's retrieval processes show that SF used abstract organizational formats to memorize lengthy random digit lists (Chase & Ericsson, 1981). These organizational schemes are analogous to the familiar schemes that people use to encode and retrieve telephone numbers or social security numbers, but were far more elaborate. In general, retrieval structures, or organized systems for using retrieval cues constitute mechanisms for effective and efficient access to information stored in LTM.

The third theoretical principle of skilled memory, the speed up principle, states that LTM encoding and retrieval operations speed up with practice, so that their speed and accuracy approach the speed and accuracy of STM storage and retrieval. More descriptive than explanatory, this principle is supported by Chase and Ericsson's (1981) finding that the time SF needed to encode a digit group dropped from about 5 seconds per group to about 1 second per group after 200 hours of practice. Such a reduction in study time is consistent with the speed up that typically occurs in cognitive and perceptual-motor skills with practice (Newell & Rosenbloom, 1981). When SF's skill was well-established, Chase and Ericsson (1981) also found that he could quickly and accurately retrieve stored information in a variety of recall tasks. For instance, when SF was probed with a digit group from a list he had just received under digit-span testing conditions, he could rapidly locate the probe's position in a schematic drawing of his retrieval structure. He could also quickly name the last digit of any digit group in a stored list when probed with the group's initial two or three digits. Overall, these findings indicate that practice had increased SF's ability to store and retrieve long random digit lists durably and with the kind of efficiency that novices store and retrieve much smaller amounts of information in STM.

According to skilled memory theory, it is possible to increase the functional capacity of working memory through practice. By learning to quickly store and retrieve information in LTM, experts increase the amount of information they can easily access for processing beyond the limited amount that can be maintained in STM. However, because it assumes that LTM storage and retrieval operations are controlled within the confines of STM, skilled memory is entirely consistent with the concept of a limited STM with general-purpose capacity. This assertion leads to at least two empirically testable claims. First, skilled memory is domain specific and involves LTM storage and retrieval for a restricted body of material. Second, storage and retrieval in skilled memory operate under the constraints of limited-capacity STM.

Ericsson, Chase, and Faloon (1980) noted that SF's cognitive processes remained constrained by STM even at exceptional levels of digit-span performance. First, the size of SF's groups were almost always three and four digits, and he never generated a mnemonic association for more than five digits. Second, he almost never kept more than six digits in his rehearsal buffer. Third, SF clustered digit groups together into supergroups. He generally included three groups in his supergroups; and, after some initial difficulty with five groups, never allowed more than four groups in a supergroup. SF's exceptional digit-span performance was domain specific and limited to digits. In one experimental session after 3 months of practice, SF was switched from digits to letters of the alphabet and exhibited no transfer: His memory span dropped back to about six consonants.

Clear evidence that SF relied on LTM storage and retrieval comes from the free-recall task regularly administered after the digit-span trials presented in a typical practice session. At the end of practice sessions he was able to recall over 84% of all digit groups presented in a session totaling 200-300 digits. Furthermore, a series of experiments (Chase & Ericsson, 1981) showed that when severe interference with STM occurred between presentation and recall of the digits, it had essentially no effect.

Of course, more than one subject must be able to acquire skilled memory if this theoret5ical construct is generalizable. SF's performance on the digit-span task must be replicated, and the mechanisms of skilled memory must be shown to underlie "exceptional" memory performance in other domains of expertise. Therefore we briefly review the evidence for skilled memory theory in a wide range of studies of exceptional memory performance. Then we extend our analysis to three different skills. We show that subjects who exhibit exceptionally skilled performance use skilled memory to cope with unusually high working memory loads that their respective tasks impose.

## SKILLED MEMORY THEORY
## AND EXCEPTIONAL MEMORY PERFORMANCE

Evidence linking the tenets of skilled memory theory to exceptional memory performance comes from our own studies of skilled memory as well as from other investigations of people with extraordinary mnemonic abilities. In this section, we briefly review earlier studies of mnemonists and their capabilities (Ericsson, 1985; Ericsson & Chase, 1982) and of retarded subjects with exceptional memory (Ericsson & Faivre, in press) to show how these findings are consistent with skilled memory theory. We also report more direct support for skilled memory theory obtained in recent studies of two runners who dramatically improved their digit span through practice (Ericsson, Fendrich, & Faivre, in preparation; Staszewski, 1988, in preparation) and other studies in which subjects were trained to attain exceptional memory performance (Kliegl, Smith, & Baltes, 1986). Our discussion of the evidence follows the format of the previous section, dealing with findings that support the meaningful encoding principle, the retrieval structure principle, and the speed up principle, in that order.

Empirical evidence consistently supports the meaningful encoding principle because studies of exceptional memory performance consistently show that it is contingent upon mnemonists' use of a rich semantic knowledge base to encode information. The two runners who developed exceptional digit spans through practice were explicitly instructed to encode digits as running times, ages, and dates (Ericsson, Fendrich, & Faivre, in preparation; Staszewski, 1988, in preparation).

Other subjects with exceptional memory were skilled in mental calculation and had extensive experience in mathematics. When tested on the digit span task, they reported using their knowledge of mathematics to encode groups of digits (Bryan, Lindley, & Harter, 1941; Mueller, 1911, 1913).

For example, Professor Rueckle (Mueller, 1911, 1913) reported memorizing six-digit sequences by first chunking each sequence as two three-digit numbers and then identifying the prime factors of these numbers. He would code 451697 as 451 = 11 × *41* & 697 = 17 × *41*, and 893047 as 893 = 19 × *47* and 047 = *47*. The mathematicians also used other knowledge such as dates and patterns, which nonmathematicians have also used (Hunt & Love, 1972). Retarded subjects with exceptional memory also reported using similar types of knowledge about numbers (Ericsson & Faivre, in press). The subjects studied by Gordon, Valentine, and Wilding (1984) and by Susukita (1933, 1934) reported using mnemonic techniques based on phonemic recoding, by which two to four digits can be recoded as words, preferably concrete nouns. Kliegl, Smith, and Baltes (1986) explicitly trained their subjects to use the phonemic recording method. Although the particular kind of knowledge varied across subjects, those with exceptional memory consistently used such knowledge in encoding presented information.

Evidence for the retrieval structure principle also comes from several sources. This evidence shows that retrieval structures can assume a variety of surface forms, but an underlying set of general principles describes their form and function. Subjects strategically assign predetermined retrieval cues to meaningfully encoded chunks of information to specify the location of the chunks within a presented sequence. When it is time to recall the presented information, they then use their retrieval structures to systematically regenerate these cues to retrieve the stored chunks in their appropriate order.

The most systematic study of retrieval structures comes from an analysis of DD, a runner who, through several years of practice on the digit span task, attained the highest span ever recorded, 106 digits (Staszewski, 1988, in preparation). Figure 9.1 shows the organization of DD's retrieval structure for 100-digit lists.

DD's hierarchical organization of the digits in a list is similar to SF's organization (Chase & Ericsson, 1981, 1982). The lowest level of the hierarchy corresponds to the locations of sublists of three or four digits that are coded as meaningful units (i.e., running times, dates, ages, etc.) At the second level, digit groups of equivalent length are grouped in relation to a higher-level functional unit, or supergroup, in which the ordinal relations "first," "middle," and "last" specify the location of each component digit-group. Supergroups, in turn, occupy specific locations within more superordinate groupings called supergroup clusters.

Analysis of DD's pauses as he recalled lists of 100 digits or more showed that longer pauses occurred at the hierarchical boundaries of this postulated structure, confirming the organizational hypothesis derived from his verbal reports (Staszewski, 1988). Another study showed that the temporal patterns of DD's list encoding reflected the same abstract structure as those characterizing his serial recall. This finding implies that the same mechanism was used both to encode and retrieve lists. In addition, cued-recall experiments showed that DD could directly access information about the location of stored

100-DIGIT LIST

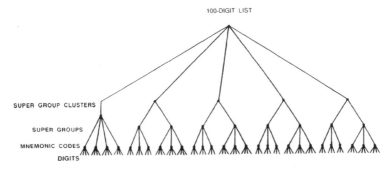

SUPER GROUP CLUSTERS

SUPER GROUPS

MNEMONIC CODES

DIGITS

FIG. 9.1.   Proposed hierarchical organization of DD's memory encoding and retrieval processes for 100-digit lists. (The first abstract level of organization contains mnemonic encodings of digit groups. The second level consists of super groups, in which the relative location of several digit groups of equal size are encoded. The third level consists of super group clusters combining several supergroups.) Source: "The Psychological Reality of Retrieval Structures: An Investigation of Expert Knowledge" by J. J. Staszewski, 1988. *Dissertation Abstracts International, 42,* 2126B.

digit groups and that the speed at which he retrieved adjacent digit groups was determined by hierarchical unit boundaries.

Similar evidence for hierarchically organized retrieval of large amounts of material was reported by G. E. Mueller (1911, 1917) in his analysis of Professor Rueckle, a mathematics professor with exceptional memory. Further correspondence between our studies of retrieval structures and Mueller's work comes from cued-recall experiments in which Rueckle could rapidly recall digit-groups when cued with just their list positions (Mueller, 1917)

Susukita (1933, 1934) described Isahara's retrieval structure, the method of loci, which consisted of a fixed sequence of about 400 physical locations, such as a brook near his house. In memorizing digits Isahara would recode a group of digits into a concrete word and then form a visual image of the word and the first physical location. The next word would be imagined in the second location and so on. At the time of recall, Isahara would use his knowledge about the fixed series of locations to retrieve the images stored there and would then decode the word to identify the presented digits. Similarly, Kliegl, Smith, and Baltes (1986) instructed their subjects to use a particular sequence of physical locations. The mnemonically trained subject studied by Gordon, Valentine, and Wilding (1984) used a similar method, relying on a previously learned sequence of concrete objects, like pegs.

The speed up principle states that with practice, normal subjects can increase the speed of storage and retrieval in LTM so that it approaches the speed of information storage and retrieval in STM. The implicit assumption that storage in LTM takes time is well-supported. Many subjects with exceptional memory are very sensitive to the rate of presentation and their digit span can be reduced to a normal level by increasing that rate (Ericsson, 1985).

Support for the speed up principle has been obtained in studies examining self-paced memorization rates of the digit-span experts at different levels of practice. Earlier studies with SF showed speed up of memorization with practice (Chase & Ericsson, 1981, 1982), as did subsequent studies with our two trained digit-span experts, DD (Staszewski, in preparation) and NB (Ericsson, Fendrich, & Faivre, in preparation). The clearest evidence comes from NB, one of the runners who attained an exceptional digit span with practice (Ericsson, Fendrich, & Faivre, in preparation), and whose encoding speed was monitored from the onset of her training. Half of NB's training sessions consisted of regular digit span trials, and the other half of self-paced memorization of 21 digits. At the first training session when her digit span was normal, NB required over 1 minute to memorize an entire 21-digit sequence. At the end of practice, when her digit span during regular trials was well over 21 digits, she could memorize 21 digits under self-paced conditions at a rate comparable to 1 digit/second, the rate at which digits were presented to her during regular trials. Recently, Kliegl, Smith, and Baltes (1986) also showed that with practice subjects can memorize digits at presentation rates 5 to 10 times faster than their rates at the beginning of practice. Hence, with practice, time for storage in LTM can be dramatically reduced, and similar reductions in retrieval times have been observed after practice.

Generally, evidence from a variety of independent studies of exceptional memory supports other claims about skilled memory. The claim that skilled memory is domain specific is clearly supported: For all subjects, exceptional memory was limited to a particular type of material, often digits (Ericsson, 1985). Although a small number of subjects exhibited memory performance for other types of materials that was consistently higher than average, their performance was usually within the range of variation for normal subjects. In a later section of the chapter, we discuss how transfer to unfamiliar materials is possible within skilled memory theory.

The claim that skilled memory operates within the capacity constraints of attention and STM is also supported. Our own studies of SF, DD, and NB as well as those of other well-known mnemonists show a striking regularity. They show that mnemonists seldom operate upon more than three or four symbols (or chunks) at a given moment, and five elements appears to be the upper limit (Ericsson, 1985, Staszewski, 1988). These numbers are quite consistent with several investigators' estimates of the working capacity of STM (Broadbent, 1975; Glanzer & Razel, 1974; Simon, 1976).

The final claim that exceptional memory involves storage in LTM was not addressed by earlier studies of mnemonists, but the two runners who developed exceptional digit spans, like SF, could consistently recall a large proportion of material presented in span trials when asked for free recall of these materials at the close of a practice session (Ericsson, Fendrich, & Faivre, in preparation; Staszewski, 1988, in preparation). Their retention of coded digit groups over the course of a session supports the claim that these materials are stored in LTM.

In sum, many investigations of exceptional memory have reported evidence consistent with the principles and characteristics of skilled memory and have documented that memory performance can be dramatically improved with practice. This improvement can be accounted for in terms of skilled memory theory.

## SKILLED MEMORY THEORY AND EXPERTISE

Our discussion of exceptional memory performance indicated that with practice and an appropriate knowledge base, normal subjects can considerably increase the amount of information that they can store in memory and then access rapidly, reliably, and flexibly. Skilled memory theory provides a plausible account of how they do so. Also, skilled memory theory can handle findings related to the skilled memory effect that are inconsistent with Chase and Simon's (1973a, 1973b) theoretical explanation.

This latter point is significant because it links the studies of exceptional memory performance to the typical person's conception of what an expert is and does. Mnemonists, individuals who can quickly learn and retain large amounts of seemingly meaningless information, are somewhat distantly related to most people's prototype of an expert. Understandably, most people relate expertise to the proficient use of meaningful materials in particular content domains. Indeed, most of our scientific knowledge about experts is based on studies using materials that most people regard as meaningful: chessboard arrangements, electronics diagrams, architectural drawings, computer programs, and physics problems, for example.

In the following three sections of this chapter, we discuss recent work that extends the generality of skilled memory theory to three new skill domains: memory for dinner orders, mental calculation, and blindfold chess. This research is distinguished from the foregoing studies of "pure" memory experts by its demonstration of how experts employ skilled memory to process meaningful materials efficiently and achieve exceptional levels of performance in specific content areas. In showing how skilled memory relates to expert performance in each area, we pay special attention to showing how retrieval structures are used to facilitate the storage and retrieval of meaningful chunks of information in LTM, because these mechanisms represent a novel and potentially powerful theoretical construct.

### Memory Skill for Dinner Orders

Taking the dinner orders of a party of customers accurately and efficiently is only one of many skills excellent waiters master. If waiters memorize dinner orders instead of writing them down, they risk serving the wrong order to a customer who is not likely to wait serenely while others enjoy their food. Furthermore, while memorizing orders, waiters still have to be willing to explain and describe menu items, accommodate customers who change their minds, and so forth. Hence, in real life, memory skills must be compatible with interruptions and many other concurrent activities that demand attention.

JC, a waiter who could memorize up to 20 complete dinner orders in an actual restaurant setting, was studied for a 2-year period by Ericsson and Polson (1988, in press). They devised a laboratory analogue in which each person at a table was represented by a card with a picture of a face. Each order was a random combination of one of eight meat entrees, one of five meat temperatures (rare to well-done), one of five salad dressings, and one of three starches (baked potato, rice, or french fries), forming a pool of 600 possible orders. In the laboratory, presentation was self-paced, and subjects indicated when the next order should be read. Tables with three, five, and eight customers were used throughout these studies.

JC's performance on the laboratory analogue of the dinner order task is shown in Fig. 9.2. His study times were dramatically faster than those of a group of college students and a group of waiters, who memorized dinner orders from tables with three to five customers. Only the group of waiters were able to approach JC's low error rate in recall. Hence even the laboratory version of the memory task shows that JC's memory skill was exceptional.

Not only was JC's performance on the memory task clearly superior to that of the other two groups of subjects, but his cognitive processes during memorization and recall were also qualitatively different. At the time of recall JC would recall all items of a category together in a clockwise fashion for all customers at a table: first all salad dressings, then all temperatures, then all steaks, and finally all starches. Thinking aloud protocols (Ericsson & Simon, 1984) from his memorization showed that as a new dinner order was presented, items of each category were encoded together with previously presented items of the same category.

JC encoded the items for each category with a different mnemonic strategy. Salad dressings were encoded as a group of the initial letters of their names (e.g., Bleu cheese, Oil-and-vinegar, Oil-and-vinegar, Thousand island = BOOT or *boot*). Because there were only three starches, repetitions were frequent, and JC encoded starches in patterns (e.g., baked potato, rice, rice, baked potato = abba). Temperatures of the meat were all ordered by the degree to which they were cooked (rare to well-done), and JC would encode these relations spatially; that is, Rare, Medium-rare, Medium-well, Rare became a linear increase from rare to medium-well (omitting medium) down to rare again, expressed by the numbers 1241. The entrees were encoded primarily by association with the position of the person ordering.

It is important to note that these encodings are configural; that is, JC needed to attend simultaneously to all or at least most of the items to access the mnemonic pattern. JC encoded up to five items in a single encoding, which is sufficient for tables of three to five people. For tables of eight people, he grouped the items for the first four and last four people together, two encodings for four items each.

Because we want to emphasize the role of retrieval structures in skilled memory, let us simply state in passing that Ericsson and Polson, (1988, in

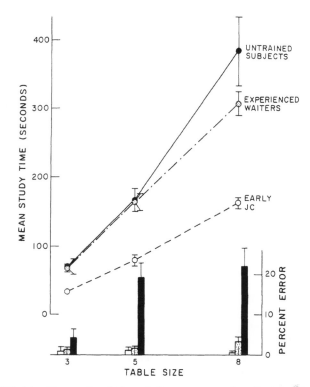

FIG. 9.2.   Mean total study times and percent errors of recall as a function of number of dinner orders (table size) to be memorized. (Untrained college students' performance [Ericsson & Polson, in press] is represented by the solid circles and bars; experienced waiters' and waitresses' performance [Crutcher & Ericsson, in preparation] by the dot-filled circles and bars, and JC's performance in Experiment 1 by the unfilled circles and bars.)

press) found extensive support for the two other principles of skilled memory, meaningful encoding, and practice-related speed up. Furthermore, Ericsson and Polson (in press) found clear evidence for storage in LTM from studies of postsession recall.

The claim that retrieval structure is an abstract entity can be supported by showing that the structure can be used for different types of information and stimuli. Further evidence could be provided by showing that the same retrieval structure can be used even when the order of presentation is dramatically varied. Ericsson and Polson (1988, in press) sought such evidence in a series of experiments.

In one experiment, JC was, as always, presented with dinner orders from customers in the standard clockwise order according to their placement around the table. This predictable order was contrasted with presentation orders, varying from trial to trial, in which the sequence of customers placing orders was randomly determined for each memory list. In both conditions of this experiment, JC recalled the dinner orders by categories, and the order of items followed the standard clockwise order. JC's accuracy of recall was very high and not different between conditions.

An analysis of JC's study times showed the only reliable difference between the two conditions occurred for study times for table sizes of eight customers. The absence of differences for table sizes of three and five customers suggest that items can be associated with the appropriate retrieval cues regardless of presentation order as long as only a single group of items for each category is involved. For table sizes of eight customers, JC used two equal groups corresponding to Customers 1-4 and Customers 5-8 for each item category. When presentation was random, he had to store and maintain items in both of these groups until all four items corresponding to one of the groups had been presented. Ericsson and Polson (in press) showed that accumulating all of the items for Customers 1-4 or Customers 5-8 and thus being able to store that group away led to a reliable decrease in JC's study time for the next dinner order. Think aloud protocols from memorization of tables with the random presentation order showed that JC immediately encoded items with their position within the retrieval structure and continued rehearsal of all items until all four items of a group had been presented (Ericsson & Polson, in press).

In two experiments, Ericsson & Polson (1988, in press) examined whether JC's memory skill would transfer to information other than dinner orders. The first experiment used lists of dinner orders and also materials with categories that matched the structural properties of categories in the dinner orders. The ordered category of meat temperatures ranging from rare to well-done was matched with a category of time intervals ranging from *second* to *week*. The five salad dressings were mapped onto five names of flowers with unique initial letters to allow for continued use of the first-letter mnemonic. The three starches were matched with three metals, and eight names of animals corresponded to the entrees.

After two or three sessions JC's performance on the new category items was nearly the same as his performance on dinner orders in the first experiment. All available indicators showed that he used the same processes for both the dinner orders and the new category material. In both conditions JC recalled the material by category, and even the order in which the categories were recalled was the same.

In the second experiment on transfer, JC was presented with items from categories in formats designed to hinder him from using his mnemonic encoding processes and his category-based storage. His performance was dramatically impaired, and in at least one condition his recall was no longer based on category but was based on the order in which the information was presented.

In sum, JC was able to use his retrieval structure in a flexible manner when the presentation order was dramatically varied. Furthermore, he was able to use the same structure to encode unfamiliar material that had a structure compatible with the mnemonic methods he used for dinner orders. With a few hours of practice on the unfamiliar material, JC's memory skill showed complete transfer. However, transfer was dramatically reduced when JC memorized material lacking a compatible structure and organization.

## Mental Calculation

Mental arithmetic is an ideal domain for exploring the generality of skilled memory theory mainly because the difficulty of mental calculation lies in the demands this task imposes on working memory. For example, an average college student has no difficulty in solving a problem such as 48,856 × 23 when external memory aids such as pen and paper can be used. The same student usually struggles to solve a simple multiplication problem like 24 × 36 when computations must be carried out mentally. The key to successful mental calculation is the ability to maintain the numbers of the problem and intermediate results in memory during periods of extended computational activity. Sophisticated strategies for managing memory are obviously required to solve problems like those given here quickly and accurately.

This section briefly summarizes some of the results from a training study in which two college students became expert mental calculators through extended laboratory practice (Staszewski, in press). At the outset of their training they were instructed to use a general strategy for multiplication used by most experts in mental calculation. One of the subjects, GG, received about 300 hours of practice over a 4-year period, and the other subject, JA, received about 175 hours of practice over 3 years. At the end of their training both subjects could maintain error rates under 10% and solve problems between 5 and 10 more quickly than they could at the beginning of the study. Generally they showed the greatest improvements in the conditions in which their solutions were initially the slowest and least accurate. Their solution times near the end of training are shown in Fig. 9.3.

The average solution times in Fig. 9.3 are organized by the number of digits in each problem. A 1 × 1 problem corresponds to the multiplication of two single digits, for example, 3 × 4, 9 × 7. A 2 × 5 problem corresponds to a two-digit number times a five-digit number, for example, 23 × 48,856, or 69 × 47,389.

Figure 9.3 also includes the solution times of a semiprofessional mental calculator, AB, for the same types of problems and presentation conditions. AB has practiced mental calculation on a daily basis for over 15 years and is recognized as one of the world's best contemporary mental calculators (Smith, 1983). AB's primary skill is in multiplying and calculating squares of numbers, and Chase (Chase & Ericsson, 1982) analyzed his procedures for squaring in detail. A comparison of AB's performance with that of the trained subjects clearly shows that both trainees achieved expert-level performance through practice. The following sections describe how they managed

Comparison of Trainees and AB

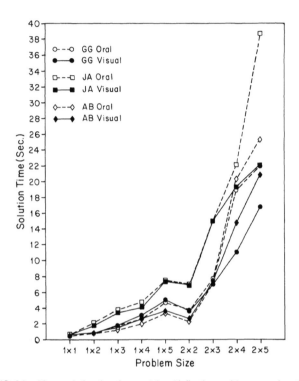

FIG. 9.3.    Mean solution time for mental multiplication problems as a function of the number of digits in the numbers multiplied. Each data point represents the solution times to 30 randomly-generated problems. Under visual presentation conditions, problem operands remain available for the subjects viewing throughout a trial. In the oral condition, problem operands are read once at the start of each trial. Source: "Skilled Memory and Expert Mental Calculation" by J. J. Staszewski, in M. T. H. Chi, R. Glaser, & M. J. Farr (Eds.), *The Nature of Expertise*. Hillsdale, NJ: Lawrence Erlbaum Associates.

the memory load imposed by this task and to what extent their strategies were congruent with the principles of skilled memory.

### Mechanisms of Expert Mental Calculation

The principle difficulty of mental calculation is remembering the operands of a problem and the intermediate results produced in the course of computing its solution. For all but the simplest of problems, novices tend to forget these critical pieces of information due to computational operations that intervene between their original encoding and later use. The speed and accuracy of experts' solutions clearly imply that they have found effective means to retain critical information. Theoretical analysis of the trainees' memory management strategies began by testing the hypothesis that task-critical information was stored in LTM. The recall paradigm repeatedly used to demonstrate the skilled memory effect was employed here. Following practice sessions in which the trainees were given 54 randomly-generated problems of varying size, they were sometimes asked to recall as many of the problems given in the session as they could.

After about 100 hours of practice, GG and JA could recall 31% and 37%, respectively, of the problems presented during daily sessions. As their training progressed, their recall improved gradually and toward the end of training, JA consistently recalled about 46% of the problems, on the average, and GG 61%. Although these results were consistent with the LTM storage hypothesis, relative to the postsession recall of the digit-span experts, the proportion of material these subjects recalled was small. Therefore, a more sensitive assessment of their reliance on LTM storage was made by testing their recognition of problems. The performance of the three experts, GG, JA, and AB, conformed to expectations: All could distinguish quite accurately between problems they had solved in a session and randomly generated distractor problems (GG 92% correct, JA 87%, AB 82%).

In addition, because it was possible to reliably infer the intermediate results GG generated in solving problems with two-digit multipliers, a recognition test was used to see if GG also stored these essential items in LTM. Results showed that his postsession recognition of these items was as accurate as his memory for problems. This further confirmed that mental calculation experts use LTM to maintain critical information.

How these expert calculators use LTM to achieve their exceptional performance can now be considered in more detail.

*Retrieval Structures.* Retrieval structures are abstract, hierarchical knowledge representations that experts develop to efficiently encode and retrieve large amounts of information in LTM. The key function of these mechanisms is to represent information in a manner that maintains serial order and supports speedy and reliable access to stored information when it is needed.

Two sources of evidence show that GG and JA use retrieval structures. One is the verbal protocols obtained from GG and JA as they performed their calculation. The second is a study examining the temporal structure of GG's responses in the studies of his postsession problem recall. Analyses of these data reveal that both GG and JA consistently coded digit strings representing problems or intermediate results in a remarkably regular and organized fashion. In a number of ways, their processes for encoding and retrieving important information parallel those used by the digit-span experts, DD and SF, to encode and retrieve random digits presented on digit-span trials.

Analyses of protocols taken as the trainees "thought aloud" while solving problems of varying size have produced several findings that confirm the role of retrieval structures in expert mental calculation. Both GG's and JA's protocols show that they consistently used abstract, hierarchically organized data structures to encode, represent, and retrieve digit strings of specific length in the course of their computations. Although clear individual differences in organization were apparent and the representational formats for digit strings varied with their length and function (i.e., problem operand, running product, or partial product), within subjects the same organizational format was nearly always used to represent strings of a specific length that served the same function.

Converging evidence that retrieval structures were used to represent problem operands in LTM comes from chronometric analyses of GG's responses in the problem-recall studies discussed earlier. If GG stored problem operands in LTM using the hypothesized abstract structures shown in the panels of Fig. 9.4, corresponding structural effects should be seen in his postsession recall of these items. Because GG recalled most problem operands in these sessions as sequences of individual digits, it was feasible to analyze the temporal structure of his output to test hypotheses about the organization of these items in memory.

Figure 9.4 shows the average time interval separating the individual digits of three, four, and five-digit multiplicands correctly recalled by GG in 20 postpractice problem recall sessions. Notice how these temporal patterns are consistent with the coding structures derived from the protocol data and depicted schematically in each panel. The plotted functions show that longer pauses separate digits located on either side of the predicted chunk boundaries.

An interesting feature of the trainee's use of retrieval structures is that they frequently use several structures simultaneously in the course of computation to maintain problem operands, running products, and partial products. Invariably, these structures are tailored to the material being stored; that is, the format used to represent a number is determined both by its magnitude and its function in a computational algorithm. Such precise adaptation of coding structures to the dimensions and computational role of to-be-remembered numbers may also serve as an important, if unintentional, strategy for combatting interference; storing task-critical information in unique structures may help the calculators to avoid confusing items held simultaneously in temporary storage.

In general, the trainees' strategic use of retrieval structures reflects their knowledge of their task environment. Their familiarity with particular solution algorithms and the intermediate knowledge states those algorithms produce enables them to anticipate future information needs and systematically code critical information in LTM in a way that facilitates its later retrieval.

***Semantic Codes in Mental Calculation.***    Consistent with previous studies of expert mental calculators, Staszewski (in press) found that JA and GG used

Pause Times in GG's Problem Recall

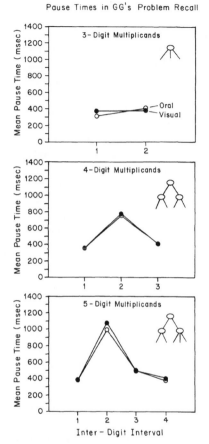

FIG. 9.4. Mean pause duration between digits in GG's recall of problem multiplicands in postsession problem recall. Included in each panel is the hypothesized structure used to encode and retrieve 3-, 4-, and 5-digit multiplicands. Source: "Skilled Memory and Expert Mental Calculation" by J. J. Staszewski, in M. T. H. Chi, R. Glaser, & M. J. Farr (Eds.), The Nature of Expertise. Hillsdale, NJ: Lawrence Erlbaum Associates.

semantic memory to recognize, encode, and efficiently solve familiar problems and subproblems. Indeed, several researchers have noted the rich knowledge bases that calculation experts exploit to achieve remarkable solution times. For example, Hunter (1968) reported that Professor Aitken, one of the world's premier mental calculators, could retrieve the factors of all three-digit and many four-digit numbers instantaneously. Bryan, Lindley, and Harter (1941) reported that another calculation expert, AG, knew "by heart" the multiplication tables up to 130 × 130, the squares of all numbers up to 130, the cubes of numbers to 100, and more. Chase (Chase & Ericsson, 1982) found that AB also drew upon a huge knowledge base of numerical facts to square multi-digit numbers with exceptional speed. Of course, these experts devoted decades of practice to their skills. With much less practice, JA and GG developed similar, if less extensive, knowledge bases of interrelated and easily accessible arithmetic facts and patterns used to facilitate their computations. In informal terms, both protocols and experimental evidence indicate that JA and GG had "expanded their multiplication tables," and, like AB, adjusted their computational strategies to their recognition of familiar patterns of information.

From a functional standpoint, Staszewski's (in press) analysis suggests that the factual knowledge bases that these experts developed support efficient calculation in two important ways. First, recognizing and coding new problems or subproblems in terms of an organized semantic network creates relatively unique and easily accessible memory codes. Second, strong associations linking problems to their products within such networks enable experts to substitute retrieval for computation as a means of solving certain problems. Notice here the parallel between expertise in mental calculation and chess. In both domains, experts develop LTM representations that are used to recognize and encode familiar patterns (Chase & Simon, 1973a, 1973b). Such encoding is reflected in the skilled memory effect. In the application of their skills, experts' recognition of such patterns then drives the selection and use of efficient processing strategies (Simon & Chase, 1973; Staszewski, in press).

One source of evidence for the trainees' recognition and exploitation of familiar numerical patterns is a qualitative change that appeared in their protocols and practice performance after about 200 practice sessions. With increasing regularity in practice sessions, the trainees began to report solutions to 1 × 2 problems in a fraction of the expected time, given problem size. Asked to retrospectively report their computational activities on such occasions, they reported knowing the answers to certain problems immediately upon their presentation. Rather than solving such problems by reducing each to a sequence of simple multiplication or addition operations involving pairs of single digits, they found they could simply retrieve answers to some problems. Just as most adults recognize that the product of 4 × 25 is 100 without engaging in a sequence of computational steps, with practice, GG and JA gradually increased the number of problems whose products they could retrieve instead of compute. The most obvious advantage of replacing computation with retrieval was shown in a study testing GG on all problems with single-digit multipliers and two-place multiplicands (Staszewski, in press). After each trial, he reported the solution strategy he used. For visually presented problems, his mean solution time was 631 msec (SE = 6) for problems on which he reported using retrieval. He averaged 1,014 msec (SE = 36) for problems on which he reported using a fully computational strategy.

This qualitative shift and the performance benefits that result extend beyond problems that call for multiplying a single-digit number by a two-digit number. Both concurrent and retrospective verbal protocols showed that JA and GG consistently recognized familiar 1 × 2's embedded within larger problems (i.e., 1 × 3 to 2 × 5 forms) immediately upon their presentation and adjusted their computational plans accordingly. Consistent with their reports, solution times for such problems tended to be faster than the solutions for problems within which familiar subproblems were not detected.

In general, the improvements in the trainees' postsession recall as a function of practice suggests that the development of a rich arithmetic knowledge base serves a mnemonic function while also affecting improvements in calculation speed. The trainees' development and use of such a knowledge base is consistent with skilled memory theory's meaningful encoding principle.

*Evidence for Speed Up.*   In order to explore the relation between memory load and performance, the manner in which problems were presented to the trainees in practice was manipulated throughout this study. Half of the problems in each practice session were presented visually and their operands remained displayed until their solutions were given. Problems on the remaining trials were read once to the trainees, forcing them to retain both problem operands in memory during their computations. Thus, oral presentation imposes a greater memory load. As expected, both trainees were considerably faster and more accurate in solving visually presented problems at the start of their training. This was especially the case for GG, who actively exploited the externally represented information in the visual condition. With practice, however, his margin of superiority in the visual condition gradually diminished and differences in average calculation speed for the two presentation conditions finally disappeared after about 500 practice sessions. This outcome implies that with practice GG developed the ability to store problem operands in LTM and retrieve their contents nearly as efficiently as he could operate upon external problem representations.

### Conclusion

Chase's analysis (Chase & Ericsson, 1982) of AB's exceptional squaring abilities suggested that his strategies for managing memory involved the use of retrieval structures and meaningful semantic codes. The results of the mental calculation training study highlighted here show that expertise in mental multiplication is an acquired skill and that the acquisition of expertise in this domain is related to the development of (a) retrieval structures, (b) memory codes for representing meaningful patterns of information, and (c) increasing efficiency in the use of the foregoing LTM mechanisms. These studies lead us to conclude that skilled memory is a major component of expertise in mental calculation.

### Chess

Chess has been a prototypical domain for studies of expertise since de Groot's (1978) and Chase and Simon's (1973a, 1973b) pioneering studies. Much of our current knowledge of expertise comes from or was inspired by these classic studies. The primary focus of this section is a special variant of chess known as blindfold chess. Apparently, chess players with a level of skill approaching that of a chess master are able to play blindfold chess essentially without practice at or close to their regular chess-playing strength. This ability is similar to the remarkably good memory of strong chess players for briefly presented chess positions shown by de Groot (1966, 1978) and Chase and Simon (1973a, 1973b). Before turning to blindfold chess, we discuss exceptional memory for briefly presented chess positions and relate it to skilled memory theory.

## Skilled Memory Theory and Memory for Chess Positions

Chase and Simon (1973a, 1973b) initially proposed that the superior memory of chess masters for briefly presented chess positions was mediated by recognition of integrated patterns of chess pieces called chunks, and pointers to these chunks that were maintained in STM. Further studies have shown that storage in STM is not necessary for recall and that the chess positions are encoded in LTM during their 5-second exposure time (Charness, 1976; Frey & Adesman, 1976). The encoding in LTM appears to be based on meaningful encoding of the relation of chess pieces. Lane and Robertson (1979) found that good chess players selecting the best move for a chess position (meaningful encoding) remembered as much about the chess configuration in a surprise recall (incidental condition) as they did when they had been told about the recall in advance (intentional condition). When the task was changed to a perceptual task that was unrelated to meaningful encoding of the chess position, like finding the number of chess pieces on light and dark squares, a large difference in memory was found between players in the intentional and incidental memory conditions.

Chase and Ericsson (1982) suggested that the superior memory of chess experts was consistent with skilled memory theory. Presented chess positions are rapidly encoded in LTM using knowledge about meaningful arrangements of chess pieces. The rapid extraction of meaningful patterns of chess pieces has been nicely demonstrated by Chase and Simon (1973a, 1973b) and Chi (1978). Chase and Simon (1973a, 1973b) assumed that chunks of chess pieces were distinct and that a given chess piece could therefore belong to only a single chunk. Chi (1978) showed that chess pieces occasionally belong to more than one chunk, a finding that suggests relations between the chunks from the same chess position. From retrospective verbal reports of grandmasters and masters after brief exposures to chess positions, de Groot (1978) found clear evidence for perception of chess pieces in chunks, or complexes, and also encodings relating chunks to each other to form a global encoding of the position. It appears necessary to assume that globally integrated encodings account for the ability of chess experts to accurately recall more than one briefly presented chess position (Frey & Adesman, 1976).

Until recently the evidence on representation of chess positions has come primarily from studies using free recall. However, Ericsson and Oliver's (1984) recent studies of blindfold chess used cued recall of information from memorized chess positions. With this technique Ericsson and Oliver were able to assess the availability of information about chess positions and to explore the role of retrieval structures in its retrieval.

### Blindfold Chess and Retrieval From Memorized Chess Positions

In blindfold chess extreme demands are made on a player's memory representation of the current chess configuration. To play blindfold chess near the level of his or her regular chess-playing ability, a chess player not only needs an accurate account of the current chess position, but also rapid and flexible access to information about the chess position that supports selection of the best possible next move.

Ericsson and Oliver (1984) investigated the possibility that flexible retrieval of information about a chess position is mediated by a retrieval structure. They studied a young male chess player, PS, who was rated just below the level of chess master. PS had played blindfold chess a couple of times prior to this series of experimental studies, and a pilot study supported his claim that he could play blindfold chess at a level close to his normal playing strength.

In the first study, PS was presented with individual chess moves on a CRT and instructed to play out the game mentally. After about 40 moves into a game, Ericsson and Oliver evaluated PS's memory for the then-current chess position. They used a notation that uniquely specified each square of a chessboard as the intersection of a column, denoted by a letter from a through h, and a row, denoted by a number from 1 to 8. Their method was to present the chess notation for one square of the chessboard, for example a4 or g2, and to ask PS to name the piece in that square or report "nothing" as fast as possible. All 64 squares of the chessboard were probed with this method in random order. For purposes of comparison, Ericsson and Oliver also had PS follow the same procedure with an actual chessboard on which he could move the pieces and see the then-current chess position at the time of the test.

Surprisingly, PS required only around 2 seconds to make a move in the blindfold condition. In fact, this response time was faster than the corresponding times for the perceptual condition. PS was also very accurate—over 95% correct—in responding to the probes in the test of his memory for the current chess position. His average latency of response to a probe for a square on the chessboard was around 2 seconds for the blindfold condition, about a second slower than his response when he could see the chess position. Considering the rapid updating of the chess position prior to testing, PS's rapid access of the contents of any square of the chessboard is remarkable. It also suggests that he can generate mental cues corresponding to any location on the chessboard to retrieve information from LTM to identify which chess piece, if any, stood in the probed location. The set of mental cues allowing selective access of information in any square of the chess board represents the retrieval structure "index" for the meaningful information related to a particular chess position.

A straightforward prediction from the use of a retrieval structure to access information from a chess position stored in memory is that considerable interference will occur if the player is required to retrieve information about two different chess positions concurrently. In another experiment, rather than mentally playing through 30 to 40 moves to reach a middle-game chess position, PS memorized two middle-game chess positions presented in sequence. His average study time for each board was 11 seconds, which incidentally corresponds to about two 5-second exposures to a given chess position. After PS had memorized the two chess positions, he was probed for the contents of the 64 squares on both boards according to one of three specific presentation orders. In the sequential condition, all squares of one position were probed in random order and then all squares of the other position. In the alternating condition, randomly selected squares from both positions were probed in a strict, alternating fashion. In the third condition, the squares probed were randomly selected from both positions.

PS's latency to report the contents of probed locations differed distinctly for these recall conditions. Probes randomly selected from the two boards took 2.4 seconds, and in this condition there was no reliable speed-up with further probes. This result is illustrated by a horizontal line in Fig. 9.5. Probes alternating between the two boards were intermediate with an average recall latency of 1.9 seconds, and in this condition there was a reliable but small decrease in recall latency, indicated by the sloping line in Fig. 9.5.

The recall latencies for the sequential condition are also plotted in Fig. 9.5. The first couple of recall latencies in this condition were indistinguishable from the recall latencies of the other condition, but after just a few successive retrievals from the same board, retrieval was very fast. In Fig. 9.5, a clear peak corresponds to the start of retrieval from the other board at Trial 65. It is remarkable that within about 3 probes from this new board, retrieval was as fast as it was for the first board, which at this point was well-entrenched in PS's mind. The retrieval times are just over 1 second, which incidentally is close to the times observed for perceptually available chess positions in the experiment previously described.

These results suggest that PS used a common retrieval structure because only a single chess position at a time can be thus accessed. Additional support for this interpretation comes from a detailed analysis of the data in the random order condition. This analysis examined runs of various lengths when PS consecutively retrieved probes from the same board. Figure 9.6 shows his recalled latency as a function of the number of times a square on the same

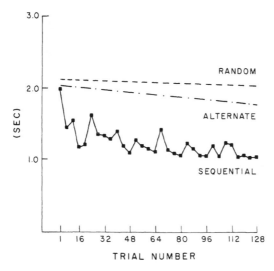

FIG. 9.5. Mean reaction time to name the piece, if any, occupying a specified square of one of the two chess positions as a function of serial order of probe and three presentation conditions.

board was recalled on the immediately preceding trials. The benefit of recalling from the same board on successive trials is clear, and it increases with further retrievals from the same board.

Another implication of the use of a retrieval structure to retrieve information from the chess position is that PS should have been able to retrieve information that was not related to the meaningful relations among chess pieces. After memorizing the board, he was probed for the number of pieces in each row and column and in all 49 possible instances of four adjacent locations forming a 2 × 2 square, for example the squares a1, a2, b1, and b2. Alternating with a randomized sequence of these complex probes were probes for the contents of individual squares. In this experiment PS was again urged to be accurate, and his accuracy was 98.5% for the complex probes and 99% for the simple probes.

Figure 9.7 shows the average retrieval time for simple location probes (1.3 seconds), 2 × 2 squares (3.9 seconds), rows (5.4 seconds), and columns (5.2 seconds). It also shows the time to report the corresponding information from a perceptually available chessboard. Although the retrieval times are impressively rapid, a considerable difference between retrieval from memory and perceptual report remains.

In a final condition PS was told to relax the accuracy criterion and concentrate on speed. The response latencies for the same types of probes are given in Figure. 9.8. The reduction in retrieval time for the complex memory probes is close to 50%. For the complex probes, the difference between perceptual and memory retrieval is reduced to 1 second, and for simple probes to about 200 msec. That is, retrieval of pieces from memory was faster than the naming of pieces in the earlier condition in which accuracy was stressed and the positions were perceptually available. How much did this speed-up cost in terms of accuracy? Essentially nothing! Accuracy remained at 99% for simple probes and was only slightly reduced to 95.1% for the complex probes.

This last experiment also made it possible to compare the mechanisms underlying retrieval from memory and from a perceptually available chess position. It is apparent that these processes are qualitatively different when the patterns of retrieval time across types of probes are compared. In the perceptually available condition PS retrieved the number of pieces faster for rows and columns than for the 2 × 2 squares, even though the number of squares considered in a row or column is twice as large as the number in a 2 × square. In the memory condition he took much longer to retrieve the number of pieces in rows and columns than to retrieve the number in 2 × squares. This finding is consistent with some form of serial processing of the individual squares. This experiment shows that PS is able to use his retrieval structure to very efficiently retrieve information from memory about a chess position. The temporal characteristics of his memory retrieval imply a dif-

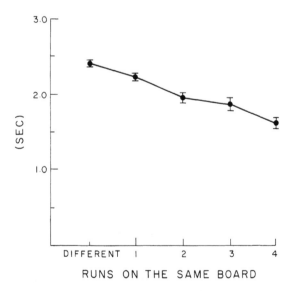

FIG. 9.6. Average reaction time in the piece-retrieval task in the random condition as a function of the number of consecutive times that the same chess position had been retrieved from an immediately preceding retrieval trial.

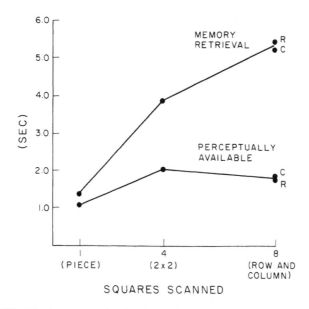

FIG. 9.7. Average reaction time in the piece-retrieval task and the piece-counting task for 2 × 2 squares and rows (R) and columns (C) for perceptually available chess positions and for memorized chess positions.

ferent set of processes than those used to perceptually extract the same information from a visually available chess position.

In another series of experiments, Ericsson and Oliver (1984, in preparation) examined the retrieval of chess-related information such as the number of black pieces attacking a square. PS's retrieval of the number of attacks appeared to be governed by a sophisticated search constrained by knowledge about the chess position. One of Ericsson and Oliver's (in preparation) last experiments tested whether PS used some of the study time to make additional encodings not normally made during a 5-second exposure as used in the original Chase and Simon (1973, 1973b) studies. In this experiment, PS was shown the chess positions for 5 seconds and immediately given the cued recall test. PS's accuracy of recall hardly dropped and was 96% correct for location of pieces. His retrieval times were almost indistinguishable from those in earlier experiments and averaged 1.4 seconds for information about individual squares.

In sum, several experiments using cued-recall procedures demonstrated that PS was able to access information about any part of the chess position within seconds. PS was particularly fast in naming the pieces in randomly determined locations of the chessboard. If allowance is made for the time necessary to perceive the probe on the CRT, PS's time for actual retrieval was consistently less than 1 second. Hence, PS appears to have associated the pieces of the chess position with retrieval cues specifying their locations and providing him with flexible access to the information about the chess position.

## Summary and Comments

Our analyses of expertise in three different content domains yielded findings that are consistent with the principles of skilled memory. In all three examples there was evidence for the experts' use of meaningful encodings drawing on existing knowledge and patterns and on the strategic use of retrieval cues at encoding and retrieval. The evidence for speed up was particularly salient for the mental calculators, but was also present in further testing of people who were already experts, such as the waiter (Ericsson & Polson, in press) and the chess master (Ericsson & Oliver, in preparation). We have consistently found that experts cope with the memory demands of their respective tasks in ways that are consistent with skilled memory theory.

It is also interesting to see the clear differences in the details of the retrieval structures for the three skills. Each of these differences can be viewed as a straightforward adaptation to the demands of the particular skill. The mental calculation experts were following very familiar algorithms and could therefore fully anticipate when and how access of information would be

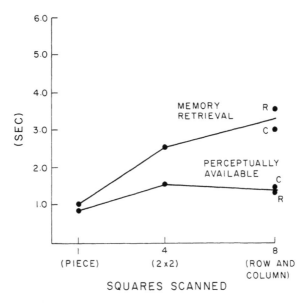

FIG. 9.8.   Average reaction time in the piece-retrieval task and the piece-counting task for 2 × 2 squares and rows (R) and columns (C) for memorized and perceptually available chess positions with an instruction to respond rapidly.

needed. The waiter, in contrast, was heavily influenced by his environment and required more flexibility in storage to anticipate the order in which information (i.e., dinner orders) would be presented. A common denominator among these experts is that all knew exactly how task-critical information should be encoded at the time of presentation so that it could be easily accessed later.

The situation was quite different for the chess master. In blindfold chess it is essential to be able to review all possible move sequences for a given chess position. Hence if a chess position were directly encoded in terms of its significant relations for a particular plan or strategy, it would be nearly impossible for the player to change in response to an opponent's unexpected moves. From Ericsson and Oliver's (1984) analyses it appears that the chess master preserved a representation of the chess position that allowed him to search and explore it as he would a perceptually available chess position.

These three case studies represent only a beginning in the analysis of the memory mechanisms associated with expertise. They demonstrate that such detailed analysis is feasible and also show the variety of skills in which skilled memory supports expert performance.

## CONCLUDING REMARKS

This chapter describes common features discovered in the skills of different experts in different areas. Our studies of exceptional memory show that the three principles of skilled memory theory characterize the exceptional skills of mnemonists trained in our laboratories. Other researchers' analyses of exceptional mnemonists indicate that these principles generalize broadly. Studies of a waiter with exceptional memory for dinner orders, mental calculation experts, and blindfold chess show that the mechanisms of skilled memory mediate the extraordinary performance of experts in these domains. This evidence and the broad empirical support for the skilled memory effect suggests that future studies examining the structures and processes that support expert performance in additional domains will likewise uncover evidence for the mechanisms proposed by skilled memory theory. At the very least, skilled memory theory offers a viable theoretical framework for guiding future studies of expert-level skills.

Skilled memory theory confronts the paradox of expertise and claims that people not only acquire content knowledge as they practice cognitive skills, they also develop mechanisms that enable them to use a large and familiar knowledge base efficiently. We argue that skilled memory enables experts to rapidly encode, store, and retrieve information within the domain of their expertise and thereby circumvent the capacity limitations that typically constrain novice performance. The result is that experts enjoy an enhanced, but not unbounded, functional working memory capacity. Evidence for the effects of limited-capacity attention and STM in expert performance indicates that these information-processing bottlenecks are not eliminated by the development of skilled memory, but the performance ceiling they impose is raised as long as experts tread familiar ground.

How do these findings advance our theoretical understanding of expertise? Chase and Simon's work provides the benchmark for measuring progress. Like their original chunking theory, skilled memory theory asserts that acquired knowledge enables experts to quickly encode and retain large amounts of information in LTM. Both theories also restrict experts' information processing advantage to information typically dealt with in particular tasks or domains. In both theories, chunking is the mechanism experts use to encode meaningful patterns of information. The two theories differ in that skilled memory theory claims that experts also have at their disposal mechanisms for indexing chunks in LTM that subsequently facilitate their rapid, reliable, and flexible retrieval. Moreover, skilled memory theory asserts, with empirical support, that LTM storage and retrieval operations mediated by the chunking and retrieval structure mechanisms speed up with practice.

We do not suggest that skilled memory theory constitutes a comprehensive theory of expertise. Rather, it is a theoretical framework used to organize and explain the most general and compelling empirical phenomena uncovered by the relatively few studies that have investigated experts and their capabilities. It provides an account of how they employ their most distinguishing asset, knowledge, to overcome basic information-processing constraints that characterize the human mind and memory and achieve extraordinary levels of performance. Although expertise certainly depends upon more than skilled memory, the evidence discussed in this chapter leads us to view skilled memory as an integral part of human expertise, and possibly its foundation.

We close by noting that our findings and conclusions are closely related to the theoretical vision of Herb Simon. Our debt to Chase and Simon's (1973a, 1973b) pioneering work on expertise should be clear. A significant assumption of that early work is that expertise can be understood within a general model of the human memory system. At the same time, Simon (1976), ever one to ground broad theorizing on a firm empirical foundation, squarely faced the challenge of integrating expert performance with contemporary models of memory:

> Perhaps the safest conclusion for us to carry away from the experiments with the delayed recall paradigm (i.e., the skilled memory effect) is that the data do not yet provide us with a convincing reason for abandoning the main outlines of the three-memory model. They do give us additional reasons, however, to look more closely at the structures and properties of long-term memory, and particularly at the special properties of the (indexing) and semantic components of that memory. They add further plausibility to the notion that storage of new information in semantic memory may be quite rapid. (p. 79)

The studies described in this chapter have taken just such a look at the structures and properties of the memory systems, particularly LTM, that mediate expert performance. These studies provide solid empirical support for skilled memory theory and suggest that skilled memory is a fundamental general component of expertise. Moreover, this work offers theoretical insights into how the general memory architecture that Simon (1976) described can accommodate many empirical phenomena related to expertise.

## REFERENCES

Anderson, J. R. (1987). Skill acquisition: Compilation of weak-method problem solutions. *Psychological Review, 94,* 192–210.

Anderson, J. R., Farrell, R. G., & Sauers, R. (1984). Learning to program in LISP. *Cognitive Science, 8,* 87–129.

Baddeley, A. D. (1976). *The psychology of memory.* New York: Basic Books.

Barsalou, L. W., & Bower, G. H. (1984). Discrimination nets as psychological models. *Cognitive Science, 8,* 1–26.

Bartlett, F. C. (1932). *Remembering: A study in experimental and social psychology.* New York: Macmillan.

Broadbent, D. E. (1958). *Perception and communication.* London: Pergamon Press.

Broadbent, D. E. (1975). The magical number seven after fifteen years. In A. Kennedy & A. Wilkes (Eds.), *Studies in long-term memory.* New York: Wiley.

Bryan, W. L., Lindley, E. H., & Harter, N. (1941). *On the psychology of learning a life occupation.* Bloomington, IN: Indiana University Publications.

Charness, N. (1976). Memory for chess positions: Resistance to interference. *Journal of Experimental Psychology: Human Learning and Memory, 2,* 641–653.

Chase, W. G., & Ericsson, K. A. (1981). Skilled memory. In J. R. Anderson (Ed.), *Cognitive skills and their acquisition.* Hillsdale, NJ: Lawrence Erlbaum Associates.

Chase, W. G., & Ericsson, K. A. (1982). Skill and working memory. In G. H. Bower (Ed.), *The psychology of learning and motivation* (Vol. 16). New York: Academic Press.

Chase, W. G., & Simon, H. A. (1973a). The mind's eye in chess. In W. G. Chase (Ed.), *Visual information processing.* New York: Academic Press.

Chase, W. G., & Simon, H. A. (1973b). Perception in chess. *Cognitive Psychology, 4,* 55–81.

Chi, M. T. H. (1978). Knowledge structures and memory development. In R. S. Siegler (Ed.), *Children's thinking: What develops?* Hillsdale, NJ: Lawrence Erlbaum Associates.

Chi, M. T. H., Feltovich, P. J., & Glaser, R. (1981). Categorization and representation of physics problems by experts and novices. *Cognitive Science, 5,* 121–152.

Chi, M. T. H., Glaser, R., & Farr, M. J. (Eds.). (in press). *The nature of expertise.* Hillsdale, NJ: Lawrence Erlbaum Associates.

Chiesi, H. L., Spilich, G. J., & Voss, J. F. (1979). Acquisition of domain-related information in relation to high and low domain knowledge. *Journal of Verbal Learning and Verbal Behavior, 18,* 257–273.

Crutcher, R. J., & Ericsson, K. A. (in preparation). *Assessing the structure of skill in memory for dinner order in experienced waiters and waitresses.*

de Groot, A. (1966). Perception and memory versus thought: Some old ideas and recent findings. In B. Kleinmuntz (Ed.), *Problem Solving* (pp. 19–50). New York: Wiley.

de Groot, A. (1978). *Thought and choice in chess.* The Hague: Mouton.

Ericsson, K. A. (1985). Memory skill. *Canadian Journal of Psychology, 39,* 188–231.

Ericsson, K. A., & Chase, W. G. (1982). Exceptional memory. *American Scientist, 70,* 607–615.

Ericsson, K. A., Chase, W. G., & Faloon, S. (1980). Acquisition of a memory skill. *Science, 208,* 1181–1182.

Ericsson, K. A., & Faivre, I. (in press). What's exceptional about exceptional abilities? In L. K. Obler & D. Fein (Eds.), *The exceptional brain.* New York: Guilford Press.

Ericsson, K. A., Fendrich, D., & Faivre, I. (in preparation). *A chronometric analysis of the acquisition of exceptional digit-span performance.*

Ericsson, K. A., & Oliver, W. (1984, November). *Skilled memory in blindfolded chess.* Paper presented at the Annual Psychonomic Society Meeting, San Antonio, TX.

Ericsson, K. A., & Oliver, W. (in preparation). *An analysis of skilled memory for chess positions in a chess master.*

Ericsson, K. A., & Polson, P. G. (1988). An experimental analysis of the mechanisms of a memory skill. *Journal of Experimental Psychology: Learning, Memory, and Cognition, 14,* 305–316.

Ericsson, K. A., & Polson, P. G. (in press). Memory for restaurant orders. In M. T. H. Chi, R. Glaser, & M. J. Farr (Eds.), *The nature of expertise.* Hillsdale, NJ: Lawrence Erlbaum Associates.

Ericsson, K. A., & Simon, H. A. (1984). *Protocol analysis.* Cambridge, MA: MIT/Bradford.

Frey, P. W., & Adesman, P. (1976). Recall memory for visually presented chess positions. *Memory & Cognition, 4,* 541–547.

Glanzer, M., & Razel, M. (1974). The size of the unit in short-term storage. *Journal of Verbal Learning and Verbal Behavior, 13,* 114–131.

Gordon, P., Valentine, E., & Wilding, J. (1984). One man's memory: A study of a mnemonist. *British Journal of Psychology, 75,* 1–14.

Hayes, J. R., & Flower, L. S. (1986). Writing research and the writer. *American Psychologist, 41,* 1078–1089.

Hitch, G. J. (1978). The role of the short-term working memory in mental arithmetic. *Cognitive Psychology, 10,* 302–323.

Hunt, E., & Love, T. (1972). How good can memory be? In A. W. Melton & E. Martin (Eds.), *Coding processes in human memory.* New York: Holt.

Hunter, I. M. L. (1968). Mental calculation. In P. C. Wason & P. N. Johnson-Laird (Eds.), *Thinking and reasoning.* Baltimore, MD: Penguin.

Jeffries, R., Turner, A. A., Polson, P. G., & Atwood, M. E. (1981). The processes involved in designing software. In J. R. Anderson (Ed.), *Cognitive skills and their acquisition.* Hillsdale, NJ: Lawrence Erlbaum Associates.

Kliegl, R., Smith, J., & Baltes, P. B. (1986). Testing-the-limits, expertise and memory in adulthood and old age. In F. Klix & H. Hagendorf (Eds.), *Proceedings of symposium in memoriam Hermann Ebbinghaus.* Amsterdam: North Holland.

Lane, D. M., & Robertson, L. (1979). The generality of levels of processing hypothesis: An application to memory for chess positions. *Memory & Cognition, 7,* 253–256.

Larkin, J. H., McDermott, J., Simon, O. P., & Simon, H. A. (1980). Expert and novice performance in solving physics problems. *Science, 208,* 1335–1342.

Lesgold, A. M. (1984). Acquiring expertise. In J. R. Anderson & S. M. Kosslyn (Eds.), *Tutorials in learning and memory* (pp. 31–60). San Francisco, CA: W. H. Freeman.

Miller, G. A. (1956). The magical number seven, plus or minus two. *Psychological Review, 63,* 81–97.

Mueller, G. E. (1911). Zur Anlyse der Gedachtnistatigkeit und des Vorstellungsverlaufes: Teil I⅓ [Studies of memory and cognitive processes: Part I] *Zeitschrift fur Psychologie, Erganzungsband 5.*

Mueller, G. E. (1913). Neue Versuche mit Rueckle [New experiments with Rueckle]. *Zeitschrift fur Psychologie und Physiologie der Sinnesorgane, 67,* 193–213.

Mueller, G. E. (1917). Zur Analyse der Gedachtnistatigkeit und des Vorstellungsverlaufes: Teil II [Studies of memory and cognitive processes: Part 2]. *Zeitschrift fur Psychologie, Erganzungsband 9.*

Newell, A., & Rosenbloom, P. S. (1981). Mechanisms of skill acquisition and the law of practice. In J. R. Anderson, (Ed.), *Cognitive skills and their acquisition.* Hillsdale, NJ: Lawrence Erlbaum Associates.

Newell, A., & Simon, H. A. (1972). *Human problem solving.* Englewood Cliffs, NJ: Prentice-Hall.

Simon, H. A. (1976). The information-storage system called human memory. In M. R. Rozenzweig & E. L. Bennett (Eds.), *Neural mechanisms of learning and memory* (pp. 79–96). Cambridge, MA: MIT Press.

Simon, H. A., & Chase, W. G. (1973). Skill in chess. *American Scientist, 61,* 394–403.

Smith, E. E., Adams, N., & Schorr, D. (1978). Fact retrieval and the paradox of interference. *Cognitive Psychology, 10,* 438–464.

Smith, S. B. (1983). *The great mental calculators.* New York: Columbia University Press.

Spilich, G. J., Vesonder, G. T., Chiesi, H. L., & Voss, J. F. (1979). Text processing of domain-related information for individuals with high and low domain knowledge. *Journal of Verbal Learning and Verbal Behavior, 18,* 275–290.

Staszewski, J. J. (1988). The psychological reality of retrieval structures: An investigation of expert knowledge (Doctoral dissertation, Cornell University, 1987). *Dissertation Abstracts International, 48,* 2126B.

Staszewski, J. J. (in press). Skilled memory and expert mental calculation. In M. T. H. Chi, R. Glaser, & M. J. Farr (Eds.), *The nature of expertise.* Hillsdale, NJ: Lawrence Erlbaum Associates.

Staszewski, J. J. (in preparation). *Engineering human expertise.*

Susukita, T. (1933). Untersuchung eines ausserordentlichen Gedaechtnisses in Japan (I) [Study of exceptional memory in Japan]. *Tohoku Psychologia Folia, 1,* 111–154.

Susukita, T. (1933). Untersuchung eines ausserordentlichen Gedaechtnisses in Japan (II) [Study of exceptional memory in Japan]. *Tohoku Psychologia Folia, 2,* 14–43.

Tulving, E., & Thomson, D. M. (1973). Encoding specificity and retrieval processes in episodic memory. *Psychological Review, 80,* 352–373.

# 10

## Expertise and Learning: How Do We Think About Instructional Processes Now That We Have Discovered Knowledge Structures?

Robert Glaser
*University of Pittsburgh*

In the 1950s, when Herb Simon and his colleagues were warming up for later feats with complex information processing systems, experimental work and theory building in learning were arenas of hot activity in behavioral science. At that time we knew more about learning than we did about the competence and expertise that learning produce. Over the last three decades, this situation has reversed. Cognitive science has devoted energies to the investigation of performance in areas such as memory, problem solving, the structure of knowledge, human development, and intelligence; investigations of how knowledge and cognitive skill are acquired have been fewer. With the advance of our science, we are also looking closely at the relationships between theory, practice, and technology—a mature science should profit from their interrelationships. With this in mind, I want to ask what our current understanding of performance can contribute to learning and instructional theory and to examine this question further by describing how the design of instruction now reflects assumptions about the acquisition of knowledge and skill.

The introduction of Newell and Simon's now classic *Human Problem Solving* (1972) laid out certain premises about the directions that the science of cognition has since taken. The stance they struck on learning and development in a section entitled "Emphasis on Performance" explained that "Turning to the performance-learning-development dimension, our emphasis on performance . . . represents a scientific bet. . . . What sort of information processing system a human becomes depends intimately on the way he develops. . . . Yet, acknowledging this, . . . we have too imperfect a view of the system's final nature." Newell and Simon saw benefits and costs of scientific patience:

> The study of learning takes its cue, then, from the nature of the performance system. If performance is not well understood, it is somewhat premature to study learning. . . . It is our judgment that in the present state of the art, the study of performance must be given precedence, even if the strategy is not costless. Both learning and development must then be incorporated in integral ways in the more complete and successful theory of human information processing that will emerge at a later stage in the development of our science. (pp. 7–8)

Then, in a section entitled "A Content-Oriented Theory," they fleshed out a conception of performance that indicated a departure that cognitive science's approach represented.

> By attempting only to describe basic universal processes used by humans . . . psychology was [earlier] ignoring a major part of its domain. The present theory is oriented strongly to content. . . . The importance of the orientation . . . is twofold. On the one hand, it removes a barrier toward extension of the theory. On the other hand, if content is a substantial determinant of human behavior . . . then information processing theories have opportunities for describing human behavior veridically that are foreclosed to theories unable to cope with content. (pp. 10–11)

Furthermore, they offered early documentation of the mystery of expertise in a telling account of the perceptual aspect of competence revealed when chess masters display automaticity in responding to chessboard features, that is, when they determine move possibilities without explicit, verbalized problem solving. "Defining the situation is an important type of information processing to understand, since it contrasts sharply with search activity, which so far has been the mainstay of the cognitive activity in analyzing a chess position. . . . There is clear evidence that this first act of definition differs substantially from all the others" (p. 761).

With these preambles, the seeds of the study of competent performance and expertise were sown. The focus was the products of learning and experience over time—the properties that characterize highly competent performance systems. This influential introduction looked ahead to a history that marks the last 25 years as an era when cognitive psychology profited from fundamental investigations in the general tasks of problem solving and in specific domains of knowledge and skill. Studies devoted to learning, transition mechanisms, and interventions that fostered the acquisition of knowledge and cognitive skills, even as a test of theory, were noticeably fewer. Only quite recently has attention to these matters increased, as Newell and Simon anticipated they would; we now look ahead to what they saw as "a later stage in the development of our science" (p. 8). The discovered properties of competence are informing investigations and theories of learning and development. Furthermore, from the view of instructional theory, these theories promise to be powerful enough to help produce the behavior whose acquisition they purport to explain.

The recognized advances in the analysis of competence and acquired knowledge and skill as they feed interest in theoretically grounded approaches to the processes, conditions, and activities of learning, set the theme of my commentary. It is defined by two questions: (a) What properties of the end state of expertise provide dimensions of acquisition that describe developing competence? (b) What principles of learning and conditions of acquisition are becoming apparent?

## COMPONENTS OF COMPETENT PERFORMANCE

Concepts that seem essential to the description of complex human behavior are now available. These include consideration of structures of knowledge and issues of knowledge accessibility; the quality of knowledge representation in problem solving; the development of automaticity and relationships between unconscious and controlled processing; the interplay of general heuristics and knowledge-derived processes; the uses and influence of mental models; and the significance of executive and self-regulatory processes (metacognition). As Feigenbaum makes clear in chapter 6 of this volume, the most impressive is the pervasive influence of structures of knowledge. In numerous domains, we have accounts of interacting organizations of information from which processes of competent cognition derive. In chapter 7 by Charness and 9 by Ericsson and Staszewski, research is presented on knowledge structures and cognitive processes that enable the efficiency, judgment, seeming intuition, and outstanding abilities displayed in highly competent performance. Yet, as I have said, we have identified properties of the state of attainment, but know less about the transformation operations that turn novice learners into increasingly competent individuals. How knowledge becomes organized and how the processes that accompany it develop with learning and experience are current fundamental questions. As with the older Piagetian account of development in children, stages are identified, but there is less to say about transition mechanisms.

Nevertheless, our advances in understanding of the nature of competence and the phenomena of expertise provide more fundamental analyses of the objectives of instruction than the behavioral objectives of older times and offer a new basis for studying learning, for designing the conditions of learning, and for assessing acquired competence. We know that, at various stages of learning, there exist different integrations of knowledge, different degrees of proceduralized and compiled skill, and differences in rapid access to memory—all of which shape the representations of tasks and differentiate levels of cognitive attainment. As they develop, these differences can signal advancing expertise or possible blockages in the course of learning. On the basis of these advances, a number of dimensions along which changes in levels of knowledge and skill occur can be identified. These dimensions define, in a general way, components of acquisition and potential criteria for a new psychometrics of developing proficiency; they become focal issues for learning theory and objectives for instructional interventions.

## Knowledge Organization and Structure

As competence is attained, elements of knowledge become increasingly interconnected, so that proficient individuals access coherent chunks of information rather than fragments. In various subject-matter domains, beginners' knowledge is spotty, consisting of isolated definitions and superficial understandings of central terms and concepts. With experience, these items of information become structured, are integrated with past organizations of knowledge, so that they are retrieved from memory rapidly in larger units. Ericsson and Staszewski's chapter explores this phenomenon by careful study of the processes that mediate superior memory performance in different domains of expertise. It appears that information is stored in LTM even for briefly presented materials, and exceptional memory retrieval in a domain of expertise is based on the structured content of stored information. Thus, structuredness, coherence, and accessibility to interrelated chunks of knowledge become targets for explanation by learning theory and objectives for instruction.

## Depth of Problem Representation

Certain forms of representation are correlated with the high levels of ability to carry out the details of a task or the steps of a problem solution. It is now well known that novices work on the basis of the surface features of a task situation or problem, whereas more proficient individuals, as they approach a problem, make inferences and identify principles that subsume its surface structure. A related phenomena is experts' qualitative analysis prior to the execution of solution procedures, which enables them to infer additional relations and constraints defined by the task situation. This representational ability of experts, which reflects organization in the knowledge base, has been replicated in a variety of domains (e.g., Chi, Glaser, & Farr, 1988). The preeminence of expert pattern recognition is emphasized in the chapter by Charness, who points out that the expert virtually "sees" a different problem than the novice. Thus, ability for fast recognition and perception of underlying principles and patterns indicates developing competence that could be assessed by appropriate tasks in verbal and graphic situations. One of the challenges for studies of learning and instruction is to understand the motivational and instructional conditions by which novices can acquire expert pattern-recognition capabilities.

## Theory and Schema Change

In the course of learning, people modify their knowledge and develop schemata that facilitate more advanced thinking. Research has described how their naive theories influence individuals' learning (e.g., McCloskey, 1983). Even after a period of instruction, and although students have learned problem-solving algorithms, these naive theories often persist and may preclude the development of performance based on more sophisticated principles. Thus, the quality of students' theories and how they are attached to procedural skills become issues for studies of learning and instruction.

Of particular significance is the process of interrogation, confrontation, conflict, and discovery whereby rules and generalizations are tested and revised (Collins & Stevens, 1982). At any level of proficiency, a form of understanding and primitive theory may be available or can be devised by a teacher or teaching device and then used as a basis for working toward more encompassing explanations. By this view, knowledge acquisition is a sequential transition through a space of theories or mental models where each model is evolved, elaborated, and then transitioned to a next higher model (White & Frederikson, 1986). Anderson, in chapter 13, begins to describe mechanisms for a form of knowledge extrapolation in which causal information is extended by analogy to new problem-solving situations.

## Proceduralized and Goal-Oriented Knowledge

Studies of expert-novice differences suggest that the course of knowledge acquisition proceeds from declarative or propositional form to a compiled procedural condition-action form. Many chapters in this volume refer to this aspect of developing competence. Novices can know a principle, or a rule, or a specialized vocabulary without knowing how and where that knowledge applies. When knowledge is accessed by experts, it is bound to these conditions of applicability. This functional knowledge is closely related to experts' knowledge of the goal structure of a problem space. Experts and novices may be equally competent at recalling specific items of information, but the experts chunk these items in memory in cause and effect sequences that relate to the goals and subgoals of problem solution and that feedback information for further action. The progression from declarative to tuned procedural and goal-oriented information is a significant dimension of developing competence.

## Automaticity to Reduce Attentional Demands

In investigations of competence, it is apparent that experts are fast, despite limits in human ability to perform competing attention-demanding tasks (Schneider, 1985). This speed has particular implications for the interaction between basic and advanced components of cognitive performance that must be integrated in the course of skill acquisition. For example, in tennis, in reading, and in medical diagnosis, where attention may alternate between basic skills and higher levels of strategy and comprehension, automaticity is crucial to good performance; component processes must work well not only as they are separately taught and tested, they must become efficient enough to work together (Lesgold & Perfetti, 1978; Perfetti & Lesgold, 1979). In the development of higher levels of proficiency, some component skills need to become automatized, so that conscious processing capacity can be devoted to higher levels, as necessary. A dimension of developing competence, then, is the level of efficiency or automaticity required for subprocesses to have minimal interference effects (i.e., to have progressed to a point where they can facilitate and be integrated into total performance).

## Metacognitive Self-Regulatory Skills

The experience of experts enables them to develop executive skills for approaching problems and monitoring performance. Experts rapidly check their progress toward problem solutions; they are more accurate at judging problem difficulty, apportioning their time, asking questions, assessing their knowledge, and predicting the outcomes of their performance (Chi, Glaser, & Rees, 1982; Larkin, McDermott, Simon, & Simon, 1980; Simon & Simon, 1978). These self-regulatory skills vary in individuals and appear to be less developed in those with performance difficulties. Superior monitoring skills reflect the domain knowledge and representational capabilities of experts, and these skills contribute to the utility of knowledge. Knowledge of a rule or procedure is enhanced by overseeing its applicability and monitoring its use. Thus, self-regulatory skills are important candidates for learning and instruction and can be significant predictors of problem-solving abilities that result in new learning.

In sum, the cognitive analysis of performance has identified outcomes of learning that characterize acquired expertise. Now, we must ask, how can this knowledge of human competence guide the development of learning theories and the design of conditions that foster learning? The answer, to some extent, lies in events around us. Work proceeds on AI machine learning that is oriented toward understanding the details of human learning, and there are the beginnings of theories of skill and knowledge acquisition in work like that of Anderson and others. Furthermore, cognitive scientists are active in designing computer teaching machines and conducting other instructional investigations. Interaction between application and theory may be our best next step in the study of learning—as George Miller recently advised, in an essay discussing G. Stanley Hall, "When the next experiment in any program of research comes to seem too trivial to justify the effort of doing it, a useful application can do wonders to revitalize and redirect the work" (Miller, 1986, p. 295).

## APPROACHES TO INSTRUCTION

As an historical note, extrapolations from older theories of learning merit attention here. These are of interest because they illustrate belief in the unidirectional movement from theory to application. Because it was a bold thing to apply theory for instructional design, the notion of a mutually correcting system between theory and development was less attended to in the past than it is in attempts of the present day.

With earlier forms of learning theory, quite direct extrapolations to instruction were attempted. For example, stimulus sampling and Markov models of learning were used for optimization studies on the conditions of paired-associate learning, including beginning word recognition in reading and foreign language vocabulary. Transitions between states of learning were assessed by changes in response probability, and the postulation of different (continuous or all-or-none) models of these changes prescribed different instructional procedures (Atkinson, 1972; Atkinson & Paulson, 1972). The work stimulated by Skinner on programmed instruction attempted very direct application of the principles of operant conditioning, using techniques of successive approximations of response requirements, the interaction and fading of stimulus supports, and contingent feedback and reinforcement. From today's perspective, it is not so much these pedagogical techniques that are to be faulted, but our weak and trivial understanding of the nature of the performance that was to be acquired.

Brief sketches of four examples illustrate how modern cognitive theory takes into account the dimensions of competence that I have listed. These examples consider: the development of knowledge structures, the use of production system models of competence to facilitate the acquisition of procedural knowledge, specifications of the conditions of practice that influence automaticity, and self-regulatory strategies that foster the acquisition of cognitive skill.

### Knowledge Networks

The analysis of information structures in the form of knowledge networks as an approach to instruction is documented as beginning with Carbonell and Collins' (1973) work with the SCHOLAR program. This was a so-called mixed-initiative Socratic tutoring program in which both the system and the student could initiate conversation by asking questions; knowledge about the domain being tutored was represented in a semantic network. From a psychological point of view, this approach assumed an ideal model of the organization of knowledge as it might exist in human memory. Such a network, specified in advance, provided the type of organization of knowledge that is to be learned by the student. Starting with such a model, instruction proceeds by the student's interrogation of this structure and by providing information about errors that reflect differences between the student's knowledge structure and the ideal structure. Diagnostic and remedial techniques were envisioned to enable the student, when interrogated, to give answers that would be forthcoming from the ideal model. The instructional idea was that the semantic network that was first rationally imposed could be revised to approximate the student's memory organization more closely, and pedagogical procedures could be determined that effectively facilitated acquisition of the desired knowledge structure.

Over the last 15 years, with the growth of AI and computer tutors, the representation of knowledge structures has seemed less simple. For example, in Clancey's (1986, in press) work on medical diagnosis, several knowledge structures are involved: a medical knowledge base, a structure of inference procedures for diagnosis, and a set of teaching rules. In addition to the AI advances and complexities involved, from the point of view of learning theory, such attempts at explicit tutoring in the context of expert knowledge structures are forcing us to discover the kinds of representations that facilitate interaction between the domain expert, the expert teacher, and the learner's abilities for knowledge acquisition. What is particularly interesting in recent developments is the emphasis on understanding in guiding learning, that is, generating explanation in the course of instruction—explanation that indicates coherence in a knowledge structure on the basis of which inferences can be made, explanation that supplies forgotten or unlearned causal connections, and explanation that relates information being processed to prior information so that learning occurs. Understanding is encouraged in programs of this kind by a new relationship between students and subject matter in which knowledge and its use become objects of interrogation and hypothesis testing.

### Procedural Performance Analysis and Cognitive Skill Compilation

A number of principled instructional ideas are explicit in other work on computer tutoring. John Anderson and his colleagues' efforts (1984, 1985) to design programs that offer a structured plan for the procedures being taught are particularly prominent. An initial design principle is to identify a production system model of how successful students solve problems and make this problem-solving procedure explicit, as well as the search and inference processes required to produce it. Information and feedback correction are given to the student during problem solving. The principle involved in providing instruction in a problem-solving context is that memory retrieval and the encoding of information are increased because the context of recall matches the context of study. Presenting information during problem solving is assumed to attach knowledge to the conditions of its applicability and its relevant goals. Klahr and Carver (in press) have described a similar kind of principled instructional design where the cognitive objective of the curriculum is for students to acquire a goal structure as defined by a hierarchical model and to increase procedural efficiency by narrowing solution search.

In these instructional systems, the knowledge underlying problem-solving skill is represented as a set of if-then goal-oriented production rules. Errors or missing rules are monitored, and, as rules are learned, a compilation process is assumed by which, with experience in the domain, sequences of rules collapse into larger macro rules. As this occurs, the computer tutor or teacher can adjust the grain size of instruction. The tutor supports a gradual approximation of expert behavior by accumulation of separate parts of the performance and by updating partial products and subgoals to reduce memory load; these partially correct solutions are accepted and shaped into more completely correct solutions, in a manner reminiscent of Skinnerian programmed instruction. However, in contrast to older efforts on theory-generated instruction, this work is especially attuned to the constructive interaction between application and the correction of theory, and we look to see how the theory of skill acquisition will change with continued instructional experimentation.

## Automatic and Controlled Processing

A program of theoretical and instructional research on automaticity in *high performance skills,* such as visual search in air traffic control and electronic troubleshooting tasks, has been conducted by Walter Schneider (1985). Schneider's guidelines for training are based on the theory that skill results from the effective interaction of automatic and controlled processes. Experimental findings show that automatic processing typically develops when subjects deal with a stimulus consistently over many trials, and controlled processing is facilitated when they deal with novel or inconsistent information. Hence, the objective of training is to develop automatic skills through performance of routine, consistent task components, as well as to develop strategies concurrently to allocate limited controlled processing to inconsistent task components. In the course of instruction, information is presented to promote consistent performances of skill in order to develop fast, low-workload processing, using many speed-stress trials. Aspects of the task are varied so that automatic skill components generalize to the class of situations in which they are appropriate. Information for a component skill is presented in a context that illustrates the larger task goal, and various component skills are intermixed to facilitate distribution of practice and knowledge of their interrelationships. Executive regulatory skills are trained so that performance can be discriminated in situations that require different speed-accuracy trade-offs and judgments of task priorities. This work is of particular significance in its attempts to unpack the venerable term *practice* and to further the development of theory and technology on unconscious and conscious processing in high levels of performance.

### Self-Regulatory Strategies

Instructional programs in reading, writing, and mathematics that attend to the development and use of self-regulatory skills for learning are described in a recent paper by Collins, Brown, and Newman (in press). In each program, the teacher serves as the instructor. The training in reading skills involves such strategies as formulating questions, generating summaries, making predictions, and attempting to clarify difficulties in interpreting text (Palincsar & Brown, 1984). The approach to writing, which resembles that taken in Hayes' discussion in chapter 8, presents writing as a recursive task in which goals emerge and are refined as part of a process that draws on strategies for planning, organizing ideas, and revision (Scardamalia, Bereiter, & Steinbach, 1984; Scardamalia & Bereiter, 1985). The instruction in mathematical problem solving involves learning to use both problem-solving heuristics appropriate to different types of problems and (improving on Polya, 1957) control strategies, such as evaluating which heuristics apply, which get you closer to solution, and which you are best able to carry out (Schoenfeld, 1985).

All three programs highlight the planning and executive or monitoring properties of competent performance. As a way of fostering self-regulatory activities, cooperative learning is emphasized where students, among themselves and with teachers as models, alternate carrying out a procedure, generating questions and solutions, critiquing courses of action, and monitoring progress. In keeping with the goal-directedness and the conditionalized nature of competent performance, these programs encourage teaching in the context of problem-solving situations. They emphasize comprehension and meaningful outcomes as the objectives of cognitive strategies.

### COMMENT AND QUESTIONS

This chapter's title asks how we think about instructional processes now that we have discovered a great deal about the nature of knowledge and cognitive skill. In response, I have commented on how cognitive analyses of human performance have influenced approaches to facilitating learning. As learning theorists, however, we appear to be at the novice stage of less than integrated bundles of knowledge, and the power of knowledge-structure generated cognitive processes (Feigenbaum's Knowledge Principle) is not as evident as a fundamental aspect of instruction as I think it will be eventually. On the other hand, the picture of the goal states of competence is rich— certainly as compared with attempts at theory-generated instruction in the S-R and statistical learning theory days. Furthermore, the articulation between research and design has taken on the character of a mature science where attempts at application enrich theory and vice versa.

The scientific bet made in 1972 to concentrate on performance and on the steady-state system is paying off, and the move to the study of the content of expertise in knowledge-rich domains has been especially fruitful. What Newell and Simon referred to as a price for leaving learning as a second step should become apparent as attempts at building learning theory and theories of instruction proceed. Progress brings work and leaves questions. As an illustration, I present an instructional puzzle and a possibility. The puzzle is the rapid pattern recognition and fast representational ability acquired by the expert. The possibility is investigation of the ways in which learners instruct themselves to elaborate structures of knowledge (somewhat akin to the observation by Ericsson and Staszewski that memory skills are not taught but developed by the subjects themselves).

In his essay in the Tuma and Reif book (1980) generated by a previous CMU conference, Simon called attention to the importance of these two issues in research on learning and instruction. He referred to the first as the perceptual skill of problem solving and problem representation, and considered the second in terms of techniques of self-instruction generated in the context of learning from examples. For the first issue, as Neil Charness indicated, the mystery remains; from an instructional point of view, the possibilities for enhancing, systematizing, or shortcutting the learning experiences that result in rapid pattern recognition and deep-principled problem representation are unclear. The phenomenon certainly requires study, perhaps by investigations in which the systematic presentation of problems make the principled bases for solution increasingly apparent, or by using Schneider-type automaticity training, or by the invention of a magic bullet for motivation that encourages extensive practice.

On the second issue, we may be making a little headway. Simon and his colleagues, and others, have been studying learning from examples for some time. Micki Chi and I, with our colleagues, Miriam Bassok, Matthew Lewis, and Peter Reimann, have also been investigating this form of learning in physics problem solving (Chi et al., in press). We find interesting differences between good and poor learners that are apparent when they study examples and subsequently when they attempt to work out new examples by reference to the examples they have studied. Our protocol analyses show that good students make elaborations on the content of a problem that serve the functions of explicating the conditions or consequences of the situation and of chunking a set of problem statements to provide a goal for a series of procedures or equations. The elaborations of good students offer more inferences about the physical concepts that underlie the problem, whereas poor students paraphrase the presented information or produce incomplete inferences. Part of the reason that poor students do not make such elaborations is that they think they do understand; they frequently do not detect their comprehension failures. In contrast, good students detect the loci of their comprehension failures, and this recognition initiates elaboration and inferencing processes. With respect to how they refer to old examples while solving new problems, poor students use examples as an analog base from which they can make syntactic mappings, whereas good students use them mainly as a memory aid for familiar procedures and as a form of reference to check their answers. Thus, good students consult examples after they have a plan or have formulated an idea about how to solve a problem, whereas the poor students use the examples as a way to find a solution. These skills are apparent, but how are they derived and how can they be enhanced? Perhaps we can prompt students to use the effective behaviors. Or can we develop a technology of designing examples that does so? The learning problem emerges, and new work on learning and instruction will be shaped by what we know about the abilities of learners for self-instruction and self-explanation.

Finally, as someone who has devoted most of a career to inquiring how learning theory and instruction can inform each other, I conclude with deep gratitude to Herb Simon. I thank him for the years of work that have led to richer descriptions of the end-states of learning and the dimensions of acquired competence than we have ever had in the history of psychological and cognitive science. And I thank him also, I think, for returning me now to where I began, as a student, with the study of learning. I had thought, for a wild youthful moment, that we had that covered once before.

## ACKNOWLEDGMENTS

Preparation of this article was supported in part by the Office of Naval Research (#N00014-84-K-0542) and the Center for the Study of Learning (OERI #G008690005).

## REFERENCES

Anderson, J. R., Boyle, C. F., & Yost, G. (1985). The geometry tutor. In *Proceedings of International Joint Conference on Artificial Intelligence-85* (pp. 1–7). Los Angeles: International Joint Conference on Artificial Intelligence.

Anderson, J. R., Farrell, R. G., & Sauers, R. (1984). Learning to program in LISP. *Cognitive Science, 8,* 87-129.

Atkinson, R. C. (1972). Optimizing the learning of a second language vocabulary. *Journal of Experimental Psychology, 96,* 124-129.

Atkinson, R. C., & Paulson, J. A. (1972). An approach to the psychology of instruction. *Psychological Bulletin, 78,* 49-61.

Carbonell, J. R., & Collins, A. (1973). Natural semantics in artificial intelligence. *IJCAI, 3,* 344-351.

Chi, M. T. H., Bassok, M., Lewis, M. W., Reimann, P., & Glaser, R. (in press). Self-explanations: How students study and use examples in learning to solve problems. *Cognitive Science.*

Chi, M. T. H., Glaser, R., & Farr, M. (Eds.). (1988). *The nature of expertise.* Hillsdale, NJ: Lawrence Erlbaum Associates.

Chi, M. T. H., Glaser, R., & Rees, E. (1982). Expertise in problem solving. In R. Steinberg (Ed.), *Advances in the psychology of human intelligence* (Vol. 1, pp. 7-75). Hillsdale, NJ: Lawrence Erlbaum Associates.

Clancey, W. J. (in press). The knowledge engineer as student: Metacognitive bases for asking good questions. In H. Mandl & A. Lesgold (Eds.), *Learning issues for intelligent tutoring systems.* New York: Springer-Verlag.

Clancey, W. J. (1986). From GUIDON to NEOMYCIN and HERACLES in twenty short lessons: ONR final report 1979-1985. *AI Magazine, 7*(3), 40-60.

Collins, A., Brown, J. S., & Newman, S. E. (in press). Cognitive apprenticeship: Teaching the the craft of reading, writing, and mathematics. In L. B. Resnick (Ed.), *Knowing, learning, and instruction: Essays in honor of Robert Glaser.* Hillsdale, NJ: Lawrence Erlbaum Associates.

Collins, A., & Stevens, A. L. (1982). Goals and strategies of inquiry teachers. In R. Glaser (Ed.). *Advances in instructional psychology* (Vol 2, pp. 65-119). Hillsdale, NJ: Lawrence Erlbaum Associates.

Klahr, D., & Carver, S. M. (in press). Cognitive objectives in a LOGO debugging curriculum: Instruction, learning, and transfer. *Cognitive Psychology.*

Larkin, J. H. McDermott, J., Simon, D. P., & Simon, H. A. (1980). Models of competence in solving physics problems. *Cognitive Science, 4,* 317-345.

Lesgold, A. M., & Perfetti, C. A. (1978). Interactive processes in reading comprehension. *Discourse Processes, 1,* 323-336.

Miller, G. A. (1986). Dismembering cognition. In S. H. Hulse & B. F. Green, Jr. (Eds.), *One hundred years of psychological research in America* (pp. 277-298). Baltimore, MD: Johns Hopkins University Press.

McCloskey, M. (1983). Naive theories of motion. In D. Gentner & A. Stevens (Eds.), *Mental models* (pp. 299-324). Hillsdale, NJ: Lawrence Erlbaum Associates.

Newell, A., & Simon, H. A. (1972). *Human problem solving.* Englewood Cliffs, NJ: Prentice-Hall.

Palincsar, A. S., & Brown, A. L. (1984). Reciprocal teaching of comprehension-fostering and monitoring activities. *Cognition and Instruction, 1*(2), 177-175.

Perfetti, C. A., & Lesgold, A. M. (1979). Coding and comprehension in skilled reading. In L. B. Resnick & P. Weaver (Eds.), *Theory and practice of early reading,* (Vol. 1, pp. 57-84). Hillsdale, NJ: Lawrence Erlbaum Associates.

Polya, G. (1957). *How to solve it: A new aspect of mathematical method* (2nd ed.). Princeton, NJ: Princeton University Press.

Scardamalia, M., & Bereiter, C. (1985). Fostering the development of self-regulation in children's knowledge processing. In S. F. Chipman, J. W. Segal, & R. Glaser (Eds.), *Thinking and learning skills: Research and open questions* (Vol. 2). Hillsdale, NJ: Lawrence Erlbaum Associates.

Scardamalia, M., Bereiter, C., & Steinbach, R. (1984). Teachability of reflective processes in written composition. *Cognitive Science, 8,* 173-190.

Schneider, W. (1985). Training high performance skills: Fallacies and guidelines. *Human Factors, 27*(3), 285-300.

Schoenfeld, A. (1985). *Mathematical problem solving.* Orlando, FL: Academic Press.

Simon, H. A. (1980). Problem solving and education. In D. T. Tuma & F. Reif (Eds.), *Problem solving and education: Issues in teaching and research* (pp. 81-96). Hillsdale, NJ: Lawrence Erlbaum Associates.

Simon D. P., & Simon, H. A. (1978). Individual differences in solving physics problems. In R. Siegler (Ed.), *Children's thinking: What develops?* (pp. 325-348). Hillsdale, NJ: Lawrence Erlbaum Associates.

White, B., & Frederiksen, J. R. (1986). *Progressions of qualitative models as a foundation for intelligent learning environments* (BBN Report No. 6277) Cambridge, MA: BBN Laboratories.

# III

## INSTRUCTION AND SKILL ACQUISITION

# 11

## Situations, Mental Models, and Generative Knowledge

James G. Greeno
*Stanford University and*
*Institute for Research on Learning*

In the 30 years since cognitive science was pioneered by Newell, Shaw, and Simon's (1957) General Problem Solver, and by Chomsky's (1957) *Syntactic Structures,* an impressive body of scientific knowledge, concepts, and methods has been developed. As the chapters in this volume attest, the assumptions and methods of the complex information-processing approach provide a viable structure for a vigorous and progressive science of knowledge and cognition. This body of scientific knowledge and practice is in good health, and the information-processing framework is strong and appropriate for continuing to construct the kinds of results and analyses that have productively formed cognitive science within this point of view.

But this chapter asks a question about the adequacy of that framework, which does not seem able to hold many of the new issues that need to be addressed. If some different framing is required, then the assumptions and methods that support our scientific practice need more work. This chapter attempts to state where that work is needed. Fortunately, bodies of scientific knowledge and practice are not like physical buildings. If a building's foundation and structure are not adequate to support new construction, the building has to be rebuilt from the ground up. In science, it is quite feasible for work in building knowledge within an existing framework to go on at the same time as and in interaction with work that is addressing significant questions about the framework's adequacy.

This chapter questions whether our science of cognition is fundamentally limited because it deals only with symbolic computation. Many criticisms of modern cognitive science focus on the essentially symbolic nature of the knowledge that we know how to analyze; Searle's (1980) famous "Chinese room" parable[1] is the most familiar. The criticisms are often taken as claims that artificial intelligence is limited, but I believe the problem predates the so-called "computational" theory of mind. The view of knowledge as a network of associations and procedures for making inferences in the mind goes back at least to the British Associationists and probably to the classical Greeks. The fundamental question addresses epistemological assumptions. We may require a different way of thinking about knowledge.

Rather than thinking that knowledge is in the minds of individuals, we could alternatively think of knowledge as the potential for situated activity. On this view, knowledge would be understood as a relation between an individual and a social or physical situation, rather than as a property of an individual. A relativized concept of knowledge would be analogous to the concept of motion in physics. The velocity and acceleration of an object in motion are not properties of the object itself, but are properties of a relation between the object and a frame of reference. We do not yet understand the dependencies of knowledge on its contexts well enough to formulate a relativistic epistemology, but such an epistemology may be needed to provide an adequate framework for analyzing cognition in practice.

The reasons for considering a relational theory of knowledge are primarily empirical. One set of findings that seems particularly persuasive (i.e., troubling for our current epistemological beliefs) come from the ethnographic study of quantitative reasoning, sometimes called "everyday math." According to our usual understanding, mathematical knowledge is what students acquire in school, and their ability to solve quantitative problems in real situations depends (a) on the knowledge they have thus acquired and (b) on their ability to "transfer" that knowledge to the situation they are in. Recent research by Carraher, Carraher, and Schliemann (1983), Lave, Murtaugh, and de la Rocha (1984; also see Lave, 1988), and Scribner (1984) makes our usual understanding problematic. Children in Brazilian street markets who have little or no relevant schooling are able to determine the prices of lottery tickets that depend on the number of permutations of four or five numbers, and adults in California compute fractions of portions of food with methods that use resources in the situations, rather than symbolic computation. These accomplishments involve knowledge of quantitative properties in the domain of objects. The reasoning is situated, in that it uses resources in the situation rather than computations on symbols to arrive at conclusions.

---

[1]In Searle's parable, a man who does not know Chinese is locked in a room whose walls are lined with baskets that contain Chinese characters. Someone outside the room sends in rules for putting characters in sequences, which the man uses to compose strings that people outside interpret as sentences and stories. We would not say that the man inside the room understands the Chinese language. He is analogous to a computer program that can construct expressions that are meaningful to us, but the program does not understand language because it has no idea what the expressions mean.

An example that has become almost canonical is from de la Rocha's study (see Lave, 1988) of individuals who had recently enrolled in the Weight Watchers diet program. An interviewer asked, "How much cottage cheese would you have if you served three-fourths of the day's allotment, which is two-thirds of a cup?" After the man muttered that the had studied calculus in college, he measured two-thirds of a cup of cottage cheese, put it on the counter, shaped it into a circle, put a horizontal and a vertical line through it, set aside one of the quadrants, and served the rest. In school, students learn the symbolic operation of multiplying fractions. The dieter's solution was not obtained by multiplying "¾ × ⅔ = ½." Instead, his action was an operation on objects in the situation he was in.

An example given by Ginsburg (1977) illustrates the point in another way. Ginsburg interviewed a child who solved addition problems by aligning numerals from the left, as in the following:

$$\begin{array}{r} 10 \\ 1 \\ \hline 20 \end{array}$$

If a question was asked about numbers of objects, however—such as "if you have 10 books and I have one book, how many books do we have altogether?"—the child gave the correct answer. It turned out that the child had two separate procedures, cued by whether "plus" or "altogether" was used in the question. Whenever a question was phrased with "plus," numerals were written down aligned at the left. Whenever a question was phrased with "altogether," correct answers were given, apparently with a counting procedure. The child's procedure for operating on written symbols, cued by "plus," happened to be incorrect, but it seems safe to assume that many children with correct procedures have little or no understanding of the relations between their symbolic operations and the world of real quantities and numbers.

Another set of examples is in the literature on naive conceptions of physics. Students learn to solve textbook problems using formulas such as "$f = ma$," but they do not use the principles that the formulas express when they reason about events in the world. Thus, when students are asked, after they have taken physics, to draw the path of the weight of a pendulum if its string is cut suddenly at different points in its swing, they often draw straight vertical lines, an answer that ignores the Newtonian principles on which $f = ma$" depends (Caramazza, McCloskey, & Green, 1981). Another example involves predicting the motion of a ball that emerges from a curved tube, which many students say will continue to be curved, rather than the straight path that is the correct Newtonian prediction (McCloskey, Caramazza, & Green, 1980).

One response to these examples is to treat them as instances of the problem of transfer, which we all know is difficult. An alternative is to ask whether there may be something more fundamental involved. Lave (1988) has argued that the structure of information in school mathematics and the structures of settings of activity are very different. Settings of activity are organized according to the social and personal goals that individuals have, the physical and social resources available, and modes of interacting with the environment that are familiar. School subjects, including mathematics, organize information according to concepts and principles of academic disciplines and with the purpose of providing a coherent conceptual structure. For example, school mathematics relates multiplication of fractions, not surprisingly, to multiplication of whole numbers and the concept of fractions, contrasts it with addition of fractions, and so on. Those relations are not salient in the kitchen; therefore, when the problem is to determine a quantity of cottage cheese, it may not be surprising if the relevant piece of mathematical knowledge is not accessed. To retrieve the relevant piece of mathematical knowledge, a person would have to activate the organized domain of mathematics and find the piece that could be used to solve the problem at hand. Instead, in de la Rocha's example, the person built a solution out of components of the situation— the counter, properties of the cheese, and an operation of separating an object into parts.

The metaphor of Simon's ant (Simon, 1969) provides a way to state the issue. The metaphor concerns the elaborate path traversed by an ant on a sandy beach. We may have taken the wrong moral from Simon's image. Generally the story is thought to indicate that a very simple set of rules in the ant's mind can account for the path, given the complexity of the terrain. A sandy beach, however, is not complex in the same way that street markets and kitchens are complex. Beaches have many ups and downs, but very little structure, at least at the grain size that is relevant to an ant. Arenas of human activity, to use Lave's (1988) term, have complex structures involving both social and physical factors. The activities of individuals are situated in the social and physical contexts in which they occur. The situated character of activity is not reflected well in information-processing models, as Suchman (1987) and others have noted. In particular, the knowledge that individuals have for acting in an environment must incorporate detailed understanding of the structural features of the environment.

One approach to structured environments, advocated by Feigenbaum (chap 6 in this volume), simply builds a representation of that structure as part of the individual's knowledge. In this approach, domain-specific knowledge is like the rest of the individual's knowledge except that it does not apply as generally. Unfortunately, this approach does not reach the difficulty, which is to understand how the ant interacts with the beach when activity with the beach involves significant interaction between the ant's knowledge and the structure of the beach. To give the ant knowledge about the beach, and then have the ant's general knowledge interact with its specific knowledge about the beach, is not the same as accounting for the ant's interaction with the beach itself.[2]

## A VIEW OF SEMANTICS

To proceed toward a more adequate framework for analyzing the cognition of situated activity and reasoning, it is helpful to have some terminology for discussing aspects of the semantics of symbolic systems. Figure 11.1 presents some helpful distinctions, from Smith (1983).

On the left of Fig. 11.1 are symbolic expressions, and on the right are entities to which the symbolic expressions refer. Examples of symbolic expressions include written or spoken instructions, such as "Put the filter in the filter holder, put ground coffee beans in the filter, and slide the filter holder under the water compartment," or an algebra formula such as "$y = 2(0.2x)^2$." The entities that are referred to in the instructions include parts of a coffee maker, a substance, and actions of a person pouring the substance and assembling a device (cf. Larkin, chap 12 in this volume). The entities that are referred to in an equation may be quantities in a concrete situation or abstract entities, such as variables and functions.

Both the symbols of an expression and the objects and persons in a physical-social situation are organized in ways that are important for meanings of symbolic objects and for the activities of individuals. Figure 11.1 indicates this, albeit too simply, by showing layers on both sides. On the symbolic side, the lower layer labelled "symbolic notations," refers to the physical objects of symbolic expressions, such as marks on a piece of paper, and the upper layer refers to the expressions as organized structures.

The main features of symbolic structures are constituent units: such as the verbs, noun phrases, prepositional phrases, etc., of English, or the coefficients, variables, terms, etc., of algebra. Symbolic structures are often represented in theories as parsed representations, shown as tree diagrams. We need not assume that human cognition includes separate cognitive representations of the structural features of expressions. Structural features need only provide ways in which human reasoners can be cognitively connected with the symbolic situations they are in; that is, individuals interact directly with the struc-

---

[2]In the view of some cognitive scientists, it is not the beach itself, but its perception (and thus acquired knowledge) of the beach that the ant must interact with. If this were the case, then the difficulty that I take to be fundamental would be much less serious. I am persuaded, however, that in normal activity in physical and social settings, we are connected directly with the environment, rather than connected indirectly through cognitive representations, and that cognitive representations come into play when normal connected activity fails in some way. This view, mainly due to Heidegger (1926/1962), and its implications for cognitive theory have been discussed by Dreyfus and Dreyfus (1986), Suchman (1987), and Winograd and Flores (1986).

tural features of situations, rather than with notations. Even so, it is useful to consider a function $\Theta_s$, that describes the relation between notations and symbolic structures. I intend $\Theta_s$, like the other functions in Fig. 11.1 and other similar diagrams, to refer to descriptions of relations, not to psychological processes.

$\Psi$ is a mapping from symbolic expressions to other symbolic expressions. This refers to the transformations that are permitted according to some set of rules. For example, in English, "John brewed some coffee" can be rewritten as "Some coffee was brewed by John" without changing the referential meaning of the expression, but "John was brewed by some coffee" is not a legitimate rewriting of the sentence. In algebra, "$2(0.2x)^2$" can be rewritten as "$2(0.04x^2)$" without changing its referential meaning, but not as "$4(0.04x^2)$." In Fig. 11.1, the function $\Psi$ is a mapping at the level of symbolic structures, not physical expressions. This reflects a hypothesis that operations on symbolic expressions apply more directly to their structural constituents than to their physical notations.

On the right side of Fig. 11.1, the lower layer contains individual objects and events, and the upper layer contains the objects as they are organized in relation to human activity. Features of structured objects include the parts and combinations of objects, as well as other properties and relations relevant to activity, such as the shape of a coffee filter that makes it appropriate for holding ground coffee. The structural features can be thought of as being in a representation, but it is also possible to think of them as features of the situation, and a particular set of structural features provides a way for individuals to be connected with the situation in the context of an activity. On this view, which is somewhat Gibsonian (Gibson, 1966), but more directly Heideggerian (Heidegger, 1926/1962), an individual in ordinary circumstances is considered as interacting with the structures of situations directly, rather than constructing representations of structural features and interacting with the representations.[3] Representations of structure can be constructed, and typically are when direct interaction with the situation is unsuccessful. As with expressions, it is useful to indicate the relation between objects and the way they are organized in an individual's interaction with them as a function, which is denoted $\Theta_d$ in Fig. 11.1.

$\mu$ is a set of operations on the objects in a situation. These are changes

---

[3]Larkin's model (chap. 12 in this volume) constructs parsed representations of symbolic expressions and objects in situations and reasons over the representations. At the same time, she assumes that construction of the representations is easy and that the model reconstructs the representations of structure whenever they are needed, rather than storing them. The view that I prefer is that those reprsentations are not constructed at all, because features in those representations are in the situation and the individual just interacts with them there. Of course, an assumption of easily constructed representations and a view of no representations agree in some of their implications. I believe, however, that there are important differences as well, including different hypotheses about learning that are suggested or implied by the two views.

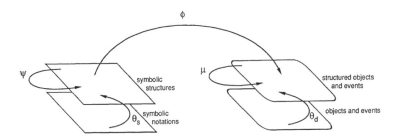

FIG. 11.1    A view of semantics (after Smith, 1983).

that can be made to occur, such as transferring ground coffee from a container to a coffee filter, or assembling or separating the parts of a coffee maker. If an algebra expression such as "$y = 2(0.2x)^2$" denotes a situation involving Tom's advertisements and customers, $\mu$ refers to changes such as increasing the number of advertisements that Tom runs. A situation might also include the option of changing the newspaper that Tom uses, which could change the function between advertisements and customers along with the value of some other quantity, such as the cost of each advertisement. In the domain of abstract denotations, $\mu$ refers to operations on entities such as mathematical functions. For example, operations on functions include differentiation. The operation of differentiating the function denoted by "$2(0.2x)^2$" results in the function denoted by "$0.16x$." (The functions themselves are abstract mathematical objects, related by the operation of differentiation. There also is an operation in $\Psi$ that transforms the symbolic expression "$2(0.2x)^2$" into the expression "$0.16x$.") Another example of operations on functions is the addition of a constant; this operation changes "$2(0.2x)^2$" into a different function, depending on the constant that is used.

In Fig. 11.1 $\mu$, a mapping in the domain of structured objects and events, is analogous to $\Psi$ in the domain of structured symbols. This reflects the hypothesis that features of structured objects provide the terms in which we interact with objects in situations. Anzai and Simon (1979) provided an example that illustrates the idea in their study of a subject learning to solve the Tower of Hanoi puzzle. The subject's first efforts involved operations on individual disks. After solving the problem once or twice, however, the subject developed the concept of a pile of disks, and formed the operation of moving a pile. Moving a pile is obviously equivalent to a sequence of moves of individual disks, but the operation on the pile applies to a structural feature of the situation, and reasoning at that level involves a different way of interacting with the objects in the problem situation than reasoning at the level of individual disks.

The function $\Phi$ refers to the mapping from symbolic expressions to objects and events that the symbols denote. The phrase "the filter" denotes an object in the coffee-making situation, "the ground coffee" denotes some material, and "put the ground coffee in the filter" denotes an action. The terms in "$2(0.2x)^2$" can refer either to quantities in some concrete situation or to abstract mathematical entities. For example, "$y = 2(0.2x)^2$" can refer to a relation among quantities in a concrete commercial situation, where $y$ is the number of customers that Tom gets, $x$ is the number of advertisements that he runs, and the equation expresses a relation between these quantities. Alternatively, the objects that are denoted may be abstract; for example, $x$ and $y$ can be understood as denoting the set of real numbers, and the equation denotes a function that maps the set onto itself.

*Coherence of $\Psi$, $\Phi$, and $\mu$.* To be useful, the operations that we perform on symbolic expressions must preserve the references of their terms and the truth of their assertions in the domain that they are about. In mathematics, some aspects of this issue of coherence are addressed in proofs of soundness of operations, and Smith (1983) discussed some general conditions on $\Psi$ and $\Phi$ that are required. Some of the coherence constraints are related to equivalence. For example, transformations from active to passive voice are allowed because they describe the same states of affairs. Simplifications of expressions in algebra are allowed (e.g., "$2(0.2x)^2$" to $2(0.04x^2)$") because they refer to the same function. And operations involved in solving equations are allowed (e.g., "$2(0.2x)^2 = 50$" to "$(0.2x)^2 = 25$") because they have the same solution set. In these cases, the issue involves $\Psi$ and $\Phi$; the alternative symbolic expressions have to denote the same object or class of situations.

Other coherence constraints involved inferences and therefore require correspondence between $\Psi$ and $\mu$, under the correspondence that $\Phi$ specifies. For example, instructions for making coffee might say "After the water stops dripping, remove the pot and serve the coffee." Some language-processing systems might need to include the inference that "Coffee will drip into the pot" and add that statement to its data. (Note that in situated langauge use, representations would ordinarily not include such inferences.) The rules for adding such statements should be valid, in that they correspond to events that will occur in the situations to which the statements refer. In algebra, the operation in $\Psi$ of expressing the derivative of a function (e.g., "$2(0.2x)^2$" to "$0.16x$") needs to provide expressions that denote the functions that they are intended to. That is, the function that the second expression denotes must really be the derivative of the function that the first expression denotes, if the symbolic operation is carried out correctly.

Smith's framework gives us terms for discussing some aspects of the epistemological problem that I raised earlier in this chapter. The examples of school-based knowledge separated from everyday reasoning show that $\Psi$ and $\mu$ may exist for students as two quite disconnected systems. The separation is illustrated dramatically by the child that Ginsburg (1977) interviewed, who had one "plus" procedure for operating on written symbols, and a different "altogether" procedure for operating on quantities and numbers. The addition algorithm, for that child, was a set of symbolic operations—part of $\Psi$—with no significant connection to objects, that is, no relation with $\mu$. That student reasoned correctly about the numbers of objects involved in an event in the world described in English, but saw no need to constrain the operations of symbolic arithmetic so the two procedures would give the same results. The examples from ethnographic research (Carraher et al., 1983; Lave, 1988) similarly illustrate abilities to reason about quantities in real situations— that is, apply operations designated by $\mu$ in Fig. 11.1—without any significant connection with knowledge of the symbolic operations of school mathematics. In the examples of naive physics, students have acquired correct knowledge of $\Psi$—their ability to solve textbook problems with formulas—but reason about events in the world incorrectly. Their inferences about the motion of objects are not informed by the Newtonian principles expressed by the formulas that they use symbolically.

The disconnection of operations with symbols from events in the world is a well-recognized educational problem, but the idea of situated cognition puts it in a new light. For example, in the case of algebra, many individuals would see the problem in something like the following terms: Students are poor at word problems, and have difficulty mapping world entities (as described in word problems) into algebraic operations that they have already mastered. The problem is with what we mean by "mastered." In the situation of schooling, the activity that students engage in and are tested in is the manipulation of symbols. The physical objects they manipulate are marks on chalkboards and paper. These are intended to be symbols that denote mathematical objects (variable, functions, and so on) and that can denote quantities in many specific situations, such as tanks that are filled and drained with pipes of specified diameters and commercial activities such as advertising and attracting customers. But the concrete situations with quantities that the symbols can denote are not present, and the students' knowledge probably does not include the mathematical abstractions of variable and function for the symbols to refer to.

I take as a framing assumption of the kind referred to in the beginning of this chapter that human cognition is situated, and that individuals make sense of the symbolic activities in which they engage. This means that students will interpret the symbolic operations that they learn as being about something, but what they are about in the students' understanding may be quite different from what we intend. Normally, language is about the objects and events in a situation in which the language is used, and learners of the language depend on the situations of language use to understand what is being said (e.g., Anderson, 1983). In most school instruction, especially in mathematics and science, the objects in the situation are notations—marks on chalkboards and pieces of paper—and the events are manipulations of those notations by a teacher and other students. Assuming that students learn that their knowledge is about the situations of learning, it should not be surprising that mathematical and scientific formulas seem to them to be about the notations, rather than about the quantities, variables, and functions that they are intended to denote.

The result could be a knowledge structure like the one diagrammed in Fig. 11.2, involving an ability to perform symbolic operations (knowledge of $\Psi$) but with a perverse semantic interpretation $\Phi'$ that maps the symbolic structures back to the notations used to express them, rather than to a domain of real objects and situations and abstract mathematical entities. It is small wonder then, that students have difficulty mapping world entities into symbolic algebraic operations that they have "mastered." If this analysis is correct, "mastery" may be nothing more than knowledge of some rules for manipulating symbols: knowledge of $\Theta_s$ and $\Psi$, It should include knowledge corresponding to $\Theta_s$ and $\Psi$, the abilities to comprehend and manipulte symbolic exressions, but it should also include knowledge corresponding to $\Phi$ and $\mu$, the relations between symbolic expressions and their denotations and the operations on objects and events that the expressions denote. If Fig. 11.2 is an accurate reflection of a student's knowledge, we would not want to say that the student has mastered algebra.

An example provided by Schoenfeld (1987) shows that school instruction can lead to an outcome with the properties shown in Fig. 11.2. Schoenfeld observed a teacher of high school geometry, whose instruction was excellent by conventional standards. In teaching construction problems, the teacher emphasized the technical requirements of accuracy in setting the compass and drawing lines, and indicated that for credit on homework, all the marks needed to be visible and accurate. Schoenfeld found that the students' knowledge for solving construction problems was knowledge about the drawings, rather than knowledge about spatial relations and constraints.

In one example, students were asked to prove that in a circle inscribed in an angle, the radii of the circle that intersect the sides of the angle are perpendicular to those sides. The diagram of the proof was still on the blackboard when the students were asked to construct a circle inscribed in an angle through a point on one of the sides of the angle. The students worked for several minutes without considering use of perpendicular lines to find the center of the circle. When Schoenfeld asked whether they considered the previous proof problem, they indicated that they believed there is no relation between the concepts involved in proofs and construction problems.

Mathematically, construction problems are solved by applying constraints that determine the locations of geometric objects. Theorems provide those constraints, which are properties of abstract mathematical objects. Ideally, students, then, should know both the symbols used in theorems of proofs (including both statements and diagrams), which denote mathematical entities and state their properties (e.g., radii of an inscribed circle are perpendicular to the angle's sides), and the symbols used in construction problems (again including both statements and diagrams), which denote the same mathematical entities. This understanding would correspond to $\Phi$ in Fig. 11.1. Instead, based on the students' performance on the construction problem Schoenfeld described, the symbols for those problems apparently referred primarily to their own notations, the drawings, the version of $\Phi'$ in Fig. 11.2 rather than involving mathematical concepts.

Another example involves solution of word problems in algebra, studied by Paige and Simon (1966). Their study investigated processes of writing formulas for word problems, in relation to a model developed by Bobrow (1968) in which a minimum of semantic reference is used. in Bobrow's model, use of semantics is limited as much as possible to terms that corefer and therefore use the same variable. Some students' performance agreed with Bobrow's model. But other students made use of quantitative constraints in the situations that the problems described, often using diagrams to express the constraints. One example involved the length of a board, cut into two pieces, with one piece $\frac{2}{3}$ as long as the whole board and the other piece 4 feet longer than the first piece. Students who used minimal semantics assigned variables to all the quantities and solved equations, while students who used more semantics recognized that the second piece could not be longer than the first. In terms of Fig. 11.1 and 11.2, the second group of students, who used diagrams successfully, had denotations of symbols that included quantitative constraints. The denotations of symbols for students whose process involved more direct translation of texts to formulas did not include such constraints. For the students, language about quantitative relations referred mainly to symbols in equations, as in Fig. 11.2, rather than quantitative relations among objects in a situation, as in Fig. 11.1.[4]

Theoretical and educational issues involved in the coherence of $\Psi$ and $\Phi$ may be quite fundamental. They may require the kind of epistemological refor-

---

[4]It seems likely that the approaches to instruction in algebra advocated by Anderson (chap. 13 in this volume) and Larkin (chap. 12 in this volume) would not be helpful in overcoming the insulation of symbolic expressions from their intended meaning. Larkin, in fact, explicitly identifies the objects of algebraic procedures as written symbols and gives them the same theoretical status as the objects in a situation where one makes coffee. Anderson and Larkin, of course, are not alone in their acceptance of a theory of mathematical cognition as the manipulation of disembodied and decontextualized symbols. For example, Brown and Burton (1978) and VanLehn (1983) analyzed subtraction procedures without regard to the meanings of numeral symbols, and my analysis of geometry problem solving (Greeno, 1978), like Anderson's (1982), and a discussion of physics problem solving by Larkin and Simon (1987), have treated cognitive processes as operating entirely over symbols, with the modest extension that the symbols include diagrams as well as statements of propositions. Some analyses (Briars & Larkin, 1984; VanLehn & Brown, 1978; Greeno, 1983; Greeno, Riley, & Gelman,1984; Kintsch & Greeno, 1985; Resnick & Omanson, in press; Riley, Greeno, & Heller, 1983) have attempted to deal with semantic relations in the form of schemata that represent relations among objects in situations. These seem like steps in the right direction, although I believe that their analyses of the structures of situations and concepts are insufficiently developed.

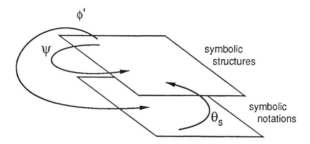

FIG. 11.2    An unintended outcome of "good" instruction.

mulation that I alluded to earlier in this chapter. Indeed, Smith's concerns with semantics have led him in more recent work to consider very general issues of correspondence between symbols and their referents (Smith, 1987a), and the properties of symbolic systems that are embedded in the situations that they are about (Smith, 1987b). If my assessment is correct, we are poorly equipped in cognitive science to address the kinds of educational questions that Lave, Schoenfeld, Caramazza et al., and others have raised, for reasons that are deeply embedded in the epistemology on which our current theories rest.

## SOME RESEARCH ON MEANING AND MODELS

A solution of the general problem of accounting for situated, generative reasoning is well beyond the scope of this chapter—I consider it a major agenda item for cognitive science that will require some years of concentrated effort. I can, however, propose the beginning of an idea that seems promising for solving some aspects of the problem.

The idea involves reasoning in the space of a mental or physical model that represents a situation that the person needs to reason about. The representation has a special property, that the objects in the representation work in ways that are like the ways that objects in the situation work. This property of behavioral similarity makes the representation useful for reasoning by simulation. Reasoning with a mental model has features that give it some of the character of situated reasoning in physical and social contexts. In this section, I describe preliminary results of two research projects that are investigating properties of such reasoning. In "An Extended View of Semantics" I present an extension of the framework discussed in the previous section and use that framework to discuss these findings and their implications.

### Mental Models in Physics Cognition

The first example is from research by Jeremy Roschelle (Roschelle & Greeno, 1987), who presented diagrams to experienced physicists and asked them "What's happening?" Figure 11.3 is one of the diagrams that Roschelle used.

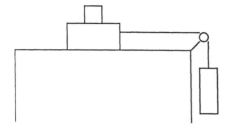

FIG. 11.3.   A physics diagram.

The protocols that Roschelle obtained provide interesting information about the interplay between knowledge of general propositions in the theory of physics and everyday causal knowledge about the world. The data, therefore, are relevant to understanding the separation between formulas and the interpretation of physical events that is evident in many students' understanding.

Faced with Fig. 11.3, one of the physicists said, "This one is very interesting because it illustrates a very important point, which is that friction isn't always in the wrong direction—or the right direction." The physicist said he had begun with a force diagram "in his head" with a friction force associated with the smallest block, pointed to the left. He also envisioned the two-block system moving to the right. If friction was in the left direction, the smallest block would have to go to the left, which contradicted the envisionment. This contradiction led to a generative reformulation of the problem. He said, "The answer is . . . that friction opposes relative motion . . . so the friction's going . . . to oppose the motion between the little mass and the big mass it's sitting on. And that happens to be to the right if the big mass is moving to the right." In the reformulation, he had constructed the frame of reference of the moving largest block and realized that to remain stationary in the frame of reference of the table, the smaller block would be moving to the left in the frame of the larger block. Then the appropriate direction for the friction force is to the right.

With regard to Fig. 11.1, the reasoning involved construction of at least two representations based on different sources of knowledge. One representation involved theoretical concepts with names such as "friction force." The standard notation for that representation is a force diagram, with arrows representing the force vectors. The other representation was more like a dynamic mental picture in which the objects in the diagram are imagined to be moving in various directions. The two representations were inconsistent. The mental force diagram implied that motion of the top block should be to the left, while in the envisionment, that object was moving to the right. We cannot tell from the protocol exactly how the conflict was resolved, but the envisionment of motion won. A revision of the theory-based representation occurred, involving addition of a frame of reference, and the friction force in the revised theory-based representation was consistent with the motion in the envisionment.

Roschelle takes this kind of interactive construction of representations as a significant theoretical problem, and is currently engaged in an effort to construct a program that simulates it. In the meantime, he has developed an instructional system that realizes the distinction in a different way (Roschelle, 1987).

In the instructional system—Roschelle calls it the "Envisioning Machine"—the display includes two windows, called the object world and the Newtonian world. Fig. 11.4 shows displays that can be constructed in the two windows.

The two windows display different representations of Newtonian motion. The lower window has objects that are like those in the physical world. There are balls and a hand, the hand can grasp and carry a ball, and it can throw a ball by releasing it while carrying it. The motions of balls are like those in the world, except that a trace is left so that the motion can be considered reflectively.

The upper window has a different set of objects, corresponding to Newtonian theory. Here, objects include circles that denote point masses and arrows that denote velocities and accelerations. Operations that can be applied to these objects are positioning the circle and changing the lengths and directions of the arrows for initial velocity and for a (constant) acceleration. One or more point-masses with associated initial velocity and acceleration arrows can be set up, and the system will move the circles in a way that agrees with the parameters, again leaving a trace of the motion(s).

Using the Envisioning Machine as an instructional system involves giving students various tasks to perform. One task is to show a motion in the object window and ask the student to set the velocity and acceleration of a motion in the Newtonian window so it matches the given "observable" motion. Other activities include setting two motions and comparing the effects of different settings. For example, there can be equal initial velocities and unequal accelerations in the same direction. Roschelle is in an early stage of investigating the effectiveness of the instructional system. Results of preliminary explorations have been quite promising, but much remains to be done.

In this regard, Roschelle's Envisioning Machine is based on a similar intuition as that of many "manipulative" models in the teaching of elementary mathematics, such as the use of rods of different lengths to teach additive relations among integers, and the use of spatial diagrams to teach the notation of fractions. The arrows in the "Newtonian world" corresponding to velocity and acceleration are manipulable symbolic objects in that representation. The manipulability of the arrows as objects in Roschelle's system that correspond to properties and relations in the object representation is sometimes present in manipulable materials but often is not. For example, with place-value blocks for arithmetic, the objects correspond to objects, not numbers, and children can manipulate the numbers only by changing the numbers of blocks, not by changing objects that represent numbers directly.

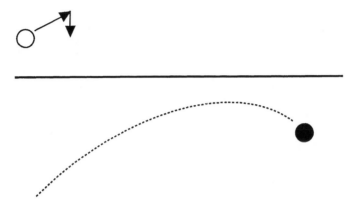

FIG. 11.4.    Displays of Roschelle's Envisioning Machine.

Another important pedagogical idea is the interaction between representations. Motions that are controlled by the velocity and acceleration vectors can be compared with motions that are produced by actions like those that we perform in the real world. Properties of motions in the Newtonian world such as "catching up" or "getting farther ahead" also can be observed and related to the theoretical concepts. This could result in a better connection between the theoretical concepts and students' interpretations of ordinary events.

My main concern in this chapter, however, is theoretical rather than instructional. I contend that the two displays of the Envisioning Machine present information that is like the information that individuals can have in their representations of situations involving the motions of objects. An important part of individuals' knowledge includes the ability to construct alternative representations and manipulate these representations to make inferences. One kind of representation is a mental model with which an individual can imagine objects moving through space along different trajectories, at different speeds, and so on. Another kind of representation uses concepts that we learn about when we study physics. This theory-based representation includes objects that may not appear in the envisionment of ordinary moving objects. The effective use of these multiple representations includes their coordination; for example, recognizing conflicts between representations and revising either representation to produce new representations that are consistent.

Regarding Fig. 11.1, the distinction between the two representations provides some clues about the problematic Φ relation between symbolic expressions and the objects they denote. Apparently, in the protocol for Fig. 11.3 and for similar acts of reasoning, the link between verbal expressions such as "friction force" and their denotations in situations crucially includes reasoning with representations that allow mental simulations of the situations. These representations for simulative reasoning are a part of the symbolic realm (i.e., they involve mental or physical objects that represent objects, properties, or relations in the physical world), but their properties differ importantly from the verbal or formal representations of language or mathematics, as we all know. The example of Roschelle's research and instructional development highlight the need for a better understanding of the relations between these representational systems. Some important insights have been provided in work on qualitative reasoning, notably by deKleer (1979), deKleer and Brown (1984), and Forbus (1984), but the issues of interactive reasoning among multiple representational systems have not been resolved.

## Meanings of Words About Quantities

The second example involves tasks that use language about quantities. Some of these tasks are word problems used in school arithmetic instruction. An example is: "Jay has three books; Kay has five more books than Jay; How many books does Kay have?" Other tasks are used in developmental research about children's understanding of quantity, such as number conservation and class inclusion. As an example, some red and blue blocks are shown, and a child is asked: "Who would have more toys to play with: someone who owned the red blocks or someone who owned the blocks?"

The research that I am conducting, along with Adele Goldberg and Walter Johnson, involves analyses of differences in the meanings of words that may characterize different children's understanding. In the development assessment tasks, children have to map the language of statements and questions onto the objects in the situation. The well-known mistake of answering "the red blocks" rather than "the blocks" if there are more red blocks than blue blocks involves a failure to map the term "the blocks" onto the set of all the blocks, or to appropriately quantify that set. In the word problems, the sets of objects such as Jay's books and Kay's books are not presented in the situation, but in some experiments counters are provided so that children can construct sets as models of the situation that the problem describes. Our analysis considers language as providing a set of specifications for constructing models, as well as referents to features of the models that have been constructed. Of course, if physical objects are not available in the situation to construct a model, children still may use a mental model in their understanding and reasoning about the problem. This would accord with analyses of understanding syllogisms by Johnson-Laird (1983) and others, as well as Fauconnier's (1985) general analyses of language understanding as the construction of mental spaces and their contents.

Our analysis of language and models has two components: a formal analysis of propositional meanings of language, and a computational analysis of the process of constructing models. We have formulated alternative hypotheses about the meanings of terms that children could understand, and we have used Montague grammar (Dowty, Wall, & Peters, 1981) to derive implications of these hypotheses for the propositional meanings of texts of problems and questions. Then we have constructed programs that take propositions as input and set goals and choose procedures for constructing models either by counting out sets of objects and modifying sets to correspond to the problem texts, or by identifying sets in situations corresponding to statements that are made. Finally, the procedures set goals and choose procedures for counting sets in the model to determine answers to questions. (Some, but not all, of the model-constructing procedures have been implemented as programs.) The general scheme is one that Walter Kintsch and I used in an earlier analysis of text processing and problem solving with word problems (Kintsch & Greeno, 1985). The analysis that Goldberg, Johnson, and I are working on now specifies the relations between word meanings and propositions more formally, and uses different assumptions about the knowledge involved in constructing and making inferences with models.

Results of the analysis include relations between references to abstract structures and processes for constructing models. We have looked at assumptions about meanings of terms that include explicit references to sets, relations between sets, and operators on sets that have numerical values and other meanings that do not include such explicit references. In effect, we have asked what difference it makes, in constructing or interpreting a model, whether or not the representation of propositions about the model includes symbols that refer explicitly to sets, relations between sets, and operators. It turns out that the differences these references make are substantial, and potentially quite important for the theory of reasoning with mental and physical models.

Regarding Fig. 11.1, the questions we have addressed in our analysis involve alternative symbolic structures with correspondingly different versions of $\Theta_s$, and a version of $\Phi$, the mapping from expressions in language to objects that the language is about. In our model, different versions of $\Theta_s$ correspond to different propositions that represent the information in texts when different word meanings are assumed. $\Phi$ corresponds to a set of procedures that arrange objects so they provide a correct model of the situation that the language describes. The objects that we consider here have the special property of representing something else, so they themselves are symbols, and I will discuss this dual role more fully in the following section.

Our hypotheses focus on the meanings of numeral terms and relational terms such as "more." We consider alternative meanings in which more advanced versions are more mathematically sophisticated. That is, they include information that corresponds to understanding some mathematical concepts and principles that the less advanced versions do not include.

One distinction involves understanding numbers as properties of sets. In this case, the more developmentally advanced version takes a phrase such as "three books" and represents a proposition that refers to a set of books with cardinality 3. The less advanced version does not refer to the set explicitly. In either case, the numeral can be an argument to a procedure that counts a set of objects, or the result of a counting operation. We have referred to the distinction as a "principle of linguistic cardinality." By this we mean that the more advanced meaning of numerals includes reference to sets that have cardinalities that the numerals name, while in the less advanced meaning numerals only denote arguments and results of counting procedures.

In our analysis of linguistic cardinality, we treat numeral terms linguistically as determiners. In general, determiners specify that objects exist; for example, a logical expression for "Jay operates a robot," is

"Jay operates a robot" $\Rightarrow \exists(x)[\text{robot}(x) \quad \text{operate}(\text{Jay},x)]$.

That is, for the sentence to be true, there has to be a robot that Jay operates.

The question about numeral-determiners is what they specify the existence of. On the less advanced reading, they specify that there are some objects that satisfy the predicates of the sentence. For example:

"Jay has three books" $\Rightarrow \exists x \exists y \exists z$ [book$(x) \wedge$ book$(y) \wedge$book$(z) \wedge$has $(\text{Jay},x) \wedge$has$(\text{Jay},y) \wedge$has$(\text{Jay},z) \wedge x \neq y \wedge x \neq z \wedge y \neq z]$.

For the sentence to be true, there have to be three objects that are books and Jay has them. On the more advanced reading, a numeral specifies the existence of a set that has the cardinality specified by the numeral. In that case,

"Jay has three books" $\Rightarrow \exists X[3(X) \wedge \forall x(x \in X \rightarrow \text{book}(x)) \wedge$
$\forall x(x \in X \rightarrow \text{has}(\text{Jay},x))]$

For this sentence to be true, there has to be a set with cardinality 3, whose members are books and Jay has them. The sentences are true in the same situations, of course, but the second version refers explicitly to the set of books, while the first version does not.

The difference in representations makes little difference when the task is simply to model a set or modify or count a set that already is modeled. Then the numeral simply specifies an argument or result of a counting procedure, and the presence of a symbol that denotes the set is not important. The difference is significant, however, when relations between sets are important. An example in word problems is the difference between a problem such as "Jay had eight books; then he lost three of them. How many of them does he have left?" and "Jay had some books; then he lost three of them and now he has five books left. How many books did he have in the beginning?" The second problem is harder than the first for first- and second-grade children, and the difference can be understood in the ease of constructing models of the two situations. In the first problem, a set of eight objects is constructed, then three of those objects are removed, and the question is answered by counting the objects that remain. These operations can be carried out just by performing counting procedures with arguments that are supplied in the text. In the second problem, the first sentence specifies a set, but does not allow its construction. There is no way to remove three blocks from a set that does not exist, and the sentence about having five blocks is the first one that allows construction of a model. The second problem, therefore, requires some inferential work that cannot be done in the model. This inferential work is quite easy if the representation includes reference to sets and relations between the sets. Then "three of them" is represented as a set with cardinality 3 that is a subset of the first set that was specified. The information in the representation includes the relations of subset-to-superset between each of the two given sets and the unknown, and the model can be constructed easily on this basis.[5]

Relations between sets also have to be understood to answer "Which is more?" questions, such as "Are there more red flowers, or more flowers, or are they the same?" Evidence provided by Markman and Siebert (1976) and by Markman (1979) indicates that the representations texts use can have significant effects on children's performance in answering questions about relative cardinalities. Markman used class and collection terms in tasks involving class inclusion, number conservation, and other quantitative comparisons. for example, with 10 blue blocks and 5 red blocks arranged in a pile, in the class condition the experimenter said, "Who would have more toys to play with: someone who owned the blue blocks or someone who owned the blocks?" In the collection condition, the experimenter asked, "Who would have more toys to play with: someone who owned the blue blocks or someone who owned the pile?" Kindergarten and first-grade children in the collection condition answered correctly about 50% more often than children in the class condition (2.8 vs. 1.8 of 4 questions).

Another meaning of numerals is involved when the numerical difference between sets is stated or requested in a question. If there are five birds and two worms, and a child is asked, "How many more birds are there than worms?" the answer is not the cardinality of any set in the situation, but is a relation between the cardinalities of two sets. The referent can be expressed as the value of an operator, $\Delta_+(X, Y) = 3$ in this case, where $X$ is the set of birds, $Y$ is the set of worms, and $\Delta_+$ is an operator that maps pairs of sets to the differences between their cardinalities. (" + " indicates that the second number is subtracted from the first.)

---

[5]This discussion assumes that the problem is solved by constructing a model with sets of objects, as young children have done in several experiments on these tasks. Different representations that might be used by older children would not raise the same difficulties; for example, if a child knew algebra and translated the texts to the equations "8 − 3 = x" and "x − 3 = 5," a differnt analysis of the process would be needed from the one I have described here.

The question of "How many more?" can be solved, of course, without a representation that refers directly to the difference between cardinalities. Indeed, most preschool children answer correctly if the problem is phrased as follows: "The birds are going to race over and each bird is going to try to get a worm. How many birds won't get a worm?" One possible solution is to construct a one-to-one match of the elements of the two sets, and then count the set of remaining birds. Some children appear to do that, but many count the smaller set, count that many out of the larger set, and count the remaining elements of the larger set to get the answer (Hudson, 1983). Another wording that is easier than "How many more?" involves equalizing the sets: "How many more worms would we need so there would be the same number of worms as there are birds?" (Carpenter & Moser, 1983). These findings indicate that children can compute the difference between two sets before they are able to answer "How many more?" questions directly. The interpretation that Goldberg, Johnson, and I give this is that a structural feature of situations, the numerical difference between sets, is denoted directly by sentences with phrases such as "three more _____ than _____" or "how many more _____ than _____." Many younger children do not understand this, and the lack of that understanding causes them to misinterpret sentences that have those phrases in them.

In an empirical study, Goldberg investigated the understanding of numerical comparisons by four- and five-year-old children. Goldberg's study rests on the hypothesis that to answer "How many more $x$'s are there than $y$'s?" requires understanding that includes an operator that takes sets to the differences between their cardinalities—the concept that we have denoted $\Delta_+ (X, Y)$ in our formal analysis. Goldberg told a story about a penguin and a bear that go fishing, receive presents, and play with marbles. (A toy penguin and bear were used to animate the story.) During the story the child was asked questions such as "How many more fish-monsters than turtles are there?" and "Are there more bear stickers than dinosaur stickers?" and "How many star fish are there?" None of the children in Goldberg's study answered any of the "How many more?" questions correctly. At the same time, all the children answered at least a majority of the "Which is more?" questions and "How many?" questions correctly. The finding is consistent with the hypothesis that "How many more?" questions require the cognitive structure of an operator that relates a pair of sets to a number, the difference between the cardinalities of the sets. On this interpretation, the children in this study had the concept of cardinality and the relation of "more than," but their understanding of language about numbers did not yet include the concept of a relation between the cardinalities of sets.

In another study about quantitative comparisons, Johnson (1988) described situations to second- and third-grade children using comparative propositions such as "Bert baked five cookies; Ernie baked three more than Bert," and asked children to construct models of the situation that was described by placing counters in front of Bert and Ernie dolls. Johnson also gave the children problems to solve, such as "Bert and Ernie had a marble shooting contest; Ernie won. Bert won seven marbles and Ernie won two more. How many marbles did Ernie win?" Both the modeling and word-problem tasks were given in different versions, with some explicit comparisons (e.g., "Ernie baked three more than Bert") and other sentences that were ambiguous (e.g., "Ernie baked three more," which could mean that Ernie baked three cookies in addition to those that Bert baked). In both the modeling tasks and the word problems, children had a strong tendency to adopt a consistent reading of the comparative conjunctions—individual children either interpreted "more than" as a comparison between two sets or interpreted "more" as a disjoint set—and therefore were incorrect when "more than" was used in the sentence. More children chose the comparative construction in the modeling tasks than in the word problems, suggesting that the presence of an external domain of objects facilitated the more complicated relational interpretation of the linguistic symbols. In the modeling tasks, 63% of the children used a comparative interpretation, while only 42% of the word problems were interpreted comparatively. In the word problems, many children adopted a simple strategy of operating on the numbers in all the problems in the same way, often by just giving the sum of the numbers in every problem. Regarding Fig 11.1, the request to model the situations involved arranging some objects so that the problem statements were accurate descriptions of a situation, according to an interpretation $\phi$. Many of the second- and third-grade children in this study apparently could understand the relational structure of the "$x$ more than $y$" phrases and used that relation when they constructed models. When they were given word problems, however, some of those children apparently resorted to a symbolic procedure, finding numbers and adding them, thus not constructing an interpretation involving relations between numbers of objects in situations. This latter process provides another illustration of the arrangement in Fig. 11.2, a self-contained symbolic system.

These findings provide an example of the role that general concepts can have in constructing and interpreting models. There are abstract concepts, in this case, sets, relations between sets (such as subset), and operations on sets (such as the difference between cardinalities) that can be part of the individual's understanding of symbolic expressions. If our interpretations are correct, these concepts play a significant role in the individual's reasoning in a model-theoretic setting.

## AN EXTENDED VIEW OF SEMANTICS

The research on mental models that I have discussed here, along with many other studies (e.g., those in Gentner & Stevens, 1983), requires some distinctions to let us begin to refine the framework for theorizing about representation and meaning that I discussed in the previous section.

## Abstract Entities

First, there is an important issue involving abstract concepts. The analysis of meanings of simple quantitative language involves abstract concepts of sets, relations, and operators. Roschelle's work on understanding physics, like other analyses of qualitative reasoning in physics (e.g., Forbus, 1984), involves abstract concepts such as velocities, accelerations, and forces.[6] Symbols for these concepts are included in formulas as well as in the English-language expressions used for discourse in the domain. An issue much discussed in epistemology and metaphysics is how these symbolic expressions are related to the physical world.

I believe it is simplest to say that the relation between the symbolic expressions and their domains of interpretations is one of reference. On this view, the symbols in theories denote entities that can correspond to structural features of concrete situations, but that also have the status of cognitive objects for purposes of theoretical reasoning.

Fig. 11.5 emphasizes the distinction between concrete and abstract entities. There is a domain of concrete objects and events that individuals are in and that affect their actions. And these objects and events are organized in our understanding. Some of the structural features of concrete objects and events correspond to concepts that are used in theoretical analyses. When individuals reason theoretically, we treat such concepts as entities and reason about them as objects.

For example, consider the situation of a class-inclusion experiment where a child is shown 10 red blocks and 5 blue blocks. The blocks are concrete objects, arranged in some way. The situation has the blocks; it also has sets of blocks, the set of red blocks, and the set of blocks. Each of the sets has a cardinality. The sets and their cardinalities are structural features of the concrete situation. Statements about the situation can be made in terms of these structural features, such as "The number of blocks is greater than the number of red blocks." Sets and numbers are also entities that we can reason about. Fifteen is greater than 10, and the union of two sets has at least as many members as either of the sets that are combined. And we can reason about specific situations using knowledge about general properties of the structures in the specific situations. For example, because the set of blocks is the union of the sets of red and blue blocks, there must be at least as many blocks as there are red blocks or blue blocks.

As another example, consider a physical setup like the diagram in Fig. 11.3, with real blocks, a table, a pulley, and a string. The concrete objects are organized, and a person can interact with them or reason about them as a system

---

[6]There is no princpled way to distinguish concrete objects from abstract entities, except via a physical theory. Indeed, modern physics has made the concept of an object as a well-defined entity problematic. What I have in mind as an object is an integral bunch of physical stuff that moves or can be moved more or less as a unit, which I take to be the commonly held view.

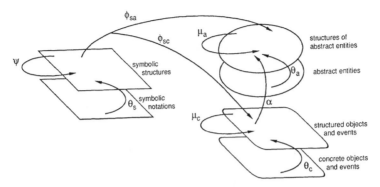

FIG. 11.5.    A view of semantics with abstract entities.

with components. For instance, the two blocks on the table are in contact with each other, and can be lifted or pushed along the table together. The motions of objects have quantitative properties such as forces. Masses, accelerations, velocities, and forces are abstract entities that we reason about theoretically in physics. Forces, masses, accelerations, and so on are also structural features of the concrete situation with blocks and the pulley. Reasoning about the situation can be done in a way that uses knowledge of the general properties of those abstract concepts.

In Fig. 11.5 there are functions $\mu_c$ and $\mu_a$ that refer to operations that can be performed on the entities in real domains. $\mu_c$ refers to things that can be done with concrete objects and events, such as pulling on a string or making a pile of blocks. Individuals acquire knowledge of the way things work, which includes capabilities to perform actions that $\mu_c$ refers to and anticipations of the results of those actions. For example, when a block is resting on another block, you can make both blocks move toward you if you pull on a string attached to the lower block, if you don't pull too hard. If you have a set of blocks designated by a location (e.g., the blocks on a particular piece of paper) and you put another block on the piece of paper, then the number of blocks in the designated set will be increased by one.

Similarly, knowledge can be acquired about the way that abstract entities work—that is, how they can be combined and decomposed, and how they interact. The capability of interacting with abstract entities—that is, manipulating them and anticipating the results of their interactions—would correspond to $\mu_a$ in Fig. 11.5. Examples of knowledge corresponding to $\mu_a$ include knowledge that when two disjoint sets are combined, another set is formed, and the cardinality of the union is the sum of the cardinalities of the subsets. Another example is knowledge that when a force is applied to an object, there is a change in the magnitude of its velocity that is proportional to the magnitude of the force.

I have blithely indicated a relation between concrete and abstract entities with an arrow labeled $\alpha$, for abstraction. But what that could mean presents fundamental theoretical problems most of which are beyond the scope of this paper and our present understanding. An important feature of the relation is that abstract conceptual entities can significantly influence the ways that we interact with situations, by focusing our cognitive connection with the situation on one set of structural features rather than another. If an individual is connected to a situation at the level of structural features, then operators on abstract entities can be applied to manipulate structural features of the situation. An operation of reducing the cardinality of a set by one can be in the repertoire of an agent and applied in a situation, as well as the operation of moving an object away from a given location. Similarly, a driver can have an operation of increasing the velocity of an automobile, as well as the operation of depressing the accelerator.

One important requirement on the $\alpha$ relation is that it includes a relation between $\mu_c$ and $\mu_a$. The mental operations we perform on abstract entities should not be arbitrary; they should correspond to the interactions of structural features of situations. The nature of this correspondence and of the cognitive processes involved in becoming capable of reasoning in and with conceptual entities are very poorly understood, although hypotheses and results provided by Holland, Holyoak, Nisbett, and Thagard (1986) are helpful and promising.

Relations between $\mu_a$ and $\Psi$ are also important and theoretically problematic. Operations on abstract entities corresponding to features of structured objects in a situation may be accompanied by symbolic expressions that denote those operations, but are surely not identical to those symbolic expressions or the operations that transform expressions. For example, the phrase "$5 - 1 = 4$" may be written or spoken to denote an operation of removing a block from a set of five. The terms "5," "1," and "4" denote properties of sets in the situation. Of course "$5 - 1 = 4$" is also a true sentence about integers, abstract entities that can be thought of as independent of the cardinalities of sets in specific situations. At the same time, "$5 - 1 = 4$" is included in $\Psi$, and can be part of a computational system or the mind of a child without being meaningfully related to sets, their cardinalities, or numbers as conceptual entities.

The analysis of language about quantities discussed earlier provides an illustration of the concepts of Fig. 11.5. The analyses formalize the idea that English phrases can denote entities in situations at different levels of abstraction. "Three books" can denote three individual books, or it can denote the set that has those three books as its members. Connecting phrases with the sets they are intended to denote can be problematic, at least in cases where relations between the sets are important as they are in class inclusion tasks. "Three more birds than worms" can denote an operator on two sets and its value, but some young children apparently lack that abstract entity—at least they do not connect the phrase to it in situations that are used in experiments and arithmetic instruction.

Examples of disconnected reasoning discussed earlier also can be discussed in terms of the distinctions in Fig. 11.5. De la Rocha's example of dividing a circle of cottage cheese into four parts involves $\mu_c$ operations on the quantities of the concrete object of cottage cheese, but not the symbolic expression "¾ × ⅔." The action of creating a fractional part of an amount of food seems unlikely to have been learned specifically by the person in the experiment. To generate this action, it seems likely that he must have understood the quantity denoted by "¾" as a structural feature of the situation, and therefore available to be the basis for the action of dividing the cottage cheese into parts. Whether the rational numbers denoted by "¾" and "⅔" were involved in the individual's operation cannot be determined, but it is not unlikely that someone who had studied calculus probably had rational numbers as conceptual entities.

Schoenfeld's (1987) example of geometry construction problems involves operations on diagrams that are not meaningfully related to abstract entities such as congruent triangles. An interesting choice is available in thinking about this example, because the diagram can be considered either as a concrete object or as a symbolic expression. If we consider the diagram as a concrete object, the students' knowledge for constructions involves operations on lines, angles, and so on, but it lacks operations on more abstract entities that are part of their knowledge for proofs. If we consider the diagram as a symbolic representation that denotes geometric objects and relations, the students' knowledge involves operations that transform symbolic expressions—that is, components of $\Psi$—without sufficient connection through $\phi$ to the geometric entities that the diagrammatic expressions are meant to denote.

## Mental and Physical Models

To consider the role of mental models in reasoning and to consider physical models as devices for learning abstract concepts, it is useful to make another distinction, which is illustrated in Fig. 11.6.

The new component of Fig. 11.6 is a domain that is designed as a model. I focus here on the model's dual standing as domains that are denoted by other symbolic expressions in English or mathematical notation, and as symbolic expressions that denote domains of concrete or abstract entities. We can consider the operations performed on the entities in the model either as $\mu_m$ or as $\Psi_m$, that is either as operations on objects and structures of a domain (denoted by linguistic expressions) or as operations on symbols (that denote other entities). Another feature is that the objects in model (of the kind I have in mind) are designed to behave in ways that support simulative reasoning. The operations that are performed on these symbolic objects have effects that are like the effects of corresponding operations on the objects that they denote.

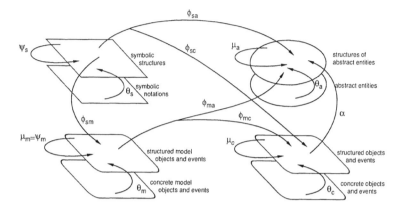

FIG. 11.6.    A view of semantics with a model.

As a simple example, consider arithmetic word problems and models that can be constructed for them by designating locations for sets and small blocks for objects. For example, a problem may be "Jay has five books; Kay has three more books than Jay. How many books does Kay have?" These words are symbolic notations, in the upper left corner of Fig. 11.6, and they are collectively understood as symbolic structures, which might include references to sets of books and a difference operator on the sets with the value 3 for the difference between the number of Kay's books and Jay's books.

In the model, a set of five blocks can be placed on a card for Jay's books. Then a set of five blocks can be placed on a card for Kay's books, and then three more blocks are placed on that second card, corresponding to the three more books that Kay has. These actions construct a model of the sort designated in the lower left corner of Fig. 11.6. The mapping $\phi_{sm}$ is the relation between meanings of the text and objects in the model, which corresponds to procedures that arrange objects in a way that satisfies the propositions. The question requires the number of blocks on the second card, a goal included in the mapping $\phi_{sm}$. The answer is obtained by counting those blocks, giving the answer "eight."

The model, with cards and blocks, stands in place of the situation that the text describes—the persons named Jay and Kay are not present, nor are there any books. The blocks correspond to books that would be present in the real situation, and $\phi_{mc}$ identifies that correspondence. The cards correspond to sets, with the relation of being on a card corresponding to the relation of being a member of a set. The sets and relations of membership are in the domain of abstract entities, and the mapping $\phi_{ma}$ identifies the correspondence between these objects in the model, and features of abstract entities that correspond to structured objects in a situation that the text describes.

The objects in the model—the blocks and the cards that the blocks are placed on—behave in ways that are like the behavior of books and persons who own them. In particular, if a set of five blocks is constructed, and then another set of blocks is constructed that has three more than the first set, the number of blocks in the second set will be the same as would be the case for books and ownership by individuals.

In Roschelle's Envisioning Machine, there are two models. The "object world" has symbols that correspond to physical objects and trajectories of motions. The "Newtonian world" has symbols that correspond to physical objects and trajectories, but also has symbols (the arrows) that correspond to velocities and accelerations. The domain of concrete objects that these models refer to has objects that move in space, and the domain of abstract entities has velocities and accelerations. The mapping from the "object world" to concrete objects takes symbols for objects to objects, and takes properties of the symbolized trajectories to properties of trajectories. The mapping from the "Newtonian world" to concrete objects and trajectories is similar. The "Newtonian world" also has symbols that are mapped to entities in the abstract domain. Unlike the symbols for sets in the blocks-and-cards model for arithmetic, the arrows that symbolize velocities and accelerations are directly manipulable by students.

Velocities and accelerations are properties of events in the physical situations that we experience in ordinary life, but they are not physical objects in those situations. Velocities and accelerations are denoted in the symbolic expressions of physics—for example in formulas such as "$v_f = v_i + gt$" and "$f = ma$." They also are denoted by the arrows in the Roschelle's model. The arrows, however, behave in ways that are like the behavior of velocities and accelerations in ordinary physical situations. For example, the velocity arrow becomes longer or shorter, depending on the direction of acceleration. Symbols such as "$v$" and "$a$" do not behave like velocities and accelerations (For example, the letter "$v$" does not increase or decrease its size on the page depending on the size and orientation of "$a$.") A conjecture about learning that underlies the use of models like Roschelle's is that acquisition of understanding of abstract entities can be facilitated by providing models with objects that students can manipulate and observe, especially when the actions that operate on the model objects, and the effects of those operations, simulate the reasoning operations and inferences that students need to acquire for the abstract entities. For example, the direction of acceleration produces curvature of the trajectory of motion, a causal relation that students should include in their reasoning.

Blocks for arithmetic word problems and arrows displayed on a computer screen provide models in which the symbols are physical objects. To account for other examples, such as the protocols that Roschelle obtained for understanding physics diagrams, we can postulate mental representations in which the symbols have properties like those in physical models of the kind

I have discussed. That is, we can assume that reasoning occurs in a mental space containing symbolic objects in the situations that the symbolic expressions represent. In the protocol given by Roschelle's physicist subject, the mental model apparently included symbols for physical objects such as blocks and a pulley, and operations on those symbols corresponding to the way that physical blocks would move in a real situation. Another aspect of the mental model involved components of a force diagram, either as a description like "friction force to the left" or perhaps as a visualized arrow. The important feature of the physicist's reasoning was the recognition that these two aspects were in conflict. The direction of the imagined force and the direction of the imagined movement were opposite, and that was known to be incompatible.

Many examples of disconnected reasoning in mathematics and physics also involve use of mental models. One such example is the child interviewed by Ginsburg (1977), who had different procedures for "plus" and "altogether" problems. Unlike the physicist in Roschelle's experiment, the child that Ginsburg interviewed did not integrate the information of her procedures for symbolic numerals and real objects and numbers. There are several differences, of course, between Roschelle's and Ginsburg's examples. One major difference is that for the physicist, technical concepts and ordinary envisionment clearly were representations of the same situation, while for the arithmetic student, numerals and descriptions of quantities were not about the same thing. If numerical procedures are to be used for inferences about situations, and if they are to be constrained by the numerical quantities in situations, then the numbers on which the procedures operate must be understood as features or objects in the situations, not as disconnected objects or symbols that exist only in the special setting of school instruction. For physicists, forces are features of and objects in situations, as are blocks and pulleys that move in space, so that an effort to represent a situation creates a need for consistency between its various representations.

The examples commonly called "misconceptions" in physics also can be seen as reasoning in which alternative representations are disconnected. Many students say that an object dropped from a flying airplane will fall straight down, but also know the statements of Newton's principles and can use theoretically correct formulas to solve textbook problems. A reasonable conjecture is that they answer questions about airplanes or pendulums on the basis of a mental model that utilizes ordinary experience, perhaps in the form of phenomenological primitives that diSessa (1983) has discussed. Recognition of forces, velocities, and accelerations as features of the situation, and constraints on the model of objects based on Newton's second law, could constrain the mental model of motion to produce a result that is consistent with the principles of scientific physics.

## CONCLUSIONS

The basic problem that I have tried to address in this chapter is the insulation of symbolic knowledge. Symbolic computation has provided formalisms and methods for representing generative knowledge that have led to a major advance in the theory of human cognition. One result is a set of concepts and methods for developing models of knowledge for school tasks, where the cognitive structures and processes needed to perform successfully are represented in an information-processing model, often in sufficient detail to run as a program. Many of us (e.g., Anderson, Boyle, Farrell, & Reiser, 1984; Greeno, 1976; Greeno, Brown, Foss, Shalin, Bee, Lewis, & Vitolo, 1986; Klahr & Carver, 1988) have designed systems for instruction in symbolic procedures that use cognitive models of task performance as a guide for developing instructional activities and assessments.

An important limitation of current models and the cognitive principles that they embody is their inability to account for performance that is highly situated. In cases that are being increasingly studied, knowledge and the structures of situations are so tightly bound together that it seems best to characterize knowledge as a relation between the knowing agent and the situation, rather than as something that the agent has inside of himself or herself. Cognitive models of the kind we know how to construct lack this relational character.

So does much of the human knowledge that students acquire in school instruction—at least that knowledge is not relational in many situations in which generative relations would be valuable. This does not imply that typical school-based knowledge is not situated. It probably is relational with respect to the situations of schooling, but not with reference to the other situations in which it would be valuable to be connected.

One theoretical question is, "What characteristics of human knowledge enable generative reasoning about novel situations that have significant structure?" The suggestion of this paper is that mental models provide an important resource. A representation is a model, in this sense, if its symbolic objects behave similarly to the objects in situations that are represented, so that operations on the objects in the model have effects like those of corresponding operations in the situations. Mental models of this kind incorporate features of the situation that can go beyond the knowledge that the individual can state in propositions or other explicit forms, and the representations of situations formed as mental models can be constrained by principles that are either known or considered as hypotheses.

This idea about mental models implies that we human reasoners have a mental capability that seems important and interesting, but is poorly understood. The capability can create mental representations that we interact with in ways that are similar to our interactions with physical and, probably, social environments. A theory of situated cognition is a major goal of current research, as I argued in this chapter, so the claim that model-based reasoning is like externally situated reasoning is hardly a solution to the theoretical problem of mental models. I suggest, however, that as we develop accounts of situated cognition for ordinary physical and social environments, we should be alert to implications of those accounts for theories of cognition involving mental models.

This idea also suggests ways of thinking about generative properties of knowledge. Suppose that mental models are acquired with significant properties of external situations and one's interactions with the situations. Suppose, further, that at least some of the properties of mental models are known implicitly in something like the way that we know how to interact with environments but lack articulate expressions of the principles of those interactions. A conclusion is that we have a resource for generative reasoning that can be used to modify the knowledge that we have in symbolic form. Simulative reasoning can be used to conduct thought experiments in which we test implications of principles that we state as propositions. The protocols that Roschelle obtained from physicists provide examples of productive interactions between alternative representations, including cognitive simulations of moving objects apparently based on ordinary experience-based knowledge. The idea also suggests an approach to thinking about the processes involved in conducting thought experiments and of their role in scientific discovery (cf. Miller, 1986).

The concern with situated cognitive activity that I have presented here has precursors in the literature on information processing, and is not unique in current research. Larkin and Simon (1987) discussed ways in which information organized in a diagram can permit more efficient processing than information expressed in sentences. They made the important points that information-processing operations, including search, can be more or less efficient depending on the organization of information in a situation and that information in a diagram may be arranged so that certain operations are easier to carry out with the spatial arrangements of information that diagrams provide. A similar point about computational efficiency was made by Dinsmore (1987) regarding information arranged in mental spaces, as Fauconnier (1985) discussed.

Simon (1975) recognized that different information-processing systems can interact in different ways with objects in an environment, and worked out a perceptual strategy for solving the Tower of Hanoi that uses information in the problem situation in its choices of moves, rather than goals that are stored in a memory stack. Larkin's model DiBS (chap. 12 in this volume) makes similar use of information in the situation, which she refers to as a display.

Issues of situated reasoning have also been addressed recently by Agre and Chapman (1987), in a program called Pengi that simulates play of a video game. Agre and Chapman's program recognizes objects that are related to its current activity and goals (e.g., "the block that the block I just kicked will collide with"). The descriptions in the program have three significant features in relation to the issues that I have discussed here: (a) they are definite descriptions—they are specifically designed to denote objects in a situation, rather than members of a context-free class; (b) they are indexical—they presuppose the situation in which they are used; (c) they are relational—objects are identified by virtue of being in activity based relations with the agent.

These analyses all contribute significantly to our understanding of important aspects of the problem of situated cognition. Analyses that relate actions to information in the situation, rather than information in memory, have begun to spell out some of the ways in which learned situated activity can be represented. A fundamental problem that remains is to understand knowledge that enables generative interactions in novel situations. I believe that the concept of mental models with entities that allow simulative reasoning may have promise for accounting for such generative knowledge, but that is certainly only a hope at this time.

I do not view the suggestions of this paper as undermining the important developments of information-processing psychology during the past two decades. My own research in this period, like that of many others, has been shaped by Herbert Simon's seminal ideas along with those of the other pioneers of cognitive science. The theoretical method of simulation programming and the empirical method of thinking-aloud protocols that Newell and Simon (1972) introduced made possible the analyses of problem-solving knowledge and processes that I and others developed in domains of high-school geometry (e.g., Greeno, 1978) and elementary-school arithmetic (e.g., Kintsch & Greeno, 1985). Like many psychologists, my work has been enriched enjoyably and productively by the opportunity to collaborate with Simon, leading to an analysis of alternative retrieval strategies for hierarchically organized information in memory (Greeno & Simon, 1974) and a review of the psychology of problem solving and reasoning (Greeno & Simon, 1988). Best of all, I benefited during the years that I was in Pittsburgh from opportunities to discuss research in progress in the fairly regular meetings held with Simon, Jill Larkin, and a group of students from the Carnegie-Mellon and Pittsburgh psychology departments, and more often than not from the pleasure of a conversation with Herb as we walked home together after the meeting of that group.

I consider the view that I have presented here toward development of a more relational epistemological framework as a suggestion that builds upon the impressive body of scientific concepts and methods that has been built using the ideas of information processing. The kind of development I have suggested would involve some different directions from those that have been developed thus far within cognitive science and would take into account some perspectives that have been developed along separate lines in the theory of representation and in ethnographic studies. I expect that the outcome of this development will involve significant restructuring of the ways in which we view cognition and learning. At the same time, we could not proceed with this next scientific effort if we did not have the results of information-processing cognitive science to build from.

## ACKNOWLEDGMENTS

Research reported here was supported by the Office of Naval Research (Project NR 667-544, for Roschelle's research), the National Science Foundation (for Johnson's research), the Sloan Foundation (for Goldberg's research), and the Institute for research on Learning (IRL). I am grateful for conversations with many colleagues at IRL about the topics of this paper, including John Seely Brown, Andy diSessa, Brigitte Jordan, Jean Lave, George Pake, Jeremy Roschelle, Alan Schoenfeld, Susan Stucky, and Etienne Wenger. Paul Duguid, Adele Goldberg, Walter Johnson, David Klahr, and Kenneth Kotovsky, contributed helpful comments, and Noreen Greeno assisted with graphic design.

## REFERENCES

Agre, P. E., & Chapman, D. (1987). Pengi: An implementation of a theory of activity. *American Association for Artificial Intelligence.*

Anderson, J. R. (1982). Acquisition of cognitive skill. *Psychological Review, 89,* 396–406.

Anderson, J. R. (1983). *The architecture of cognition.* Cambridge, MA: Harvard University Press.

Anderson, J. R., Boyle, C. F., Farrell, R. G., & Reiser, B. J. (1984). *Cognitive principles in the design of computer tutors* (Tech. Rep. No. ONR-84-1). Pittsburgh: Carnegie-Mellon University, Advanced Computer Tutoring Project.

Anzai, Y., & Simon, H. A. (1979). The theory of learning by doing. *Psychological Review, 86,* 124–140.

Bobrow, D. G. (1968). Natural language input for a computer problem-solving system. In M. Minsky (Ed.), *Semantic information processing.* Cambridge, MA: MIT Press.

Briars, D. J., & Larkin, J. H. (1984). An integrated model of skill in solving elementary word problems. *Cognition and Instruction, 1,* 245–296.

Brown, J. S., & Burton, R. R. (1978). Diagnostic models for procedural bugs in basic mathematical skills. *Cognitive Science, 2,* 155–192.

Caramazza, A., McCloskey, M., & Green, B. (1981). Naive beliefs in "sophisticated" subjects: Misconceptions about trajectories of objects. *Cognition, 2,* 117–123.

Carpenter, T. P., & Moser, J. M. (1983). The acquisition of addition and subtraction concepts. In R. Lesh & M. Landau (Eds.), *Acquisition of mathematics concepts and processes* (pp. 7–44). New York: Academic Press.

Carraher, T., Carraher, D., & Schliemann, A. (1983). *Mathematics in the streets and in schools.* Recife, Brazil: Universidade Federal de Pernambuco.

Chomsky, N. (1957). *Syntactic structures.* The Hague: Mouton.

deKleer, J. (1979). Qualitative and quantitative reasoning in classical mechanics. In P. H. Winston & R. H. Brown (Eds.), *Artificial intelligence: An MIT perspective* (Vol. 1, pp. 11-32). Cambridge, MA: The MIT Press.

deKleer, J., & Brown, J. S. (1984). A qualitative physics based on confluences. *Artificial Intelligence, 24,* 7-84.

Dinsmore, J. (1987). Mental spaces from a functional perspective. *Cognitive Science, 11,* 1-21.

diSessa, A. A. (1983). Phenomenology and the evolution of intuition. In D. Gentner & A. Stevens (Eds.), *Mental models* (pp. 15-33). Hillsdale, NJ: Lawrence Erlbaum Associates.

Dowty, D. R., Wall, R. E., & Peters, S. (1981). *Introduction to Montague semantics.* Dordrecht: D. Reidel.

Dreyfus, H. L., & Dreyfus, S. E. (1986). *Mind over machine.* New York: The Free Press.

Fauconnier, G. (1985). *Mental spaces: Aspects of meaning construction in natural language.* Cambridge, MA: MIT Press/Bradford Books.

Forbus, K. D. (1984). Qualitative process theory. *Artificial Intelligence, 24,* 95-168.

Gentner, D., & Stevens, A. L. (Eds.). (1983). *Mental models.* Hillsdale, NJ: Lawrence Erlbaum Associates.

Gibson, J. J. (1966). *The senses considered as perceptual systems.* Boston: Houghton, Mifflin.

Ginsburg, H. (1977). *Children's arithmetic: The learning process.* New York: D. Van Nostrand.

Greeno, J. G. (1976). Cognitive objectives of instruction: Theory of knowledge for solving problems and answering questions. In D. Klahr (Ed.), *Cognition and instruction* (pp. 123-160). Hillsdale, NJ: Lawrence Erlbaum Associates.

Greeno, J. G. (1978). A study of problem solving. In R. Glaser (Ed.), *Advances in Instructional Psychology* (vol. 1, pp. 13-75). Hillsdale, NJ: Lawrence Erlbaum Associates.

Greeno, J. G. (1983). Forms of understanding in mathematical problem solving. In S. G. Paris, G. M. Olson, & H. W. Stevenson (Eds.), *Learning and motivation in the classroom* (pp. 83-112). Hillsdale, NJ: Lawrence Erlbaum Associates.

Greeno, J. G., Brown, J. S., Foss, C. Shalin, V., Bee, N. V., Lewis, M. W., & Vitolo, T. M. (1986). Cognitive principles of problem solving and instruction. Berkeley, CA: School of Education, University of California, Berkeley.

Greeno, J. G., Riley, M. S., & Gelman, R. (1984). Conceptual competence and children's counting. *Cognitive Psychology, 16,* 94-143.

Greeno, J. G., & Simon, H. A. (1974). Processes for sequence production. *Psychological Review, 81,* 187-198.

Greeno, J. G., & Simon, H. A. (1988). Problem solving and reasoning. In R. C. Atkinson, R. J. Hernstein, G. Lindzey, & R. D. Luce (Eds.), *Stevens' handbook of experimental psychology* (rev. ed.). New York: Wiley.

Heidegger, M. (1962). *Being and time.* New York: Harper & Row. (Original German version, 1926)

Holland, J. H., Holyoak, K. J., Nisbett, R. E., & Thagard, P. R. (1986). *Induction: Processes of inference, learning, and discovery.* Cambridge, MA: MIT Press.

Hudson, T. (1983). Correspondences and numerical differences between disjoint sets. *Child Development, 54,* 84-90.

Johnson, W. A. L. (1988). *Mental models as mediators of language comprehension and domain knowledge in word problem solving.* Unpublished doctoral dissertation, University of Pittsburgh, Pittsburgh.

Johnson-Laird, P. N. (1983). *Mental models: Towards a cognitive science of language, inference, and consciousness.* Cambridge, MA: Harvard University Press.

Kintsch, W., & Greeno, J. G. (1985). Understanding and solving word arithmetic problems. *Psychological Review, 92,* 109-129.

Klahr, D., & Carver, S. M. (1988). Cognitive objectives in a LOGO debugging curriculum: Instruction, learning, and transfer. *Cognitive Psychology, 20,* 362-404.

Larkin, J. H., & Simon, H. A. (1987). Why a diagram is (sometimes) worth ten thousand words. *Cognitive Science, 11,* 65-100.

Lave, J. (1988). *Cognition in practice.* Cambridge: Cambridge University Press.

Lave, J., Murtaugh, M., & de la Rocha, O. (1984). The dialectic of arithmetic in grocery shopping. In B. Rogoff & J. Lave (Eds.), *Everyday cognition: Its development in social context* (pp. 67–94). Cambridge, MA: Harvard University Press.

Markman, E. M. (1979). Classes and collections: Conceptual organization and numerical abilities. *Cognitive Psychology, 11,* 395–411.

Markman, E. M., & Siebert, J. (1976). Classes and collections: Internal organization and resulting holistic properties. *Cognitive Psychology, 8,* 516–577.

McCloskey, M., Caramazza, A., & Green B. (1980). Curvilinear motion in the absence of external forces: Naive beliefs about the motion of objects. *Science, 210,* 1139–1141.

Miller, A. I. (1986). *Imagery in scientific thought.* Cambridge, MA: MIT Press.

Newell, A., Shaw, J. C., & Simon, H. A. (1957). *Preliminary description of the general problem solving program I (GPS I)* (CIP Working Paper 7). Pittsburgh: Carnegie-Mellon University.

Newell, A., & Simon, H. A. (1972). *Human problem solving.* Englewood Cliffs, NJ: Prentice-Hall.

Paige, J. M., & Simon, H. A. (1966). Cognitive processes in solving algebra word problems. In B. Kleinmuntz (Ed.), *Problem solving.* New York: Wiley.

Resnick, L. B., & Omanson, S. F. (in press). Learning to understand arithmetic. In R. Glaser (Ed.), *Advances in instructional psychology* (vol. 3). Hillsdale, NJ: Lawrence Erlbaum Associates.

Riley, M. S., Greeno, J. G., & Heller, J. I. (1983). Development of children's problem-solving ability in arithmetic. In H. P. Ginsburg (Ed.), *The development of mathematical thinking* (pp. 153–196). New York: Academic Press.

Roschelle, J. (1987). *Envisionment, mental models, and physics cognition.* Paper presented at the International Conference on Artificial Intelligence and Education, Pittsburgh, PA.

Roschelle, J., & Greeno, J. G. (1987). Mental models in expert physics reasoning (Rep. No. GK-2). Berkeley, CA: University of California School of Education.

Schoenfeld, A. H. (1987). When good teaching leads to bad results: The disasters of "well taught" mathematics courses. In P. L. Peterson & T. L. Carpenter (Eds.), *Educational Psychologist, 23,* 145–166.

Scribner, S. (1984). Studying working intelligence. In B. Rogoff & J. Lave (Eds.), *Everyday cognition: Its development in social context* (pp. 9–40). Cambridge, MA: Harvard University Press.

Searle, J. R. (1980). Minds, brains, and programs. *The Behavioral and Brain Sciences, 3,* 417–457.

Simon, H. A. (1969). *The sciences of the artificial.* Cambridge, MA: MIT Press.

Simon, H. A. (1975). The functional equivalence of problem solving skills. *Cognitive Psychology, 7,* 268–288.

Smith, B. C. (1983). *Reflection and semantics in a procedural language* (MIT/LCS/TR-272). Cambridge, MA: MIT Laboratory for Computer Science.

Smith, B. C. (1987a). *The correspondence continuum.* CSLI Report (CSLI-87-71), Center for the Study of Language and Information, Stanford University.

Smith, B. C. (1987b). *The semantics of clocks.* CSLI Report, Center for the Study of Language and Information, Stanford University.

Suchman, L. (1987). *Plans and situated actions.* New York: Cambridge University Press.

VanLehn, K. (1983). *Felicity conditions for human skill acquisition: Validating an AI-based theory* (Report No. CLS-21). Palo Alto, CA: Xerox Palo Alto Research Center.

VanLehn, K., & Brown, J. S. (1978). Planning nets: A representation for formalizing analogies and semantic models of procedural skills. In R. E. Snow, P. A. Federico, & W. Montague (Eds.), *Aptitude, learning, and instruction, Volume 2: Cognitive process analyses of learning and problem solving* (pp. 95–138). Hillsdale, NJ: Lawrence Erlbaum Associates.

Winograd, T., & Flores, F. (1986). *Understanding computers and cognition: A new foundation for design.* Norwood, NJ: Ablex.

# 12

## Display-Based Problem Solving

Jill H. Larkin
*Carnegie-Mellon University*

Problem solving is often done in the context of an external display. Often there are the physical objects that are part of a problem situation. Alternatively the solver may construct equations and diagrams as an aid to solving the problem. The purpose of this chapter is to describe a model that explicates the role of these displays, particularly for simple every-day problems and for school mathematics and science. In many of these tasks, skillful use of the display seems to be the dominant problem-solving process. This display-based model of problem solving both explains why certain tasks are easy and why particular mistakes are common.

This kind of display-based problem solving is not the only, or even the most important, process in more complex problem solving. But even for complex problems, use of a display may reduce the complexity of the mental processes required.

Simon (1975) provides the first, and a very clear analysis of this kind of processing in the "sophisticated perceptual" strategy he describes for the Tower of Hanoi puzzle. In contrast to the search, trial, and error of a beginner on the problem, and to the heavy mental computation required by other strategies, for this strategy, each move is directly cued by the visible state of the physical puzzle. The pieces of the puzzle serve as an external record of the problem state, and operators are cued by this external record. Therefore each step requires only looking at the display, and doing what it suggests, without more effortful mental calculation or storage.

Simon also addresses problem solving with external displays in a paper with Paige (1966), which shows that the problem solving of algebra problems is better for subjects who draw diagrams. They also begin to suggest the mechanisms of this advantage—an appropriate diagram can substitute easy perceptual judgments (e.g., which part of a board is longer) for more effort-ful and error-prone logical judgments.

Larkin and Simon (1987) elaborate these ideas demonstrating that for some problems, a good diagram can provide at least two major advantages: First it can greatly shorten the search that would be required to use a verbal state-ment of the same problem. Second, the solver may be able to substitute quick perceptual judgments (e.g., whether two lines intersect) for more difficult logical inferences. These advantages, however, depend on the problem solver having operators that are matched to the display being used. As Simon (1969) commented, computational efficiency depends on the data structure, the pro-gram that operates on it, and the match between them.

This work suggests that diagrams, and other external displays (e.g., the pieces of the Tower of Hanoi) can play an important role in problem solving. This paper pursues further the role of external displays by considering a class of problems that we solve so routinely and easily we may not even think of them as problems. Consider, for example, brewing coffee, a "problem" many of us can solve reliably even with the diminished capacities of early morning. Figure 12.1 shows some of the processes that are part of my personal coffee-making procedure. Lines run toward the left from a process to its prerequisite processes. For example, if coffee is to result, one can't put the filter assembly into the coffee maker until one has put in a filter and has coffee grounds on the filter.

Inside the dotted line are the central processes that are actually required to make coffee. Outside this line are tasks I often perform along with coffee making, like miscellaneous kitchen cleanup, and feeding the cat. These are included merely to illustrate that coffee making doesn't overload cognitive capacity, but allows simultaneous response to stimuli (e.g., the cat's request to be fed or the disgraceful state of the counter).

How are so many components performed reliably, always obeying the many ordering constraints? Furthermore, why does it seem to take so little cognitive effort—I can perform it reliably while talking on the phone or thinking about writing this chapter. The process also suffers little from interruption. I can leave the process to take in the paper, and return easily without becoming confused about what I'm doing. The process is easy to modify. Am I out of filters? A paper towel will do. Am I ambivalent about the decaffeinated regular choice? I can mix the two kinds of beans. Finally, whatever the men-tal processes are, they are not organized as a sequential algorithm. I, and everyone I have watched perform this task, perform it in many orders.

In short, to understand easy tasks like coffee brewing, the following features need to be explained for a task with many component parts that must be performed in a constrained but variable order.

1. The process is easy.
2. It is largely error-free (although as discussed later, particular errors do occur).

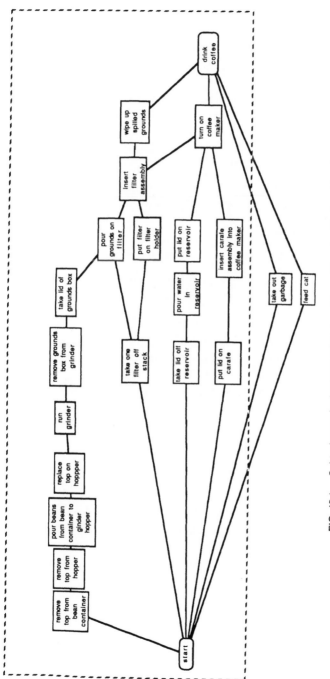

FIG. 12.1.   Subtasks required to brew coffee from beans. Lines leading into a box from the left connect to prerequisite tasks.

3. It is not degraded by interruption.
4. The steps are performed in a variety of orders.
5. The process is easily modified.
6. Performing the task smoothly and easily requires learning—the novice coffee brewer makes many mistakes and often doesn't produce the desired cup of coffee.

What kinds of tasks have these features—effortless, largely error-free performance of a task with many components that must be done according to stringent constraints (although not in a single fixed order)? Certainly many everyday tasks (getting dressed, driving to work, shopping for food) have exactly these characteristics. But they are also true for competent performance of many school tasks. As a second example, consider solving a linear equation such as the following:

$$-3 - 4(2x - 9) = 7 + 5x$$

For most of us, who are essentially experts on this task, our performance shares many aspects with that of brewing coffee.

1. The process is easy.
2. It is largely error-free (although errors do occur, again different ones for more and less experienced people (Carry, Lewis, & Bernard, 1980; Lewis, 1981; Sleeman, 1982, 1984)).
3. This task also is not badly disturbed by interruption, especially if one has completed writing one step before responding to the interruption. But even if interrupted within a step, as in the following sequence, most of us could probably recover:

$$-3 - 4(2x - 9) = 7 + 5x$$
$$- 4(2x - 9) = 10$$

The $-3$ at the left has disappeared and the 7 on the right has become a 10. All numbers are accounted for except the $5x$, which must have been left unwritten at the interruption. There is a constraint that all parts from one step must be accounted for in the next step.
4. Equation solving is commonly done in many orders. In the preceding example, some of us might start by adding 3 to both sides, and others by "clearing" the parentheses.
5. When done by skilled solvers the equation-solving process is easily modified and extended. Little difficulty is caused by changes of letters, the inclusion of fractions, decimals, or powers, or the inclusion of other variables.
6. The smooth easy performance of experts requires learning.

This chapter first describes a computer-implemented model that accounts for these six features by letting the problem solver make extensive use of the external display, the filters and pots of the coffee task and the sequences of symbols in the algebra task, and finally the disks of the Tower of Hanoi. After describing the model, the next section discusses why certain tasks like these can be reliably easy and relatively error-free, and what kinds of errors are still common. The final section suggests some practical applications of the model.

## DESCRIPTION OF THE MODEL

The model is a production system, a set of condition-action pairs, together with a working memory. Conceptually, the computer-implemented working memory is divided into two kinds of elements: those reflecting external real-world objects and those reflecting elements held internally in the solvers' short-term memory. Like all production systems, the model acts when the conditions of some production are satisfied by the contents of working memory, here by a combination of external objects and internal items. The associated actions then change working memory. Again these changes can either be changes to the physical world (e.g., pouring water from a carafe), or to the internal world of the solver (e.g., setting the subgoal to get coffee beans). When working memory has been altered in either of these ways, ordinarily the conditions of some new production are satisfied, and its actions are then implemented. Cycles like this repeat until the problem is solved or until no production is satisfied. The computer model, called "DiBS" for Display-Based Solver is implemented using ExperOps5 on a Macintosh Plus.

DiBS is constructed to use external objects as the major component of its data structure. This lets DiBS clearly explicate the role of display-based problem solving. Then this simple model can be compared with human performance to assess under what circumstances display-based processes may dominate and when they may be mixed with other processes using internal data structures more extensively.

### Basic Mechanisms of Display Based Problem Solving

DiBS reflects the following mechanism: When a solver looks at a display, various visible objects suggest or cue information about where they ought to be placed in order to solve the problem. In assembling a coffee maker, one either knows the equipment, and has an internal memory tag cued by each object indicating where it should go. In solving linear equations, one knows that ultimately the numbers must be on the right and a single instance of the variable on the left. In the Tower of Hanoi one knows that the disks must all be placed, in descending order of size, on the goal peg.

Sometimes DiBS cannot move an object to the place where it "wants" to be. There are two possible reasons—either the object DiBS wants to move has something on top of it, or the location where the object should go has something on top of it. In this situation, DiBS moves the blocking object, and then returns to execute the original goal of moving the first object to its desired location.

As illustrated in the following section, different problem situations require different knowledge about how to get rid of offending blockages, but the same basic mechanism applies to all three, and certainly could readily be extended to other tasks involving assembly physical objects, or manipulating symbol arrays.

## Data Structures

As an OPS program DiBS' data structures are implemented as elements (lists) in a working memory. Each of these elements corresponds to an object visible in the external world. The elements in the list describe the attributes of the object (e.g., its name and location). For simplicity, DiBS works in just one spatial direction—it has an orientation, which turns out to be vertical in all of the examples here. The attribute "below" specifies any object located immediately below the given object.

One attribute (called want_below) in DiBS' data elements does not ordinarily correspond to visible features of the external world. This attribute represents internal knowledge cued by seeing the external physical object. For example, when I see a filter_holder,[1] I know I want a filter above it. However, such knowledge is sometimes represented externally. Commercial coffee makers designed for use by many people often have labels indicating the desired state as in "Pour water in here," and "Filter must be in place before starting machine."

The animistic idea that objects "want" to be below other objects reflects the structure of the program. Problem solving is driven by looking at an object and thinking where it ought to go. Although the knowledge of where this object "wants" to go is in the head of the solver, it is attached to the data structure of the object. In this way, every time the solver attends to an object, this information is available.

## The Program

The DiBS program has the following main parts, reflecting the general strategy discussed in the preceding section.

---

[1]When terms correspond exactly to those used in the program, they are written as they appear in the program, as in the single object "filter_holder," not filter holder.

### Whenever Possible, Move and Object
### Where it Wants to Be.

The details of moving in different problem spaces require slightly different productions. But all these productions have the content of saying if it is known that an objects wants to be below another object, and if there are no objects blocking either the object to be moved or the place to which it would be moved, then move the object.

### Remove Blockages

The second group of productions deals with cases where either an object that wants an object on top of it, or the object that is wanted is blocked by an additional object. These productions remove these blocking objects, putting them elsewhere. Again there are special considerations in various cases and in various problems—fluids must be moved onto another object, not dumped on the counter. In the Tower of Hanoi, disks can only go on larger disks, and it is unfruitful to undo the move that has just been made. In algebra, the 4 in the following equation:

$$3(4 - 2x) = 7$$

is wanted on the right-hand side because it is a number. But unblocking it requires applying the distributive principle.

### Combinations

Solving linear equations also requires some special rules for arithmetic combination. Replacing $3 \times 4$ by 12 is different from placing a coffee filter on a filter holder. In the former, two objects actually disappear and are replaced by a new one. In the latter the objects retain their identity, but change location. Some similar treatment would be required for chemistry or cooking, where flour, milk, and sugar can disappear and are replaced by cake.

### Recognizing That the Problem is Solved

A final set of productions checks that every object is where it wants to be, and declares the problem solved.

### Explaining Actions

To facilitate following DiBs work, each production, as it executes, writes an English description of its action, and the conditions that cued that action. This produces an interpretable record of the problem-solving actions.

## ILLUSTRATIONS OF USING EXTERNAL DATA
## STRUCTURES TO SOLVE PROBLEMS

We look here at some examples showing how the basic mechanisms described in the preceding section apply to three situations: brewing coffee, solving linear equations, and solving the Tower of Hanoi puzzle. The solution to the latter problem is compared with the perceptual strategy of Simon (1975).

### Brewing Coffee

Figure 12.2 shows a typical array of coffee-brewing equipment laid out on a counter. Table 12.1a shows this data structure coded as OPS working-memory elements for DiBS. Each of these elements is a list of attribute-value pairs. In Table 12.1a, the first line (underlined) lists the attributes that may be possessed by an any object in DiBS' data structures. Below this line working-memory objects are listed with values corresponding to the equipment array shown in Fig. 12.2. Additionally the values for "want__below" specify knowledge about how the coffee maker should be assembled—knowledge not directly present in the external world but cued by seeing the objects.

Table 12.1b shows the sequence of productions that execute as DiBS works on the coffee task and the English statements describing the action and the conditions cueing that action. In brief, the solution consists of placing objects where their "want__below" attribute indicates they should go, and moving some blocking objects out of the way in order to do this. For example, to get the water from the carafe into the reservoir, both the carafe lid and the reservoir lid must be removed.

### Linear Equations

To support the idea that display-based problem solving is important in both routine and common school tasks, DiBS also has knowledge for solving linear equations, as well as knowledge for brewing coffee. The two examples differ in that one task is abstract and the display consists of marks on paper, whereas the other is concrete and the display consists of real objects resting on a counter. Of course the model needs some different domain-specific knowledge for each of these two cases, but the main features of its operation are the same.

We consider how DiBS uses a written linear equation like the following:

$$-3 - 4(2x - 9) = 7 + 5x$$

as an external display for the task of solving the equation.

Figure 12.3 shows schematically DiBS' data structure for a linear equation. The leaves of the tree are the external parts of the data structure, the physically written numbers and symbols. At the top of the tree, under the root "equation" node, are the nodes called lhs and rhs two sides of the equa-

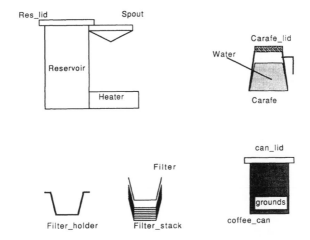

FIG. 12.2.  External display for brewing coffee

tion. Below them are nodes for the four top-level terms of the equation. The second term has two factors, one of which is itself made up of two terms.

For simplicity, terms are always jointed by " + " and factors by "x". Therefore, in DiBS' data structure − 3 − 4(2x − 9) is replaced by − 3 + − 4(2x + ⁻9). This simplification is not essential to the arguments made here, but makes the programs much simpler and easier to present. The notation − 9 with the elevated negative sign indicates the number negative nine, and avoids ambiguity with subtraction of a positive nine.

Notice that every node in the tree corresponds to a collection of external written symbols that could readily be identified by any competent human solver, who could perform tasks like: Underline the right hand side; Circle the terms in the left hand side; Name the factors of the second term. Therefore it is plausible that the nodes in Fig. 12.3 correspond to internal parts of the data structure of a competent solver.

Table 12.2a shows how DiBS represents the data structure shown in Fig. 12.3. The elements are exactly the nodes of the tree. For ease of implementation, both $x$__terms (like 2x) and numbers (like 5) have values that are numbers. The $x$__terms and numbers can be distinguished because numbers want to be below the rhs node, whereas $x$__terms want to be below the lhs node.

Table 12.2b shows the sequence of productions that execute as DiBS solves the equation, together with the English statements written by each production. In brief, the solution consists of moving − 3 to the rhs, because it wants to be there, and is not blocked from moving. Also 5x is free to be moved to the lhs. Then ⁻3 and 7 are combined to give:

TABLE 12.1
Trace of DiBS' Procedure for Brewing Coffee

(a) The Initial Data Structure

| Name | Type | Value | Below | Want_below |
|------|------|-------|-------|------------|
| filter_holder | solid | | | filter |
| filter | solid | | grounds | |
| filter_stack | solid | | filter | |
| reservoir | solid | | res_lid | water |
| res_lid | solid | | | |
| carafe | solid | | water | carafe_lid |
| water | fluid | | carafe_lid | res_lid |
| carafe_lid | solid | | | |
| grounds_can | solid | | grounds | can_lid |
| grounds | fluid | | can_lid | spout |
| can_lid | solid | | | |
| heater | solid | | | carafe |
| spout | solid | | | |

(b) Trace of Brewing Coffee

1. put_an_object_where_it_wants_to_be_coffee_1

   filter_holder wants to be below filter
   moving filter_holder beneath filter
   filter_stack no longer below filter

2. solid_object_blockage_1

   water is below carafe_lid but wants to be below res_lid
   moving carafe_lid off of water

3. solid_object_blockage_2

   reservoir wants to be below water and is instead below res_lid
   res_lid is a solid
   moving res_lid off of reservoir

4. put_an_object_where_it_wants_to_be_coffee_1

   reservoir wants to be below water
   moving reservoir beneath water
   carafe no longer beneath water

5. put_an_object_where_it_wants_to_be_coffee_2

   water wants to be below res_lid

and is not already there
moving res_lid onto water

6. put_an_object_where_it_wants_to_be_coffee_2

   carafe wants to be below carafe_lid
   and is not already there
   moving carafe_lid onto carafe

7. solid_object_blockage_1

   grounds is below can_lid but wants to be below spout
   moving can_lid off of grounds

8. put_an_object_where_it_wants_to_be_coffee_1

   filter wants to be below grounds
   moving filter beneath grounds
   can no longer beneath grounds

9. put_an_object_where_it_wants_to_be_coffee_2

   grounds wants to be below spout
   moving grounds beneath spout

10. put_an_object_where_it_wants_to_be_coffee_2

    heater wants to be below carafe
    moving heater beneath carafe

$$-5x + {}^-4(2x + {}^-9) = 10$$

Now ⁻9 is blocked from being moved to the rhs because it lies under the factor node p4. This cues execution of the production that carries out the distributive principle, yielding:

$$-5x + {}^-8x + 36 = 10$$

All terms are now free to move, and when this has happened the equation is:

$${}^-13x = {}^-26$$

A final production capturing special algebra knowledge is cued by the existence of just two terms, each in their desired place. This production changes the coefficient of $x$ to 1 and the value of the rhs number to

$${}^-26/{}^-13 = 2.$$

The equation is now $x = 2$, and the done production recognizes that there are just two items, each in their proper place, and that the value of the x_term is 1. This is the criterion for solution, and the program halts.

## The Tower of Hanoi

DiBS' method for solving the Tower of Hanoi is essentially similar to the "perceptual" strategy of Simon (1975). Like that strategy it uses as part of its data structure external display (for the three-disk version), and thereby avoids any need for keeping track (internally) of any long goal stack. This display consists of three disks, initially arranged in decreasing size on one

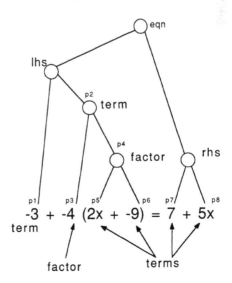

FIG. 12.3 Linear equation grouped with higher representing composites of lower nodes.

TABLE 12.2
Trace of DiBS' Solution of a Linear Equation

(a) The Initial Data Structure

| Name | Type | Value | Below | Want_below |
|------|------|-------|-------|-----------|
| p1 | term | −3 | lhs | rhs |
| p2 | term | | lhs | |
| p3 | factor | −4 | p2 | rhs |
| p4 | factor | | p2 | |
| p5 | term | 2 | p4 | lhs |
| p6 | term | −9 | p4 | rhs |
| p7 | term | 7 | rhs | rhs |
| p8 | term | 5 | rhs | lhs |

(b) Trace of the Solving Process

| p1 | | p3 | p5 | p6 | p7 | p8 |
|----|---|----|----|----|----|----|
| −3 | + | −4 | (2x | + | −9) | = 7 + 5x |

1. put_an_object_where_it
   _wants_to_be_alg
   p1, value −3 wants to be below
   rhs
   moving p1 below rhs

2. combine_add
   combining terms of value −3
   and −7 on rhs

3. put_an_object_where_it
   _wants_to_be_alg
   p8, value 5 wants to be below
   lhs
   moving p8 below lhs

| | | p2 | | |
|---|---|----|----|---|
| | | | p4 | |
| p8 | | p3 | p5 | p6 | p7 |
| −5x | + | −4 | (2x | + | −9) | = 10 |

4. uncover_alg
   taking apart the mixed term p2
   with coefficient −4 and number
   2 and x_term −9

| p8 | | p5 | | p6 | | p7 |
|----|---|----|---|----|---|----|
| −5x | + | −8x | + | 36 | = | 10 |

5. combine_add
   combining terms of value −5
   and −8 on lhs

6. put_an_object_where_it
   _wants_to_be_alg
   p6, value 36 wants to be below
   rhs
   moving p8 below rhs

7. combine_add
   combining terms of value −36
   and 10 on rhs

| p5 | p7 |
|----|----|
| −13x | + −26 |

8. last_x_term
   dividing both sides by −13

9. done_alg
   all variables are below lhs
   and all numbers are below rhs
   only two terms remain
   therefore done

of three pegs. The problem is to move them all to a goal peg, moving the disks one at a time, never placing a larger disk on a smaller. Table 12.3a shows the DiBS data structure written as OPS working-memory elements. The data structure for the Tower of Hanoi is, not surprisingly, more similar to that of the coffee equipment than to that of the linear equation. The linear equation data structure contained elements corresponding to groups of objects.

In the coffee and Tower of Hanoi tasks, each element of the data structure corresponds to a single external object.

For consistency with the other problems, the pegs in the Tower of Hanoi are objects that want to have certain disks on them. One might imagine, instead of pegs, flat spots on a table, that want to acquire certain disks.

The production

put__an__object__where__it__wants__to__be__coffee__1

used in the coffee task also serves to move a disk from one peg to another. The problem-solving strategy is involved in attaching to each disk a tag indicating what peg currently wants to have it.

Briefly, this strategy has the following components:

If there is nothing else to do let the largest disk become wanted by the top of the "fixed" disks already placed on the goal peg.

If a disk A is wanted by another place, and there is a blocking disk B on top of it, make B wanted by something which has nothing on top of it, which is not the place where you want to move A, and is not on top of A and B.

If an object X (peg or disk) wants a disk Y on top of it, but X already has something on top of it, then make Y wanted by an object which has nothing on top of it, which is not on top of Y or X.

When a disk is placed on the goal peg c, on top of the next-larger disk, relabel it a "fixed__disk" so that it can no longer be recognized by any of the productions that move disks.

Table 12.3b shows how the productions reflecting these strategies interact with move productions already used by the coffee task in order to solve the three-disk Tower of Hanoi problem.

## DiBS AND HUMAN PROBLEM SOLVING

Having described DiBS' components and how it works, we return to the six features of human solutions described in the preceding section and ask how this model can account for these features.

A central feature of all the DiBS solutions discussed is that very little must be held in internal working memory. Many attributes of the data structure are attributes of external objects. These need not be stored internally but can be observed from the environment. Others are associated directly with an object, so that the object may well serve as a helpful cue to remembering the attribute.

With this background, let us see how DiBS might account for the following six features of human display-based problem solving listed in the introduction.

TABLE 12.3
Trace of DiBS's Solution to the Three-disk Tower of Hanoi Problem.

### (a) The Initial Data Structure

| Name | Type | Value | Below | Want_below |
|------|------|-------|-------|------------|
| d3 | disk | 3 | d2 | d2 |
| d2 | disk | 2 | d1 | d1 |
| d1 | disk | 1 | nil | nil |
| a | pole | | d3 | nil |
| b | pole | | nil | |
| c | pole | | nil | d3 |

### (b) Trace of the Solving Process

```
  d1
  d2
  d3
  a     b     c
```

1. no_goals
   the largest disk is wanted on
   the goal pec c

2. assign_goal_1
   object b wants disk d2 on top
   of it

3. assign_goal_1
   object c wants disk d1 on top
   of it

4. put_an_object_where_
   it_wants_to_be _coffee_1
   c wants to be below d1
   moving c beneath d1
   d2 no longer beneath d1

5. put_an_object_where_it
   _wants_to_be _coffee_1
   b wants to be below d2
   moving b beneath d2
   d3 no longer beneath d1

6. assign_goal_2
   object d2 wants disk d1 on top
   of it

7. put_an_object_where_it_
   wants_to_be _coffee_1
   c wants to be below d3
   moving c beneath d3
   a no longer beneath d3

```
  d1
  d2       d3
  a     b     c
```

8. fixing_done_disks_on_goal_peg
   disk d3 is in its final
   location
   calling it fixed_disk to avoid
   moving it again

9. recurse
   set goal to place the largest
   remaining disk d2
   onto the top of the fixed_disk
   pile

10. assign_goal_1
    object a wants disk d1 on top
    of it

11. put_an_object_where_it
    _wants_to_be_coffee_1
    a wants to be below d1
    moving a beneath d1
    d2 no longer beneath d1

12. put_ann_object_where_it
    _wants_to_be _coffee_1
    d3 wants to be below d2
    moving d3 beneath d2
    b no longer beneath d2

```
              d2
  d1          d3
  a     b     c
```

13. fixing_done_disks_on_goal_peg
    disk d2 is in its final
    location
    calling it fixed_disk to avoid
    moving it again

14. recurse
    set goal to place the largest remaining
    disk d1
    onto the top of the fixed_disk
    pile

*(Continued)*

TABLE 12.3
*(continued)*

| | |
|---|---|
| 15. put__an__object__where__<br>it__wants__to__be __coffee__1<br>d2 wants to be below d1<br>moving d2 beneath d1<br>a no longer beneath d1 | 13. fixing__done__disks__on__goal__peg<br>disk d1 is in its final<br>location<br>calling it fixed__disk to avoid<br>moving it again |

| | | d1 | | 14. done__toh |
|---|---|---|---|---|

```
                    d1
                    d2
                    d3
   a      b         c
```

14. done__toh
all disks are fixed disks in
their goal location

1. Because DiBS places very little load on internal working memory to hold either goals or problem-state information, for a human this process should seem introspectively **easy.**

2. DiBS follows a process that should be **resilient against errors.** Working memory losses are not important. If errors are made, they are encoded in the display. On the next cycle, DiBS may simply be able to continue from the current state. It could also use special error-correction procedures, although none of these have been implemented.

3. If it is interrupted, at worst DiBS looses internal information not yet reflected by altering the display. Therefore there is **little cost for interruption.**

4. DiBS has little strategic knowledge—it performs any legal action suggested by the display, working around roadblocks when it must. It therefore has no preference for one sequence of actions over another. The particular sequence chosen may depend on exactly where in the display attention is focused, or, as discussed later, on efforts to work around special difficulties.

5. Because DiBS can find any currently legal step, it easily **modifies its procedure to work around difficulties,** and on different occasions will solve the same problem with different orders of steps.

6. Display-based problem solving **requires learning.** Domain specific productions are required to get useful information from the display and to generate knowledge of where an object "wants" to go.

In summary, DiBS uses an external display as the major part of its data structure and so produces behavior with major features similar to those of humans working similar tasks.

## When is Problem Solving Based on Displays?

The examples considered are extreme in that they can be done with little reliance on internal memory and extensive use of an external display for both goal and problem-state information. Much problem solving has less reliance on displays. Operationally, the difference is the extent to which information can be held internally, in either short- or long-term memory. Ericsson, Chase, and Faloon (1980) described mechanisms through which information can quickly be attached to long-term memory structures. Display-based problem solving seems unlikely to be an isolated special form of reasoning, but one technique among several that may be used. As previously discussed, it has many advantages, but there are times when a good display doesn't exist. A good example is the planning of a sentence or a few lines of code in a computer program. The information being assembled is stored internally. If interrupted, one largely loses this information. The reasoning is subject to errors—often one writes a faulty sentence or piece of code, only detecting the error when it is written.

## Errors of Display-Based Problem Solving

As we have seen, display-based problem solving is resistant to many errors because the display makes the process largely independent of internal memory failures. There is, however, considerable evidence, much gathered using the Tower of Hanoi and its isomorphs that the nature of the display can greatly affect problem difficulty (Hayes & Simon, H.A., 1976, 1977; Kotovsky, Hayes, & Simon, 1985). This section discusses common human errors in the algebra and coffee-brewing tasks, and suggests how these errors are related to the nature of the displays.

### Parsing Errors in Algebra

In algebra, the DiBS data structure consisted of objects corresponding to single symbols (e.g., 9) and to meaningful groups of symbols [e.g., $4(9x - 5)$]. Suppose a solver did not have these group elements in the data structure, but instead viewed an equation as simply a string of individual symbols. I call errors resulting from this situation *parsing* errors, because they result from developing an internal data structure that does not appropriately capture the important features of the external display.

The following two errors are among the most common made by students (Sleeman, 1982).

1. $$^-3 + {}^-4(2x + {}^-9) = 7 + 5x$$
   "Move" the $^-9$ to the right side to obtain either
   $$^-3 + {}^-4(2x) = 5x + 16$$
   $$^-3 + {}^-4(2x) = 5x + {}^-2,$$
   depending on correct application of the algebraic move operator.

2. $$^-3 + {}^-4(2x + {}^-9) = 7 + 5x$$
   Combine the $^-4$ and 2, neglecting the grouping function of parentheses, to obtain

$$-3 + {}^-8x + {}^-9 = 7 + 5x$$

Display-based problem solving gives a parsimonious explanation of these common errors if one assumes that students prone to these errors do not construct the tree structure shown in Fig. 12.3, but instead use simply a string with parentheses ignored.

Running DiBS on a display parsed in this way produces exactly the two common errors already listed. In string representation the $-9$ is just as moveable as the $-3$, and it is quickly moved to the goal location at the right of the equal sign. The substring " $-4(2x$" is parsed as an assembly containing two numbers that can be further assembled, making progress towards the goal of only one number. Table 12.4 shows DiBS' production of these two errors.

### Errors Due to Hidden State Information

I have collected about 100 errors from two sources over the last 8 months—asking people about errors in making coffee, and observing guests using the equipment in my kitchen. About 70 of these errors are isomorphs of the following:

> While on vacation, I was making drip coffee in a thermos bottle. I put hot water into the bottle to preheat it. But then when I came to make the coffee, I put the filter on top and poured through new water, forgetting that the old water was there. So weak coffee went all over the counter.

This error has many variants:

> "We used to have a pot (or cone filters) so small that we had to pour the water in twice in order to fill the coffee pot. Then we got a bigger pot (or bigger filters cone filters), and the first many times we used them we still poured in water twice and overfilled the pot. (In both cases the coffee pot was not transparent.)
>
> We have two coffee pots, one clear and one solid. When we use the solid one, we sometimes forget that the water has already been poured in and . . .

I believe this common set of errors is produced because the display conceals crucial information about its state (the contents of the coffee pot). Because the display fails to provide adequate information about the problem state, the advantages of display-based problem solving are lost. If the solver is interrupted or experiences a working memory loss, this information cannot be recovered easily from the display, and the preceding kind of error results.

A second set of coffee-making errors is analogous to novices' incorrect parsing of equations. The most obvious cases are those in which someone cannot disassemble or assemble some piece of equipment (observed both for my grinder, and for the espresso machine of a friend). I also have observed

TABLE 12.4
Trace of DiBS' Solution of a Linear Equation,
with a String (rather than a tree) Data Structure

(a) The Initial Data Structure

| Name | Type | Value | Below | Want_below |
|------|------|-------|-------|------------|
| p1 | | −3 | | rhs |
| op1 | op | + | | |
| p3 | | −4 | | rhs |
| op2 | op | • | | |
| p5 | | 2 | | lhs |
| op3 | op | + | | |
| p6 | | −9 | | rhs |
| p7 | | 7 | | rhs |
| op | op | + | | |
| p8 | | 5 | | lhs |

(b) Trace Showing Production
of Two Common Human Errors

| p1 | | p3 | p5 | p6 | | p7 | | p8 |
|----|----|----|----|----|----|----|----|----|
| −3 | + | −4 | (2x | + | −9) | = | 7 | + | 5x |

1. put_an_object_
   where_it_wants_to_be_alg

   p6, value −9 wants to be below
   rhs
   moving p6 below rhs

2. combine_add

   combining terms of value 7
   and 9 on rhs

| p1 | | p3 | p5 | p7 | | p8 |
|----|----|----|----|----|----|----|
| −3 | + | −4• | (2x | = | 16 | + | 5x |

3. combine_multiply

   combining factors of value −4
   and 2 on lhs

| p1 | | p5 | p7 | | p8 |
|----|----|----|----|----|----|
| −3 | + | −8x | = | 16 | + | 5x |

one case in which a guest assembled the grinder omitting the lid to the grounds hopper. When she turned on the grinder, it blew grounds all over the kitchen. This error is analogous to algebra errors in which a visually small display element (parentheses) is ignored. Here the lid is small, and when inserted in the grinder, the hopper appears to have a cover (just not a grounds-tight one).

### Knowledge-Lack Errors

In the context of display-based problem solving, errors based on the display are particulary interesting. However, there are errors which have nothing to do with the display, but with lack of knowledge of how to implement the domain-specific operators. In algebra, the simplest and most common error is to move a term (e.g., +4) across the equal sign as if it were a bag of coffee, paying no attention to the mathematical meaning of the "+" sign. The correct move operator for moving across the equal sign consists of taking minus, the inverse operator of plus, and then subtracting 4 from both sides.

In coffee making too, implementing operators can be the source of error. About half the reported errors deal with misjudging quantities, for example: (a) "I meant to have a lot of milk in my last cup of coffee in the afternoon, but I forgot and didn't leave enough space." or, (b) Remembering the quantities of coffee and water, and/or the quantitative setting on dials is a great difficulty for anyone who doesn't use particular equipment regularly.

In summary, I've identified two kinds of errors common in display-based problem: (a) the solver may fail to encode essential features of the display (parsing errors), and (b) the solver may lack needed domain-specific knowledge. When the display hides crucial information (as in the opaque reservoir of a coffee maker) errors are particularly likely.

## POTENTIAL APPLICATIONS

In discussing the model of display-based problem solving, I have considered displays specified for the user. The coffee display is the physical equipment available. The algebra display is the set of marks conventionally used to represent equations. The model, however, describes a general hypothesis about how humans use displays in solving problems. Based on this model therefore, one can suggest guidelines that should make displays more or less difficult to use. There are existing guidelines and philosophies for designing certain kinds of displays (Bertin, 1983; Tufte, 1983), these are not based on psychological theory (Kosslyn, 1985).

The central premise of display-based problem solving is that the external display is the main representation of the current problem state. If various internal goals or annotations are lost, they can always be reconstructed from the display. As discussed more extensively in Larkin and Simon (1987), there is a crucial interaction between the nature of the display and the program that operates on it. A good display supports an efficient, robust problem-solving process. The discussion here suggests that the following features are useful.

First, show all essential features of the current problem state. DiBS cannot solve problems for which this is not the case, and the major errors found in coffee making occurred where the display hid a crucial aspect of the problem state (usually whether the pot was full). There is also suggestive evidence that many errors in algebra occur because the solver does not "see" the relevant groupings, but interprets the display as a string of symbols.

Also, left inferences be made through perceptual rather than logical processes. Perceptual judgments (e.g., comparisons of length, judging whether two lines cross) are easy. Logical inferences are difficult and error prone. Therefore, in designing a good display for problem solving, one would like to let as much of the work as possible be done by perceptual rather than logical inferences.

This idea can often be applied to developing good displays of scientific data where the reader's problem is to make certain inferences based on the data. For example, consider the following array of numbers:

| Seed Batch | Inside Storages | |
| --- | --- | --- |
| Number | Mean | SD |
| 191 PRIOR | .176 | (.301) |
| POST | .006 | (.024) |
| 302 PRIOR | .400 | (.490) |
| POST | .805 | (.206) |
| 337 PRIOR | .133 | (.340) |
| POST | 1.000 | (.004) |
| 284 PRIOR | .876 | (.004) |
| POST | .000 | (.000) |
| 283 PRIOR | .500 | (.500) |
| POST | .069 | (.136) |
| 273 PRIOR | .500 | (.500) |
| POST | .973 | (.075) |

They concern probably usages of various sites in an archaeological dig. The numbers describe the probabilities that a particular spot was used for a given activity. The two probabilities are those assigned before and after the application of a novel statistical technique (see Kadane & Hastorf, 1988).

The interesting questions about this reseasrch are: "Did the novel analysis change the estimations of what the structures were used for?" These questions are quite difficult to answer based on the numerical array previously illustrated.

A better display would let the reader observe and compare estimates and estimate changes perceptually. Figure 12.4 uses vectors to represent the difference between the initial and final estimates for usage of each site. The heads of the vectors are at the final estimates, and the tails initial estimates.

This representation makes it very easy to make relevant inferences about the data and its analysis.

Generally, considerations of the psychological processes that a display should support could lead to better design in a variety of areas. I have, for example, recently seen a coffee maker with a clear panel down the side of its reservoir. Algebra students might be aided by special display, emphasizing the relevant symbol groups (Larkin, 1988). Such considerations should certainly be a part of the growing efforts to design easily used human-computer interfaces.

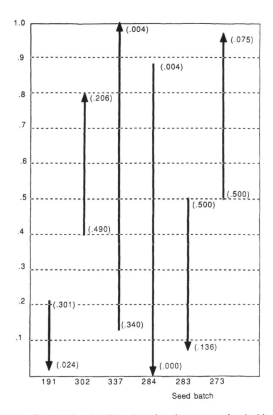

FIG. 12.4. Estimated probabilities that a location was used as inside storage based on seeds gathered at six locations. The tails of the arrows indicate the estimates before a particular statistical technique was applied, and the heads the estimate after this technique was applied. Standard errors of each estimate are shown next to the heads and tails.

## CONCLUSION

Most models of problem solving, and many experimental studies of it, characterize only reasoning occurring inside the head. This paper suggests that in many tasks, an external display may be an extremely important information storage resource. Displays include both configurations of real objects (e.g., coffee makers and grinders) and the pencil marks making up an artificial display such as an algebra equation or a graph.

The DiBS (display-based solver) model described here describes the mechanisms of display-based problem solving for both a real-object and a paper-and-pencil display. The main features of this model is that all important results are immediately reflected in a change in the display. Processing like this can explain why some tasks (like the tree used as examples here) are almost effortless for skilled people—there is little storage in working memory and the model recovers easily from working-memory failures. DiBS also explains a common class of errors that result from misinterpreting the display.

In other tasks, display-based problem solving may play only a partial role, with important information storage also in internal short-term or long-term memory. But the ease and reliability of display-based problem solving suggests that it is a powerful technique to be exploited wherever possible.

DiBS' mechanisms and its typical errors suggest that guidelines for designing useful displays are based on making the display a clear and regularly updated representation of the problem state, and letting important parts of problem solving be done by perceptual rather than logical inference.

## ACKNOWLEDGMENTS

This work was supported by a grant from John Simon Guggenheim Memorial Foundation and by grants MDR 8470166 and R118600412 from NSF. My thanks to Fred Reif, Bruce Sherwood, and Don Ploger for their particularly useful comments on an earlier draft. The editors David Klahr and Kenneth Kotovsky made excellent suggestions used extensively in preparing the final draft.

## REFERENCES

Bertin, J. (1983). *Semiology of graphs* (W. J. Berg, trans.) Madison, WI: University of Wisconsin Press.

Carry, L. R., Lewis, C., & Bernard, J. E., (1980). *Psychology of equation solving: An information processing study.* Technical Report Department of Curriculum & Instruction, University of Texas at Austin.

Ericsson, K. A., Chase, W. G., & Faloon, S. (1980). Acquisition of a memory skill. *Science, 208,* 1181–1182.

Hayes, J. R., & Simon, H. A. (1976). The understanding process: Problem isomorphs. *Cognitive Psychology, 8,* 165–190.

Hayes, J. R., & Simon, H. A. (1977). Psychological differences among problem isomorphs. In N. J. Castellan, G. R. Pisoni, & G. R. Potts (Eds.), *Cognitive Theory* (Vol. 2). Hillsdale, NJ: Lawrence Erlbaum Associates.

Kadane, J. B., & Hastorf, C. (in press). Bayesian paleoethnobotony. In J. M. Bernardo, M. deGroot, D. Lindley, & A. M. F. Smith (Eds.), *Bayesian statistics 3.* Oxford: Oxford University Press.

Kosslyn, S. M. (1985). Graphics and human information processing: A review of five books. *JASA, 80* (391), 499–512.

Kotovsky, K., Hayes, J. R., & Simon, H. (1985). Why are some problems hard? Evidence from Tower of Hanoi. *Cognitive Psychology, 17,* 248–294.

Larkin, J. H. (1988). Robust performance in algebra: The role of the problem representation. *Proceedings of the Research Agenda Project in Algebra, Athens, GA, 1987.* National Council of Teachers of Mathematics.

Larkin, J. H., & Simon, H. A. (1987). Why a diagram is (sometimes) worth 10,000 words. *Cognitive Science, 11,* 65–100.

Lewis, C. (1981). Skill in algebra. In J. Anderson (Ed.), *Cognitive skills and their acquisition* (pp. 85–110). Hillsdale, NJ: Lawrence Erlbaum Associates.

Paige, J. M., & Simon, H. A. (1966). Congitive processes in solving algebra word problems. In B. Kleinmuntz (Ed.), *Problem solving.* New York: Wiley.

Simon, H. A., & Barenfeld, M. (1969). Information processing analysis of perceptual processes in problem solving. *Psychological Review, 76,* 473–483.

Simon, H. A. (1975). The functional equivalence of problem solving skills. *Cognitive Psychology, 7,* 266–268.

Sleeman, D. (1984). An attempt to understand students' understanding of basic algebra. *Cognitive Science, 8* (4), 387–413.

Sleeman, D. (1982). Assessing aspects of competence in basic algebra. In D. Sleeman & J. S. Brown (Eds.), *Intelligent Tutoring Systems* (pp. 185–200). New York: Academic Press.

Tufte, E. R. (1983). *The visual display of quantitative information.* Cheshire, CT: Graphics Press.

# 13

## The Analogical Origins of Errors in Problem Solving

John R. Anderson
*Carnegie-Mellon University*

Problem solving and learning have long been among Herb Simon's intellectual interests. The major argument of this chapter is that people learn problem solving skills in domains like mathematics and computer programming by analogy. Specifically, when solving a current problem they analogize to the solutions of previous problems (done by them or others). The idea of learning by doing has long been an idea of Simon's (e.g., Anzai & Simon, 1979) and recently Herb has been looking in detail at learning from examples (Zhu & Simon, 1987). This chapter looks at systematic pattern errors that occur in students' interactions with intelligent tutors and argues that these errors arise through the analogy process. The implication is that not only errors but successful learning occurs by analogy. In fact, most analogies appear to be successful as witnessed by the fact that such systematic errors are relatively rare.

We have been working on intelligent tutors to teach students problem solving skills in the domains of generating proofs in geometry (Anderson, Boyle, & Yost, 1985), writing LISP programs (Reiser, Anderson, & Farrell, 1985), and solving algebraic manipulation problems (Lewis, Milson, & Anderson, 1987). Student errors are the most important events in terms of guiding the tutorial dialogues. They are very good signals that the student is in need of help. Other cues do not seem so reliable. Latency of response and requests for help are the two other cues that we have considered in addition to errors. Long latencies may only mean that the student has been distracted and students are notoriously unwilling to ask for help. On the other hand an error comes close to being a necessary and sufficient condition for tutorial intervention. They are the primary signal used by almost all tutorial systems that have been built (e.g., consider Sleeman & Brown, 1982).

Errors can have different etiologies. One class of error is the *slip*, which is characterized by the fact that the subject does not reliably make that error and can self-correct when the error is pointed out. In our work on tutoring, slips appear to decrease in frequency with practice and increase with working memory load. We (Anderson & Jeffries, 1985) argued that slips can be traced to losses from working memory of critical information for solving a problem. Thus, when memory load goes up, slips increase. The decrease in slips with practice reflects a growth in effective working-memory capacity with expertise (Chase & Ericsson, 1982).

A second category of errors that has been discussed (e.g., McCloskey, 1983) is *importations of prior misconceptions into a new domain*. Physics is one domain that has many such errors. However, they have not been a significant category of error in our work given that we are working in domains for which students do not have an abundance of prior conceptions.

A third category of errors, which is the focus of this chapter, is *within-domain misconceptions*. These are misconceptions that arise, not because of prior beliefs that the student has, but as a consequence of the learning that takes place in the domain. These are perhaps the most interesting errors because they reflect on the nature of the learning process itself. Also in contrast to the first category of errors they challenge the tutor. It is not enough to simply point out the error because the student cannot self-correct easily. The tutor must explain to the student something about what the error is and what is required for a correct answer.

A very elegant set of analyses have been done by Brown and VanLehn (1980) and VanLehn (1983) on within-domain misconceptions in multicolumn subtraction. Brown and VanLehn's basic argument was that these errors arose when students tried to bridge points in their problem solving where they had inadequate knowledge. These points are called *impasses* and the bridging process produces *repairs*. If students believe their repairs, a permanent misconception appears and if they do not, an inconsistent pattern of "bug migration" appears. The analysis to be offered here has a lot in common with their analysis. Its major point of departure is that it conceives of the repair process as rather simpler than what Brown and VanLehn proposed. This chapter argues that these errors are caused by making analogies to misleading examples of problem solution.

This chapter begins with a sketch of the basic learning processes that we think are at work in the subjects we have tutored. Basically, this involves students doing a causal analysis of the examples and trying to extend that analysis analogically. The most straightforward way errors can occur in this analogy process is for students to choose an inappropriate example to map to the current solution. This is certainly not the only way misunderstandings can arise and it is of interest to get a sense of what fraction of student errors may be explained in this fashion. Therefore, I present a list of some of the dominant misconceptions that students have displayed interacting with our tutors and consider how many can be interpreted in this fashion. Then, I speculate on how many of subtraction errors, which were the focus of Brown and VanLehn's analysis, can be so explained. Finally, I compare this analysis of the source of errors with the analysis offered by VanLehn (1983, 1985).

## THE PUPS THEORY OF LEARNING

We have developed a simulation program called PUPS (Penultimate Production System—Anderson & Thompson, in press), which embodies our current theory of learning. It is somewhere between an elaboration and a successor of the ACT* theory that I developed a few years ago (Anderson, 1983). It differs from that theory mainly in the emphasis it gives to analogy in the knowledge acquisition process. Data from sources such as Pirolli (1985) convinced us that analogy is very important to the learning process. Such research finds constant reference by subjects to examples when they are faced with learning a new concept. This chapter provides another converging set of data.

In the PUPS theory, learning progresses from concrete examples to abstract principles through four stages:

1. Examples are encoded into declarative structures that record their perceptually available form and attributes. Thus, if we see someone type ( + 4 2) into a CommonLISP system and the system responds 6, PUPS would encode this with something like the following structures:[1]

   | | |
   |---|---|
   | event1: | isa typing |
   | | form (type person1 message computer) |
   | message: | isa list |
   | | form (list + four two) |
   | two: | isa integer |
   | | form (text 2) |
   | four: | isa integer |
   | | form (text 4) |
   | event2: | isa response |
   | | form (print computer six screen) |
   | six: | isa integer |
   | | form (text 6) |

2. The example is "understood." This involves placing the components of the structure into a causal framework. Thus, the student might infer that the first event caused the second. This information gets encoded in function slots of the examples.

---

[1]The general format of these PUPS structures is structure name plus a list of attributes. In the first structure "event1" is the structure name and "isa typing," "form (type person1 message computer)," and "context CommonLISP" are the attributes. Each attribute consists of a relation like "isa" plus a value like "typing" or "(type person1 message computer)."

3. When an appropriate problem arises, an attempt is made to analogically extrapolate the understanding of the example to produce a solution to the current problem.
4. Successful extrapolations are encoded as production rules.

As for the first step of processing, I am simply assuming that our perceptual system (perhaps including the linguistic system) can deliver an encoding of the forms and attributes of things in our environment. Steps 2 and 3 are far from trivial and occupy most of our attention. Step 4 receives some analysis.

## Step 2: Causal Induction

The first step in using an example is to understand its causal structure. For instance, what is the relationship between event1 and event2 in the previous example? The majority of our adult causal ascriptions flow from theories we have already acquired, but people are quite capable of making these ascriptions in the absence of a domain theory. Thus, most people would think event1 caused event2 in the absence of any knowledge about LISP or computers. It is from these pretheoretical inferences that domain theories eventually arise. There are at least three well-documented factors inducing people to perceive one thing as causing another in the absence of an existing theory (Lewis, 1986; Shultz, 1982; Siegler, 1976). Each of these can be fairly easily justified as a rational basis for making causal ascriptions:

1. Contiguity. People tend to perceive something as the cause the closer in time and space it is to the effect with the strong discontinuous provision that effects cannot precede their causes.
2. Similarity. People tend to perceive something as a cause the more similar it is to the effect. It is difficult to specify an all-encompassing metric for similarity, but for our purposes the important feature is that two things are more similar if they overlap in a number of components. For instance, suppose we observe two events involving an unknown computer system—the user points to an icon of an apple and he points to an icon of a dog. After both of these events a third event happens— the icon of the apple disappears. We are more likely to think the cause of the third event is the pointing to the apple icon than the dog icon (Lewis, 1986). This is because both cause and effect involve the apple icon.
3. Regularity. If a cause has been accompanied fairly regularly by an effect and the effect has seldom occurred in the absence of the cause, we are likely to perceive a causal relationship. Note perception of causality does not demand a perfect predictive relationship. There can always be extenuating circumstances.

It is an open question just how these three factors should be computed and combined to produce an attribution of a causal relationship. One can imagine doing psychological research by creating somewhat artificial situations to test for refined predictions of one scheme versus another. However, typically causal attributions are highly overdetermined. For instance, suppose we have no knowledge of computers and that we see (+ 4 2) typed into the computer and see 6 as a response. We would decide that the typing caused the 6 on the basis of contiguity, similarity (6 is the sum of 4 and 2), or by statistical trials noting the regularity of the relationship.

Causal information is stored in special slots of PUPS knowledge structures. Thus, if we were to take our earlier example and embellish it with causal information it would look like:

```
eventl:    isa typing
           form (type person1 message computer)
           cause (event2)
           context CommonLISP

message:   isa list
           form (list + four two)

event2:    isa response
           form (print computer six screen)

four:      is a integer
           form (text 4)

fact:      isa addition-fact
           form (sequence four plus two is six)

two:       isa integer
           form (text 2)

six:       isa integer
           form (text 6)
```

I have also included the addition fact that 4 + 2 = 6, which is critical to being able to extrapolate this event. The form slot is used to record the physical form of the object or event, and cause slots record the causal position of these objects.

In many situations it is useful to compose causal relationships into higher order relationships for compact representation. This composed information is stored under function slots. Thus, rather than having the event1 cause event2 and event2 be the printing of the message on the screen, we might represent event1 as:

```
eventl:    isa typing
           form (type person1 message computer)
           function (display computer six)
           context CommonLISP
```

where (display X Y) means (cause (print X Y screen)). The original development of analogy by Anderson and Thompson (in press) was with respect to function slots and not cause slots. In the remaining discussion we continue this practice.

### Knowledge Extrapolation

Knowledge extrapolation involves trying to extend a causal analysis to a new situation. Suppose, for instance, one wanted to predict what would happen when (+ 5 7) was typed into CommonLISP. Analogical extrapolation in PUPS (Anderson & Thompson, in press) allows one to map the past example onto the current example provided the categories (isa slots) of the objects are the same. In this case, 4 from the past example would map onto 5, 2 onto 7, and 6 onto 12. Thus, PUPS could predict the computer would display 12. In effect, PUPS has extracted the following rule from the example:

```
IF        = structure:   isa typing
                         form (type  =person  =message  =computer)
          = message:     isa list
                         form (list +  =num1  =num2)
          = fact:        isa addition-fact
                         form (sequence  =num1 plus  =num2 is
                          =num3)
THEN      = structure:   function (display  =computer  =num3)
```

The rule above is a production rule that predicts the function of = structure given its form. PUPS can also create problem-solving productions in which the form necessary to achieve a function is specified:

```
IF        goal:         isa typing
                        function (display  =computer  =num3)
          =fact:        isa addition-fact
                        form (sequence  =num1 plus  =num2 is
                         =num3)
THEN      goal:         form (type  =person  =message  =computer)
          =message:     isa list
                        form (list +  =num1  =num2)
```

These analogical extrapolations depend on two basic assumptions:

1. One can map one member of a category to another. Thus, we are able to replace 4, 2, and 6 by variables (implicitly restricted to integers). Anderson and Thompson (in press) called this the *no function in identity principle*, because it asserts that elements from the same category appearing in analogous positions in form slots will appear in analogous

positions in function slots. The assumption is that elements of the same category and in the same position in the form will have the same functional relationships.

2. One is able to trace paths through the function and form slots of structures to find paths of connections from the condition side to the action side of a production. Thus, in the aforementioned rule we find a path from = num3 through the addition fact that relates it to = num1 and = num2 in the action side. We call this the *principle of elaboration*.

For more discussion of both principles, see Anderson & Thompson (in press).

Although we often talk about knowledge extrapolation in terms of the rules extracted from an example, it is only evoked when there is an example and a target problem to map it to. The rule is just a specification of the mapping from the example to the target. Thus, availability of an appropriate example is key. Much of the research of Ross (1984) on analogy turns on manipulating variables that make the example more or less available in the target context. The hypothesis that recent examples are highly available for analogy is the key to our analysis of errors.

### Knowledge Compilation

The processes of causal inference and knowledge extrapolation produce general production rules that can be used for prediction and problem solving. Those rules that prove successful get permanently recorded as production rules. Anderson (in press) observed dramatic 2-1 reductions in time and speed from the first occasion that a rule is used to later occasions. Pirolli (1985) noted subjects made analogies to examples only the first time they needed a piece of knowledge. Later trials only produce very gradual improvements. I have assumed that this reflects the compilation of a production rule on the first trial that can then be used more efficiently in later trials. This chapter is not very concerned with these compiled rules. Our concern is with the analogical processes that first produce the target rules.

## SOURCES OF ERRORS IN PUPS

Given this general picture of learning where can systematic errors arise? There are in fact multiple ways that PUPS can make errors. However, this chapter is devoted to exploring what seems to be the most probable way that it would make systematic errors—which is to map an example inappropriately to the problem. Typically this is because the example that is chosen is inappropriate for solving the target problem, but it is also possible that an appropriate example is selected but mapped inappropriately. Either of these cases will be put under the heading of "misleading example." As evidence of how obvious this is as an error mechanism I can report that the most frequent criticism I get from people to whom I describe PUPS goes like this: "Yes, it works all right if you choose just the right example and encode it just right but how can you assume people always do this?"

The major goal of the remainder of the chapter is to look at systematic errors in our three tutors and see how many can be interpreted as mistaken examples. I have culled from our protocols cases where at least 30% of the students make the same error at the same point (the 30% is calculated as a percentage of all responses, not just errors). This consistency of the error suggests it is not a slip. Unfortunately for the current purposes, errors tend not to be repeated across problems in the tutors. This is because subjects are immediately corrected. Thus, we do not see in our tutor interactions the kind of consistent bugs that Burton and Brown (1982) found in subtraction. The reason is that they did not intervene tutorially. If we had not intervened, the error we see might become a permanent part of the student's repertoire. However, because we do intervene, we cannot use consistency of error pattern as a basis for diagnosing systematic errors. This is why we resort to a criterion like 30% same errors because it is highly unlikely that this consistency would occur through slips.[2] However, this criterion means we will not see the bizarre and rare errors Burton and Brown were able to document.

It would probably be possible to conjure up some example under some encoding that could serve as an analogical basis for any error we observed. Thus, the mere fact that we can explain an error by analogy to an example is not very compelling evidence that it actually occurred because of analogy. One has to judge the reasonableness of the encoding of the example from which the analogy flowed. I think the encodings we offer are far from strained and, indeed, are quite compelling—perhaps even obvious. Our analysis is more compelling if it turns out that examples that serve as the source of the analogy occur in the vicinity of the error. According to the PUPS theory, examples just processed should still be active and hence highly available for analogy. Our tutoring paradigm allows us to determine what examples a student has studied in the vicinity of an error. This is where our data base is at an advantage over the one used by Burton and Brown. They have no record of the learning context in which the error first appeared. With our tutors we have a very good record.

What we do is show that the majority of the errors we see can be interpreted as bad analogies to close-by examples. What we do not know yet is whether PUPS predicts analogy errors that in fact are not observed—what Brown and VanLehn (1980) would call *star bugs*.

The 30% criterion was chosen because it gave us about 10 consistent errors for each of our three tutors (LISP, geometry, and algebra). In each of

---

[2]The assumption is that working memory failures are slips at random and produce a wide range of different responses and would not concentrate at one place in the protocol.

the sample data sets we are looking at about 500 interactions. Thus, these consistent errors only occur on about 2% of the possible occasions. This small number testifies to the rather low error rates on the tutors (from 10% to 25% of all interactions are errors, depending on tutors) and the fact that most errors are relatively idiosyncratic to a subject. Thus, these events that we are examining are statistically exceptional in the tutor interactions. The research strategy here is to use exceptional events to tell us what is happening in the learning process. As we said earlier, our assumption is that analogy usually produces successful learning and we are examining the rare occasions where it does not work.

## ERRORS WITH THE LISP TUTOR

In the case of the LISP tutor I present a list of all errors meeting the 30% threshold that occurs in lessons 2 and 3 of the tutor. Lessons 2 and 3 are analyzed rather than lesson 1 because lesson 1 has some peculiar properties due to start-up with the LISP tutor.

### First

Lesson 2 concerns how to write LISP functions. The very first problem is specified to the students as: "Define a function called *first*. Given any list, it returns the first element of that list. For example, (first '(a b c)) returns a." Given that this function is totally redundant with the LISP function CAR, this is really just an exercise in function definition. The following is the correct code:

```
(defun first (lis)
    (car lis))
```

A full 30% of the subjects make the following error:

```
(defun first (lis)
    (car (lis)))
```

Anderson, Farrell, and Sauers (1984) discussed at length a simulation of a protocol of a subject making this error. In that simulation it came from an inappropriate analogy to the following function definition:

```
(defun f-to-c (temp)
    (quotient (difference temp 32) 1.8))
```

The first argument to the function quotient is in parentheses and the subject places the argument in parentheses in writing f-to-c. This is an error in the representation of the example. The subject is not representing the fact that the parentheses in the *f-to-c* example are to hold an embedded function call not just an argument. An important observation for current purposes is that the f-to-c example is used to illustrate a function definition and so the example is occurring immediately prior to coding first.

In informal interviews with students, we have also noticed some who make this error out of analogy to the parameter list in the first line of the function definition. In fact, many teachers have complained that students are confused because the parameters in LISP definitions are placed in parenthesis and the arguments to functions are not. This is another case of an error by analogy to an inappropriate example. The student either does not encode or ignores that a list is used for specifying parameters and not for holding arguments to functions. In this case the subject is using one piece of the code as an analog for another piece of the code.

## Replace

The function that follows first is called *second* and it is supposed to return the second element of the list. This does not display a comparably consistent error. The next function does however. It is specified to the student as: "Write a function *replace* that replaces the first element of a list with a new element. The function takes two parameters—the new element and the list. For example, (replace 'rings '(ties hats pants)) returns (rings hats pants)." The correct code is:

$$\text{(defun replace (item lis)}$$
$$\text{(cons item (cdr lis)))}$$

A full 55% of the students start out trying to define the function:

$$\text{(defun replace (variable).} \ldots$$

*Variable* stands for whatever variable name they choose. The relevant fact is that the two previous function definitions both involved a single list parameter. This is further evidence that some subjects are not understanding what the parameter list is about and inappropriately map it here. Our guess is that subjects incorrectly conjecture that each parameter must separately be placed in parentheses. We would predict that subjects would have encoded a second parameter in a second list. That is, their code would have taken the form:

$$\text{(defun replace (item) (lis)}$$

with a list for each parameter. Unfortunately, the tutor stops them after their first error and so we do not see how they would have continued the code. The important observation about this analysis of the error and others like it is that it attributes the error to incorrectly understanding an example and, consequently, inappropriately mapping that example.

## Sqr

The next function to display a high consistent error pattern is specified to the student as "Define a function called sqr that returns a list of the perimeter and the area of a square, given the length of one side. For example, (sqr 2) returns (8 4)" The following is the correct code:

```
(defun sqr (side)
    (list (times side 4) (times side side)))
```

A full 35% of the subjects started their code as follows:

```
(defun sqr (side)
    (times
```

*List* is missing. This error has no obvious analog and so stands as the first example of an error that cannot be explained by analogy to a close-by example. It is an instance of what we have called a *part error.* That is, subjects never had to code a list answer before and we assume this 35% could not figure out how to achieve that. What they did was to proceed to code that part of the answer that they did know how to code—namely the circumference of a square. Subjects have a tendency to do part of a problem if they cannot do it all.

## Ends

The next function that produces a high error rate is specified to the students as "Define a function called ends, that has one argument and returns a list containing the first and last items in that argument. For example, (ends '(a b c d)) returns (a d)." The following is one form of the correct code:

```
(defun ends (lis)
    (list (car lis) (car (last lis))))
```

A full 50% of the subjects tried the following code:

```
(defun ends (lis)
    (list (car lis) (last lis)))
```

This argument could be classified as a part error—subjects did not know how to code the first of a list and so they coded just the list—(last lis) returns a *list* of the last element of the list. However, this does not seem very plausible. Subjects have coded car successfully many times (including in this function) and this is the first time they used last. More likely it represents a misunderstanding of what last does. Our guess is that subjects do not know what last does—that they believe it returns the last element rather than a list of the last element. We have observed many students firmly assert that last returns the last element despite the fact that they have read instruction and seen examples to the contrary. This misunderstanding of last may come from interpreting it as analogous to car, which does return the first element rather than the first list. This error is an interesting case. Under this analysis it has its origin in analogy, but it is not an analogy of the problem to a nearby example. Rather it is an analogy of the instruction about last to the knowledge about car. Thus, we cannot count this as a supporting case for our hypotheses although the error may stem from analogy.

## Snoc

The next function to produce a high error rate is *snoc,* which is specified to students as: "Write a function called *snoc* that is the opposite of *cons.* Instead of inserting an item into the front of the list, it inserts the item at the end. For example, (snoc 'd '(a b c)) returns (a b c d). Write this function without using append." The following is the correct code:

(defun snoc (item lis)
    (reverse (cons item (reverse lis)))))

A full 70% of the students start their code for this function:

(defun snoc (item lis)
    (cons . . . .

It is unlikely that this is a part error stemming from an inability to use reverse because they have already used it a number of times successfully. The interesting feature of this example is that the instruction itself implicitly references an example of cons. The error could derive from analogy to this implicit example. We assume students represent the body of the function they are to write as follows:

problem: isa lispcode
    function (insert item lis end)

and their representation of the implicit *cons* example is:

example: isa lispcode
    function (insert item lis front)
    form (cons item lis)

The implicit example has the insert at the front where the problem has the insert at the end. Perhaps they intended to reverse the arguments to cons or perhaps they choose to ignore the mismatch between cons and their current problem.

## Samesign

The third lesson is on predicates, logical operators, and conditionals. The first function to produce a high consistent error was described to the students as: "Define samesign. It takes two numbers as arguments, and returns *t* if both arguments have the same sign. That is, if both arguments are zero, both positive, or both negative, the function should return *t*. For example, (samesign 0 0) returns *t*, (samesign -2 -5) returns *t*, and (samesign -2 3) returns nil." At this point students should have known about the logical functions *and* and *or* but not *cond*. Thus the code we expected was:

```
(defun samesign (num 1 num2)
    (or (and (greaterp num1 0)(greaterp num2 0))
        (and (greaterp 0 num1)(greaterp 0 num2))
        (and (zerop num1)(zerop num2))))
```

Or some equivalent variant. Eighty percent of the students started their coded displaying the following error:

```
(defun samesign (num1 num2)
    (greaterp . . .
```

That is, they ignored the *or* and the *and*. Because this was the first exercise in *or* and *and* we assume they just did not know how to use them. This is the third case where there is no obvious analog to a nearby example for making the error. This seems like another part error where the subject is again trying to write that part of the code they know how to—namely coding predicates.

## Carlis

The first function to use conditional structure was *carlis*. It was specified to the subject "Define *carlis*. It takes one argument. If the argument is a non-empty list, then *carlis* returns the first element of that list. But if the argument is the empty list, then *carlis* returns the empty list. If the argument is an atom, *carlis* returns just that atom. Hint: Be careful how you order your tests. Remember that nil is both an atom and a list. For example, (carlis '(cat rabbit)) returns cat, (carlis 'george) returns george, and (carlis nil) returns nil." The correct code for carlis is:

```
(defun carlis (object)
    (cond ((null object) nil)
          ((atom object) object)
          (t (car object))))
```

or some variant. This problem produced the following two high frequency errors:

```
(defun carlis (object)
    (cond (null object) nil)
          ((atom object) object)
          ((listp object) (car object))))
```

The first error, made by 30% of the subjects is to type just a single left parenthesis before null.[3] This is the first time they have had to code two left parentheses in a row and we assume the many examples of a single left parenthesis dominate. The second error, made by 80% of the students, is to use a predicate in the test for the final clause—(listp object). Although semantically it is not an error, the tutor treats it as a stylistic error and the example function students studied involved a *t* for the last clause. However, the two previous lines in this function provide more recent examples of coding tests and we assume these are the sources of the mistake. Basically, their status as appropriate for only nonfinal tests is not being represented or ignored by students.

This error and the next we discuss are both stylistic. They do not represent code that will not work, but rather solutions that are less than optimal by reasonably well-accepted criteria. Numerous people have questioned mixing these in with true errors. Therefore, it is important to be explicit why such mixing is appropriate for our current purposes. The goal here is not to pass evaluative judgment on the student's behavior or to grade it. The goal is to understand the origin of that behavior by focusing on cases where it deviates from the tutor's prescriptions. For these purposes a stylistic deviation that arises from analogy is every bit as interesting as a true error. Both indicate that analogy is in control of the learning process.

## Numline

The next function to produce a high error rate is *numline*. It is specified to the student as "Define a function called *numline*. It takes one argument that is a number and returns a two element list. The first element of the list is *t* if the number is 0 and nil otherwise. The second element of the list is *t* if the number is negative and nil otherwise. For example, (numline -5) returns (nil *t*)." The target code for this function is:

```
(defun numline (item)
   (list (zerop item) (< item 0)))
```

This function just occurs after a series of functions, all coded with cond. Fifty percent of the students produce the same response, which is to try to code the function as follows:

```
(defun numline (item)
   (cond . . .
```

This might lead to a function that works, but it is clearly nonoptimal (which is what the tutor tells them). It seems that it is again analogy to the recent previous functions that produce this mistake.

---

[3]The single parenthesis error is immediately corrected by the LISP tutor, which is why they know not to make the error before *atom*.

## LISP Errors: A Concluding Remark

We have now reviewed the nine dominant high frequency errors in lessons two and three with the LISP tutor. Two of these are explainable as part errors and another six as inappropriate selection of a recent example. The ninth error may arise from a misanalogy in the understanding of the instruction about *last*. I think the relatively simple genesis of these errors is interesting given what a complex domain LISP programming is supposed to be.

## ERRORS WITH THE GEOMETRY TUTOR

In the case of the geometry tutor I present an analysis of all above 30% errors that occur in the first chapter. This is a chapter mainly devoted to relating algebraic operations on geometry measurements to some basic geometry concepts like congruence. The high school students who go through this material often find it frustratingly subtle. If we were designing a geometry course we would not begin it with such material, but our tutor was compelled to follow the textbook sequence.

Before going through the individual errors I should say a little about the geometry tutor, although for details consult Anderson, Boyle, & Yost (1985) and Anderson, Boyle, Corbett, & Lewis (in press), Fig. 13.1 shows a completed geometry proof as it appears on the tutor screen. It takes the form of a graph structure connecting a set of premises on the bottom to the conclusion to be proven at the top. Students interact with the tutor by picking a set of premises, stating a rule to apply to the premises, and then stating the conclusion that follows.

In my discussion of the errors, for brevity's sake I present descriptions abstracted away from many of the details of interaction. I just describe the diagram, the premises, the to-be-proven conclusion, and the nature of the error without reference to the exact screen images.

### Addition Postulate

The first geometric rule introduced to the student is the addition postulate: if $a = b$ and $c = d$, then $a + c = b + d$. Figure 13.2 shows the three problems on which students practice this postulate. The first two cause no difficulties—students combine the two premises to establish the conclusion. However, 80% of the students make the same error on the third problem. They try to apply the postulate to all three premises at once. Whether this really should be counted as an error is problematical, but the tutor and the text restrict the addition postulate to two premises. What is remarkable is the number of students who make the opposite inference. I think the error quite definitely comes from analogy to this training sequence, but the in-

358

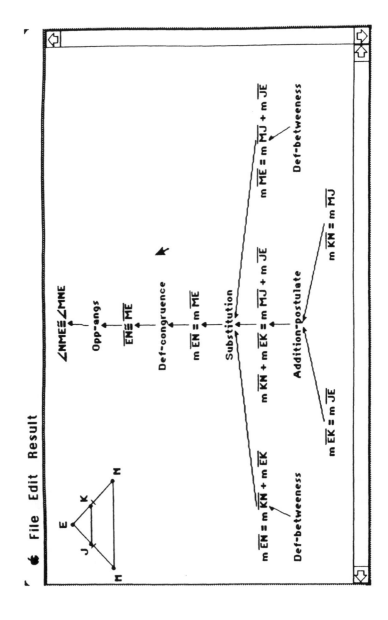

FIG. 13.1.    An example of a completed proof on the geometry tutor. The conclusion is at the top of the series and the initial premises are at the bottom of the screen.

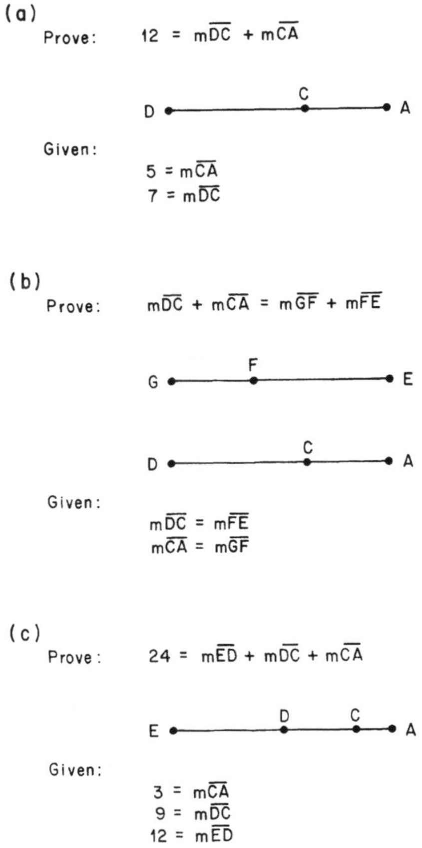

(a)

Prove:    $12 = m\overline{DC} + m\overline{CA}$

D •————————•——————• A
                    C

Given:

$5 = m\overline{CA}$
$7 = m\overline{DC}$

(b)

Prove:    $m\overline{DC} + m\overline{CA} = m\overline{GF} + m\overline{FE}$

G •————————•——————————• E
                  F

D •————————————•————————• A
                    C

Given:

$m\overline{DC} = m\overline{FE}$
$m\overline{CA} = m\overline{GF}$

(c)

Prove:    $24 = m\overline{ED} + m\overline{DC} + m\overline{CA}$

E •————————————•——•——• A
                      D    C

Given:

$3 = m\overline{CA}$
$9 = m\overline{DC}$
$12 = m\overline{ED}$

FIG. 13.2.   The first three problems in the geometry tutor. (a) and (b) are problems that cause few errors, (c) produces a high-frequency error.

teresting observation is that PUPS, as it is currently implemented, does not make the analogy from two of a kind to three of a kind. This points in a direction that we have to develop the PUPS analogy system.

## Reflexive Postulate

The postulate to follow addition is subtraction and it does not promote a similarly consistent pattern of errors. However, the next postulate, the reflexive postulate, asserting a quantity is equal to itself, does. Figure 13.3 shows the first problem involving this rule. It requires subjects to first establish $m$DC $= m$DC and then use subtraction. The peculiar feature about establishing that $m\overline{DC} = m\overline{DC}$ through the reflexive postulate is that this postulate requires no premises. Eighty percent of the subjects first choose the one premise given and try to apply some rule to it. There is no obvious rule that students

Prove: $m\overline{CA} = m\overline{ED}$

FIG. 13.3. In this problem, students try to apply a rule to $m\text{DC} + m\text{CA} = m\text{ED} + m\text{DC}$ rather than first establishing $m\text{DC} = m\text{DC}$ by the reflexive postulate.

E •————D——C————• A

Given: $m\overline{DC} + m\overline{CA} = m\overline{ED} + m\overline{DC}$

can apply to this premise and so their rule-posting behavior is quite variable—the majority try to post the reflexive rule as applying to this premise but others post the addition rule, others the subtraction rule, others just quit the inference, and others ask for help. Thus, they make the error of selecting the premise and then try a host of different behaviors to get out of corner they have painted themselves into. This seems a clear analogy to their pattern of responding with the tutor up until this point where they have always had to choose a premise.

## Definition of Congruence

The fourth rule is the definition of congruence. It asserts that segments with equal measure are congruent. Figure 13.4 shows a problem that produces two common errors. Almost all subjects again select the premise on the screen rather than using the no-premise reflexive rule. Secondly, when subjects establish that $m\text{DC} = m\text{DC}$, they then combine this and the given premise by the subtraction postulate but choose as the conclusion the statement on the screen involving congruences rather than the fact that $m\text{CA} = m\text{ED}$, which has to be converted into the congruence. The obvious analog to this problem is the problem in Fig. 13.3, which occurred three problems earlier. The students are simply mapping one to the other, ignoring the difference between congruence and equality.[4]

## Substitution

The next rule introduced allows students to substitute an equal term in another equality. Figure 13.5 shows the first problem that students have to solve with this rule. It involves using the definition of congruence to go in the other direction and convert $\overline{HN} \cong \overline{SM}$ into $m\text{HN} = m\text{SM}$. Seventy percent of the students pick both statements without first converting, and try substituting

---

[4]The reader may well consider why this distinction between equality of measure and congruence is being enforced in the geometry curriculum. Without defending the distinction, let me state the rationale: Congruence means that objects will be the same after rotation, reflection, and translation. Equality means the identity of two numerical measures. The distinction becomes important in later chapters where two objects (e.g., triangles) can be equal in some measure (e.g., area) but not congruent.

Prove:    $\overline{CA} \cong \overline{ED}$

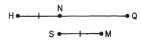

Given:

$m\overline{DC} + m\overline{CA} = m\overline{ED} + m\overline{DC}$

FIG. 13.4.    A problem that produces two high-frequency errors in the geometry tutor.

---

Prove: $12 = m\overline{SM} + m\overline{NQ}$

Given:

$\overline{HN} \cong \overline{SM}$
$12 = m\overline{NQ} + m\overline{HN}$

FIG. 13.5.    In this problem, students fail to convert $\overline{HN} \cong \overline{SM}$ into $m$HN = $m$SM before applying the substitution rule.

---

Prove:    $\overline{CA} \cong \overline{GF}$

G •————————• F   E •————————• D

C •————————• A

Given:

$m\overline{CA} = m\overline{ED}$
$m\overline{ED} = m\overline{GF}$

FIG. 13.6.    Subjects tend to combine the two equalities by transitivity and conclude the congruence statement.

the congruence statement into the measure statement. Again it is to be explained as students confusing equality and congruence. This time the analogy is to the example that is used to illustrate substitution in the instruction, which does not require such a conversion. This is what they have studied just prior to solving the problem.

### Transitivity

The next rule is transitivity and Fig. 13.6 shows the first problem on which 40% of the students make the same error. Perhaps the reader can guess what it is: Students combine the two equalities by transitivity and conclude the congruence. Again the analogy is being made to the instructional example that is being used to illustrate the transitivity of equality.

### Midpoint

The next rule is definition of midpoint. Without burdening the reader with the problems, let me just say students do well on the first two problems but once again overextend their knowledge on the third problem, which requires discriminating between congruence and equality.

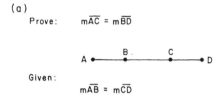

(a)

Prove:    $m\overline{AC} = m\overline{BD}$

Given:

$m\overline{AB} = m\overline{CD}$

FIG. 13.7. (a) Most students conclude $m$AB + $m$BC = $m$AC and $m$BC + $m$CD = $m$BD and then try unsuccessfully to use these conclusions as premises for a rule. Students make an error on (b) by using (a) as an analogy. They fail to establish congruence as a separate step from equality of measure.

(b)

Prove:    $\overline{OY} \cong \overline{RN}$

Given:

$\overline{NY} \cong \overline{RO}$

## Betweenness

The next rule is the definition of betweenness, which says that three points A, B, C, are collinear with B in between if and only if $m$AB + $m$BC = $m$AC. The first four problems involving this rule are rather uneventful and then subjects come upon the problem in Fig. 13.7a, which high school students always find very difficult. Most students are able to analogize to their past four solutions and make the inferences that $m$AB + $m$BC = $m$AC and that $m$BC + $m$CD = $m$BD. Then the majority of students select these two premises, which is an error—no useful rule will apply to these premises. Having selected them, what they next try to do is unsystematic. Some students abort the inference; some try subtraction, some try addition, some try substitution, and so forth. This is the only high frequency error in our geometry protocols that does not seem to have an explanation as an analogy to some example. In some sense subjects feel that these two premises must be enough to establish the conclusion.

After this problem, the tutor repeats a number of similar problems. Figure 13.7b shows the third in the sequence (i.e., there is one problem between Fig. 13.7a and Fig. 13.7b). Students learn inference pattern required, but then make a systematic error in Fig. 13.7b. Again ignoring the difference between congruence and equality, they try to directly apply an algebraic rule to the congruence $\overline{NY} \cong \overline{RO}$ without first converting it to an equality.

## Concluding Remarks About Geometry

We have looked at nine common errors in geometry and found that all but one of them can be explained as an analogy to a close-by example. The majority (5) of these analogy errors turn on subjects failing to block an analogy by observing the distinction between equality and congruence. It should be stressed that this confusion is well-known in high school geometry and is not a product of the tutor. In fact, it is to the tutor's credit that it eventually gets students to respect the difference between equality and congruence. Many high school teachers have just given in and do not require students to make the distinction.

## ERRORS WITH THE ALGEBRA TUTOR

The algebra tutor currently teaches a course that reviews prealgebra (fractions, signed numbers, distribution), solving linear equations in one unknown, polynomials, and solving quadratics. We have analyzed the nine errors that occurred above the 30% threshold in the prealgebra curriculum. Interactions with the algebra tutor involve selecting an operator, passing its arguments, and then producing a result. Most of our high-frequency errors involve calculating the result. Almost always it appears that the error can be explained as an analogy to the immediately preceding problem.[5] Therefore, we present our results in terms of correct answer on the preceding problem and then common error on the current problem.

### Reciprocal

One of the early prealgebra skills that students are taught involves finding the reciprocal of a fraction. The following two are the key problems:

correct prior: reciprocal (-3/4) = -4/3
common error: reciprocal (1/4) = 4/1 (rather than 4)

Fifty-five percent of the students make this error although they have been told to enter their answer in simplest possible form. The analogical source of this error is apparent. Again, it is an interesting question in just what sense this is an error. However, our task is not to judge the rules of the game but to observe where students deviate from these rules.

### Greatest Common Factor

The next operation to produce a high-frequency common error involves finding the greatest common factor (GCF) of two numbers

---

[5]It is interesting to consider why the algebra errors can always be traced to the immediately preceding example, whereas in geometry the examples were as much as three back. This is because the immediately preceding problem in geometry and LISP was often not capable of being mapped to the next problem whereas, given our problem sequence, it was almost always possible to make such a mapping in the case of algebra.

correct prior: GCF (44, 28) = 4
common error: GCF (81, 54) = 9 (rather than 27)

Thirty-five percent of the students make this error. In the prior examples when the two numbers have a common factor in the multiplication table (44 = 4 × 11; 28 = 4 × 7) the common factor is the greatest common factor. Subjects appear to be extrapolating this erroneous pattern to the current case and coming up with 9 since 81 = 9 × 9 and 54 = 9 × 6.[6]

## Fraction Addition

Another prealgebra skill reviewed by the tutor is fractional arithmetic. The following example produces the high error rate:

correct prior: ADD (3/28, 5/7) = 23/28
common error: ADD (1/21, 7/6) = 51/42 (rather than 17/14)

Forty percent of the students make this error. This is the first case of an example from fraction addition where the result needed simplification. We assume that by analogy to the previous problems some subjects were omitting the simplification step when it was needed.

## Variable Combination

Another lesson involves representing the product of a constant and a variable. This produces the following two problem sequence:

correct prior: Varcombine (-10, X) = -10X
common error: Varcombine ( -1, Y) = -1Y (rather than -Y)

Fifty-five percent of the students make this error. This is the first case of combining a variable with 1 or -1.

From this example students learn the special case rule involving 1 and apply it correctly until they come across the following pair, which involves multiplying parenthesized expressions by constants.

correct prior: Varcombine (-31, (-1X + 17)) = -31(-1X + 17)
common error: Varcombine ( -1, (4/5Z - 3)) = -1(4/5Z - 3)
(rather than -(4/5Z - 3))

Forty-five percent of the students made this error. By accident the prior example had gotten into the tutor in a form where the special case rule for 1 was violated. Many students promptly copied this pattern for the next ex-

---

[6]One might argue that this error is due to subjects abrogating search for a greatest factor too early and not due to the prior example. However, students had opportunity many times before to make the error (including giving 2 as the answer to the prior example). The striking fact is this is the first time this error appears with any frequency.

ample. This is probably the case where the student's behavior least deserves the classification "error." However, for our purposes it reinforces how much of the students' behavior is analogically based.

## Factor

The next operator that produces a common error involves factoring out a common product.

> correct prior: factor (5 * 3X + 5 * 1) = 5(3X + 1)
> common error: factor (5 * 3Z + 5) = 5(3Z + 5)
>                             (rather than 5(3Z + 1))

Thirty-five percent of the students make this error. This sequence of two was an informally constructed sequence designed to get students to extract the pattern by analogy. However, in making the mapping from the prior example to the target problem subjects map both the 5 and the 1 into the 5 producing the error observed.

## Expandexpression

Expandexpression is an operator that rewrites an expression in terms of products involving a specific term. It produces the following sequence:

> correct prior: Expandexpression (5 + 20X, 5) = 5 * 1 + 5 * 4X
> common error: Expandexpression (18 + 6Y, 6) = 6 * 3 + 6 * 1Y
>                             (rather than 6 * 3 + 6 * Y)

Thirty-five percent of the students make this error. This is another case of subjects failing to take into account the special case nature of 1 in their analogies. Note that this error had laid dormant through many opportunities in prior problems but arises anew when students face a new algebraic operator.

## Factor

The next operator to produce a consistent error pattern involves factoring a sum. This error pattern involves choosing a wrong suboperator rather than wrong result.

> prior example: Factor (-14Z + 7)
>                 GCF (-14,7) = 7
>                 Expandexpression (-14Z + 7, 7)
> common error: Factor (-6 - 8 X)
>                 GCF (-6, - 8) = -2
>                 Expandexpression (-6 - 8X, 2)
>                 (rather than Expandexpression (-6 - 8X, -2))

The first step in factoring is to find the greatest common factor of the two integers and the second step is to use expandexpression with the expression and the greatest common factor. The problem that produces the error is the first case where the greatest common factor is negative. Fifty percent of the students choose to pass a positive integer as the argument to expandexpression by analogy to the previous problems.

## Adding Terms

The following is the final problem to produce a consistent error pattern:

prior example: ADD (-3/2Z, 5/2Z) = Z
common error: ADD (2X, -2X) = X rather than 0

Forty percent of the students make the error illustrated. It seems unlikely that this is just an analogy error. This error has been analyzed by other researchers as a failure to properly parse the problem (Matz, 1982). Students analyze the 2 and the -2 cancelling each other leaving the X. Their problem is that they do not know how to combine the 0 that results and the X. This is not a problem due to analogy to the prior example.

## SUMMARY

Table 13.1 presents a summary of our analysis of the high-frequency errors in the three domains. Clearly there is a preponderance of analogical errors. Given the informal nature of our classification, there is room for disputing particular analyses of particular errors. However, such disputes would not take away from the conclusion of a heavy proportion of analogical errors. On the other hand, in absolute frequency such errors are rare. This suggests that in most cases where analogy is at work it produces the right result.

## EINSTELLUNG

The reader may have noted the similarity between the errors we are observing and those errors that have been called *Einstellung errors* (Luchins, 1942). This is the phenomenon that states when students have had a run of success with a particular solution pattern they are likely to try to repeat that pattern on a problem where it is no longer appropriate. In fact, in the PUPS theory, Einstellung errors are to be attributed to choosing inappropriate examples for analogy. This contrasts with the explanation that had been offered in ACT* and by others (e.g., Lewis, 1978) that saw Einstellung errors as being produced by composing together sequences of production rules. The problem with this explanation has always been that the tendency to make this error is very much

TABLE 13.1
Classification of High Frequency Errors

|  | Analogy-Based | Not Analogy-Based |
|---|---|---|
| LISP | 6 | 3 |
| Geometry | 8 | 1 |
| Algebra | 8 | 1 |
| Total | 22 | 5 |

under conscious control. For instance, Luchins was able to cut these down by 50% just with the admonition "Don't be blind." The demonstration also never works in my class if I introduce it as an example of where people get tricked in problem solving. Composed production rules are not the sort of things in most theories that are subject to such conscious control. On the other hand, it is perfectly plausible that subjects interpreted Luchins' "Don't be blind" instructions as instructions not to use the obvious recent example pattern that had been working.

## COMPARISONS WITH VANLEHN'S THEORIES

As a final point it is worth comparing what I am saying here with VanLehn's analysis of errors. He has produced two theories of the origins of bugs. The earlier is the repair theory that he developed with Brown (Brown & VanLehn, 1980) and the more recent is the step theory he developed for his dissertation (VanLehn, 1983). These are complimentary not alternative hypotheses. Step theory attributes bugs to an inductive process of learning from examples, whereas repair theory attributes bugs to repairs that students invent when they come to impasses in their problem solving.

VanLehn has already compared my analogy-based explanation with inductive-based explanation of step theory. He comments, "Although I have not investigated example-exercise analogy in detail, I expect it to behave indistinguishably from learning by generalizing examples" (VanLehn, 1985, p. 19). I think he is right in that there is no difference between analogy from examples generally considered and induction from examples generally considered. It is the case that PUPS and his step theory are not identical, but then I think we both admit that our theories are not sufficient to produce the full class of inductive/analogical errors. The one thing that the analogy perspective of the PUPS theory emphasizes is that one should be able to observe students making mappings between examples and problems and learning from these mappings. A dominant feature of protocols from students' learning is the presence of these analogical mappings. As we noted in the introduction, it was protocol data from subjects that first led us to our theory of analogically based instruction.

On the other hand, repair theory does contrast with the predictions of PUPS analogy. It is interesting to look at the domain most associated with VanLehn, subtraction bugs, and classify those according to whether they seem to have an analogical explanation or a repair explanation. There are bugs that Brown and VanLehn cannot explain with their repair model but that are naturally explained as analogy errors due to wrong selection of an example. There are errors that can be explained either way. There are errors for which the Brown and VanLehn explanation seems much more plausible than any analogy-to-wrong-example explanation I have been able to think of. Finally, there are errors that neither model can explain. I discuss examples of each.

### Add Instead of Subtract

The error of addition instead of subtraction has an obvious analogical explanation where the student relaxes the constraint on the sign and uses an addition example as an analogy for a subtraction example. On the other hand, it is not possible to explain this bug as a repair. I think this error is very plausibly explained in analogical terms because it is known that children who can do subtraction perfectly when presented with a sheet of all subtraction problems will make add-instead-of-subtract errors when those subtraction problems are intermixed with addition problems. Such mixed addition and subtraction problems provide students with erroneous analogs in close proximity to the subtraction problems.

### Carry Instead of Borrow

Equally explainable in terms of analogy is the error where students perform subtraction correctly except that they carry when they should borrow. Again it cannot be explained by repair theory.

### Smaller-From-Larger

Certainly the most common subtraction bug, and one that I have anguished much over with my son, is the smaller from larger bug illustrated:

$$
\begin{array}{r} 93 \\ -37 \\ \hline 64 \end{array}
\quad\text{which has the obvious analog -}\quad
\begin{array}{r} 7 \\ 3 \\ \hline 4 \end{array}
$$

In PUPS terms one can represent the problem of finding the digit in the units column as:

```
Goal: isa number
      function (difference 3 7)
      form ????
```

and the example:

> example: isa number
> function (difference 7 3)
> form (text 4)

Cast this way there is actually a problem explaining the error in PUPS because PUPS respects the order of the arguments to a relation like *difference* and will not make the analogy. Thus, the feature that has to be relaxed here is the argument order. However, despite the fact that PUPS will not, it is more than plausible that children are willing to relax this order. Most kids, and, I suspect most adults (certainly the ones I have tested), when asked "what the difference between 3 and 7" will respond 4, not − 4 or impossible. In fact, memory of examples where it is heard "the difference between 3 and 7 is 4" could serve for PUPS as the analog that would allow it to make the argument reversal.

The Brown and VanLehn explanation of this affirms that students reverse the order of the arguments when they hit an impasse. The difference is that they do not tie it to any specific example of subtraction. Presumably, the two points of view could be separated by careful experimental data.

## Borrow-No-Decrement

This error is illustrated below:

$$
\begin{array}{r}
62 \\
-44 \\
\hline
28
\end{array}
$$

This is produced in repair theory by deleting the decrement rule associated with borrowing from a column. It would be produced in PUPS by not encoding the decrement in an example and hence not learning the rule. This is really a very subtle difference and, if the two accounts could be separated at all, it would require taking protocols to find out what students attend to in the examples they learn from.

## Zero Instead of Borrow

This error is illustrated below:

$$
\begin{array}{r}
42 \\
-16 \\
\hline
30
\end{array}
\quad \text{could be analogy to} \quad
\begin{array}{r}
42 \\
-12 \\
\hline
30
\end{array}
$$

However, I think it is implausible to suppose there is very often such a near-by analog. The standard repair explanation, that the student starts to count down from 2 and hits zero, is much more plausible. I think if the student were going to look for an analog to deal with this dilemna, the smaller-from-larger bug would be produced. Thus, this is one example of a number where I find the repair explanation definitely more compelling.

## Subtract-Top-From-Bottom

Just to document an error that neither analysis can handle well consider the following subtraction error, which has apparently been documented in at least one kid's behavior:

$$\begin{array}{r} 81 \\ -27 \\ \hline 46 \end{array}$$

In this error the student chooses to subtract the top number from the bottom. Thus, 6 is written as the difference of 7 and 1. The student borrows a mysterious 1 to convert the 2 to 12 and then subtracts 8 from it to get 4. Apparently this error has stumped all attempts at explanation.

## CONCLUSIONS

Although I hate chapters that end with calls for more research, it is essential to end on such a note. This chapter has really been a plausibility argument. We need to extend the PUPS simulation to establish that it can generate the full class of analogy errors. More important, once it does, we need to expose it to the full curriculum that students see to determine if there are overgeneration problems. That is, will the PUPS analogy mechanism produce errors that we do not see in students protocols? The point of such an exercise is not so much to establish that PUPS per se is correct but to establish more precisely the sense in which these are analogy errors.

## ACKNOWLEDGMENTS

The research reported on this paper was supported by ONR contract N00014-87-K-0103 and NSF grant MDR-8470337.

## REFERENCES

Anderson, J. R. (1983). *The architecture of cognition.* Cambridge, MA: Harvard University Press.
Anderson, J. R., & Jeffries, R. (1985). Novice LISP errors: Undetected losses of information from working memory. *Human-Computer Interaction, 22,* 403–423.

Anderson, J. R., & Thompson, R. (in press). Use of analogy in a production system architecture. In S. Vosniadou & A. Ortony, (Eds.), *Similarity and analogy*. New York: Cambridge University Press.

Anderson, J. R. Boyle, C. F., & Yost, G. (1985). The geometry tutor. In *Proceedings of International Joint Conference on Artificial Intelligence-85* (pp. 1-7). Los Angeles: International Joint Conference on Artificial Intelligence.

Anderson, J. R., Boyle, C. F., Corbett, A. T., & Lewis, M. W. (in press). Cognitive modelling and intelligent tutoring. *Artificial Intelligence*.

Anderson, J. R., Farrell, R. G., & Sauers, R. (1984). Learning to program in LISP. *Cognitive Science, 8,* 87-129.

Anzai, Y., & Simon, H. A. (1979). The theory of learning by doing. *Psychological Review, 86,* 124-140.

Brown, J. S., & VanLehn, K. (1980). Repair theory: A generative theory of bugs in procedural skills. *Cognitive Science, 4,* 379-426.

Burton, R. R., & Brown, J.S. (1982). An investigation of computer coaching for informal learning activities. In D. Sleeman & J. S. Brown (Eds.), *Intelligent tutoring systems* (pp. 79-98). New York: Academic Press.

Chase, W. G., & Ericsson, K. A. (1982). Skill and working memory. In G. H. Bower (Ed.), *The psychology of learning and motivation*. New York: Academic Press.

Lewis, C. H. (1978). *Production system models of practice effects*. Unpublished doctoral dissertation, University of Michigan, Ann Arbor.

Lewis, C. H. (1986). Understanding what's happening in system interactions. In D. A. Norman & S. W. Draper (Eds.), *User centered system design: New perspectives in human-computer interaction*. Hillsdale, NJ: Lawrence Erlbaum Associates.

Lewis, M. W., Milson, R., & Anderson, J. R. (1987). Designing a intelligent authoring system for high school mathematics ICAI: The teachers apprentice project. In Greg Kearsley (Ed.), *Artificial intelligence and instruction: Applications and methods*. Reading, MA: Addison-Wesley.

Luchins, A. S. (1942). Mechanization in problem solving. *Psychological Monographs, 54,* (248).

Matz, M. (1982). Toward a process model for high school algebra. In D. Sleeman & J. S. Brown (Eds.), *Intelligent tutoring systems*. New York: Academic Press.

McCloskey, M. (1983). Intuitive physics. *Scientific American, 24,* 122-130.

Pirolli, P.L. (1985). *Problem solving by analogy and skill acquisition in the domain of programming*. Unpublished Ph.D. thesis, Carnegie-Mellon University.

Reiser, B. J., Anderson, J.R., & Farrell, R. G. (1985). Dynamic student modelling in an intelligent tutor for LISP programming. In *Proceedings of International Joint Conference on Artificial Intelligence-85* (pp. 8-14). Los Angeles: International Joint Conference on Artificial Intelligence.

Ross, B. H. (1984). Remindings and their effects in learning a cognitive skill. *Cognitive Psychology, 16,* 371-416.

Shultz, T. R. (1982). Rules of causal attribution. *Monographs of the Society for Research in Child Development, 47*(1, Serial No. 194).

Siegler, R. S. (1976). The effects of simple necessity and sufficiency relationships in children's causal inferences. *Child Development, 47,* 1058-1063.

Sleeman, D., & Brown, J. S. (Eds.). (1982). *Intelligent tutoring systems*. New York: Academic Press.

VanLehn, K. (1983). *Felicity conditions for human skill acquisition: Validating an AI-based theory* (Tech. Rep. No. CIS-21). Palo Alto, CA: Xerox Parc.

VanLehn, K. A. (1985). *Arithmetic procedures are induced from examples* (Tech. Rep. No. ISL-12). Palo Alto, CA: Xerox Palo Alto Research Center.

Zhu, X. & Simon, H. A. (1987). Learning mathematics from examples and by doing. *Cognition and Instruction, 4,* 137-166.

# IV

## SCIENCE AND THOUGHT

# 14

# The Scientist as Problem Solver

Herbert A. Simon
*Carnegie-Mellon University*

The thesis of this chapter can be stated succinctly, simply be replacing the "as" in its title by "is a": The Scientist is a problem solver. If the thesis is true, then we can dispense with a theory of scientific discovery—the processes of discovery are just applications of the processes of problem solving. However, because the thesis is not obvious to everyone, and because the topic of scientific discovery has interest in its own right, perhaps it is worthwhile to say a little more about it.

In a recent book (Langley, Simon, Bradshaw, & Zytkow, 1987), my co-authors and I have said a great deal more about discovery, and Deepak Kulkarni and I have added yet another chapter in a paper published in *Cognitive Science* (Kulkarni & Simon, 1988). There is no need to repeat these accounts here beyond a brief summary of what we concluded and how we supported our conclusions. We concluded that the thesis is, indeed, valid. As evidence, we adduced careful reports of a substantial number of historical scientific discoveries, together with computer simulations that, starting with essentially the same initial conditions as the human discoverers, made the same discoveries. Thus, the computer programs contained a set of processes that were sufficient for making the discoveries, and thereby provided a possible explanation for the success of the human scientists.

Our explorations of the histories of scientific discoveries have made it eminently clear to us that scientists set themselves many different kinds of tasks. These include tasks of formulating significant scientific problems, of discovering interesting phenomena, of finding the laws that are hidden in data (with and without the help of theories for guiding the search), of inventing new representations for phenomena and their accompanying theories, of inferring the logical consequences of theories and testing them, of designing experiments, of finding explanatory mechanisms to account for empirical generalizations, and of inventing new instruments for observation and measurement. Undoubtedly there are others.

What is common to all of these tasks is that they appear to employ the same general kinds of problem-solving processes as chessplayers employ in choosing moves, subjects in the laboratory in solving the Tower of Hanoi or the Missionaries and Cannibals problem, physicians in making diagnoses, computer salesmen in configuring systems for clients, architects in designing houses, or organic chemists in synthesizing new molecules. Mostly, they engage in heuristic search in a number of problem spaces: the spaces of theories and experiments mentioned by Klahr and Dunbar (chap. 4 in this volume), but also spaces of problems, of phenomena, of representations, of instruments, and others.

Moreover, the insight that is supposed to be required for such work as discovery turns out to be synonymous with the familiar process of recognition; and other terms commonly used in the discussion of creative work— such terms as *judgment, creativity,* or even *genius*—appear either to be wholly dispensable or to be definable, as insight is, in terms of mundane and well-understood concepts.

Until rather recent times, much of the published work about scientific discovery has consisted of anecdotes, frequently autobiographical, about specific discoveries and their finders. If discovery requires creativity, or even genius, it would be immodest for anyone to claim that he or she had made a discovery, and futile to try to describe how it had been done. But if discovery is plain, garden-variety problem solving, then there is no immodesty, and perhaps not even futility, in adding to the anecdotal evidence. I use this opportunity to think aloud, albeit retrospectively, about some of my own scientific work, and to see whether it, too, fits the problem-solving mold.

I say "albeit retrospectively," but a disputatious philosopher might argue that backward predictions are really the only ones we can trust when we are dealing with a theory of human behavior. After all, he could say, when we make forward predictions, our scientists may have been influenced by the very theories of discovery we are trying to test. The theory may fit their behavior only because they have read about BACON or DALTON, and think they will do better science if they simulate those programs. We avoid that danger of spurious verification by predicting events from a time when the theory did not exist.

## FORMULATING PROBLEMS

It is usually thought that a prerequisite to answering a question is to state it. Or, to change the metaphor, for something to be found, something must have been lost. But is that always true? When one finds a vein of gold, was it Nature who lost it? If we can find gold we haven't lost, perhaps we can answer questions we haven't asked.

Let's try again. We may find gold (even gold we haven't lost) by searching for it. But that means that the question has already been asked: "Where can we find some gold?" But what about the gold we find when we are not looking for gold; when we are engaged in some quite different activity (gathering wildflowers on the mountain, say)? At the very least, we must *notice* the gold; it must attract our attention, distracting us from the flowers. Do we account for this by postulating a need for gold? Or will an attention-attracting propensity of shiny yellow objects do the job? And how is the attraction of these yellow objects enabled by our distractibility from the flower-gathering task?

Now let's return from gold-seeking to problem-seeking. If we take our metaphor seriously, it suggests that one way to find a problem, and perhaps even its solutions, is to try to solve some other problem. That doesn't tell us where the other problem came from; but one problem at a time! We are dealing with the phenomenon of surprise. Searching for wildflowers, we are surprised to see something shining and golden in the rocks. To be surprised, we must attend to the surprising phenomenon. Hence the dictum of Pasteur: "Accidents happen to the prepared mind." And now we have a new problem: How does a mind become prepared? If I am to follow the time-honored tradition of using autobiographical anecdotes as the evidence for my theory of discovery, perhaps it is time for the first anecdote.

My first piece of scientific work, begun as a paper in an "independent projects" course at the University of Chicago in the winter and spring of 1935, was a study of the administration of public recreation in the City of Milwaukee (Simon, 1935). Never mind why that was a problem: it was relevant to a research project of my professor, Jerry Kerwin, on the relations of school boards with city governments. A standard topic in studies of organizations is the budget process, which in this case involved the division of funds between playground maintenance, administered by one organizational unit, and playground activity leadership, administered by another. How does one arrive at this division (which was a frequent subject of dispute)?

My previous study of economics provided a ready hypothesis: Divide the funds so that the next dollar spent for physical maintenance will produce the same return as the next dollar spent for leaders' salaries. I saw no evidence that anyone was viewing the decision in this way. Was I surprised? Perhaps, initially, but on reflection, I didn't see how it could be done. How were the values of better activity leadership to be weighed against the values of more attractive and better-maintained neighborhood playgrounds?

Now I had a new research problem: How do human beings reason when the conditions for rationality postulated by the model of neoclassical economics are not met—for example, when no one can define the appropriate utility function, or suggest how the contribution of expenditures to utility is to be measured? After further investigation of the particular situation before me, I thought I could see a rather simple pattern of the mental processes. Those who were organizationally responsible for playground supervision wanted more money spent for leadership; those who were responsible for the physical condition of the playgrounds wanted more spent for maintenance. Generalizing, people in organizations bring decision problems within reasonable bounds by identifying with the partial (and more nearly operational) goals that are the particular responsibility of their own organizational units (Simon, 1947, chap. 10).

Of course this is only a partial answer. It defined and labeled the phenomenon of *organizational identification,* a concept that has proved valuable in administrative theory, but it did not explain how higher levels of the organization adjudicated between the claims arising from competing identifications at the lower levels. That subject has subsequently been addressed by other researchers, among them John P. Crecine, who wrote his dissertation on this topic some 30 years after the events I am describing (Crecine, 1969).

The broader question—how do people make decisions when the conditions for the economists' global rationality are not met (or even when they are)?—remains an active frontier of research today, although large pieces of an answer have been provided through research by cognitive scientists on problem solving. Here the central concept is what economists call *bounded rationality,* and what cognitive scientists would more likely label *computational constraints on human thinking.* A large part of the answer explains that, when people don't know how to optimize, they may very well be able to satisfice—to find good-enough solutions. And good-enough solutions can often be found by heuristic search (Simon, 1955, 1982).

Now what does this anecdote say about finding problems as an essential component in the process of scientific discovery? One thing it says is that a problem I found in 1935 has lasted me for 52 years. I have never had to find another. More accurately this very broad problem of accounting for human rationality has served as a powerful generator for an endless series of subproblems (e.g., how do people solve the Tower of Hanoi problem, how do they choose chess moves, how do they make scientific discoveries?) (Newell, & Simon, 1972; Simon, 1979, sections 4, 7; Langley et al., 1987).

Another lesson to be drawn from the anecdote is that scientific discovery is incremental. An explanation for a particular act of discovery must take everything that has gone before as initial conditions. What we seek to explain is how these initial conditions led to the next step—in this case how my knowledge of elementary price theory, and Jerry Kerwin's desire to know how the school board and the public works department cooperated to provide public recreation service in Milwaukee, led me to observe a phenomenon that initially surprised me; and how that surprise led to new observations that could be explained by the concepts of identification and bounded rationality. Steps taken 20 years later led from bounded rationality to statisficing, and from satisficing to heuristic search.

Third, the anecdote adds another to the long list of examples where surprise was a key element in discovery. But what was "prepared" about this particular mind? My training in economics, and the evocation of that training in the context of a budget situation, disclosed a contradiction between what theory taught me ought to be happening and what my eyes and ears showed me to be actually happening. Without the training in economics the observed behavior would have appeared entirely "natural." Without the observations, I could have continued in the happy illusion that the neoclassical theory of utility maximization explains human behavior in the domain of budgeting. And because my exposure to the economics profession was still rather minimal, I had not acquired the habit, so common in that profession, of ignoring the real world when it contradicts the theory.

Nothing mystical, Nothing Magical. Can we simulate it? The heuristics indeed resemble quite closely those of KEKADA, the program that Deepak Kulkarni and I have used to simulate the research strategy of Hans Krebs, who found the chemical path for the *in vivo* synthesis of urea, a program that has now been generalized to other discoveries (Kulkarni & Simon, 1988). The program experiences surprise when its expectations are not met, and reacts to its surprise by seeking explanations for the surprising phenomena. But now I am waving my hands. (Or am I hand simulating?) We have not yet investigated what heuristics would have to be added to KEKADA in order to simulate the discovery of bounded rationality. But I think I might have saved myself a lot of work in 1935 if I had had KEKADA to advise me.

## LAWS FROM DATA

In our book, *Scientific Discovery* (Langley et al., 1987), my colleagues and I gave primary attention to the problems of inducing generalizations, quantitative and qualitative, from empirical data. Our programs, BACON and DALTON, were systems for inducing qualitative laws.

Data are not the only possible initial conditions for the induction of new laws; theories can also be used, in conjunction with data or independently. In our BACON simulations, we showed that, by incorporating in BACON heuristics that search for symmetries and conservation laws, we could substantially improve the efficiency with which it found laws in empirical data. In the limit, it may be possible to find a descriptive law directly, by deriving it from a more fundamental explanatory law. For example, Newton showed that Kepler's Third Law of Planetary Motion (the period of revolution of a planet varies as the 3/2 power of its distance from the Sun) could be derived mathematically from the inverse square law of gravitational attraction. (But note that Newton was working backward from the law that Kepler had already discovered by data-driven search.)

Before one can find mathematical functions that fit empirical data, one must have appropriate data that look as though a smooth mathematical function could generate them. it's the recipe for rabbit stew all over again; first catch the rabbit. Examples of such data have been much easier to come by in the physical sciences than in the biological or social sciences. When we find social science data of this kind, we should prize them.

On only one occasion in my life have I run into such data, and I cannot recall exactly when I first encountered them—possibly as early as about 1936 in Lotka's *Elements of Physical Biology* (1924), a fascinating book that the economist Henry Schultz always called to the attention of his students. Lotka reported data, compiled by one Dr. J. C. Willis, showing that when the number of species belonging to each genus in some order of plants or animals (beetles, say) are counted, and the genera are then arranged in order, according to the number of their species, the genus with the $n$th largest number of species will have about $1/n$ as many species as the genus with the largest number.

Similarly, when the frequencies with which different words appear in a book are counted, and words are then arranged in order of their frequency, the $n$th most frequent word will occur about $1/n$ times as frequently as the most frequent word. Moreover, about half of all the words that occur in a book will occur exactly once, about one sixth exactly twice, one twelfth three times, and so on. These relations hold for books in any alphabetic language, and the departures from regularity are small.

Other data show a similar regularity in the populations of cities in the United States: The $n$th largest city is about $1/n$ times as large as New York. These regularities are easily seen if the data are plotted on log-log paper, whereupon they fall on a straight line with a slope of minus one.

What does one do with regularities like this—regularities that, at first blush, can only be described as astonishing? What one does (or should do) is to behave in a BACON-like fashion until one finds a formula that fits the data. Then, like DALTON, one should see if one can postulate a mechanism whose operation would produce the regularity described by the formula.

I wish I could say that this was my immediate response to the data. Memory fails me. I recall my fascination with them, but not whether I pondered over them, and if I did, for how long. I do recall that, when I returned to Chicago after 1942, I thought about them again—I have a clear picture of sitting in the biology library in the University of Chicago, reading a paper referenced in Lotka's book. I also recall mentioning my interest in the matter to Allen Newell while visiting him and his wife, Noël, in their Santa Monica apartment between 1952 and 1954. But I was doing many other things during these years. The startling data on word frequencies and city sizes were not a constant preoccupation, but were more like a recurring itch that needed to be scratched occasionally.

Sometime during 1954 I found the answer. My recollections of just how I found it are sketchy, with no scraps of paper to bolster my memory, but a few aspects of the discovery are recoverable now. First, I looked for a function to fit the data. I was especially impressed by the regularity of the word-frequency data at the low end of the frequency range. The simple fractions seemed to point to a formula involving ratios of integers. In fact, the simple formula, $f(i) = 1/[i(i + 1)]$, gives the required numbers, $\frac{1}{2}$, $\frac{1}{6}$, $\frac{1}{12}$, and so on. For large $i$, we have approximately, $f(i) = 1/i^2$. The rank, which is simply the integral of the frequency, will then give $F(i) = 1/i$, so that on a logarithmic scale the relation between rank and frequency will be linear with a slope of $-1$.

Finding an equation that fits these magic numbers sets the stage for a new problem: finding an explanation for the equation, a plausible mechanism that will provide a rationale for the phenomena. My recollections of how I did this are even sketchier than my recollections about the previous stage. The ratios of integers were again the key. Where can you get ratios of integers? ratios of factorials are one possible source: $\frac{1}{6}$ can be written as the product of $\frac{1}{2}$ and $\frac{1}{3}$, and $\frac{1}{12}$ as the product of $\frac{1}{2}$, $\frac{1}{3}$, and $\frac{3}{4}$. In general, the formula $(i-2)!/i!$ produces the required numbers. The next step is likely to occur only to someone who has a little mathematical knowledge, and who sees in these ratios of factorials something like the Beta function, or at least sees the kinds of expressions one is accustomed to encounter in problems on combinations and probabilities. (In fact, I discovered that the beta function was what I wanted by searching through my copy of Peirce's *A Short Table of Integrals,* where I vaguely remembered having seen some ratios of factorials.)

Are there any other reasons for thinking that the situation may call for a probability model? Indeed there are. What do word frequency distributions and city size have in common? Nothing very obvious, unless they can be viewed as instantiations of the same urn scheme. So let us see whether we can interpret the formula as representing the steady state of some stochastic process.

Here I recall being aided by a metaphor. If we think of a book as being created word by word, and if a word is added that has already occurred $k$ times, the number of words occurring $k + 1$ times each will be increased by one, and the number of words occurring $k$ times each decreased by one. For a steady-state equilibrium, the rate at which words are created that had previously occurred $k$ times must be equal to the rate at which words are created that had previously occurred $k - 1$ times. In this way, the $k$ urn will be replenished as rapidly as it is depleted. At some point I began to visualize this as a cascade, with successive pools of water each maintained at a constant level by flow in from the pool above, and flow out to the pool next below. Working back from our answer—the distribution that we know describes the phenomena—it is not too hard to show that the equilibrium condition requires that the probability of creating a word that has already occurred $k$ times must be proportional to $k$.

We are ready for the final step: to interpret the probability assumption. In the case of word distributions, it can be interpreted to mean that the chance of a word being chosen as the next word in a text is proportional, because of association, to the frequency with which it has been used already, and also proportional, because of long-term associations stored in memory, to the frequency with which it is used in the language. In the case of city sizes, it can be interpreted to mean that birth and death rates are approximately independent of city size, whereas the probability that a city will be the target for any given migration is also proportional to its size (Simon, 1955).

I don't propose to defend these interpretations here. My purpose is to understand the process that reached them. If my account, through the filter of 30 to 50 years of forgetting, has any relation to reality, then we see a process for arriving at the initial formula that looks very BACON-like, followed by working-backward search processes that are guided by the evocation of prestored mathematical and real-world knowledge—BACON as the front end to an expert system.

Again, my hands are waving wildly. You will not have failed to notice that I have not accounted at all for the cascade metaphor, yet at some time it was evoked and helped me to formulate the steady-state relations. So there is still work to be done on the theory of discovery; still theses to be written and papers published. But I see in this little history, or imagined history, no magic and no mystery. Each step appears to proceed, if not inexorably at least plausibly, from the preceding one.

If the data cried out so loudly for explanation, and if the discovery process proceeded in such a plausible succession of steps, why did not others discover this law and its stochastic explanation? Indeed they did. The first was G. Udny Yule, the English statistician, who in 1924 published "A mathematical theory of evolution, based on the conclusions of Dr. J. C. Willis, F. R. S." Yule constructed a model very similar to the one I have just described to explain Willis' data, mentioned earlier, on the distribution of species among genera. (I could have been led to this paper by a footnote in Lotka, but I wasn't.) A second was the English economist, D. G. Champernowne, who published "A model of income distribution" in 1953, describing a quite similar process. A third was B. Mandelbrot, who, in 1953, published "An informational theory of the statistical structure of language." There were some differences between Mandelbrot's model and mine, which later occasioned heated dispute between us (which enlivens the pages of *Information and Control*; Mandelbrot 1959, 1961a, 1961b; Simon 1960, 1961a, 1961b), but the basic ideas were closely related.

In 1955, I learned about all these partial anticipations when I searched the literature and inquired among my friends prior to publishing my own paper on the topic (Simon, 1955).

That still isn't quite the end of the story, for again, the solution of one scientific problem created a host of new problems. In the book by Yuji Ijiri and myself, *Skew Distributions and the Sizes of Business Firms* (1977), you can find a series of essays applying the same stochastic mechanism, and generalized versions of it, to the task of understanding the size distributions of business firms and the economic implications of these distributions.

## REPRESENTATIONS

Mention of the cascade metaphor that I used to find the stochastic process underlying word-frequency and city-size distributions raises the question of representations. What kinds of representations are used by scientists in thinking about their research problems, and where do these representations come from? One hallowed form of the question is whether scientists (and others) think in words, or whether thoughts take some quite different shape—whether, for example, they employ "mental pictures."

### Words and Pictures

The French mathematician, Jacques Hadamard, in his delightful essay, *The Psychology of Invention in the Mathematical Field* (1945), comes down heavily on the side of images and against words. Among the many distinguished mathematicians and scientists testifying for him is Albert Einstein, who in a letter to Hadamard stated that "the words or the language, as they are written or spoken, do not seem to play any role in my mechanism of thought. The psychical entities which seem to serve as elements in thought are certain signs and more or less clear images which can be 'voluntarily' reproduced and combined."

What is good enough for Hadamard and Einstein is good enough for me. I, too, have difficulty in finding any presence of words when I am thinking about difficult matters, especially mathematical ones. Even as I sit here at the keyboard, composing this chapter, I cannot really detect the words in my thoughts (or much of anything else, for that matter) until they come out the ends of my fingers. But perhaps I am not thinking, but just recording previously composed ideas that reside somewhere in my subconscious mind.

Even if we do think in images rather than words, neither Hadamard nor Einstein nor I had much success in describing just what these images were or how they were represented in a biological structure like the brain. However, I believe that Jill Larkin and I have recently made substantial progress in explaining these matters (in "Why a Diagram is (Sometimes) Worth Ten Thousand Words," Larkin & Simon, 1987). In order to deal with the difficulties one by one, we fudged a bit, alleging that we were talking about diagrams on paper rather than mental pictures; but most of our argument carries over in a straightforward way. The basic ideas, which I will not elaborate upon here, are (a) that in the course of transforming verbal propositions into images, many things are made explicit that were previously implicit and hidden, and (b) that (learned) inference operators facilitate making additional inferences from the images in computationally efficient ways.

We also show, as a byproduct of our analysis, that diagrams are representable as list structures (alias "schemas," "scripts," "frames," "labeled directed graphs," etc.), hence are programmable in standard list-processing languages, hence are readily seen to be representable in systems of neuronlike structures. Because the surface structures and the semantics of natural languages can also be represented as list structures, we can conclude that propositions and pictures (or at least diagrams) can use common representational machinery—that both are best viewed as specializations of a common list-structure mode of representation. [I did not wish to deny that we may *also*, as Kosslyn (1980, and also Chap. 1 in this volume) argued, possess a specialized raster-like organ for more literal representation of visual images—a mind's eye. But I would prefer to put that question aside here.]

Now just as there has been a debate as to whether we use words or images in our thoughts, so there has been a debate (perhaps the same debate) as to whether our internal representations of problems look like collections of propositions or like models of the problem situations. Each of these views has been held by an important segment of the cognitive science community, and the two segments do not often communicate with each other, except sometimes to quarrel.

One segment, under the banner of "let language lead the way," takes verbal reasoning as its metaphor for the problem-solving process, and thinks of reasoning as some kind of PROLOG-like theorem-proving procedure. The book by Miller and Johnson-Laird called *Language and Perception* (1976) is an excellent representative of this point of view, although Johnson-Laird, in his more recent book, *Mental Models* (1987), takes a long step of apostacy toward the alternative viewpoint. That he does without any apparent awareness that he is moving into well-explored ground exemplifies the mutual insulation of the two segments.

The second segment of the cognitive science community uses heuristic search through a problem space (a mental model of the task domain) as its metaphor for problem solving. *Human Problem Solving* (1972) adheres strictly to this viewpoint. It has been claimed, by Pylyshyn (1973) among others, that the two viewpoints cannot be distinguished operationally, but this claim rests on a confusion between the informational equivalence and the computational equivalence of representations. Even if two representations contain exactly the same information, it may be far cheaper, computationally, to make some of this information explicit using one representation than using the other.

The incorrectness of the claim of computational equivalence is demonstrated by the examples given in the Larkin-Simon paper already mentioned, as well as by extensive experimental work with Hayes and Kotovsky that demonstrates enormous differences in the difficulty of problems that are isomorphic, but represented differently (See Simon, 1979, Section 7; Kotovsky, Hayes, & Simon, 1987).

## Representing a Dynamic System

I am afraid that I have been diverted from my main topic, which is providing anecdotal evidence about the problem-solving processes used in scientific discovery. Let me return with an example that I present rather sketchily, to avoid technical detail. Economists frequently use what they call *partial equilibrium analysis,* in which they avoid talking about everything at once by making a host of *ceteris paribus* assumptions. They examine the impact of a disturbance on a small segment of the economy while assuming no interaction with the rest of the economy.

If challenged on the legitimacy of what they are doing, economists using partial equilibrium methods may defend themselves by saying that, of course, interactions are not completely absent but they are small, hence unimportant. That is an argument we know not only in economics, but throughout all of science. But is it a satisfactory argument? Small effects, persisting over a long period of time, may integrate into large effects.

Thoughts of these kinds (represented as words or as images?) went through my mind while I read, in the early 1950s, a paper by Richard Goodwin, "Dynamical Coupling with Especial Reference to Markets Having Production Lags," published in *Econometrica* in 1947. Again, I cannot claim any clear recollection of the precise steps I took to formulate and solve the problem that this paper evoked. I did conceive of it as a matter of analyzing the behavior of a large dynamic system divided into sectors, with strong interactions among the components in each sector, and weak interactions among the sectors. I remember also that I worked very hard for several months to get answers, and that I worked, without paper and pencil, while taking long walks.

My representation, at least much of the time, was an image of the matrix of coefficients of such a dynamic system—hardly surprising, because this is the way dynamic systems are normally represented in mathematics books. At some point, I saw that the rows and columns of the matrix could be permuted so that the new matrix would consist of a number of diagonal blocks with large coefficients in them, and only small coefficients in the matrix outside the diagonal blocks. The matrix was "nearly block diagonal." The image was vague, in that the number of blocks and their sizes were not seen in detail. If forced to give numbers, I might say that there could have been three blocks, each three rows by three columns in size—but the answer is surely a fabrication.

At some later point in time, I acquired a metaphor. I visualized a building divided into rooms, each of which was divided, in turn into cubicles. You can see a diagrammatic interpretation of my metaphor in *The Sciences of the Artificial* (1981, p. 212). We start out with an extreme disequilibrium of temperature, each cubic foot of each cubicle being at a different temperature from its neighbors.

Several things now seemed obvious. Throughout each cubicle, a constant temperature would be established very rapidly by exchange of heat between adjoining volumes. At some later time, each room would attain a constant temperature by heat diffusion through the walls of the cubicles. At a still later time, the entire building would reach a constant temperature by exchange of heat between the thicker walls of the rooms.

Moreover, because of the differences in the durations involved, each of these processes of equilibrium—within cubicles, among cubicles, and among rooms—can be studied independently of the others. In studying the equilibration of each cubicle, we can ignore the other cubicles. In studying the equilibration of rooms, we can represent each cubicle by its average temperature, and ignore the other rooms. In studying the equilibration of the building, we can represent each room by its average temperature. As a result, the mathematics of the problem can be simplified drastically.

There still were some difficult mathematical steps from this picture of the situation to rigorous proofs of the (approximate) validity of the simplification, but the result to be attained was clear. The reasoning I have described was carried out mainly in the summer of 1956, and incorporated, together with the mathematics, in a paper written with Albert Ando later that year, and published in 1961 (Simon & Ando, 1961).

I can throw no further light on the source of the heat-exchange metaphor, or on how, if at all, I drew inferences from the image of the nearly block diagonal matrix. Block diagonal matrices were not unfamiliar to me, for they had played an important role in the theoretical work I had done on causal ordering in 1952 and 1953 (Simon, 1952, 1953). The mathematics required for the proofs, which was fairly standard, would have been evoked, I think, in the mind of any mathematician who had put the problem in the form we did. Our results were rediscovered by some Russian mathematicians in the late 1960s (Korolyuk, Polischuk, & Tomusyak, 1969), but apparently had not been known earlier.

Our theorems and methods (which may be used to invert matrices that are nearly block diagonal) have attracted the attention of numerical analysts, and of natural scientists who are concerned with hierarchically organized systems. The aggregation method we introduced has also now been recognized to be closely related to the so-called "renormalization" procedures that play an important role in several parts of physics, and which were also invented quite independently of our method.

Even with this sketchy account, the discovery process appears quite unremarkable. The problem was found in the literature (Goodwin's paper), and it can be represented in a quite standard way by matrices having a certain special structure. The metaphor, by showing how such a system would behave, made clear the nature of the theorems to be proved. Although nothing is revealed about the source of the metaphor, it is not at all esoteric. The proofs, although intricate, would not pose any great difficulty for a professional mathematician. A case of normal problem-solving, we would have to conclude.

## FINDING AN EXPLANATORY MODEL

The last two sections provided two examples of the process of finding an explanatory model—a model for the rank-frequency relation, and a model of nearly decomposable dynamic systems. However, the reader may be interested in an example a little closer to home. How could one discover an explanatory model of human problem solving? One answer might be: "By observing some problem solving behavior closely and inducing the model directly from your observations."

Explanatory theories take a variety of forms. For example, the behavior of gases is commonly explained by supposing that they consist of a cloud of energetic particles, interacting with each other in accordance with the laws of mechanics. Magnetic attraction between two bodies is explained by a field of magnetic force in the space between them.

One very common form of explanation, in both natural and social science, employs systems of differential equations or difference equations to determine the values of the time derivatives of system variables. At any given time, the system is supposed to be in a specified *state,* and the differential equations then determine to what state it will be moved a moment later. Thus, in mechanics, the state is defined in terms of positions and velocities, and the differential equations show how the action of forces to produce accelerations brings about a continuing change in state through time.

Building an explanatory model involves a choice among these or other representations of the phenomena. Will it be a particle model or a continuum model? Will it represent static equilibrium, a steady state, or dynamic change? The representation has to be chosen prior to, or simultaneously with, the induction of the model from the data.

When Allen Newell, Cliff Shaw, and I began the construction of a theory to explain problem solving, around 1955, we were already committed to a representation. In fact, it was our recognition that such a representation had become available with the invention of the digital computer that motivated us to undertake the study of human thinking. A reader can find detailed accounts of the background for this recognition in Newell and Simon (1972, p. 873–886) and in McCorduck (especially chaps. 3 and 6).

What we observed—we have told the story before (Newell & Simon, 1972)—was that the program of a computer is formally equivalent to a set of difference equations. At each operation cycle, the program determines the new state of the machine as a function of its previous state (the contents of all its memories) together with any new input it has received. Moreover, these difference equations were not limited to manipulating numbers, but could process symbols of any kind.

The explanatory task, then, was to find a dynamic theory of the processes of problem solving in the form of a computer program. The data we could muster on the behavior of human problem solvers had to be examined for clues as to the nature of that program. This requirement provided very strong guidelines both for the kinds of data that would be valuable (preferably data that followed the course of problem solution as closely and minutely as possible), and for the best ways of examining the data (searching out the succession of "actions" the problem solver executed, and the cues that motivated each action).

Of course, there was more to the representation than simply the specification that it be a computer program. It had to contain symbol structures that could represent the structures in human memory, which were known to be, in some sense, associative. The important point was that there was a continuing two-way interaction between the gradual construction of the representation and the construction of the theory that used it. Sometimes programming convenience (or necessity) dictated choices, sometimes psychological requirements. Some aspects of the representation that were initially conceived mainly to meet programming needs (for example, the list-processing languages and data structures in the form of lists and description lists), were later seen to have psychological interpretations as networks of associations.

The empirical part of the undertaking, which I discuss later in connection with the topic of experimental design, went hand in hand with the design of the representation of the explanatory model.

Once some experience had been gained with information-processing models in the form of computer programs, they became a readily available tool for building theories of other aspects of human thinking. So, Kotovsky and I, interested in explaining simple law-discovery processes as a first step toward a theory of scientific discovery, naturally framed our model as a computer program in a list processing language, capable of discovering and extrapolating the patterns of Thurstone letter-sequence problems (Simon & Kotovsky, 1963, and Kotovsky & Simon, 1973). No alternative representations were even considered.

In the past few years, with the availability of a whole new menu of variants: production systems, models of memory with spreading activation, connexionist models, SOAR, the PROLOG language—choices of representation have again become an important and difficult part of the model-building process. Comparisons among these alternative architectures will be high on the research agenda in the next decade.

## DESIGNING GOOD EXPERIMENTS

Experiments are supposed to be aimed at testing hypotheses or, better yet, choosing between contending hypotheses ("critical" experiments). That an experiment meets one or both of these aims is neither a necessary not a sufficient condition for its being a good experiment.

It is not a sufficient condition because testing weak-tea hypotheses of the form, "variable $X$ affects variable $Y$," or its negation, is not usually very interesting, and does not often contribute much to our understanding of the world. (But if I continue in this vein, I will trespass on Allen Newell's (1973) noted "Twenty Questions" essay.)

Testing stronger quantitative hypotheses (e.g., the periods of the planets are as the 3/2 power of their distances from the Sun) is much more interesting, and very interesting indeed if the hypotheses are closely connected with broad explanatory theories (e.g., with the inverse square law of gravitation).

We are on safer ground if we aim experiments at testing *models* instead of testing *hypotheses,* but when we do that, we must remember to throw away the whole standard apparatus of significance tests, which is no longer applicable. [I cannot pause here to defend this dictum, which will sound like heresy to psychologists, but is nearly unanimously accepted by mathematical statisticians. My reasons, and pointers to the literature, can be found in Gregg & Simon (1967).] We must also remember that models are multicomponent creatures, and when our data don't fit a model, we are faced with a difficult diagnostic task to determine what to change—or whether to discard the entire model.

So much for sufficiency, but what about necessity? Is model-testing the only reason for experimenting? Surely not. One good reason for running an experiment—or for spending one's time just observing phenomena closely—is that you may be surprised. The best things that come out of experiments are things that we didn't expect to come out—especially those that we couldn't even have imagined, in advance, as possibilities. Of such stuff are many Nobel Prizes made. (See Klahr & Dunbar, chap. 4 in this volume, for subjects who search without hypotheses.)

Lest I be accused of advocating planning experiments by casting dice, let me suggest that there are heuristics for planning both kinds of experiments, experiments to test models and experiments to generate surprise. (Of course, an experiment designed to test a model may also produce a surprise.) Let me illustrate both sorts of heuristics with some examples. I begin with the more traditional model-testing category.

## Testing Models

A few years ago, I found occasion to begin the study of the Chinese language. I did it just for fun, and because I planned to visit China, but to put a more solemn face on things, I called it "exposing myself to new phenomena." That allowed me to do some of it on company time, with a good conscience. Finding myself in China, working with Chinese psychologists, we decided to replicate with Chinese language materials some standard short-term memory experiments. The motive was to test a model. Does Chinese have a magical number (Miller, 1956)? And is it seven? The answer to both questions was "yes"—no great surprise.

Meanwhile, I had learned a striking fact about the Chinese language (no surprise to my Chinese colleagues, but a surprise to me). A Chinese college graduate can recognize about 7,000 Chinese characters (hanzi). Each character is pronounced with a single syllable. But in the Chinese language there are only about 1,200 distinct syllables (even taking account of tone distinction.). Hence, on average, there are about six homophones for each character.

Somehow (intuition or recognition at work), I remembered that short-term memory was generally thought to be acoustical in modality, but only because of Conrad's rather indirect evidence that errors in recall generally involved similarity in sound rather than similarity in appearance. In Chinese, we could put the acoustical hypothesis to direct test. After establishing that the STM span is about six or seven unrelated and nonhomophonic characters, we presented the same subjects with strings of visually distinct homophonic characters. The result was dramatic—the STM spanned dropped to about two, confirming Conrad's result (Zhang & Simon, 1985; Yu, et al., 1985).

A similar methodological predisposition for testing models underlies the experiments that Bill Chase and I did on memory for chess positions, building on the earlier work of de Groot and others (Chase & Simon, 1973a, 1973b). Here the question was whether the differences in chess memory between experts and novices could be accounted for by differences in their vocabularies of "chunked" chess patterns. The answer that came out of our experiments was "qualitatively yes, but quantitatively no," an answer that, if slightly disappointing, was much sharper than if we had simply asked whether experts' chunks were larger than novices'.

The qualified affirmative answer has led to much subsequent research, which is gradually giving us a more precise model of how chunks are constructed and organized in memory. This research is strongly represented in this volume by the chapters by Charness, and Ericsson and Staszewski, (7 and 9)and closely related questions are examined by Carpenter and Just (chap. 2) in their use of eye movements and a memory model to study the role of working memory in reading.

The experiments with Chase on chess memory, like those with Chinese characters, were designed by asking what quantitative predictions a current model made and how we could make the measurements necessary for testing these predictions. The problem-solving search, if there was one, took place in the space of the characteristics of the task domain, and was facilitated by looking for "surprising" or "interesting" features of the domain. In the Chinese language case, the surprising feature was found first, and the model it was relevant to was found second. In the chess case, the order was reversed.

The experiments just described all have an experimental and a control condition, just as a well-designed experiment is supposed to. In the Chinese language experiments we compared homophonic with nonhomophonic strings of characters. In the chess experiments, we compared the performance of experts with the performance of novices, and chess positions from well-played games with random positions. The expert-novice dichotomy has also served me in good stead in some more recent experiments on problem solving in physics (Larkin et al., 1980; Simon & Simon, 1978), and has been used by Hayes (chap. 8 in this volume) and his colleagues in research on writing. An incidental benefit of using this paradigm is that being able to point to clearcut experimental and control conditions seems to soothe the savage breast of referee and editor.

## Problem Isomorphs

To conclude my list of experimental manipulations, I mention just one other, which has provided us with almost unlimited mileage—the idea of problem isomorphs. Its history is as obscure as that of many of the other things I have been talking about. I think I invented the idea of problem isomorphs about 1969, or a little earlier; for I do not have any evidence of earlier mention by myself or anyone else. I have a conjecture about its antecedents, but it is a reconstruction, not a recollection, although my colleague, John Michon, without prompting corroborated it.

Saul Amarel was one of the first researchers in artificial intelligence to point out that changing the representation of a problem—the problem space and operators—could sometimes greatly facilitate its solution. Amarel, Newell, and I participated in a semester-long seminar at CMU in 1966, the main topic of which was problem representation. Now it is only a small step (at least by hindsight) from the idea that a subject can solve a problem easily by finding the right representation to the idea than an experimenter can make a problem harder or easier for a subject by presenting it in one or another guise.

So much for the antecedents. Some problem isomorphs—problems with identical task domains and legal-move operators, but described by difference sets of words—were a topic of discussion in the Understand Seminar (alias the Cognitive Science Seminar), which has run weekly in the psychology department at Carnegie-Mellon University for 20 years. The first example was number scrabble, an isomorph of tic-tac-toe; and John Michon then added another member, JAM, to this set. John R. Hayes rapidly became the most prolific and ingenious designer of problem isomorphs, providing us with somewhere between a dozen and two dozen isomorphs of the Tower of Hanoi puzzle, most of which have been used in one or more experiments (Hayes & Simon, 1974, 1977; Simon & Hayes, 1976).

We have used isomorphs to discover what characteristics of a problem, other than the size of the task domain, account for its difficulty. Early work in problem solving, our own included, had focused on the combinatorial explosion of search as the main source of problem difficulty. Yet we had found that the Tower of Hanoi, with a relatively small and easily exhaustible domain, and the Missionaries and Cannibals puzzle, with a tiny one, could occupy human adults for 15 minutes or 30 minutes before they found a solution.

The idea that only the size of the task domain could affect problem difficulty sometimes died hard. One referee for a funding agency gave a project proposal low marks because he or she thought that, on these grounds, our experiments could have only negative results, because all isomorphs must be of the same difficulty. (At the time we were told of this objection, we had already demonstrated differences in average solution times to various isomorphs of the Tower of Hanoi in the ration of 16:1.) Our theoretical account of problem difficulty is still very incomplete, although we have been able to model some of the phenomena (Kotovsky, Hayes, & Simon, 1985; Kotovsky & Fallside, chap. 3 in this volume). [The UNDERSTAND program, for example, constructs different representations of problems when presented with different isomorphs (Hayes & Simon, 1974).]

The experimental strategy here is clear, deriving from the single idea of isomorphism—and that idea has at least a plausible lineage. The power of the idea would be enhanced if we had more systematic ways of designing isomorphs with specific features designed in advance to test particular putative sources of difficulty.

## Experimenting Without an Independent Variable

The experiments described up to this point all compare performance under two or more different conditions—they involve manipulation of an independent variable. When I examine my publications beyond the limited set already mentioned, to my embarrassment I find that this fundamental condition for sound experimentation is seldom met in them. What have I been up to? What can I possibly have learned from ill-designed experiments? The answer (it surprised me) is that you can test theoretical models without contrasting an experimental with a control condition. And apart from testing models, you can often make surprising observations that give you ideas for new or improved models.

Let me start with an example of the latter kind. Many summers ago (about 1965) Jeffrey Paige and I decided to take thinking-aloud protocols from high-school students solving algebra word problems (Paige & Simon, 1966). Our main motivation, I think, was just to see how they did it—what processes they used. Perhaps we had in mind comparing their behavior with Bobrow's STUDENT program (subsequently published in Bobrow, 1968), which solved such problems. Or perhaps we thought we might build a program ourselves that would do a better job of simulating the human processes. If those were our intentions, my memory does not retain them.

Jeff conceived of a fine idea (at least, I have always remembered it as his). We constructed some "impossible" problems—problems that could not be given a real physical interpretation because their solutions involved boards of negative length or nickels that were worth more than dimes. We then asked our subjects to set up the equations corresponding to the problem statement, but not to solve them.

The outcome was wholly unanticipated. Our subjects fell into three groups, rather consistently over the set of three problems. Some set up the equations that corresponded literally with the verbal statements of the problems. Some translated the problems inaccurately, always ending up with equations that corresponded to a realizable physical situation. Some said, "Isn't there a contradiction?"—meaning, "I draw inferences from the problem statements that conflict with my knowledge of the real world."

Because we were trying to get as dense a set of data as we could, in order to trace processes in detail, we had asked the subjects both to think aloud and to draw diagrams of the problem situations. The diagrams drawn by subjects in the first group were generally incomplete and unintegrated, and did not reveal the "contradiction." The diagrams drawn by subjects in the second group misrepresented the situations in just the way their equations did—so as to make them physically realizable. The subjects in the third group drew diagrams that revealed the contradictions.

The direction of the causal arrow is not clear, but one can take these results as at least presumptive evidence that subjects in the second and third groups used imagery to represent the information from the word problems before translating into the language of algebra. Subjects in the first group gave evidence of translating directly to equations using only syntactic information.

With this kind of information in hand, one can begin to construct models for the simulation of these sorts of behavior, and to explore what other predictions could be made about systems behaving in these ways. The ISAAC program, written by Gordon Novak to solve physics problems presented in natural language, is an example of a system that uses an internal diagram of the problem situation to mediate between the verbal stimulus and the equations it finally constructs (Novak, 1976). The UNDERSTAND program that John R. Hayes and I constructed, around 1972, to show how verbal problem instructions could be converted into inputs appropriate for a GPS-like problem solver, also borrowed this insight from the algebra experiments (Hayes & Simon, 1974). All of this work was antecedent to the current investigations, mentioned earlier, of representation and imagery.

But the most massive set of examples of the experimental strategy of "just looking" is to be found in *Human Problem Solving*. Density of data was the name of the game, and protocol analysis the way of playing it. In 1956, the *Logic Theorist* (LT) demonstrated the feasibility of solving difficult problems by highly selective heuristic search (Newell & Simon, 1956). But is that the way people did it? The *General Problem Solver*, LT's successor, was our answer—a heuristic search system that used means-end analysis as its principal heuristic (Newell & Simon, 1972).

Both Al Newell and I agree that the core of GPS was extracted from a particular protocol that we can identify. We also agree as to the week in the summer of 1957 when it was done. On the details, the evidence is not wholly concordant, but sometime, when we have leisure to examine the papers we have preserved, we may get it all straightened out (see McCorduck, 1979, p. 212). The main lesson is clear: GPS, a theory of human problem solving, was extracted by direct induction from the thinking aloud protocol of a laboratory subject, without benefit of an experimental and a control condition.

What, in addition to luck, entered into the result? First, as I have pointed out in an earlier section, we already knew that we wished to represent our model as a computer program in a list-processing language. Second, a data gathering method was used that obtained the densest record of the subject's behavior that we knew how to get. We were able to discover what he had done each few seconds of time during which he worked on the task. Third, some care had been taken in selecting the task. It had already been used by O. K. Moore and his colleagues at Yale, and we had access to both their experience and their data. The task was symbolic, hence made for easy verbalization, and seemed to call for a minimum of picture visualization. It was a hard enough task to evoke genuine problem-solving behavior from intelligent subjects.

Application of these criteria to the selection of problem-solving tasks accounts for a substantial fraction of the knowledge that has been collected about problem-solving processes during the past 30 years, and a substantial part of the theoretical efforts that have succeeded in building models to account for behavior in many kinds of tasks. The metaphor of chess, cryptarithmetic and the Tower of Hanoi serving as the sweet peas, Drosophila and E. coli of cognitive science is as near to literal truth as it is to fancy.

Do these experiments really lack independent variables? Can't we consider the task domain or the subject to be just that? Of course we can, but to no particular end. The principal knowledge we gained from these experiments did not come out of comparisons between tasks or subjects. It came out of painstakingly analyzing individual protocols and inducing from them the processes that problem solvers employed in their work. Once this had been done, we could test the generality of our results by comparing over tasks and over subjects. But detailed longitudinal analysis of the behavior of single subjects was the foundation stone for the information processing theories we have built of what goes on in human problem solving.

If the methodology troubles us, it may be comforting to recall that detailed longitudinal analysis of the behavior of a single solar system was the foundation stone for Kepler's Laws, and ultimately for Newton's. Perhaps it is not our methodology that needs revising so much as the standard textbook methodology, which perversely warns us against running an experiment until precise hypotheses have been formulated and experimental and control conditions defined. How do such experiments ever create surprise—not just the all-too-common surprise of having our hypotheses refuted by fact, but the delight-provoking surprise of encountering a wholly unexpected phenomenon? Perhaps we need to add to the textbooks a chapter, or several chapters, describing how basic scientific discoveries can be made by observing the world intently, in the laboratory or outside it, with controls or without them, heavy with hypotheses or innocent of them.

## THE SCIENTIST AS A SATISFICER

My economist friends have long since given up on me, consigning me to psychology or some other distant wasteland. If I cannot accept the true faith of expected utility maximization, it is not the fault of my excellent education in economics—in fact, the education was repeated four times, often enough even for a slow learner. First, as a high school student, I read the works of Richard Ely and Henry George in order to meet the arguments of opposing debating teams on such issues as the tariff or the single tax. Then, at the University of Chicago, I learned price theory from Henry Simonds and Walrasian equilibrium and econometrics from Henry Schultz.

Next, at Berkeley, my colleagues, Kenneth May and Ronald Shepard, students of Griffith Evans, revealed to me the inference-drawing powers of the second-order conditions of maximization; while I learned about Neyman-Pearson statistics from Jerzy Neyman himself. Finally, on returning to Chicago, I was exposed to Samuelson's *Foundations* and Hicks on value in the brilliant discussions at the Cowles Commission seminars among Jascha Marschak, Tjalling Koopmans, Ken Arrow, Larry Klein, Franco Modigliani, Gerard Debreu, and other superbly keen and well-informed minds.

Alas, it did not take. My traumatic exposure in 1935 to the budgeting process in the Milwaukee recreation department had immunized me against the idea that human beings maximize expected utility, and had made me an incorrigible satisficer. And that same imprinting experience supplied me with the problem—the cornucopia of problems—that has kept me occupied ever since. I have sketched the theory of scientific discovery to which my study of these problems has led me. It is not a theory of global rationality, but a theory of human limited computation in the face of complexity. It views discovery as problem solving, and problem solving as heuristic search, and heuristic search as the only fit activity for a creature of bounded rationality.

Some scientists believe that theories should be judged by their ability to make correct predictions. This chapter provides some tests of the predictive power of this problem-solving theory of discovery. The anecdotes I have provided from my own scientific life are instances where it gives pretty good accounts of the processes that are visible in my research.

It describes me, like KEKADA, formulating a new problem in response to my surprise at encountering an unexpected phenomenon. It traces my BACON-like progress toward discerning a lawful regularity in data, and the evocation of knowledge, in expert-system style, to find an explanation for the regularity. It accounts for my use of diagrams to gain a grasp of complex phenomena in a dynamic system. It illuminates how the availability of representations and the invention of new ones has influenced my efforts to construct explanations. It characterizes a number of my strategies for designing experiments, and perhaps even explains why I am frequently unconcerned about such things as "experimental controls" or even independent variables.

Of course I am exercising poetic license in talking of predictions. A comprehensive SIMPLE SIMON has not been programmed; only pieces of him exist. It would be more defensible to talk of explanatory accounts rather than predictions. But you will not be misled by the metaphor, which is as useful as one can expect a metaphor to be.

The information processing theory of discovery that I have been describing has one other virtue. It is not only a descriptive theory, but a normative one as well. Not only does it predict (explain) my behavior successfully, but, unbeknownst to me, it has served me for 52 years as a reliable set of heuristics for conducting research. Quite unwittingly, I have been following the instruction of BACON, of STAHL, of GLAUBER, of DALTON, and of KEKADA. I couldn't have had better guidance.

However, one heuristic that has been of first importance to my work is missing from these programs. I mention it, because you too may find it useful. If you want to make interesting scientific discoveries, be sure to acquire as many good friends as possible, who are as energetic, intelligent, and knowledgeable as they can be. Form partnerships with them whenever you can. Then sit back and relax. You will find that all the programs you need are stored in your friends, and will execute productively and creatively as long as you don't interfere too much.

## ACKNOWLEDGMENTS

This research was supported by the Personnel and Training Programs, Psychological Sciences Division, Office of the Naval research, under Contract No. N00014-86-K-0768. Reproduction in whole or in part is permitted for any purpose of the United States Government. Approved for public release; distribution unlimited.

## REFERENCES

NOTE: "MOT" is an abbreviation for Simon (1979).

Bobrow, D. G. (168). Natural language input for a computer problem-solving system. In M. Minsky (Ed.). *Semantic information processing* (pp. 135–215). Cambridge, MA: MIT Press.

Champernowne, D. G. (1953). A model of income distribution. *Economic Journal, 63,* 318–351.

Chase, W. G., & Simon, H. A. (1973a). Perception in chess. *Cognitive Psychology, 4,* 55–81. (Reprinted in MOT chap. 6.4.)

Chase, W. G., & Simon, H. A. (1973b). The mind's eye in chess. In W. G. Chase (Ed.), *Visual information processing.* New York: Academic Press. (Reprinted in MOT, chap. 6.5.)

Crecine, J. P. (1969). *Governmental problem-solving: A computer simulation of municipal budgeting.* Chicago, IL: Rand-McNally.

Goodwin, R. M. (1947). Dynamical coupling with especial reference to markets having production lags. *Econometrica, 15,* 181–204.

Gregg, L. W., & Simon, H. A. (1967). Process models and stochastic theories of simple concept formation. *Journal of Mathematical Psychology, 4,* 246–276. (Reprinted in MOT, chap. 5.4.)

Hadamard, J. (1945). *The psychology of invention in the mathematical field.* Princeton: Princeton University Press.

Hayes, J. R., & Simon, H. A. (1974). Understanding written problem instructions. In L. W. Gregg (Ed.), *Knowledge and cognition.* Hillsdale, NJ: Lawrence Erlbaum Associates. (Reprinted in MOT, chap. 7.1.)

Ijiri, Y., & Simon, H. A. (1977). *Skew distributions and the sizes of business firms.* Amsterdam: North Holland.

Johnson-Laird, P. N. (1983). *Mental models.* Cambridge, MA: Harvard University Press.

Korolyuk, V. S., Polischuk, L. I., & Tomusyak, A. S. (1969). A limit theorem for semi-markow processes (In Russian). *Kibernetika, 5,* 144–145.

Kosslyn, S. M. (1980). *Image and mind.* Cambridge, MA: Harvard University Press.

Kotovsky, K., & Simon, H. A. (1973). Empirical tests of a theory of human acquisition of concepts for sequential patterns. *Cognitive Psychology, 4,* 399–424. (Reprinted in MOT, chap. 5.2.)

Kotovsky, K., Hayes, J. R., & H. A. Simon (1985). Why are some problems hard? *Cognitive Psychology, 17,* 248–294.

Kulkarni, D., & Simon, H. A. (1988). *The processes of scientific discovery: The strategy of experimentation. Cognitive Science, 12,* 139–176.

Langley, P. W., Simon, H. A., Bradshaw, G., & Zytkow, J. (1987). *Scientific discovery: Computational explorations of the creative processes.* Cambridge, MA: MIT Press.

Larkin, J. H., McDermott, J., Simon, D., & Simon, H. A. (1980). Expert and novice performance in solving physics problems. *Science, 208,* 1335–1342.

Larkin, J. H., & Simon, H. A. (1987). Why a diagram is (sometimes) worth 10,000 words. *Cognitive Science, 11,* 65–100.

Lotka, A. J. (1924). *Elements of physical biology.* Baltimore, MD: Williams & Wilkins.

Mandelbrot, B. (1953). An informational theory of the statistical structure of language. In Willis Jackson (Ed.). *Communication Theory* (pp. 486–502). London: Butterworths.

Mandelbrot, B. (1959). A note on a class of skew distribution functions: Analysis and critique of a paper by H. Simon. *Information and Control, 2,* 90–99.

Mandelbrot, B. (1961a). Final note on a class of skew distribution functions. *Information and Control, 4,* 198–216.

Mandelbrot, B. (1961b). Post Scriptum to Professor Simon's "Reply." *Information and Control, 4,* 300–304.

McCorduck, P. (1979). *Machines who think.* San Francisco, CA: W. H. Freeman.

Miller, G. A. (1956). The magical number seven, plus or minus two. *Psychological Review, 63,* 81–97.

Miller, G. A., & Johnson-Laird, P. N. (1976). *Language and perception.* Cambridge, MA: Harvard University Press.

Newell, A. (1973). You can't play 20 questions with Nature and win. In William G. Chase (Ed.), *Visual information processing,* New York: Academic Press.

Newell, A., & Simon, H. A. (1972). *Human problem solving.* Englewood Cliffs, NJ: Prentice-Hall.

Novak, G. S. Jr. (1976). *Computer understanding of physics problems stated in natural language* (Tech. Rep. No. NL-30). Austin, TX: Department of Computer Sciences, University of Texas.

Paige, J. M., & Simon, H. A. (1966). Cognitive processes in solving algebra word problems. In B. Kleinmuntz (Ed.), *Problem solving.* New York: Wiley. (Reprinted in MOT, chap. 4.4)

Peirce, B. O. (1929). *A short table of integrals* (3rd rev. ed.) Boston, MA: Ginn & Company.

Pylyshyn, Z. W. (1973). What the mind's eye tells the mind's brain. *Psychological Bulletin, 80,* 1–24.

Simon, H. A. (1935). *Administration of public recreational facilities in Milwaukee.* Unpublished manuscript. (Quoted in *Administrative Behavior,* 211–212).

Simon, H. A. (1947). *Administrative behavior.* New York: Macmillan.

Simon, H. A. (1952). On the definition of the causal relation. *The Journal of Philosophy, 49,* 517–528.

Simon, H. A. (1953). Causal ordering and identifiability. In W. C. Hood & T. C. Koopmans (Eds.), *Studies in econometric methods.* New York: Wiley.

Simon, H. A. (1955). A behavioral model of rational choice. *Quarterly Journal of Economics, 69,* 99–118. (Reprinted in MOT, chap. 1.1.)

Simon, H. A. (1955). On a class of skew distribution functions. *Biometrika, 52,* 425–440.

Simon, H. A. (1960). Some further notes on a class of skew distribution functions. *Information and control, 3,* 80–88.

Simon, H. A. (1961a). Reply to "Final Note" by Benoit Mandelbrot. *Information and Control, 4*, 217-223.

Simon, H. A. (1961b). Reply to Dr. Mandelbrot's post scriptum. *Information and Control, 4*, 305-308.

Simon, H. A., & Ando, A. (1961). Aggregation of variables in dynamic systems. *Econometrica, 29*, 111-138.

Simon, H. A., & Hayes, J. R. (1976). The understanding process: Problem isomorphs. *Cognitive Psychology, 8*, 165-190. (Reprinted in MOT chap. 7.2.)

Simon, H. A., & Kotovsky, K. (1963). Human acquisition of concepts for sequential patterns. *Psychological Review, 70*, 534-546. (Reprinted in MOT, chap. 5.1.)

Simon, D. P., & Simon, H. A. (1978). Individual differences in solving physics problems. In R. S. Siegler (Ed.), *Children's thinking: What develops?* Hillsdale, NJ: Lawrence Erlbaum Associates.

Simon, H. A. (1979). *Models of thought.* New Haven, CT: Yale University Press.

Simon, H. A. (1981). *The sciences of the artificial.* Cambridge, MA: MIT Press.

Simon, H. A. (1982). *Models of bounded rationality* (Vol. 1-2). Cambridge, MA: MIT Press.

Yu, B., Zhang, W., Jing, Q., Peng, R., Simon, H., & Zhang, G. (1985). STM capacity for Chinese and English language materials. *Memory & Cognition, 13*, 202-207.

Yule, G. U. (1924). A mathematical theory of evolution, Based on the conclusions of Dr. J. C. Willis, F.R.S. *Philosophical Transactions,* 21-83.

Zhang, G., & Simon, H. A. (1985). STM capacity for Chinese words and idioms: Chunking and acoustical loop hypotheses. *Memory & Cognition, 13*, 193-201.

# 15
## Putting It All Together

Allen Newell
*Carnegie-Mellon University*

I carefully chose my title—"putting it all together"—intending it to have multiple meanings. First, Herbert Simon has indeed put it all together over the course of his career. Thus, this is a suitable title for the chapter that concludes a celebration of his cumulative work. But second, this title could be an echo of my William James lectures, *Unified Theories of Cognition,* given the Spring of 1987 at Harvard. Thus, this is a suitable title to provide a lead in for me to write about what preoccupies me these days—always a good thing for a commentator to do. Third, the title could refer to putting the chapters of this volume all together. After all, I am officially a discussant—and the final one at that. So I could do what I was hired to do.

Three separate meanings might be thought to pose three alternatives, and thus a choice between them for the main line of a commentary. In fact, I believe they can be put together into a single exposition. For all three parts support the same point, namely, that our field is moving toward putting it all together. Indeed, I hope that the very act of my writing a commentary in this integrative mode will be seen to symbolize the need for us all to be synthetic—to put cognition together. However, paper being a linear medium, it is necessary to put the parts together, one after the other—first Herbert Simon, then William James, and then the volume. But that too can show that serial is as effective as parallel integration, and perhaps even more so.[1]

---

[1]There is a whimsical tradition in computer science of self-referential acronyms. Thus *FINE,* an Emacs-like editor on Digital's Tops20 systems stands for *Fine Is not Emacs*; and *Gnu,* which is a prefix for a family of systems such as *Gnu-Emacs,* stands for *Gnu is Not Unix.* In this tradition, the acronym for this paper is *PIAT,* which clearly stands for *PIAT Is All Together.* It is left as an exercise for the reader to find out how many multiple meanings there really are in this title.

## HERBERT SIMON

It might be thought that I am an especially good choice as commentator on Herb's career, having worked with him for so long. However, there is a difficulty. Herb had it all put together at least 40 years ago—and I've only known him for 35. The central idea is *bounded rationality*—there are limits on man as a decision maker and these limits, especially those of cognitive processing in all its varied forms, loom large in man's behavior. Everything that Simon has done has stemmed from the working out of this idea. This central scientific proposition has remained without revision.

A look, however superficial, through Simon's contributions to cognitive science, clearly shows this (see Table 15.1). Each of these scientific topics— from the direct expression of a theory of bounded rationality, through symbol systems, to induction, chunking, task-acquisition, and onto spatial reasoning—all have to do with how humans deploy their limited processing capabilities so as to do their best with what they've got. The fact that these parts of cognitive science have proven to have so much scientific substance, reflects how much our human actions are shaped by processing limitations.

It is an interesting side note that Herb did not succumb to the temptation of a capacity theory. A common response to limited processing is to posit a resource, call it *rationality juice*. A person has only a limited supply of this juice, and what is used for purpose $P$ cannot be used for purpose $Q$. Then, the analyst regains the ability to apply optimization theory by assuming that the person will always distribute his limited rationality juice optimally among his options. Many have succumbed to positing such overall resource limits (by this or any other name). In my opinion, it has shielded them from discovering the real character of the mechanisms of cognition, which have shape as well as volume. Instead, Herb went for the details of the specific mechanisms involved. There is nothing in Herb's story that I know of that says why this happened. But it is fortunate that it occurred, as the array in Table 15.1 bears witness.

I do not have to make the case at this point in the volume for how much Herb has put it all together. All of the chapters that have preceded me have done this job in greater or lesser detail. Even Herb's own chapter helps us see how all the pieces fit together. Still, I would like to add one example of my own. In 1975, in our joint talk accepting the ACM Turing Award, Herb and I chose to talk about *Symbols and Search* (Newell & Simon, 1976). We presented this as a *retrospective* account, not as a *prospective* scientific claim. The central role of search was clear to Herb (and myself as his colleague) by 1956, the central role of symbols by 1960. Indeed, we took the field to have understood these notions by the 1960s. That seems a long time ago, and it is. If anything constitutes the central dogma of cognitive science, it is these two ideas. They would seem to constitute the fountainhead of the subsequent research.

TABLE 15.1
Topics in Cognitive Science to Which Simon and his Colleagues
Have Contributed (With Representative Citations)

---

**Theory of Bounded Rationality**

    Adaptive systems (Simon, 1955a; Simon, 1956; Simon, 1980b)
    Decomposable systems (Ando, Fisher & Simon, 1963)

**Problem Solving**

    Search (Baylor & Simon, 1966; Simon & Kadane, 1975)
    Human problem solving (Newell, Shaw & Simon, 1957; Newell & Simon, 1972)
    Word problems (Paige & Simon, 1966)
    Protocol analysis (Ericsson & Simon, 1984)

**Symbol Systems**

    List processing (Newell & Shaw, 1957; Newell & Simon, 1976)
    Architectures (Shaw, Newell, Simon & Ellis, 1959)
    Semantic nets (Quillian, 1967)

**Learning**

    **Verbal learning and EPAM (Simon & Feigenbaum, 1964; Simon & Gilmartin, 1973)**
    **ADaptive production systems (Anzai & Simon, 1979; Neves, 1981)**

**Induction and Concept Formation**

    Patterns (Gregg & Simon, 1967; Simon & Kotovsky, 1963; Simon & Lea, 1974; Williams, 1969)

**Emotion (Simon, 1967)**

**Chunking**

    Size and rates of chunks (Simon, 1974; Gilmartin, Newell & Simon, 1976)
    STM (Zhang & Simon, 1985)

**Expertise**

    Chess perception (Simon & Barenfeld, 1959; Chase & Simon, 1973, Simon & Gilmartin, 1973)
    Physics (Larkin, McDermott, Simon & Simon, 1980)

**Task Acquisition**

    Language (Coles, 1967; Simon & Siklossy, 1972)
    Games, UNDERSTAND (Simon & Hayes, 1976; Williams, 1965)

**Scientific Discovery**

    BACON, GLAUBER, STAHL, DALTON (Langley, Simon, Bradshaw & Zytkow, 1987)
    KEKADA (Kulkarni & Simon, 1988)

**Representation**

    Spatial reasoning and external memory (Larkin & Simon, 1987)

---

Note, however, that these two items are not at the top of Table 15.1. The topmost node of this generation tree of scientific knowledge is a *model of man*. The correct model of man as intendedly rational was already in place early on—indeed during the 5 years before I got to know Herb. Symbols and search are already the working out of this model, a refinement of it. Ed Feigenbaum is correct, in his contribution to this volume, when he takes as key two very early papers of Simon that set out this model of bounded rationality (Simon, 1955a, 1956).

When I say that Herb has long since had it all put together, am I saying that Herb has known all these years all the science that the rest of us are still struggling to discover? Not at all. Being right in science does not mean knowing everything, or learning nothing new, or even not being surprised. Being right means being on the main path—the cumulative path. Along the main path, scientific revolutions occur in the metastructure of science or in its sociology, but not in the trenches. Consider the move from classical Newtonian mechanics to quantum theory. Since Kuhn (1962), all of us have learned to talk and think about this as a revolution. And indeed it was. But we must be careful to understand where the revolution occurred. It occurred in our overall views, in our big picture, in our heuristics. To be sure, there were technical developments—powerful and elegant ones. But they did not sweep the old away. Indeed, all of classical mechanics resides, alive and rosy well, within the new non-Newtonian view. If the French Revolution had been like this, it would have chosen the King to be the Minister of the Interior.

So I think Herb would agree with Ed Feigenbaum's comment that there has been a big shift toward knowledge intensive systems and toward understanding the powerful role played by having the right (or wrong) knowledge. I certainly would. But I doubt that Herb was surprised at the changed course of events. Each thing in its own time—bounded rationality, search, symbols, knowledge, architecture, learning, . . . . The reader must guess the next term in the sequence, for it is not predetermined, only constrained by a sort of scientific readiness. Indeed, the emergence of the focus on knowledge was not a surprise to me, but it surely was a major development. I rejoice that Ed and his colleagues at Stanford found the path and that it turned out to lead so far so fast.

Thus Herb, with a serenity and prescience that some of the rest of us lack, has always seen the field whole—has seen it as the unfolding of a single central idea. It has allowed him to move from topic to topic within the area, always assured that the particular bit of the cathedral he happens to work on will add to the total structure—will help put it all together.

## UNIFIED THEORIES OF COGNITION

As I noted at the beginning, I have just finished a spring-full of lectures on unified theories of cognition (Newell, 1987). Let me introduce my concern with this topic, which relates strongly to putting it all together, by going back to a paper I gave at the Eighth Carnegie Symposium on Cognition (Newell, 1973b), organized by Bill Chase on visual information processing (Chase, 1973). The paper, itself a commentary just like this one, was entitled *You Can't Play 20 Questions with Nature and Win: Projective Comments on the Papers of This Symposium.*

The situation, as it seemed to me in 1972, was that the cognitive view was in place and well taken. Recall that this was before the cognitive science movement of the late 1970s, although after Ulric Neisser's deservedly famous book *Cognitive Psychology* (1967). There was a great accumulation of experimental data, especially chronometric data. Indeed I was being called upon to comment on the papers of Mike Posner (1973), Lynne Cooper and Roger Shepard (1973), David Klahr (1973), and Bill Chase and Herb Simon (1973); and I also managed to squeeze in a reference to some other presenters as well (Bransford & Johnson, 1973; Clark, Carpenter, & Just, 1973). This was as shining a collection of experimental luminaries as one could choose to read psychology by. Yet, despite the really fine examples of new data and penetrating analysis at that meeting, I feared for theoretical progress. It seemed to me, as I put it at the time, that the field did its theory by dichotomies, trying to find a general question to pose and then designing an experiment to settle *that* question, yes or no, and so move on down to the next subquestion. This is the classical strategy of 20 questions. And I did not think it would get us to the science of cognition that we all wanted.

I went on to describe some ways to try to put it together. One could create complete processing models. One could analyze complete tasks for all of the psychological phenomena they contain. One could take a single model and apply it to many different tasks across the psychological spectrum. In each case, at the heart of the enterprise is a cognitive model or detailed theory that provides the groundwork for an integration that is missing from the strategy of 20 questions.

Herb was pretty unhappy with my paper, though he didn't say much to me about it. However, the depth of his feeling was evident when he entitled his own commentary in the Fifteenth Carnegie Symposium on Cognition (1979), *How to Play Twenty Questions with Nature and Win* (Simon, 1980b). Indeed, many people have reacted to my little paper, and reactions continue right up to the present day. (It is a bit disconcerting to find that it is one's commentary papers that seem to be the most widely read.) Most everyone (though not quite all) take it as pure criticism and even disillusionment—as showing that some commentators (to wit, me) believe that cognitive psychology is in deep trouble. Most everyone (again, not quite all) ignore or never notice that I also proposed three positive steps—that I was concerned with moving psychology toward a course that I judged would help put it all together. I even produced a companion paper (which was actually part of the same commentary, but split off for purposes of publication) that took a technical step toward architectures, namely *Production Systems: Models of Control Structures* (Newell, 1973a).

Herb, I have no doubt, understood me, and in fact his essay 7 years later bears that out. That essay reveals that he simply prefers a different metaphor. In concluding his discussion of the papers that were his assignment, Herb described them as ". . . three fine examples of bricklaying for a cathedral that is beginning to take shape" (Simon, 1980a, p. 547). I have no trouble with the latter metaphor. One of the great things about metaphors is that they can be put on and taken off with the weather, like so many sweaters. So it is easy to abandon the 20-questions metaphor and put on the cathedral metaphor. In its terms, then, I was just trying to get the truckloads of bricks to go to the right construction site.

My goal for my commentary this time is to assert that it is coming together—or that the cathedral looks in good shape, rising majestically skyward. Or whatever other metaphor pleases you. The prognosis looks excellent to me and I have acted upon that assessment by undertaking my current scientific project, which is to move the field toward unified theories of cognition. To which we can now turn.

## The Architecture as the Unified Theory

Let us start with a familiar notion—the architecture—sketched out in Fig. 15.1. An architecture is the fixed structure that realizes a symbol system. It is what makes possible the hardware–software distinction—a structure that can be programmed with content (encoded in some representation), which can itself control behavior. As the figure shows, intelligent systems are constructed in levels. The two levels of main interest for cognitive science are the symbol level and above it the knowledge level (Newell, 1982). The knowledge level abstracts away from all representation and processing, to reflect only what the system has acquired about its environment that permits it to deploy its resources to attain its goals. Knowledge-level systems are just a way of describing a real system, of course. Thus, such a system is also always describable in more physical terms—with the representation and processing accounted for. Such systems are symbol-level systems (Newell, 1980).

The symbol level is that of data structures with symbolic operations on them, being carried out under the guidance of plans, programs, procedures, or methods. These are organizations of processing that are rationally ordered to the attainment of the goals of the system—that do the work that makes it true that the system uses whatever it knows to attain its goals. A symbol system, also, is just a way of describing a real system, so that this same system is also always describable in terms of some physical substrate.

This substrate (or rather, its design) is the architecture. In current digital computers it is a register-transfer level system, but in biological systems it is some organization of neural circuits. As George Miller said in his chapter, the separation of hardware from software was Simon's essential simplification—it was at the heart of the conceptual position Simon had taken. George is absolutely right. To say that a system has an architecture is another way of saying that it admits of being programmed, which is to say that it admits of the hardware-software distinction.

Unified theories of cognition are architectures. That is a key point. It is

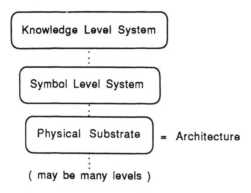

FIG. 15.1. The architecture and system levels.

the architecture, changing only slowly over time, that provides the communality that shows up amid the diversity of behavior of a single human. It is the communality of the architecture across all humans that makes the behavior of all humans similar in many ways. To use the slogan of this commentary: It is the architecture that keeps it all together. Thus, to propose a unified theory of cognition is to propose a cognitive architecture.

This volume sports a veritable showcase of cognitive architectures—enough so that I've listed them in Table 15.2. First there is CAPS, the cognitive architecture that lies behind the work on working memory in the context of reading, discussed by Marcel Just and Pat Carpenter (Thibadeau, Just, & Carpenter, 1982). Next, there are various unadorned productions systems. Neil Charness used an informal production system for his hand simulations; Jill Larkin used a version of Ops5 (ExperOps5). John Anderson's work on errors was built entirely around his use of PUPS, a production-system based architecture that is the high-level successor to ACT* (Anderson, 1983). BRIAN, the topic of Steve Kosslyn's chapter is special in a couple of ways. Not only is it a neural architecture, but the focus of his chapter is to *establish* BRIAN as a viable candidate architecture. The other speakers *use* their architectures in explicating whatever scientific story they tell. Finally there is Soar, the architecture by John Laird, Paul Rosenbloom, and myself (Laird, Newell, & Rosenbloom, 1987). Its inclusion in the list provides a living example of a *writing act*—the written analogue of a speech act. The list contains the cognitive architectures discussed in this volume, and Soar joins that group by virtue of my having added its name to that list, and discussing the addition as a writing act.

This list indicates the shift in cognitive science towards integrated theoretical attempts and away from dichotomies. These authors seek *systems of mechanisms* that explain the behavior of subjects on their tasks. In general they use their systems for explanation, rather than just propose or analyze

TABLE 15.2
Specific Symbolic Architectures in Residence in This Volume

| |
|---|
| **CAPS** ( Just & Carpenter ) |
| **Unadorned Production Systems** |
| Informal hand simulation    ( Charness )<br>ExperOps5    ( Larkin ) |
| **PUPS** ( Anderson ) |
| **BRIAN** ( Kosslyn, Sokolov, & Chen ) |
| **Soar**    ( Laird, Newell & Rosenbloom ) |

them. The mileage obtained by using an architecture seems to me quite evident. This is certainly what I had in mind 15 years ago. This represents real progress. I congratulate the authors of these chapters, one and all. They themselves will have to answer whether my 20-questions carp helped nudge them in this direction, so that particular essay can claim to have played a positive role in the evolution of our science, rather than just the negative, critical role that so many commentators have assigned to it. Actually, I care much less about that than about the fact of the case, namely, that cognitive science is outgrowing the 20-questions games of its youth.

However, I am left with some questions, though these are mostly to the other participants. To Kevin Dunbar and David Klahr, and also to Anders Ericsson and Jim Staszewski—Why not use an architecture as the basis for detailed processing models? It seems to me the complexity of both your tasks cries out for it. It would help to see through all of that complexity. Likewise, to Ken Kotovsky and David Fallside—Why not use an architecture? It would make lots of difference to the questions you ask. Finally, to Marcel Just and Pat Carpenter—Why not make more use of CAPS? It sits behind your models already, and I think it could play a much more explicit and important role.

Three factors modulate this assertion of the centrality of architecture to theories of cognition. First, in adaptive systems, the nature of the task has a strong determining effect on behavior (Simon, 1980b). Therefore, in so far as humans do similar tasks (seek similar goals in similar environments), they also behave similarly. Second, the knowledge available determines how an intelligent system behaves. Therefore, in so far as humans have the same knowledge in doing the same tasks, they also behave similarly. Third, the knowledge they have is determined by their prior experiences, including those we call education and socialization. Therefore, once again, in so far as humans are educated and socialized similarly, they will behave similarly.

At their strongest, these modulations imply that systems are describable at the knowledge level, so that their only commonalities are those of knowledge, goals, and the surrounding and constraining environment. This is the important plank in Ed Feigenbaum's general research stance, which he has made the central substantive theme of his chapter in this volume. Much vanishes at the knowledge level—most of what we think of as psychology and also the architecture. More precisely, the architecture still has a job to do, but it never shows its face. Now, in fact, the architecture is very much in evidence (and with its psychology). The modulations do not render it imperceptible. There is more here than meets Ed Feigenbaum's eye.

Herb has championed a particular middle ground here, namely that a small number of parameters define the effects of architecture and thus express the ways in which human rationality is bounded even beyond the limits of knowledge that stem from social, educational and organizational locality. Primary among these are basic limits on the speed and concurrency of processing, short-term memory, and the acquisition of new long-term knowledge (Newell & Simon, 1972; Simon, 1979a, Parts 1 and 2). Such a view focusses on the parameters and keeps the rest of the architectural structure essentially in the background. As Herb has shown in many analyses, there is substantial power in this approximation.

My own view at the moment is that more architectural detail will be found relevant to a useful model of human behavior. In this regard, Table 15.3 shows a favorite list of mine—all the constraints that jointly bear on the human architecture to make it what it is. The dimension of flexibility, including symbolic, abstract, and linguistic abilities, is what computation provides. It is what leads on to the notions of universal computation, knowledge is all, and ultimately that the architecture is immaterial, merely the turtle on which the towers of elephants stand that hold up the world—so far down as to be consignable to mythology.

But flexibility and its associated constraints are only part of the story. Other constraints also play a strong role in shaping human cognition—to behave in real time, to learn and develop continuously, and to be realizable by evolutionary processes operating on a neural technology, built on a genetic substrate. The architecture reflects these requirement as well. In doing so, it affects the way flexibility is realized and limited. These constraints shape the architecture in specific ways that may show in behavior.

Let me focus on just one of these—the temporal constraint. The time scale at which things happen is a critical characteristic. Consider Table 15.4, another favorite of mine, the time scale of human action. It also shows the systems hierarchy. Each level is a quite different system, starting from organelles at the bottom of the figure, up through neural circuits to the cognitively behaving individual and on up to social systems and beyond. This is a true systems hierarchy, in which each system is composed of the components of the level below—neurons out of organelles, neural circuits out of neurons, and so forth. Each level is larger in size and runs slower than the level below, an inevitable consequence of having the level below as components. Interestingly, each

TABLE 15.3
Multiple Constraints on the Nature of the Architecture

| |
|---|
| 1. Behave flexibly as a function of the environment |
| 2. Exibit adaptive ( rational, goal-oriented ) behavior |
| 3. Operate in real time |
| 4. Operate in a rich, complex, detailed environment |
|     4.1 Perceive an immense amount of changing detail<br>    4.2 Use vast amounts of knowledge<br>    4.3 Control a motor system of many degrees of freedom |
| 5. Use symbols and abstractions |
| 6. Use language, both natural and artificial |
| 7. Learn from the environment |
| 8. Acquire capabilities through development |
| 9. Live autonomously within a social community |
| 10. Exhibit awareness and a sense of self |
| 11. Be realizable as a neural system |
| 12. Arise through evolution |

system level is only about a factor of 10 larger and slower than its components. This is just about the *minimum* factor that is required for building up a new system—it is necessary to have a few components to interact and to give them a few operation times to pass the interactions around, before new behaviors emerge. That the systems levels pile up about as fast as possible should come as no surprise to most of us here, since it is (in part) a reflection of considerations Herb put forth so cogently 25 years ago in his *Architecture of Complexity* (Simon, 1962). The systems that we see around us are hierarchical, because hierarchies are stable and because unstable systems do not survive. Delving into the argument a bit shows that ceteris paribus the smaller the systems level, the more stable.

I want to call your attention to the *cognitive band,* starting above neural circuits, which are at ~10 *ms,* and moving up to the first observable cognitive behavior, at about 1 *s.* The *real-time constraint on cognition* is that the human must produce genuine cognitive behavior in ~1 *s,* out of components that have ~10 *ms* operation times. This is only about 100 operation times to get from the basic circuitry to behavior. Put in terms of system levels, 100 operation times is only two levels, each of 10 operations (that is, 100 = 10 × 10 = 10 operations of components, each of which take 10 operations of its components). To be explicit, there is *hardly any time at all* to produce complex behavior. This constraint has been widely noted. The connectionists in particular have used it as an argument for why the architecture has to be massively parallel (Feldman & Ballard, 1982)— and why clunky old serial symbolic architectures are simply out of the race. However, much more follows from it than the need for parallelism. It is binding enough to shape many aspects of the cognitive architecture.

Figure 15.2 shows the levels of the cognitive band whose existence and structure can be inferred from the real-time constraint on cognition, given the neural-circuit level on the low end and the representational and computational requirements on the high end (Newell, 1986, 1987, lecture 3). Let me take just a sentence apiece to indicate these levels, without going through the argument. The bottom level of the cognitive band provides *symbolic access.* The next level up provides the most *elementary deliberation,* comprising multiple accesses of memory to accumulate the considerations that enter into a deliberate selection of an action. The next level provides *simple operations,* composed of sequences of deliberations—simple, because the operations themselves must be immediately realizable, hence, pre-existing (although selected from an available repertoire). The top level of the cognitive band admits composing a response or result by working with operations which

**TABLE 15.4**
Timescale of Human Action

## TIMESCALE OF HUMAN ACTION

| Scale (secs) | Time Units | System | World (theory) |
|---|---|---|---|
| $10^7$ | months | | |
| $10^6$ | weeks | | SOCIAL BAND |
| $10^5$ | days | | |
| $10^4$ | hours | Task | |
| $10^3$ | 10 mins | Task | RATIONAL BAND |
| $10^2$ | minutes | Task | |
| $10^1$ | 10 sec | Unit task | |
| $10^0$ | 1 sec | Operations | COGNITIVE BAND |
| $10^{-1}$ | 100 ms | Deliberate act | |
| $10^{-2}$ | 10 ms | Neural circuit | |
| $10^{-3}$ | 1 ms | Neuron | NEURAL BAND |
| $10^{-4}$ | 100 μs | Organelle | |

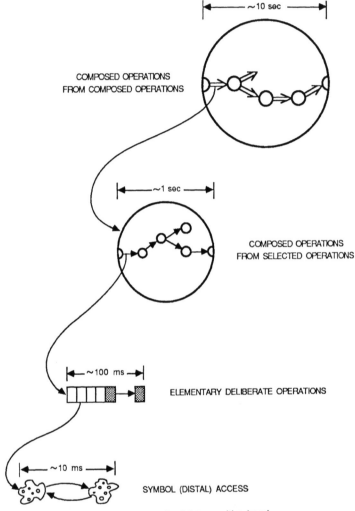

FIG. 15.2.    Levels of the cognitive band.

themselves are composed and hence can be adapted to the task at hand. This is the first level that admits full problem spaces, that is spaces with operators adapted to the task at hand.

As the system builds on up from this top cognitive level, employing ever more complex operations, we begin to move into the world that Ed Feigenbaum champions—the world of *intendedly rational* behavior. Increasingly there is enough computational space to permit the knowledge available in the system to be the strongest determinant of the system's response. Adaptation has the opportunity to be effective. The structure of the behaving system is dictated not by the architecture but by the structure of the task as perceived by the agent. It becomes a different world than what the cognitive psychologist normally studies. However, as Herb repeatedly emphasizes, it never becomes quite what the economists wish for, where *only* the objective external economic situation counts. It remains only intendedly rational, subject to the limits of knowledge and computing power.

But back at the level of cognitive machinery, it is not this way. Indeed, it will be observed that the system arrives at the level of immediate action (∼1 *s*) before it is able to deploy other than simple pre-existing operations to compose its response. The real-time constraint on cognition does not provide time for more.[2]

Let me note some of the consequences of Fig. 15.2. A chief one is that the time-mapping from cognition to neural systems is fixed in terms of orders of magnitude. Symbol access takes ∼10 *ms*. It could not take ∼100 *ms*, because there would never be time for cognitive behavior at ∼1 *s*. Elementary deliberation occurs at ∼100 *ms*. This is as soon as it can occur, given ∼10 *ms* for symbolic access, and as late as it can occur, given the requirement for behavior at ∼1 *s*. Simple operations occur at ∼1 *s*, and immediate reactive behavior must result from such processes.

The significance of such a mapping, however approximate, should not be underestimated. For years, cognitive psychology has enjoyed the luxury of considering its analysis to be one that floats entirely with respect to how it might be realized in the brain. This has been both a reflection of the long standing chasm between brain and behavior and a contributor to it. Figure 15.2 signifies that era is coming to an end. Of course, the era is not ending *because* of the figure. A look at the architecture discussed by Steve Kosslyn shows how much the neurophysiological and the behavioral are converging. However, I believe that the structure of Fig. 15.2 goes a long way toward seeing how we must map results from neural and cognitive descriptions into each other. The floating kingdom has finally been grounded.

The yield of Fig. 15.2 is not limited to just the temporal mapping. From it, plus the considerations behind it, comes the basic recognitional character of the symbolic level, the existence of automaticity at the ∼100 *ms* level, problem spaces, and the existence of a process that continually converts experience into recognitions. The arguments are of course speculative. But, importantly, they are not tied to any specific architecture. Rather, they serve to provide constraints that the human cognitive architecture must satisfy, and thus help to guide our search for it.

---

[2]The compulsive force behind the constraint—why overt behavior *must* occur by ∼1 s rather than ∼10 or ∼100 s—would appear to be evolutionary. If organisms can respond this fast, given their technology (here, neural technology), then they must. For whoever gets there fastest survives.

## Soar: A Candidate Cognitive Architecture

Figure 15.2 sets the stage for a brief description of Soar, as a candidate theory of the human cognitive architecture. Soar has been around for some time as an AI architecture for general problem solving and learning (Laird, Newell, & Rosenbloom, 1987; Laird, Rosenbloom, & Newell, 1986). Soar is based on many of the mechanisms that have played a major role in information processing theories, such as problem spaces and production systems. Thus, from the start, Soar has been an architecture that is roughly commensurate with what we know of human cognition. But further development and analysis have convinced us that Soar is a serious candidate for the architecture of human cognition in detail as well as in overall character (Newell, 1987). Soar is an architecture for putting it all together.

Figure 15.3 enumerates the main mechanisms in Soar. The top four items set the outer context, being aspects shared by all comprehensive cognitive-science theories of human cognition. Soar operates as a controller of the human organism, hence is a complete system with perception, cognition and motor components. This already takes mind in essentially functional terms—as the system that arose to control the gross movements of a mammal in a mammalian world. Soar is goal-oriented with knowledge of the world, which it uses to attain its goal. This knowledge is represented by a symbol system, which means that computation is used to create representations, extract their implications for action, and implement the chosen actions. Thus, Soar is an architecture, with most of the knowledge in the total system embodied in the content that the architecture makes meaningful and accessible.

The rest of the items describe Soar from the bottom up, temporally speaking. Soar comprises a large *recognition memory*. This is realized by an Ops5-like production system (Forgy, 1981), with a set of productions each of whose conditions is matched against the elements in working memory, leading to the execution of the actions of the successful instantiations. The productions execute very rapidly, within about 10 *ms*. Although in AI and cognitive science, productions are usually taken to correspond to operators (deliberately deployed actions), here they correspond to associational memory. Thus, production actions behave like a memory retrieval. They only enter new elements into working memory; they cannot modify or delete what is there; and there is no conflict resolution (of the kind familiar from Ops5). Each production operates independently—an isolated memory access and retrieval.

The next level of organization, which occurs within ∼100 *ms*, consists of the *decision cycle*. This comprises a sequence of retrievals from long-term memory (i.e., a sequence of concurrent production firings) that assemble from memory what is immediately accessible and relevant to the current decision context. This sequence ultimately terminates, when no more knowledge is forthcoming (in practice it quiesces quickly). Then a *decision procedure* makes a choice of the next step to be taken. This changes the decision context, so

1. Controller  -  Perception-Cognition-Motor

2. Knowledge and Goals

3. Representation, Computation, Symbols

4. An architecture plus content

5. Recognition memory  (about 10 ms )

6. Decision cycles - Automatic  ( about 100 ms )

7. Problem spaces and operators  ( about 1 sec )

8. Impasses and Subgoals

9. Chunking  ( about 10 s )

10. Intended rationality  ( 100 sec and up )

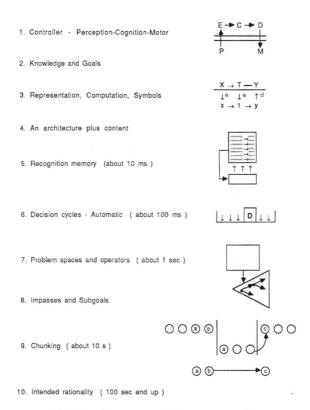

FIG. 15.3.    Soar as a unified theory of cognition.

that the cycle can repeat to make the next decision. At the 100 *ms* level, cognitive life is an endless sequence of assembling the available knowledge and using it to make the next deliberate choice.

The decisions taken at the 100 *ms* level implement search in *problem spaces,* which comprise the next level of organization, namely, at the ∼1 *sec* level. Soar organizes all its goal-oriented activity in problem spaces, from the most problematical to the most routine. It performs a task by creating a space within which the attainment of the task can be defined as reaching some state, and where the moves in the spaces are the operations that are appropriate to performing the task. The problem then becomes which operators to apply and in what order to reach the desired state. The search in the problem space is governed by the knowledge in the recognition memory. If Soar has the appropriate knowledge and if it can be brought to bear when needed, then Soar can just put one operator in front of another, to step its way directly to task attainment. If the memory contains little relevant knowledge or it can't be accessed, then Soar must search the problem space, leading to the familiar combinatorial explosion.

Given that the problem-space organization is built into the architecture, the decisions to be made at any point are always the same—what problem space to work in; what state to use (if more than one is available); and what operator to apply to this state to get a new state, on the way to a desired state. Making these choices is the continual business of the decision-cycle. Operators must actually be applied, of course—life is not all decision making. But applying operators is just another task, which therefore occurs by going into another problem space to accomplish the implementation. The recursion bottoms out when an operator becomes simple enough to be accomplished within a single decision cycle, by a few memory retrievals.

The decision procedure that actually makes the choice at each point is a simple, uniform process that can only use whatever knowledge has accumulated via the repeated memory searches. Some of this knowledge is in the form of *preferences* about what to choose—that one operator is preferred to another, that a state is acceptable, that another state is to be rejected. The decision procedure takes whatever preferences are available and extracts from them the decision. It adds no knowledge of its own.

There is no magic in the decision cycle—it can extract from the memory only what knowledge is there, and it may not even get it all; and the decision procedure can select only from the options thereby produced and by using the preferences thereby obtained. Sometimes this is sufficient and Soar proceeds to move through its given space. Sometimes—often, as it turns out—the knowledge is insufficient or conflicting. Then the architecture is unable to continue—it arrives at an *impasse*. This is like a standard computer trying to divide by zero. Except that, instead of aborting, the architecture sets up a *subgoal* to resolve the impasse. For example, if several operators have been proposed but there is insufficient information to select one, then a *tie impasse* occurs, and Soar sets up a subgoal to obtain the knowledge to resolve the tie, so it can then continue.

Impasses are central to Soar. They drive all of Soar's problem solving. Soar simply attempts to execute its top level operators. If this can be done, Soar has attained what it wanted to do. Failures along the way imply impasses. Resolving these impasses, which occur in other problem spaces, can lead to other impasses, hence to subproblem spaces, and so on. The entire subgoal hierarchy is generated by Soar itself, in response to its inability at performance time to attain its objectives. The different types of impasses generate the full variety of goal-driven behavior familiar in AI systems—operator implementation, operator instantiation, operator selection, precondition satisfaction, state rejection, and so forth.

In addition to problem solving, Soar learns continuously from its experience. The mechanism is called *chunking*. Every time Soar encounters and resolves an impasse, it creates a new production (the chunk) to capture and retain that experience. If the situation ever recurs, the chunk will fire, making available the information that was missing on the first occasion. Thus, Soar will not even encounter an impasse on a second pass.

The little diagram at the right of *chunking* at the bottom of Fig. 15.3 sketches how this happens. The view is looking down on working memory, with time running from left to right. Each little circle is a data element that encodes some information about the task. Starting at the left, Soar is chugging along, with productions putting in new elements and the decision procedure determining which next steps to take. At the vertical line an impasse occurs. This sets a new context and then behavior continues. Finally, Soar produces an element that resolves the impasse (the circled *c* at the second vertical line), after which behavior continues in the original context. The chunk is then built, with an action corresponding to the element *c* that resolved the impasse and with conditions corresponding to the elements prior to the impasse that led to the resolution (the circled *a* and *b*). This captures the result of the problem solving to resolve the impasse, and does so in a way that permits it to be evoked again to avoid that particular impasse.

Chunking operates as an automatic mechanism that continually caches all of Soar's goal-oriented experience, without detailed interpretation or analysis. As described, it appears to be simply a practice mechanism—a way to avoid redoing the problem solving to resolve prior impasses, thus speeding up Soar's performance. However, the conditions of the productions reflect only a few of the elements in working memory at the time of the impasse. Thus, chunks *abstract* from the situation of occurrence, and can apply in different situations, as long as the specific conditions apply. This provides a form of *transfer* of learning. Although far from obvious, this mechanism in fact generates a wide variety of kinds of learning (Steier, Laird, Newell, Rosenbloom, Flynn, Golding, Polk, Shivers, Unruh, & Yost, 1987), enough to conjecture that chunking might be the only learning mechanism Soar needs. Chunks get built in response to solving problems (i.e., resolving impasses). hence, they correspond to activities at about the 1 *sec* level and above. The chunk, of course, is a production, which is an entity down at the memory access level at about 10 *ms*.

The higher organization of cognitive activity arises from top-level operators not being implementable immediately with the information at hand. Thus, they must be implemented in subspaces with their own operators, which themselves may require further subspaces. Each descent into another layer of subspaces means that the top-level operators take longer to complete— that is, are at a higher level. Thus the timescale of organized cognitive activity climbs above what can be called the region of cognitive mechanism and into the region of intendedly rational behavior. Here, enough time is available for the system to do substantial problem solving and use more and more of its knowledge. Here, the organization of cognition becomes increasingly dictated by the nature of the task and the knowledge available, rather than by the structure of the architecture.

There are limits to the extent of the means-ends structure that a human builds up at a given moment, in response to impasses. The really long-term organization of behavior cannot arise just from piling up the goal hierarchy. Soar does not yet incorporate any theory of what happens as the hours grow, disparate activities punctuate one another, and sleep intervenes to let the world of cognition start afresh each morning.

What can be gleaned from such a rapid-fire tour through Soar? Certainly not an assessment of whether it is an effective theory of human cognition. However, perhaps it can be glimpsed that Soar is an architecture that spans the entire range of psychological functions—well, not quite the entire range yet, but it is reaching in that direction, with its modeling of behavior from the $\sim$10 *ms* level on up to into the rational band of $\sim$1,000 *s*, namely, the time it takes humans to solve problems such as designing algorithms (Steier & Newell, 1988). This lets me make my point—that cognitive science is on the threshold of obtaining architectures that will provide the basis for comprehensive theories. This is a major step toward being able to put it all together.

## THE CHAPTERS OF THIS VOLUME

Having made my point about the central integrative role of architectures, let me finally turn to the chapters of this volume. My job, of course, is to put them all together. Actually, I will avoid my obligation directly, by turning the point around and asking what these chapters tell us about putting it together. Thus, I will keep to my central theme. But as a consequence, I will not criticize the chapters as studies in their own terms.

It is not a single activity to put science together. Cognitive science, like any science, has multiple aspects: methodology, foundations, the heartland, and the borders. The chapters of this volume say something about putting matters together in each of these aspects.

### Methodologies

Cognitive psychology has developed many methodologies for studying human behavior. It inherits the basic methodologies of controlled experimentation, statistical design and data analysis from its ancestral psychological tradition. But it has also been prolific in creating new methodologies and sharpening existing ones. Table 15.5 lists a number of examples. The first four—task analysis, mental chronometry, simulation, and protocol analysis—are solidly in place. They all go back to the first decade of the cognitive revolution. Actually, I like George Miller's remark in his chapter that the behaviorists were the revolutionaries, so the events commencing in the 1950s should be taken as the counter-revolution. I have so labeled the figure, for the counter is nowhere more apparent than in the methodologies that are used. Interestingly, protocol analysis, perhaps the epitome of the countermove, has taken a long time to become widely practiced. The last six methodologies are also familiar, but their

TABLE 15.5
Methodologies of the Cognitive Counter-Revolution

| | | |
|---|---|---|
| 1. | [ TA ] | Task analysis  ( including AI systems ) |
| 2. | [ RT ] | Mental chronometry |
| 3. | [ Sim ] | Simulation |
| 4. | [ PA ] | Protocol analysis |
| 5. | [ Arch ] | Architecture |
| 6. | [ SS ] | Special subjects:  neurological deficits, experts |
| 7. | [ CA ] | Comparative analysis:  Novice / Expert,  Child / Adult |
| 8. | [ EM] | Eye movements |
| 9. | [ QEA] | Qualitative error  analysis |
| 10. | [ ET ] | Experimental  training |

use is much more specialized and scattered. Indeed, the fifth one—theorizing within a theoretically specified architecture—has hardly begun. As I have just borne witness, it is my own current project to try to help it along.

Methodologies partition a field as surely as theoretical ideas. Indeed, the tensions within cognitive science have on occasion been laid to the different methodologies of its subdisciplines—psychology with its experimental subjects, linguistics with its individual informants, philosophy with its imagined situations and artificial intelligence with its designed programs. Within psychology, topics become identified with particular methodologies and develop their own special groups of investigators. One need only note the way error measures and a few experimental paradigms dominated verbal learning for years, or the specialized territory occupied by eye movements research over the years, with its own special conferences and books (Fisher, Monty, & Senders, 1981; Groner, Menz, Fisher, & Monty, 1983; Monty & Senders, 1976; Senders, Fisher, & Monty, 1978).

Table 15.6 shows the methodologies used by the research reported in the volume. Of course, they use a wide variety of the methods; that is only to be expected. More interesting, there is a strong tendency towards the use of multiple methodologies, substantially more than two. I take this as a sign of integration—less purity and more power. It is an interesting step toward putting it together to be able to relate the observations from many different sources. One is tempted to reach for some analogy to the use of multiple knowledge sources in AI, as a mark of intelligence. But the causal arrow probably goes the other way.

### Foundations

Foundational issues were addressed by both Ed Feigenbaum and Jim Greeno. I have strong opinions about what each said—but that is a hallmark of foundational issues. One issue from each seems relevant to putting cognitive science together.

TABLE 15.6
Multiple Methodologies in the Studies of This Conference

| | |
|---|---|
| Kosslyn | Sim, Arch, SS |
| Just-Carpenter | RT, PA, Arch, EM |
| Kotovsky-Fallside | TA, RT |
| Dunbar-Klahr | TA, PA, CA |
| Feigenbaum | TA ( Foundations ) |
| Charness | TA, PA, SS, Arch |
| Hayes | PA, CA |
| Ericsson-Staszewski | RT, PA, SS, ET |
| Greeno | ( Foundations ), PA |
| Larkin | TA, Sim, Arch, QAE |
| Anderson | TA, Sim, Arch, QAE |
| Simon | ( Theory applications ), SS |

## Preparation versus Deliberation

Although I agree with much of what Ed says in his chapter, I wish to differ with him on what he calls the knowledge versus search display. I present my version of it in Fig. 15.4. The axes are labeled *preparation* along the vertical, and *deliberation* along the horizontal. The diagram refers to the means by which a system performs a task. Preparation is the extent to which the system draws on what it has prepared in advance of the task. Deliberation is the extent to which the system processes information once the task is set—engages in searching problem spaces, or reasons from what it knows, or whatever you want to call it. The curves represent equal-performance isobars. That is, different choices of how much to draw on prepared material and how much to compute once the task is set can yield the same performance—more preparation and less deliberation versus less preparation and more deliberation.

This graph is a variant of the familiar store-versus-compute tradeoff (Berliner & Ebeling, in press). It is also often called the knowledge vs search graph, which is the term Ed uses. But the latter phrase is something of a misnomer. Both axes represent knowledge—knowledge that comes from stored memory structures (what has been prepared) and knowledge that comes from computation during the decision process. The axes, however, are not measured in knowledge abstractly. Stored knowledge is measured in amount of structure (number of rules or number of memory bits) and acquired knowledge is measured in situations examined or processed.

This tradeoff is fundamental to information processing systems. Different systems embody different strategies and end up in different places on the diagram. Although the graph refers to the division used for a given task, systems typically treat all their tasks similarly. Thus, a system itself can be located at a point in the space in the middle of the cluster of its task points.

Thus, Fig. 15.4 shows the characteristics of various types of AI systems—the early AI search-oriented systems, which had small knowledge and modest search, expert systems which have more knowledge (up to $\sim 10^4$ rules currently) but do less search. Hitech, Hans Berliner's high-master chess machine (Berliner & Ebeling, in press) is way out at the extreme of deliberation, with $\sim 10^7$ situations examined per external move, and with only a small amount of recognitional knowledge.

This diagram is part of the foundations of AI and cognitive science. It provides a fundamental view of how information processing systems can differ and yet be related to each other. It tells us that systems, such as Hitech, are not an entirely unrelated way of attaining task performance (to be classified as brute force), but rather a different part of the total space of information processing systems. This is a space of architectures we need to explore in understanding intelligence. Exactly the same considerations enter into systems such as Hitech as into other systems in the space. For instance, once the architecture of a system is fixed, whether for a human or Hitech, the amount of deliberation becomes fixed. Then the system can improve only by vertical movement in the space. Indeed, Hitech has moved from a low expert to a high master entirely by adding recognition knowledge. As noted above, the total amount of recognition knowledge involved is quite small—it is as if the hyperbolic character of the diagram really applied and the isobars are squeezed tightly together as one moves out toward asymptotically high search.

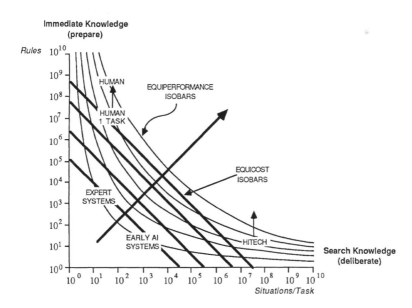

FIG. 15.4.    Preparedness vs. deliberation tradeoff.

As another instance, it is possible to have systems that move back and up along an isobar (i.e., decreasing deliberation and increasing preparation). Soar, with its chunking, is such a system. It appears much more difficult to move in the other direction. In fact, I do not know any systems that do so in any substantial way. This seems to be the crux of Ed's criticism—that a Mycin cannot extend search and do with less knowledge. Indeed, that is true. In the short run we run out of knowledge just as we run out of time. And we can only search the spaces we know about (more knowledge). Time scale, as always, is crucial. Thus, the just-noted continual movement by chunking from search to knowledge does not occur within a single performance, but takes place over many trials. Furthermore, new knowledge can be generated by extended thought if the spaces are available that can support it. That Mycin does not have such spaces—that, in the parlance of expert systems, it is a *shallow* system, not a *deep* one—only reveals that Mycin and most early-generation expert systems, were primarily explorations in what could be attained with only stored knowledge. They are no more to be taken as the shape of a generally intelligent system than are the early AI search systems. Fully intelligent systems will do extended search to add to their knowledge, just as mathematicians do in searching for proofs.

### Sufficiency of Physical Symbol Systems

I also agree with much of what Jim Greeno says in his chapter. In particular, I think there is much to be learned about how humans deal with external environments and how they use the environment to keep track of what they are doing and to perform computations for them, both implicitly and explicitly. There are many signs that more attention is being paid to such things. One is the strong emphasis placed on situated action, such as the Center for the Study of Language and Information at Stanford and nearby West Coast research centers. At the present conference, Jill Larkin's analysis of coffee making fits within this focus rather explicitly. Topics become ripe for exploration in particular epochs. I agree that this one seems ready now, and I hope the immediate future will see a major increase in our understanding of how cognitive agents work in intimate concert with the world.

But Greeno goes somewhat further than that, and grounds this shift in a need for a new philosophical view of symbols and how they refer to the external world. In that, he seems to me to be wrong, though undoubtedly not wrong that some scientists perceive it that way. I fail to see that the current conceptual apparatus is inadequate for dealing with situated action and close-coupled interaction with the outside world, at least of the kind that Greeno is discussing. This is the aspect of Greeno's chapter that is relevant to my theme of putting it together. Arguments for shifts in the foundations are often meant to signal, not a way of putting it together, but a way of producing a new start. Greeno, good scientist that he is, specifically acknowledges the way the new future grows out of the past. Still, I wish to quarrel a bit.

To be specific, the concept of symbols that has developed in computer science and AI over the years is not inadequate in any way that I understand. It does not need extending in some special way to deal with the external world. It is not especially inward looking. Symbols, as that concept occurs in physical symbol systems (Newell, 1980), designate entities in an external world, including actions to be taken to effect changes out there. No implicit notions of context freedom exist to plague the formulation, so as to pose difficulties to being indexical or relative or operating off concurrently perceived external structure.

At first blush, I cannot imagine how one would think otherwise. For example, such symbols are used as a matter of course by the Navlab autonomous land vehicle (a van that drives itself around Schenley Park next to Carnegie-Mellon), which views the road in front of it through TV eyes and sonar ears, and controls the wheels and speed of the vehicle to navigate along the road and between the trees (Thorp, Herbert, Kanade, & Shafer, 1987). The symbols that float everywhere through the computational innards of this system refer to the road, grass and trees in an epistemologically adequate, though sometimes empirically inadequate, fashion. These symbols are the symbols of the physical symbol system hypothesis (Newell & Simon, 1976), pure and simple.

Well, maybe I can imagine how one might think otherwise. Here is one possibility. The mechanics of symbols are built around the *access* relation, which permits the system, upon encountering a symbol token in the course of processing a symbolic expression, to access the additional structures that are related to the meaning of the tokened symbol. Those symbol structures are still internal to the computational system. These structures will, in general, contain additional symbol tokens leading to further access to other symbol structures. Around and around it goes, but it seems to stay inside forever. So it seems that symbols are right where Guthrie accused Tolman of leaving his rats—forever lost in thought (Guthrie, 1953). But the access relation is *not* the relation of designation to objects and relations in the world outside, although it is an essential support. Designation comes about because of two additional features. First, some of the symbols arise from transduction from the external world and initiate transduction back to the actions of the system (both to further internal processing and to the external world). The TV eyes of the NavLab van give rise via recognition systems to internal symbols and other internal symbols move the wheels, accelerator and brake shoes. But within this, the structures and the processing can be arranged so the internal structures behave according to the external environment—so that internal symbols can stand for *tree1* and *tree2*, and also the generic *tree*.

Here is another possibility. Although not directly stated, there exists a strong undercurrent in Greeno's chapter of identification of symbols with propositional expressions and what can be articulated (see especially the concluding section). Mental models are counterposed to symbolic expressions; abstract entities that have simple mappings to the external situation are seen as distinct from symbols and symbolic structures; and, in an acknowledged shadowing of Gibson, *direct* coupling with the world in normal activity is taken to bypass the need for representation altogether. This suggests that the emphasis on situated action is in part a reaction to the current flurry of logicist interpretations of artificial intelligence (Genesereth & Nilsson, 1987). However, the theory of symbols that has arisen in computer science is certainly not tied to such an interpretation.[3]

Now, I should not get myself exercised about Feigenbaum's and Greeno's foundational interpretations—nor they about mine. Foundations are always contentious. (Sometimes it feels like that is what foundations are for.) General views of a science can be taken as heuristic. Differences in such views often lead people to explore different paths, but only occasionally do they keep them from doing good science. So, I am exceeding glad over Feigenbaum's concern with knowledge, and trust it will lead him towards getting us examples of systems with much more knowledge than we have had the courage to build to date. So, I am exceeding glad over Greeno's concern with action situated in the world, and trust it will lead him towards getting representations with the right sorts of model structure.

## The Heartland

The heartland of a science is where the real work gets done in putting the science together. It is in the accumulation of a network of specific techniques for making predictions and explanations, and in our attempts at constructing an encompassing cathedral-like theory, that progress is made—or fails to be made, so leaving matters in wait until some better next generation of scientists finds a way.

### More Architectural Issues

I need to return to the topic of architectures. My initial discussion focused on their role in putting cognitive science together, using Soar as an exemplar. But as noted in Table 15.2 there are lots of other candidate architectures, many on exhibit in this volume. The individualized production systems used by Larkin and by Charness are not really candidates. However, ACT*/PUPS is certainly a candidate and CAPS could form the basis for one if its scope were expanded. And, although the proposal of Kosslyn and his colleagues is too nascent to be a serious candidate yet, it reminds us that the architecture sits at the boundary of the cognitive and neural bands, a place notorious for not

---

[3]The William James lectures discuss the relation of mental models to symbol structures and problem spaces in detail (Newell, 1987, lecture 7; Polk & Newell, 1988).

fitting together. So, with all these architectures around, does all this fit together? Or is it just another centrifugal research area—soon to bespatter all participants, and reveal that, once more, psychology is not yet ready to get it together.

At the present time lots of architectures must exist and coexist. We do not know enough to put together a single candidate architecture—not yet. So, although I am personally attempting to develop Soar into a prime candidate, I neither wish nor recommend that work stop on others. Thus, my proposal is not that there be one unified theory, embodied in an architecture, but that each and every cognitive theory should be a full-bodied architecture that can integrate results from across the breadth of cognitive phenomena. This pluralism was also a theme in my William James Lectures, accounting for the plural *theories* in its title (Newell, 1987).

The main force toward convergence will come through the successful coverage of a wide array of disparate phenomena. Of course, it is an act of scientific faith that two theories cannot explain in detail hundreds of disparate regularities across the breadth of cognition without being fundamentally the same under the skin. But we need not face that eventuality until we generate it. Actually, I cannot imagine a more exciting situation than having two unified cognitive theories (how about a dozen, while we're at it), each of which makes strong quantitative predictions across perception, memory, reasoning, immediate response, knowledge acquisition, skill learning, and motor behavior— but which are also radically incommensurate. We would be the wonder of the scientific world! Even the most radical such event in scientific history— the wave-particle duality—required only a few years for a satisfactory technical synthesis to emerge, once the phenomena covered became diverse, with the quantum formulation. Of course, philosophical, heuristic, and popular commentary about incommensurability of the duality continued to swirl for a much longer time. But the right place to measure the progress of science is in the living technique, not in the commentary.

In fact, the nonconvergence issue does not look to me like a major threat. Examination of the candidate architectures shows them to have an immense communality of mechanism. ACT* and Soar are both built around production systems, which is to say an associational recognition system. They both work with symbolic data structures as representations, gain their directionality through goal hierarchies, and employ problem spaces as the way of formulating tasks. CAPS shares the use of symbolic structures and production systems. Some of the other aspects exist in CAPS only in rudimentary form, since it has been used mostly for the vertical integration of a single complex skill (reading), so problem spaces and goals are not really necessary in their full-blown glory.

Certainly there are differences. Table 15.7 shows some between ACT* and Soar. ACT* has both a declarative and procedural memory; Soar has only the procedural one. ACT* does not have any higher levels of organization

TABLE 15.7
Soar and ACT*

|  | ACT* | Soar |
|---|---|---|
| Memory | Declarative<br>Procedural | Procedural |
| Higher<br>Organization | None | Multiple<br>Problem spaces |
| Goals | Deliberate<br>learned | Impasse created |
| Control | Activation<br>variable rate | All-or-none<br>cycles |
| Learning | Compilation<br>composition<br>proceduralizaton | Chunking |
|  | Tuning<br>strengthening<br>discrimination<br>generalization |  |
|  | Declarative augmentation |  |

than its production system: Soar is organized in hierarchies of problem spaces, and will probably acquire additional higher organization. ACT* creates its goals deliberately, by positing them as actions in productions; Soar creates its subgoals automatically by impasses. ACT* controls processing by a continuous quantity (activation) which determines a variable rate of computation; Soar uses multiple production firings in the decision cycle. ACT* learns by means of multiple learning mechanisms; Soar uses only chunking.

On the surface, these differences look very large. But the rate of convergence is pretty striking. Soar and ACT* are the two best examples in the world of general chunking systems. When Soar goes to take in information from the outside, which is in declarative form, its mechanism for assimilation looks like a variant of the interpretation scheme of ACT* (Yost, 1988). Activation seems like a major difference. But along comes PUPS, which preserves much that is important in ACT*, but abstracts away from activation. The most striking difference of all would seem to be the separate declarative memory in ACT*, especially if one takes the rhetoric of ACT* seriously (Anderson, 1983, p. 21). But Soar has developed ways of learning and recalling declarative data. This mechanism, *data chunking* (Rosenbloom, Laird, & Newell, 1987; Rosenbloom, Laird, & Newell, in press), is built from chunking, but constitutes a separate subsystem with its own special properties. It becomes hard to say whether Soar has one learning mechanism or two. Now, for the life of me, I don't want to say that Soar and ACT* are simply the same! I do want to say that they look to me to be variant explorations of the same underlying mechanisms.

I would rather view multiple unified theories as more like an insurance policy on our getting one or two that are successful. Do you realize how much effort it will be to get a unified theory of cognition, with its supporting architecture and detailed explanations and predictions? At issue is not just scientific creativity—many will believe they have creative ideas for an architecture that differs from those currently in existence. The issue is person-years of efforts—hundreds of person-years to get an architecture beyond the talk stage, beyond the prototype stage, and into genuine contention. Maybe none of us will have the stamina. There are just too many phenomena out there to be covered by a unified theory.

A comprehensive architecture, such as ACT*, CAPS or Soar, contains many mechanisms that have been the object of a good deal of study in cognitive science, for instance production systems and problem spaces. These architectures capture rather easily the phenomena that these mechanisms have been used to explain in other studies. However, by the same turn, these architectures do not contain other mechanisms that have played a role in cognitive research. Thus, far from putting things together, it might seem like these architectures are devices for partitioning the whole field. In some sense, this must be so. To incorporate production systems directly and not, say schemas, is to favor one set of theoretical mechanisms over another, and thus to divide the field, at least in the short term. The situation is no worse than with any other theoretical choice, of course, but it still contrasts with my casting comprehensive architectures as ways to bring the field together.

My own solution to the tension described above is to emphasize the obligation of a candidate cognitive architecture to deal with the phenomena that important excluded mechanisms have been central to explaining. The whole point of a comprehensive architecture is to have it treat *all* the major phenomena of cognition. It is certainly the wrong turn to have the candidates partition the space of cognitive phenomena, so they talk past each other—as if emulating the worst sort of Kuhnian paradigms.

Consider, for example, that most of the architectures in this volume are built around production systems. They do not embody explicitly a notion of *schema* or *frame*. How then will they be responsive to the considerations that gave rise to these notions, and have made of schemas and frames important concepts in cognitive science?

Let us start with the evident truth that knowledge is organized. The items of knowledge relevant to the analysis of a scene or the performance of an action within a task context is strongly interrelated—they cluster around the scene or event. Furthermore, human action makes equally evident that it partakes of this organized knowledge, rapidly, effectively and in substantial quantities. It is incumbent on theories of cognition to capture this phenomena.

*Schemas* are a proposed solution to the imperative of the organization of knowledge in action that the human evinces. The term schema has a long and variegated history, having roots in Head's (1920) motor schemas, Bartlett's

(1932) strongly memorial structures and in Piaget's (1952) action schemas. All these are highly general and diffuse theoretical constructs. The notion of schema became grounded when data structures and programs were created to capture this construct—the frames of Minsky (1975), the conceptual dependency structures of Schank (Schank & Ableson, 1977), and the schemas of Norman and Rumelhart (Norman, Rumelhart, & LNR Research Group, 1975).[4] With these developments we finally obtain operational notions that proffer actual solutions.

The key feature of this operational concept of schema is positing a fixed data structure and variablizing a fixed set of places in the structure (the slots). The schema is completely rigid about the frame, while being open (or open, subject to a set of constraints) about a fixed, predetermined (i.e., rigid) set of aspects. Thus, they are devices of specific but limited adaptability.

The argument for this solution is that it holds together the in-the-large organization of related knowledge that is so evident in human behavior. This is stated clearly by Minsky:

> It seems to me that the ingredients of most theories both in artificial intelligence and in psychology have been on the whole too minute, local, and unstructured to account—either practically or phenomenologically—for the effectiveness of common sense thought. The "chunks" of reasoning, language, memory, and "perception" ought to be larger and more structured, and their factual and procedural contents must be more intimately connected in order to explain the apparent power and speed of mental activities. (Minsky, 1975, p. 211)

But this large-grain-size argument seems to me misplaced. It confuses structure with behavior. It says that if humans cluster knowledge, then the internal representation must be a pre-existing fixed structure that is that cluster. This will, of course, capture some of the action, especially in non-dynamic situations where there is no way to determine how or when the knowledge was assembled, but only that it governs the current behavior.

We need to ask how a production-based cognitive architecture is to respond to this same imperative. Such a system has a declarative representation— usually over objects defined as collections of attributes and values, where the values can themselves can be objects. This is reminiscent of schemas and frames, though it predates them considerably (Newell & Shaw, 1957). However, it has none of their characteristic additional apparatus—defaults, inheritance hierarchies, attached procedures, and so forth.

Collections of productions then provide the functional equivalent of complex schema or frame structures. Each production provides a link, when instantiated. Inheritance occurs by productions automatically executing on the

---

[4]Semantic nets do not quite belong to this family, and they only became so with developments such as partitioned semantic nets (Hendrix, 1977).

results of others and so can march up a concept hierarchy in a context-dependent way. In Soar, for example, such a sequence occurs in a single elaboration phase (see Figure 15.3), in an essentially automatic way. Simple attached procedures can be realized by other productions (again, in Soar, within a single decision cycle). Complex attached procedures are realized by break outs into the full power of the problem solver.

From the description I have given, it is possible to see a structure in a production system that could correspond to schemas. It has certain properties that move it in what seems the desirable direction—it is dynamic and generated on the fly in response to the local situation. Its most striking feature is its high disaggregation compared to the standard implementations of schemas. Its units are productions, which correspond to the smallest parts of the data structures of schemas and frames. We know these are the units, and not something effectively larger, from the unit of learning being the production (whether in Soar or ACT*).

But all this is simply opinion, though a commentator is nothing if not a purveyor of opinions. It is meant to be an invitation to architectures that are built around production systems to address in a general and principled way how to do what schemas can do. The invitation is issued by means of a pointer to the type of phenomena where the current data-structured instantiation of a schema might reveal its limitations and where the more finely decomposed recognition systems might show a difference.

### The Foothills of Rationality

All science has a strong tendency to work from the simple to the complex, from the more controlled to the less. However, a certain amount of scientific activity always occurs throughout the spectrum, of course, driven by interest and need. For cognitive science, there have always been arguments that complexity itself was of the essence, and even that simpler was not always easier. However, that does not gainsay the general trend. Even though the higher mental processes constituted a major focus of the earliest years of the cognitive revolution—the problem solving and organized decision-making that was Herb Simon's special concern—psychology has kept primarily to the low road of work in memory and immediate responses amenable to chronometric analysis. To give yet one more (oft noted) example: Over the years research in reading has moved from the letter, to the word, to the sentence, to the paragraph (most recently), and still has ahead the page, chapter, book, encyclopedia and library.

We talk of the complexity of a task and its associated behavior, but in fact this is strongly linked to the time scale of behavior (see Table 15.4 again). At the scale of $\sim 1$ $s$, where behavior is immediate, the architecture is much in evidence. As the scale grows, more time becomes available for processing and deliberation, and the human moves toward rational behavior—that is to say, toward being characterizable by goals and the knowledge available—the world Feigenbaum declares all important.

It takes time for the human to bring to bear all that he or she knows about a problem at hand, and it never completely happens (or mathematics would be easy). The peaks of rationality always rise up on the temporal horizon just another ridge or two away. Much real behavior takes place on the foothills of rationality, in the range from $\sim 10$ $s$ to $\sim 10^4$ $s$ (a few hours). Cognitive psychology—I should say modern experimental psychology—has located itself at immediate behavior and only gradually moves up the scale. Such movement, then, becomes an indicator of putting it together. It is only possible to deal with larger time scales by bringing to bear considerations from many subareas of cognition. After all, the subject is bringing them to bear, so it stands to reason that the scientist must as well.

Table 15.8 shows how we are moving up to foothills of rationality. I have plotted on the timescale chart the phenomena that each contributor to the volume is primarily dealing with (by last-name initials of the authors). They cluster up at the intendedly rational band, in the 1 to 10-minute range. This is, of course, partly a CMU specialty. But the papers from, say, the Eighth Symposium in 1973 (where the 20 questions commentary was given) would cluster between 1 and 10 $s$, two orders of magnitude lower. I take this figure as evidence of my theme that it is being put together. Of course, as befits empirical data, there are exceptions. Steve Kosslyn is focused on basic architectural issues, below 1 $s$, on the border rather than in the heartland. And we have had to add the historical band above $10^8$ $s$, to take care of Herb's reflections on himself as subject.

Even as we move up the foothills, the processing limits show through in many ways. As Herb has constantly maintained, only a few parameters seem to suffice to express the effect of the architecture. These include the rate of cognitive processing, the size of STM, the size of a chunk and the rate of chunking. Observe, to pick up on an earlier theme, that this is a highly differentiated and structured set of functional parameters. It contrasts sharply with what I caricatured earlier as rationality juice, a set of anonymous and homogeneous resources or capacities. Herb's view, besides having much truth on its side, also has much to recommend it in our attempt to put it all together. For it says that a small number of constants suffice to carry out analysis over a wide range of behavior—over the whole band of intendedly rational behavior, and maybe more.

It is our task as cognitive psychologists to characterize the ways in which the underlying architecture shows through in the foothills—to find out what structures need to be used and what parameters need to be measured. Success in the venture gradually stitches together all the parts. A lot of the research presented at this conference can be seen this way. Let me just pick two examples, where I have something concrete to say.

First, Kotovsky and Fallside note that their current data confirms their

TABLE 15.8
Timescale of Action Considered in the Volume

TIMESCALE  OF  HUMAN  ACTION

| Scale (secs) | Time Units | System | World (theory) |
|---|---|---|---|
| $10^{10}$ | centuries | | |
| $10^9$ | decades | | HISTORICAL BAND |
| $10^8$ | years | S | |
| $10^7$ | months | | |
| $10^6$ | weeks | | SOCIAL BAND |
| $10^5$ | days | | |
| $10^4$ | hours | | |
| $10^3$ | 10 mins | D K | RATIONAL BAND |
| $10^2$ | minutes | K F, A, F / C, H, G, L, E S | |
| $10^1$ | 10 sec | J C | |
| $10^0$ | 1 sec | | COGNITIVE BAND |
| $10^{-1}$ | 100 ms | K S C | |
| $10^{-2}$ | 10 ms | | |
| $10^{-3}$ | 1 ms | | NEURAL BAND |
| $10^{-4}$ | 100 µs | | |

earlier finding (Kotovsky, Hayes, & Simon, 1985), also on the Tower of Hanoi, of a long explanatory phase with a short final phase, which starts again from the beginning. They attribute this to the difficulty in performing the operators, which inhibits effective problem solving, until this is learned during the initial phase). This of course is not the primary concern of their paper, but I find it interesting. It reminded me of some of the work in cryptarithmetic that Herb and I did (Newell & Simon, 1972). I reproduce the problem behavior graph of *S3* on DONALD + GERALD in Fig. 15.5. It will be observed that it falls into two phases, a long initial one (76%). and a short final one (24%), where the subject starts over one more time and goes much further than he ever had before.

It is not evident that the explanation of operator difficulty works here.

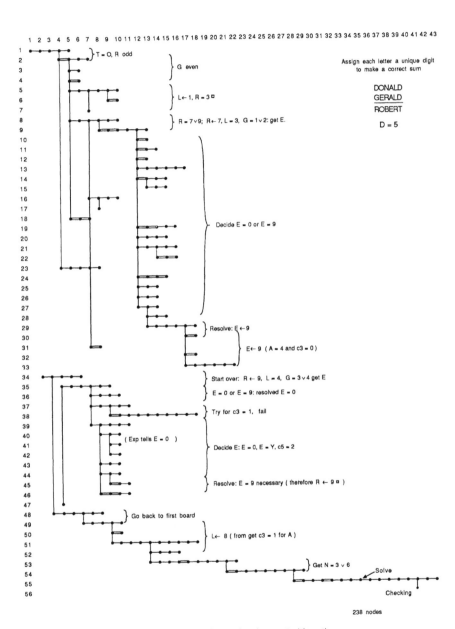

FIG. 15.5. Progressive deepening in cryptarithmetic.

430

There is a difficulty all right, indicated by the repeated returns to one particular state. This happens to be the E + O = E column. It is indeed a puzzlement and, roughly speaking, when *S3* gets it straight he is able to solve the problem. But *S3* does not really seem to be learning how to apply operators in the sense of Kotovsky and Fallside.

What seems a better description of the cryptarithmetic behavior is that the subject engages in *progressive deepening*. This is a search strategy in which one passes over the same task again and again, each pass acquiring some new item of information. The strategy was first defined by de Groot (1965) in chess. But it has much wider currency. It seems to be what is going on in Fig. 15.5. I might conjecture that it is going on in the situations described by Kotovsky and Fallside, although it is a little hard to be sure.

It might also be going on in some of sentence construction situations that Dick Hayes describes in his chapter. He notes that subjects compose left to right, adding what he calls sentence parts at the leading edge. But they do in fact repeat and correct what they do, and their behavior has some of the typical look of progressive deepening. It is not really possible to tell, because the studies are not focused on the exact question. But the illustrative fragment of typical protocol given by Hayes looks like Fig. 15.6 when drawn as a problem behavior graph. We can see clearly the repetitions that constitute the hallmark of progressive deepening.

Progressive deepening seems to be even more widespread. David Steier, in attempting to construct a system for designing algorithms in Soar (Steier

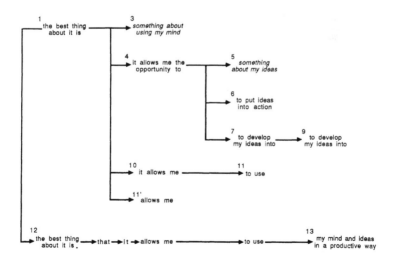

FIG. 15.6.   Problem behavior graph of sentence generation (after Hayes).

& Newell, 1988), has looked in some detail at protocols (Kant & Newell, 1984). What he finds is a form of progressive deepening, applied to a design task, rather than an information-gathering task. Design, of course, invariably involves successive refinements to be successive deepenings. In fact, progressive deepening provides the *control* of what to refine, by going over and over again what one has done, finding the next item of relevant information (when evaluating or analyzing) or finding the next place where the design should be extended or refined.

What does this have to do with the architectural features that show through in the foothills? Progressive deepening is a pattern of behavior that appears to arise from the architecture. The standard argument is that it is a response to memory limitations. In this regard, it is interesting to note that the method is still essentially unknown in AI, where the architectures have very different memory properties. Consequently, the ubiquity of progressive deepening is in fact a geological feature of the foothills—an example of the regularities that we need to discover. It is not clear yet that this is the case, but there are hints all around.

The second example is a major point of Dunbar and Klahr's chapter, namely, that two problem spaces are involved in their discovery task. They give a detailed account of these two spaces, showing how they illuminate what is going on in their complex task. George Miller, in his chapter, picked up on the issue of multiple spaces, focusing on the relations of the spaces to each other and whether search could be concurrent. In fact, there are many more than two spaces involved. Table 15.9 gives a list, whomped up by a little arm-chair task analysis on my part.

What does the number of problem spaces have to do with the architectural features of the foothills? I think Soar provides a clue. With Soar, we have finally found out how to have multiple problem spaces. Not one or two problem spaces, but problem spaces all the way down. Furthermore, this is driven by the architecture—scratch an impasse, get another problem space. The proliferation of spaces may be modulatable ever so slightly by deliberation, but not much. Thus, the multiple problem-space character of a task is not a strategy choice for an intelligent agent or even a task characteristic. Multiple problem spaces are a feature of the foothills, created by the nature of the cognitive architecture. That multiple spaces show up in the work of Dunbar and Klahr, or of Simon and Lea (1974) before them, is not a discovery of a specific feature of their tasks. Rather, the analysis these authors performed was thorough enough to dig out the spaces that are there. Good for them. But multiple spaces are there for all tasks in the foothills, if one just learns how to look for them.

## The Borders

To put it all together requires more than just becoming unified within the heartland, though that is certainly task enough. Cognitive science has especially many borders, for the study of man is one of the great intellectual ger-

TABLE 15.9
Multiple Spaces for Scientific Discovery in the Bigtrack World

| |
| --- |
| Hypothesis space |
| Experimentation space |
| Experimental design space  ( program synthesis ) |
| Experiment task environment space   ( predict Bigtrack ) |
| Observation space   ( Bigtrack's behavior ) |
| Data analysis space   ( was the experiment supported? ) |
| Underlying mechanism space   ( constrain hypothesis space ) |
| Prior literature space   ( what has prior theory said ) |

rymanders. Along some borders, what is required is simply to understand how things are transformed in crossing them. Along other borders, however, serious intellectual work must be done, if cognitive science is to attain any substantial unification. The contributions to the volume provide the opportunity to touch on an issue on each of two key borders, the neural band below and the social band above.

### The Neural Band

One senses that integration along the neural border cannot be far off. This seemingly forever impenetrable border has been a feature of our scientific landscape for so long, with periodic bursts of hope and optimism, that it is difficult to know how to read the signs. Certainly, the enthusiasm for connectionism is running strong and there are additional signs as well, as Kosslyn's chapter—our lone entry from that research frontier—again attests. More certain than even the enthusiasm on the upland side of the border is the immense progress being made on the other side. Massive detail and analysis continues to build a reasonably consistent picture. The various wild alternative speculations that seemed always to be with us, seem to have finally damped down—e.g., the action is not really in the neural circuits at all, but in the glial cells, or in the macromolecules. The sense of hopelessness at not having a single viable neural candidate for the engram has given way to active investigation of a range of intriguing phenomena, such as long-term potentiation (Lynch, McGaugh, & Weinberger, 1984). Neural anatomical functional specificity is way up, which makes projects such as Kosslyn's important enterprises.

The auguries for my own project of putting it all together are surely conflicting here. On the one hand, integration across this nether border cannot but help the cause. I have already noted with approval the grounding of the floating kingdom. All cognitive functions are now to be tied to an absolute time scale—recognition memory accesses at $\sim$10 $ms$, elementary deliberations at $\sim$100 $ms$, and so forth. The big implication is the potential of neural data to be brought to bear everywhere. This can only be a great thing, the ability to bring more constraints to bear (recall Table 15.3).

On the other hand, to hear it from the connectionists, theirs is a movement to sweep symbolic cognition away. The success of neuroscience will bring with it success at the cognitive level, but not the integration of the cognitive science that I have been extolling throughout this essay. For it is a new paradigm that will take over. It is to be a revolution à la Français, with no ministries available. Or so they say.

I am rather partial to revolutions in the fashion of Darwin or Bohr. As I indicated earlier, revolutions within the world of paradigm science have this benign character in which, whatever the cover story, the techniques and the results continue to accumulate.

In fact, I believe that neuroscience-inspired architectures, whether of the connectionist stripe or the more functional variety of Kosslyn, are worth pursuing. It is only by such means that we will find out the implications of neural technology. The proposition that unified theories of cognition take the form of architectures holds for whatever architectural structure one considers.

I would argue that connectionist architectures should strive towards being unified theories of cognition, just like the rest of us. Good results on some special corner of phenomena is a good thing to have, and indeed is necessary. But it only means a theory has joined the microtheories, of which psychology has now quite a few. We need unified theories that cover the full gamut of psychological phenomena. Connectionists architectures must strive towards the same extended coverage that the symbolic architectures will be attaining.

### The Social Band

The border looking upward toward social behavior has a quite different character for individual psychology than the border looking downward toward neurophysiology. For one, a different foot wears the reductionist shoe, and when the other shoe drops, as it must in both cases, it will land on a different toe. Furthermore, both individual and social psychology belong to the same field, the really marshy boundaries being the crossovers from social psychology to sociology and anthropology. This makes the border considerably more permeable, and historically there has been lots of traffic between individual psychology and social psychology.

Still the interpretation of cognition and the social band does not seem to me in very good shape currently. It is not for lack of trying, and by demand pull, rather than technology push, which would seem to be the right way for it to happen. But we have now had a decade of work in *social cognition*, as this attempt has come to be called. There has been no lack of enthusiasm and no lack of effort. The Seventeenth Carnegie Symposium on Cognition (Clark & Fiske, 1982) provided a mid-term report, which was pretty upbeat. But somehow it hasn't happened. A symposium now would not have much really new to say over the early 1980s. This is no place to make a real diagnosis. My carom shot, for what it is worth, is that social cognition successfully moved to variables of internal processing and internal memory. But they still kept the comparative-statistics methodology. They never moved to consider *mechanisms of cognition* in the social setting—not in the way Herb did when he went after all those topics in cognition listed in Table 15.1.

So psychology will have to try it again in a different way with a new set of ideas about how it might work. One of the great things about science is there is no ultimate defeat. It is the land of eternal regrouping until success is attained. My belief, consistent with my diagnosis above, is that we must deal with models of the human social actor as a system of mechanisms. But I have little faith in my own preferences here.

In thinking about the task on this border, I noted that Herb was off by himself in the timescale chart of Table 15.8, far away from the rest of us. This led me to list in Table 15.10 the fields in which Simon has made his contributions. There are lots of them, but that is not my point. Note how many are social sciences. Herb has been working across this upper boundary throughout his whole career. In fact, his most notable accomplishments, those for which he was given his Nobel Prize, are the application of the model of intendedly rational behavior to economics—one of the social sciences far off from social psychology, the object of my attention here.

Even so, Herb has not been able to abolish that border. Indeed, much of his work in these social sciences occurred early in his career. Then I went back to the lonesome outpost high up in Table 15.8. The reason Herb is out there is his most recent work on the psychology of scientific discovery (Langley, Simon, Bradshaw, & Zytkow, 1987). That research is a curious mixture of detailed simulations of individual attainment and significance within the historical timescale. Could it be that Herb is pioneering a new way to finally get what we know about cognition into the social band?

## CONCLUSION

It makes no sense to summarize a summary of something, itself a summary event. But a conclusion to a concluding essay is still conscionable. I have been upbeat in the extreme about the prospects of cognitive science being able to put it all together. I have seen in the contributions to this volume many signs that this is happening. I can think of no better way to honor Herb Simon for the immense part he has played in initiating the cognitive revolution and in giving it substance and sustenance through its first 4 decades, than a volume that bears witness to the maturing of cognitive science into a unified cumulating science. Such an eventuality will not surprise him, of course. Nor will he see in it any paradigm shifts, however startling the changes may seem to other observers. For it will be a continuation of the path he has been

TABLE 15.10
The Fields of Simon's Contributions (With Representative Citations)

Artificial Intelligence (Simon, 1963)

Cognitive Psychology

Comnputer Science (Newell, Perlis, & Simon, 1967)

Design (Simon, 1969)

Economics (Simon, 1979b; Simon, 1982)

Econometrics (Ijiri & Simon, 1977)

History of Science (Langley, Simon, Bradshaw & Zytkow, 1987)

Operations Research and Management Science (Holt, Modigliani, Muth, (Simon, 1960)

Organization Theory (Simon, 1957; March & Simon, 1958)

Philosophy and Foundations (Simon, 1947; Simon & Rescher, 1966)

Philosophy of Science (Simon, 1970)

Political Science (Simon, 1954)

Public Administration (Simon, Smithburg, & Thompson, 1950)

Social Psychology (Simon & Guetzkow, 1955)

| Statistics | (Simon, | 1955b) |
|---|---|---|

scouting for us. And it will reveal that he has been on the main path all along. That is the best present there can be for a true scientist.

## ACKNOWLEDGMENTS

This research was sponsored by the Office of Naval Research (ONR), under contract number N00014-86-K-0678. The views and conclusions contained in this document are those of the author and should not be interpreted as representing the official policies, either expressed or implied, of the Office of Naval Research.

## REFERENCES

Anderson, J. R. (1983). *The architecture of cognition.* Cambridge, MA: Harvard University Press.

Ando, A., Fisher, F., & Simon, H. A. (1963). *Essays on the structure of social science models.* Cambridge, MA: MIT Press.

Anzai, Y., & Simon, H. A. (1979). The theory of learning by doing. *Psychological Review, 86,* 124–140.

Bartlett, F. C. (1932). *Remembering: A study in experimental and social psychology.* Cambridge, England: Cambridge University Press.

Baylor, G. W., & Simon, H. A. (1966). A chess mating combinations program. *Proceedings of the 1966 Spring Joint Computer Conference, 28,* 431–447.

Berliner, H., & Ebeling, C. (in press). Pattern knowledge and search: The SUPREM architecture. *Artificial Intelligence.*

Bransford, J. D., & Johnson, M. K. (1973). Considerations of some problems of comprehension. In W. G. Chase, (Ed.), *Visual information processing.* New York: Academic Press.

Chase, W. G. (Ed.). (1973). *Visual information processing.* New York: Academic Press.

Chase, W. G., & Simon, H. A. (1973). The mind's eye in chess. In W. G. Chase, (Ed.), *Visual information processing.* New York: Academic Press.

Chase, W. G., & Simon, H. A. (1973). Perception in chess. *Cognitive Psychology, 4,* 55-81.

Clark, H. H., Carpenter, P. A., & Just, M. A. (1973). On the meeting of semantics and perception. In W. G. Chase, (Ed.), *Visual information processing.* New York: Academic Press.

Clark, M. S., & Fiske, S. T. (Eds.). (1982). *Affect and cognition.* Hillsdale, NJ: Lawrence Erlbaum Associates.

Coles, L. S. (1967). *Syntax Directed Interpretation of Natural Language.* Unpublished doctoral dissertation, Carnegie Institute of Technology, Pittsburgh.

Cooper, L. A., & Shepard, R. N. (1973). Chronometric studies of the rotation of mental images. In W. G. Chase, (Ed.), *Visual information processing.* New York: Academic Press.

de Groot, A. (1965). *Thought and choice in chess.* The Hague: Mouton.

Ericsson, K. A., & Simon, H. A. (1984). *Protocol analysis: Verbal reports as data.* Cambridge, MA: MIT Press.

Feldman, J. A., & Ballard, D. (1982). Connectionist models and their properties. *Cognitive Science, 6,* 205-254.

Fisher, D. F., Monty, R. A., & Senders, J. W. (Eds.). (1981). *Eye movements: Cognition and visual perception.* Hillsdale, NJ: Lawrence Erlbaum Associates.

Forgy, C. L. (1981). *OPS5 User's Manual* (Tech. Rep.). Pittsburgh: Carnegie-Mellon University, Computer Science Departments.

Genesereth, M. R., & Nilsson, N. J. (1987). *Logical foundations of artificial intelligence.* Los Altos, CA: Morgan Kaufman.

Gilmartin, K. J., Newell, A., & Simon, H. A. (1976). A program modeling short-term memory under strategy control. C. M. Cofer (Ed.), *The structure of human memory.* San Francisco, CA: W. H. Freeman.

Gregg, L. W., & Simon, H. A. (1967). Process models and stochastic theories of simple concept formation. *Journal of Mathematical Psychology, 4,* 246-276.

Groner, R., Menz, C., Fisher, D. F., & Monty, R. A. (Eds.). (1983). *Eye, movements and psychological functions: International views.* Hillsdale, NJ: Lawrence Erlbaum Associates.

Guthrie, E. R. (1953). *The psychology of learning.* New York: Harper & Row.

Head, H. (1920). *Studies in neurology.* Oxford, England: Oxford University Press.

Hendrix, G. G. (1977). Expanding the utility of semantic networks through partitioning. *Proceedings of the 5th International Joint Conference on Artificial Intelligence.* Menlo Park, CA: AAAI.

Holt, C. C., Modigliani, F., Muth, J., & Simon, H. A. (1960). *Planning production, inventories, and work force.* Englewood Cliffs, NJ: Prentice-Hall.

Ijiri, Y., & Simon, H. A. (1977). *Skew distributions and the sizes of business firms.* Amsterdam, The Netherlands: North-Holland Publishing Company.

Kant, E., & Newell, A. (1984). Problem solving techniques for the design of algorithms. *Information Processing and Management, 20,* 97-118.

Klahr, D. (173). Quantification processes. In W. G. Chase, (Ed.), *Visual information processing.* New York: Academic Press.

Kotovsky, K., Hayes, J. R., & Simon, H. A. (1985). Why are some problems hard? Evidence from the Tower of Hanoi. *Cognitive Psychology, 17,* 248-294.

Kuhn, T. (1962). *Scientific revolutions.* Chicago, IL: University of Chicago Press.

Kulkarni, D., & Simon, H. A. (in press). Processes of scientific discovery: The strategy of experimentation. *Cognitive Science.*

Laird, J. E., Newell, A., & Rosenbloom, P. S. (1987). Soar: An architecture for general intelligence. *Artificial Intelligence, 33*(1), 1-64.

Laird, J. E., Rosenbloom, P. S., & Newell, A. (1986). Chunking in Soar: The anatomy of a general learning mechanism. *Machine Learning, 1*, 11-46.

Langley, P., Simon, H. A., Bradshaw, G. L., & Zytkow, J. M. (1987). *Scientific discovery: Computational explorations of the creative processes*. Cambridge, MA: MIT Press.

Larkin, J. H., & Simon, H. A. (1987). Why a diagram is (sometimes) worth 10,000 words. *Cognitive Science, 11*, 65-100.

Larkin, J. H., McDermott, J., Simon, D., & Simon, H. A. (1980). Expert and novice performance in solving physics problems. *Science, 208*, 1335-1342.

Lynch, G., McGaugh, J. L., & Weinberger, N. M. (Eds.). (1984). *Neurobiology of Learning and Memory*. New York: Guilford Press.

March, J. G., & Simon, H. A. (1958). *Organizations*. New York: Wiley.

Minsky, M. (1975). A framework for the representation of knowledge. In P. Winston (Ed.), *The psychology of computer vision*. New York: McGraw-Hill.

Monty, R. A., & Senders, J. W. (Eds.). (1976). *Eye movements and psychological processes*. Hillsdale, NJ: Lawrence Erlbaum Associates.

Neisser, U. (1967). *Cognitive psychology*. New York: Appleton-Century-Crofts.

Neves, D. M. (1981). *Learning procedures from examples*. Unpublished doctoral dissertation, Carnegie-Mellon University, Pittsburgh.

Newell, A. (1973a). Productions systems: Models of control structures. In W. G. Chase, (Ed.), *Visual information processing*. New York: Academic Press.

Newell, A. (1973b). You can't play 20 questions with nature and win: Projective comments on the papers of this symposium. In W. G. Chase, (Ed.), *Visual information processing*. New York: Academic Press.

Newell, A. (1980). Physical symbol systems. *Cognitive Science, 4*, 135-183.

Newell, A. (1982). The knowledge level. *Artificial Intelligence, 18*, 87-127.

Newell, A. (1986). *Scale counts in cognition*. APA Scientific Contribution Award Lecture, American Psychology Association Convention.

Newell, A. (1987). *Unified theories of cognition*. The William James Lectures. Harvard University, Spring 1987. (Available in videocassette, Psychology Department, Harvard).

Newell, A., Perlis, A. J., & Simon, H. A. (1967). What is computer science? *Science, 155*, 1373-1374.

Newell, A., & Shaw, J. C. (1957). Programming the Logic Theory Machine. *Proceedings of the 1957 Western Joint Computer Conference, 11*, 230-240.

Newell, A., Shaw, J. C., & Simon, H. A. (1957). Empirical explorations of the Logic Theory Machine: A case study in heuristics. *Proceedings of the 1957 Western Joint Computer Conference*, Western Joint Computer Conference.

Newell, A., & Simon, H. A. (1972). *Human problem solving*. Englewood Cliffs, NJ: Prentice-Hall.

Newell, A., & Simon, H. A. (1976). Computer science as empirical inquiry: Symbols and search. *Communications of the ACM, 19*(3), 113-126.

Norman, D. A., Rumelhart, D. E., & LNR Research Group. (1975). *Explorations in cognition*. New York: Freeman.

Paige, J. M., & Simon, H. A. (1966). Cognitive processes in solving algebra word problems. In B. Kleinmuntz (Ed.), *Problem solving*. New York: Wiley.

Piaget, J. (1952). *The origins of intelligence in children*. New York: International Universities Press.

Polk, T. A., & Newell, A. (1988). Modeling human syllogistic reasoning in Soar. *Proceedings Cognitive Science Annual Conference—1988*. Cognitive Science Society.

Posner, M. I. (1973). Coordination of internal codes. In W. G. Chase, (Ed.), *Visual information processing*. New York: Academic Press.

Quillian, R. (1967). *Semantic memory*. Unpublished doctoral dissertation, Carnegie Institute of Technology, Pittsburgh.

Rosenbloom, P. S., Laird, J. E., & Newell, A. (1987). Knowledge-level learning in Soar. *Proceedings of the American Association of Artificial Intelligence - 1987*. Los Altos, CA: Morgan Kaufman.

Rosenbloom, P. S., Laird, J. E., & Newell, A. (in press). The chunking of skill and knowledge. In H. Bouma & B. A. G. Elksendorn (Eds.), *Working models of human perception*. London: Academic Press.

Schank, R., & Ableson, R. (1977). *Scripts, plans, goals and understanding*. Hillsdale, NJ: Lawrence Erlbaum Associates.

Senders, J. W., Fisher, D. F., & Monty, R. A. (Eds.). (1978). *Eye movements and the higher psychological functions*. Hillsdale, NJ: Lawrence Erlbaum Associates.

Shaw, J. C., Newell, A., Simon, H. A., & Ellis, T. O. (1959). A command structure for complex information processing. *Proceedings of the 1958 Western Joint Computer Conference, 13*, 119-128.

Simon, H. A. (1947). The axioms of Newtonian mechanics. *The Philosophical Magazine, 38*, 888-905.

Simon, H. A. (1954). Bandwagon and underdog effects and the possibility of election predictions. *Public Opinion Quarterly, 18*, 245-253.

Simon, H. A. (1955a). A behavioral model of rational choice. *Quarterly Journal of Economics, 69*, 99-118.

Simon, H. A. (1955b). On a class of skew distribution functions. *Biometrika, 42*, 425-440.

Simon, H. A. (1956). Rational choice and the structure of the environment. *Psychological Review, 63*, 129-138.

Simon, H. A. (1957). *Administrative behavior (2nd ed.)*. New York: Macmillan.

Simon, H. A. (1962). The architecture of complexity. *Proceedings of the American Philosophical Society, 26*, 467-482.

Simon, H. A. (1963). Experiments with a heuristic compiler. *Journal of the Association for Computing Machinery, 10*, 493-506.

Simon, H. A. (1967). Motivational and emotional controls of cognition. *Psychological Review, 74*, 29-39.

Simon, H. A. (1969). *The sciences of the artificial*. Cambridge, MA: MIT Press.

Simon, H. A. (1970). The axiomization of physical theories. *Philosophy of Science, 37*, 16-26.

Simon, H. A. (1974). How big is a chunk? *Science, 183*, 482-488.

Simon, H. A. (1979a). *Models of thought*. New Haven, CT: Yale University Press.

Simon, H. A. (1979b). Rational decision making in business organizations (Nobel Lecture). *American Economic Review, 69*, 493-513.

Simon, H. A. (1980a). Cognitive science: The newest science of the artificial. *Cognitive Science, 4*, 33-46.

Simon, H. A. (1980b). How to play twenty questions with nature and win. In R. Cole (Ed.), *Perception and production of fluent speech*. Hillsdale, NJ: Lawrence Erlbaum Associates.

Simon, H. A. (1982). *Models of bounded rationality*. (2 volumes). Cambridge, MA: MIT Press.

Simon, H. A., & Barenfeld, M. (1969). Information-processing analysis of perceptual processes in problem solving. *Psychological Review, 76*, 473-483.

Simon, H. A., & Feigenbaum, E. A. (1964). In information-processing theory of some effects of similarity, familiarization, and meaningfulness in verbal learning. *Journal of Verbal Learning and Verbal Behavior, 3*, 385-396.

Simon, H. A., & Gilmartin, K. (1973). A simulation of memory for chess positions. *Cognitive Psychology, 5*, 29-46.

Simon, H. A., & Guetzkow, H. (1955). A model of short- and long-run mechanisms involved in pressures toward uniformity in groups. *Psychological Review, 62*, 56-68.

Simon, H. A., & Hayes, J. R. (1976). The understanding process: Problem isomorphs. *Cognitive Psychology, 8*, 165-190.

Simon, H. A., & Kadane, J. B. (1975). Optimal problem-solving search: All-or-none solutions. *Artificial Intelligence, 6*, 235-247.

Simon, H. A., & Kotovsky, K. (1963). Human acquisition of concepts for sequential patterns. *Psychological Review, 70*, 534-546.

Simon, H. A., & Lea, G. (1974). Problem solving and rule induction: A unified view. In L. W. Gregg (ed.), *Knowledge and cognition*. Hillsdale, NJ: Lawrence Erlbaum Associates.

Simon, H. A., & Rescher, N. (1966). Cause and counterfactual. *Philosophy of Science, 33,* 323–340.

Simon, H. A., & Siklossy, L. (Eds.). (1972). *Representation and meaning: Experiments with information processing systems.* Englewood Cliffs, NJ: Prentice-Hall.

Simon, H. A., Smithburg, D. W., & Thompson, V. A. (1950). *Public administration.* New York: Knopf.

Steier, D. E., Laird, J. E., Newell, A., Rosenbloom, P. S., Flynn, R. A., Golding, A., Polk, T. A., Shivers, O. G., Unruh, A., & Yost, G. R. (1987). Varieties of learning in Soar: 1987. In *Proceedings of the Fourth International Workshop on Machine Learning.* Los Altos, CA: Morgan Kaufman.

Steier, D., & Newell, A. (1988). Integrating multiple sources of knowledge into Designer-Soar, an automatic algorithm designer. *Proceedings American Association of Artificial Intelligence—1988.* American Association of Artificial Intelligence.

Thibadeau, R., Just, M. A., & Carpenter, P. A. (1982). A model of the time course and content of reading. *Cognitive Science, 6,* 157–203.

Thorp, C. E., Herbert, M., Kanade, T., & Shafer, S. (1987). Vision and navigation for the Carnegie-Mellon Navlab. In J. Traub, B. J. Groog, B. W. Lampson, & M. J. Nilsson (Eds.), *Annual review of computer science, 2,* Palo Alto, CA: Annual Reviews.

Williams, D. S. (1969). *Computer program organization induced by problem examples.* Unpublished doctoral dissertation, Carnegie-Mellon University, Pittsburgh.

Williams, T. G. (1965). *Some studies in game playing with a digital computer.* Unpublished doctoral dissertation, Carnegie Institute of Technology, Pittsburgh.

Yost, G. (1988). *TAQ reference manual.* Pittsburgh: Carnegie-Mellon University, Soar Project, Computer Science Department.

Zhang, G., & Simon, H. A. (1985). STM capacity chinese words and idioms: Chunking and the acoustical loop hypothesis. *Memory and Cognition, 13,* 193–201.

# Epilogue

# How It All Got Put Together
# A Story[1]

Allen Newell
*Carnegie-Mellon University*

Once upon a time when the world was young,
  Oh best beloved.
There came to the banks of the Monongogo river,
  All muddy and brown,
  Oh best beloved,
A djinn who was one thing on the inside
  But many things on the outside.

And he camped by the banks of the Monongogo river,
  All muddy and brown,
  Oh best beloved.
And he stayed and stayed and he never went away.

And he did his magic there.

He had many hands, each hand with many fingers,
  Oh best beloved.
More hands and fingers than you and I.
  More hands than you have fingers,
  More fingers on each hand than you have toes.

---

[1]Told on the occasion of the Twenty-first Carnegie-Mellon Sympsoium on Cognition, a festschrift for Herbert A. Simon, 30 May 1987.

Each hand played a tune on a magic flute,
   Oh best beloved.
And each fluted tune floated out on a separate flight.
   And each was a tune for a separate dance,
   And each was heard in a separate place,
   And each was heard in a separate way,
   And each was merged in the dance it swayed.

But it was still all the same tune,
   For that was the magic of the djinn.

Now, best beloved, listen near—
Each separate place, when the world was young,
Danced in a way that was all its own,
Different from all of the others.

But the melody told of how it could be
That creatures out of an ancient sea,
By dancing one dance on the inside,
Could dance their own dance on the outside,
   Because of the place where they were in—
      All of its ins and outs.
For that was the magic of the djinn.

And little by little, each swayed a new way,
Taking the melody each its own way,
But hearing the melodies far away
   From other places with separate dances,
   But the very same melody
That told the dance to be done on the inside.
So, each started to step in the very same way,
   Putting together one dance on the inside
   For many dances on the outside.

So the melody grew, and it drifted back
To the Monongogo river, all muddy and brown.
   And the river can clear and sweet.

Ah, best beloved, I must tell the truth.
The river is not yet clear and sweet,
   Not really so.
Because putting together is a task forever.
   And no one—not even a djinn with kilohands and megafingers,
      All of which play a different-same tune—
Can put all things together in a single breath,
   Not even a breath of fifty years.

It is not all put together yet,
   And it never shall be,
   For that is the way of the world.

But even so, when the world was young,
   Was the time of the need for the single tune
   To guide the dance that would move together
   All of the steps in all of the places.

And it happened by the banks of the Monongogo river,
   All muddy and brown,
   Best beloved.
   And the river will never be the same.

Just so.

# Author Index

**A**

Abelson, R., 426, *439*
Adams, N., 236, *267*
Adesman, P., 256, *266*
Agre, P. E., 315, *316*
Albright, T. D., 13, *28*
Amsel, E., 109, 113, 138, *142*
Amsterdam, J. B., 4, 5, 7, 8, 9, 10, 11, 17, 21, *28*
Andersen, R. A., 8, *26*
Anderson, J. A., 12, *27*
Anderson, J. R., 37, *67*, 69, 105, *108*, 196, 206, *207*, 235, 238, *265*, 276, *280*, *281*, 293, 295n, 313, *316*, 343, 345, 347, 348, 349, 351, 357, *370*, *371*, 405, 424, *436*
Ando, A., 386, *398*, 401, *436*
Annett, J., 11, *26*
Anzai, Y., 291, *316*, 343, *371*, 401, *436*
Assumpcao, P. P., 196, *207*
Atkinson, J. W., 205 *207*
Atkinson, R. C., 37, *67*, 275, *281*
Attneave, F., 9, *26*
Atwood, M. E., 235, *266*
Austin, G. A., 109, *141*


**B**

Baddeley, A. D., 42, 60, *67*, 153, *161*, 236, *265*

Ballard, D., 408, *437*
Baltes, P. B., 241, 242, 243, 244, *266*
Barenfeld, M., *341*, 401, *439*
Barsalou, L. W., 236, *265*
Bartlett, F. C., 109, *141*, 235, *265*, 425–426, *436*
Bassok, M., 69, *107*, 279, *281*
Baumgardner, M. H., 112, *142*
Baylor, G. W., 401, *436*
Bee, N. V., 313, *317*
Bender, D. B., 13, *27*
Benson, D. F., 14, *27*
Benton, A., 8 *27*
Bereiter, C., 210, 211, *232*, 278, *278*
Berliner, H., 183, *207*, 418, 419, *436*
Bernard, J. E., 322, *340*
Bertin, J., 337, *340*
Bever, T. G., 56, *67*
Bhaskar, R., 69, *107*
Bienkowski, M., 64, *68*
Blackwood, E., 196, *207*
Blaustein, A., 225, 228, *233*
Bloom, B. S., 205, *207*
Bobrow, D. G., 177, *181*, *316*, 392, *396*
Bond, S. J., 217, *234*
Boorstin, D., 181, *181*
Bovair, S., 69, 81, *107*
Bower, G. H., 236, *265*
Boyle, C. F., 276, *280*, 313, *316*, 343, 357, *371*
Bracewell, R. J., 210, *232*

Bradshaw, G. L., 109, 132, 141, *142,* 375, 378, 379, *397,* 401, 435, 436, *438*
Bradshaw, J. L., 4, *27*
Bransford, J. D., 403, *437*
Briars, D. J., 295n, *316*
Broadbent, D. E., 159, *161,* 236, 238, 244, *265*
Brown, J. S., 278, *281,* 295n, 300, 313, *316, 317, 318,* 343, 344, 350, 366, *371*
Bruner, J. S., 109, *141*
Bryan, W. L., 241, 253, *265*
Bryden, M. P., 4, *27*
Buchanan, B. G., 170, 175, 177, 180, *181, 182*
Bukstel, L., 193, 196, *207*
Bundesen, C., 6, *28*
Burns, D., 56, *68*
Burton, R. R., 295n, *316,* 350, *371*

**C**

Campbell, D. J., 205, *208*
Campbell, K. M., 205, *208*
Caramazza, A., 287, *316, 318*
Carbonell, J. R., 275, *281*
Carey, L., 211, 213, 215, 228, *233*
Carey, S., 11, *141, 142*
Carpenter, P. A., 36, 38, 39, 40, 41, 42, 43, 45, 49, 57, 65, *67, 68,* 403, 405, *437, 440*
Carpenter, T. P., 304, *316*
Carraher, D., 286, 293, *316*
Carraher, T., 286, 293, *316*
Carry, L. R., 322, *340*
Carver, S. M., 69, *107,* 128, *142,* 277, *281,* 313, *317*
Case, R., 60, *67,* 112, *142*
Cave, K. R., 6, 7n, *27*
Champernowne, D. G., 382, *396*
Chapman, D., 315, *316*
Charness, N., 183, 184, 185, 187, 190, 193, 194, 196, 199, *207,* 238, 256, *265*
Chase, W. G., 54, *67,* 183, 184, 188, 189, 192, *207, 208,* 214, 226, 227, *233,* 235, 236, 237, 238, 239, 240, 241, 242, 244, 245, 249, 254, 255, 256, 262, *265, 266, 267, 268,* 334, *340,* 344, *371,* 390, *396,* 401, 402, 403, *437*
Chi, M. T. H., 197, *207,* 235, 236, 256, *265,* 272, 274, 279, *281*
Chiesi, H. L., 235, *265, 267*
Chomsky, N., 285, *316*
Clancey, W. J., 276, *281*
Clark, H. H., 403, *437*

Clark, M. S., 434, *437*
Cohen, A., 11, *28*
Cohen, P. R., 110, *142*
Coles, L. S., 401, *437*
Collins, A., 273, 275, 278, *281*
Cooper, L. A., 403, *437*
Corbett, A. T., 357, *371*
Cowey, A., 6, *27*
Crecine, J. P., 378, *396*
Crutcher, R. J., 247, *265*
Curran, T., 216, *233*

**D**

Daneman, M., 41, 42, 43, 45, *67*
Deci, E. L., 205, *207*
Dee-Lucas, D., 41 *67*
de Groot, A. D., 184, 188, 190, *207,* 227, *233,* 235, 255, 256, *265,* 431, *437*
deKleer, J., 300, *317*
de la Rocha, O., 286, *318*
Dennis, M., 11, *27*
De Renzi, E., 3, 4, 15, *27*
Desimone, R., 6, 13, 19, *28*
Deutsch, G., 4, *29*
Dinsmore, J., 314, *317*
diSessa, A. A., 312, *317*
Dowty, D. R., 301, *317*
Dreyfus, H. L., 289n, *317*
Dreyfus, S. E., 289n, *317*
Duffy, T., 216, *233*
Dunbar, K., 110, 111, 111n, 132n, *142*

**E**

Ebeling, C., 418, 419, *436*
Ellis, T. O., 401, *439*
Elo, A. E., 183, 185, *207*
Emig, J., 209, *233*
Engle, R. W., 193, 196, *207*
Ericsson, K. A., 54, *67,* 141, 142, 189, 198, *207,* 235, 236, 237, 238, 239, 240, 241, 242, 243, 244, 246, 247, 248, 249, 255, 256, 257, 258, 262, 263, 264, *265, 266,* 334, *340,* 344, *371,* 401, *437*
Ernst, G. W., *181*
Essick, G. K., 8, *26*

**F**

Faglioni, P., *27*
Faivre, I., 241, 242, 244, *266*

Falkenhainer, B., 139, *142*
Faloon, S., 54, *67*, 235, 238, 239, 240, *266*, 334, *340*
Farr, M., 236, *265*, 272, *281*
Farrell, R. G., 235, *265*, 276, *281*, 313, 343, 351, *370*, *371*
Fauconnier, G., 300, 314, *317*
Feigenbaum, E. A., 110, *142*, 166, 170, 171, 175, 177, 179, 179n, 180, *181*, *182*, 206, *207*, 401, *439*
Feldman, J. A., 5, 6, 9, 13, *27*, 166, 171, *181*, 408, *437*
Feltovich, P. J., 235, *265*
Fendrich, D., 241, 244, *266*
Fisher, D. F., 417, *437*, *439*
Fisher, F., 401, *436*
Fiske, S. T., 434, *437*
Flavell, J. H., 111–112, *142*
Flesch, R. F., 60, *67*
Flores, F., 289n, *318*
Flower, L. S., 209, 211, 213, 215, 225, 228, *233*, 235, *266*
Flynn, R. A., 4, 5, 7, 8, 9, 10, 11, 17, 21, *28*, 415, *440*
Forbus, K. D., 300, 306, *317*
Ford, M., 56, *67*
Forgy, C., 35, *67*, 412, *437*
Foss, C., 313, *317*
Frederiksen, J. R., 273, *282*
Frey, P. W., 256, *266*
Frey, R. L., 195, 202, *207*
Friedlander, A., 215, 225, *233*
Friedrich, F. J., 11, *28*

**G**

Galanter, E., 211, *233*
Gazzaniga, M. S., 13, 14, *27*
Gelade, G., 6, *29*
Gelernter, H., 170, *181*
Gelman, R., 295n, *317*
Genesereth, M. R., 422, *437*
Gentner, D., 69, *107*, 305, *317*
Geschwind, N., 14, *27*
Gibson, J. J., 290, *317*
Gick, M. L., 69, 94, *107*
Gilmartin, K., 401, *437*, *439*
Ginsburg, H., 287, 292, 312, *317*
Glanzer, M., 238, 244, *267*
Glaser, R., 197, *207*, 235, 236, *265*, 272, 274, 279, *281*
Golding, A., 415, *440*

Goldstein, I., 171, *181*
Goodnow, J. J., 109, *141*
Goodwin, R. M., 385, *396*
Gordon, P., 242, 243, *266*
Gray, W. D., 69, *107*
Green, B., 287, *316*, *318*
Greeno, J. G., 295n, 296, 301, 313, 315, *317*, *318*
Greenwald, A. G., 112, *142*
Gregg, L. W., 155, *161*, 389, *396*, 401, *437*
Gregory, R. L., 9, *27*
Groen, G. J., 197, *208*
Groner, R., 417, *437*
Gross, C. G., 6, 13, *27*, *28*
Guetzkow, H., 436, *439*
Guthrie, E. R., 421, *437*

**H**

Haas, C., 211, 213, 218, 222, 233, *233*
Hadamard, J., 383, *396*
Hansen, J. R., 170, *181*
Hardyck, C., 4 *27*
Harre, R., 112, *142*
Harter, N., 241, 253, *265*
Hasher, L., *207*
Hastie, R., 21, *28*
Hastorf, C., 338, *340*
Hayes, J. R., 69, 71, 77, 78, 81, 87, 88, 105, *107*, *108*, 209, 211, 213, 215, 217, 222, 225, 226, 228, 232, *233*, *234*, 235, *266*, 334, *340*, 384, 391, 392, 393, *396*, *397*, 398, 429, *437*, *439*
Hayes, P., 177, *181*
Hayes-Roth, F., 196, *208*
Hayward, R. W., 14, *28*
Head, H., 425, *437*
Heidegger, M., 289n, 290, *317*
Heller, J. I., 295n, *318*
Hendrix, G. G., 426n, *437*
Herbert, M., 421, *440*
Hinton, G. E., 12, *27*
Hiscock, M., 11, *28*
Hitch, G., 42, 60, *67*, 153, *161*, 238, *266*
Holding, D. H., 184, 192, 193, *208*
Holland, J. H., 308, *317*
Holt, C. C., 436, *437*
Holtzman, J. D., 13, *27*
Holyoak, K. J., 69, 94, *107*, 308, *317*
Hudson, T., 304, *317*
Hughes, H. C., 13, *27*
Hunt, E., 242, *266*

Hunter, I. M. L., 253, *266*

**I**

Ijiri, Y., 382, *397,* 436, *437*
Inhelder, B., 109, 111, 112, *142*
Inhoff, A. W., 11, *28*

**J**

Jackson, J. H., 3, 15, *27*
James, W., 31, *67*
Janik, C. J., 217, *234*
Jarvella, R. J., 64, 66, *67*
Jeffries, R., 235, *266,* 344, *370*
Jing, Q., 390, *398*
Johnson, M. K., 403, *437*
Johnson, W. A. L., 304, *317*
Johnson-Laird, P. N., 157n, *161,* 300, *317,*
    384, *397*
Jones, R. K., 18, *27*
Judd, C. H., 69, *107*
Just, M. A., 36, 38, 39, 40, 41, 49, 57, 65,
    *67, 68,* 403, 405, *437, 440*

**K**

Kadane, J. B., 338, *340,* 401, *439*
Kanade, T., 421, *440*
Kant, E., 432, *437*
Kantar, E., 196, *208*
Karmiloff-Smith, A., 109, *142*
Katona, G., 69, *107*
Kaufer, D., 211, 213, 225, *233*
Kearse, A. L., 195, 202, *207*
Keil, F. C., 111, *142*
Keren, G., 193, *208*
Kieras, D., 69, 81, *107*
Kimball, J. P., 40, *68*
Kimura, D., 14, *27*
Kinsbourne, M., 11, 13, *27, 28*
Kintsch, W., 61, *68,* 295n, 301, 315, *317*
Klahr, D., 35, *68,* 69, *107,* 110, 111, 111n,
    113n, 128, 132n, *142,* 277, *281,* 313,
    *317,* 403, *437*
Klahr, P., 196, *208*
Kliegl, R., 241, 242, 243, 244, *266*
Kohn, B., 11, *27*
Korolyuk, V. S., 386, *397*
Kosslyn, S. M., 4, 5, 5n, 6, 7, 7n, 8, 9, 10,
    11, 14, 15, 17, 18, 21, 26, *27, 28,* 337,
    *340,* 384, *397*

Kotovsky, K., 69, 71, 77, 78, 87, 88, 105,
    *107,* 334, *340,* 384, 388, 392, *397, 398,*
    401, 429, *437, 439*
Kuhn, D., 109, 111, 112, 113, 138, *142*
Kuhn, T., 402, *437*
Kulkarni, D., 109, 110, 112, 132, *142,* 375,
    379, *397,* 401, *437*

**L**

Laird, J. E., 405, 412, 415, 424, *437, 438,*
    *439, 440*
Lane, D. M., 256, *266*
Langley, P., 35, *68,* 109, 132, 141, *142,* 375,
    378, 379, *397,* 401, 435, 436, *438*
Larkin, J. H., 235, *266,* 274, *281,* 295n, 314,
    *316, 317,* 320, 337, 338, *341,* 383, 390,
    *397,* 401, *438*
Larkin, W., 56, *68*
Larsen, A., 6, *28*
Laughlin, S. A., 14, *28*
Lave, J., 286, 287, 288, 293, *318*
Lea, G., 110, 132, 141, *143,* 158, *161,* 401,
    432, *440*
Lederberg, J., 175, 177, 180, *181, 182*
LeDoux, J. E., 14, *27*
Leiman, J. M., 64, *68*
Leippe, M. R., 112, *142*
Lenat, D., 110, *142,* 179, 179n, *181*
Lenneberg, E. H., 11, 16, *28*
Lesgold, A. M., 235, *266,* 274, *281*
Levine, D. N., 16, *28*
Levine, L., 229, *233*
Levy, J., 14, *28*
Lewis, C., 322, *340, 341*
Lewis, C. H., 346, 366, *371*
Lewis, M. W., 279, *281,* 313, *317,* 343, *371*
Liebert, R. M., 112, 140, *143*
Lindley, E. H., 241, 253, *265*
Lindsay, R., 175, *182*
LNR Research Group, 426, *438*
Lotka, A. J., 380, *397*
Love, T., 242, *266*
Loveland, D. H., 170, *181*
Lowe, D. G., 7, 7n, *28*
Luchins, A. S., 366, *371*
Lynch, G., 433, *438*
Lynch, J. C., 9, *28*

**M**

Macko, K. A., 7, *28*
Mandelbrot, B., 382, *397*

March, J. G., 436, *438*
Marcus, M. P., 40, *68*
Markman, E. M., 303, *318*
Marr, D., 5, *28*
Mateer, C., 14, *28*
Matz, M., 365, *371*
Maunsell, J. H. R., 6, 12, *29*
Mazur, J. E., 20, *28*
Mazzocchi, F., 14, *28*
McCarthy, J., 158, *161*
McClelland, J. L., 13, *28*
McCloskey, M., *281,* 287, *316, 318,* 344, *371*
McConkie, G. W., 63, *68*
McCorduck, P., 165n, 171, 177, *181, 182,*
    387, 393, *397*
McCulloch, W. S., 146, *161*
McDermott, J., 35, *67,* 235, *266,* 274, *281,*
    390, *397,* 401, *438*
McDonald, J. L., 41, *68*
McGaugh, J. L., 433, *438*
McLean, R. S., 155, *161*
Menz, C., 417, *437*
Miller, A. I., 314, *318*
Miller, G. A., 37, 62, *68,* 152n, 155, *161,*
    211, *233,* 236, 238, *266,* 275, *281,* 384,
    389, *397*
Milner, B., 3, 11, 18, *28*
Milson, R., 343, *371*
Minsky, M., 120, 132, *142,* 426, *438*
Mishkin, M., 6, 7, *27, 28, 29*
Modigliani, F., 436, *437*
Monty, R. A., 417, *437, 438, 439*
Moran, J., 6, 13, 19, *28*
Moser, J. M., 304, *316*
Mostow, D. J., 196, *208*
Mountcastle, V. B., 9, *28, 29*
Mueller, G. E., 241, 242, 243, 244, *266*
Murtaugh, M., 286, *318*
Muth, J., 436, *437*

**N**

Naeser, M. A., 14, *28*
Neches, R., 35, *68*
Neisser, U., 9, *28,* 403, *438*
Nelson, J., 222, *233*
Nettleton, N. C., 4, *27*
Neumann, J. von, 146, *161*
Neves, D. M., 401, *438*
Newell, A., 32, 35, 36, *68,* 70, 94, *107,* 146,
    *161,* 167, 170, *181, 182,* 185, 194, *208,*
    209, *233,* 236, 238, 240, *267,* 269–271,

*281,* 285, 315, *318,* 378, 387, 388, 393,
    *397,* 399, 400, 401, 402, 403, 404, 405,
    407, 409, 412, 415, 421, 422n, 423, 424,
    426, 429, 432, 436, *437, 438, 439, 440*
Newman, S. E., 278, *281*
Nii, H. P., 177, *181*
Nilsson, N. J., 71, *107,* 422, *437*
Nisbett, R. E., 308, *317*
Norman, D. A., 426, *438*
Nottebohm, F., 14, *28*
Novak, G. S., Jr., 393, *397*

**O**

Oliver, W., 257, 258, 262, 263, 264, *266*
O'Loughlin, M., 109, 113, 138, *142*
Omanson, S. F., 295n, *318*
Orasanu, J. M., 69, *107*
Osgood, C. E., 94, *107*

**P**

Paige, G., 319, *341*
Paige, J. M., 295, *318,* 392, *397,* 401, *438*
Palincsar, A. S., 278, *281*
Papert, S., 69, *107,* 171, *181*
Patel, V. L., 197, *208*
Paulson, J. A., 275, *281*
Peirce, B. O., *397*
Peng, R., 390, *398*
Perfetti, C. A., 274, *281*
Perlis, A. J., 436, *438*
Peters, S., 301, *317*
Pfau, H. D., 193, *208*
Phelps, E., 111, 112, 113, *142*
Piaget, J., 109, 111, 112, *142,* 426, *438*
Pirolli, P. L., 345, 349, *371*
Pitts, W., 146, *161*
Polischuk, L. I., 386, *397*
Polk, T. A., 415, 422n, *438, 440*
Polson, P. G., 235, 246, 247, 248, 263, *266*
Polya, G., 278, *281*
Posner, M. I., 11, *28,* 403, *438*
Pratkanis, A. R., 112, *142*
Pribram, K., 211, *233*
Pritchard, R. D., 205, *208*
Pylyshyn, Z. W., 384, *397*

**Q**

Quillian, R., 401, *438*

**R**

Rasmussen, T., 3, 11, 18, *28*
Razel, M., 238, *266*
Reddy, R., 36, *68*
Rees, E., 197, *207*, 274, *281*
Reimann, P., 279, *281*
Reiser, B. J., 313, *316*, 343, *371*
Rescher, N., 436, *440*
Resnick, L. B., 295n, *318*
Reynolds, R. I., 184, *208*
Richard, I. A., 151, *161*
Riley, M. S., 295n, *317*, *318*
Robertson, L., 256, *266*
Rocha-Miranda, C. E., 13, *27*
Roschelle, J., 296, 298, *318*
Rosenbloom, P. S., 185, *208*, 240, *267*, 405, 412, 415, 424, *437*, *438*, *439*, *440*
Ross, B. H., 69, *107*, 349, *371*
Ruger, H. A., 69, *107*
Rumelhart, D. E., 12, *28*, 426, *438*
Ryan, R. M., 205, *207*

**S**

Saariluoma, P., 184, *208*
Sass, D., 216, *233*
Sauers, R., 235, *265*, 276, *281*, 351, *371*
Scardamalia, M., 210, 211, *232*, 278, *281*
Schank, R., 426, *439*
Schliemann, A., 286, 293, *316*
Schneider, W., 274, 277, *282*
Schoenfeld, A., 278, *282*, 294, 309, *318*
Schorr, D., 236, *267*
Schriver, K., 211, 213, 215, 217, 225, 228, *233*
Schwartz, E. L., 13, *28*
Scribner, S., 286, *318*
Searle, J. R., 285, *318*
Seidenberg, M. S., 64, *68*
Senders, J. W., 417, *437*, *438*, *439*
Shafer, S., 421, *440*
Shalin, V., 313, *317*
Sharp, C. A., 14, *29*
Shaw, J. C., 285, *318*, 401, 426, *438*, *439*
Shepard, R. N., 403, *437*
Shiffrin, R. M., 37, *67*
Shivers, O. G., 415, *440*
Shortliffe, E. H., *181*
Shrager, J., 113n, 139, *142*
Shultz, T. R., 346, *371*
Siebert, J., 303, *318*
Siegel, R. M., 8, *26*

Siegler, R. S., 112, 140, *143*, 346, *371*
Siklossy, L., 401, *440*
Simon, D. P., 195, *208*, 235, *266*, 274, *281*, *282*, 390, *397*, *398*, 401, *438*
Simon, H. A., 3, 5, 26, *28*, 32, 35, 36, 61, *68*, 70, 71, 77, 78, 81, 87, 88, 94, 105, *107*, *108*, 109, 110, 112, 132, 141, *142*, *143*, 145, 146, 147, 148–150, 152, 152n, 153, 156–157, 158, 159–160, *161*, 166, 167, 172, *182*, 183, 184, 188, 189, 192, 194, 195, 198, 206, *207*, *208*, 209, 214, 226, 227, 232, *233*, *234*, 235, 236, 237, 238, 245, 246, 254, 255, 256, 262, 265, *265*, *266*, *267*, 269–271, 274, 279, *281*, *282*, 285, 291, 295, 295n, 314, 315, *316*, *317*, *318*, 319, 320, 326, 329, 334, 337, *340*, *341*, 343, *371*, 375, 377, 378, 379, 382, 383, 384, 385, 386, 387, 388, 389, 390, 391, 392, 393, *396*, *397*, *398*, 400, 401, 402, 403, 404, 406, 407, 408, 421, 429, 432, 435, 436, *436*, *437*, *438*, *439*, *440*
Singley, M. K., 69, 105, *108*
Sleeman, D., 322, 334, *341*, 343, *371*
Smith, B. C., 289, 291, 292, 296, *318*
Smith, E. E., 236, *267*
Smith, J., 241, 242, 243, 244, *266*
Smith, S. B., 69, *108*, 249, *267*
Smithburg, D. W., 436, *440*
Spilich, G. J., 235, *265*, *267*
Spilka, R., 225, 228, *233*
Springer, S. P., 4, *29*
Staszewski, J. J., 241, 242, 243, 244, 249, 250, 252, 253, 254, *267*
Steier, D. E., 415, 431–432, *440*
Steinbach, R., 278, *281*
Sternberg, S., 153, *161*
Stevens, A. L., 273, *281*, 305, *317*
Stratman, J., 215, 228, *233*
Suchman, L., 288, 289n, *318*
Summers, J. J., 14, *29*
Sussman, H. M., 14, *29*
Susukita, T., 242, 243, *267*
Swaney, J. H., 217, *234*
Swinney, D. A., *68*

**T**

Talbot, W. H., 9, *28*
Tanenhaus, M. K., 64, *68*
Thagard, P. R., 308, *317*
Thibadeau, R. H., 36, 38, *68*, 405, *440*

Thomson, D. M., 239, *267*
Thompson, R., 345, 347, 348, 349, *371*
Thompson, V. A., 436, *440*
Thorndike, E., 69, 81, *108*
Thorp, C. E., 421, *440*
Tomusyak, A. S., 386, *397*
Toulmin, S. E., 225, *234*
Treisman, A. M., 6, *29*
Truscott, A. F., 195, 202, *207*
Tschirgi, J. E., 113, *143*
Tufte, E. R., 337, *341*
Tulving, E., 239, *267*
Turner, A. A., 235, *266*
Tyler, S. W., 225, *234*

**U**

Ungerleider, L. G., 6, 7, *28, 29*
Unruh, A., 415, *440*

**V**

Valentine, E., 242, 243, *266*
Van Essen, D., 6, 12, *29*
VanLehn, K., 295n, *318,* 344, 345, 350, 366, 367, *371*
Vesonder, G. T., 235, *267*
Vignolo, L. A., 14, *28*
Vipond, D., 61, *68*
Vitolo, T. M., 313, *317*
Voss, J. F., 225, *234,* 235, *265, 267*
Vygotsky, L., 109, *143*

**W**

Wall, R. E., 301, *317*
Wang, G., 4, 5, 7, 8, 9, 10, 11, 17, 21, *28*

Wason, P. C., 112, *143,* 157n, *161*
Waterman, D. A., 170, *182*
Weinberger, N. M., 433, *438*
Westbury, J. R., 14, *29*
Whitaker, H. A., 11, *27*
White, B., 273, *282*
White, M. J., 4, *29*
Wilding, J., 242, 243, *266*
Williams, D. S., 401, *440*
Williams, T. G., 401, *440*
Winograd, T., 289n, *318*
Wishbow, N., 225, 226, 227, *234*
Woodworth, R., 69, 81, *108*
Woolley, J. D., 57, *68*

**Y**

Yengo, L. A., 225, *234*
Yin, T. C. T., 9, *28, 29*
Yost, G., 276, *280,* 343, 357, *371,* 415, 424, *440*
Yu, B., 390, *398*
Yule, G. U., 382, *398*

**Z**

Zacks, R. T., *207*
Zangwill, O., 14, *29*
Zatz, L. M., 14, *28*
Zhang, G., 390, *398,* 401, *440*
Zhang, W., 390, *398*
Zhu, X., 390, *398*
Zhu, X., 343, *371*
Zimba, L. D., 13, *27*
Zola, D., 63, *68*
Zytkow, J. M., 109, 132, 141, *142,* 375, 378, 379, *397,* 401, 435, 436, *438*

# Subject Index

## A

Abstract concepts, 306–309
Activation of visual representations, 9–10
ACT*, 405, 422–425
Algebra
  linear equations, 322, 326–329, 334–335
  word problems, 295, 319
Architectures, see cognitive architectures
Automaticity, 274, 277–278
Artificial Intelligence, 149, 165–180
  Role of knowledge, 171–177
  Simon's contribution, 166–169
Associative memory in object recognition, 9
Asymmetries in transfer, 78–80

## B

BigTrak, 113–114
Blindfold chess, 257
BRIAN (Bilateral Recognition and Imagery
  Adaptive Networks), 16–25, 405
Bridge, 193–196
Bounded rationality, 400

## C

CAPS (Concurrent Activation-based Production System), 36, 405, 422–423
Causal induction in PUPS, 346–348
Cerebral lateralization, see Hemispheric
  lateralization

Chess, 184
  acquisition of skill, 185–192
  memory for chess positions, 256–257
Chunking, 61–62, 188, 272
  in bridge, 193,
  in chess, 188–190, 237–238, 256
Coffee brewing problem, 320, 326, 335–336
Cognitive architectures, 404–411, 422–427
  ACT*, 405, 42–425
  BRIAN, 405
  CAPS, 405, 422–423
  constraints on, 407–408
  Soar, 405, 412–416, 422–425
Cognitive Science, 416–435
  foundations, 417–422
  methodologies, 416–417
Competent performance, see skill acquisition
Compilation, 349
Computer simulations, 146–150
  of neural networks, 146
Concept formation, 109–110
Connectionist architectures, 434
Control of speech output, 14
Control of visual search patterns, 14–15
Cryptarithmetic, 168–169, 429–431

## D

DENDRAL, 173–175
Development of scientific reasoning,
  111–113, 139–140

Diagrams, 319–320, 383
DiBS (Display-Based Solver), 323–325
Digit span, 239, 244
Display-based problem solving, 319–340
  errors in, 334–337
  in everyday tasks, 320–322, 326–329
  in solving equations, 322, 326–329,
    334–335
  in solving the tower of Hanoi, 329–
    331
  production-system model of, 323–325
  comparison to human performance,
    331–333
Dorsal system, 8–9

## E

Einstellung errors, 366–367
Embedded clauses, 56–57
Encoding, see storage processes
Envisioning machine, 298–300
EPAM (Elementary Perceiver and
  Memorizer), 206
Errors, 344–345
  analogical mapping errors, 349–351
  in algebra, 363–366
  in geometry, 357–363
  in LISP, 351–357
  Einstellung, 366
  in display-based problem solving,
    334–337
Everyday mathematics knowledge, 286–
  288
Experimental design, 388–394
  for hypothesis testing, 388–389
  for model testing, 389–390
  using problem isomorphs, 391–392
Experimentation strategies, 112–113,
  137–139, 392–394
Expertise, 183–206
  at mental calculation, 249–255
  at taking dinner orders, 245–249
  in chess, 184–192, 256–263
  in memory, 235–265
  in writing, 209–232
  role of knowledge, 224–231, 236–238, 241,
    252–255
  see also skill acquisition
Explanatory models, 386–388
External display, see display-based problem
  solving
Eye fixations, 46

## F

Feature detection, 8
Feedback
  role in BRIAN, 20–21
  role in hemispheric lateralization, 15–16,
    20–21
Formal operations, 112
Frames, 120, 132

## G

Gaze durations, 40–41
Generative knowledge, 285–314
GRI (Generalized Rule Inducer), 110, 132

## H

Hemispheric lateralization, 3–26
  by inhibition of hemispheric processing,
    13
  by training with feedback, 12–13, 15–16
  innate bilateralization, 14
  of speech, 14
  of visual search, 14–15
Heuristic knowledge, 168
Hierarchical organization in memory,
  see retrieval structures
Hypothesis testing, 137–138
  in visual recognition, 9–10
  see also experimentation

## I

Individual differences,
  in children's search strategies, 131
  in eye fixations while reading, 46
  in hemispheric lateralization, 4
  in planning in bridge, 202–204
  in planning for writing, 211–213
  in reading comprehension, 50–53
  in reading span, 43, 44–52, 57
  in revision of text, 215–216
  in scientific reasoning, 124–125
Inducing laws from data, 379–382
  BACON, 379
  DALTON, 379
Information processing approaches in
  cognitive psychology, 147–150
Insight, 376
Intelligence 169–172

competence/performance distinction,
  170–171
dimensions of, 169–170
knowledge-based intelligence, 171–175,
  178–180
Instruction, 275
as symbol manipulation, 294–296
development of automaticity, 277–278
teaching self-regulatory strategies, 278
via knowledge networks, 275–276
via proceduralization and compilation,
  276–277
Isomorphs, 157
tower of Hanoi, 71

**K**

KEKADA, 379
Knowledge
and artificial intelligence, 171–177
and expertise, 224–231, 236–238, 241, 252–255
compilation, 349
everyday math knowledge, 286–288
extrapolation, in PUPS, 348–349
generative, 285–314
heuristic, 168
importance of task environment, 285–289
Knowledge-is-power hypothesis, 178–180
networks, 275–276
Knowledge-based intelligence, 171–175, 178–180

**L**

Language about quantities, 300–305
Learning, see skill acquisition
Lexical access, 46–49
LT (Logic Theorist), 393

**M**

Mental calculation, 241–242, 249–255
Method of loci, 243
Mnemonic strategies, 246
Monster problems, 72–73
Move operators,
in Tower of Hanoi, 72–77
role in transfer, 77–80
MYCIN, 173, 174, 175, 420

**N**

Newtonian physics, 298–299

Number scrabble game, 156–157
Numerical comparison, 303–305

**O**

Object recognition, see Visual recognition

**P**

Pattern activation in vision, 7–8
Pattern recognition, 204
in bridge, 204
in chess, 256
see also chunking
Physical symbol system hypothesis, 167, 178
sufficiency of, 420–421
Planning
in bridge, 199–202
in writing, 211–213
influence of social environment,
  222–224
influence of writing medium, 218–222
moves in Monster problems, 75–77
Problem solving
and search, 167–169, 174–177
and transfer, 69–107
by analogy, 343–370
display-based, 319–340
Problem space, see also problem
  representation
in Tower of Hanoi, 71–72
Problem representation, 69, 272–273
and transfer, 81–95
in scientific reasoning, 383–386
Proceduralization, 273
Production systems, 35
of display-based problem solving,
  323–325
of learning by analogy,
of planning in bridge, 199–202
PUPS, 345–351, 405

**R**

Readability of text, 60–61
READER, 34–36
Reading comprehension and working
  memory, 31–67,
immediacy of interpretation during comprehension, 39–42
levels of processing, 32, 62–66
storage demands during comprehension, 39

Reading comprehension (*continued*)
  see also working memory
Reading span
  and reading ability, 44-46
  and reading comprehension, 43-52
Reading span task, 43
Reasoning, 296-312
  reasoning about abstract concepts,
    306-309
  reasoning about quantities, 300-305
  reasoning with a mental model, 296-300,
    309-312
  reasoning with physical models, 309-312
Repair theory
  comparison with PUPS, 367-370
Response compatibility, 94
Retrieval structures, 239, 245-249, 251-252
  for blindfold chess, 258-262
  for digit span, 242
  for mental calculation, 251-252
  for recall of chess positions, 256-257
Revision, 215-218

**S**

Schemas, 425-427
  see also frames
Scientific discovery, 375-396
  see also scientific reasoning
Scientific reasoning, 109-141
  as search, 110, 376
  hypothesis-space search, 125-127
  experiment-space search, 122-123
  Development of, 111-113, 139-140
    Piagetian view, 111-112
  in adults, 114-127
  in children, 127-131
  models
    BACON, 379
    DALTON, 379
    GRI (Generalized Rule Inducer), 110, 132
    SDDS (Scientific Discovery as Dual
      Search), 132-136
  use of representations, 383-386
Search, 158-160
  in scientific discovery, 376, 384
  of experiment space, 122-123
  of hypothesis space, 125-127
  visual, 14-15
  in problem solving, 167-169, 174-177
Semantic knowledge
  in mental calculation, 252-254

Self-regulation, 274, 278
Semantics
  of abstract concepts, 306-309
  of structured objects and events, 290-296
  of symbol systems, 289-296
Sentence generation, 213-215
Seriality of speech, 32
Short-term memory, see working memory
Skill acquisition, 204-207, 272-280
  and automaticity, 274
  and knowledge organization, 272
  and problem representation, 272-273
  and self-regulatory processes, 274-275
  in chess, 185-192
  instructional issues, 205-206, 275-278
  motivational issues, 205
  proceduralization, 273
Skilled memory theory, 238-265
  and memory expertise, 245-263
  principles of skilled memory, 238-245
  role of knowledge, 239, 241, 252-255
  role of practice, 240, 243, 255
Soar architecture, 405, 412-416, 422-425
Social cognition, 434-435
Star bugs, 350
Storage processes, 239, 242, 245-249,
    252-252, 334-335
  see also chunking
STUDENT, 392
Symbol structures, 289-209
Syntax processing in reading, 52-58

**T**

Tower of Hanoi
  display-based problem solving of, 319,
    329-331
  isomorphs, 71
  solution patterns on, 86-88
  problem difficulty, 71-72
  problem space, 71-72
  solution patterns, 73-77
Transfer, 69-107
  between Tower of Hanoi isomorphs, 77-93
  locus on transfer, 88-93
  role of move operators, 77-80
  role of problem representation, 81-95,
    153-157
  role of stimulus overlap, 93-104
  of memory skill, 248-249
  role of representational similarity,
    153-157

Tutors
  algebra, 363–366
  geometry, 357–363
  LISP, 351–357

**U**

UNDERSTAND, 151–152, 393
Unified theories of cognition, 402–416

**V**

Ventral System, 7–8
Visual buffer, 6
Visual recognition, 4–11
  attention in, 6, 11
  location recognition, 8–9
  shape recognition, 7–8

**W**

Working Memory, 31–67, 59–62, 150–153
  capacity, 36–39
    limitations, 37–38, 42
    measures of, 61–62
    of skilled readers, 43
  definition, 32, 34
  in the READER model, 34–36
  load
    in syntactic processing, 55–60
    and reading comprehension, 46–69
Writing, 209–232
  and revision, 215–218
  relation of planning to writing quality,
    211–213
  role of topic knowledge, 228–231
  sentence generation, 213–215
  writing environment, 218–224

Printed and bound by CPI Group (UK) Ltd, Croydon, CR0 4YY

17/10/2024

01775685-0012